Real-Time Software Design for Embedded Systems

This textbook takes the reader from use cases to complete software architectures for real-time embedded systems using SysML, UML, and MARTE and shows how to apply the COMET/RTE design method to real-world problems. The author covers key topics such as use cases for real-time systems, state machines for real-time control, architectural patterns for distributed and hierarchical real-time control and for real-time component-based software architectures, performance analysis of real-time designs using real-time scheduling, and timing analysis on single- and multiple-processor systems.

Five complete case studies illustrating design issues include a light rail control system, a railroad crossing control system, a microwave oven control system, and an automated highway toll system.

Organized as an introduction followed by several self-contained chapters, the book is perfect for experienced software engineers wanting a quick reference at each stage of the analysis, design, and development of large-scale real-time embedded systems, as well as for advanced undergraduate or graduate courses in computer science, software engineering, systems engineering, and computer engineering programs.

Hassan Gomaa is Professor and former chair of the Department of Computer Science at George Mason University. Gomaa has more than thirty years of experience in software engineering, in both industry and academia. He has taught short in-depth industrial courses on real-time software design in North America, Europe, Japan, and South Korea. He has published more than 200 technical papers and is the author of four other textbooks on software design, including *Software Modeling and Design* and *Designing Software Product Lines with UML*.

REAL-TIME SOFTWARE DESIGN FOR EMBEDDED SYSTEMS

Hassan Gomaa

George Mason University

CAMBRIDGE
UNIVERSITY PRESS

Shaftesbury Road, Cambridge CB2 8EA, United Kingdom

One Liberty Plaza, 20th Floor, New York, NY 10006, USA

477 Williamstown Road, Port Melbourne, VIC 3207, Australia

314–321, 3rd Floor, Plot 3, Splendor Forum, Jasola District Centre, New Delhi – 110025, India

103 Penang Road, #05–06/07, Visioncrest Commercial, Singapore 238467

Cambridge University Press is part of Cambridge University Press & Assessment, a department of the University of Cambridge.

We share the University's mission to contribute to society through the pursuit of education, learning and research at the highest international levels of excellence.

www.cambridge.org
Information on this title: www.cambridge.org/9781107041097

First published 2016

A catalogue record for this publication is available from the British Library

Library of Congress Cataloging-in-Publication data
Gomaa, Hassan, author.
Real-time software design for embedded systems / Hassan Gomaa, George Mason University.
    pages cm
Includes bibliographical references and index.
ISBN 978-1-107-04109-7 (hardback)
1. Computer software – Development.   2. Embedded computer systems – Programming.   3. Real-time data processing.   I. Title.
QA76.76.D47G649   2015
005.3–dc23   2015026051

ISBN   978-1-107-04109-7   Hardback

To Gill, William and Neela, Alex and Nicole,
Amanda and Neil, and Edward

Contents

Preface		*page* xv
Annotated Table of Contents		xix
Acknowledgments		xxv

Part I   Overview

1   Introduction   3
1.1	The Challenge	3
1.2	Real-Time Embedded Systems and Applications	3
1.3	Characteristics of Real-Time Embedded Systems	5
1.4	Distributed Real-Time Embedded Systems	7
1.5	Cyber-Physical Systems	9
1.6	Requirements for Real-Time Software Design Method for Embedded Systems	10
1.7	COMET/RTE: A Real-Time Software Design Method for Embedded Systems	10
1.8	Visual Modeling Languages: UML, SysML, and MARTE	11
1.9	Summary	11

2   Overview of UML, SysML, and MARTE   12
2.1	Model-Driven Architecture with SysML and UML	12
2.2	Use Case Diagrams	14
2.3	Classes and Objects	14
2.4	Class Diagrams	15
2.5	Interaction Diagrams	17
2.6	State Machine Diagrams	19
2.7	Package Diagrams	20
2.8	Concurrent Sequence and Communication Diagrams	20
2.9	Deployment Diagrams	23
2.10	Composite Structure Diagrams	24

2.11   UML Extension Mechanisms and Profiles   26
2.12   SysML   27
2.13   MARTE Profile   28
2.14   Timing Diagrams   29
2.15   Tool Support for UML, SysML, and MARTE   30
2.16   Summary   31

3   Real-Time Software Design and Architecture Concepts   32
3.1   Object-Oriented Concepts   32
3.2   Information Hiding   34
3.3   Inheritance   36
3.4   Active and Passive Objects   37
3.5   Concurrent Processing   37
3.6   Cooperation between Concurrent Tasks   39
3.7   Information Hiding Applied to Access
       Synchronization   42
3.8   Runtime Support for Real-Time Concurrent
       Processing   43
3.9   Task Scheduling   45
3.10   Software Architecture and Components   47
3.11   Summary   48

Part II   Real-Time Software Design Method

**4   Overview of Real-Time Software Design Method for
    Embedded Systems   51**
4.1   COMET/RTE System and Software Life Cycle model 51
4.2   Phases in COMET/RTE Life Cycle model   52
4.3   Comparison of the COMET/RTE Life Cycle with
       Other Software Processes   56
4.4   Survey of Design Methods for Real-Time Embedded
       Systems   57
4.5   Multiple Views of System and Software Architecture 59
4.6   Summary   60

**5   Structural Modeling for Real-Time Embedded Systems with
    SysML and UML   61**
5.1   Static Modeling Concepts   62
5.2   Categorization of Blocks and Classes using
       Stereotypes   66
5.3   Structural Modeling of the Problem Domain with
       SysML   66
5.4   Structural Modeling of the System Context   69
5.5   Hardware/Software Boundary Modeling   72
5.6   Structural Modeling of the Software System Context 72
5.7   Defining Hardware/Software Interfaces   76
5.8   System Deployment Modeling   77
5.9   Summary   78

6 Use Case Modeling for Real-Time Embedded Systems   79
  6.1   Use Cases   79
  6.2   Actors   80
  6.3   Identifying Use Cases   85
  6.4   Documenting Use Cases in the Use Case Model   87
  6.5   Specifying Nonfunctional Requirements   88
  6.6   Examples of Use Case Descriptions   88
  6.7   Use Case Relationships   92
  6.8   The *Include* Use Case Relationship   92
  6.9   The *Extend* Use Case Relationship   94
  6.10 Use Case Packages   98
  6.11 Summary   99

7 State Machines for Real-Time Embedded Systems   100
  7.1   State Machines   101
  7.2   Examples of State Machine   103
  7.3   Events and Guard Conditions   103
  7.4   Actions   105
  7.5   Hierarchical State Machines   113
  7.6   Cooperating State Machines   118
  7.7   Inherited State Machines   119
  7.8   Developing State Machines from Use Cases   121
  7.9   Example of Developing a State Machine from a Use Case   122
  7.10 Summary   125

8 Object and Class Structuring for Real-Time Embedded Software   126
  8.1   Object and Class Structuring Criteria   126
  8.2   Object and Class Structuring Categories   127
  8.3   Object Behavior and Patterns   128
  8.4   Boundary Classes and Objects   129
  8.5   Entity Classes and Objects   136
  8.6   Control Classes and Objects   137
  8.7   Application Logic Classes and Objects   139
  8.8   Summary   141

9 Dynamic Interaction Modeling for Real-Time Embedded Software   143
  9.1   Object Interaction Modeling   144
  9.2   Message Sequence Description   145
  9.3   Approach for Dynamic Interaction Modeling   145
  9.4   Stateless Dynamic Interaction Modeling   146
  9.5   Examples of Stateless Dynamic Interaction Modeling   147
  9.6   State Dependent Dynamic Interaction Modeling   150
  9.7   Example of State Dependent Dynamic Interaction Modeling: Microwave Oven System   154
  9.8   Summary   162

10   Software Architectures for Real-Time Embedded Systems   163
   10.1   Overview of Software Architectures   164
   10.2   Multiple Views of a Software Architecture   166
   10.3   Transition from Analysis to Design   170
   10.4   Separation of Concerns in Subsystem Design   172
   10.5   Subsystem Structuring Criteria   175
   10.6   Decisions about Message Communication between
          Subsystems   181
   10.7   Summary   183

**11   Software Architectural Patterns for Real-Time Embedded
Systems**   184
   11.1   Software Design Patterns   184
   11.2   Layered Software Architectural Patterns   186
   11.3   Control Patterns for Real-Time Software
          Architectures   190
   11.4   Client/Service Software Architectural Patterns   194
   11.5   Basic Software Architectural Communication
          Patterns   197
   11.6   Software Architectural Broker Patterns   203
   11.7   Group Message Communication Patterns   206
   11.8   Documenting Software Architectural Patterns   209
   11.9   Applying Software Architectural Patterns   209
   11.10 Summary   210

**12   Component-Based Software Architectures for Real-Time
Embedded Systems**   211
   12.1   Concepts for Component-Based Software
          Architectures   212
   12.2   Designing Distributed Component-Based Software
          Architectures   212
   12.3   Component Interface Design   213
   12.4   Designing Composite Components   217
   12.5   Examples of Component-Based Software
          Architecture   218
   12.6   Component Structuring Criteria   221
   12.7   Design of Service Components   223
   12.8   Distribution of Data   227
   12.9   Software Deployment   228
   12.10 Design of Software Connectors   229
   12.11 Summary   232

13   Concurrent Real-Time Software Task Design   233
   13.1   Concurrent Task Structuring Issues   234
   13.2   Categorizing Concurrent Tasks   234
   13.3   I/O Task Structuring Criteria   235
   13.4   Internal Task Structuring Criteria   242
   13.5   Task Priority Criteria   248

13.6   Task Clustering Criteria   249
13.7   Design Restructuring by Using Task Inversion   256
13.8   Developing the Task Architecture   257
13.9   Task Communication and Synchronization   258
13.10   Task Interface and Task Behavior Specifications   264
13.11   Summary   265

14   Detailed Real-Time Software Design   266
14.1   Design of Composite Tasks   266
14.2   Synchronization of Access to Classes   274
14.3   Designing Monitors   278
14.4   Designing Connectors for Inter-Task Communication   284
14.5   Task Event Sequencing Logic   291
14.6   Detailed Real-Time Software Design in Robot and
        Vision Systems   293
14.7   Implementing Concurrent Tasks in Java   295
14.8   Summary   296

15   Designing Real-Time Software Product Line Architectures   297
15.1   Software Product Line Engineering   298
15.2   Problem Description of Microwave Oven SPL   299
15.3   Requirements Modeling for Software Product Lines   299
15.4.   Analysis Modeling for Software Product Lines   303
15.5   Design Modeling for Software Product Lines   308
15.6   Summary   310

Part III   Analysis of Real-Time Software Designs

**16   System and Software Quality Attributes for Real-Time
        Embedded Systems   313**
16.1   Scalability   313
16.2   Performance   315
16.3   Availability   315
16.4   Safety   316
16.5   Security   317
16.6   Maintainability   318
16.7   Modifiability   319
16.8   Testability   320
16.9   Traceability   321
16.10   Reusability   322
16.11   Summary   323

17   Performance Analysis of Real-Time Software Designs   324
17.1   Real-Time Scheduling Theory   325
17.2   Real-Time Scheduling for Aperiodic Tasks and Task
        Synchronization   330
17.3   Generalized Real-Time Scheduling Theory   331
17.4   Performance Analysis Using Event Sequence
        Analysis   336

17.5   Performance Analysis Using Real-Time Scheduling
        Theory and Event Sequence Analysis   338
17.6   Advanced Real-Time Scheduling Algorithms   339
17.7   Performance Analysis of Multiprocessor Systems   340
17.8   Estimation and Measurement of Performance
        Parameters   343
17.9   Summary   345

18   Applying Performance Analysis to Real-Time Software
Designs   346
18.1   Example of Performance Analysis Using Event
        Sequence Analysis   346
18.2   Example of Performance Analysis Using Real-Time
        Scheduling Theory   351
18.3   Example of Performance Analysis Using Real-Time
        Scheduling Theory and Event Sequence Analysis   354
18.4   Design Restructuring   367
18.5   Summary   368

Part IV   Real-Time Software Design Case Studies for Embedded
Systems

19   Microwave Oven Control System Case Study   371
19.1   Problem Description   371
19.2   Structural Modeling   372
19.3   Use Case Modeling   373
19.4   Object and Class Structuring   377
19.5   Dynamic State Machine Modeling   379
19.6   Dynamic Interaction Modeling   383
19.7   Design Modeling   395
19.8   Performance Analysis of Real-Time Software Design   403
19.9   Component-Based Software Architecture   406
19.10   Detailed Software Design   413
19.11   System Configuration and Deployment   415

20   Railroad Crossing Control System Case Study   417
20.1   Problem Description   417
20.2   Structural Modeling   418
20.3   Use Case Modeling   422
20.4   Dynamic State Machine Modeling   426
20.5   Object and Class Structuring   429
20.6   Dynamic Interaction Modeling   429
20.7   Design Modeling   435
20.8   Performance Analysis of Real-Time Software Design   441
20.9   Component-Based Software Architecture   443
20.10   System Configuration and Deployment   450

21   Light Rail Control System Case Study   451
21.1   Problem Description   451

21.2	Structural Modeling	452
21.3	Use Case Modeling	455
21.4	Dynamic State Machine Modeling	464
21.5	Subsystem Structuring	471
21.6	Object and Class Structuring	471
21.7	Dynamic Interaction Modeling	474
21.8	Design Modeling	486
21.9	Subsystem Integrated Communication Diagrams	486
21.10	Design of Distributed Light Rail System	487
21.11	Component-Based Software Architecture	495
21.12	System Configuration and Deployment	499

22 Pump Control System Case Study — 500

22.1	Problem Description	500
22.2	Structural Modeling	501
22.3	Use Case Modeling	501
22.4	Object and Class Structuring	504
22.5	Dynamic State Machine Modeling	504
22.6	Dynamic Interaction Modeling	506
22.7	Design Modeling	507

23 Highway Toll Control System Case Study — 513

23.1	Problem Description	513
23.2	Use Case Modeling	514
23.3	Software System Context Modeling	516
23.4	Object and Class Structuring	516
23.5	Dynamic State Machine Modeling	517
23.6	Dynamic Interaction Modeling	517
23.7	Design Modeling	519

Appendix A: Conventions Used in This Textbook   525

Appendix B: Catalog of Software Architectural Patterns   530

Appendix C: Pseudocode Templates for Concurrent Tasks   551

Appendix D: Teaching Considerations   557

Glossary   559

Bibliography   573

Index   581

Preface

OVERVIEW

This book describes a comprehensive concurrent object-oriented and component-based method for the real-time software design of distributed embedded systems and the cyber components of cyber-physical systems.

The book starts with a discussion of the characteristics of real-time embedded systems and a description of the important concepts in the design of these systems. It then describes a detailed object-oriented and component-based method for developing architectural and detailed designs of real-time embedded software. The design method and the impact of design decisions are further illustrated through the use of detailed case studies covering a range of real-time embedded systems. All examples and case studies are documented using the industry standard UML, SysML, and MARTE visual modeling languages and notations.

The book is aimed at both the professional market and the academic market, particularly at the graduate level. It assumes a basic background in UML and object-oriented principles, although a brief overview is given of each.

WHAT THIS BOOK PROVIDES

There are various textbooks on the market describing general object-oriented analysis and design concepts and methods. However, real-time and embedded systems have special needs, which are only treated superficially in these books. Other books describe real-time systems in general or provide a survey-based approach. The focus of this book is on real-time software design for embedded systems. Because real-time systems are usually embedded, the method described in the book takes a systems-engineering perspective addressing system-wide issues involving both hardware and software.

This book provides a comprehensive treatment of the application of object-oriented and component-based concepts to the analysis and design of complex real-time and embedded software. The distinguishing features of this book are that it:

1. Describes fundamental concepts in the software design of object-oriented real-time and embedded systems. This includes concurrent tasks; the

object-oriented concepts of information hiding, classes, and inheritance; distributed component technology; software architectures; finite state machines; and performance analysis of real-time software designs using real-time scheduling.

2. Describes in considerable detail a concurrent object-oriented analysis and design method for real-time and embedded software that is suitable for use in large and complex industrial software development efforts.

3. Seamlessly and systematically integrates several important design concepts for real-time software design, including concurrency, objects, components, services, architectural design patterns, software product lines, and real-time scheduling.

4. Presents several detailed case studies, illustrating different characteristics of real-time and embedded software systems, providing a step-by-step description of how to proceed from real-time systems requirements analysis to detailed software design. All case studies are documented using the SysML, UML 2, and MARTE visual modeling languages and notations.

5. Provides appendixes on a catalog of architectural design patterns and pseudocode templates for detailed task design and includes a glossary and a bibliography, as well as teaching considerations on how to teach industrial and academic courses based on it.

INTENDED AUDIENCE

This book is intended for both professional and academic audiences. The professional audience includes systems engineers, software engineers, computer engineers, analysts, architects, designers, programmers, project leaders, technical managers, and quality assurance specialists, who are involved in the design and development of large-scale real-time and embedded software systems in industry and government. The academic audience includes senior undergraduate and graduate-level students in computer science, software engineering, systems engineering, and computer engineering, as well as researchers in the field.

WAYS TO READ THIS BOOK

This book may be read in various ways. It can be read in the order in which it is presented, in which case Chapters 1 through 3 provide introductory concepts; Chapter 4 provides an overview of the COMET/RTE real-time software design method for embedded systems; Chapters 5 through 18 provide an in-depth treatment of real-time software design; and Chapters 19 through 23 provide detailed case studies.

Alternatively, some readers may wish to skip some chapters, depending on their level of familiarity with the topics discussed. Chapters 1 through 3 are introductory and may be skipped by experienced readers. Readers familiar with software design concepts may skip Chapter 3. Readers particularly interested in real-time software design can proceed directly to the description of COMET/RTE, starting in Chapter 4. Readers who are not familiar with UML, SysML, or MARTE can read Chapter 2 in conjunction with Chapters 4 through 18.

Experienced software designers may also use this book as a reference, referring to various chapters as their projects reach a particular stage of the requirements, analysis, or design process. Each chapter is relatively self-contained. For example, at different times one might refer to Chapter 5 for a discussion of structural modeling using SysML and UML, Chapter 6 for a description of use cases, and to Chapter 7 for a description of state machines. Chapter 10 can be referenced for an overview of real-time software architectures; Chapter 11 and Appendix B for software architectural patterns; Chapter 12 for component-based software architectures; and Chapter 13 for concurrent real-time task design with MARTE. Chapter 15 can be consulted for software product line design; Chapter 16 for system and software quality attributes; and Chapters 17 and 18 for performance analysis of real-time software designs. One can also improve one's understanding of how to use the COMET/RTE method by reading the case studies in Chapters 19–23, because each case study explains the decisions made at each step of requirements, analysis, and design.

Hassan Gomaa
George Mason University
November 2015
Email: hgomaa@gmu.edu
www: http://mason.gmu.edu/~hgomaa

Annotated Table of Contents

PART I: OVERVIEW

Chapter 1. Introduction

This chapter provides an overview of real-time embedded systems and applications and then describes the major characteristics of real-time embedded systems, both centralized and distributed. This chapter also provides an overview of the emerging field of cyber-physical systems, for which real-time software is a critical component. This chapter then introduces COMET/RTE, the design method for real-time embedded systems described and applied in the book.

Chapter 2. Overview of UML, SysML, and MARTE

This chapter describes the main features of the UML, SysML, and MARTE visual modeling languages and notations that are particularly suited for real-time design using the COMET/RTE method. The purpose of this chapter is not to be a full exposition of UML, SysML, and MARTE, because several detailed books exist on these topics, but rather to provide a brief overview of each, in particular those parts that are used by COMET/RTE.

Chapter 3. Real-Time Software Design and Architecture Concepts

This chapter describes key concepts in the software design of concurrent object-oriented real-time embedded systems as well as important concepts for developing the architecture of these systems. The concurrent processing concept is introduced and the issues of communication and synchronization between concurrent tasks are described. Some general design concepts are also discussed from the perspective of their applicability to real-time design, including object-oriented design concepts of information hiding and inheritance, software architecture, and software components. This chapter also briefly discusses technology issues related to real-time software design, including real-time operating systems and task scheduling.

PART II: REAL-TIME SOFTWARE DESIGN METHOD

Chapter 4. Overview of Real-Time Software Design Method for Embedded Systems

This chapter provides an overview of the software design method for real-time embedded systems called COMET/RTE (*C*oncurrent *O*bject *M*odeling and Archi-tectural Design Me*t*hod for *R*eal-*T*ime *E*mbedded systems), which uses the SysML, UML, and MARTE visual modeling languages and notations. This chapter also describes the iterative system and software life cycle of COMET/RTE and how it compares to other life cycles. It then describes the main steps in using COMET/RTE.

Chapter 5. Structural Modeling for Real-Time Embedded Systems with SysML and UML

This chapter describes how structural modeling can be used as an integrated approach for system and software modeling of embedded systems consisting of both hardware and software components, using SysML and UML. This chapter describes structural modeling of the problem domain, structural modeling of the hardware/software system context, hardware/software boundary modeling, struc-tural modeling of the software system context, defining hardware/software interfaces, and system deployment modeling.

Chapter 6. Use Case Modeling for Real-Time Embedded Systems

This chapter describes how use case modeling can be applied to real-time embedded systems from both systems engineering and software engineering perspectives. After an overview of the basic principles of use cases, it provides a more in-depth focus on capturing the functional and nonfunctional requirements for real-time and embed-ded systems. It also explains the difference between system and software use cases and actors.

Chapter 7. State Machines for Real-Time Embedded Systems

This chapter describes state machine modeling concepts, which are particularly important for reactive real-time systems. This chapter covers events, states, condi-tions, actions and activities, entry and exit actions, composite states, and hierarchi-cal state machines with sequential and orthogonal substates. The issues of devel-oping cooperating state machines, inheritance in state machines, and deriving state machines from use cases are also addressed.

Chapter 8. Object and Class Structuring for Real-Time Embedded Software

This chapter describes the identification and categorization of software classes and objects, in particular the role the class plays in the real-time software, including boundary, control, and entity classes. It also describes the corresponding behavior pattern for each category of object.

Chapter 9. Dynamic Interaction Modeling for Real-Time Embedded Software

This chapter describes dynamic interaction modeling concepts. Interaction diagrams are developed for each use case, including the main scenario and alternative scenarios. Specific discussions on state dependent real-time embedded systems cover dynamic interaction modeling for state dependent object interactions. This chapter describes how state machines and interaction diagrams relate to each other and how to make them consistent with each other.

Chapter 10. Software Architectures for Real-Time Embedded Systems

This chapter introduces software architectural concepts for distributed real-time embedded systems. Issues in Software Architectural Design are described. The benefits of developing multiple views of a software architecture are explained. This chapter also provides an introduction to software components and component-based software architectures. The transition from requirements and analysis to architectural design is carefully explained. Separation of concerns in subsystem design and subsystem structuring criteria are also described. This is followed by designing subsystem message communication interfaces.

Chapter 11. Software Architectural Patterns for Real-Time Embedded Systems

The role of architectural design patterns in developing the real-time software architecture is described. An overview of software architectural patterns is presented, including architectural structure and communication patterns. Architectural patterns for real-time systems are described, including layered patterns, real-time control patterns, client/service patterns, brokering patterns, and event-based subscription/notification patterns.

Chapter 12. Component-Based Software Architectures for Real-Time Embedded Systems

This chapter describes how a distributed real-time architecture is designed as a component-based software architecture, which can be deployed to multiple nodes in a distributed environment. Component design issues are described, including composite and simple components, component interface design with provided and required interfaces, ports, and connectors. The design of service components and distributed software connectors are also described. Component configuration and deployment issues are explained.

Chapter 13. Concurrent Real-Time Software Task Design

This chapter describes the design of concurrent tasks using the MARTE real-time modeling notation. Concurrent task structuring is described, including event-driven tasks, periodic tasks, and demand driven tasks. Task clustering of objects is also described. Design of task interfaces is described, including synchronous and asynchronous message communication, event synchronization, and communication through passive objects. The implications of different types of message communication on the concurrent behavior of the software architecture are described.

Chapter 14. Detailed Real-Time Software Design

This chapter describes the detailed design of concurrent tasks. The design of composite tasks with nested passive classes is described. Task synchronization of access to passive classes is described using mutual exclusion, multiple readers and writers, and monitors. The design of connectors for inter-task communication is explained. The implementation of concurrent tasks as Java threads is briefly described.

Chapter 15. Designing Real-Time Software Product Line Architectures

This chapter describes the characteristics of real-time software product lines. The important concepts of feature modeling, and modeling commonality and variability, are explained. How to model variability in use cases, static and dynamic models, and software architectures is explained. The chapter goes on to describe how to model common and variable components in software product line architectures. The engineering of software applications from product line artifacts is explained.

PART III: ANALYSIS OF REAL-TIME SOFTWARE DESIGNS

Chapter 16. System and Software Quality Attributes for Real-Time Embedded Systems

This chapter describes system and software quality attributes and how they are used to evaluate the quality of the real-time embedded system and software architecture. System quality attributes include scalability, performance, availability, safety, and security. Software quality attributes include maintainability, modifiability, testability, traceability, and reusability. This chapter also discusses how the COMET/RTE real-time design method supports the system and software quality attributes.

Chapter 17. Performance Analysis of Real-Time Software Designs

This chapter presents methods for analyzing the performance of real-time embedded software designs. It describes two approaches for analyzing the performance of a design, real-time scheduling theory and event sequence analysis, which are then combined to analyze a concurrent multitasking design. Advanced real-time scheduling algorithms, including deadline monotonic scheduling, dynamic priority scheduling, and multiprocessor scheduling, are described. Practical approaches for analyzing the performance of multiprocessor systems including multicore systems are also described. Estimation and measurement of performance parameters are discussed.

Chapter 18. Applying Performance Analysis to Real-Time Software Designs

This chapter applies the real-time performance analysis concepts and theory described in Chapter 17 to the real-time design of a Light Rail Control System.

Real-time scheduling theory and event sequence analysis are both applied to analyze the performance of the concurrent multitasking design. The performance of the design executing on single-processor and multiprocessor systems is also analyzed and compared.

PART IV: REAL-TIME SOFTWARE DESIGN CASE STUDIES FOR EMBEDDED SYSTEMS

Chapter 19. Microwave Oven Control System Case Study

This chapter describes how the COMET-RTE design method is applied to the design of the embedded real-time software for a consumer product – a microwave oven control system.

Chapter 20. Railroad Crossing Control System Case Study

This chapter describes how the COMET-RTE design method is applied to the design of the embedded real-time software for a safety critical railroad crossing control system.

Chapter 21. Light Rail Control System Case Study

This chapter describes how the COMET-RTE design method is applied to the design of an embedded light rail control system, in which the automated control of driverless trains must be done safely and in a timely manner.

Chapter 22. Pump Control System Case Study

This chapter describes a concise case study of how the COMET-RTE design method is applied to the design of the embedded real-time software for a pump control system.

Chapter 23. Highway Toll Control System Case Study

This chapter describes a concise case study of how the COMET-RTE design method is applied to the design of the distributed embedded real-time software for a highway toll control system.

APPENDIX A. CONVENTIONS USED IN THIS TEXTBOOK

The conventions for naming requirements, analysis, and design artifacts are described. The conventions used for message sequence numbering on interaction diagrams are described.

APPENDIX B. CATALOG OF SOFTWARE ARCHITECTURAL PATTERNS

Each architectural structure and communication pattern is described using a standard design pattern template.

APPENDIX C. PSEUDOCODE TEMPLATES FOR CONCURRENT TASKS

The pseudocode for several different kinds of concurrent tasks is provided.

APPENDIX D. TEACHING CONSIDERATIONS

An outline is given for teaching academic (both graduate and senior undergraduate) courses and industrial courses.

GLOSSARY
BIBLIOGRAPHY
INDEX

Acknowledgments

I gratefully acknowledge the reviewers of earlier drafts of the manuscript for their constructive comments. Hakan Aydin very carefully reviewed Chapter 17 on performance analysis and made several valuable and insightful comments. Kevin Mills and Rob Pettit provided very thorough and constructive reviews of several chapters. The anonymous reviewers provided many helpful comments. I am very grateful to the students in my software modeling and design, real-time software analysis and design, and reusable software architecture courses at George Mason University for their enthusiasm, dedication, and valuable feedback. Many thanks are due to Aparna Keshavamurthy, Ehsan Kouroshfar, Carolyn Koerner, Nan Li, and Upsorn Praphamontripong, for their hard work and careful attention producing the figures. I am also very grateful to the Cambridge University Press editorial and production staff, including Lauren Cowles, and the production staff at Aptara.

I gratefully acknowledge the Software Engineering Institute (SEI) for the material provided on real-time scheduling, on which parts of Chapter 17 are based. I also gratefully acknowledge the permission given to me by Pearson Education, Inc., to use material from my earlier textbooks, *Designing Concurrent, Distributed, and Real-Time Applications with UML,* © *2000 Hassan Gomaa, Reproduced by permission of Pearson Education, Inc.,* and *Designing Software Product Lines with UML,* © *2005 Hassan Gomaa, Reproduced by permission of Pearson Education, Inc.*

Last, but not least, I would like to thank my wife, Gill, for her encouragement, understanding, and support.

PART I

Overview

1

Introduction

This book describes how to design the real-time software for embedded systems. This chapter provides an overview of real-time embedded systems and applications and then describes the major characteristics of real-time embedded systems, both centralized and distributed. This chapter also provides an overview of the emerging field of cyber-physical systems, for which real-time software is a critical component. This chapter then introduces COMET/RTE, the real-time software design method for embedded systems described and applied in this book, which uses the Unified Modeling Language (UML), Systems Modeling Language (SysML), and MARTE (Modeling and Analysis of Real-Time Embedded Systems) visual modeling languages and notations.

1.1 THE CHALLENGE

In the twenty-first century, a growing number of commercial, industrial, military, medical, and consumer products are real-time embedded software intensive systems, which are either software controlled or have a crucial software component to them. These systems range from microwave ovens to Blu-ray™ video recorders, from driverless trains to driverless automobiles to aircraft that "fly by wire," from submarines that explore the depths of the oceans to spacecraft that explore the far reaches of space, from process control systems to factory monitoring and control systems, from robot controllers to elevator controllers, from city traffic control to air traffic control, from "smart" sensors to "smart" phones, from "smart" networks to "smart" grids, an ever-growing volume of mobile and pervasive systems – the list is continually growing. These systems are concurrent, real-time, and embedded. Many of them are also distributed. Real-time software is a critical component of these systems.

1.2 REAL-TIME EMBEDDED SYSTEMS AND APPLICATIONS

A *real-time embedded system* is a real-time computer system (hardware and software) that is part of a larger system (called a *real-time system* or *cyber-physical system*) that typically has mechanical and/or electrical parts, such as an airplane or

3

(UML Deployment Diagram)

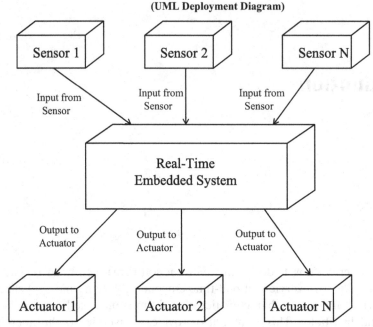

Figure **1.1.** Real-time embedded system.

automobile. A real-time embedded system interfaces to the external environment through sensors and actuators, as depicted in Figure 1.1. An example of a real-time embedded system is a robot controller that is a component of a robot system consisting of one or more mechanical arms, servomechanisms controlling axis motion, multiple sensors to provide inputs to the system from external devices, and multiple actuators to control external devices.

Real-time systems are computer systems with timing constraints. The term *real-time system* usually refers to the whole system, including the real-time application, real-time operating system, and the real-time I/O subsystem, with special-purpose device drivers to interface to a variety of sensors and actuators. Although the emphasis in this book is on designing real-time software, in order to develop high-quality real-time software, it is necessary to consider the complete real-time system, since many software quality attributes, such as performance, availability, safety, and scalability, are heavily dependent on the total hardware/software system.

Real-time systems are often complex because they have to deal with multiple independent sequences of input events and produce multiple outputs. Frequently, the order of incoming events is not predictable. In spite of input events having arrival rates and sequences that might vary significantly and unpredictably with time, the real-time system must be capable of responding to these events in a predictable manner within timing constraints specified in the system requirements.

Real-time systems are frequently classified as hard real-time systems or soft real-time systems. A *hard real-time system*, such as a driverless car or train, has time-critical deadlines, such as an emergency stop in front of an obstacle, which must always be met in order to prevent a disastrous system failure. A hard real-time system in which a system failure could be catastrophic is also called a safety-critical system (Kopetz 2011). A *soft real-time system*, such as an interactive Web-based system, is

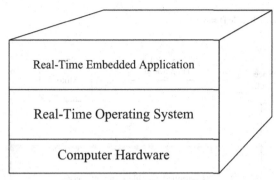

Figure 1.2. Layered architecture of a real-time embedded system.

a real-time system in which missing timing deadlines occasionally, such as response time to a user input, is considered undesirable but not catastrophic.

A real-time embedded system can be designed to have a layered system architecture, as shown in Figure 1.2, consisting of the real-time embedded application, the real-time operating system (with the likely addition of special-purpose device drivers), and the computer hardware.

1.3 CHARACTERISTICS OF REAL-TIME EMBEDDED SYSTEMS

Real-time embedded systems (both centralized and distributed) have several characteristics that distinguish them from other software systems:

a) **Interaction with the external environment**. A real-time embedded system interacts with an external environment that is to a large extent nonhuman. For example, the real-time system might be controlling machines or manufacturing processes, or it might be monitoring chemical processes and reporting alarm conditions.

b) **Sensors and actuators**. Interaction with the external environment necessitates sensors for receiving data from the external environment and actuators for outputting data to and controlling the external environment (see Figure 1.1).

A **sensor** is a device that detects events or changes in a physical property (e.g., temperature) or entity (e.g., switch) and converts the measurement (e.g., of temperature) or event (e.g., switch on) into an electrical or optical signal. For example, a thermocouple is a sensor that converts a measurement of temperature into an analog voltage. An analog-to-digital converter then converts the analog voltage into digital inputs to a real-time computer system (Kopetz 2011, Lee and Seshia 2015).

An **actuator** is the means by which a real-time computer system can control an external device or mechanism. Many actuators are devices that convert electrical energy (e.g., in the form of a current) into some kind of motion, for example to open or close a door, or to switch a light on or off.

c) **Measuring time**. A real-time system models the passage of time from the past through the present and into the future. An **event** occurs at an instant of time (conceptually lasting zero time). A **duration** is an interval of time between two

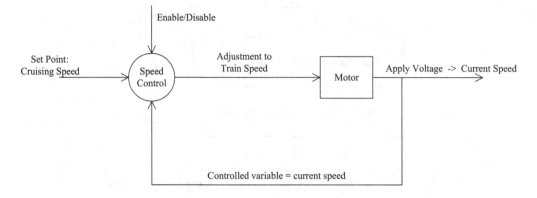

Note: This figure does not conform to the UML notation.

Figure 1.3. Speed control algorithm for automatically controlled train.

events, a starting event and a terminating event. A **period** is a measurement of recurring intervals of the same duration.

There are different units of time in a real-time system. **Execution time** is the CPU time taken to execute a given task on a CPU (or CPUs in a multiprocessor system). **Elapsed time** is the time to execute a task from start to finish, which consists of the task execution time in addition to **blocked time**, which is waiting time when the task is not using the CPU, including waiting for I/O operations to complete, waiting for messages or responses to arrive, waiting to be assigned the CPU, and waiting for entry into critical sections. **Physical time** (or real-world time) is the total time for a real-time command to be completed, for example, to stop a train, which includes the elapsed times of the software tasks involved and then the much longer time required to stop the train physically by applying the brakes and gradually slowing down to a halt.

d) **Timing constraints**. Real-time systems have timing constraints; in particular, they must process events within a given time frame. Whereas in an interactive system, a human might be inconvenienced if the system response is delayed, a delay in a real-time system might be catastrophic. For example, inadequate response in an air traffic control system could result in a midair collision of two aircraft. The required response time will vary by system, ranging from milliseconds in some cases to seconds or even minutes in others.

e) **Real-time control**. A real-time embedded system often involves real-time control. That is, the real-time system makes control decisions based on input data and the current state, without any human intervention. A driverless train has to control the motion of the train automatically, starting from a stationary position, increasing and decreasing speed, cruising at constant speed, slowing down or stopping in the presence of obstacles, and stopping at stations along the route.

In some real-time embedded systems, the control function can be viewed as a process control problem (Kopetz 2011), as shown in Figure 1.3. For example, consider the speed control algorithm in an automatically controlled driverless train. The speed control algorithm has a *set point*, which is the target cruising speed, and a *controlled variable*, which is the current speed of the train.

The speed control algorithm compares the set point with the controlled variable with the goal of increasing or decreasing the current speed of the train as required to make the current speed equal to the cruising speed, plus or minus some small delta value. The positive or negative speed adjustments are converted into electrical voltage and applied to the electric motor, which in turn increases or decreases the speed of the train. A train speed sensor measures the current speed of the train – the controlled variable – and sends the measured speed to the software at regular intervals.

f) **Reactive systems**. Many real-time systems are reactive systems (Harel and Politi 1998). They are event driven and must respond to external stimuli. It is usually the case in reactive systems that the response made by the system to an input stimulus is state dependent; that is, the response depends not only on the stimulus itself but also on what has previously happened in the system, which is captured as the current state of the system.

g) **Concurrency**. Concurrent tasking is an effective solution to the design of real-time embedded systems because it reflects the natural parallelism that exists in the real-time problem domain, in which there are typically many real-world events occurring in parallel. For example, in an air traffic control system, the system is monitoring several aircraft, so many activities are occurring in parallel. Changes in weather conditions can lead to unexpected loads and unpredictable patterns of behavior in the system. A design emphasizing concurrent tasks is clearer and easier to understand because it is a more realistic model of the problem domain than a sequential program. In *multiprocessing systems*, such as *multicore systems*, concurrent tasks can take advantage of multiple CPUs, since any given task can execute in parallel with other tasks executing on other CPUs.

1.4 DISTRIBUTED REAL-TIME EMBEDDED SYSTEMS

Many real-time systems are also distributed. A distributed real-time embedded system executes in an environment consisting of multiple nodes that are in locally or geographically separated locations. In the example given in Figure 1.4, each node consists of a real-time embedded subsystem. Locally separated nodes are connected to each other by means of a *local area network*, while geographically separated nodes are connected to each other by means of a *wide area network*.

A distributed real-time embedded system has the following advantages:

Distributed control. Instead of being centralized, control is distributed among several interconnected nodes in configurations that can be hierarchical or peer-to-peer.

Improved availability. Operation is feasible in a reduced configuration in cases in which some nodes are temporarily unavailable. It is advantageous to design the system such that it has no single point of failure.

Flexible configuration. A given system can be configured in different ways by selecting the appropriate number of nodes for a given instance of the system.

Localized control and management. A distributed subsystem, executing on its own node, can be designed to be autonomous, so it can to a large extent execute independently relative to other subsystems on other nodes.

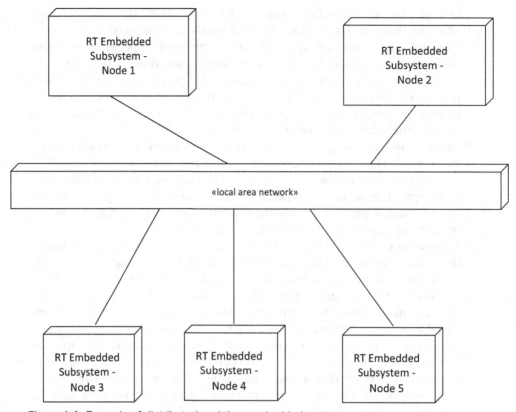

Figure 1.4. Example of distributed real-time embedded system.

Incremental system expansion. If the system gets overloaded, the system can be expanded by adding more nodes.

Load balancing. In some systems, the overall system load can be shared among several nodes and can be dynamically adjusted with varying loads.

Figure 1.5 depicts an example of a layered architecture for a distributed real-time embedded system in which the distributed nodes are interconnected by means of a local area network. Each node consists of several layers, which are the real-time embedded application software, middleware, real-time operating system, and communication software, with the computer and network hardware at the lowest layer. Compared to Figure 1.2, there are additional middleware and communication software layers, as well as additional network hardware in the hardware layer. The communication software allows distributed nodes to communicate with each other using network protocols, such as the Internet Protocol (IP). Middleware is a software layer that lies above the operating system and communication software to provide a uniform platform above which distributed applications can run (Bacon 2003), for example, to provide message communication between applications executing on different nodes. Distributed operating systems often integrate the middleware into the operating system.

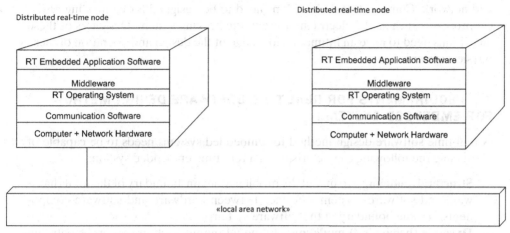

Figure 1.5. Example of layered architecture of a distributed real-time embedded system.

1.4.1 The Internet of Things

The **Internet of Things** (IoT) is a concept of interconnecting physical things to the Internet. This is achieved by connecting remote sensors and actuators to the Internet, with the objective of providing remote access to sensor data and remote control of physical devices over the Internet (Kopetz 2011). RFID is a technology that can be used to enable the connection of physical things (referred to as smart objects) to the Internet. A low-cost electronic RFID tag is attached to a physical product, allowing the product to become a smart object that can be uniquely identified over the Internet. The IoT provides a means for integrating real-time embedded systems with the Internet.

1.5 CYBER-PHYSICAL SYSTEMS

A National Science Foundation vision statement describes **cyber-physical systems** (CPS) as "smart networked systems with embedded sensors, processors and actuators that are designed to sense and interact with the physical world, and support real-time, guaranteed performance in safety-critical applications. In CPS systems, the joint behavior of the 'cyber' and 'physical' elements of the system is critical – computing, control, sensing and networking can be deeply integrated into every component, and the actions of components and systems must be safe and interoperable" (Lee and Seshia 2015).

The design of cyber-physical systems considers the design and integration of both the embedded cyber system and the physical processes. Furthermore, the real-time software design of cyber systems, which monitor and control the physical processes, is critical in the design of cyber-physical systems.

The automated driverless train described in Section 1.3 is an example of both an embedded system and a cyber-physical system. In the design of the train CPS, the design of physical systems such as the electric motor, braking system, speed control system, and transmission, etc. have to be considered in addition to the design of the embedded cyber system consisting of the computer hardware, real-time software, and network. Computational algorithms need to be designed for controlling physical processes such as the electric motor and the braking system. Designers of these algorithms need to have an intimate knowledge of the design and operation of these physical systems.

1.6 REQUIREMENTS FOR REAL-TIME SOFTWARE DESIGN METHOD FOR EMBEDDED SYSTEMS

A real-time software design method for embedded systems needs to be capable of addressing the following characteristics of a real-time embedded system:

- **Structural modeling** – to model the problem domain, boundary of the total (hardware and software) system, interface between hardware and software components, and the boundary of the software system.
- **Dynamic (behavioral) modeling** – to model the interaction sequences between system and software artifacts at the requirements, analysis, and design levels.
- **State machines** – to react to external events as determined by both the input and the current state of the system.
- **Concurrency** – to handle multiple input sequences and unpredictable loads by modeling activities that execute in parallel with each other.
- **Component-based software architecture** – to provide an architecture consisting of concurrent object-oriented components and connectors, such that components can be deployed to different nodes in a distributed environment.
- **Performance analysis of real-time designs** – to analyze the performance of the real-time system before its implementation to provide an early determination of whether the system will meet its performance goals.

These requirements are all addressed by the COMET/RTE real-time software design method for embedded systems described in this book. How these requirements are addressed by COMET/RTE is described in Chapter 4. An overview of COMET/RTE is given next.

1.7 COMET/RTE: A REAL-TIME SOFTWARE DESIGN METHOD FOR EMBEDDED SYSTEMS

This book describes a software modeling and architectural design method called COMET/RTE (*C*oncurrent *O*bject *M*odeling and Architectural Design *Met*hod for **R**eal-**T**ime Embedded Systems), which is tailored to the needs of real-time embedded systems. COMET/RTE is an iterative use case–driven and object-oriented method that addresses the requirements, analysis, and design modeling phases of the system and software development life cycle.

Structural modeling is used to analyze the problem domain from a systems engineering perspective, identifying the static structure of the total hardware/software system and then the boundary between hardware and software. *Requirements modeling* is used to determine the functional and nonfunctional requirements of the system. In *use case modeling*, the functional requirements are described in terms of actors and use cases. In *analysis modeling* for real-time embedded systems, the emphasis is on *dynamic modeling*. The use cases are realized to describe the objects that participate in the use case and their interactions. The state dependent parts of the system are analyzed using state machines. In *design modeling*, the software architecture is developed, addressing issues of distribution, concurrency, and object orientation. Concurrent components use a blend of object-oriented and concurrency concepts to enable the distribution of components among several nodes in a distributed configuration.

1.8 VISUAL MODELING LANGUAGES: UML, SYSML, AND MARTE

The Unified Modeling Language (UML) is a standardized visual modeling language and notation for describing software requirements and designs. For the UML notation to be applied effectively, however, it needs to be used with an object-oriented analysis and design method. Although UML is sufficient for modeling most software applications, it needs to be supplemented for modeling real-time embedded systems. The Systems Modeling Language (SysML) is used to model the total hardware/software system from a systems engineering perspective. MARTE provides UML extensions for modeling real-time systems.

Modern object-oriented analysis and design methods are model-based and use a combination of use case modeling, static modeling, state machine modeling, and object interaction modeling. Almost all modern object-oriented methods (such as COMET, as described in Gomaa 2011) use the UML notation for describing software requirements, analysis, and design models (Booch et al. 2005; Fowler 2004; Rumbaugh et al. 2005). This book describes how COMET/RTE can be used to design real-time embedded systems using a blend of the UML, SysML, and MARTE modeling languages and notations.

1.9 SUMMARY

This chapter has described the characteristics of real-time embedded systems and applications. It has provided overviews of the COMET/RTE design method for real-time embedded systems and of its use of visual modeling languages and notations. Chapter 2 provides an overview of the UML, SysML, and MARTE modeling language and notations, in particular those parts that are used by COMET/RTE. Chapter 3 describes the fundamental design concepts on which concurrent object-oriented design for real-time embedded systems is based. It describes object-oriented concepts, the concurrent tasking concept including task communication and synchronization, as well as operating system support for concurrent tasks. Chapter 4 provides an overview of the COMET/RTE design method as well as the system and software life cycle for real-time embedded systems. Chapters 5 through 18 describe the details of the method, and Chapters 19 through 23 describe case studies of applying COMET/RTE to design real-time embedded systems.

A comprehensive and wide ranging textbook on real-time systems is Kopetz (2011). Other informative textbooks on real-time systems are Burns and Wellings (2009), Laplante (2011), Lee and Seshia (2015), and Li and Yao (2003).

2

Overview of UML, SysML, and MARTE

The notation used for the COMET/RTE method is the Unified Modeling Language (UML), supplemented with the Systems Modeling Language (SysML) and Modeling and Analysis of Real-Time Embedded Systems (MARTE). This chapter provides a brief overview of these three related visual modeling notations.

The Object Management Group (OMG) maintains UML and SysML as standards. The UML notation has evolved since it was first adopted as a standard in 1997. A major revision to the standard was the introduction of UML 2.0 in 2003. Since then there have been further minor changes, and the latest version of the standard is UML 2.4. The versions of the standard before UML 2 are referred to as UML 1.x, and the current version is generally referred to as UML 2. SysML is based on UML 2, using some parts of UML 2 and extending it in other areas for systems modeling. MARTE is a more recent UML profile for real-time embedded systems. Each of these notations is of a significant size, and it is therefore beneficial for the real-time system modeler to pick and choose carefully among the multitude of diagrams and stereotypes provided by these notations.

The UML notation has grown substantially over the years and supports many diagrams. SysML and MARTE extend the modeling notations further. The approach taken in this book is to use only those parts of the UML and SysML notation that provide a distinct benefit to the design of real-time embedded systems, and to use the parts of MARTE that can be most usefully blended with UML and SysML for the design of these systems. This chapter describes the main features of the UML, SysML, and MARTE notations that are particularly suited for real-time design using the COMET/RTE method. The purpose of this chapter is not to be a full exposition of UML, SysML, and MARTE, because several detailed books exist on these topics, but rather to provide a brief overview of each. The main features of each of the diagrams used in this book are briefly described, but lesser-used features are omitted.

2.1 MODEL-DRIVEN ARCHITECTURE WITH SysML AND UML

In the OMG's view, "modeling is the designing of software applications before coding" (OMG 2015). The OMG promotes model-driven architecture as the approach in which UML models of the software architecture are developed prior to implementation. According to the OMG, UML is methodology-independent; UML is a notation for describing the results of an object-oriented analysis and design developed via the methodology of choice.

SysML can be used to model the total hardware/software embedded system to help design the hardware/software interface, and then UML can be used to model the software system in more detail. MARTE is a UML profile that is a real-time extension of UML that supports concepts for real-time embedded systems (Selic and Gerard 2014).

A UML model can be either a platform-independent model (PIM) or a platform-specific model (PSM). The PIM is a precise model of the software architecture before a commitment is made to a specific platform. Developing the PIM first is particularly useful because the same PIM can be mapped to different platforms, such as .NET, J2EE, Web Services, or a RTE platform. A typical real-time embedded platform might consist of one or more processors connected by a high-speed system bus or local area network, interfacing to several sensors and actuators.

The approach in this book is to use the concept of model-driven architecture to develop a component-based software architecture, which is expressed as a UML PIM. The PIM is then mapped to a PSM deployed to a specific configuration, the performance of which can then be analyzed using real-time scheduling, as described in Chapter 17.

2.1.1 UML Diagrams

The UML diagrams used in this book for real-time embedded system development are:

- **Use case diagram**, briefly described in Section 2.2.
- **Class diagram**, briefly described in Section 2.4.
- **Sequence diagram**, briefly described in Section 2.5.1.
- **Communication diagram**, which in UML 1.x was called the *collaboration diagram*, briefly described in Section 2.5.2.

Sequence and communication diagrams can also be used for modeling concurrent systems, as briefly described in Section 2.8.

- **State machine diagram** (also referred to as a *statechart*), briefly described in Section 2.6.
- **Composite structure diagram**, briefly described in Section 2.10, is used for modeling distributed components in a UML PIM.
- **Package diagram**, briefly described in Section 2.7.
- **Deployment diagram**, briefly described in Section 2.9.
- **Timing diagram**, briefly described in Section 2.14, is a time-annotated sequence diagram.

How these UML diagrams are used by the COMET/RTE method is described in Chapters 5 through 18 and in the case studies described in Chapters 19 through 23 of this book.

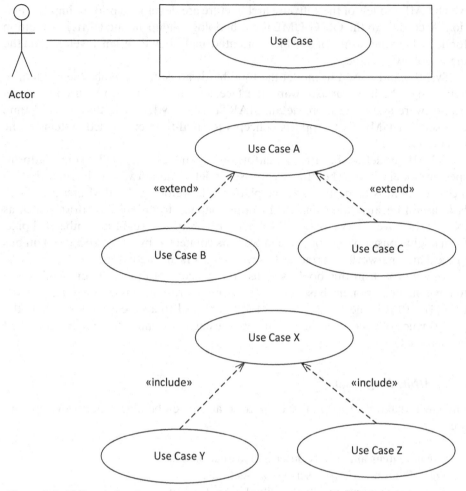

Figure 2.1. UML notation for a use case diagram.

2.2 USE CASE DIAGRAMS

A **use case** defines a sequence of interactions between the actor(s) and the system. An *actor* is external to the system and is depicted as a stick figure on a use case diagram. The system is depicted as a box. A use case is depicted as an ellipse inside the box. Communication associations connect actors with the use cases in which they participate. Relationships among use cases are defined by means of *include* and *extend* relationships. The notation is depicted in Figure 2.1.

2.3 CLASSES AND OBJECTS

Classes and objects are depicted as boxes in the UML notation, as shown in Figure 2.2. The class box always holds the class name. Optionally, the attributes and operations of a class may also be depicted. When all three are depicted, the top compartment of the box holds the class name, the middle compartment holds the attributes, and the bottom compartment holds the operations.

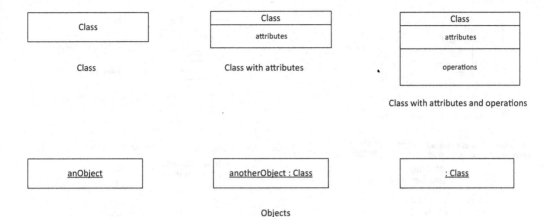

Figure 2.2. UML notation for objects and classes.

To distinguish between a class (the type) and an object (an instance of the type), an object name is shown underlined. An object can be depicted in full with the object name separated by a colon from the class name – for example, anObject : Class. Optionally, the colon and class name may be omitted, leaving just the object name – for example, anObject. Another option is to omit the object name and depict just the class name after the colon, as in : Class. Classes and objects are depicted on various UML diagrams, as described in Section 2.4.

2.4 CLASS DIAGRAMS

In a **class diagram**, classes are depicted as boxes, and the static (i.e., permanent) relationships between them are depicted as lines connecting the boxes. The following three main types of relationships between classes are supported: associations, whole/part relationships, and generalization/specialization relationships, as shown in Figure 2.3. A fourth relationship, the dependency relationship, is often used to show how packages are related, as described in Section 2.7.

2.4.1 Associations

An **association** is a static, structural relationship between two or more classes. An association between two classes, which is referred to as a *binary association*, is depicted as a line joining the two class boxes, such as the line connecting the ClassA box to the ClassB box in Figure 2.3a. An association has a name and optionally a small black arrowhead to depict the direction in which the association name should be read. On each end of the association line joining the classes is the multiplicity of the association, which indicates how many instances of one class are related to an instance of the other class. Optionally, a stick arrow may also be used to depict the direction of navigability, such as shown in the association from ClassA to ClassC in Figure 2.3a.

The **multiplicity** of an association specifies how many instances of one class may relate to a single instance of another class (Figure 2.3b). The multiplicity of an association can be exactly one (1), optional (0..1), zero or more ($*$), one or more (1..$*$), or

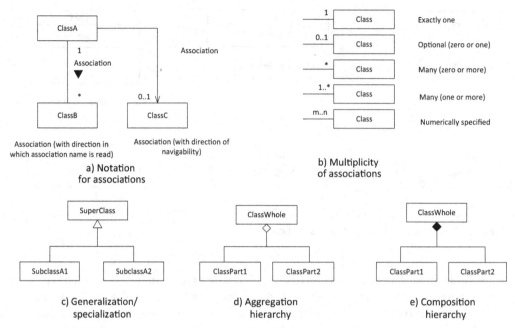

Figure 2.3. UML notation for relationships on a class diagram.

numerically specified (m..n), where *m* and *n* have numeric values. Associations are described in more detail with examples in Chapter 5.

2.4.2 Aggregation and Composition Hierarchies

Aggregation and composition hierarchies are **whole/part** relationships. The composition relationship (shown by a black diamond) is a stronger form of whole/part relationship than the aggregation relationship is (shown by a hollow diamond). The diamond touches the aggregate or composite (Class Whole) class box (see Figures 2.3d and 2.3e). More detail with examples is provided in Chapter 5.

2.4.3 Generalization/Specialization Hierarchy

A generalization/specialization hierarchy is an **inheritance** relationship. A generalization is depicted as an arrow joining the subclass (child) to the superclass (parent), with the arrowhead touching the superclass box (see Figure 2.3c).

2.4.4 Visibility

Visibility refers to whether an element of the class is visible from outside the class, as depicted in Figure 2.4. Depicting visibility is optional on a class diagram. **Public visibility**, denoted with a + symbol, means that the element is visible from outside the class. **Private visibility**, denoted with a – symbol, means that the element is visible only from within the class that defines it and is thus hidden from other classes. **Protected visibility**, denoted with a # symbol, means that the element is visible from within the class that defines it and within all subclasses of the class.

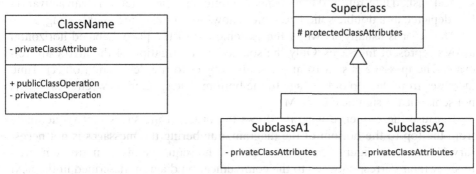

Figure 2.4. UML notation for visibility on a class diagram.

2.5 INTERACTION DIAGRAMS

UML has two kinds of interaction diagrams, which depict how objects interact: the sequence diagram and the communication diagram. On these interaction diagrams, objects are depicted in rectangular boxes. However, **object names are not underlined**. The main features of these diagrams are described in Sections 2.5.1 and 2.5.2. Sequence diagrams and communication diagrams depict similar, although not necessarily identical, information, but do so in different ways.

2.5.1 Sequence Diagrams

A sequence diagram depicts cooperating objects dynamically interacting with each other in time sequence, as shown in Figure 2.5. A **sequence diagram** is a two-dimensional diagram in which the objects participating in the interaction are depicted horizontally, the vertical dimension represents time, and the sequence of message interactions is depicted from top to bottom. Starting at each object box is a

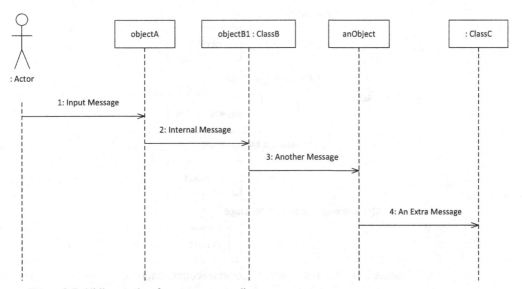

Figure 2.5. UML notation for a sequence diagram.

vertical dashed line, referred to as a *lifeline*. Optionally, each lifeline has an activation bar, depicted as a double solid line, which shows when the object is executing.

The actor is usually shown at the extreme left of the page. Labeled horizontal arrows represent messages. Only the source and destination of the arrow are relevant. The message is sent from the source object to the destination object. Time increases from the top of the page to the bottom. The spacing between messages is not semantically significant in UML.

Because the sequence diagram shows the order of messages sent sequentially from the top to the bottom of the diagram, numbering the messages is not necessary. However, in Figure 2.5, the messages on the sequence diagram are numbered to show their correspondence to the communication diagram described in the next section.

In addition to depicting specific scenarios, sequence diagrams can be extended to depict multiple scenarios on the same diagram by incorporating loops and alternative sequences, as described in Chapter 9.

2.5.2 Communication Diagrams

A different way of illustrating the interaction among objects is to show them on a **communication diagram**, which shows the objects participating in the interaction and the sequence of messages passed among them. Objects are shown as boxes, and lines joining boxes represent object interconnection. Labeled arrows adjacent to the arcs indicate the name and direction of message transmission between objects. The sequence of messages passed between the objects is numbered. The notation for communication diagrams is illustrated in Figure 2.6. An iteration, as illustrated for message 3 in Figure 2.6, is indicated by an asterisk (∗), which means that a message may be sent more than once. A conditional message means that the message is only sent if the condition shown in square brackets is true.

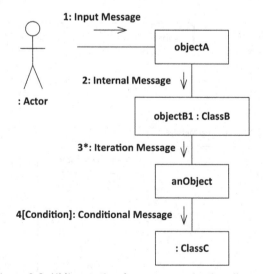

Figure 2.6. UML notation for a communication diagram.

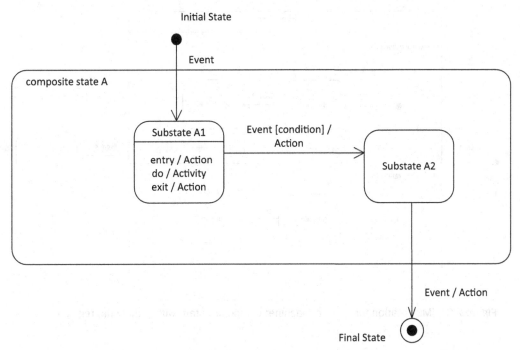

Figure 2.7. UML notation for a state machine: composite state with sequential substates.

2.6 STATE MACHINE DIAGRAMS

In the UML notation, a state transition diagram is referred to as a **state machine** diagram or *statechart diagram*. In this book, the shorter term **state machine** is generally used. In the UML notation, states are represented by rounded boxes, and transitions are represented by arcs that connect the rounded boxes, as shown in Figure 2.7. The initial state of the state machine is depicted as an arc originating from a small black circle. Optionally, a final state may be depicted by a small black circle inside a larger white circle, sometimes referred to as a *bull's eye*. A state machine may be hierarchically decomposed such that a composite state is broken down into substates.

On the arc representing the state transition, the notation *Event [Condition]/ Action* is used. The **event** causes the state transition. The optional Boolean **condition** must be true, when the event occurs, for the transition to take place. The optional **action** is performed as a result of the transition. Optionally, a state may have any of the following:

- An **entry action**, performed when the state is entered
- An **activity**, performed for the duration of the state
- An **exit action**, performed on exit from the state

Figure 2.7 depicts a composite state A decomposed into sequential substates A1 and A2. In this case, the state machine is in only one substate at a time; that is, first substate A1 is entered and then substate A2. Figure 2.8 depicts a composite state B decomposed into orthogonal regions BC and BD. In this case the state machine is in each of the orthogonal regions, BC and BD, at the same time. Each orthogonal region is

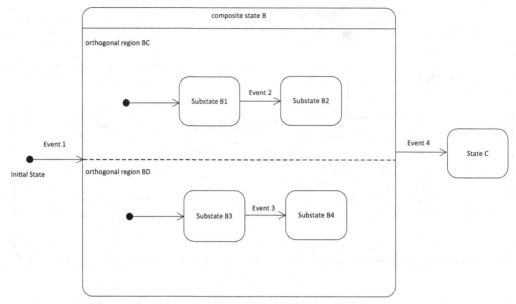

Figure 2.8. UML notation for a state machine: composite state with orthogonal regions.

further decomposed into sequential substates. Thus, when the composite state B is initially entered, each of the substates B1 and B3 is also entered.

2.7 PACKAGE DIAGRAMS

In UML, a **package** is a grouping of model elements – for example, to represent a system or subsystem. A package diagram is a structural diagram used to model packages and their relationships, as shown in Figure 2.9. A package is depicted by a folder icon, a large rectangle with a small rectangle attached on one corner. Packages may also be nested within other packages. Possible relationships between packages are dependency (shown in Figure 2.9) and generalization/specialization relationships. Packages may be used to contain classes, objects, or use cases.

2.8 CONCURRENT SEQUENCE AND COMMUNICATION DIAGRAMS

An **active object** – also referred to as a *concurrent object*, *process*, *thread*, or *task* – has its own thread of control and executes concurrently with other objects. By contrast, a **passive object** has no thread of control. A passive object executes only when another object (active or passive) invokes one of its operations.

In UML, active objects are depicted on concurrent interaction diagrams, either **concurrent sequence diagrams** or **concurrent communication diagrams**. On a concurrent sequence or communication diagram, an active object is depicted as a rectangular box with two vertical parallel lines on the left- and right-hand sides; a passive object is depicted as a regular rectangular box. An example is given in Figure 2.10, which depicts the notation for active and passive objects. Also shown is the notation for multiple instances of an object, which is used when more than one object can be instantiated from the same class. The multiplicity indicator (e.g., 1..*) is depicted in

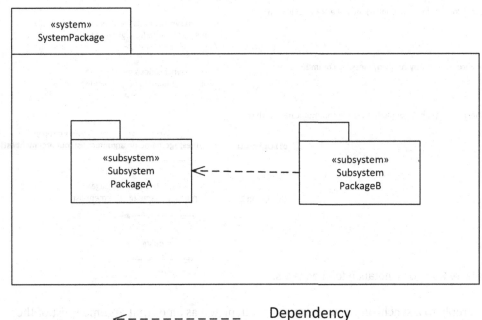

Dependency

Figure 2.9. UML notation for packages.

the upper right-hand corner of the rectangular box and can be omitted if the multiplicity is 1.

2.8.1 Message Communication on Concurrent Communication Diagrams

Message interfaces between tasks on concurrent communication diagrams are either **asynchronous** or **synchronous**. For synchronous message communication, two possibilities exist: (1) synchronous message communication with reply and (2) synchronous message communication without reply.

The UML notation for message communication is summarized in Figure 2.11. Asynchronous messages are depicted with a stick arrowhead while synchronous messages are depicted with a black filled arrowhead. The contents of the message are depicted as an input argument list of the message as depicted in Figure 2.11 a) and b).

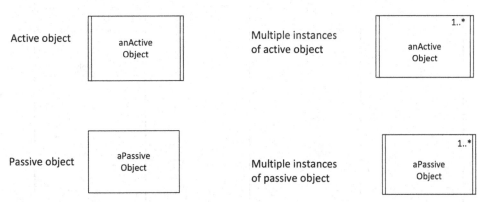

Figure 2.10. UML notation for active and passive objects.

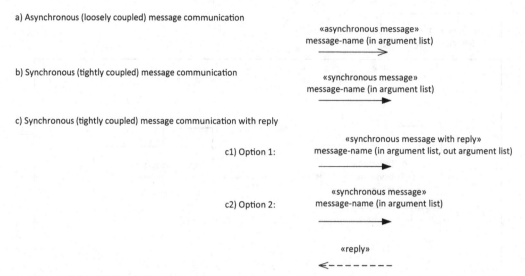

a) Asynchronous (loosely coupled) message communication

«asynchronous message»
message-name (in argument list)

b) Synchronous (tightly coupled) message communication

«synchronous message»
message-name (in argument list)

c) Synchronous (tightly coupled) message communication with reply

c1) Option 1:

«synchronous message with reply»
message-name (in argument list, out argument list)

c2) Option 2:

«synchronous message»
message-name (in argument list)

«reply»

Figure 2.11. UML notation for messages.

A reply to a synchronous message can be depicted as an output argument list of the original message as illustrated in c1) option 1 in Figure 2.11. Alternatively, the reply can be depicted as a dashed arrow with a stick arrowhead as illustrated in c2) option 2 in Figure 2.11.

Figure 2.12 and 2.13 respectively depict concurrent versions of interaction diagrams, namely the concurrent sequence and concurrent communication diagram.

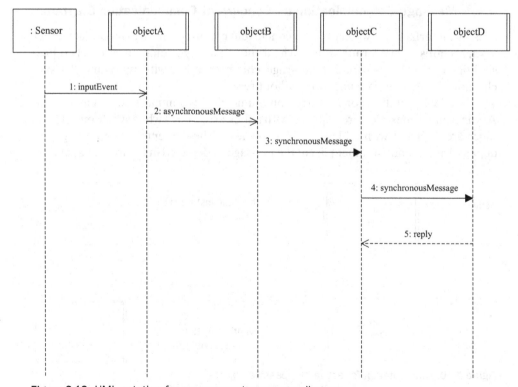

Figure 2.12. UML notation for a concurrent sequence diagram.

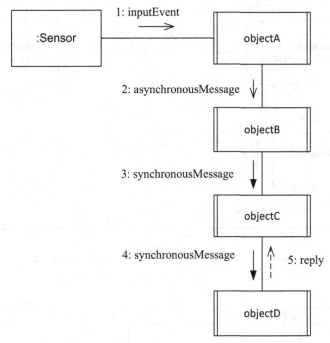

Figure 2.13. UML notation for a concurrent communication diagram.

Each diagram depicts active objects and the various kinds of message communication between them. In both diagrams, objectA, after receiving an input event from an external sensor, sends an asynchronous message (message #2) to objectB, which in turn sends a synchronous message (message #3 without reply) to objectC, which in turn sends a synchronous message (#4) to objectD, which then responds by sending a reply (#5).

2.9 DEPLOYMENT DIAGRAMS

A **deployment diagram** shows the physical configuration of the system in terms of physical nodes and physical connections between the nodes, such as network connections. A node is shown as a cube, and the connection is shown as a line joining the nodes. A deployment diagram is essentially a class diagram that focuses on the system's nodes (Booch et al. 2005).

In this book, a node usually represents a computer node, with an optional constraint (see Section 2.10.3) describing how many instances of this node may exist. The physical connection has a stereotype (see Section 2.10.1) to indicate the type of connection, such as «local area network» or «wide area network». Figure 2.14 shows two examples of deployment diagrams: In the first example, nodes are connected via a wide area network (WAN); in the second, they are connected via a local area network (LAN). In the first example, the ATM Client node (which has one node for each ATM) is connected to a Bank Server that has one node. Optionally, the objects that reside at the node may be depicted in the node cube. In the second example, the network is shown as a node cube. This form of the notation is used when more than two computer nodes are connected by a network.

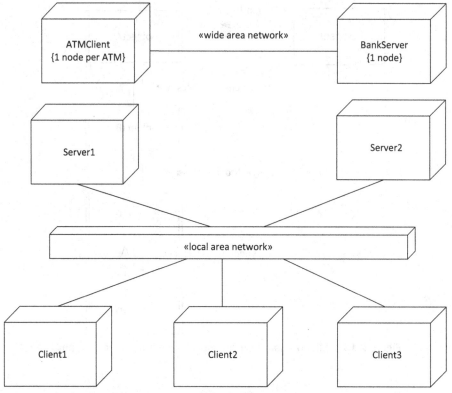

Figure 2.14. UML notation for a deployment diagram.

2.10 COMPOSITE STRUCTURE DIAGRAMS

Composite structure diagrams are used to depict component-based software architectures consisting of components and their interfaces. An **interface** specifies the externally visible operations of a class, service or component without revealing the internal structure (implementation) of the operations. Since the same interface can be implemented in different ways, an interface can be modeled separately from a component that realizes (i.e., implements) the interface.

An interface can be depicted with a different name from the class or component that realizes the interface. To improve clarity across UML diagrams, the name of an interface starts with the letter I. There are two ways to depict an interface: simple and expanded. In the simple case, the interface is depicted as a little circle with the interface name next to it. The class or component that provides the interface is connected to the small circle, as shown in Figure 2.15a.

In the expanded case, the interface is depicted in a rectangular box, as shown in Figure 2.15b, with the stereotype «interface» and the interface name in the first compartment. The operations of the interface are depicted in the third compartment. The second compartment is left blank (note that in other texts, interfaces are sometimes depicted with the middle compartment omitted). An example of an interface is IBasicAlarmService, which provides two operations, one to read alarm data and one to post new alarms.

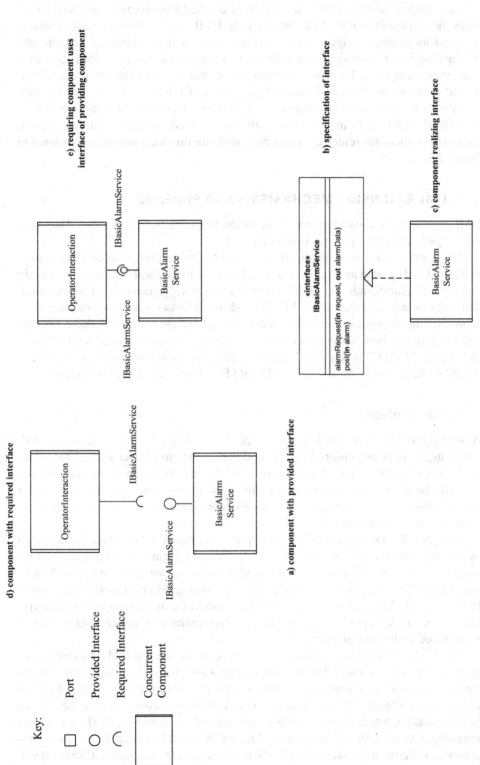

Figure 2.15. UML notation for components and interfaces.

25

The component that realizes the interface is called BasicAlarmService, which provides the implementation of the interface. In UML, the realization relationship is depicted as shown in Figure 2.15c (dashed arrow with a triangular arrowhead). A required interface is depicted with a small semi-circle notation with the interface name next to it. The class or component that requires the interface is connected to the semi-circle, as shown in Figure 2.15d. To show that a component with a required interface uses a component with a provided interface, the semi-circle (sometimes referred to as a socket) with the required interface is drawn around the circle (sometimes referred to as a ball) with the provided interface, as shown in Figure 2.15e.

2.11 UML EXTENSION MECHANISMS AND PROFILES

UML provides three mechanisms to allow the language to be extended. These are *stereotypes*, *tagged values*, and *constraints*.

These extension mechanisms are also used to create UML *profiles*. Rumbaugh defines a UML **profile** as a "coherent set of extensions applicable to a given domain or purpose" (Rumbaugh et al. 2005). Two relevant UML profiles for real-time embedded systems are SysML and MARTE. SysML addresses systems modeling concepts that are important for embedded systems because models of these systems need to consider how hardware components and software components interface to each other. MARTE is relevant because it addresses real-time concepts. SysML is described further in Section 2.12, and MARTE is described further in Section 2.13.

2.11.1 Stereotypes

A **stereotype** defines a new building block that is derived from an existing UML modeling element but tailored to the modeler's problem (Booch et al. 2005). This book makes extensive use of stereotypes. Several standard stereotypes are defined in UML. In addition, a modeler may define new stereotypes. This chapter includes several examples of stereotypes, both standard and COMET-specific. Stereotypes are indicated by guillemets (« »).

In Figure 2.1, two specific kinds of dependency between use cases are depicted by the stereotype notation: «include» and «extend». Figure 2.9 shows the stereotypes «system» and «subsystem» to distinguish between two different kinds of packages. Figure 2.11 uses stereotypes to distinguish among different kinds of messages. In UML, a modeling element can also be depicted by more than one stereotype. Therefore, different, possibly orthogonal, characteristics of a modeling element can be depicted with different stereotypes.

The UML stereotype notation allows a modeler to tailor a UML modeling element to a specific problem. In UML, stereotypes are enclosed in guillemets usually within the modeling element (e.g., class or object) as depicted in Figure 2.16a, in which the class Sensor Input is depicted as a «boundary» class to distinguish it from Elevator Control, which is depicted as a «control» class. However, UML also allows stereotypes to be depicted as symbols. One of the most common such representations was introduced by Jacobson (1992) and is used in the Unified Software Development Process (USDP) (Jacobson et al. 1999). Stereotypes are used to represent «entity» classes, «boundary» classes, and «control» classes. Figure 2.16b depicts the

a) Standard UML notation for depicting stereotypes

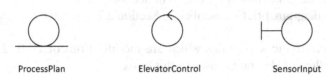

«entity» ProcessPlan	«control» ElevatorControl	«boundary» SensorInput

b) Alternative notation for stereotypes used in Unified Software Development Process

ProcessPlan   ElevatorControl   SensorInput

Figure 2.16. UML notation for stereotypes.

Process Plan «entity» class, the Elevator Control «control» class, and the Sensor Input «boundary» class using the USDP's stereotype symbols.

2.11.2 Tagged Values

A **tagged value** extends the properties of a UML building block (Booch et al. 2005), thereby adding new information. A tagged value is enclosed in braces in the form {tag = value}. Commas separate additional tagged values. For example, a class may be depicted with the tagged values {version = 1.0, author = Gill}, as shown in Figure 2.17.

2.11.3 Constraints

A **constraint** specifies a condition that must be true. In UML, a constraint is an extension of the semantics of a UML element to allow the addition of new rules or modifications to existing rules (Booch et al. 2005). For example, for the Account class depicted in Figure 2.17, the constraint on the attribute balance is that the balance can never be negative, depicted as {balance > = 0}. Optionally, UML provides the Object Constraint Language (Warmer and Kleppe 1999) for expressing constraints.

2.12 SysML

SysML is a general-purpose visual modeling language for modeling systems requirements and designs. It has been approved as a standard by OMG. As with UML,

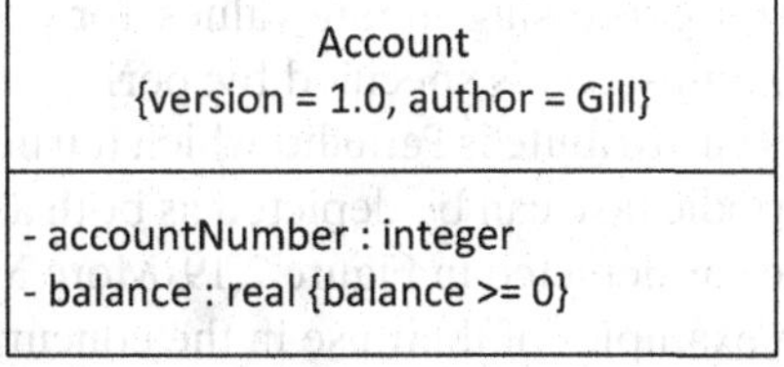

Account {version = 1.0, author = Gill}
- accountNumber : integer - balance : real {balance >= 0}

Figure 2.17. UML notation for tagged values and constraints.

SysML is methodology-independent. SysML is based on a subset of UML 2 with extensions for systems modeling.

From UML 2, SysML incorporates the following diagrams without change, which are used in this book:

- **Use case diagram**, briefly described in Section 2.2.
- **State machine diagram**, briefly described in Section 2.6.
- **Sequence diagram**, briefly described in Section 2.5.1.
- **Package diagram**, briefly described in Section 2.7.

SysML also introduces diagrams which are modifications of UML 2 diagrams. Of these, the following diagram is used in this book:

- **Block definition diagram**, which is a modification of the class diagram and is briefly described next.

2.12.1 Block Definition Diagrams

SysML uses block definition diagrams to depict the system in terms of blocks, which are hardware, software, or people structural elements. SysML blocks are static structural elements that are based on UML classes and extend the capabilities of UML classes (Friedenthal et al. 2015). The block notation is compatible with the class notation, which means that UML class diagrams in which classes have the stereotype «block» are used as SysML block definition diagrams.

Thus, a block definition diagram is equivalent to a class diagram in which the classes have been stereotyped as blocks. This allows a block definition diagram to represent and depict the same modeling relationships as a class diagram, in particular associations, whole/part (composition or aggregation) relationships, and generalization/specialization relationships. Thus, composite relationships are used to depict how a real-world embedded system is composed of blocks. The modeling notation for block definition diagrams is given in Figure 2.18, which is essentially the same notation as in Figure 2.3, except for the classes stereotyped as blocks.

2.13 MARTE PROFILE

MARTE is a UML profile developed explicitly for real-time embedded systems. It provides several stereotypes for modeling elements in these systems. Examples depicted in Figure 2.19 are stereotypes for a hardware device, which is depicted as «hwDevice», a timer device, which is referred to as a timer resource and depicted as «timerResource», and a software task, which is referred to as a software schedulable resource and depicted as «swSchedulableResource».

MARTE also allows for expressing timing values, for example a timer resource can have a period of 100 milliseconds specified by: period = (100, ms). The «timerResource» stereotype has an attribute is Periodic, which if true means that the timer is recurring. A software periodic task can be depicted as both a «timerResource» and a «swSchedulableResource» as depicted in Figure 2.19. More MARTE stereotypes are given in Chapter 13, with examples of their use in the concurrent design of real-time embedded systems.

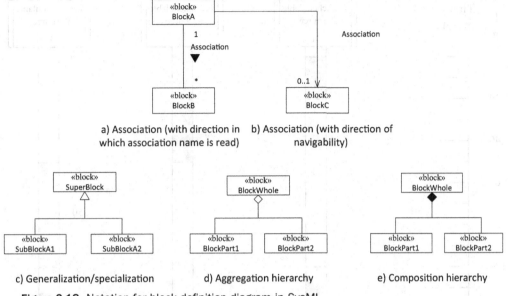

a) Association (with direction in   b) Association (with direction of
which association name is read)   navigability)

c) Generalization/specialization   d) Aggregation hierarchy   e) Composition hierarchy

Figure 2.18. Notation for block definition diagram in SysML.

2.14 TIMING DIAGRAMS

A **timing diagram** is a time annotated sequence diagram, which is a sequence diagram that depicts a time-ordered execution sequence of a collection of concurrent tasks. Time is explicitly labelled on the left hand side of the page, uniformly increasing from the top of the page to the bottom in equally spaced intervals. The lifelines depict the tasks as active throughout, with the shaded portions identifying when tasks are executing on a CPU and for how long. Depending on whether there is one or more CPUs in the configuration, the timing diagram can explicitly depict parallel execution of tasks on multiple CPUs. If there is only one CPU, as in the example in

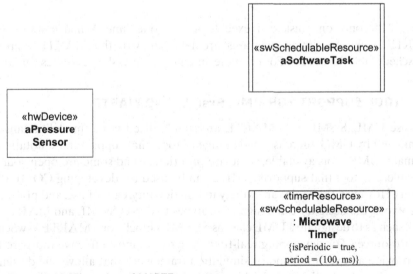

Figure 2.19. Examples of MARTE stereotypes.

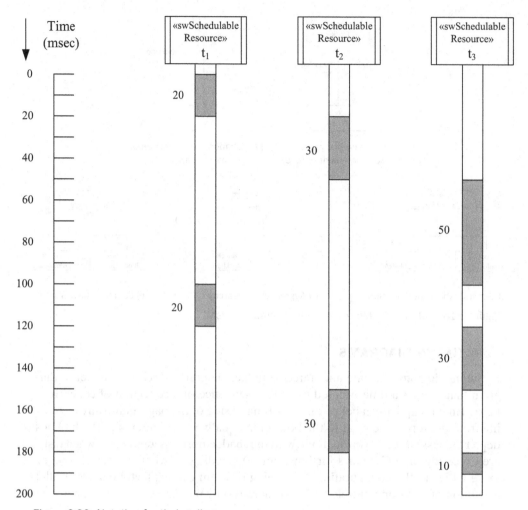

Figure 2.20. Notation for timing diagram.

Figure 2.20, only one task can execute at any one time. When combined with MARTE, tasks on timing diagrams are labelled with the MARTE stereotype «swSchedulableResource». For example, in Figure 2.20, task t_1 executes for 20 msec.

2.15 TOOL SUPPORT FOR UML, SysML, AND MARTE

Because UML, SysML, and MARTE are standardized visual modeling languages maintained by OMG, there is a wide range of tools that support these notations. Of the many UML tools available, some are proprietary and some are open source. In principle, any tool that supports UML 2 can be used for developing COMET/RTE designs. However, the tools vary widely in functionality, ease of use, and price. Using stereotypes, the designer can assign stereotypes to depict SysML and MARTE concepts, such as to designate a UML class as a SysML «block» or a MARTE «swSchedulableResource». For developing real-time designs, the most effective tools are those that provide an execution and/or simulation framework that allows the designer to dynamically execute the model. This enables the designer to validate the design by iteratively detecting and correcting design flaws, and hence have greater confidence in the design before it is implemented and deployed.

2.16 SUMMARY

This chapter has briefly described the main features of the UML, SysML, and MARTE notations and the main characteristics of the diagrams using these notations in this book. Appendix A describes the naming conventions used in this book for classes and objects.

For further reading on UML, Fowler (2004) and Ambler (2005) provide introductory material. More detailed information can be found in Booch et al. 2005 and Eriksson et al. 2004. A comprehensive and detailed reference to UML is Rumbaugh et al. 2005. For further reading on SysML, Friedenthal et al. (2015) is a very informative book. For further reading on MARTE, Selic and Gerard (2014) is an outstanding and very clear explanation of MARTE.

3

Real-Time Software Design and Architecture Concepts

This chapter describes key concepts in the software design of concurrent object-oriented real-time embedded systems as well as important concepts for developing the architecture of these systems. First, object-oriented concepts are introduced, with the description of objects and classes, as well as a discussion of the role of information hiding in object-oriented design and an introduction to the concept of inheritance. Next, the concurrent processing concept is introduced and the issues of communication and synchronization between concurrent tasks are described. These design concepts are building blocks in designing the software architecture of a real-time embedded system: the overall structure of the system, its decomposition into components, and the interfaces between these components.

Section 3.1 provides an overview of object-oriented concepts. Section 3.2 describes information hiding and how it is used in software design. Section 3.3 describes inheritance and generalization/specialization relationships. Section 3.4 describes active and passive objects, while Section 3.5 provides an overview of concurrent processing. Section 3.6 describes cooperation between concurrent tasks, including mutual exclusion, task synchronization, and the producer/consumer problem. Section 3.7 describes how information hiding is applied to access synchronization. Section 3.8 provides an overview of runtime support for concurrent processing, while Section 3.9 describes task scheduling. Finally, Section 3.10 provides an overview of software architecture and the concepts of components and connectors.

3.1 OBJECT-ORIENTED CONCEPTS

An **object** is a real-world physical or conceptual entity that provides an understanding of the real world and hence forms the basis for a software solution. A real-world object can have physical properties (they can be seen or touched); examples are a door, motor, or lamp. A conceptual object is a more abstract concept, such as an account or transaction.

From a design perspective, an object packages both data and procedures that operate on the data. The procedures are usually called operations or methods. Some approaches, including the UML notation, refer to the operation as the specification of a function performed by an object and the method as the implementation of the

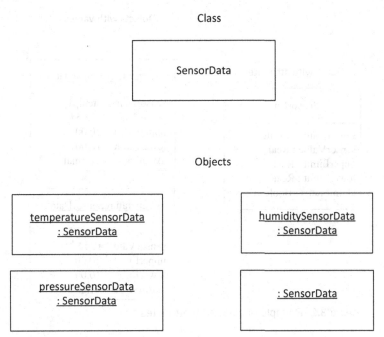

Figure 3.1. Example of classes and objects.

function (Rumbaugh, Booch, and Jacobson 2005). In this book, we will use the term **operation** to refer to both the specification and the implementation, in common with Gamma et. al. (1995), Meyer (2000), and others.

The *signature* of an operation specifies the operation's name, the operation's parameters, and the operation's return value. An object's **interface** is the set of operations it provides, as specified by the signatures of the operations.

A **class** is an object type; for example, the class train represents all trains of a given type. An object is an instance of a class. Individual objects, which are instances of the class, are instantiated as required at execution time, for example, a specific temperature sensor or a specific train.

Figure 3.1 depicts a class called Sensor Data and two objects, temperature Sensor Data: Sensor Data and pressure Sensor Data: Sensor Data, which are instances of the class Sensor Data. The objects humidity Sensor Data: Sensor Data and: Sensor Data are also instances of the class Sensor Data.

An **attribute** is a data value held by an object in a class. Each object has a specific value of an attribute. Figure 3.2 shows a class with attributes. The class Sensor Data has five attributes, namely sensor Name, sensor Value, upper Limit, lower Limit, and alarm Status. Two objects of the Sensor Data class are shown, namely temperature Sensor Data1 and temperature Sensor Data2. Each object has specific values of the attributes. For example, the sensor Value of the first object is 12.57 while the sensor Value of the second object is 24.83. The alarm Status of the former object is Normal while and the alarm Status of the latter is High.

An **operation** is the specification of a function performed by an object. An object has one or more operations. The operations set, retrieve, or modify the values of one or more attributes maintained by the object. Operations may have input and

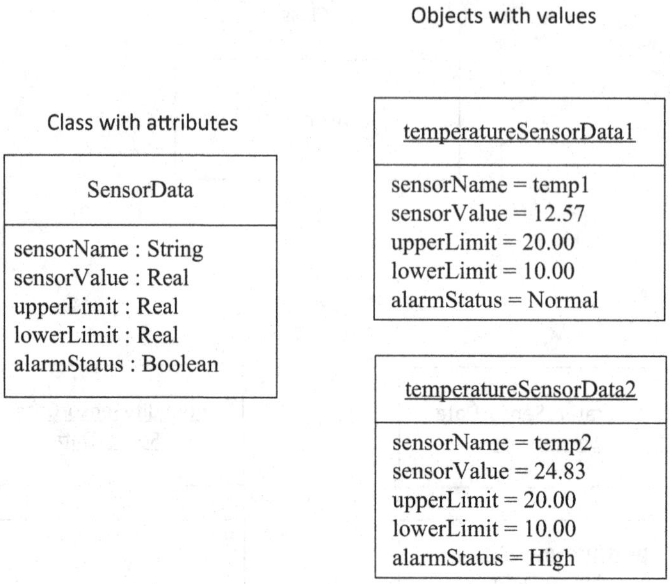

Objects with values

Class with attributes

SensorData
sensorName : String sensorValue : Real upperLimit : Real lowerLimit : Real alarmStatus : Boolean

temperatureSensorData1
sensorName = temp1 sensorValue = 12.57 upperLimit = 20.00 lowerLimit = 10.00 alarmStatus = Normal

temperatureSensorData2
sensorName = temp2 sensorValue = 24.83 upperLimit = 20.00 lowerLimit = 10.00 alarmStatus = High

Figure 3.2. Example of class with attributes.

output parameters. For example, the class Analog Sensor Repository (Figure 3.3) has the operations read Analog Sensor and update Analog Sensor.

3.2 INFORMATION HIDING

Information hiding is a fundamental software design concept relevant to the design of all software systems. Early systems were frequently error-prone and difficult to modify because they made widespread use of global data. Parnas (1972, 1979) showed that by using information hiding, software systems could be designed to be substantially more modifiable by greatly reducing or – ideally – eliminating global data. Parnas advocated information hiding as a criterion for decomposing a software system into modules.

3.2.1 Information Hiding in Object-Oriented Design

Information hiding is a basic concept of object-oriented design. Information hiding is used in designing the class, in particular when deciding what information should

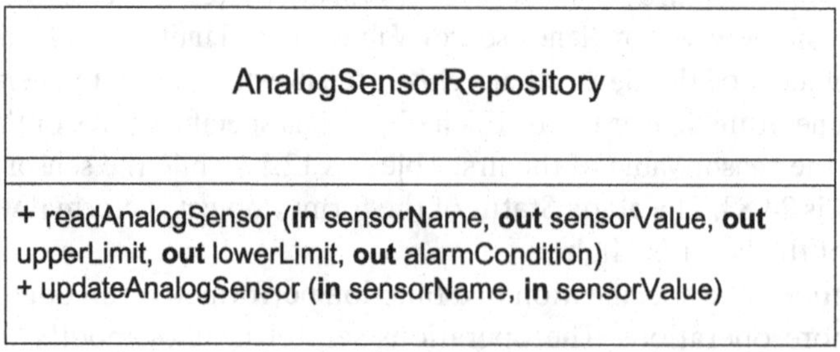

AnalogSensorRepository
+ readAnalogSensor (**in** sensorName, **out** sensorValue, **out** upperLimit, **out** lowerLimit, **out** alarmCondition) + updateAnalogSensor (**in** sensorName, **in** sensorValue)

Figure 3.3. Example of class with operations.

be visible and what information should be hidden. Those parts of a class that need not be visible to other classes are hidden. Hence, if the internals of the class change, only this class is impacted. The term **encapsulation**is also used to describe hiding information by a class or object.

With information hiding, the information that could potentially change is encapsulated (i.e., hidden) inside a class. External access to the information can only be made indirectly by invoking operations – access procedures or functions – that are also part of the class. Only these operations can access the information directly. Thus the hidden information and the operations that access it are bound together to form an **information hiding class**. The specification of the operations (i.e., the name and the parameters of the operations) is called the **interface** of the class. The class interface is also referred to as the *abstract interface*, *virtual interface*, or *external interface* of the class. The interface represents the visible part of the class, that is, the part that is revealed to other classes.

Two examples of applying information hiding in software design are given next. The first example is information hiding applied to the design of internal data structures, and the second is information hiding applied to the design of interfaces to I/O devices.

3.2.2 Information Hiding Applied to Internal Data Structures

A potential problem in application software development is that an important data structure, one that is accessed by several objects, might need to be changed. Without information hiding, any change to the data structure is likely to require changes to all the objects that access the data structure. Information hiding can be used to hide the design decision concerning the data structure, its internal linkage, and the details of the operations that manipulate it. The information hiding solution is to encapsulate the data structure in an object. The data structure is only accessed directly by the operations provided by the object.

Other objects may only indirectly access the encapsulated data structure by calling the operations of the object. Thus if the data structure changes, the only object impacted is the one containing the data structure. The external interface supported by the object does not change; hence, the objects that indirectly access the data structure are not impacted by the change. This form of information hiding is called **data abstraction**.

An example of data abstraction is the Analog Sensor Repository class depicted in Figure 3.3. Whether the repository is implemented as a linked list, array, or some other data structure, the implementation is hidden inside the class and is not visible in the interface. If a decision is made to change the data structure, for example, from an array to a linked list, this change only impacts the implementation of the class and is not visible to, and hence does not affect, other classes that depend on this class.

3.2.3 Information Hiding Applied to Interfacing to I/O Devices

Information hiding can be used to hide the design decision of how to interface to a specific I/O device. The solution is to provide a virtual interface to the device that hides the device-specific details. If the designer decides to replace the device with a different one having the same overall functionality, the internals of the object will

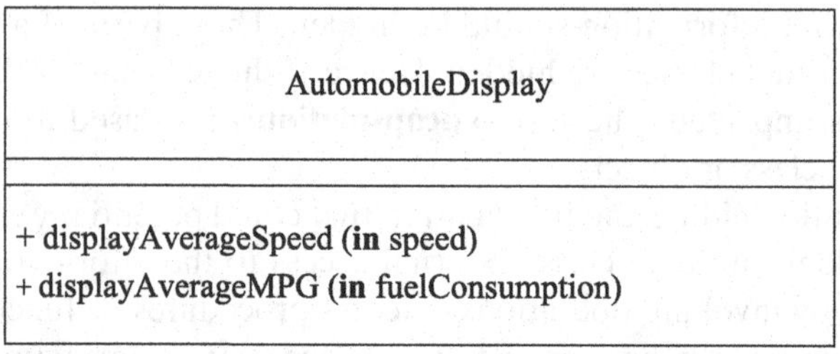

<table>
<tr><td>AutomobileDisplay</td></tr>
</table>

+ displayAverageSpeed (**in** speed) + displayAverageMPG (**in** fuelConsumption)

Figure 3.4. Information hiding applied to I/O device interface.

need to change. In particular, the internals of the object's operations need to change because they must deal with the precise details of how to interface to the real device. However, the virtual interface, represented by the specification of the operations, remains unchanged, as shown in Figure 3.4; hence, the objects that use the device interface will not need to change.

As an example of information hiding applied to I/O devices, consider an output display used on an automobile to display the average speed and fuel consumption. A virtual device can be designed that hides the details of how to format data for and how to interface to the mileage display.

The operations supported are

```
displayAverageSpeed (in speed)
displayAverageMPG (in fuelConsumption)
```

Details of how to position the data on the screen, special control characters to be used, and other device-specific information are hidden from the users of the object. If we replace this device with a different device having the same general functionality, the internals of the operations need to change, but the virtual interface remains unchanged. Thus, users of the object are not impacted by the change to the device.

3.3 INHERITANCE

Inheritance is a useful abstraction mechanism in analysis and design. Inheritance naturally models objects that are similar in some but not all respects, thus having some common properties but other unique properties that distinguish them. Inheritance is a classification mechanism that has been widely used in other fields. An example is the taxonomy of the animal kingdom, in which animals are classified as mammals, fish, reptiles, and so on. Cats and dogs have common properties that are generalized into the properties of mammals. However, they also have unique properties: a dog barks and a cat mews.

Inheritance is a mechanism for sharing and reusing code between classes. A child class inherits the properties (encapsulated data and operations) of a parent class. It can then adapt the structure (i.e., encapsulated data) and behavior (i.e., operations) of its parent class. The parent class is referred to as a **superclass** or *base class*. The child class is referred to as a **subclass** or *derived class*. The adaptation of a parent

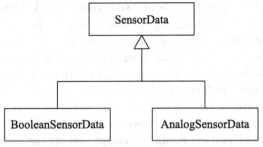

Figure 3.5. Example of inheritance.

class to form a child class is referred to as *specialization*. Child classes may be further specialized, allowing the creation of class hierarchies, also referred to as **generalization/specialization** hierarchies.

Class inheritance is a mechanism for extending an application's functionality by reusing the functionality specified in parent classes. Thus, a new class can be incrementally defined in terms of an existing class. A child class can adapt the encapsulated data (referred to as instance variables) and operations of its parent class. It adapts the encapsulated data by adding new instance variables. It adapts the operations by adding new operations or by redefining existing operations. It is also possible for a child class to suppress an operation of the parent; however, this is not recommended because the subclass no longer shares the interface of the superclass.

An example of inheritance for a real-time embedded system is the design of a Sensor Repository for storing current values of factory sensors, as shown in Figure 3.5. Sensor Data is designed as a superclass that is specialized into two subclasses, Boolean Sensor Data and Analog Sensor Data.

3.4 ACTIVE AND PASSIVE OBJECTS

So far, this chapter has described the characteristics of passive classes and objects. In fact, a class or object can be designed to be *active* or *passive*. An active object is an autonomous object that executes independently of other active objects.

Active objects are also referred to as *concurrent objects*, *concurrent tasks*, or *threads*. A **concurrent object** (**active object**) has its own thread of control and can initiate actions that affect other objects. A **passive object**, which is an instance of a passive class, has no thread of control. Passive objects have operations that are invoked by concurrent objects. Passive objects can invoke operations in other passive objects. An operation of a passive object, once invoked by a concurrent object, executes within the thread of control of the concurrent object. In a **concurrent application**, there are typically several concurrent objects, each with its own thread of control.

3.5 CONCURRENT PROCESSING

A concurrent task represents the execution of a sequential program or a sequential component in a concurrent program. Each task deals with one sequential thread of execution; thus, no concurrency is allowed within a task. However, overall system concurrency is obtained by having multiple tasks executing in parallel. The tasks often execute asynchronously (i.e., at different speeds) and are relatively independent of each other for significant periods of time. From time to time, the tasks need to communicate and synchronize their operations with each other. The UML notation for concurrent tasks is depicted in Section 2.8.

The body of knowledge on cooperating concurrent tasks has grown substantially since Dijkstra's seminal work (1968). Among the significant early contributions was Hoare 1974, who developed the monitor concept that applies information hiding to task synchronization. Several algorithms were developed for concurrent task communication and synchronization, such as the multiple readers and writers algorithm, the dining philosophers algorithm, and the banker's algorithm for deadlock prevention. Because concurrent processing is such a fundamental concept, it has been described in many textbooks. Some of the best sources of information on concurrency are books on operating systems, such as Silberschatz et. al. (2013), Tanenbaum (2014). Two excellent references are Bacon (2003), which describes concurrent systems, both centralized and distributed, and Magee and Kramer (2006), which describes concurrent programming with Java.

3.5.1 Advantages of Concurrent Tasking

The advantages of using concurrent tasking in real-time software design are:

- Concurrent tasking is a natural model for many real-world applications because it reflects the natural parallelism that exists in the problem domain, where several activities are often happening simultaneously.
- Structuring a concurrent system into tasks results in a separation of concerns about *what* each task does from *when* it does it. This usually makes the system easier to understand, manage, and develop.
- A system structured into concurrent tasks can result in an overall reduction in system execution time. On a single processor, concurrent tasking results in improved performance by allowing I/O operations to be executed in parallel with computational operations. With the use of multiple processors, such as multicore systems, improved performance is obtained by having different tasks actually execute in parallel on different processors.
- Structuring the system into concurrent tasks allows greater scheduling flexibility because time-critical tasks with hard deadlines can be given a higher priority than less critical tasks.
- Identifying the concurrent tasks early in the design can allow an early performance analysis to be made of the system. Many tools and techniques (for example, real-time scheduling) use concurrent tasks as a fundamental component in their analysis.

3.5.2 Heavyweight and Lightweight Processes

The term *process* is used in operating systems as a unit of resource allocation for the processor (CPU) and memory. The traditional operating system process has a single thread of control and thus no internal concurrency. Some modern operating systems allow a process, referred to as a **heavyweight process**, to have multiple **threads** of control, thereby allowing internal concurrency within a process. The heavyweight process has its own allocated memory. Each thread of control, also referred to as a **lightweight process**, shares the same memory with the heavyweight process. Thus the multiple threads of a heavyweight process can access shared data in the process's memory, although this access must be synchronized.

The terms "heavyweight" and "lightweight" refer to the context switching overhead. When the operating system switches from one heavyweight process to another, the context switching overhead is relatively high, requiring CPU and memory allocation. With the lightweight process, context switching overhead is low, involving only CPU allocation.

Process terminology varies considerably in different operating systems, although the most common is to refer to the heavyweight process as a process (or task) and the lightweight process as a thread. For example, the Java virtual machine usually executes as an operating system process supporting multiple threads of control (Magee and Kramer 2006). However, some operating systems do not recognize that a heavyweight process actually has internal threads and only schedule the heavyweight process to the CPU. The process then has to do its own internal thread scheduling.

Bacon uses the term **process** to refer to a dynamic entity that executes on a processor and has its own thread of control, whether it is a single threaded heavyweight process or a thread within a heavyweight process (Bacon 2003). This book uses instead the term **task** to refer to such a dynamic entity. The task corresponds to a thread within a heavyweight process (i.e., one that executes within a process) or to a single threaded heavyweight process. Many of the issues concerning task interaction apply whether the threads are in the same heavyweight process or in different heavyweight processes. Task scheduling and context switching are described in more detail in Section 3.9.

3.6 COOPERATION BETWEEN CONCURRENT TASKS

In the design of concurrent systems, several problems need to be considered that do not arise when designing sequential systems. In most concurrent applications, it is necessary for concurrent tasks to cooperate with each other in order to perform the services required by the application. The following three problems commonly arise when tasks cooperate with each other:

1. **The mutual exclusion problem**. This occurs when tasks need to have exclusive access to a resource, such as shared data or a physical device. A variation on this problem, in which the mutual exclusion constraint can be relaxed in certain situations, is the multiple readers and writers problem, as described in Chapters 12 and 14.
2. **Task synchronization problem**. Two tasks need to synchronize their operations with each other. Task synchronization involves one task waiting for an event that is signaled by a different task.
3. **The producer/consumer problem**. This occurs when tasks need to communicate with each other in order to pass data from one task to another.

Communication between tasks is often referred to as inter-process communication (IPC).

These problems and their solutions are described next.

3.6.1 Mutual Exclusion Problem

Mutual exclusion arises when it is necessary for a shared resource to be accessed by only one task at a time. With concurrent systems, more than one task might simultaneously wish to access the same resource. Consider the following situations:

- If two or more tasks are allowed to write to a printer simultaneously, output from the tasks will be randomly interleaved and a garbled report will be produced.
- If two or more tasks are allowed to write to a data repository simultaneously, inconsistent and/or incorrect data will be written to the data repository.

To solve this problem, it is necessary to provide a synchronization mechanism to ensure that access to a critical resource by concurrent tasks is mutually exclusive. A task must first acquire the resource, that is, get permission to access the resource, use the resource, and then release the resource. When task A releases the resource, another task B may now acquire the resource. If the resource is in use by A when task B wishes to acquire it, B must wait until A releases the resource.

The classical solution to the mutual exclusion problem was first proposed by Dijkstra (1968), using binary semaphores. A binary semaphore is a Boolean variable that is accessed only by means of two atomic (i.e., indivisible) operations, **acquire (semaphore)** and **release (semaphore)**. Dijkstra originally called these the P (for acquire) and V (for release) operations.

The indivisible acquire (semaphore) operation is executed by a task when it wishes to acquire a resource. The semaphore is initially set to 1, meaning that the resource is free. As a result of executing the acquire operation, the semaphore is decremented by 1 to 0 and the task is allocated the resource. If the semaphore is already set to 0 when the acquire operation is executed by task A, this means that another task, say B, already has the resource. In this case, task A is suspended until task B releases the resource by executing a release (semaphore) operation. As a result, task A is allocated the resource. It should be noted that the task executing the acquire operation is suspended only if the resource has already been acquired by another task. The code executed by a task while it has access to the mutually exclusive resource is referred to as the **critical section** or **critical region**.

3.6.2 Example of Mutual Exclusion

An example of mutual exclusion is a shared sensor data repository, which contains the current values of several sensors. Some tasks read from the data repository in order to process or display the sensor values, and other tasks poll the external environment and update the data repository with the latest values of the sensors. To ensure mutual exclusion in the sensor data repository example, a sensor Data Repository Semaphore is used. Each task must execute an *acquire* operation before it starts accessing the data repository and execute a *release* operation after it has finished accessing the data repository. The Pseudocode for acquiring the sensor Data

Repository Semaphore to enter the critical section and releasing the semaphore is as follows:

```
acquire (sensorDataRepositorySemaphore)
Access sensor data repository[this is the critical section.]
release (sensorDataRepositorySemaphore)
```

The solution assumes that during initialization, the initial values of the sensors are stored before any reading takes place.

In some concurrent applications, it might be too restrictive to only allow mutually exclusive access to a shared resource. Thus, in the sensor data repository example just described, for a writer task to have mutually exclusive access to the data repository is essential. However, it is permissible to have more than one reader task concurrently reading from the data repository, providing there is no writer task writing to the data repository at the same time. This is referred to as the multiple readers and writers problem (Bacon 2003; Silberschatz et. al. 2013; Tanenbaum 2014). This problem may also be solved by using semaphores and is described further in Chapter 14.

3.6.3 Task Synchronization Problem

Event synchronization is used when two tasks need to synchronize their operations without communicating data between the tasks. The source task signals an event. The destination task waits for the event and is suspended until the event arrives. In UML, the two tasks are depicted as active objects with an asynchronous event signal sent from the sender task to the receiver task, as depicted in Figure 3.6.

Task synchronization may also be achieved by means of message communication as described next.

3.6.4 Producer/Consumer Problem

A common problem in concurrent systems is that of producer and consumer tasks. The producer task produces information, which is then consumed by the consumer task. For this to happen, data needs to be passed from the producer to the consumer. In a sequential program, a calling operation (procedure) also passes data to a called operation. However, control passes from the calling operation to the called operation at the same time as the data.

In a concurrent system, each task has its own thread of control and the tasks execute asynchronously. It is therefore necessary for the tasks to synchronize their operations when they wish to exchange data. Thus, the producer must produce the

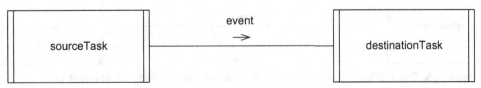

Figure 3.6. Task synchronization with event signals.

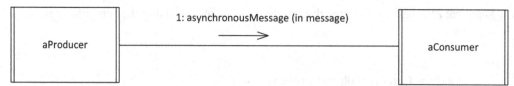

Figure 3.7. Asynchronous message communication between concurrent tasks.

data before the consumer can consume it. If the consumer is ready to receive the data but the producer has not yet produced it, then the consumer must wait for the producer. If the producer has produced the data before the consumer is ready to receive it, then either the producer has to be held up or the data needs to be buffered for the consumer, thereby allowing the producer to continue.

A common solution to this problem is to use message communication between the producer and consumer tasks. Message communication between tasks serves two purposes:

1. Transfer of data from a producer (source) task to a consumer (destination) task.
2. Synchronization between producer and consumer. If no message is available, the consumer has to wait for the message to arrive from the producer. In some cases, the producer waits for a reply from the consumer.

Message communication between tasks may be synchronous or asynchronous. The tasks may reside on the same node or be distributed over different nodes in a distributed application.

With asynchronous message communication, the producer sends a message to the consumer and continues without waiting for a response, as depicted in UML in Figure 3.7. With synchronous message communication with reply, the producer sends a message to the consumer and then immediately waits for a response, as depicted in UML in Figure 3.8. Chapter 11 provides a detailed description of message communication patterns including synchronous and asynchronous message communication.

3.7 INFORMATION HIDING APPLIED TO ACCESS SYNCHRONIZATION

The solution to the mutual exclusion problem described previously is error-prone. It is possible for a coding error to be made in one of the tasks accessing the shared data, which would then lead to serious synchronization errors at execution time. Consider, for example, the mutual exclusion problem described in Section 3.6.2. If the acquire and release operations were reversed by mistake, the Pseudocode would be

Figure 3.8. Synchronous message communication with reply between concurrent tasks.

release (sensorDataRepositorySemaphore)
Access sensor data repository [*should be critical section*]
acquire (sensorDataRepositorySemaphore)

As a result of this error, the task enters the critical section without first acquiring the semaphore. Hence, it is possible to have two tasks executing in the critical section, thereby violating the mutual exclusion principle. Instead, the following coding error might be made:

acquire (sensorDataRepositorySemaphore)
Access sensor data repository [*should be critical section*]
acquire (sensorDataRepositorySemaphore)

In this case, a task enters its critical section for the first time but is then not able to leave because it is trying to acquire a semaphore it already possesses. Furthermore, it prevents any other task from entering its critical section, thus provoking a **deadlock**, where no task is able to proceed.

In these examples, synchronization is a global problem that every task has to be concerned about, which makes these solutions error-prone. By using information hiding, the global synchronization problem can be reduced to a local synchronization problem, making the solution less error-prone. With this approach, only one information hiding object need be concerned about synchronization, as described in Chapters 11 and 14. An information hiding object that hides details of synchronizing concurrent access to data is also referred to as a *monitor* (Hoare 1974), as described in Chapter 14.

3.8 RUNTIME SUPPORT FOR REAL-TIME CONCURRENT PROCESSING

Runtime support for concurrent processing can be provided by:

- **Kernel of an operating system**. This has the functionality to provide services for concurrent processing. In some modern operating systems, a micro-kernel provides minimal functionality to support concurrent processing, with most services provided by system level tasks.
- **Runtime support system** for a concurrent language.
- **Threads package**. This provides services for managing threads (lightweight processes) within heavyweight processes.

With sequential programming languages, such as C, C++, Pascal, and Fortran, there is no support for concurrent tasks. To develop a concurrent multitasked application using a sequential programming language, it is therefore necessary to use a kernel or threads package.

With concurrent programming languages, such as Ada and Java, the language supports constructs for task communication and synchronization. In this case, the language's runtime system provides the services and underlying mechanisms to support inter-task communication and synchronization.

3.8.1 Operating System Services

The following are typical services provided by an operating system kernel:

- **Task scheduling** – allocation of tasks to the CPU using a scheduling algorithm.
- **Inter-task communication using messages**.
- **Mutual exclusion using semaphores**.
- **Event synchronization using signals**. Alternatively, messages may be used for synchronization purposes.
- **Interrupt handling and basic I/O services**.
- **Memory management**. This handles the mapping of each task's virtual memory onto physical memory.

Examples of widely used operating systems with kernels that support concurrent processing are several versions of Unix, Linux, and Windows.

With an operating system kernel, the *send message* and *receive message* operations for message communication and the *wait* and *signal* operations for event synchronization are direct calls to the kernel. Mutually exclusive access to critical sections is ensured by using the *wait* and *signal* semaphore operations, which are also provided by the kernel.

3.8.2 Real-Time Operating Systems

Much of the operating system technology for concurrent systems is also required for real-time systems. Most real-time operating systems support a kernel or microkernel, as described previously. However, real-time systems have special needs, many of which relate to the need for predictable behavior. It is more useful to consider the requirements of a real-time operating system than to provide an extensive survey of available real-time operating systems, because the list changes on a regular basis. Thus, a real-time operating system must:

- Support multitasking.
- Support priority preemption task scheduling. This means each task needs to have its own priority. The task scheduling algorithm assigns the CPU(s) to the highest priority task(s) as soon as it is ready, for example, after it receives a message for which it was waiting.
- Provide task synchronization and communication mechanisms.
- Provide a memory-locking capability for tasks. In hard real-time systems, it is usually the case that all concurrent tasks are memory resident. This is to eliminate the uncertainty and variation in response time introduced by paging overhead. This memory-locking capability allows all time-critical tasks with hard deadlines to be locked in main memory so that they are never paged out.
- Provide a mechanism for priority inheritance, as described in Chapter 17. When a task, task A, enters a critical section, its priority must be temporarily raised to the

highest priority of all tasks that are capable of entering this critical section. Otherwise, task A is liable to get preempted by a higher priority task, which is then unable to enter its critical section because of task A; hence, the higher priority task would block indefinitely.

■ Have a predictable behavior (for example, for task context switching, task synchronization, and interrupt handling). Thus, there should be a predictable maximum response time under all anticipated system loads.

3.9 TASK SCHEDULING

On single processor (CPU) or multiprocessor systems, the operating system kernel has to schedule concurrent tasks for one or more CPUs. The kernel maintains a Ready List of all tasks that are ready to use a CPU. Various task scheduling algorithms have been designed to provide alternative strategies for allocating tasks to a CPU, such as round-robin scheduling and priority preemption scheduling.

3.9.1 Task Scheduling Algorithms

The goal of the round-robin scheduling algorithm is to provide a fair allocation of resources. Tasks are queued on a FIFO basis. The top task on the Ready List is allocated to a CPU and given a fixed unit of time called a "time slice." If the time slice expires before the task has blocked (for example, to wait for I/O or wait for a message), the task is suspended by the kernel and placed on the end of the Ready List. The CPU is then allocated to the task at the top of the Ready List. In a multiprocessor system, the number of tasks that could be in Executing state is equal to the number of processors.

However, in real-time systems, round-robin scheduling is not satisfactory. A fair allocation of resources is not a prime concern, and tasks need to be assigned priorities according to the importance of the operations they are executing. Thus, time-critical tasks need to be certain of executing before their deadlines elapse. A more satisfactory scheduling algorithm for real-time systems is priority preemption scheduling. Each task is assigned a priority and the Ready List is ordered by priority. The task(s) with the highest priority is assigned to a CPU. A task will then execute until it blocks or is preempted by a higher priority task (which has just become unblocked). Tasks with the same priority are assigned to a CPU on a FIFO basis. It should be noted that priority preemption scheduling does not use time slicing.

3.9.2 Task States

Consider the various states a task goes through from creation to termination, as depicted on the state machine in Figure 3.9. These states are maintained by a multitasking kernel that uses a priority preemption scheduling algorithm.

When a task is first created, it is placed in Ready state, during which time it is on the Ready List. When it reaches the top of the Ready List, it is assigned to a CPU, at which time it transitions into Executing state. The task might later be preempted by another task and reenter Ready state, at which time the kernel places it on the Ready List in a position determined by its priority.

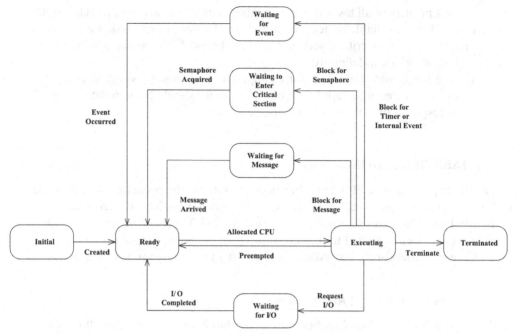

Figure 3.9. State machine for a concurrent task.

Alternatively, while in Executing state, the task may block, in which case it enters the appropriate blocked state. A task can block while waiting for I/O, while waiting for a message from another task, while waiting for a timer event or an event signaled by another task, or while waiting to enter a critical section. A blocked task reenters Ready state when the reason for blocking is removed – in other words, when the I/O completes, the message arrives, the event occurs, or the task gets permission to enter its critical section.

3.9.3 Task Context Switching

When a task is suspended because of either blocking or preemption, its current context or processor state must be saved. This includes saving the contents of the hardware registers, the task's program counter (which points to the next instruction to be executed), and other relevant information. When a task is assigned to a CPU, its context must be restored so it can resume executing. This whole process is referred to as *context switching*.

In a shared memory multiprocessing environment, an instance of the kernel usually executes on each processor. Each processor selects the task at the top of the Ready List to execute. Mutually exclusive access to the Ready List is achieved by means of a hardware semaphore typically implemented by means of a *Test and Set Lock* instruction. Thus, the same task can execute on different processors at different times. In some multiprocessing environments, threads of the same multithreaded process can concurrently execute on different processors. More information on task scheduling is given in books on operating systems, such as those by Silberschatz et. al. (2013) and Tanenbaum (2014).

3.10 SOFTWARE ARCHITECTURE AND COMPONENTS

A software architecture (Shaw and Garlan 1996; Bass, Clements, and Kazman 2013; Taylor et al. 2009) separates the overall structure of the system, in terms of components and their interconnections, from the internal details of the individual components.

A software architecture can be described at different levels of detail. At a high level, it can describe the decomposition of the software system into subsystems. At a lower level, it can describe the decomposition of subsystems into modules or components. In each case, the emphasis is on the external view of the subsystem/component, that is the interfaces it provides and requires, and its interconnections with other subsystems/components.

The software quality attributes of a system should be considered when developing the software architecture. These attributes relate to how the architecture addresses important nonfunctional requirements, such as performance, security, and maintainability, and are described in Chapter 16.

A software architecture can be described from different views, as discussed in Chapter 4. It is important to ensure that the architecture fulfills the software requirements, both functional (what the software has to do) and nonfunctional (how well it should do it). It is also the starting point for the detailed design and implementation, when typically the development team is much larger.

3.10.1 Components and Component Interfaces

The term component is used in different ways. It is often used in a general sense to mean a module in modular systems. There is a more precise definition of a component that is part of a component-based software architecture.

A **component** is a self-contained, usually concurrent, object with a well-defined interface, capable of being used in different applications from that for which it was originally designed. In distributed applications, a component is a basic unit of deployment and distribution, as described in Chapter 12. To fully specify a component, it is necessary to define it in terms of the operations it *provides* and the operations it *requires*. Such a definition is in contrast to conventional object-oriented approaches, which describe an object only in terms of the operations it provides. However, if a preexisting component is to be integrated into a component-based system, it is just as important to understand – and therefore to represent explicitly – both the operations that the component requires and those that it provides. Components are described in more detail in Chapter 12.

3.10.2 Connectors

In addition to defining the components, a software architecture must define the connectors that join the components. A **connector** encapsulates the interconnection protocol between two or more components. Different kinds of message communication between components include **asynchronous** and **synchronous** communication. The interaction protocols for each of these types of communication can be encapsulated in a connector. For example, although asynchronous message communication between components on the same node is logically the same as between components on different nodes, different connectors would be used in the two cases. In the former case, the connector could use a shared memory buffer; the latter case would use a different connector that sends messages over a network. Connectors are described in more detail in Chapter 12.

3.11 SUMMARY

This chapter has described key concepts in the software design of concurrent object-oriented real-time embedded systems as well as important concepts for developing the architecture of these systems. The object-oriented and concurrent tasking concepts introduced here form the basis of several of the forthcoming chapters. From a design perspective, class design is described in Chapter 14. Concurrent tasking and inter-task communication aspects are addressed in more detail from two perspectives. A large-grained perspective is given in Chapter 12 on the software architecture of distributed applications. A smaller-grained perspective on task design is described in Chapters 13 and 14. Issues relating to synchronization of access to information-hiding classes are addressed in more detail in Chapter 14. Software architecture is described in more detail in Chapter 10. Architectural structure and communication patterns are described in Chapter 11. Software quality attributes are described in Chapter 16.

PART II

Real-Time Software Design Method

4

Overview of Real-Time Software Design Method for Embedded Systems

Model-based systems engineering (Buede 2009, Sage 2000) and model-based software engineering (Booch 2007, Gomaa 2011, Blaha 2005) are recognized as important engineering disciplines in which the system under development is modeled and analyzed prior to implementation. In particular, embedded systems, which are software intensive systems consisting of both hardware and software components, benefit considerably from a combined approach that uses both system and software modeling. As described in Chapter 2, the modeling languages used in this book are SysML for systems modeling and UML for software modeling.

This chapter provides an overview of the real-time software design method for embedded systems called COMET/RTE (Concurrent Object Modeling and Architectural Design Method for Real-Time Embedded systems), which uses the SysML, UML, and MARTE notations. Section 4.1 starts with an overview of the COMET/RTE systems and software life cycle. Section 4.2 describes each of the main phases of COMET/RTE. Section 4.3 compares the COMET/RTE life cycle with the Unified Software Development Process, the spiral model, and agile software development. Section 4.4 provides a survey of design methods for real-time embedded systems. Finally, Section 4.5 gives an introduction to the multiple view modeling and design of real-time embedded software architectures described in this textbook.

4.1 COMET/RTE SYSTEM AND SOFTWARE LIFE CYCLE MODEL

This section presents an overview of the COMET/RTE method from a system and software life cycle perspective. COMET/RTE starts with a systems structural analysis and modeling of the total system (hardware, software, people), which leads to defining the boundary between the system and the external environment and to designing the hardware/software interface. This is followed by an iterative software development process, which is both use case–based and object-oriented. The COMET/RTE life cycle model, which is depicted in Figure 4.1, is highly iterative and encompasses both system and software modeling. Iteration is between successive phases, as well as iterating back through multiple phases using an incremental development approach.

Studies have shown that errors in requirements engineering and software architectural design are usually the last to be discovered and the most costly to fix

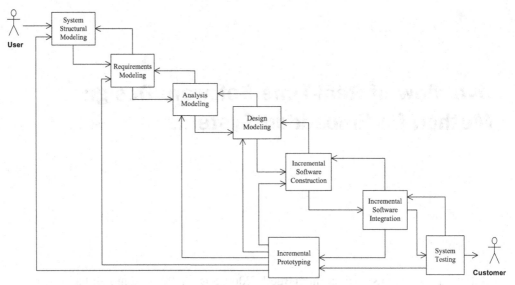

Figure 4.1. COMET/RTE life cycle model.

(Boehm 2006), and this is particularly the case for real-time embedded systems. COMET/RTE focuses on requirements and design within an iterative system and software life cycle, as described in this section.

4.2 PHASES IN COMET/RTE LIFE CYCLE MODEL

This section provides an overview of the main phases of the COMET/RTE method from a system and software life cycle perspective.

4.2.1 System Structural Modeling

System modeling focuses on static structural modeling of the total system using SysML to get a better understanding of the system. The following steps consider the total system perspective, consisting of hardware, software, and people, without consideration of what functionality is carried out in hardware and what functionality in software. The details of these steps are provided in Chapter 5.

a) Structural Modeling of the Problem Domain

Structural modeling of the problem domain involves static modeling of real-world entities, including relevant systems, relevant users, physical entities, and information entities, and determining the relationships between them. Structural modeling of the problem domain is carried out using SysML block definition diagrams.

b) Structural Modeling of the System Context

Structural modeling of the system context involves explicitly determining the boundary between the total system, which is treated as a black box, and the external environment. In considering the total hardware/software system, users and external systems are external to the system, while both hardware and software entities are inside the system. This static structural model requires developing a *system context block definition diagram* using SysML.

c) Hardware/Software Boundary Modeling

This step involves the decomposition of the total system into hardware and software components. Each hardware component is identified and its interface to the software system is determined. If the software system is to interface to other existing systems or new systems under development, then each of these systems is depicted as a component.

d) Software System Context Modeling

Once the hardware/software boundary has been determined, the next step addresses developing the software system context model. This step involves determining the boundary of the software system, in particular how the software system interfaces to the hardware components that are external to the software system. This static structural model requires developing a *software system context block definition diagram* using SysML.

e) System Deployment Modeling

Develop a deployment diagram depicting the deployment of system (hardware and software) components, in particular how components are allocated to physical nodes. Deployment modeling is particularly useful for distributed real-time embedded systems.

4.2.2 Requirements Modeling

During the **requirements modeling** phase, both the functional and nonfunctional requirements of the system are determined. A use case model is developed in which the functional requirements of the system are described in terms of actors and use cases. A narrative description of each use case is developed. User inputs and active participation are essential to this effort. If the requirements are not well understood, a *throwaway prototype* (Gomaa 2011) can be developed to help clarify the requirements.

The activities in requirements modeling are:

- **Develop use cases**. The system and software functional requirements of the system are described in terms of use cases and actors. The use case descriptions are a behavioral view; the relationships among the use cases give a structural view. Use case modeling is described in Chapter 6.
- **Develop nonfunctional requirements**. Addressing nonfunctional requirements (also referred to as quality requirements) is also important at the requirements phase. The UML notation does not specifically address this activity. However, the use case modeling approach can be supplemented to address nonfunctional requirements, as described in Chapter 6.

4.2.3 Analysis Modeling

In the **analysis modeling** phase, static and dynamic models of the software system are developed. The static model defines the structural relationships among problem domain classes, as described in Chapter 5. Object structuring criteria are used to determine the objects to be considered for the analysis model. A dynamic interaction model is then developed. In the dynamic state machine model, state-dependent parts of the system are designed using state machines. In the dynamic interaction model, the use cases from the requirements model are realized to show the objects that participate in each use case and how they interact with each other. Objects and their interactions are depicted on interaction diagrams, either sequence diagrams or communication diagrams.

Dynamic modeling is particularly important for real-time embedded systems, since it is important to determine the dynamic reaction of the system to the different sequences of external events. In most real-time systems, static modeling is much simpler than dynamic modeling and can be largely or even completely addressed during system structural modeling.

In the analysis model, the analysis of the problem domain is considered. The activities are:

- **Static modeling**. This is a structural view of the information provided in the system. Classes are defined in terms of their attributes, as well as their relationship with other classes. Static modeling is described in Chapter 5.
- **Dynamic state machine modeling**. The state dependent view of the system is defined using hierarchical state machines. Designing state machines is described in Chapter 7.
- **Object structuring**. Determine the objects that participate in each use case. Object structuring criteria are provided to help determine the software objects in the system, which can be entity objects, boundary objects, control objects, and application logic objects. State machines are encapsulated in state dependent control objects. Object structuring is described in Chapter 8. After the objects have been determined, the dynamic relationships between objects are depicted in the dynamic interaction model.
- **Dynamic interaction modeling**. The use cases are realized to show the interaction among the objects participating in each use case. Interaction diagrams, either sequence diagrams or communication diagrams, are developed to depict how objects communicate with each other to execute each use case. Chapter 9 describes both stateless dynamic interaction modeling and state-dependent dynamic interaction modeling, in which the interaction among the state dependent control objects and the state machines they execute is explicitly modeled.

4.2.4 Design Modeling

In the **design modeling** phase, the real-time software architecture of the system is designed, in which the analysis model, with its emphasis on the problem domain, is mapped to the design model, with its emphasis on the solution domain. Subsystem structuring criteria are provided to structure the system into subsystems, which are considered as composite objects. Special consideration is given to designing distributed subsystems as configurable concurrent components that communicate with each other using messages. Each subsystem is then designed. For the design of real-time embedded systems, it is necessary to consider concurrent tasking concepts in addition to object-oriented concepts of information hiding, classes, and inheritance.

For designing real-time software architectures, the following activities are performed:

- Transition from analysis to design. The *use case–based interaction diagrams* (developed during dynamic interaction modeling) are integrated to produce *integrated communication diagrams*. The transition from analysis to design is described in Chapter 10.
- Make decisions about subsystem structure and interfaces; develop the overall software architecture; structure the application into subsystems. Subsystem design is described in Chapter 10.
- Make decisions about what software architectural and design patterns to use in the software architecture. Software architectural patterns are described in Chapter 11.
- Make decisions about how to structure the distributed application into distributed subsystems, in which subsystems are designed as configurable components, and define the message communication interfaces between the components. Designing component-based software architectures is described in Chapter 12.
- For each subsystem, structure the system into concurrent tasks (active objects). During task structuring, tasks are structured using the task structuring criteria, and task interfaces are defined. Designing concurrent tasks is described in Chapter 13.
- Make decisions about the characteristics of messages, in particular, whether they are asynchronous or synchronous (with or without reply). Architectural communication patterns are described in Chapter 11 and applied in Chapters 12 and 13.
- Develop the detailed software design, in which tasks that contain nested passive objects are designed, detailed task synchronization issues are addressed, connector classes are designed to encapsulate the details of inter-task communication, and each task's internal event sequencing logic is defined. Detailed software design is described in Chapter 14.
- Incorporate system and software quality into the software architecture. System and software quality attributes, and how to incorporate them into a real-time software architecture, are described in Chapter 16.
- Analyze the performance of the real-time software design before it is implemented using real-time scheduling and/or event sequence analysis, to determine whether the design meets its performance requirements. Performance analysis of concurrent real-time software designs is described in Chapter 17.

4.2.5 Incremental Software Construction

After completion of the software architectural design, an *incremental software construction* approach is taken. This approach is based on selecting a subset of the system to be constructed for each increment. The subset is determined by choosing the use cases to be included in this increment and the objects that participate in these use cases. Incremental software construction consists of the detailed design, coding, and unit testing of the classes in the subset. This is a phased approach by which the software is gradually constructed and integrated until the whole system is built.

4.2.6 Incremental Software Integration

During *incremental software integration*, the integration testing of each software increment is performed. The integration test for the increment is based on the use cases selected for the software increment. Integration test cases are developed for each use case. Integration testing is a form of white box testing, in which the interfaces between the objects that participate in each use case are tested.

Each software increment forms an *incremental prototype*. After the software increment is judged to be satisfactory, the next increment is constructed and integrated by iterating through the *incremental software construction* and *incremental software integration* phases. However, if significant problems are detected in testing the software increment, further iteration through the *requirements modeling, analysis modeling*, and *design modeling* phases might be necessary.

4.2.7 System Testing

System testing includes the functional and nonfunctional testing of the system – namely, testing the system against its functional and nonfunctional requirements. This testing is black box testing, that is, it is conducted without knowledge of the system internals and is based on test cases developed from the use cases. Thus, functional test cases are built for each use case. Any software increment that is to be released to the customer needs to go through System Testing before release.

4.3 COMPARISON OF THE COMET/RTE LIFE CYCLE WITH OTHER SOFTWARE PROCESSES

This section briefly compares the COMET/RTE life cycle with the Unified Software Development Process (USDP), the spiral model, and agile software development. The COMET/RTE method can be used in conjunction with either the USDP or the spiral model. Some agile approaches can be used usefully with COMET/RTE, but others should be avoided.

4.3.1 Comparison of COMET/RTE with Unified Software Development Process

The Unified Software Development Process, as described in (Jacobson, Booch, and Rumbaugh 1999, Kruchten 2003, Kroll and Kruchten 2003) emphasizes process and – to a lesser extent – method. The USDP provides considerable detail about the life cycle aspects and some detail about the method to be used. The COMET/RTE method is compatible with USDP. The workflows of the USDP are the requirements, analysis, design, implementation, and test workflows.

Several phases of the COMET/RTE software life cycle correspond to workflows of the USDP. The Requirements Modeling, Analysis Modeling and Design Modeling phases of COMET/RTE correspond to the first three workflows of the USDP. The COMET/RTE *incremental software construction* phase corresponds to the USDP implementation workflow. The *incremental software integration* and *system testing* phases of COMET/RTE map to the test workflow of USDP. COMET/RTE separates these activities because *integration testing* is viewed as a development team activity, whereas a separate test team should carry out *system testing*.

4.3.2 Comparison of COMET/RTE with the Spiral Model

The COMET/RTE method can also be used with the *spiral model* (Boehm 1988), which is a risk driven process model consisting of four activities (depicted in four quadrants) that are iteratively carried out. During the project planning for a given cycle of the spiral model (first quadrant), the project manager decides what specific technical activity should be performed in the third quadrant, which is the product development quadrant. The selected technical activity, such as requirements modeling, analysis modeling, or design modeling, is then performed in the third quadrant. The risk analysis activity, performed in the second quadrant, and cycle planning, performed in the fourth quadrant, determine how many iterations are required through each of the technical activities.

4.3.3 Comparison of COMET/RTE with Agile Methods

Agile methods have become widely used in software development (Beck 2005, Cockburn 2006, Sutherland 2014). As Meyer (2014) points out in his insightful assessment of agile methods, there is the good, the hype, and the ugly. This assessment is particularly important when time-critical and safety-critical software systems are being developed. In particular, agile software development largely avoids upfront requirements and design activities.

Substituting agile *user stories* (Cohn 2006) for a requirements specification is not an effective solution for real-time embedded software. Starting from a sketchy design instead of a well-designed software architecture is also inadequate for real-time software development. However, some agile approaches can be used effectively in real-time software development after the requirements have been specified and software architecture has been designed. Thus, agile approaches have some similarities to the iterative development approaches used in COMET/RTE, USDP and the spiral model. In particular, the agile emphasis on team communication and frequent team meetings, short iterations, frequent integration, and emphasis on software testing including regression testing, can be used effectively in real-time software development.

4.4 SURVEY OF DESIGN METHODS FOR REAL-TIME EMBEDDED SYSTEMS

This section provides a survey and description of the evolution of design methods for real-time embedded systems. For the design of these systems, a major contribution came in the late seventies with the introduction of the MASCOT notation (Simpson 1979) and later the MASCOT design method (Simpson 1986). Based on a data flow approach, MASCOT formalized the way tasks communicate with each other, via either channels for message communication or pools (information hiding modules that encapsulate shared data structures).

The 1980s saw a general maturation of software design methods, and several system design methods were introduced. Parnas's work with the Naval Research Lab, in which he explored the use of information hiding in large-scale software design, led to the development of the Naval Research Lab (NRL) Software Cost Reduction Method (Parnas, Clements, and Weiss 1984). Work on applying Structured Analysis and Structured Design to concurrent and real-time systems led to the development of Real-Time Structured Analysis and Design (RTSAD) (Ward 1985, Hatley 1988) and the Design Approach for Real-Time Systems (DARTS) (Gomaa 1984, 1986) methods.

Another software development method to emerge in the early 1980s was Jackson System Development (JSD) (Jackson 1983). JSD was one of the first methods to advocate that the design should model reality first and, in this respect, predated the object-oriented analysis methods. The system is considered a simulation of the real world and is designed as a network of concurrent tasks, in which each real-world entity is modeled by means of a concurrent task. JSD also defied the then-conventional thinking of top-down design by advocating a scenario-driven behavioral approach to software design. This approach was a precursor of object interaction modeling, an essential part of modern object-oriented development.

The early object-oriented analysis and design methods emphasized the structural issues of software development through information hiding and inheritance but neglected the dynamic issues and hence were less useful for real-time design. A major contribution by the Object Modeling Technique (Rumbaugh et al. 1991) was to clearly demonstrate that dynamic modeling was equally important. In addition to introducing the static modeling notation for the object diagrams, OMT showed how dynamic modeling could be performed with statecharts (hierarchical state transition diagrams originally conceived by Harel [1996, 1998]) for showing the state-dependent behavior of active objects and with sequence diagrams to show the sequence of interactions between objects.

The Concurrent Design Approach for Real-Time Systems (CODARTS) method (Gomaa 1993) built on the strengths of earlier concurrent design, real-time design, and early object-oriented design methods. These included Parnas's NRL Method, Booch's Object-Oriented Design Method (described in Booch 2007), JSD, and the DARTS method by emphasizing both information hiding module structuring and task structuring. In CODARTS, concurrency and timing issues are considered during task design and information hiding issues are considered during module design.

Octopus (Awad, Kuusela, and Ziegler 1996) is a real-time design method based on use cases, static modeling, object interactions, and statecharts. By combining concepts from Jacobson's use cases with Rumbaugh's static modeling and statecharts, Octopus anticipated the merging of the notations that is now the UML. For real-time design, Octopus places particular emphasis on interfacing to external devices and on concurrent task structuring.

ROOM – Real-Time Object-Oriented Modeling – (Selic, Gullekson, and Ward 1994) is a real-time design method that is closely tied in with a Computer Assisted Software Engineering tool called ObjecTime. ROOM is based around actors, which are active objects that are modeled using a variation on statecharts called

ROOMcharts. A ROOM model, which has been specified in sufficient detail, may be executed. Thus, a ROOM model is operational and may be used as an early prototype of the system. ObjecTime is a precursor of executable design modeling frameworks, which (as described in Chapter 2) are particularly effective for developing real-time systems.

Buhr (see Buhr and Casselman 1996) introduced an interesting concept called the use case map (based on the use case concept) to address the issue of dynamic modeling of large-scale systems. Use case maps consider the sequence of interactions between objects (or aggregate objects in the form of subsystems) at a larger grained level of detail than do communication diagrams.

For UML-based real-time software development, Douglass (1999, 2004) has described how UML can be applied to real-time systems. The 2004 book describes applying the UML notation to the development of real-time systems. The 1999 book is a detailed compendium covering a wide range of topics in real-time system development.

An early version of the COMET/RTE method described in this book is the original COMET method (Gomaa 2000), which used UML 1.0 and was oriented toward the design of concurrent, real-time, and distributed applications.

4.5 MULTIPLE VIEWS OF SYSTEM AND SOFTWARE ARCHITECTURE

Real-time system and software architectures can be considered from different perspectives, which are referred to as different views. Kruchten (1995) introduced the 4+1 view model of software architecture, in which he advocated a multiple view modeling approach for software architectures, in which the use case view is the unifying view (the 1 view of the 4+1 views).

This book describes and depicts the different modeling views of a real-time system and software architecture using the UML, SysML, and MARTE visual notations. The modeling views, which address the requirements for a real-time software design method outlined in Chapter 1, are:

- **Structural view**. The structural view of the total hardware/software system architecture is depicted on SysML block definition diagrams in terms of blocks and relationships. The structural view of the software architecture is depicted on UML class diagrams in terms of classes and relationships. Relationships can be associations, whole/part relationships (compositions or aggregations), or generalization/specialization relationships. This view is similar to the logical view in the 4+1 view model.
- **Use case view**. This view is a functional requirements view, which is an input to develop the software architecture. Each use case describes the sequence of interactions between one or more actors (external users or entities) and the system. This view is the same as the use case view, which is the 1 view, in the 4+1 view model.
- **Dynamic interaction view**. This view describes the architecture in terms of objects as well as the message communication between them. This view can also be used to depict the execution sequence of specific scenarios. Depicted on UML interaction diagrams, either sequence or communication diagrams.

- **Dynamic state machine view**. This view depicts the internal control and sequencing of a control object using a state machine. Depicted on UML state machine diagrams.
- **Structural component view**. This view depicts the software architecture in terms of components, which are interconnected through ports, which in turn support provided and required interfaces. Depicted on UML structured class diagrams. This view is similar to the development view in the 4+1 view model.
- **Dynamic concurrent view**. This view depicts the software architecture as concurrent components (tasks), executing on distributed nodes and communicating by messages. Depicted on UML concurrent communication diagrams. This view is similar to the process view in the 4+1 view model.
- **Deployment view**. This view depicts a specific configuration of the distributed architecture with components assigned to hardware nodes. Depicted on UML deployment diagrams. This view is similar to the physical view in the 4+1 view model.
- **Timing view**. This view analyzes the concurrent tasks composing the real-time software architecture from a timing perspective. This analysis considers each task's execution time on the target platform, as well as its elapsed time as it competes for resources with other tasks, and whether it will meet its hard deadlines.

4.6 SUMMARY

This chapter has described the COMET/RTE system and software life cycle for the development of real-time embedded systems. The chapter then described each of the main phases of the COMET/RTE method. The chapter then compared the COMET/RTE life cycle with the Unified Software Development Process, the spiral model, and agile software development, which was followed by a survey and description of the evolution of design methods for real-time systems. It then described the different modeling views of the COMET/RTE method. Each of the steps in the COMET/RTE method is described in more detail in the subsequent chapters of this textbook.

5

Structural Modeling for Real-Time Embedded Systems with SysML and UML

This chapter describes how *structural modeling* can be used as an integrated approach for system and software modeling of embedded systems consisting of both hardware and software components. The structural view of a system is a *static modeling* view, which does not change with time. *A static model* describes the static structure of the system being modeled, first the static structure of the total hardware/software system followed by the static structure of the software system.

Since a *class* is a software concept describing a software element, a more general term is needed to refer to a system element. SysML uses the concept of a *block* as a system structural element, which is a broader modeling concept than a class that can be used to refer to a hardware, software, or person structural element. In this chapter, the term *structural element* is used to refer to either a block or class.

The SysML *block definition diagram* notation is used to depict the static model of the total hardware/software system and the UML *class diagram* notation is used to depict the static model of the software system. SysML block definition diagrams and UML class diagrams were first introduced in Chapter 2. For system modeling, this chapter describes system-wide structural modeling concepts including blocks, attributes of blocks, and relationships between blocks. For software modeling, this chapter describes software structural modeling concepts including classes, attributes of classes and relationships between classes. Software design concepts such as class operations (methods) are deferred to software class design as described in Chapter 14.

The objective of the model-based approach described in this chapter is to clearly delineate between total system (i.e., hardware and software) modeling and strictly software modeling, with a well-defined transition between the two modeling activities. This chapter starts with a brief description of static modeling, in particular the relationships between structural elements (blocks or classes) in Section 5.1. Three types of relationship are described: *associations*, *composition* and *aggregation* relationships, and *generalization/specialization* relationships. After the introduction to static modeling, this chapter addresses the categorization of blocks and classes using stereotypes in Section 5.2, structural modeling of the problem domain with SysML in Section 5.3, structural modeling of the system context in Section 5.4, hardware/software boundary modeling in Section 5.5, structural modeling of the software system context in Section 5.6, and defining hardware/software interfaces in Section 5.7. Finally, system deployment modeling is described in Section 5.8.

5.1 STATIC MODELING CONCEPTS

This section provides an overview of static modeling concepts, which are used in the structural modeling of embedded systems. A *static model* defines the structural elements of a system in terms of blocks in the total hardware/software system and classes in the software system, as well as the attributes of the structural elements and the relationships between them. The concepts of objects and classes, as well as class attributes and operations, are described in Chapter 3. This section describes the three main types of relationships between *structural elements* (whether *system blocks* or *software classes*): associations, whole/part relationships, and generalization/specialization relationships. The relationships described in this section apply equally to relationships between UML classes and to relationships between SysML blocks. More information on the static modeling notation is given in Chapter 2. The following subsections describe each type of relationship in turn.

5.1.1 Associations

An **association** is a static, structural relationship between two or more structural elements. The **multiplicity** of an association specifies how many instances of one structural element can relate to a single instance of another structural element. The multiplicity of an association may be:

- **One-to-one (1..1)**. In a one-to-one association between two structural elements, the association is one-to-one in both directions.
- **One-to-many (1..*)**. In a one-to-many association, two structural elements have a one-to-many association in one direction and a one-to-one association in the opposite direction.
- **Numerically specified (m..n)**. A numerically specified association is an association that refers to a specific range of numbers.
- **Optional (0..1)**. In an optional association, two structural elements have a zero-to-one association in one direction and a one-to-one association in the opposite direction. This means that there might not always be a link from an instance of one structural element to an instance of the other.
- **Many-to-many (*)**. In a many-to-many association, two structural elements have a one-to-many association in each direction.

An example of structural elements that depicts classes and their associations in a factory automation system is given in Figure 5.1. A workflow plan defines the steps for manufacturing a part of a given type; it contains several manufacturing operations, where each operation defines a single manufacturing step. Consequently, there is a one-to-many association between the Workflow Plan class and the Manufacturing Operation class. A work order defines the number of parts to be manufactured of a given part type. Thus the Work Order class has a one-to-many association with the Part class. Because a workflow plan defines how all parts of a given part type are manufactured, the Workflow Plan class also has a one-to-many association with the Part class. The attributes of these classes are also shown in Figure 5.1. For example,

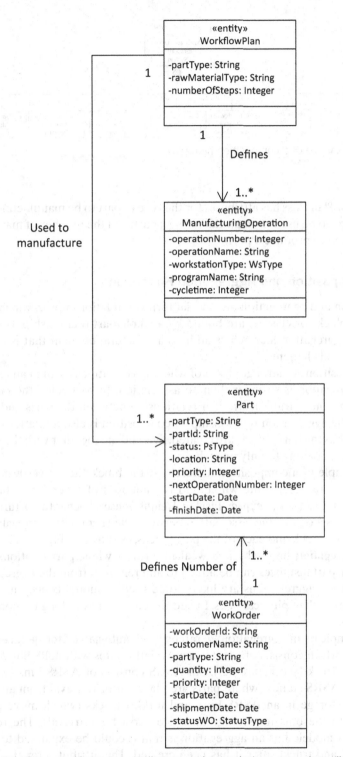

Figure 5.1. Example of classes, attributes, and associations on a class diagram.

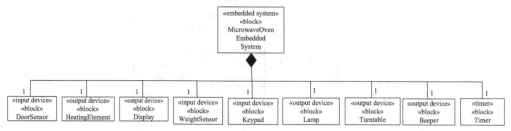

Figure 5.2. Example of a composition hierarchy.

the Workflow Plan class has attributes for the type of part to be manufactured, the raw material type to be used for manufacturing a part, and the number of manufacturing steps required to produce a part.

5.1.2 Composition and Aggregation Hierarchies

Composition and aggregation are special forms of relationships in which structural elements (blocks or classes) are bound by a **whole/part** relationship. Both composition and aggregation hierarchies address a structural element that is made up of other structural elements.

A composition is a stronger form of whole/part relationship than an aggregation, and an aggregation is stronger than an association. In particular, the **composition** relationship demonstrates a stronger relationship between the parts and the whole than does the aggregation relationship. A composition is also a relationship among instances. Thus the part objects are created, live, and die together with the whole. The part object can belong to only one whole.

An example of a composition hierarchy is the block Microwave Oven Embedded System, which represents the whole and is composed of several part blocks: Door Sensor, Heating Element, Keypad, Display, Weight Sensor, Beeper, Lamp, Turntable, and Timer. There is a one-to-one association between the Microwave Oven Embedded System composite block and each of the part blocks, as shown in Figure 5.2.

The **aggregation** hierarchy is a weaker form of whole/part relationship. In an aggregation, part instances can be added to and removed from the aggregate whole. For this reason, aggregations are likely to be used to model conceptual structural elements rather than physical ones. In addition, a part may belong to more than one aggregation.

An example of an aggregation hierarchy is the Automated Storage & Retrieval System (ASRS), which consists of one-to-many relationships with ASRS Bin, ASRS Stand, and Forklift Truck (see Figure 5.3). An ASRS consists of ASRS bins (where parts are stored), ASRS stands (where parts are placed after retrieval from an ASRS bin or prior to storage in an ASRS bin), and forklift trucks (which move parts from the stands to the bins for storage and vice versa for retrieval). The reason that the ASRS is modeled as an aggregation is that it could be expanded to add more bins, stands, and trucks after it has been created. The attributes for the three part classes are also depicted in Figure 5.3. For example, ASRS Bin has attributes for the bin #, the ID of the part located in the bin, and the status of the bin (occupied or empty).

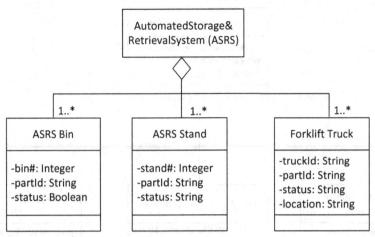

Figure 5.3. Example of an aggregation hierarchy.

5.1.3 Inheritance and Generalization/Specialization

Inheritance is a useful abstraction mechanism in structural modeling and design. Inheritance permits modeling of structural elements that are similar in some but not all respects, thus having some common properties but other unique properties that distinguish them. Inheritance is a classification mechanism that has been widely used in other fields. An example is the taxonomy of the animal kingdom, in which animals are classified as mammals, fish, reptiles, and so on. Cats and dogs have common properties that are generalized into the properties of mammals. However, they also have unique properties: A dog barks and a cat mews.

The following description is in terms of software classes, but it can also be applied to system blocks. **Inheritance** is a mechanism for sharing properties between classes. A child class inherits the properties (e.g., encapsulated data) of a parent class. It can then modify the structure (i.e., attributes) of its parent class by adding new attributes. The parent class is referred to as a **superclass** or *base class*. The child class is referred to as a **subclass** or *derived class*. The adaptation of a parent class to form a child class is referred to as *specialization*. Child classes may be further specialized, allowing the creation of class hierarchies, also referred to as **generalization/specialization** hierarchies.

Consider an example from a factory automation system given in Figure 5.4. There are three types of factory workstations – receiving workstations, line workstations, and shipping workstations – so they are modeled as a generalization/specialization hierarchy; that is, the Factory Workstation class is specialized into three subclasses: Receiving Workstation, Shipping Workstation, and Line Workstation. All factory workstations have attributes for workstation name, workstation ID, and location, which are therefore attributes of the superclass and are inherited by the subclasses. Since factory workstations are physically laid out in an assembly line, the Receiving Workstation class has a next workstation ID, the Shipping Workstation has a previous workstation ID, while a Line Workstation has both a previous workstation ID and a next workstation ID. Because of these differences, previous and next workstation IDs are attributes of the subclasses, as shown in Figure 5.4.

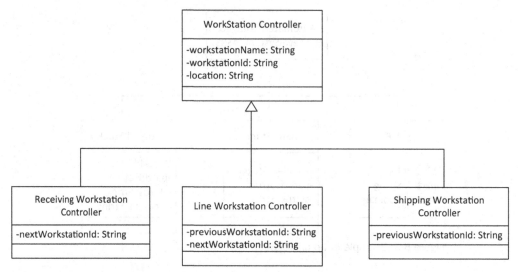

Figure 5.4. Example of a generalization/specialization hierarchy.

5.2 CATEGORIZATION OF BLOCKS AND CLASSES USING STEREOTYPES

This section describes how blocks and classes can be categorized (i.e., grouped together) using a classification approach. The dictionary definition of *category* is "a specifically defined division in a system of classification." Whereas classification based on inheritance is an objective of object-oriented modeling, it is essentially tactical in nature. Thus, classifying the Factory Workstation class into a Receiving Workstation, Shipping Workstation, and Line Workstationis a good idea because Receiving Workstation, Shipping Workstation, and Line Workstation have some properties (e.g., attributes) in common and others that differ. Categorization, however, is a strategic classification – a decision to organize classes into certain groups because most software systems have these kinds of classes and categorizing classes in this way helps to better understand the system being developed.

In UML and SysML, stereotypes are used to distinguish among the various kinds of modeling elements. A **stereotype** is a subclass of an existing modeling element (for example an application or external class), which is used to represent a usage distinction (for example the kind of application or external class). In the UML notation, a stereotype is enclosed by guillemets, like this: «input device».

Examples shown in Figure 5.5 from the microwave oven system are the input devices Door Sensor and Weight Sensor, the output devices Heating Element and Lamp, and the timer Oven Timer.

5.3 STRUCTURAL MODELING OF THE PROBLEM DOMAIN WITH SysML

Structural modeling of the problem domain for real-time embedded systems refers to modeling the external entities that interface to the embedded system to be developed, as well as the hardware and software structural elements of the embedded

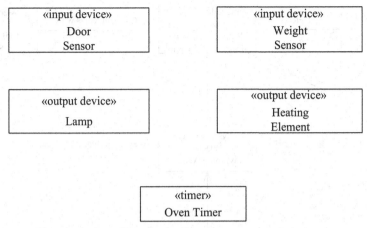

Figure 5.5. Example of UML modeling elements and their stereotypes.

system. In this structural modeling, the embedded system refers to the total hardware/software system, consisting of hardware elements, such as sensors and actuators, and software elements. The software system refers to the software elements, in particular the software components that compose the software system to be developed.

5.3.1 Modeling Real-World Entities in the Problem Domain

With structural modeling of the problem domain for real-time embedded systems, the designer uses SysML block definition diagrams (see Section 2.12) to depict real-world structural elements (such as hardware elements, software elements, or people) as blocks and defines the relationships among these blocks. A block definition diagram is equivalent to a class diagram in which the classes have been stereotyped as blocks, thereby allowing a block definition diagram to depict the same modeling relationships as a class diagram.

In structural modeling of the problem domain, the initial emphasis is on modeling real-world entities to create a conceptual static model, which includes relevant systems, users, physical entities and information entities. Relevant real-world entities in the problem domain of embedded systems include:

1. **Physical entity**. A physical entity is an entity in the problem domain that has physical characteristics – that is, it can be seen or touched. Such entities include physical devices, which are often part of the problem domain in embedded applications. For example, in the railroad crossing system, the train is a physical entity that must be detected by the system. Other relevant physical entities controlled by the system are the railroad crossing barrier, the warning flashing lights, and the audio warning alarm.
2. **Human user**. A human user of the system interacts with the system, providing inputs to the system and receiving outputs from the system. For example, the microwave user is a human user.
3. **Human observer**. A human observer views the outputs of the system but does not interact directly with the system, that is, does not provide any inputs to the system. An example of a human observer is a vehicle driver or pedestrian

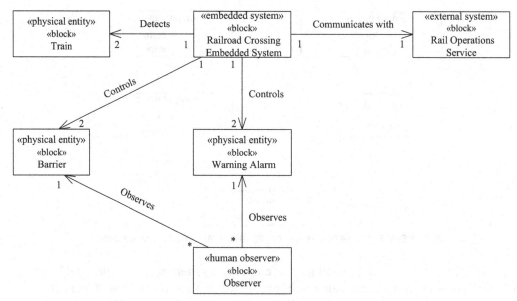

Figure 5.6. Example of conceptual structural model of problem domain.

who is alerted of the imminent train arrival by the closing of the barrier, the flashing lights, and the audio alarm.

4. **Relevant system**. A relevant system is the system to be developed or any other system that interfaces to it. Relevant systems can be *embedded systems, information systems*, or *external systems*.

5. **Information entity**. An information entity is a conceptual data-intensive entity that is often persistent – that is, long-living. Information entities are particularly prevalent in information systems (e.g., in a banking application, examples include accounts and transactions) but may also be needed by some real-time systems (for example to store status information or system configuration information). Information entities are modeled as UML classes as described in Section 5.3.3.

An example of a conceptual structural model of the problem domain is shown in the block definition diagram for the Railroad Crossing Embedded System in Figure 5.6. From a total system perspective, the problem domain for Railroad Crossing Embedded System consists of the following blocks:

- Railroad Crossing Embedded System, which is the *embedded system* to be developed;
- Train, which is a *physical entity* detected by the system;
- Barrier, which is a *physical entity* controlled by the system and which consists of a barrier actuator and a barrier sensor;
- Warning Alarm, which consists of Warning Lights and Warning Audio and which is a *physical entity* controlled by the system;
- Observer (who waits at the railroad crossing), which is an *observer* of the system;
- Rail Operations Service, which is an *external system* that is notified of the status of the railroad crossing.

5.3.2 Modeling the Embedded System

In embedded systems, in which there are several physical devices such as sensors and actuators, block definition diagrams can help with modeling these real-world devices. In the microwave oven system, for example, it is useful to model real-world devices (such as the door, heating element, weight sensor, turntable, beeper, display, keypad, lamp, and timer), their associations, and the multiplicity of the associations. Composite blocks are often used to show how a real-world composite modeling element, such as the Microwave Oven Embedded System composite block (see Figure 5.2), is composed of other blocks. Individual blocks are categorized as input devices, output devices, timers, and systems and are depicted on block definition diagrams using stereotypes. An example of a structural model is for the Microwave Oven System, which is an embedded system described in the case study in Chapter 19.

5.3.3 Modeling Information Entities as Entity Classes

Information Entities are modeled as entity classes, which are depicted as UML classes with the stereotype «entity». Entity classes are conceptual data-intensive classes. Some entity classes store persistent (i.e., long-lasting) data that, during execution, is typically accessed by several objects. Entity classes are particularly prevalent in information systems; however, many real-time and distribution applications have significant data-intensive functionality.

During static modeling of the problem domain, the emphasis is on determining the entity classes that are defined in the problem, their attributes, and their relationships. For example, in a Factory Automation System, there are parts, workflow plans, manufacturing operations, and work orders all mentioned in the problem description. Each of these real-world conceptual entities is modeled as an entity class and depicted with the stereotype «entity», as depicted in Figure 5.1. The attributes of each entity class are determined and the relationships among entity classes are defined, as described in Section 5.1.

5.4 STRUCTURAL MODELING OF THE SYSTEM CONTEXT

It is very important to understand the *system context*, that is the scope of a computer system – in particular, what is to be included inside the system and what is to be excluded from the system. Context modeling explicitly identifies what is inside the system and what is outside. Context modeling can be done at the total system (hardware and software) level or at the software system (software only) level. The system context is determined after modeling and understanding the problem domain, as described in Section 5.3.

A **system context diagram** is a block definition diagram that explicitly depicts the boundary between the system (hardware and software), which is modeled as one block, and the external environment. By contrast, a **software system context diagram** explicitly shows the boundary between the software system, also modeled as one block, and the external environment, which now includes the hardware.

When developing the system context (which is depicted on a block definition diagram) it is necessary to consider the context of the total hardware/software system before considering the context of the software system. In considering the total hardware/software system, only users and external system modeling elements are outside the system, while hardware and software modeling elements are internal to the system. Thus, I/O devices are part of the hardware of the system and are therefore part of the total hardware/software system.

5.4.1 Modeling External Entities of the Embedded System

When modeling an embedded hardware/software system, many of the real-world entities described in Section 5.3.1 are external entities that interface to the embedded system. Possible external entities are:

1. **External physical entity**. A physical entity is an external entity that the system has to detect and/or control. For example, in the railroad crossing system, the train is an external physical entity that has to be detected by the system. Other external physical entities, which are controlled by the system, are the railroad crossing barrier, the warning flashing lights, and the audio warning alarm.Some external physical entities, such as smart devices, might provide input to or receive output from the system.
2. **External system**. An external system is a separate system that interfaces to and communicates with the system under development. An external system might be an existing system that was previously developed or a new system that is to be developed by a different organization. An external system typically sends input messages to the system under development and/or receives output messages from the system.
3. **External user**. An external user is a human user of the system who interacts with the system, providing inputs to the system and receiving outputs from the system. For example, the microwave user is an external user.
4. **External observer**. An external observer is a human being who views the outputs of the system but does not interact directly with the system, that is, does not provide any inputs to the system. An example of an external observer is a vehicle driver or pedestrian who is alerted of the imminent train arrival by the closing of the barrier, the flashing lights, and the audio alarm.

Using the SysML notation, the system context is depicted showing the hardware/software system as an aggregate block with the stereotype «embedded system». The external environment is depicted in terms of external entities, depicted as blocks, to which the system has to interface. Stereotypes are used to differentiate between the different kinds of external blocks. For the system context diagram, an external block could be an «external system», «external physical entity», «external user», or an «external observer».

5.4.2 Modeling Associations on the System Context Diagram

The associations between the embedded system block and the external blocks are depicted on the system context diagram, showing in particular the multiplicity of the associations between the external blocks and the embedded system. These can be *one-to-one* or *one-to-many* associations. In addition, each association is given a standard name, which describes what the association is between the embedded system and the external block. The standard association names on system context block diagrams are *Inputs to, Outputs to, Communicates with, Interacts with, Detects, Controls,* and *Observes*. Note that in some cases, there is more than one standard association name between an external block and the embedded system, if different associations between them are possible. These associations are used as follows:

«embedded system» *Outputs to* «external user»
«external physical entity» *Inputs to* «embedded system»
«embedded system» *Detects* «external physical entity»
«embedded system» *Controls* «external physical entity»
«external observer» *Observes* «embedded system»
«external user» *Interacts with* «embedded system»
«external system» *Communicates with* «embedded system»

Examples of associations on system context block diagrams are as follows:

Factory Automation System *Outputs to* Operator
Smart Device *Inputs to* Factory Automation System
Railroad Crossing System *Detects* Train
Railroad Crossing System *Controls* Barrier
Observer *Observes* Barrier
User *Interacts with* Microwave Oven System
Railroad Crossing System *Communicates with* Rail Operations System

5.4.3 Example of System Context Diagrams

As an example of a system context diagram, consider the Railroad Crossing Embedded System, which is depicted on the block definition diagram in Figure 5.7, which is derived from Figure 5.6. Whereas the conceptual structural model in Figure 5.6 is a model of the problem domain, the Figure 5.7 focuses on the boundary of the system to be developed, The Railroad Crossing Embedded System is categorized as an «embedded system» «block». From a total system perspective, the system interfaces to four external blocks:

- Train, which is an *external physical entity* detected by the system;
- Barrier, which is an *external physical entity* controlled by the system and which consists of a barrier actuator (to raise or lower the barrier) and barrier sensor (to detect that the barrier has been raised or lowered;
- Warning Alarm, which consists of Warning Lights and Warning Audio and which is an *external physical entity* controlled by the system;
- Rail Operations Service, which is an *external system* that is notified of the status of the railroad crossing.

Note that Observer (vehicle driver, cyclist, or pedestrian who stops at the railroad crossing) is an *external observer* of the system.

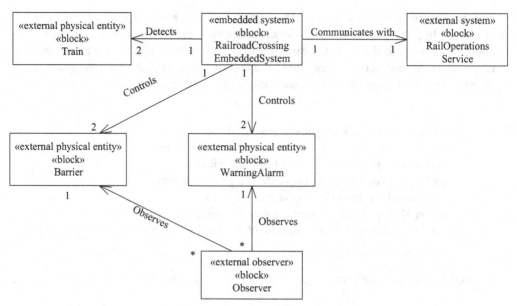

Figure 5.7 System context diagram for Railroad Crossing Embedded System.

5.5 Hardware/Software Boundary Modeling

To determine the boundary between the hardware and software blocks in preparation for modeling the software system context diagram, the modeler starts with the system context diagram and then determines the decomposition into hardware and software blocks.

From a software engineering perspective, some external blocks are modeled in the same way as in the systems engineering perspective, while others are modeled differently. In the former category are external system blocks and external users who interact with the system using standard I/O devices; these external blocks are depicted on the software system context diagram in the same way as on the system context diagram.

External blocks that are modeled differently from a software engineering perspective are external physical entity blocks that often do not physically connect to a system, and therefore need sensors or actuators to make the physical connection. As described in Section 5.4.2, the association between the embedded system and such a physical entity is *detects* and/or *controls*. Detection of physical entities is done by means of sensors while control of physical entities is done by means of actuators. Consider the external physical entities in the Railroad Crossing Embedded System. The arrival of a train is detected by an arrival sensor and the departure is detected by a departure sensor.

5.6 STRUCTURAL MODELING OF THE SOFTWARE SYSTEM CONTEXT

As described in Section 5.4, the system context diagram depicts the systems and users that are external to the total hardware/software system, which is modeled as one composite block. The hardware blocks (such as sensors and actuators) and software blocks are internal to the system and are therefore not depicted on the system context

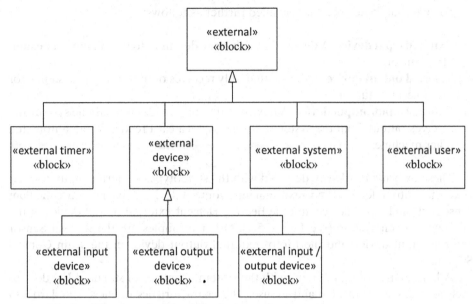

Figure 5.8. Classification of external blocks by stereotype.

diagram. Together with the hardware/software boundary modeling described in the previous section, this is the starting point for the software context modeling.

A **software system context diagram** is a block definition diagram that explicitly depicts the boundary between the software system, which is modeled as one block with the stereotype «software system», and the external environment. The software system context diagram is determined by analyzing the external blocks that connect to the software system. In particular, physical hardware devices (such as sensors and actuators) are external to the software system.

The software system is depicted on the software system context diagram as an aggregate block with the stereotypes «software system» «block», and the external environment is depicted as external blocks to which the software system has to interface.

5.6.1 Modeling External Entities of the Software System

For a real-time embedded system, it is desirable to identify low-level external blocks that correspond to all the external elements that the system has to interface to and communicate with, including physical I/O devices, external timers, external systems, and external users. External blocks are categorized by stereotype, as described in Section 5.7. Figure 5.8 depicts the classification of external blocks using inheritance, in which stereotypes are used to distinguish among the different kinds of external blocks. Thus, an external block is classified as an «external user» block, an «external device» block, an «external system» block, or an «external timer» block. Only external users and external systems can be external to the total system. Hardware devices and timers are part of the total (hardware and software) system but are external to the software system. Thus Figure 5.8 categorizes external blocks from the software system's perspective.

An external device block is classified further as follows:

- **External input device**. A device that only provides input to the system – for example, a sensor;
- **External output device**. A device that only receives output from the system – for example, an actuator;
- **External input/output device**. A device that both provides input to the system and receives output from the system – for example, a card reader for an automated teller machine.

These external blocks are depicted with the stereotypes «external input device», «external output device», and «external input/output device». Examples are the Door Sensor external input device and the Heating Element external output device in the microwave oven system (see Figure 5.9). Other examples are the Arrival Sensor external input device and the Motor external output device in the Train Control System.

A human user often interacts with the system by means of standard I/O devices such as a keyboard/display and mouse. The characteristics of these standard I/O devices are of no interest because they are handled by the operating system. The interface to the user is of much greater interest in terms of what information is being output to the user and what information is being input from the user. For this reason, an external user interacting with the system via standard I/O devices is depicted as an «external user». An example is the Factory Operator in the factory automation system.

A general guideline is that a human user should be represented as an external user block only if the user interacts with the system via standard I/O devices. However, if the user interacts with the system via application-specific I/O devices, these I/O devices should be represented as external I/O device blocks.

An «external timer» block is used if the application needs to keep track of time and/or if it needs external timer events to initiate certain actions in the system. External timer blocks are frequently needed in real-time embedded systems. An example from the Microwave Oven System is the external Timer. It is needed because the system needs to keep track of elapsed time to determine the cooking time for food placed in the oven and count down the remaining cooking time, which it displays to the user. When the time remaining reaches zero, the system needs to stop cooking. In the Train Control System, time is needed to compute the speed of the train. Sometimes the need for periodic activities only becomes apparent during design.

An «external system» block is needed when the system interfaces to other systems, to either send data or receive data. Thus, in the Factory Automation System, the system interfaces to two external systems: the Pick & Place Robot and the Assembly Robot.

5.6.2 Modeling Associations on the Software System Context Diagram

The associations between the software system aggregate block and the external blocks are depicted on the software system context diagram, showing in particular the multiplicity of the associations and the name of the association. The standard association names on software system context diagrams are *Inputs to, Outputs*

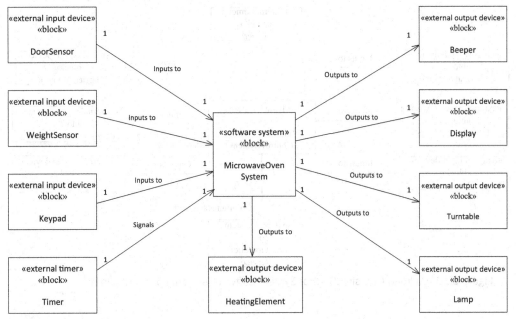

Figure 5.9. Microwave Oven System software system context diagram

to, *Communicates with*, *Interacts with*, and *Signals*. These associations are used as follows:

«external input device» *Inputs to* «software system»
«software system» *Outputs to* «external output device»
«external user» *Interacts with* «software system»
«external system» *Communicates with* «software system»
«external timer» *Signals* «software system»

Examples of associations on software system context diagrams are as follows:

Door Sensor *Inputs to* Microwave Oven Software System
Microwave Oven Software System *Outputs to* Heating Element
Factory Operator *Interacts with* Factory Automation Software System
Pick & Place Robot *Communicates with* Factory Automation Software System
Clock *Signals* Microwave Oven Software System

5.6.3 Examples of Software System Context Modeling

An example of a software system context diagram is depicted in the block definition diagram in Figure 5.9, which shows the external blocks to which the Microwave Oven System has to interface. From the total system perspective – that is, both hardware and software – the microwave oven user is external to the system, whereas the I/O devices, which include the door sensor, weight sensor, heating element and lamp,

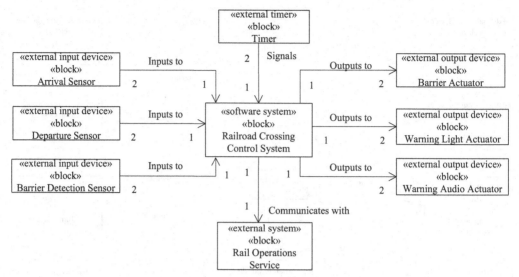

Figure 5.10. Railroad Crossing Control System software system context diagram.

are part of the system. The software system context diagram is modeled from the perspective of the software system to be developed, the Microwave Oven System, which is depicted with the stereotypes «software system» «block».

From the software system point of view, the hardware sensors and actuators are external to the software system and interface to the software system. Thus the blocks outside the software system are the external input and output devices, and the external timer, as depicted in Figure 5.9. In the example, there are three external input device blocks: the Door Sensor, the Weight Sensor, and the Keypad. There are also five external output device blocks, the Heating Element, Display, Beeper, Turntable, and Lamp, as well as one timer, namely Timer. There is one instance of each of these external blocks for a given microwave oven. This example is described in more detail for the Microwave Oven Control System case study in Chapter 19.

A second example of a software system context diagram is from the Railroad Crossing Control System, as depicted in Figure 5.10. This system has three external input devices representing different sensors: Arrival Sensor, Departure Sensor, and Barrier Detection Sensor. There are three output devices representing different actuators: Barrier Actuator, Warning Light Actuator, and the Warning Audio Actuator. There is also an external Timer. This example is described in more detail for the Railroad Crossing Control System case study in Chapter 20.

5.7 DEFINING HARDWARE/SOFTWARE INTERFACES

In defining the hardware/software boundary, it is also necessary to define the interface between each hardware input and output device and the software system. For example, in the Railroad Crossing Control System, the Arrival Sensor input device sends arrival event inputs to the software system. The software system sends switch on and switch off outputs to the Warning Light Actuator output device. Specification of the hardware/software boundary needs to clearly describe the function of each I/O device and its interface to the software system. The template for an I/O specification is:

Table 5.1. I/O Device Boundary Specification

Device name	Device type	Device function	Inputs from device	Outputs to device
Arrival Sensor	Input	Signals when train arrives	Arrival Event	
Departure Sensor	Input	Signals when train departs	Departure Event	
Barrier Detection Sensor	Input	Signals when barrier has been raised or lowered	Barrier Lowered Event, Barrier Raised Event	
Barrier Actuator	Output	Raises and lowers barrier		Raise Barrier, Lower Barrier
Warning Light Actuator	Output	Switches warning lights on and off		Switch On, Switch Off
Warning Audio Actuator	Output	Switches audio warning on and off		Switch On, Switch Off

Name of I/O device:
Type of I/O device:
Function of I/O device:
Inputs from device to software system:
Outputs from software system to device:

An I/O device boundary specification can also be depicted as a table. Examples of input and output device boundary specifications for the Railroad Crossing Control System (Figure 5.10) are given in Table 5.1.

5.8 SYSTEM DEPLOYMENT MODELING

The next step is to consider the physical deployment of the system (hardware and software) blocks of the embedded system. One possible configuration for the Distributed Light Rail System is depicted in the UML deployment diagram in Figure 5.11, in which the system blocks of the distributed embedded system are deployed to different physical nodes, which are connected by means of a wide area network.

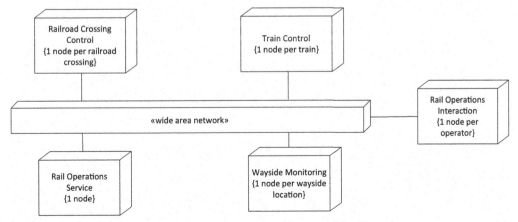

Figure 5.11. Deployment diagram for Distributed Light Rail Embedded System.

The blocks are Railroad Crossing Control, which has one node per railroad crossing, Train Control, which has one node per train, Wayside Monitoring, which has one node per wayside location, Rail Operations Service, which has one node, and Rail Operations Interaction, which has one node per operator.

5.9 SUMMARY

This chapter has described how *structural modeling* using SysML and UML can be used as an integrated approach for system and software modeling of embedded systems consisting of both hardware and software modeling elements. This chapter started by describing some of the basic concepts of static modeling, including using blocks to depict system modeling elements and classes to depict software modeling elements, as well as defining the relationships between structural modeling elements. Three types of relationships have been described: *associations*, *composition/aggregation* relationships, and *generalization/specialization* relationships. This chapter then described categorization of blocks using stereotypes, structural modeling of the problem domain, system context modeling, developing the hardware/software boundary of a system, software system context modeling, designing the interface between hardware and software blocks, and system deployment modeling. The categorization of software classes using stereotypes is described in Chapter 8.

6

Use Case Modeling for Real-Time Embedded Systems

Use case modeling is widely used for specifying the functional requirements of software systems. This chapter describes how use case modeling can be applied to real-time embedded systems from both a systems engineering and a software engineering perspective. With use case modeling, the system is viewed as a black box, so that only the external characteristics of the system are considered. Both functional and nonfunctional requirements need to be described for embedded systems. Functional requirements address the functionality that the system needs to provide. Nonfunctional requirements, sometimes referred to as quality attributes, address quality of service goals for the system, which are particularly important for real-time embedded systems. Although use case modeling is typically only used for specifying functional requirements, this chapter describes how it can be extended to specify nonfunctional requirements. Several examples of use case modeling for embedded systems are given in this chapter.

Section 6.1 gives an overview of use case modeling. Section 6.2 then describes actors and their role in use case modeling from both systems engineering and software engineering perspectives. The important topic of how to identify use cases is covered in Section 6.3. Section 6.4 describes how to document use cases. Section 6.5 describes how to specify nonfunctional requirements, which is particularly important for real-time embedded systems. Section 6.6 gives detailed examples of use case descriptions from both systems engineering and software engineering perspectives. Section 6.7 then describes use case relationships; modeling with the *include* relationship is described in Section 6.8; modeling with the *extend* relationship is described in Section 6.9. Finally, use case packages for structuring large use case models are described in Section 6.10.

6.1 USE CASES

In the use case modeling approach, functional requirements are defined in terms of **actors**, which are external to the system, and **use cases**. A **use case** defines a sequence of interactions between one or more **actors** and the system. The **use case model** describes the functional requirements of the system in terms of the actors and use cases. In particular, the use case model considers the system as a black box and

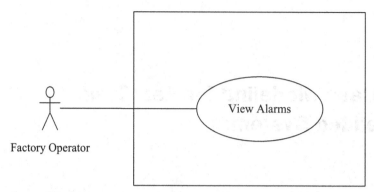

Figure 6.1. Example of actor and use case.

describes the interactions between the actor(s) and the system in a narrative textual form consisting of actor inputs and system responses. The system is treated as a black box, that is, dealing with **what** the system does in response to the actor's inputs, not the internals of **how** it does it.

For real-time embedded systems, both use cases and actors can be modeled from a systems engineering perspective or from a software engineering perspective. As these perspectives are different for real-time embedded systems, this chapter describes both perspectives.

A use case always starts with input from an actor. A use case typically consists of a sequence of interactions between the actor and the system. Each interaction consists of an input from the actor followed by a response from the system. Thus, an actor provides inputs to the system and the system provides responses to the actor. The system is always considered as a black box, so that its internals are not revealed. Whereas a simple use case might only involve one interaction between an actor and the system, a more typical use case will consist of several interactions between the actor and the system. More complex use cases might also involve more than one actor.

An example of a simple use case model in which there is no difference between the system and software perspectives is given in Figure 6.1. In this example, there is one use case, View Alarms, and one actor, Factory Operator, who is a human actor. In View Alarms, the operator requests to view factory alarms, and the system responds by displaying the current alarms to the operator.

6.2 ACTORS

An **actor** characterizes an external entity (i.e., outside the system) that interacts with the system. In the use case model, **actors** are the only external entities that interact with the system. In other words, actors are outside the system and not part of it. An actor interacts with the system by providing inputs to the system or by responding to outputs from the system.

An actor represents a role played in the application domain. An actor represents the role played by all external instances of the same type, such as all users of the same type. For example, in the View Alarms use case (Figure 6.1), there are several factory operators who are represented by the Factory Operator actor. Thus, Factory Operator models a user type, and individual factory operators are instances of the actor.

6.2.1 Actors in Real-Time Embedded Systems

In many information systems, humans are the only actors. For this reason, the UML notation depicts an actor using a stick figure. However, in real-time embedded systems, there are other types of actors in addition to or in place of human actors. In fact, in embedded systems, the nonhuman actors are frequently more important than human actors. External I/O devices and timer actors are particularly prevalent in embedded systems. I/O device actors are needed because the system interacts with the external environment through sensors and actuators. Timer actors are needed because many functions in real-time systems need to be performed periodically.

An external entity that is purely passive, that is, only receives outputs from the system and never responds to these outputs, is not considered an actor in some use case modeling approaches. However, with embedded systems, it is important to explicitly consider the interactions with each external device, whether input or output. It is therefore preferable to explicitly incorporate passive output devices into the use case models when modeling embedded systems from a software engineering perspective, as described in Section 6.2.5.

6.2.2 Systems and Software Engineering Perspectives on Actors

For systems in which the actors are usually entirely human, such as information systems and Web-based systems, there is little or no difference between the systems and software engineering perspectives of the use case model. However, in real-time embedded systems, there can be significant differences between the system and software engineering perspectives.

Consider the case of a train that does not interact directly with the system because its arrival and departure are detected by sensors. From a systems engineering perspective, the train is the actor because it is a physical entity that is external to and detected by the system, whereas the arrival and departure sensors are internal to the total (hardware/software) system and therefore are not actors. However, from a software engineering perspective, the arrival and departure sensors are actors because they are external to the software system and provide inputs to it. Thus, depending on which perspective is taken for real-time embedded systems, systems or software engineering, the actors are usually different, and consequently the use cases are described differently.

6.2.3 Primary and Secondary Actors

A **primary actor** initiates a use case. Thus, the use case starts with an input from the primary actor to which the system has to respond. Other actors, referred to as **secondary actors**, may also participate in the use case by providing inputs and receiving outputs. A primary actor in one use case can be a secondary actor in another use case. At least one of the actors must gain value from the use case; usually this is the

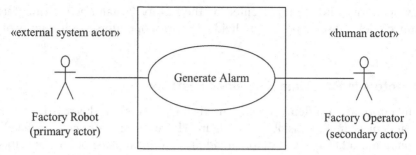

Figure 6.2. Example of primary and secondary actors, as well as external system actor.

primary actor. If there is only one actor in the use case, then that actor is also the primary actor.

In real-time embedded systems, however, where the primary actor can be an external I/O device or timer, the primary beneficiary of the use case can be a secondary human actor who receives some information from the system or a human observer who only observes but does not interact with the system.

An example of primary and secondary actors is shown in Figure 6.2. The Factory Robot actor (an external computer system) initiates the Generate Alarm use case by sending monitoring data to the system. The system determines that there is an alarm condition, which it displays to the factory operator. In this use case, the Factory Robot is the primary actor that initiates the use case, and the Factory Operator is a secondary actor that receives the alarm and hence gains value from the use case. However, Factory Operator is a primary actor in the View Alarms use case (Figure 6.1), in which the operator requests to view alarm data.

6.2.4 Modeling Actors from a Systems Engineering Perspective

From a systems engineering perspective, an actor can be a human user (either as an active participant in the use case or as an observer), an external system, or a physical entity.

A human actor frequently interacts with the system via standard I/O devices, such as a keyboard, display, or mouse. However, in real-time embedded systems, a human actor might interact with the system indirectly via nonstandard I/O devices, such as various sensors. From a systems engineering perspective, the human is the actor and the I/O devices are internal to the hardware/software system.

Consider an example of a human actor who interacts with the system using standard I/O devices. In the factory monitoring system, the Factory Operator is a human actor who interacts with the system via standard I/O devices, such as a keyboard, display, or mouse, as shown in Figures 6.1 and 6.2. An example of a human actor who interacts with the system by using several nonstandard I/O devices is a user of a microwave oven, as shown in Figure 6.3. To cook food, the user interacts with the system by using several I/O devices, including a door sensor, weight sensor, and keypad, in addition to an oven heater, oven display, and oven timer. Modeling the Cook Food use case from a systems engineering perspective, the user is the actor.

An observer is a human user who passively views the system but does not participate in the use case by providing any inputs. For example, in Railroad Crossing

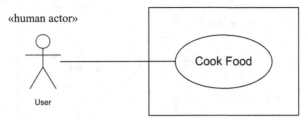

Figure 6.3. Example of human actor.

System, a driver is an observer who stops when the warning lights are flashing but does not affect the system in any way.

An actor can also be an **external system actor** that either initiates (as primary actor) or participates (as secondary actor) in a use case. An example of an external system actor is the Factory Robot in the Factory Monitoring System. The Factory Robot initiates the Generate Alarm use case, as shown in Figure 6.2, by sending an alarm to the system. The system receives the alarm and sends alarm data that is displayed to factory operators. The Factory Operator is a secondary actor in this use case.

An example of a **physical entity actor** is a Train actor, as shown in Figure 6.4. From a systems engineering perspective, the train is the primary actor of the Arrive at Railroad Crossing and Depart from Railroad Crossing use cases, since it is the arrival of the train that triggers the first use case and the departure of the train that triggers the second use case.

6.2.5 Modeling Actors from a Software Engineering Perspective

From a software engineering perspective, some actors are modeled in the same way as in the systems engineering perspective while others are modeled differently. In the former category are external system actors and human users who interact with

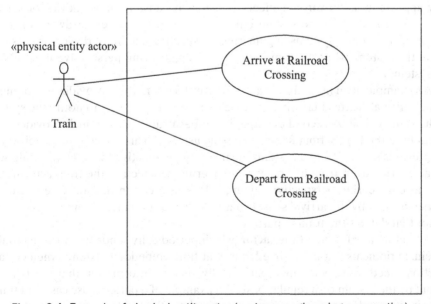

Figure 6.4. Example of physical entity actor (systems engineering perspective).

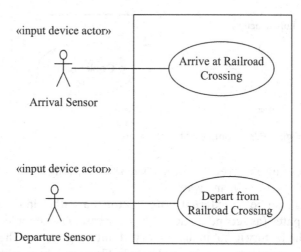

Figure 6.5. Example of input device actors (software engineering perspective).

the system using standard I/O devices. Actors that are modeled only from a software engineering perspective are input device actors and timer actors.

A physical entity actor in the systems engineering view is typically replaced by one or more input device actors when viewing the system from a software engineering perspective, since it is the input devices (such as sensors) that detect the presence of a physical entity. From a systems engineering perspective, the physical entity is the actor and the I/O devices are internal to the hardware/software system.

Furthermore, a human actor in the systems engineering view who interacts with the system indirectly via nonstandard I/O devices, such as various sensors, is typically replaced in the software engineering view by one or more I/O device actors. Thus, an actor can be an **input device actor** or an **input/output device actor**. Typically, the input device actor interacts with the system via a sensor. The reason why this kind of actor only appears in a software engineering view is because an input device or sensor is external to the software system but is internal to the larger hardware/software system. Thus, from a systems engineering perspective, the input device or sensor is inside the system, whereas from the software engineering perspective it is outside the system.

An example of an input device actor is Arrival Sensor, which provides sensor input to the Arrive at Railroad Crossing use case (shown in Figure 6.5) to notify the system of the train arrival. A second example is the Departure Sensor, which provides sensor input to the Depart from Railroad Crossing use case. This use case was depicted in the previous section from a systems engineering perspective in which the Train was the actor. However, from a software engineering perspective, the train actor in the systems engineering perspective (Figure 6.4) is replaced in the software engineering perspective by the arrival sensor that detects the train arrival and the departure sensor that detects the train departure.

An actor can also be a **timer actor**, which periodically sends timer events to the system. Periodic use cases are needed in real-time embedded systems when certain functions need to be performed periodically, such as information that needs to be output by the system on a regular basis. An example of a periodic use case and timer actor is given in Figure 6.6. The Timer actor initiates the Display Time of Day use case,

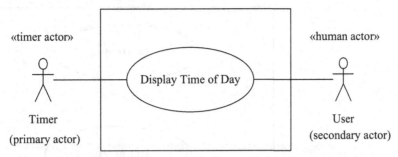

Figure 6.6. Example of timer actor (software engineering perspective).

which periodically (every minute) computes and updates the time-of-day clock and displays its value to the user. In this case, the timer is the primary actor, and the user is the secondary actor. This is an example of the secondary actor gaining value from the use case.

6.2.6 Generalization and Specialization of Actors

In some systems, different actors might have some roles in common but other roles that are different. In this situation, the actors can be generalized, so that the common part of their roles is captured as a generalized actor and the different parts by specialized actors. For an example, consider the actors in a factory automation system depicted in Figure 6.7. The Factory Robot actor captures the generalized role played by all factory robots. However, the Pick & Place Robot and Assembly Robot actors are modeled as specialized roles, which inherit the common role of all robots from Factory Robot and extend this with specialized roles for the specific types of robot.

6.3 IDENTIFYING USE CASES

To determine the use cases in the system, it is useful to start by considering the actors and the interactions they have with the system. Each use case describes a sequence of

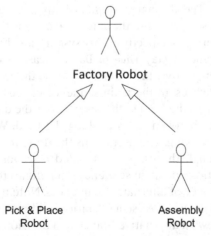

Figure 6.7. Example of generalization and specialization of actors.

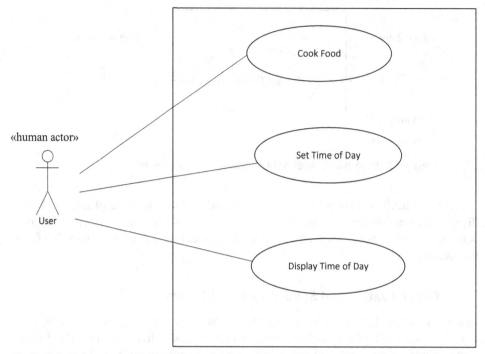

Figure 6.8. Use case model for Microwave Oven System (systems engineering perspective).

interactions between the actor(s) and the system. In this way, the functional requirements of the system are defined in terms of the use cases, which constitute a functional specification of a system.

A use case starts with input from the primary actor. The main sequence of the use case describes the most common sequence of interactions between the actor and the system. There may also be branches off the main sequence of the use case, which address less frequent interactions between the actor and the system. These deviations from the main sequence are executed only under certain circumstances – for example, if the actor makes an incorrect input to the system. Depending on the application requirements, these alternative sequences through the use case might join up later with the main sequence. The alternative sequences are also described in the use case.

Consider the use case model for the microwave oven system, which is viewed from a systems engineering perspective. This system has three use cases: the Cook Food, Set Time of Day, and Display Time of Day use cases (see Figure 6.8). From a systems engineering perspective, the primary actor is the user who wishes to cook food and not the I/O devices. In the main sequence of the Cook Food use case, the user opens the door, places the food in the oven, closes the door, selects the cooking time, and presses **Start**. The oven starts cooking the food. When the cooking time elapses, the oven stops cooking. The user opens the door and removes the food.

Each sequence through the use case is called a scenario. A use case usually describes several scenarios, one main sequence (sometimes referred to as the sunny day scenario) and a number of alternative sequences. Note that a scenario is a complete sequence through the use case, so a scenario could start out executing the main sequence and then follow an alternative branch at a decision point. In the Cook Food use case, there are several alternative scenarios to the main sequence sunny day scenario. For example, one scenario is that the user might open the door before cooking is finished, in which case cooking is stopped. In another scenario, the user might press **Cancel** or might press **Start** when the door is open.

6.3.1 Use Case Structuring Guidelines

When developing use cases, it is important to avoid a functional decomposition in which several small use cases describe individual functions of the system rather than describing a sequence of events that provides a useful result to the actor.

Although careful application of use case relationships can help with the overall organization of the use case model, use case relationships should be employed judiciously. Small inclusion use cases corresponding to individual functions (such as Open Door, Update Display, and Start Cooking) should be avoided. These functions are too small, and making them separate use cases would result in a functional decomposition with fragmented use cases in which the use case descriptions would be only a sentence each and not a description of a sequence of interactions. The result would be a use case model that is overly complex and difficult to understand – in other words, a problem of not being able to see the forest (the overall sequence of interactions) for the trees (the individual functions)!

6.4 DOCUMENTING USE CASES IN THE USE CASE MODEL

Use cases are documented in the use case model as follows:

- **Use case**. Each use case is given a name.
- **Summary**. This section briefly describes the use case, typically in one or two sentences.
- **Dependency**. This optional section describes whether the use case depends on other use cases, that is, whether it includes or extends another use case.
- **Actors**. This section names the actors in the use case. There is always a primary actor who initiates the use case. In addition, there might be one or more secondary actors who also participate in the use case.
- **Preconditions**. This section specifies one or more conditions that must be true at the start of use case, from the perspective of this use case.
- **Main sequence**. The bulk of the use case is a narrative textual description of the main sequence of the use case, which is the most usual sequence of interactions between the actor and the system. The description is in the form of the input from the actor, followed by the response of the system.
- **Alternative sequences**. This section provides a textual description of the alternative sequences that branch off from the main sequence. The descriptions of each alternative sequence, as well as the step in the main sequence at which the alternative branches off, need to be documented.
- **Nonfunctional requirements**. This section provides a textual description of the nonfunctional requirements, which could include one or more of performance requirements, safety requirements, availability requirements, and security requirements. (Refer to Section 6.5 for more information about nonfunctional requirements).
- **Postcondition**. This section specifies the condition(s) that is always true at the end of the use case, if the main sequence has been followed, from the perspective of this use case.

■ **Outstanding questions**. This section documents any questions about the use case for discussions with stakeholders.

6.5 SPECIFYING NONFUNCTIONAL REQUIREMENTS

Nonfunctional requirements address quality-of-service goals of the system, in other words how well the functional requirements are fulfilled. Nonfunctional requirements are particularly important for embedded systems and include performance requirements, safety requirements, availability requirements, and security requirements. An example of a nonfunctional requirement for the Authenticate Operator use case is the security requirement that the operator ID and password must be encrypted. An example of a nonfunctional requirement for the Cook Food use case is the performance requirement that the system must respond to the timer inputs within 100 milliseconds. An example of a nonfunctional safety requirement for a furnace is that if the temperature of the furnace exceeds a certain limit, which indicates a safety hazard of overheating, the furnace should be switched off. If the nonfunctional requirements apply to a group of related use cases, then they can be documented as such.

The nonfunctional requirements are specified in a separate section of the use case, as described in Section 6.4. Nonfunctional requirements include:

a) **Performance requirements** are system throughput and/or response time goals. For example: System shall respond to timer inputs within 100 milliseconds.

b) **Safety requirements** are requirements to protect against injury. For example: System shall switch off the furnace if temperature exceeds a pre-specified hazard level.

c) **Availability requirements** address the extent to which the system is operational for users. For example: System shall be operational 99.9 percent of required time.

d) **Security requirements** are requirements to protect information and system resources. For example: System shall encrypt operator ID and password.

e) **Scalability requirements** address the capability of system to grow beyond initial system deployment. For example: CPU, main memory, and secondary storage shall be capable of an expansion of 30 percent after initial system deployment.

f) **Configuration requirements** address decisions that can be made about the software system at deployment time. For example: There is a choice of language for displaying messages. The display language is set during system configuration.

6.6 EXAMPLES OF USE CASE DESCRIPTIONS

6.6.1 Example of Use Case from a Systems Engineering Perspective

This section gives an example of a use case description from a systems engineering perspective for the Cook Food use case (see Figure 6.8) from the microwave oven system. From this perspective, the actor is the human user, rather than the I/O devices used by the user, since the human user is outside the total system whereas the I/O devices are part of the hardware/software system. The use case description is given for the main sequence of the use case, followed by a description of the alternative sequences. In this use case, the steps in the main sequence are numbered. Each alternative sequence identifies the step number at which the alternative applies. A non-functional configuration requirement is also described.

Use case: Cook Food.
Summary: User puts food in oven, and microwave oven cooks food.
Actors: User
Precondition: Microwave oven is idle.
Main Sequence:
1. User opens the door.
2. System switches on the oven light.
3. User puts food in the oven and closes the door.
4. System switches off the oven light.
5. User presses the **Cooking Time** button.
6. System prompts for cooking time.
7. User enters cooking time on the numeric keypad and presses **Start**.
8. System starts cooking the food, starts the turntable, and switches on the light.
9. System continually displays the cooking time remaining.
10. System timer detects that the cooking time has elapsed.
11. System stops cooking the food, switches off the light, stops the turntable, sounds the beeper, and displays the end message.
12. User opens the door.
13. System switches on the oven light.
14. User removes the food from the oven and closes the door.
15. System switches off the oven light and clears the display.

Alternative Sequences:
Step 3: User presses **Start** when the door is open. System does not start cooking.
Step 5: User presses **Start** when the door is closed and the oven is empty. System does not start cooking.
Step 5: User presses **Start** when the door is closed and the cooking time is equal to zero. System does not start cooking.
Step 5: User presses **Minute Plus**, which results in the system adding one minute to the cooking time. If the cooking time was previously zero, **System** starts cooking, starts the timer, starts the turntable, and switches on the light.
Step 7: User opens door before pressing the **Start** button. System switches on the light.
Step 9: User presses **Minute Plus**, which results in the system adding one minute to the cooking time.
Step 9: User opens door during cooking. System stops cooking, stops the turntable, and stops the timer. The user closes the door (system then switches off the light) and presses **Start; System** resumes cooking, resumes the timer, starts the turntable, and switches on the light.

Step 9: User presses **Cancel**. System stops cooking, stops the timer, switches off the light, and stops the turntable. User may press **Start** to resume cooking. Alternatively, user may press **Cancel** again; system then cancels timer and clears display.

Configuration requirement:

Name: Display Language.

Description: There is a choice of language for displaying messages, which is set during system configuration. The default is English. Alternative mutually exclusive languages are French, Spanish, German, and Italian.

Postcondition: Microwave oven has cooked the food.

The main sequence for the use case, which describes the sequence of actor inputs to the system and the system's responses, should be relatively straightforward to develop. However, the alternative sequences are often trickier to develop, because so many of the system actions are state dependent. Figuring out all the alternatives of a state dependent use case is helped considerably by supplementing the use case with a state machine design, as described in the next chapter. The biggest contribution the alternatives section of the use case description can provide is to point out all the alternative events initiated by the actors that need to be addressed. Determining the details of how the system should react to these events can then be done with the aid of a state machine.

6.6.2 Example of Use Case from a Software Engineering Perspective

This section gives an example of a use case description from a software engineering perspective for the Arrive at Railroad Crossing use case (see Figure 6.9) from the Railroad Crossing Control System. From this perspective, the actors are the I/O devices (which are outside the software system but inside the total hardware/software system) rather than the train physical entity; in particular, it is the arrival sensor that detects the arrival of the train. The use case description is given for the main sequence of the use case, followed by a description of the alternative sequences. Nonfunctional requirements for safety and performance are also specified.

Use case: Arrive at Railroad Crossing.

Summary: Train approaches railroad crossing. The system lowers the barrier, switches on the warning lights, and switches on the audio warning alarm.

Actors:

- Primary actor: Arrival Sensor.
- Secondary actors: Barrier Detection Sensor, Barrier Actuator, Warning Light Actuator, Warning Audio Actuator, Rail Operations Service, Barrier Timer.

Precondition: The system is operational, and there is either no train or one train in the railroad crossing.

Main Sequence:

1. Arrival Sensor detects the train arrival and informs the system.

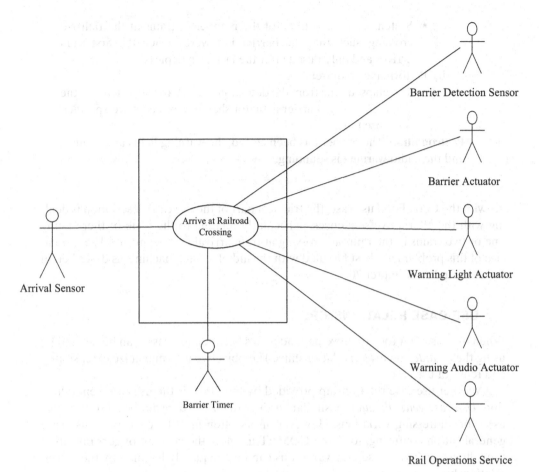

Figure 6.9. Use case model for Railroad Crossing Control System (software engineering perspective).

2. System commands each Barrier Actuator to lower a barrier, each Warning Light Actuator to switch on the flashing lights, and each Warning Audio Actuator to switch on the audio warning.
3. Barrier Detection Sensor detects that a barrier has been lowered and informs the system.
4. System sends a train arrival message to Rail Operations Service.

Alternative Sequences:

Step 2: If there is another train already at the railroad crossing, skip steps 2 and 3.

Step 3: If Barrier Timer notifies the system that the lowering timer has timed out, the system sends a safety warning message to the Rail Operations Service.

Nonfunctional Requirements:

a) Safety requirements:
   - Barrier lowering time shall not exceed a pre-specified time. If timer times out, the system shall notify Rail Operations Service.

- System shall keep track of the number of trains at the railroad crossing, such that the barrier is lowered when the first train arrives and only raised after the last train departs.

b) Performance requirement:

- The elapsed time from the detection of train arrival to sending the command to the barrier actuator shall not exceed a pre-specified response time.

Postcondition: The barrier has been closed, the warning lights are flashing, and the audio warning is sounding.

As with the Cook Food use case, the trickiest part of the use case description is dealing with the alternative sequences, particularly relating to the issue of there being one or two trains in the railroad crossing at train arrival and departure. The intricacies of this problem are best handled with the aid of a state machine, as described in the case study in Chapter 20.

6.7 USE CASE RELATIONSHIPS

When use cases get too complex, dependencies between use cases can be defined by using the *include* and *extend* relationships. The objective is to maximize extensibility and reuse of use cases.

Another use case relationship provided by the UML is the use case generalization. *Use case generalization* is similar to the *extend* relationship because it is also used for addressing variations. However, users often find the concept of use case generalization confusing, so in the COMET method, the concept of generalization is confined to classes. Use case variations can be adequately handled by the *extend* relationship.

6.8 THE *INCLUDE* USE CASE RELATIONSHIP

After the use cases for an application are initially developed, common sequences of interactions between the actor and the system can sometimes be determined that span several use cases. These common sequences of interactions reflect functionality that is common to more than one use case. A common sequence of interactions can be extracted from several of the original use cases and made into a new use case, which is called an **inclusion use case**.

Inclusion use cases reflect functionality that is common to more than one use case. When this common functionality is separated into an inclusion use case, the inclusion use case can be reused by several base (executable) use cases. An inclusion use case is executed in conjunction with a base use case, which includes, and hence executes, the inclusion use case. In programming terms, an inclusion use case is analogous to a library routine and a base use case is analogous to a program that calls the library routine.

An inclusion use case might not have a specific actor. The actor is in fact the actor of the base use case that includes the inclusion use case. Because different base use cases use the inclusion use case, it is possible for the inclusion use case to be used by different actors.

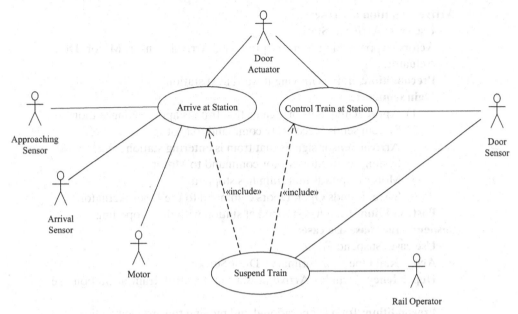

Figure 6.10. Example of inclusion use cases and *include* relationships.

6.8.1 Example of *Include* Relationship and Inclusion Use Cases

As an example of inclusion use cases, consider a Light Rail Control System (see case study described in Chapter 21), which is described from a software engineering perspective. In particular, there is a use case, Suspend Train, which includes the Arrive at Station and Control Train at Station inclusion use cases (this example is a simplified version of that in Chapter 21). Suspend Train has one human actor, the Rail Operator, who commands a train to go out of service, and one input device actor, Door Sensor. Suspend Train includes the Arrive at Station use case, which has two input device actors, the Approaching Sensor (to detect when the train is nearing the station) and the Arrival Sensor (to detect when the train is entering the station) as well as two output device actors, Motor (to first decelerate and then stop the train) and Door Actuator (to open the train doors). SuspendTrain then includes the Control Train at Station, which has one input device actor, the Door Sensor, which detects when the train doors have opened, and the Door Actuator, which, after an interval, is commanded to close the train doors. The use case descriptions of the three use cases are given next.

Control Train at Station use case:
 Use case: Control Train at Station.
 Actors: Door Sensor (primary), Door Actuator.
 Precondition: Train is stopped at station with doors opening.
 Main sequence:
  1) Door Sensor sends Doors Opened message.
  2) After time interval, System sends Close Doors command to the Door Actuator.
 Postcondition: Train is stopped at station with doors closing.

Arrive at Station use case:
> **Use case**: Arrive at Station.
> **Actors**: Approaching Sensor (primary), Arrival Sensor, Motor, Door Actuator.
> **Precondition**: Train is moving toward next station.
> **Main sequence**:
> > 1) Approaching Sensor signals that train is approaching station
> > 2) System sends Decelerate command to Motor.
> > 3) Arrival Sensor signals that train is entering station
> > 4) System sends Stop Motor command to Motor.
> > 5) Motor responds that train has stopped.
> > 6) System sends Open Doors command to the Door Actuator.
>
> **Postcondition**: Train has stopped at station with doors opening.

Suspend Train base use case:
> **Use case**: Suspend Train.
> **Actor**: Rail Operator (primary), Door Sensor.
> **Dependency**: Includes Arrive at Station, Control Train at Station use cases.
> **Precondition**: Train is operational and moving toward next station.
> **Main sequence**:
> > 1) Rail Operator sends suspend train operation command to System.
> > 2) Include Arrive at Station use case.
> > 3) Include Control Train at Station use case.
> > 4) Door Sensor sends Doors Closed message to System.
>
> **Postcondition**: Train is stationary at station and out of service.

6.8.2 Structuring a Lengthy Use Case

The *include* relationship can also be used to structure a lengthy use case. The base use case provides the high-level sequence of interactions between actor(s) and system. Inclusion use cases provide lower-level sequences of interactions between actor(s) and system. An example of this is the Manufacture High-Volume Part use case (see Figure 6.11), which describes the sequence of interactions in manufacturing a part. This process involves receiving the raw material for the part to be manufactured (described in the Receive Part use case), executing a manufacturing step at each factory workstation (described in the Process Part at High-Volume Workstation use case), and shipping the manufactured part (described in the Ship Part use case).

6.9 THE *EXTEND* USE CASE RELATIONSHIP

In certain situations, a use case can get very complex, with many alternative branches. The *extend* relationship is used to model alternative paths that a use case might take under certain conditions. A use case can become too complex if it has too many alternative, optional, and exceptional sequences of interactions. A solution to this problem is to split off an alternative or optional sequence of interactions into a separate use case. The purpose of this new use case is to extend the old use case, if the

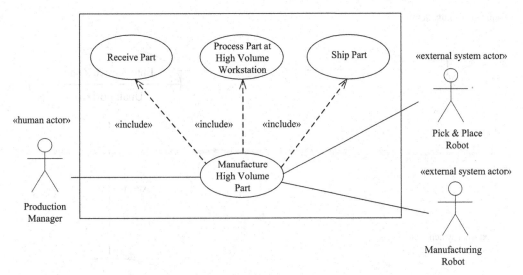

Figure 6.11. Example of multiple inclusion use cases and *include* relationships.

appropriate condition holds. The use case that is extended is referred to as the **base use case**, and the use case that does the extending is referred to as the **extension use case**.

Under certain conditions, a base use case can be extended by a description given in the extension use case. A base use case can be extended in different ways, depending on which condition is true. The *extend* relationship can be used as follows:

- To show a conditional part of the base use case that is executed only under certain circumstances
- To model complex or alternative paths.

It is important to note that the base use case does not depend on the extension use case. The extension use case, however, depends on the base use case and executes only if the condition in the base use case that causes it to execute is true. Although an extension use case usually extends only one base use case, it is possible for it to extend more than one. A base use case can be extended by more than one extension use case.

6.9.1 Extension Points

Extension points are used to specify the precise locations in the base use case at which extensions can be added. An extension use case may extend the base use case only at these extension points (Fowler 2004, Rumbaugh et al. 2005).

Each extension point in the base use case is given a name. The extension use case has one insertion segment (usually the main sequence of the extension use case) for the extension point. This segment is inserted at the location of the extension point in the base use case. The *extend* relationship can be conditional, meaning that a condition is defined that must be true for the extension use case to be invoked. Thus it is possible to have more than one extension use case for the same extension point, but with each extension use case satisfying a different condition.

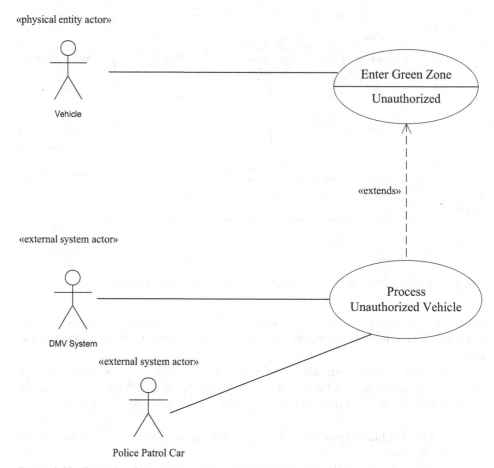

Figure 6.12. Example of an *extend* relationship and an extension use case.

A segment defines a behavior sequence to be executed when the extension point is reached. When an instance of the use case is executed and reaches the extension point in the base use case, if the condition is satisfied, then execution of the use case is transferred to the corresponding segment in the extension use case. Execution transfers back to the base use case after completion of the segment.

An extension point with multiple extension use cases can be used to model several alternatives in which each extension use case specifies a different alternative. The extension conditions are designed such that only one condition can be true, and hence only one extension use case selected, for any given situation.

The value of the extension condition is set during runtime execution of the use case because at any one time, one extension use case could be chosen, and at a different time an alternative extension use case could be chosen. In other words, the extension condition is set during runtime of the use case and can change during execution.

6.9.2 Example of Extension Point and Extension Use Cases

Consider the following example for a green zone system (Figure 6.12). The green zone is an area in the center of the city in which there is restricted access by motor vehicles. Vehicles entering the green zone have a green zone permit number encoded on a RFID (radio frequency ID) transponder, which is displayed on the windshield of the vehicle. When the vehicle enters the green zone, a remote transponder detector reads the permit number RFID and transmits it to the Green Zone Monitoring System. This functionality is handled by the base use case, Enter Green Zone. However, a car entering the green zone without a permit is handled by an extension use case, Process Unauthorized Vehicle. The extension point is called Unauthorized (Figure 6.12) and is located in an alternative sequence of the Enter Green Zone use case for handling unrecognized or missing permit numbers. The use cases are described from a systems engineering perspective, so the primary actor is the Vehicle (not the sensors that detect the vehicle), and the secondary actors for the extension use case are the external DMV System and Police Patrol Car.

Enter Green Zone base use case
   Use case: Enter Green Zone.
   Summary: Vehicle enters restricted Green Zone; System starts tracking the vehicle.
   Actor: Vehicle.
   Precondition: Green Zone entry point is clear.
   Main Sequence:
      1. Vehicle approaches green zone entry point.
      2. System detects vehicle entering the green zone.
      3. System reads vehicle permit number RFID.
      4. System checks that permit number is valid.
      5. System stores the following information: permit number, entry time/date, entry location.
   Alternative Sequence:
   Step 4: Unauthorized (i.e., unrecognized or missing permit number): Extend with *Process Unauthorized Vehicle* use case.
   Postcondition:
   Vehicle has entered green zone.

Process Unauthorized Vehicle extension use case
   Use case: Process Unauthorized Vehicle.
   Summary: The license number of the unauthorized vehicle is detected, decoded, and sent to the police.
   Actor: Vehicle (primary), Police Patrol Car (secondary), DMV System (secondary).
   Dependency: Extends *Enter Green Zone* use case.
   Precondition: Vehicle has an invalid or nonexistent permit number.
   Description of insertion segment:
      1. System takes photograph of vehicle license plate.
      2. System uses an image processing algorithm to analyze the photograph and extract the state name and vehicle license number.
      3. System sends a message to the DMV system of the vehicle's state containing the vehicle license number and requesting owner name and address.
      4. The DMV system sends a message to the system containing the name and address of the vehicle owner.

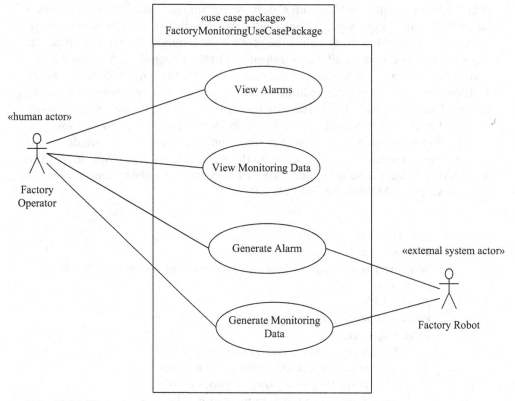

Figure 6.13. Example of use case package.

5. The system issues and prints a fine to be sent by mail to the vehicle owner.

Postcondition: The unauthorized vehicle has been detected and a fine has been issued.

Alternative sequence:

Step 2: The license plate cannot be decoded (because of bad photograph, bad weather, covered license plate); System sends alert message to the Police Patrol Car.

6.10 USE CASE PACKAGES

For large systems that have to deal with a large number of use cases, the use case model can become unwieldy. A good way to handle this scale-up issue is to introduce a **use case package** that groups together related use cases. In this way, use case packages can represent high-level requirements that address major subsets of the functionality of the system. Because actors often initiate and participate in related use cases, use cases can be grouped into packages based on the major actors that use them. Nonfunctional requirements that apply to a group of related use cases could be assigned to the use case package that contains those use cases.

Figure 6.13 shows an example of a use case package for the Factory Automation System, namely the Factory Monitoring Use Case Package, encompassing four use cases.

The Factory Operator is the primary actor of the View Alarms and View Monitoring Data use cases and a secondary actor of the other use cases. The Factory Robot is the primary actor of the Generate Alarm and Generate Monitoring Data use cases.

6.11 SUMMARY

This chapter has described the use case approach to specifying the functional requirements of the system from both systems engineering and software engineering perspectives. It has described the concepts of actor and use cases. It has also described use case relationships, in particular, the *extend* and *include* relationships. Furthermore, use case modeling can be supplemented with state machine modeling to provide a more precise specification for state dependent real-time embedded systems, as described in Chapter 7.

Use cases developed from a systems engineering perspective are less detailed than use cases developed from a software engineering perspective. The former use cases can be developed earlier in the COMET/RTE life cycle, in particular before hardware/software boundary modeling and software system context modeling, as described in Chapter 5.

The use case model has a strong influence on subsequent software development. Thus, use cases are realized in the analysis model during dynamic interaction modeling, as described in Chapter 9. For each use case, the objects that participate in the use case are determined by using the object structuring criteria described in Chapter 8, and the sequence of interactions between the objects is defined. Software can be incrementally developed by selecting the use cases to be developed in each phase of the project, as described in Chapter 4. Integration and system test cases should also be based on use cases.

7

State Machines for Real-Time Embedded Systems

State machines (also referred to as *finite state machines*) are used for modeling control and sequencing in a system. This is particularly important for real-time embedded systems, which are usually highly state dependent. In particular, the actions of a state dependent system depend not only on the inputs to the system but also on what happened previously in the system, which is captured as a state. A state machine can be used to depict the states of a system, subsystem, component, or object. Notations used to define state machines are the state transition diagram, state machine diagram, statechart, and state transition table. In highly state dependent systems, these notations help substantially to understand the complexity of these systems.

A state machine specification is typically more precise and understandable than a textual or use case description. State machines can enhance or even replace use case descriptions of requirements by providing more precise specifications. In particular, state machines are essential for specifying systems with significant state dependent behavior.

In the UML notation, a state transition diagram is referred to as a *state machine diagram*. The UML state machine diagram notation is based on Harel's statechart notation (Harel and Gery 1996; Harel and Politi 1998). In this book the terms *state machine* and *state machine diagram* are used interchangeably. This chapter refers to a traditional state transition diagram, which is not hierarchical, as a *flat state machine* and uses the term *hierarchical state machine* to refer to the concept of hierarchical state decomposition, a concept introduced by Harel. A brief overview of the state machine notation is given in Chapter 2 (Section 2.6).

This chapter starts by considering the characteristics of flat state machines and then describes hierarchical state machines. To show the benefits of hierarchical state machines, this chapter starts with the simplest form of flat state machine and gradually shows how it can be improved upon to achieve the full modeling power of hierarchical state machines. The process of developing state machines from use cases is then described. Several examples are given throughout the chapter from two case studies, the Microwave Oven and Train Control state machines.

Section 7.1 describes events and states in state machines. Section 7.2 introduces the Microwave Oven Control state machine example. Section 7.3 describes events and guard conditions, while Section 7.4 describes state machine actions. Section 7.5

describes hierarchical state machines, both sequential and orthogonal. Section 7.6 describes cooperating state machines, while state machine inheritance is described in Section 7.7. The process of developing state machines from use cases is then described in Sections 7.8 and 7.9.

7.1 STATE MACHINES

A **state machine** is a conceptual machine with a finite number of states. The state machine can be in only one of the states at any specific time. A **state transition** is a change in state that is caused by an input event. In response to an input event, the state machine might transition to a different state. Alternatively, the event has no effect and the state machine remains in the same state. The next state depends on the current state as well as on the input event. Optionally, an output action might result from the state transition.

A state machine can be used to depict the state of a system, subsystem, or component. However, in object-oriented systems, a state machine (even if it describes the state of a system) should always be encapsulated in a class, as described in Chapter 8.

7.1.1 Events

An **event** occurs at a point in time; it is also known as a discrete event, discrete signal, or stimulus. An event is an atomic occurrence (i.e., not interruptible) and conceptually has zero duration. Examples of events are Door Opened, Item Placed, Timer expired, and Cruising Speed Reached.

Events can depend on each other. For example, in a microwave oven, the event Door Opened always precedes the event Item Placed for a given sequence of events. In this situation, the first event (Door Opened) causes a transition into the state (Door Open), while the next event (Item Placed) causes the transition out of that state; the precedence of the two events is reflected in the state that connects them, as shown in Figure 7.1. However, events can be completely independent of each other. For example, the event Train x Departed from New York is independent of the event Train y Departed from Washington.

An event can originate from an external source, such as Door Opened (which is the result of the user opening the oven door), or the event can be internally generated by the system, such as Cruising Speed Reached.

A **timer event** is a special event, specified by the keyword **after**, which indicates that an event will occur after an elapsed time identified by an expression in parentheses, such as **after** (ten seconds) or **after** (elapsed time). On a state machine, the timer event causes a transition out of a given state. The elapsed time is measured from the time of entry into that state (e.g., when the timer is started) until exit from the state, which is caused by the timer expiration event.

State machines are assumed to observe *run to completion* semantics. This means that each event is executed to completion before starting the next event. Thus, if two events arrive at essentially the same time, one event is selected and processed completely before the next event is selected. Executing an event includes executing any hierarchical or orthogonal transitions and actions resulting from the event.

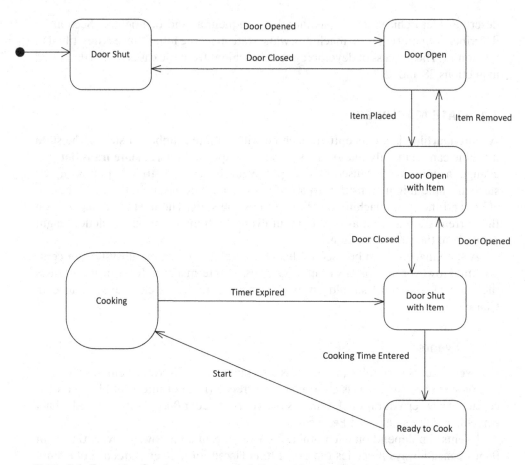

Figure 7.1. Example of main sequence of state machine (partial state machine).

7.1.2 States

A **state** represents a recognizable situation that exists over an interval of time. Whereas an **event** occurs at a point in time, a state machine is in a given state over an interval of time. The **current state** is the name given to the state that the state machine is currently occupying. The arrival of an event at the state machine usually causes a transition from one state to another. Alternatively, an event can have a null effect, in which case the state machine remains in the same state. In theory, a state transition takes zero time to occur. In practice, the time for a state transition to occur is negligible compared to the time spent in the state.

Some states represent the state machine waiting for an event from the external environment, for example the state Ready to Cook is the state in which the state machine is waiting for the user to press the Start button, as shown in Figure 7.1. Other states represent situations in which the state machine is waiting for a response from another part of the system. For example, Cooking is the state in which food is being cooked and the next event is an internal timer event that is generated when the cooking timer expires.

The initial state of a state machine is the state that is entered when the state machine is activated. For example, the initial state in the Microwave state machine is the Door Shut state, as identified in UML by the arc originating from the small black circle in Figure 7.1.

7.2 EXAMPLES OF STATE MACHINE

As an example of a state machine, consider the partial state machine for the Microwave Oven, which is taken from the microwave oven system case study and shown in Figure 7.1. The state machine follows the main sequence described in the Cook Food use case (see Chapters 6 and 19) and shows the different states for cooking food. The initial state is Door Shut. When the user opens the door, the state machine transitions into the Door Open state. The user places an item in the oven, causing the state machine to transition into the Door Open with Item state. When the user closes the door, the state machine then transitions into the Door Shut with Item state. After the user inputs the cooking time, the Ready to Cook state is entered. When the user presses the **Start** button, the state machine transitions into the Cooking state. When the timer expires, the Door Shut with Item state is reentered. The user then opens the door and the state machine transitions back to Door Open with Item state. The user removes the food and the state machine transitions to the Door Open state. From there, if the user closes the door, the state machine transitions back to the Door Shut state.

The above description closely follows the use case description and describes the states entered and exited during the execution of the main sequence of the Cook Food use case. A state machine can also depict alternative state transitions out of a state. It is possible to have more than one transition out of a state, with each transition caused by a different event. Consider the alternative state transition out of Cooking state. If, instead of the timer expiration causing the transition from Cooking state, the user opens the door during cooking (see Figure 7.2), the state machine would then transition to the Door Open with Item state. From this state, the user could then either close the door (transition to Door Shut with Item state) or remove the item (transition to Door Open state). These alternative state transitions are clearly visible in the state machine and are more precisely described than in a textual use case description.

In some cases, it is also possible for the same event to occur in different states and have different effects. For example, in Figure 7.2, if the door is opened in Door Shut state, the state machine transitions to Door Open state. If the door is opened in Door Shut with Item state, the state machine transitions to Door Open with Item state. However, if the door is opened in Cooking state, the transition is also to Door Open with Item state. In addition, on this transition out of Cooking state, cooking is stopped. This issue is discussed further in Section 7.4.

7.3 EVENTS AND GUARD CONDITIONS

It is possible to specify conditional state transitions through the use of guard conditions. This can be achieved by combining events and guard conditions in defining state transitions. The notation used is *Event [Condition]*. A condition is a Boolean expression given in square brackets with a value of True or False, which holds for some period of time. When the event arrives, it causes a state transition, provided that the guard condition is True. Conditions are optional.

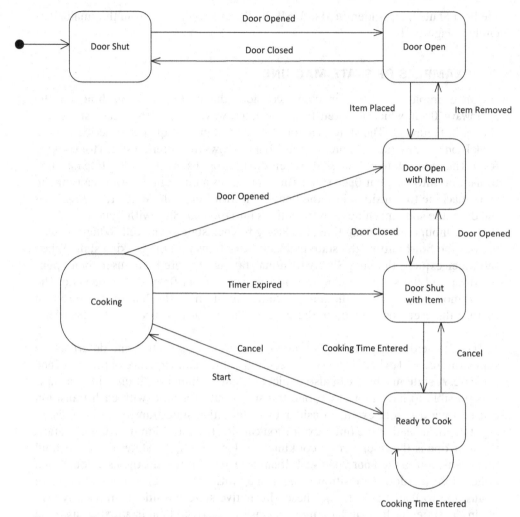

Figure 7.2. Example of alternative state transitions on state machine (partial state machine).

In some cases, an event does not cause an immediate state transition, but its impact needs to be remembered because it will affect a future state transition. The fact that an event has occurred can be stored as a condition that can be checked later.

Examples of guard conditions in Figure 7.3 are Zero Time and Time Remaining in the microwave state machine. Two of the transitions out of the Door Open with Item state are Door Closed [Zero Time] and Door Closed [Time Remaining]. Thus the transition taken depends on whether the user has previously entered the time or not. If the condition Zero Time is true when the door is closed, the state machine transitions to Door Shut with Item, waiting for the user to enter the time. If the condition Time Remaining is true when the door is closed, the state machine transitions to the Ready to Cook state. (It should be noted that these conditions can be depicted as states on a separate state machine as described in Section 7.5.5).

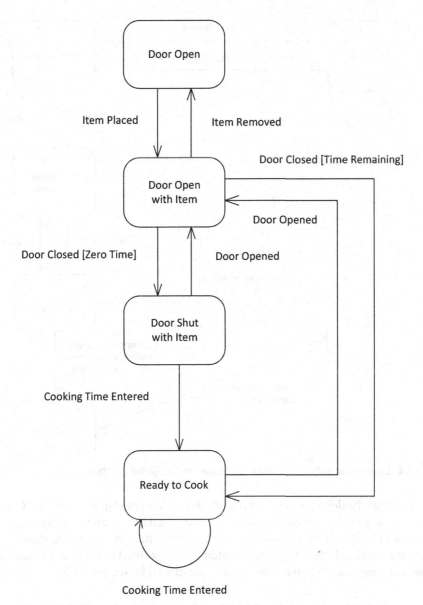

Figure 7.3. Example of events and conditions (partial state machine).

7.4 ACTIONS

Associated with a state transition is an optional output **action**. An action is a computation that executes as a result of a state transition. While an event is the cause of a state transition, an action is the effect of the transition. An action is triggered at a state transition. It executes and then terminates itself. The action executes instantaneously at the state transition; thus conceptually an action is of zero duration. In practice, the duration of an action is very small compared to the duration of a state.

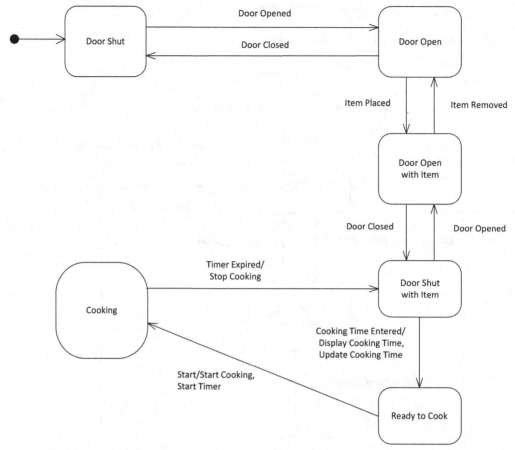

Figure 7.4. Example of actions in main sequence (partial state machine).

Actions can be depicted on state transitions, as described in Section 7.4.1. Certain actions, namely entry and exit actions, can be depicted more concisely as being associated with the state rather than with the transition into or out of the state. Entry actions are triggered when the state is entered, as described in Section 7.4.2, and exit actions are triggered on leaving the state, as described in Section 7.4.3.

7.4.1 Actions on State Transitions

A transition action is an action that is a result of a transition from one state to another – it could also happen if the state machine transitions back to the same state. To depict a transition action on a state machine, the state transition is labeled *Event/Action* or *Event [Condition]/Action*.

As examples of actions, consider the Microwave state machine of Figure 7.1 with the actions added, as shown in Figure 7.4. Consider the situation when the user presses the start button and the machine is in the Ready to Cook state. The state machine transitions into the Cooking state. The actions are to start the timer and start cooking.

There can be more than one action associated with a transition. Since the actions all execute simultaneously, there must not be any interdependencies between the actions. Thus, in the above example, the actions to start the timer and start cooking

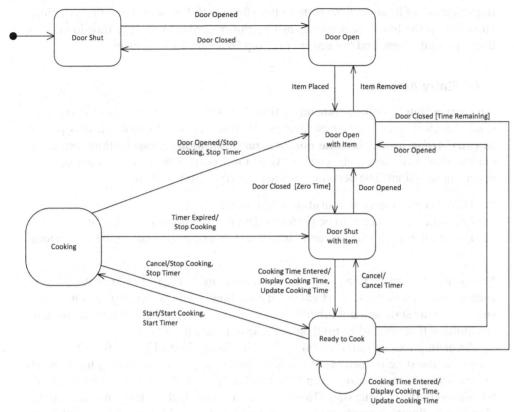

Figure 7.5. Example of alternative state transitions and actions (partial state machine).

are independent of each other. However, it is not correct to have two simultaneous actions, such as Compute Change and Display Change. Since there is a sequential dependency between the two actions, the change cannot be displayed before it has been computed. To avoid this problem, introduce an intermediate state called Computing Change. The Compute Change action is executed on entry to this state and the Display Change action is executed on exit from this state.

An example of a state machine with alternative state transitions and actions is shown in Figure 7.5. In particular, there are three alternative state transitions out of Cooking state, which have different resulting actions. From Cooking state, if the timer expires, the transition is to Door Shut with Item state, and the action is to Stop Cooking. By contrast, if the door is opened, the transition is to Door Open with Item, and the actions are Stop Cooking (as before) and Stop Timer. Stop Timer is necessary in the door opened scenario because there will be a non-zero cooking time left if the door is opened before the timer expires. If cooking is later resumed, the oven will cook for the remaining time. The same two actions are also executed if the user presses Cancel, although the transition is to Ready to Cook state.

The same event can occur in different states. Depending on the individual state, the actions could be same or different. Figure 7.5 gives an example of the Door Opened event, which can occur in four different states. In each scenario, the transition is to a different state; in three scenarios (transition out of Door Shut state to Door Open state, transition out of Door Shut with Item state to Door Open with Item state, and transition out of Ready to Cook state to Door Open with Item state) there is no action. However, in the fourth scenario, transition out of Cooking state, the transition is to Door Open with Item, and the actions are Stop Cooking and Stop Timer.

7.4.2 Entry Actions

An **entry action** is an instantaneous action that is performed on transition into the state. An entry action is represented by the reserved word **entry** and is depicted as **entry**/*Action* inside the state box. Whereas transition actions (actions explicitly depicted on state transitions) can always be used, entry actions should only be used in certain situations. The best time to use an entry action is when:

- There is more than one transition into a state.
- The same action needs to be performed on *every* transition into this state.
- The action is performed on entry into this state and not on exit from the previous state.

In this situation, the action is only depicted once inside the state box, instead of on each transition into the state. However, if an action is only performed on some transitions into the state and not others, then the entry action must not be used. Instead, transition actions should be used on the relevant state transitions.

An example of an entry action is given in Figure 7.6. In Figure 7.6a, actions are shown on the state transitions. If the **Start** button is pressed (resulting in the Start event) while the microwave oven is in the Ready to Cook state, the state machine transitions to the Cooking state. There are two actions, Start Cooking and Start Timer. However, if Minute Pressed event arrives (to cook the food for one minute) while in Door Shut with Item state, the state machine will also transition to the Cooking state. However, in this case the actions are Start Cooking and Start Minute. Thus, in the two transitions into Cooking state, one action is the same (Start Cooking) but the second is different. An alternative decision is to use an entry action for Start Cooking as shown in Figure 7.6b. On entry into Cooking state, the entry action Start Cooking is executed because this action is executed on every transition into the state. However, the Start Timer action is shown as an action on the state transition from Ready to Cook state into Cooking state. This is because the Start Timer action is only executed on that specific transition into Cooking state and not on the other transition. For the same reason, on the transition from Door Shut with Item state into Cooking state, there is a transition action Start Minute. Figures 7.6a and 7.6b are semantically equivalent to each other but Figure 7.6b is more concise.

7.4.3 Exit Actions

An **exit action** is an instantaneous action that is performed on transition out of the state. An exit action is represented by the reserved word **exit** and is depicted as **exit**/*Action* inside the state box. Whereas transition actions (actions explicitly depicted on state transitions) can always be used, exit actions should only be used in certain situations. The best time to use an exit action is when:

- There is more than one transition out of a state.
- The same action needs to be performed on *every* transition out of the state.

a) Actions on state transitions

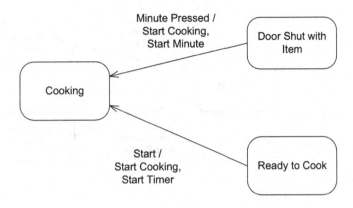

b) Entry action

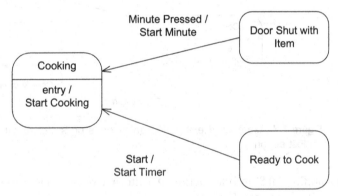

Figure 7.6. Example of entry action. (a) Actions on state transitions. (b) Entry action.

- The action is performed on exit from this state and not on entry into the next state.

In this situation, the action is only depicted once inside the state box, instead of on each transition out of the state. However, if an action is only performed on some transitions out of the state and not others, then the exit action must not be used. Instead, transition actions should be used on the relevant state transitions.

An example of an **exit action** is given in Figure 7.7. In Figure 7.7a, actions are shown on the state transitions out of Cooking state. Consider the action Stop Cooking. If the timer expires, the microwave oven transitions from the Cooking state to the Door Shut with Item state and the action Stop Cooking is executed (Figure 7.7a). If the door is opened, the oven transitions out of the Cooking state into Door Open with Item state. In this transition, two actions are executed, Stop Cooking and Stop Timer. Thus, in both transitions out of Cooking state (Figure 7.7a), the action Stop Cooking is executed. However, when the door is opened and the transition is to Door Open with Item state,

a) Actions on state transitions

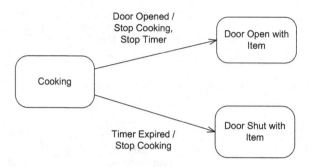

b) Exit action

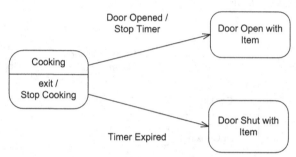

Figure 7.7. Example of exit action. (a) Actions on state transitions. (b) Exit action.

there is an additional Stop Timer action. An alternative design is shown in Figure 7.7b, where an exit action Stop Cooking is depicted. This means that whenever there is a transition out of Cooking state, the exit action Stop Cooking is executed. In addition, in the transition to Door Open with Item state, the transition action Stop Timer will also be executed. Having the Stop Cooking action as an exit action instead of an action on the state transition is more concise, as shown in Figure 7.7b. The alternative of having transition actions, as shown in Figure 7.7a, requires the Stop Cooking action to be explicitly depicted on each of the state transitions out of the Cooking state. Figures 7.7a and 7.7b are semantically equivalent to each other but Figure 7.7b is more concise.

Figure 7.8 depicts an alternative version of the Microwave Oven Control state machine in which the transition actions to Start Cooking and Stop Cooking on Figure 7.5 are replaced by an entry action in Cooking state to Start Cooking and an exit action to Stop Cooking.

7.4.4 **Activities**

In addition to actions, it is also possible to have an *activity* executed as a result of a state transition. An **activity** is a computation that executes for the duration of a state. Thus, unlike an action, which takes no time, an activity executes for a finite amount

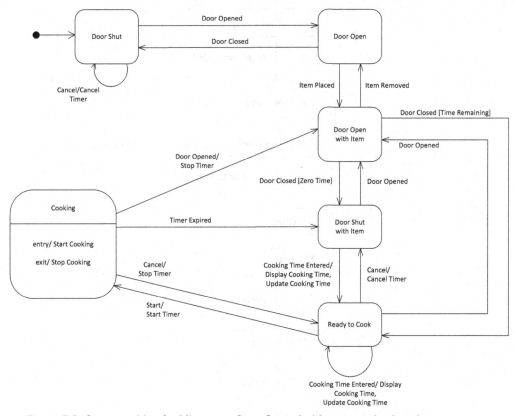

Figure 7.8. State machine for Microwave Oven Control with entry and exit actions.

of time. An activity is enabled on entry into the state and disabled on exit from the state. The cause of the state change, which results in disabling the activity, is usually an input event from a source that is not related to the activity. However, in some cases, the activity itself generates the event that causes the state change.

An activity is depicted as being associated with the state in which it executes. This is achieved by showing the activity in the state box and having a dividing line between the state name and the activity name. The activity is depicted as **do / Activity**, where **do** is a reserved word. This means the activity is enabled on entry into the state and disabled on exit from the state.

For examples of activities, consider an Automobile Cruise Control state machine. Consider the transition from Initial state into Accelerating state, as shown in Figure 7.9. An activity – namely, Increase Speed – is enabled on entry into Accelerating state. This activity executes for the duration of this state and is disabled on exit from this state. The activity is depicted as **do / Increase Speed**.

If a transition from one state to another has a combination of actions, enabled activities, and disabled activities, there are specific rules about the order in which these occur:

1. First, the activity in the state being exited is disabled.
2. Second, the action(s) is executed (if one exists).
3. Third, the activity in the state being entered is enabled.

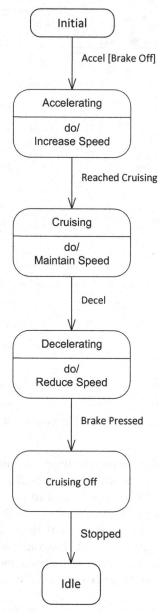

Figure 7.9. Example of state machine with activities (partial state machine).

For example, consider the Reached Cruising event that causes a transition from Accelerating state to Cruising state. First, the activity Increase Speed is disabled, and then the activity Maintain Speed is enabled and remains active throughout Cruising state. The semantics of this state transition are:

- Increase Speed is disabled on exit from Accelerating state.
- Maintain Speed is enabled on entry into Cruising state.

Figure 7.9 depicts three activities in total: besides Increase Speed and Maintain Speed, there is the activity Reduce Speed, which executes in Decelerating state.

7.5 HIERARCHICAL STATE MACHINES

One of the potential problems of flat state machines is the proliferation of states and transitions, which makes the state machine very cluttered and difficult to read. A very important way of simplifying state machines and increasing their modeling power is to introduce *composite* states, which are also known as superstates, and the hierarchical decomposition of state machines. With this approach, a *composite* state at one level of a state machine is decomposed into two or more substates on a lower-level state machine.

The objective of hierarchical state machines is to exploit the basic concepts and visual advantages of state transition diagrams, while overcoming the disadvantages of overly complex and cluttered diagrams, through hierarchical structuring. Note that any hierarchical state machine can be mapped to a flat state machine, so for every hierarchical state machine there is a semantically equivalent flat state machine.

There are two main approaches to developing hierarchical state machines. The first approach is a top-down approach to determine major high-level states, sometimes referred to as modes of operation. For example, in an airplane control state machine, the modes might be Taking Off, In Flight, and Landing. Within each mode, there are several states, some of which might in turn be composite states. The second approach is to first develop a flat state machine and then identify states that can be aggregated into composite states, as described in Section 7.5.3.

7.5.1 Sequential State Decomposition

State machines can often be significantly simplified by the hierarchical decomposition of states, in which a composite state is decomposed into two or more interconnected sequential substates. This kind of hierarchical decomposition is referred to as *sequential state decomposition*. The notation for state decomposition also allows both the composite state and the substates to be shown on the same diagram or, alternatively, on separate diagrams, depending on the complexity of the decomposition.

An example of hierarchical sequential state decomposition is given next. Figure 7.10 depicts a flat state machine with six states, including the Accelerating, Cruising, and Approaching states. Figure 7.11a depicts an equivalent state machine using hierarchical sequential state decomposition, in which there is a composite state called In Motion, which is decomposed into three substates, namely the Accelerating, Cruising, and Approaching substates. (On the hierarchical state machine, the composite state is the outer rounded box, which contains the name of the composite state at the top left. The substates are shown as inner rounded boxes). When the state machine is in the In Motion composite state, it is in one (and only one) of the substates. Hierarchical sequential state decomposition results in a *sequential state machine*, in which the substates are entered sequentially. Figure 7.11a depicts the same hierarchical state machine but this time without its substates. This depiction is referred to as a high-level state machine.

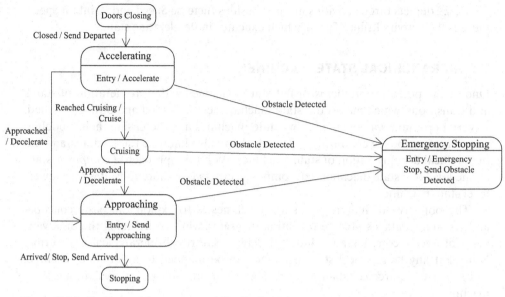

Figure 7.10. Example of flat state machine for Train Control (partial state machine).

7.5.2 Composite States

Composite states can be depicted in two ways on state machines, as described next. A composite state can be depicted with its internal substates, as shown for the In Motion composite state in Figure 7.11a. Alternatively, a composite state can be depicted as a black box without revealing its internal substates, as shown in Figure 7.11b. It should be pointed out that when a composite state is decomposed into substates, the transitions into and out of the composite state must be preserved. Thus, there is one state transition into the In Motion composite state and two transitions out of it, as shown in both Figures 7.11a and 7.11b.

Each transition into the composite state In Motion is, in fact, a transition into one (and only one) of the substates on the lower-level state machine, namely the Accelerating substate. Each transition out of the composite state has to actually originate from one (and only one) of the substates (Accelerating, Cruising, or Approaching) on the lower-level state machine.

7.5.3 Aggregation of State Transitions

The hierarchical state machine notation also allows a transition out of every one of the substates on a state machine to be aggregated into a transition out of the composite state. Careful use of this feature can significantly reduce the number of state transitions depicted on a state machine diagram.

In the flat state machine in Figure 7.10, the Obstacle Detected event can occur in any one of the Accelerating, Cruising, or Approaching states, in which case the state machine transitions to the Emergency Stopping state. With the hierarchical state machine in Figure 7.11a, instead of depicting the Obstacle Detected event as causing a transition out of each of the Accelerating, Cruising, or Approaching substates, it is more concise to show this event causing the transition out of the composite state In

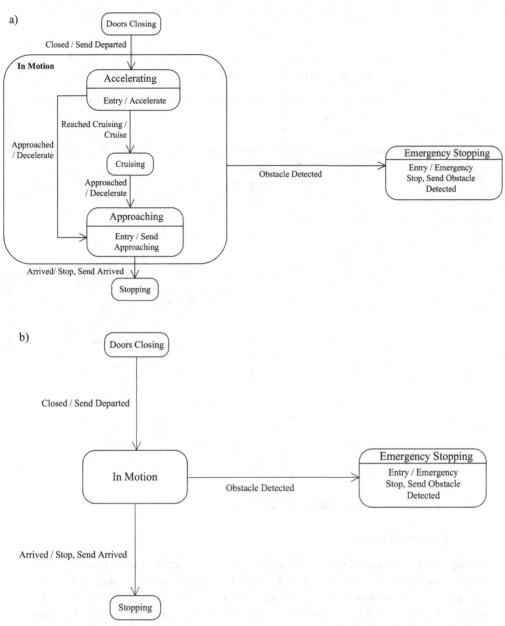

Figure 7.11. Example of hierarchical state machine for Train Control. (a) Hierarchical state machine depicted with its substates. (b) High-level depiction of hierarchical state machine without its substates.

Motion, as depicted in Figure 7.11a. The transitions out of the three substates (of the In Motion composite state) are not explicitly shown on Figure 7.11a, even though an individual Obstacle Detected event would actually occur in one of these substates and cause the transition to the Emergency Stopping state. However, the advantage is the simplification of the state machine due to the significant reduction in state transition arcs.

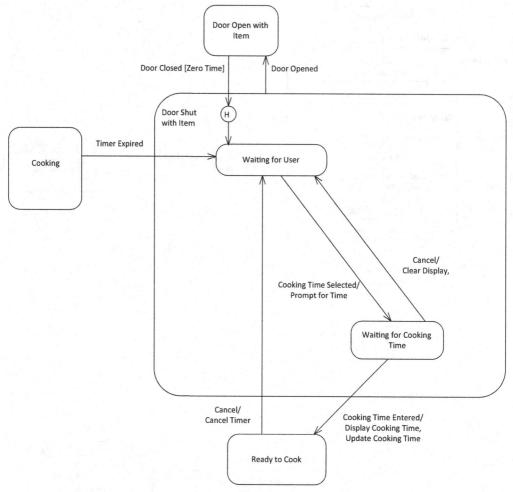

Figure 7.12. Example of history state in hierarchical state machine.

7.5.4 History State

The history state is another useful characteristic in hierarchical state machines. Indicated by an *H* inside a small circle, a **history state** is a pseudostate within a sequential composite state, which means that the composite state remembers its previously active substate after it exits. Thus, when the composite state is reentered, the previously active substate is entered.

An example of sequential state decomposition with a history state is given in Figure 7.12, in which the Door Shut with Item composite state is decomposed into the Waiting for User and Waiting for Cooking Time substates. The history state is used to remember which of these two substates the composite state (Door Shut with Item) is in, when an event transitions the state machine out of the composite state. Thus, the previous substate is reentered when the Door Shut with Item composite state is reentered. For example, if the composite state is in the Waiting for User substate when the door is opened, the state machine will transition to Door Open with Item. When the door is closed (and assuming zero time), the Door Shut with Item composite state is reentered, and in particular the Waiting for User substate is reentered. However,

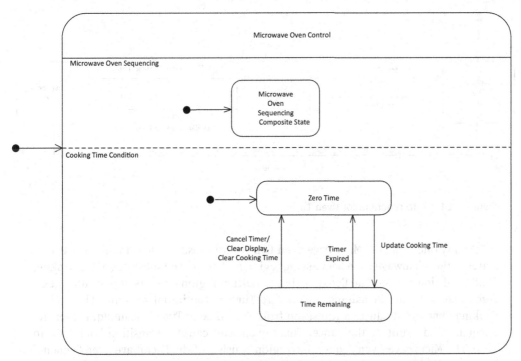

Note: Microwave Oven Sequencing composite state is decomposed into Microwave Oven Control state machine in Figure 7.8

Figure 7.13. Example of orthogonal state machine.

if the composite state is in the Waiting for Cooking Time substate when the door is opened, then that substate is reentered when the door is closed. Without the history state, this behavior would be more difficult to model.

7.5.5 Orthogonal State Machines

Another kind of hierarchical state decomposition is *orthogonal state decomposition*, which can be used to model different views of the same object's state. With this approach, a high-level state on one state machine is decomposed into two (or more) orthogonal regions. The two orthogonal regions are shown separated by a dashed line. When the higher-level state machine is in the composite state, it is simultaneously in one of the substates on each of the lower-level orthogonal regions.

Although an orthogonal state machine can be used to depict concurrent activity within the object containing the state machine, it is better to use this kind of decomposition to show different perspectives of the same object that are not concurrent. Designing active objects with only one thread of control is much simpler and is strongly recommended. Where true concurrency is required, use separate active objects and define each object with its own state machine.

An example of using an orthogonal state machine to depict guard conditions is given in Figure 7.13 for the microwave oven state machine. The Microwave Oven Control state machine is decomposed into two orthogonal regions: one for sequencing the events and actions in the oven (Microwave Oven Sequencing), and the other for Cooking Time Condition. The two regions are depicted on a high-level state machine, with a dashed line separating them.

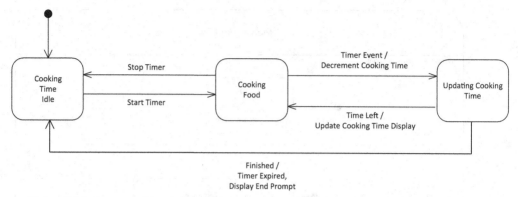

Figure 7.14. State machine for Oven Timer.

At any one time, the Microwave Oven Control composite state is in one of the substates of the Microwave Oven Sequencing region and one of the substates of the Cooking Time Condition region. The Cooking Time Condition region consists of two substates – Zero Time and Time Remaining – with Zero Time as the initial substate. The Update Cooking Time event causes a transition from Zero Time to Time Remaining. Either the Timer Expired event or the Cancel Timer event can cause a transition back to Zero Time. The Microwave Oven Sequencing region consists of the Microwave Oven Sequencing Composite State, which is decomposed to depict the sequence of states the oven goes through while handling a user request to cook food, as shown in Figure 7.8. The current state of the Microwave Oven Control state machine is the union of the current substates in each of the Microwave Oven Sequencing and the Cooking Time Condition regions.

The Zero Time and Time Remaining substates of the Cooking Time Condition region (see Figure 7.13) are the guard conditions checked in the Microwave Oven Sequencing region when the Door Closed event is received while in the Door Open with Item substate (see Figure 7.8). Cancel Timer is an action (cause) in the Microwave Oven Sequencing region and an event (effect) on the Cooking Time Condition region, which causes a transition to the Zero Time state. Update Cooking Time is also an action on the former region and an event on the latter. Timer Expired is an event in both regions.

7.6 COOPERATING STATE MACHINES

State machines can model concurrent processes by using cooperating state machines. With this approach, the control problem is divided between two separate state machines, which cooperate with each other. The cooperation is by means of an action on one state machine that propagates as an event to the other state machine, and vice versa.

An example of this is used in the Microwave Oven problem, which uses two cooperating state machines, namely the Microwave Oven Control (Figure 7.8) and Oven Timer (Figures 7.14) state machines. Oven Timer is used to control decrementing the cooking time down to zero and notifying Microwave Oven Control when the timer expires. The initial state of Oven Timer is Cooking Time Idle. Cooking food is initiated by the transition of Microwave Oven Control from Ready to Cook state into Cooking state, which results in the Start Cooking entry action and the Start Timer transition action. The Start

Timer action in the Microwave Oven Control state machine propagates as an event of the same name to the Oven Timer state machine, causing the latter to transition from Cooking Time Idle state to Cooking Food state. Each second, a Timer Event causes an Oven Timer action to decrement the cooking time by cycling through the Updating Cooking Time transient state and back to Cooking Food state. When the cooking time remaining reaches zero, the Finished event causes the Oven Timer state machine to transition from Updating Cooking Time state to Cooking Time Idle state. An action on this transition is Timer Expired, which propagates as an event of the same name back to the Microwave Oven Control state machine. This event causes Microwave Oven Control to transition from Cooking state to Door Shut with Item and the resulting action is Stop Cooking. It should be noted that the Stop Timer action in the Microwave Oven Control state machine also propagates as an event of the same name to the Oven Timer state machine, causing the latter to transition from Cooking Food state to Cooking Time Idle state.

7.7 INHERITED STATE MACHINES

Inheritance can be used to introduce change to a state machine. When a state machine is specialized, the child state machine inherits the properties of the parent state machine; that is, it inherits the states, events, transitions, actions, and activities depicted in the parent state machine model. The child state machine can then modify the inherited state machine as follows:

1. **Add new states**. The new states can be at the same level of the state machine hierarchy as the inherited states. Furthermore, new substates can be defined for either the new or the inherited states. In other words, a state in the parent state machine can be decomposed further in the child state machine. It is also possible to add new orthogonal states – that is, new states that execute orthogonally with the inherited states.
2. **Add new events and transitions**. These events cause new transitions to new or inherited states.
3. **Add or remove actions and activities**. New actions can be defined that are executed on transitions into and out of new or inherited states. Exit and entry actions, as well as new activities, can be defined for new or inherited states. It is also possible to remove predefined actions and activities, although this should be done with care and is generally not recommended.

The child state machine must not delete states or events defined in the parent. It must not change any composite state/substate dependency defined in the parent state machine.

Examples of Inherited State Machines

As an example of an inherited state machine, consider the Microwave Oven Control class from the microwave oven system, which specifies the state machine of the same name. The Microwave Oven Control state machine is depicted in Figures 7.8. The Microwave Oven Control state machine is then specialized to provide the additional features for the Enhanced Microwave Oven Control child state machine. The specialization of the Microwave Oven Control state dependent control superclass to produce

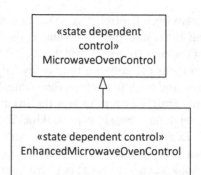

Figure 7.15. Example of inheritance of a state dependent control class.

the Enhanced Microwave Oven Control subclass is depicted in the class diagram of Figure 7.15.

The state machine for the Enhanced Microwave Oven Control class is shown in Figure 7.16. Consider the impact of the following extensions incorporated into the specialized state machine, which are referred to as features:

- TOD Clock
- Turntable
- Light
- Beeper
- Minute Plus

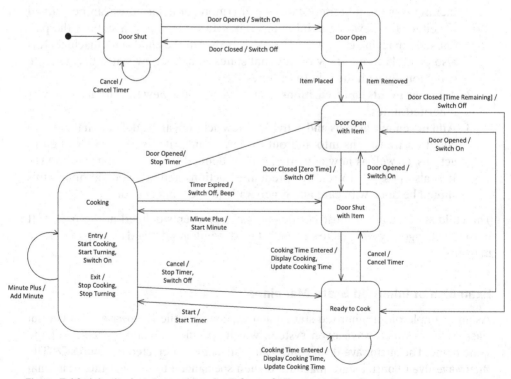

Figure 7.16. Inherited state machine for Enhanced Microwave Oven Control.

Example of new states added. To support the TOD (time-of-day) Clock feature, the inherited Door Shut state is specialized to create three new substates (see Chapter 19).

Example of new transitions added. To support the Minute Plus feature, a new Minute Plus transition (see Figure 7.16) is introduced from the Door Shut with Item state to the Cooking state, since pressing the Minute Plus button when the door is shut with an item inside it results in the oven cooking the food for a minute. If the Minute Plus button is pressed while the food is cooking, there is a transition from Cooking state back to itself.

Example of new actions added (see Figure 7.16). To support the Turntable feature, two new actions are provided: Start Turning (which is executed on entry into the inherited Cooking state) and Stop Turning (which is executed on exit from the Cooking state). To support the Light feature, two new actions are provided: Switch On, which is both an entry action (into the inherited Cooking state) and a transition action (between other inherited states), and the Switch Off transition action. To support the Beeper feature, the Beep transition action is added.

7.8 DEVELOPING STATE MACHINES FROM USE CASES

This section describes a systematic approach to develop a state machine from a use case. The approach starts with a typical scenario given by the use case, that is, one specific path through the use case. This scenario should be the main sequence through the use case, involving the most usual sequence of interactions between the actor(s) and the system. Now consider the sequence of external events given in the scenario. Usually, an input event from the external environment causes a transition to a new state, which is given a name corresponding to what happens in that state. If an action is associated with the transition, the action occurs in the transition from one state to the other. If an activity is to be performed in that state, the activity is enabled on entry to the state and disabled on exit from the state. Actions and activities are determined by considering the response of the system to the input event, as given in the use case description.

Initially, a flat state machine is developed, which follows the event sequence given in the main scenario. The states depicted on the state machine should all be externally visible states. That is, the actor should be aware of each of these states. In fact, the states represent consequences of actions taken by the actor, either directly or indirectly. This is illustrated in the detailed example given in the next section.

To complete the state machine, determine all the possible external events that could be input to the state machine. Do this by considering the description of alternative paths given in the use case. Several alternatives describe the reaction of the system to alternative inputs from the actor. Determine the effect of the arrival of these events on each state of the initial state machine; in many cases, an event could not occur in a given state or will have no impact. However, in other states, the arrival of an event will cause a transition to an existing state or some new state that needs to be added to the state machine. The actions resulting from each alternative state transition also need to be considered. These actions should already be documented in the alternative sequences section of the use case description as the system reaction to alternative input events. However, for complex state machines, the actions may not have been fully worked out and documented in the use cases, in which case the actions need to be fully designed for the state machine(s).

7.9 EXAMPLE OF DEVELOPING A STATE MACHINE FROM A USE CASE

As an example of a state machine developed from a use case, consider how the Microwave Oven Control state machine is developed from the Microwave Oven use case, which is taken from the microwave oven system case study.

7.9.1 Develop State Machine for Main Sequence of Use Case

The state machine needs to follow the interaction sequence described in the Cook Food use case (see Chapters 6 and 19) and show the different states for cooking food. In general, user inputs should correspond to input events that cause state transitions. System responses should correspond to actions on the state machine.

The precondition given for the use case is Microwave Oven Is Idle with Door Shut. We therefore decide that the initial state should be called Door Shut. The first step of the use case states that the user opens the door and in response the system switches the oven light on. The user then puts food in the oven and closes the door. These use case steps consist of three input events from the user: open the door, insert the food, and close the door, which we treat as follows:

- When the user opens the door, the state machine needs to transition into a new state, which we name the Door Open state. This causes the state machine action to switch on the light.
- When the user places an item in the oven, the state machine needs to transition again; we name the new state Door Open with Item state.
- When the user closes the door, the state machine transitions into a third state, which we name the Door Shut Waiting for User state, and a resulting action is to switch off the light. Note that we designate a different state from the initial Door Shut state in order to differentiate between the states of Door Shut with Item in the oven and Door Shut without an item.

In the next use case step, the user presses the Cooking Time button, so the microwave needs to transition to a new state, which we name Door Shut Waiting for Cooking Time. Step 6 of the use case states that the system prompts for cooking time. As this prompt is a system response, the system output in the use case needs to be an output action on the state machine. After the user inputs the cooking time, the oven is ready to start cooking, so we name the next state Ready to Cook. When the user presses the **Start** button, the oven starts cooking the food, so we designate the next state the Cooking state. Step 8 of the use case states that the system starts cooking the food. For this to happen, the system needs to start the timer, start cooking the food, start turning the turntable, and switch on the light. All these concurrent actions need to be specified on the state machine as a result of the Start transition. Since there are several actions that result from entering the Cooking state (Start Cooking, Start Turning, Switch on Light), these actions are designed as entry actions. However, Start Timer is designed as

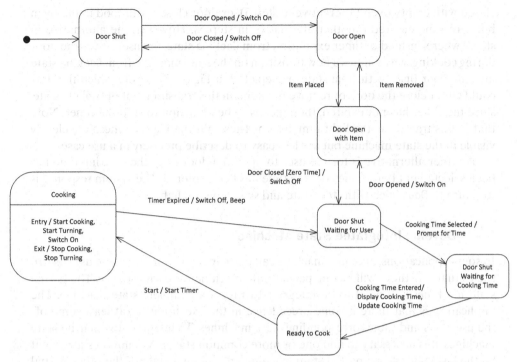

Figure 7.17. State machine for Microwave Oven Control (main sequence of Cook Food use case).

a transition action because it is does not happen on every transition into the Cooking state (as depicted in Figure 7.16).

When the timer expires, the state machine reenters the Door Shut Waiting for User state. Actions on this transition need to be to stop cooking the food, stop turning the turntable, switch off the light, and beep. Two actions that result from leaving the Cooking state are designed as exit actions (Stop Cooking and Stop Turning). The other two actions, Switch off Light and Beep, are designed as transition actions as these actions do not happen on every transition out of Cooking state (as explained in the next section and depicted in Figure 7.16).

Continuing with the main sequence, the user then opens the door and the state machine transitions back to Door Open with Item state, with the action to switch on the light. The user removes the food, which causes the state machine to transition back to Door Open state. Finally, the user closes the door and the state machine transitions back to the initial Door Shut state, with the action to switch off the light. This sequence of transitions on the state machine is depicted in Figure 7.17.

7.9.2 Consider Alternative Sequences of Use Case

The state machine so far corresponds to the main sequence through the Cook Food use case and describes the states entered and exited during the execution of the use case. Next we must consider the alternative sequences in the use case description. Some of the alternatives are events that occur in states in which they are prohibited from causing a transition and therefore correspond to null transitions. Examples are user pressing START with the door open (alternative in step 3 of the use case), door closed with empty oven (alternative in step 5), or door closed with food in the oven but zero time entered (another alternative in step 5). However, the alternative in step 9 where, instead of timer expiration from Cooking state, the user opens the door during cooking, necessitates a new transition on the state machine from Cooking state into the Door Open with Item state, as depicted in Figure 7.16, from which the user could either close the door or remove the item. In this transition out of Cooking state, since the timer has not expired, there needs to be an action to stop the timer. Note that in this transition, the light remains on. These alternative sequences are clearly visible in the state machine but are less easy to describe precisely in a use case.

Another alternative is for the user to open the door after the cooking time has been selected but before the cooking time has been entered. The system response is to return to Door Open with Item state and switch on the light.

7.9.3 Develop Integrated State Machine

In some applications, one state machine can participate in more than one use case. In such situations, there will be one partial state machine for each use case. The partial state machines will need to be integrated to form a complete state machine. The implication is that there is some precedence in the execution of (at least some of) the use cases and their corresponding state machines. To integrate two partial state machines, it is necessary to find one or more common states. A common state might be the last state of one partial state machine and the first state of the other partial state machine. However, other situations are possible. The integration approach is to integrate the partial state machines at the common state, in effect superimposing the common state of the second state machine on top of the same state on the first state machine. This can be repeated as necessary, depending on how many partial state machines need to be integrated. An example of this state machine integration is given for the Light Rail Control System case study in Chapter 21.

7.9.4 Develop Hierarchical State Machine

It is usually easier to initially develop a flat state machine before trying to develop a hierarchical state machine. After completing the flat state machine by considering alternative events, look for ways to simplify the state machine by developing a hierarchical state machine. Look for states that can be aggregated because they constitute a natural composite state. In particular, look for situations where the aggregation of state transitions simplifies the state machine.

For the integrated flat state machine of the Microwave Oven, the decision is made to aggregate the Waiting for User and Waiting for Cooking Time states into the Door Shut with Item composite state, as described in Section 7.5.4 and shown in Figure 7.12. This decision results in:

- Waiting for User and Waiting for Cooking Time becoming substates of the Door Shut with Item composite state.
- The aggregation of transitions out of each of these substates into a transition out of the composite state, when the door is opened.
- The creation of a history state to allow reentry to the substate that was previously active.

Furthermore, an orthogonal state machine can be developed to depict guard conditions for the microwave oven state machine, as depicted in Figure 7.13. The Microwave Oven Control state machine is decomposed into two orthogonal regions: one to depict the sequencing of the events and actions in the oven (Microwave Oven Sequencing), and the other to depict the Cooking Time Condition, as described in Section 7.5.5.

7.10 SUMMARY

This chapter has described the characteristics of flat state machines, including events, states, guard conditions, actions, and activities. This was followed by a description of hierarchical state machines, including sequential state decomposition, history states, and orthogonal state machines. Cooperating state machines and state machine inheritance were also described. The process of developing a state machine from a use case was then described in detail. It is also possible for a state machine to support several use cases, with each use case contributing to some subset of the state machine. Such cases are often easier to model by considering the state machine in conjunction with the object interaction model, in which a state dependent object executes the state machine, as described in Chapter 9. Several other examples of state machines are given in the case studies.

8

Object and Class Structuring for Real-Time Embedded Software

After structural modeling and defining the use case and state machine models, the next step is to determine the software classes and objects in the real-time embedded system. Using a model-based approach, the emphasis is on software objects that model real-world objects in the problem domain. Furthermore, since concurrency is so fundamental to real-time software design, an important issue that is addressed at this stage is whether the objects are concurrent or not. Another key issue described in this chapter is the behavior pattern of each category of object.

This chapter provides guidelines, in particular structuring criteria, on how to determine the classes and objects in the system. As with system structural modeling (see Chapter 5), software classes and objects are categorized by using stereotypes. Section 8.1 gives an overview of object and class structuring while Section 8.2 describes object and class structuring categories. Section 8.3 describes object behavior and patterns. Section 8.4 describes the different kinds of boundary classes and objects. Section 8.5 describes entity classes and objects, which were first introduced in Chapter 5. Section 8.6 describes the different kinds of control classes and objects. Section 8.7 describes application logic classes and objects.

8.1 OBJECT AND CLASS STRUCTURING CRITERIA

In software applications, a class is categorized by the role it plays in the application. Object and class structuring criteria are provided to assist the designer in structuring a system into its constituent classes and objects. The approach used for identifying objects is to look for real-world objects in the problem domain and then design corresponding software objects that model the real world. After the objects have been identified, the interactions among objects are depicted in the dynamic model on *sequence diagrams* or *communication diagrams*, as described in Chapter 9.

Classes are categorized in order to group together classes with similar characteristics. Figure 8.1 shows the categorization of application classes using inheritance. As described in Chapter 5, stereotypes (See Sections 5.2 and 5.6) are used to distinguish among the various kinds of classes. Application classes are categorized according to their role in the application, in particular «boundary» class, «entity» class, «control» class, or «application logic» class. Because an object is an instance of a class, an object

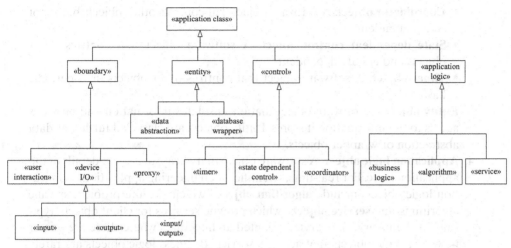

Figure 8.1. Classification of application classes by stereotype.

has the same stereotype as the class from which it is instantiated. Thus, the categorization described in this section applies equally to classes and objects.

The classification process depicted in Figure 8.1 is analogous to classifying books in a library, with major classes such as fiction and nonfiction, and further classification of fiction into classics, mysteries, adventure, and so on and nonfiction into biography, autobiography, travel, cooking, history, and other categories. It is also analogous to the taxonomy of the animal kingdom, which is divided into major categories (mammal, bird, fish, reptile, and so on) that are further divided into subclasses (e.g., cat, dog, and monkey are subclasses of mammal).

8.2 OBJECT AND CLASS STRUCTURING CATEGORIES

Objects and classes are categorized according to the roles they play in the application. There are four main object and class structuring categories, as shown in Figure 8.1: boundary classes, entity classes, control classes, and application logic classes. Most applications will have classes from each of the four categories. Real-time embedded systems are likely to have several device I/O boundary classes to interface to the various sensors and actuators. Because real-time systems are highly state dependent, they are also likely to have complex state dependent control classes. The four main object and class structuring categories (Figure 8.1) are summarized below and are described in detail in Sections 8.4 through 8.7.

1. **Boundary object**. Software object that interfaces to and communicates with the external environment. Boundary objects are further categorized as:
   - **Device I/O boundary object**. Software object that receives input from and/or outputs to a hardware I/O device.
   - **Proxy object**. Software object that interfaces to and communicates with an external system or subsystem.
   - **User interaction object**. Software object that interacts with and interfaces to a human user.
2. **Control object**. A control object that provides the overall coordination for a collection of objects. Control objects are further categorized as:

- **Coordinator object**. A software object that controls other objects but is not state dependent.
- **State dependent control object**. A software object that controls other objects and is state dependent
- **Timer object**. A software object that controls other objects on a periodic basis.
3. **Entity object**. A software object that encapsulates information and provides access to the information it stores. Entity objects are classified further as data abstraction or wrapper objects.
4. **Application logic object**. A software object that encapsulates the details of the application logic. For real-time, scientific, or engineering applications, application logic objects include **algorithm objects**, which execute problem-specific algorithms, and **service objects**, which provide services for client objects, typically in client/server or service-oriented architectures where there are one or more real-time objects that access a service. Business logic objects are rarely used in real-time systems.

In most cases, what category an object fits into is usually obvious. However, in some cases, it is possible for an object to satisfy more than one of the above criteria. For example, an object could have characteristics of both an entity object, in that it encapsulates some data, and an algorithm object, in that it executes an algorithm. In such cases, allocate the object to the category it seems to fit best in. Note that it is more important to determine all the objects in the system than to be unduly concerned about how to categorize a few borderline cases.

8.3 OBJECT BEHAVIOR AND PATTERNS

During object and class structuring, two important decisions can be made about object behavior; the first concerns the concurrent nature of the object, and the second concerns the behavior pattern of the object.

Because concurrency is so fundamental to real-time software design, during object structuring, a first attempt can be made to determine whether each software object is concurrent or not. As a general rule, apart from entity objects, each object is initially considered to be concurrent; that is, each object is considered active with a separate thread of control and can therefore execute in parallel with other objects. Entity objects are considered passive. A passive object does not have a thread of control and can therefore only execute when one of its operations is invoked by another object. The initial assumption concerning inter-object communication is that all communication between concurrent objects is asynchronous, whereas all communication with a passive object is synchronous, that is, corresponding to an operation call, as described in Chapter 3. Additional concurrency decisions are made during concurrent task design, including revising initial design decisions, for example by using task clustering or a different inter-task communication pattern, as described in Chapter 13. An example of two concurrent robot objects interacting with each other using asynchronous communication (as described in Chapter 2) is given in Figure 8.2a, while an example of two concurrent objects accessing a passive sensor data repository entity object using read and write operation invocation is given in Figure 8.2b. For more details of the communication patterns, refer to Chapter 11.

a) Communicating Concurrent objects

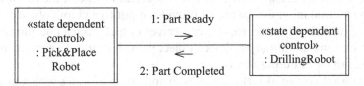

b) Concurrent objects communicating with passive object

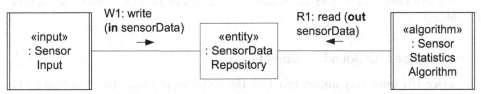

Figure 8.2. a. Example of communicating concurrent objects. **b.** Example of concurrent objects communicating with a passive object.

Another important decision taken during object and class structuring is that for each object structuring criterion, there is a corresponding object behavioral pattern, which describes how the object interacts with its neighboring objects. It is useful to understand the object's typical pattern of behavior, because when this category of object is used in an application, it is likely to interact in a similar way with the same kinds of neighboring objects. Each behavioral pattern is depicted on a UML communication diagram (first introduced in Chapter 2) as depicted in the next several figures.

8.4 BOUNDARY CLASSES AND OBJECTS

This section describes the characteristics of the three different kinds of software boundary objects that interface to and communicate with the external objects, namely device I/O boundary objects, proxy objects, and user interaction objects. In each case, an example is given of a boundary object, followed by an example of a behavioral pattern in which a boundary object communicates with neighboring objects in a typical interaction sequence.

8.4.1 External Objects and Software Boundary Objects

Boundary objects are software objects that interface to and communicate with the external objects that are outside the system (see Section 5.6). To help determine the boundary objects in the system, it is necessary to consider the external objects to which they are connected. In fact, identifying the external objects that communicate with and interface to the system helps identify the boundary objects. Each external object communicates with a boundary object in the system. External objects interface to software boundary objects as follows:

■ An **external device object** provides input to and/or receives output from a **device I/O boundary object**. An external device represents an I/O device type. An external I/O device object represents a specific I/O device, that is, an instance of the device type. An external device object can be one of the following:

- An external input device object provides input to an input object.
- An external output device object receives output from an output object.
- An external input/output device object provides input to and receives output from an input/output object.

- An **external system object** interfaces to and communicates with a **proxy object**. An external smart (i.e., software-intensive) device object also interfaces to and communicates with a smart device proxy object.
- An **external timer** object signals to a software **timer object**.
- An **external user object** interfaces to and interacts with a **user interaction object**.

8.4.2 Device I/O Boundary Objects

A **device I/O boundary object** provides the software interface to a hardware I/O device. Device I/O boundary objects are needed for nonstandard application-specific I/O devices, which are more prevalent in real-time embedded systems. Standard I/O devices are typically handled by the operating system and so do not need special-purpose device I/O boundary objects developed as part of the application.

A physical object in the application domain is a real-world object that has some physical characteristics – for example, it can be seen and touched. For every real-world physical object that is relevant to the problem, there should be a corresponding software object in the system. For example, in the Microwave Oven System, the door sensor and heating element are relevant real-world physical objects because they interact with the software system. However, the oven casing is not a relevant real-world object, because it does not interact with the software system. In the software system, the relevant real-world physical objects are modeled by means of software objects, such as the door sensor interface and heating element interface software objects.

Real-world physical objects usually interface to the system via sensors and actuators. These real-world objects provide inputs to the system via sensors or are controlled by (receive outputs from) the system via actuators. Thus, to the software system, the real-world objects are actually I/O devices that provide inputs to and receive outputs from the system. Because the real-world objects correspond to I/O devices, the software objects that interface to them are referred to as device I/O boundary objects.

For example, in the Microwave Oven System, the microwave door is a real-world object that has a sensor (input device) that provides inputs to the system. The heating element is a real-world object that is controlled by means of an actuator (output device) that receives outputs from the system.

An **input object** is a device I/O boundary object that receives input events or data from an external input device. In common with all boundary objects, an input object is assumed to be concurrent. Figure 8.3 shows an example of an input class Door Sensor Input and an instance of this class, a Door Sensor Input object, which receives door sensor inputs from an external hardware Door Sensor input device. Figure 8.3 also shows the hardware/software boundary, as well as the stereotypes for the hardware «external input device» and the software «input» objects. Thus, the input object

a) Example of input class

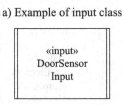

b) Example of behavioral pattern for an input object

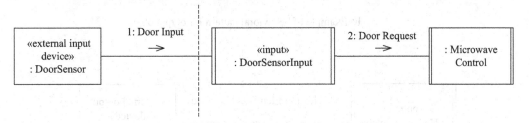

Hardware / software boundary

Figure 8.3. Example of input class and object.

provides the software interface to the external hardware input device. Because boundary objects are assumed to be concurrent, the input object is depicted using the UML notation for a concurrent object.

An **output object** is a device I/O boundary object that sends output to an external output device. As with all boundary objects, an output object is assumed to be concurrent. Figure 8.4 shows an example of an output class called Heating Element Output, as well as an instance of this class, a Heating Element Output object, which sends outputs to an external real-world object, the Heating Element Actuator external output device. The Heating Element Output software object sends Switch On and Switch Off heating commands to the hardware Heating Element Actuator. Figure 8.4 also shows the hardware/software boundary.

A hardware I/O device is a device that both sends inputs to the system and receives outputs from the system. The corresponding software class is an I/O class, and a software object that is instantiated from this class is an I/O object. An **input/output (I/O) object** is a device I/O boundary object that receives input from and sends output to an external I/O device. This is the case with the ATM Card Reader I/O class shown in Figure 8.5a and its instance, the ATM Card Reader I/O object (see Figure 8.5b), which receives ATM card input from the external I/O device, the ATM Card Reader. In addition, ATM Card Reader I/O sends eject and confiscate output commands to the card reader.

Each software boundary object should hide the details of the physical interface to the real-world object from which it receives input or to which it provides output. However, a software object should model the events experienced by the real-world object to which it corresponds. The events experienced by the real-world object are inputs to the system, in particular, to the software object that interfaces to it. In this way, the software object can simulate the behavior of the real-world object. In the case of a real-world object that is controlled by the system, the software object generates an output event that determines the behavior of the real-world object.

a) Example of output class

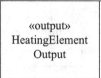

b) Example of behavioral pattern for output object

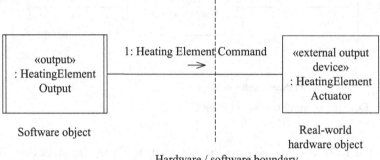

Figure 8.4. Example of output class and object.

a) Example of input/output class

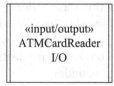

b) Example of behavioral pattern for input/output object

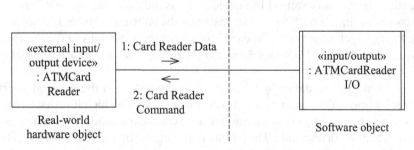

Figure 8.5. Example of I/O class and object.

a) Example of proxy class

«proxy»
Pick&Place
RobotProxy

b) Example of behavioral pattern for a proxy object

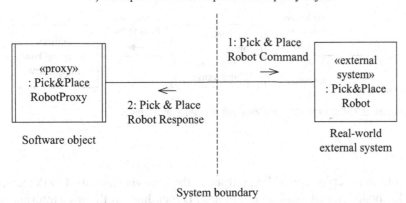

Figure 8.6. Example of proxy class and object.

8.4.3 Proxy Objects

A **proxy object** interfaces to and communicates with an external system or smart device. Although an external system can be very different from a smart device, the behavior of the two types of proxy object is similar. The proxy object is the local representative of the external system or smart device and hides the details of "how" to communicate with the external system or smart device. A proxy object is assumed to be concurrent.

An example of a proxy class is a Pick & Place Robot Proxy class. An example of a behavioral pattern for a proxy object is given in Figure 8.6, which depicts a concurrent Pick & Place Robot Proxy object that interfaces to and communicates with the external Pick & Place Robot. The Pick & Place Robot Proxy object sends pick and place robot commands to the Pick & Place Robot. The real-world robot responds to the commands.

Each proxy object hides the details of how to interface to and communicate with the particular external system. A proxy object is more likely to communicate by means of messages to an external, computer-controlled system, such as the robot in the above example, rather than through sensors and actuators, as is the case with device I/O boundary objects. However, these issues are not addressed until the design phase.

8.4.4 User Interaction Objects

This section addresses real-time embedded systems that need to interact with human users. A **user interaction object** communicates directly with a human user, receiving

a) Example of user interaction class

b) Example of behavioral pattern for user interaction object

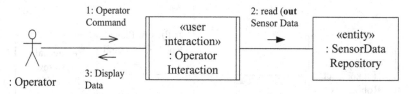

Figure 8.7. Example of user interaction class and object.

input from the user and providing output to the user via standard I/O devices, such as the keyboard, visual display, and mouse. Depending on the user interface technology, the user interface could be very simple (such as a command line interface) or it could be more complex (such as a graphical user interface [GUI] object). A user interaction object may be a composite object composed of several simpler user interaction objects. This means that the user interacts with the system via several user interaction objects such as windows and menus. Such objects are depicted with the «user interaction» stereotype. However, it is initially assumed that only the composite user interaction object is concurrent. Further design of user interaction objects is addressed during concurrent task design in Chapter 13.

An example of a simple user interaction class called Operator Interaction is depicted in Figure 8.7. An instance of this class is the Operator Interaction object (see Figure 8.7), which is depicted in a typical behavioral pattern for user interaction objects. The object accepts operator commands from the operator actor; requests sensor data from an entity object, Sensor Data Repository; and displays the data it receives to the operator. More complex user interaction objects are also possible. For example, the Operator Interaction object could be a composite user interaction object composed of several simpler user interaction objects. This would allow the operator to receive dynamic updates of workstation status in one window, receive dynamic updates of alarm status in another window, and conduct an interactive dialog with the system in a third window. Each window is composed of several GUI widgets, such as menus and buttons.

8.4.5 Depicting External Entities and Boundary Classes

Chapter 5 described how to develop a **software system context diagram**, which shows all the external entities, which are depicted as blocks (Section 5.6), that interface to

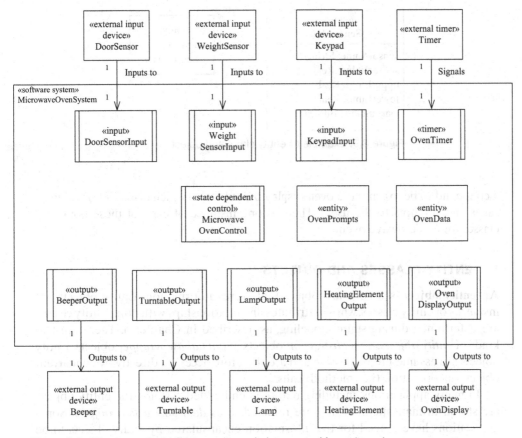

Figure 8.8. Microwave Oven System external classes and boundary classes.

and communicate with the software system. It is useful to expand this diagram to show the boundary classes that communicate with the external blocks. The boundary classes are software classes inside the software system. The software system is depicted with the stereotype «software system», and the boundary classes, which are part of the software system, are shown inside the software system. Each external block, which is external to the software system, has a one-to-one association with a boundary class. Thus, starting with the external blocks, as depicted on the software system context diagram, helps determine the boundary classes.

Starting with the software system context diagram for the Microwave Oven System, we determine that each external block communicates with a boundary class (see Figure 8.8). The software system contains the boundary classes that interface to the external blocks. In this application, there are eight device I/O boundary classes. The device I/O boundary classes are the three input classes, the Door Sensor Input, which sends inputs when the oven door is opened or closed, the Weight Sensor Input, which sends item weight inputs, and the Keypad Input, which sends keypad inputs from the user. The five output classes are the Heating Element Output class (which receives commands to switch the heater on and off), Lamp Output class (which receives commands to switch the lamp on and off), Turntable Output class (which receives commands to start and stop the turntable), Beeper Output class (which receives

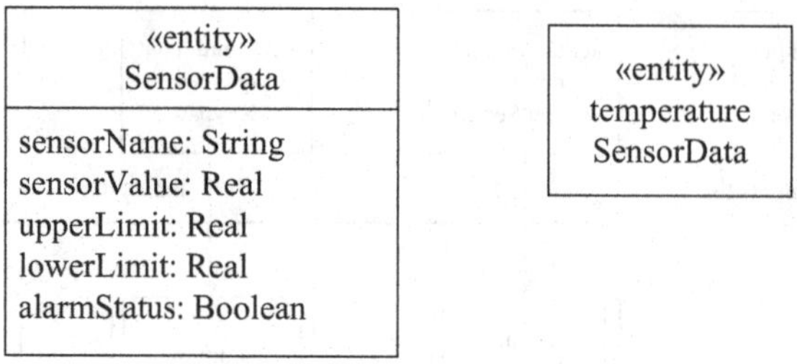

«entity» SensorData
sensorName: String sensorValue: Real upperLimit: Real lowerLimit: Real alarmStatus: Boolean

«entity» temperature SensorData

Figure 8.9. Example of entity class and object.

a command to beep), and the Oven Display Output class (which displays textual messages and prompts to the user). There is one instance of each of these boundary classes for a microwave oven.

8.5 ENTITY CLASSES AND OBJECTS

An **entity object** is a software object that stores information. Entity objects are instances of entity classes, whose attributes and relationships with other entity classes are determined during static modeling, as described in Chapter 5. There are two kinds of *entity objects*: *data abstraction* objects and *database wrapper* objects. Entity objects are assumed to be passive and are therefore accessed directly by concurrent objects via operation (i.e., method) calls.

In many applications, including real-time embedded systems, the entity objects are stored in main memory and are referred to as *data abstraction objects*. Some applications have a need for the information encapsulated by entity objects to be stored in a file or database. In these cases, the entity object is persistent, meaning that the information it contains is preserved when the system is shut down and then later powered up.

Persistent entity classes are often mapped to a database in the design phase. In this case, the data is stored in the database and access to it is by means of database wrapper objects. Database wrapper objects encapsulate how to access persistent data, which is stored on long-term storage devices, such as on files and data bases stored on disks. However, the data encapsulated by data abstraction objects is stored in main memory and is therefore not persistent.

Database wrapper objects are, in general, less frequently used in real-time embedded systems. For example, they might be used during initialization to retrieve system configuration data or before system shutdown to store data previously gathered. However, data accessed at initialization time or stored during run time execution is more likely to be obtained from or stored at a service object, as described in Section 8.7.2. For these reasons, unless explicitly stated otherwise, an entity object in this book refers to a data abstraction object. Thus the following examples all relate to entity objects that are data abstraction objects.

An example of an entity class from a sensor monitoring example is the Sensor Data class (see Figure 8.9). This class stores information about analog sensors. The attributes are sensor Name, sensor Value, upper Limit, lower Limit, and alarm Status. An example of an instance of this class is the temperature Sensor Data object. An example of a Sensor Data Repository entity object is shown in Figure 8.7 and described in Section 8.4.4. The Microwave System depicted in Figure 8.8 has two entity objects, Oven Data and Oven Prompts.

8.6 CONTROL CLASSES AND OBJECTS

A **control object** provides the overall coordination for a group of objects, which could be boundary or entity objects A control object is analogous to the conductor of an orchestra, who orchestrates (controls) the behavior of the other objects. In particular, a control object decides when, and in what order, other objects participate in an interaction sequence, notifying each object when and what to perform. Depending on the characteristics of the object and interaction sequence, the control object may be state dependent. There are three kinds of control objects, as described next.

8.6.1 State Dependent Control Objects

A **state dependent control** object is a control object whose behavior varies in each of its states. A state machine is used to define the behavior of a state dependent control object, as described in Chapter 7. This section only gives a brief overview of state dependent control objects, which are described in much more detail in Chapter 9.

Although a whole system can be modeled by means of a state machine (see Chapter 7), in object-oriented analysis and design, a state machine is encapsulated inside one object. In other words, the object is state dependent and is always in one of the states of the state machine. In an object-oriented model, the state dependent parts of a system are defined by means of one or more state machines, where each state machine is encapsulated inside its own object. If the state machines need to communicate with each other, they do so indirectly since the objects that contain them send messages to each other, as described in Chapter 9.

A state dependent control object receives incoming events that cause state transitions and generates output events that control other objects. The output event generated by a state dependent control object depends not only on the input received by the object but also on the current state of the object. An example of a state dependent control object is from the Microwave Oven System, where the control and sequencing of the microwave oven is modeled by means of a state dependent control object, Microwave Oven Control object (see Figures 8.8 and 8.10), which is defined by means of the Microwave Oven Control state machine. In the example, Microwave Oven is shown receiving inputs from an input object, Door Sensor Input and controlling two output boundary objects, Heating Element Output and Oven Display Output.

In a control system, there are usually one or more state dependent control objects. It is also possible to have multiple state dependent control objects of the same type. Each object executes an instance of the same state machine, although each object is likely to be in a different state. An example of this is the Light Rail Control System, which has several trains, where each train has an instance of the state dependent control class, Train Control, as shown in Figure 8.11using the 1..* notation (see Chapter 2) to depict multiple instances of an object. Each Train Control object executes its own instance of the Train Control state machine and keeps track of the state of the local train. More information about state dependent control objects is given in Chapter 9.

a) Example of state dependent control class

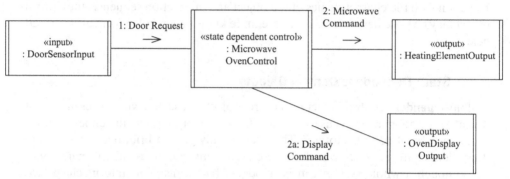

b) Example of behavioral pattern for state dependent control object

Figure 8.10. Example of state dependent control class and object.

8.6.2 Coordinator Objects

A **coordinator object** is an overall decision-making object that determines the overall sequencing for a collection of objects. A coordinator object makes the overall decisions and decides when, and in what order, other objects participate in the interaction sequence. A coordinator object makes its decision based on the input it receives and is not state dependent. Thus an action initiated by a coordinator object depends only on the information contained in the incoming message and not on what previously happened in the system.

An example of a coordinator class is the Hierarchical Coordinator, which is depicted in Figure 8.12a. The instance of this class, the Hierarchical Coordinator, coordinates several state dependent control objects. The coordinator provides high-level coordination by deciding the next job for each control object and sending a command directly to the control object. The coordinator also receives status responses from the control objects (see Figure 8.12b).

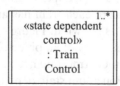

Figure 8.11. Example of multiple instances of state dependent control object.

a) Example of coordinator class

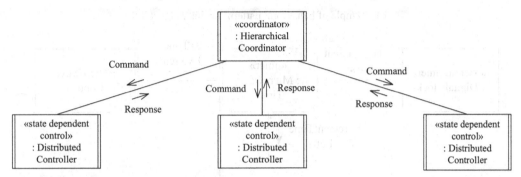

b) Example of behavioral pattern for coordinator object

Figure 8.12. Example of coordinator class and object.

8.6.3 Timer Objects

A **timer object** is a control object that is activated by an external timer, for example, a real-time clock or operating system clock. The timer object either performs some action itself or activates another object to perform the desired action.

An example of a timer class, Microwave Timer, is given in Figure 8.13. An instance of this class, the timer object Microwave Timer, is activated by a timer event from an external timer, the Digital Clock. It decrements the cooking time in the entity object Oven Data, and if the time left is zero, the timer object sends a Timer Expired message to the Microwave Control object. It is also possible for a timer object to have its own local state machine, in which case the timer object is state dependent. The Microwave Timer in Figure 8.13 is a state dependent timer object because it behaves differently in different states, as described in Chapter 19.

8.7 APPLICATION LOGIC CLASSES AND OBJECTS

Application logic classes and objects are needed when it is desirable to hide the application logic separately from the data being manipulated because it is considered likely that the application logic could change independently of the data. This section describes two kinds of application logic objects, namely algorithm objects and service objects. Another kind of application logic object is the business logic object (Gomaa 2011), which is typically only used in business applications and is therefore omitted from this discussion.

8.7.1 Algorithm Objects

An **algorithm object** encapsulates an algorithm used in the problem domain. This kind of object is more prevalent in real-time, scientific, and engineering domains.

a) Example of timer class

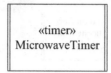

b) Example of behavioral pattern for timer object

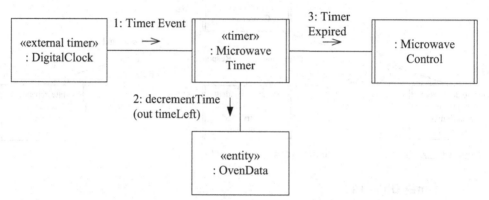

Figure 8.13. Example of a timer class and object.

Algorithm objects are used when there is a substantial algorithm used in the problem domain that can change independently of the other objects. Simple algorithms are usually operations of an entity object, which operate on the data encapsulated in the entity object. However, in many scientific and engineering domains, complex algorithms need to be encapsulated in separate objects because they are frequently improved independently of the data they manipulate, for example, to improve performance or accuracy.

An example from a Light Rail Control System is the Cruiser algorithm class. An instance of this class, the Cruiser object, calculates what adjustments to the speed should be made by comparing the current speed of the train with the cruising speed (see Figure 8.14). The algorithm is complex because it must provide gradual acceleration or deceleration of the train as needed, so as to provide a smooth ride.

An algorithm object frequently encapsulates data it needs for computing its algorithm. This data may be initialization data, intermediate result data, or threshold data, such as maximum or minimum values.

An algorithm object frequently has to interact with other objects in order to execute its algorithm, for example, Cruiser. In this way, it resembles a coordinator object. However, unlike a coordinator object, whose main responsibility is to supervise other objects, the prime responsibility of an algorithm object is to encapsulate and execute the algorithm.

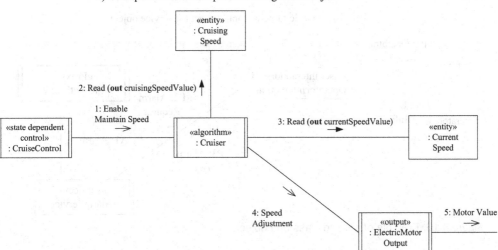

Figure 8.14. Example of algorithm class and object.

8.7.2 Service Objects

A **service object** is an object that provides a service for other objects. Although these objects are usually provided in client/server or service-oriented architectures and applications, it is possible for a real-time embedded system to make use of a service, for example to read configuration data or store status data. Client objects make requests to the service object, which the service object will respond to. A service object never initiates a request; however, in response to a service request, it might seek the assistance of other service objects. Service objects play an important role in service-oriented architectures, although they are used in other architectures as well, such as client/server architectures and component-based software architectures. A service object could be designed to encapsulate the data it needs to service client requests; alternatively, it could be designed to access another entity object(s) that encapsulates the data.

An example of a real-time service class is the Alarm Service class given in Figure 8.15a, from a factory automation example. An example of executing an instance of this class, the Alarm Service object, is also shown in Figure 8.15b. The Alarm Service object provides support for storing and viewing various factory alarms. In the example, a Robot Proxy object sends alarms received from an external robot to Alarm Service. The Operator Interaction object requests Alarm Service to view alarms.

8.8 SUMMARY

This chapter has described how to determine the software objects and classes in the real-time software system. Object and class structuring criteria were provided, and

a) Example of service class

b) Example of behavioral pattern for service object

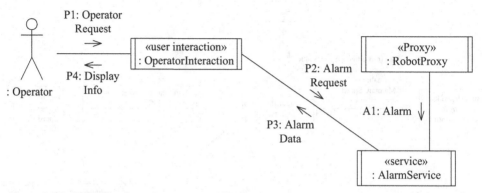

Figure 8.15. Example of service class and object.

the objects and classes were categorized by using stereotypes. The emphasis is on problem domain objects and classes, which are to be found in the real world, and not on solution domain objects, which are determined at design time. The initial object structuring decisions assume that boundary, control, and application logic objects are concurrent, while entity objects are assumed to be passive. These decisions can be revisited at design time if necessary, as described in Chapter 13.

The object and structuring criteria are usually applied to each use case in turn during dynamic interaction modeling, as described in Chapter 9, to determine the objects that participate in each use case. The sequence of interaction among the objects is then determined. Subsystem (that is, composite object) structuring criteria are described in Chapter 10. The design of concurrent tasks using task structuring criteria, as well as message communication between concurrent tasks, is described in Chapter 13, while the design of the operations provided by passive classes and synchronization of access to these classes is described in Chapter 14.

9

Dynamic Interaction Modeling for Real-Time Embedded Software

Dynamic modeling provides a dynamic (also referred to as behavioral) view of a system in which control and sequencing is considered, either within an object (by means of a state machine) or among objects (by analysis of object interactions). *Dynamic state machine modeling* is described in Chapter 7. This chapter describes *dynamic interaction modeling* among objects. However, for state dependent control objects, this chapter also describes how state machines are used to help determine state dependent object interactions. Please note that all references to *system* in this chapter are to the *software system*.

Dynamic interaction modeling is based on the realization of the use cases developed during use case modeling. For each use case, it is necessary to determine how the objects that participate in the use case dynamically interact with each other. The object structuring criteria described in Chapter 8 are applied to determine the objects that participate in each use case. This chapter describes how, for each use case, an interaction diagram is developed to depict the objects that participate in the use case and the sequence of messages passed between them. The interaction is depicted on either a sequence diagram or a communication diagram. A textual description of the object interaction is also provided in a message sequence description.

There are two main kinds of dynamic interaction modeling. *Stateless dynamic interaction modeling* is applied if the interaction sequence does not involve a state dependent control object. *State dependent dynamic interaction modeling* is applied if at least one of the objects is a state dependent control object, in which case the interaction is state dependent and necessitates the execution of a state machine. State dependent dynamic interaction modeling is particularly important in real-time embedded systems, because object interactions in these systems are frequently state dependent.

For large systems, a preliminary determination of the subsystems is usually necessary – for example, based on geographical distribution, as in distributed component-based systems described in Chapter 12. The analysis is then conducted to determine the object communication in each subsystem. Subsystem structuring is carried out in more depth during the design phase as described in Chapter 10.

Section 9.1 gives an overview of object interaction modeling. Section 9.2 describes message sequence descriptions. Section 9.3 introduces an approach for dynamic interaction modeling, which can be either state dependent or stateless, depending on whether the object communication is state dependent or not. Section 9.4 describes a systematic approach for stateless dynamic interaction modeling with two examples of this approach provided in Section 9.5. Section 9.6 describes a systematic approach for state dependent dynamic interaction modeling with an example of this approach provided in Section 9.7. Appendix A describes the convention for message sequence numbering on interaction diagrams.

9.1 OBJECT INTERACTION MODELING

For each use case, the objects that realize the use case dynamically cooperate with each other and are depicted on either a UML sequence diagram or a UML communication diagram. An introduction to these interaction diagrams was given in Chapter 2, Sections 2.5 and 2.8. Further examples of using sequence and communication diagrams are given in the examples in Sections 9.5 and 9.7. Following from Chapter 8, objects are depicted as concurrent (active) objects except for entity objects, which are depicted as passive objects.

9.1.1 Analysis and Design Decisions in Object Interaction Modeling

During analysis modeling, an interaction diagram (sequence diagram or communication diagram) is developed for each use case; only objects that participate in the use case are depicted. The sequence of messages depicted on the interaction diagram should be consistent with the sequence of interactions between the actor and the system already described in the use case.

In the analysis model, messages represent the information passed between objects. At the analysis stage, all messages passed between concurrent (active) objects are assumed to be asynchronous, while all communication with a passive entity object is assumed to be synchronous. During design, we might decide that two different messages arriving at a passive object invoke different operations – or alternatively, the same operation, with the message name being a parameter of the operation. However, these decisions are postponed to the design phase. At the analysis stage, it is assumed that all messages passed between concurrent objects are asynchronous, but this initial decision can be reversed at design time.

9.1.2 Sequence Diagrams and Communication Diagrams in Object Interaction Modeling

COMET/RTE uses a combination of communication and sequence diagrams. Communication diagrams are used primarily to present the layout and interconnections among the objects participating in the use case, while sequence diagrams are used to depict the details of the sequence of messages passed between the interacting objects. Sequence diagrams are particularlyhelpful for intricate object interactions and for timing diagrams, as described in Chapter 17.

An important step in the transition from analysis to design is to integrate the interaction diagrams developed during object interaction modeling, in order to create the first version of the software architecture of the system, as described in Chapter 10. This can be done more readily with communication diagrams than with sequence diagrams. If sequence diagrams are used for dynamic interaction modeling, it is necessary to ensure that, during the transition to design, every object interaction on each sequence diagram is mapped to the integrated communication diagrams to ensure that the integration is complete.

9.1.3 Generic and Instance Forms of Interaction Diagrams

A **scenario** is one specific sequence of object interactions, which is typically depicted on an interaction diagram. In particular, a scenario with its specific message sequence can be used to depict the realization of one interaction sequence (main or alternative) of a use case.

The two forms of an interaction (sequence or communication) diagram are the generic form and the instance form. The *generic form* (also called *descriptor form*) describes all possible interactions in which the objects might participate and so can include loops, branches, and conditions. The generic form of an interaction diagram can be used to describe both the main sequence and the alternative sequences of a use case. The *instance form* is used to depict a specific scenario, either the main sequence or an alternative sequence of a use case. Using the instance form requires several interaction diagrams to fully depict a given use case, one diagram for the main sequence and one diagram for each alternative sequence. Examples of instance and generic forms of interaction diagrams, both communication diagrams and sequence diagrams, are given in the examples in Sections 9.5 and 9.7.

9.2 MESSAGE SEQUENCE DESCRIPTION

A **message sequence description** is supplementary documentation, which is useful to provide with an interaction diagram. It is developed as part of the dynamic model and describes how the analysis model objects participate in each use case as depicted on an interaction diagram. The message sequence description is a textual description of what happens when each message arrives at a destination object depicted on a communication diagram or sequence diagram. The message sequence description uses the message sequence numbers that appear on the interaction diagram. It describes the sequence of messages sent from source objects to destination objects and describes what each destination object does with a message it receives. The message sequence description usually provides additional information that is not depicted on an interaction diagram. For example, every time an entity object is accessed, the message sequence description can provide additional information, such as which attributes of the object are referenced. Examples of message sequence descriptions are given in Section 9.5.

9.3 APPROACH FOR DYNAMIC INTERACTION MODELING

Dynamic interaction modeling is an iterative approach to help determine how the analysis objects interact with each other to realize each use case. A first attempt is made to determine the objects that participate in a use case, using the object structuring criteria described in Chapter 8. Next, the way in which these objects collaborate to execute the use case is analyzed. This analysis might demonstrate a need to define additional objects and/or additional interactions.

Dynamic interaction modeling can be either state dependent or stateless, depending on whether the object communication is state dependent. Section 9.4 describes stateless dynamic interaction modeling. State dependent dynamic interaction modeling is described in Section 9.6.

9.4 STATELESS DYNAMIC INTERACTION MODELING

This section describes the main steps in the **stateless dynamic interaction modelingapproach** starting from the use case (described in Chapter 6). The first step is to consider the objects needed to realize the use case, using the object structuring criteria described in Chapter 8. There will need to be at least one boundary object to receive inputs from the actor. A stateless control object, such as a coordination or timer object, is needed if some coordination and decision-making is required. An entity object is needed if information has to be stored or retrieved. Next, determine the sequence of message communication among the objects, following the interaction sequences described in the use case. The details are as follows:

1. **Analyze use case model**. For dynamic modeling, consider each interaction between the primary actor and the system, as described in the main sequence of the use case. The primary actor starts the interaction with the system through an external input. The system responds to this input with some internal execution and then typically provides a system output. The sequence of actor inputs and system responses is described in the use case. Start by developing the interaction sequence for the scenario described in the main path of the use case.

2. **Determine objects needed to realize use case**. This step requires applying the object structuring criteria (see Chapter 8) to determine the software objects needed to realize the use case, both boundary objects (2a below) and internal software objects (2b below).

2a. **Determine boundary object(s)**. Consider the actor (or actors) that participates in the use case; determine the external objects (external to the system) through which the actor communicates with the system, and the software objects that receive the actor's inputs.

   Considering the inputs from each external object to the system. For each external input event, consider the software object required to process the event. A software boundary object (such as an input object or user interaction object) is needed to receive the input from the external object. On receipt of the external input, the boundary object does some processing and typically sends a message to an internal (i.e., non-boundary) object.

2b. **Determine internal software objects**. Consider the main sequence of the use case. Using the object structuring criteria, determine the internal software objects that participate in the use case, such as control or entity objects.

3. **Determine message communication sequence**. For each input event from the external object, consider the communication required between the boundary object that receives the input event and the subsequent objects – entity or control objects – that cooperate in processing this event. Draw a sequence diagram or communication diagram showing the objects participating in the use case and the sequence of messages passing between them. This sequence typically starts with an external input from the actor (external object) to the boundary

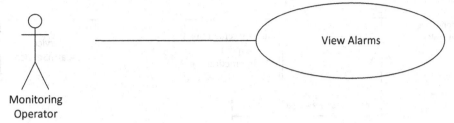

Figure 9.1. Use case diagram for the View Alarms use case.

object, followed by a sequence of messages among the participating software objects, through to a boundary object that provides an external output to the actor (external object). Repeat this process for each subsequent interaction between the actor(s) and the system. As a result, additional objects might be required to participate, and additional message communication, along with message sequence numbering, might need to be specified.

4. **Determine alternative sequences**. Consider the different alternatives, such as error handling, which are described in the *alternatives* section of the use case. Then consider what objects need to participate in executing the alternative branches and the sequence of message communication among them.

In the case of a periodic activity – for example, a report that is generated periodically – it is necessary to consider a software timer object that is activated by a timer event from an external hardware timer. The software timer object triggers an entity object or algorithm object to perform the required activity. In a periodic use case, the external timer is the actor and the software timer object is the control object. Each significant system output, such as a report, requires an object to produce the data and then typically send the data to a boundary object, which outputs it to the external environment.

9.5 EXAMPLES OF STATELESS DYNAMIC INTERACTION MODELING

Two contrasting examples are given of stateless dynamic interaction modeling. The first example starts with the use case for View Alarms, in which the primary actor is a human user. The second example starts with the use case for Send Status, in which the primary actor is an external timer. Both examples follows the four steps for dynamic modeling described in Section 9.4, although because they are simple examples, there are no alternative sequences. An example of alternative sequences is given in Section 9.7.

9.5.1 View Alarms Example

1. Develop Use Case Model
There is one actor in the View Alarms use case, Monitoring Operator, who can request to view the status of alarms, as shown in Figure 9.1. The use case description is briefly described as follows:

Use case: View Alarms.
Actor: Monitoring Operator.

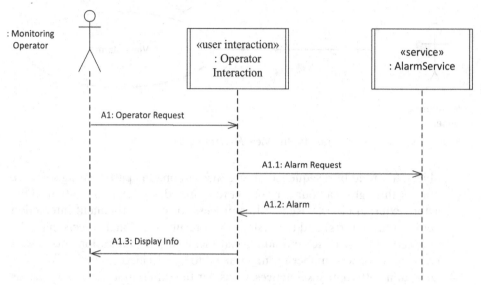

Figure 9.2. Sequence diagram for the View Alarms use case.

Summary: The monitoring operator views current alarms and acknowledges that the cause of an alarm is being addressed.

Precondition: The monitoring operator is logged in.

Main sequence:
1. **Monitoring Operator** requests to view the current alarms.
2. The system displays the current **alarms**. For each alarm, the system displays the name of the alarm, alarm description, location of alarm, and severity of alarm (high, medium, low).

Postcondition: Outstanding alarms have been displayed.

2. Determine Objects Needed to Realize Use Case

Because View Alarms is a simple use case, only two objects participate in the realization of the use case, as shown in the sequence diagram in Figure 9.2 and the communication diagram in Figure 9.3. The required objects can be determined by a careful reading of the use case, as shown in **bold** in the above use case. These are a user interaction object called Operator Interaction, which receives inputs from and send outputs to the actor, and a service object called Alarm Service, which provides access to the alarm repository and responds to alarm requests. Figures 9.2 and 9.3 depict the same information but in different ways, as described in Section 2.5.

3. Determine Message Communication Sequence

The message communication sequence among the objects, depicted in Figures 9.2 and 9.3, is an elaboration of the interaction sequence between the actor and the system described in the use case. Appendix A describes the convention for message sequence numbering on interaction diagrams. The Monitoring Operator makes a request (message A1) to the user interaction object, Operator Interaction, which in turn makes a request (message A1.1) to the service object, Alarm Service. The service object responds (message A1.2) with the desired information, which the user

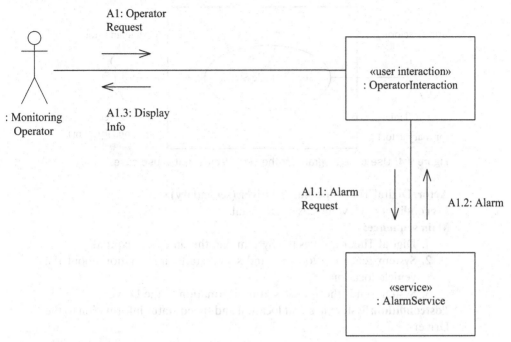

Figure 9.3. Communication diagram for the View Alarms use case.

interaction object displays to the operator (message A1.3). The message interaction sequence is described as follows:

A1:   Monitoring Operator requests an alarm handling service – for example, to view alarms or to subscribe to receive alarm messages of a specific type. The request is sent to Operator Interaction.

A1.1:   Operator Interaction sends the alarm request to Alarm Service.

A1.2:   Alarm Service performs the request – for example, read the list of current alarms or add the name of this user interaction object to the subscription list – and sends a response to the Operator Interaction object.

A1.3:   Operator Interaction displays the response – for example, alarm information – to the operator.

9.5.2 Send Vehicle Status Example

1. Develop Use Case Model

The next example describes a periodic scenario, which is initiated by a timer. There are two actors in the Send Vehicle Status use case, the primary actor is a timer actor called Digital Timer, which periodically initiates the interaction sequence, while the secondary actor is a human actor called Driver, who views the vehicle status, as shown in Figure 9.4.

The use case description is briefly described as follows:

Use case: Send Vehicle Status.
Summary: The vehicle sends status information about its location and speed to the driver.

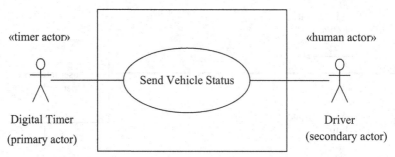

Figure 9.4. Use case diagram for the Send Vehicle Status use case.

Actor: Digital Timer (primary), Driver (secondary).
Precondition: The vehicle is operational.
Main sequence:
1. Digital Timer notifies the System that the timer has expired.
2. System reads the location and speed status information about the vehicle location.
3. System sends the vehicle status information to the Driver.

Postcondition: System has sent location and speed status information to the Driver.

2. Determine Objects Needed to Realize Use Case

The software objects that realize this use case are the Vehicle Timer (which receives timer events from the external Digital Timer), Vehicle Data, which stores location and speed status information, and Vehicle Display Output, which sends vehicle status to the external Driver.

3. Determine Message Communication Sequence

The sequence diagram for the Send Vehicle Status use case is shown in Figure 9.5 and the communication diagram in Figure 9.6, both of which depict the same message communication scenario.

The message sequence starts with the external timer event from the external Digital Timer, and is described next:

1. Digital Timer sends Timer Event to Vehicle Timer.
2. Vehicle Timer reads speed and location data from Vehicle Data.
3. Vehicle Timer sends Vehicle Status message to Vehicle Display Output.
4. Vehicle Display Output sends Vehicle Status to external Driver.

9.6 STATE DEPENDENT DYNAMIC INTERACTION MODELING

State dependent dynamic interaction modeling addresses the situations in which interactions among objects are state dependent. A state dependent interaction involves at least one state dependent control object that, by executing a state machine (as described in Chapter 7) provides the overall control and sequencing of its interactions with other objects. In more complex interactions, it is possible to have more than one state dependent control object, each of which executes a separate state machine.

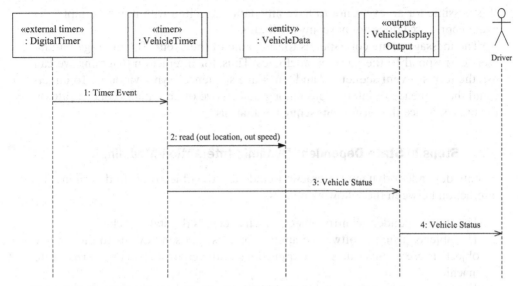

Figure 9.5. Sequence diagram for the Send Vehicle Status use case.

This section gives a detailed description of state dependent dynamic interaction modeling and is followed by an example of the approach.

9.6.1 Messages and Events

State dependent dynamic modeling relies heavily on both messages and events. It is important to understand how messages relate to events. A **message** consists of an **event** together with the data that accompanies the event, referred to as the *attributes* of the message. For example, the event approachingStation has two attributes, which are the data items that accompany the event. These are stationID and platform#. The message is depicted as

message = event (message attributes);
for example:
approachingStation (stationID, platform#)

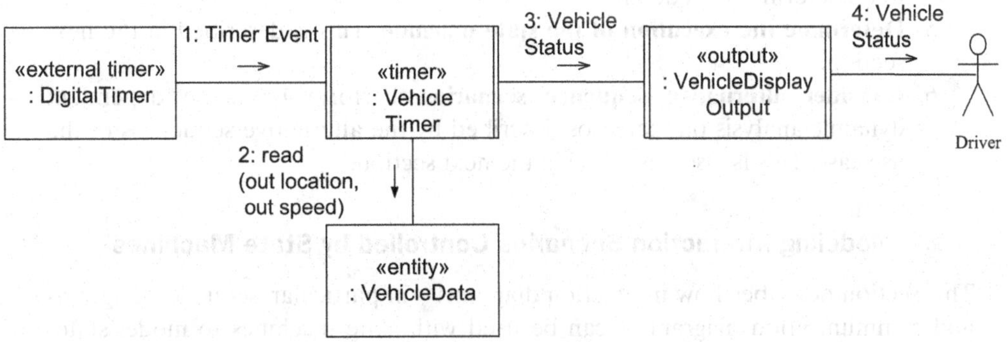

Figure 9.6. Communication diagram for the Send Vehicle Status use case.

It is possible for an event not to have any data associated with it; for example, the event door Closed does not have any attributes.

The message name corresponds to the name of the event. The message parameters correspond to the message attributes. Thus, for interaction diagrams, we can use the terms "event sequence" and "message sequence" synonymously. To understand the sequence of interactions among objects, we often initially concentrate on the events; hence the term **event sequence analysis**.

9.6.2 Steps in State Dependent Dynamic Interaction Modeling

In state dependent dynamic interaction modeling, the objective is to determine the interaction between the following objects:

- The state dependent control object, which executes the state machine.
- The objects (usually software boundary objects)that send events to the control object. These events cause state transitions in the control object's internal state machine.
- The objects that provide and execute the actions and activities, which are triggered by the control object as a result of the state transitions.
- Any other objects that participate in realizing the use case.

The interaction among these objects is depicted on a communication diagram or sequence diagram.

The main steps in the state dependent dynamic interaction modeling approach are as follows. The sequence of interactions needs to reflect the main sequence of interactions described in the use case:

1. **Determine the boundary object(s).** Consider the objects that receive the inputs sent by the external objects in the external environment.
2. **Determine the state dependent control object**. There is at least one state dependent control object, which executes the state machine. Others might also be required.
3. **Determine the other software objects**. These are software objects that interact with the control object, by executing actions or activities, or boundary objects.
4. **Determine object interactions in the main sequence scenario**. Carry out this step in conjunction with step 5 because the interaction between the state dependent control object and the encapsulated state machine it executes needs to be determined in detail.
5. **Determine the execution of the state machine**. This is described in the next section.
6. **Consider alternative sequence scenarios**. Perform the state dependent dynamic analysis on scenarios described by the alternative sequences of the use case. This is also described in the next section.

9.6.3 Modeling Interaction Scenarios Controlled by State Machines

This section describes how interaction diagrams – in particular, sequence diagrams and communication diagrams – can be used with state machines to model state-dependent interaction scenarios, as outlined in steps 5 and 6 above.

A message on an interaction diagram consists of an event and data that accompanies the event. Consider the relationship between messages and events in the case of a state dependent control object that executes its internal state machine. When a message arrives at the control object on an interaction diagram, the event part of the message causes the state transition on the state machine. The action on the state machine is the result of the state transition and corresponds to the output event depicted on the interaction diagram. In general, a *message* on an interaction diagram (communication or sequence diagram) is referred to as an *event* on a state machine; in descriptions of state dependent dynamic scenarios, however, for conciseness only the term *event* is used.

A source object sends an event to the state dependent control object. The arrival of this input event causes a state transition on the state machine. The effect of the state transition is one or more output events. The state dependent control object sends each output event to a destination object. An output event is depicted on the state machine as an action (which can be a state transition action, an entry action, or an exit action), an enable activity, or a disable activity.

To ensure that the interaction diagram and state machine are consistent with each other, the equivalent interaction diagram *message* and state machine *event* are given the same name. Furthermore, for a given state dependent scenario, it is necessary to use the same event sequence numbering on both diagrams. Using the same sequence numbers ensures that the scenario is represented accurately on both diagrams and can be reviewed for consistency.

An initial state machine might have already been developed to get a better understanding of the state dependent parts of the system, as described in Chapter 7. At this stage, the initial state machine probably needs further refinement. If the state machine was developed prior to the interaction diagram, it needs to be reviewed to see if it is consistent with the interaction diagram and, if necessary, modified.

Developing the interaction diagram and the state machine is usually iterative; each input event (to the control object and its state machine) and each output event (from the state machine and control object) need to be considered in sequence. They can actually be further broken down as follows:

1. The arrival of an event at the state dependent control object (often from a boundary object) causes a state transition. For each state transition, determine all the actions and activities that result from this change in state. Remember that an action is executed instantaneously, whereas an activity executes for a finite amount of time – conceptually, an action is executed at a state transition, and an activity executes for the duration of the state. When triggered by a control object at a state transition, an action executes instantaneously and then terminates itself. An activity is enabled by the control object on entry into the state and disabled by the control object on exit from the state.

   Determine all the objects that execute the identified actions and activities. It is also necessary to determine if any activity should be disabled.
2. For each triggered or enabled object, determine what messages it generates and whether these messages are sent to another object or output to the external environment.
3. Depict the incoming external event and the subsequent internal events on both the state machine and the interaction diagram. The events are numbered to

show the sequence in which they are executed. The same event sequence numbers are used on the interaction diagram, state machine, and sequence diagram, as well as on the message sequence description that describes the object interactions.

When the state dependent dynamic analysis has been completed for the main sequence, the alternative sequences need to be considered as follows:

1. Analyze the alternative branches described in the use case to develop additional states and transitions in the state machine. For example, alternative branches are needed for error handling.
2. To complete the state dependent dynamic analysis, it is necessary to walk through the object interaction scenarios to ensure that:
   * The state machine has been driven through every state and every state transition at least once.
   * Each action and activity has been performed at least once, so that each state dependent action has been triggered and each state dependent activity has been enabled and subsequently disabled.

9.7 EXAMPLE OF STATE DEPENDENT DYNAMIC INTERACTION MODELING: MICROWAVE OVEN SYSTEM

As an example of state dependent dynamic interaction modeling, consider the following example from the Microwave Oven System, the Cook Food use case, which is described in Chapter 6, Section 6.6.1. The software objects that participate in the realization of this use case are determined by applying the class and object structuring criteria described in Chapter 8. As described in Section 8.4, there is a need for software boundary objects, since the user interacts with the system via several external devices, in particular input and output objects.

a) To communicate with the external input devices, the corresponding input objects are Door Sensor Input, Weight Sensor Input, and Keypad Input.
b) To communicate with the external output devices, the corresponding output objects are Heating Element Output, Lamp Output, Turntable Output, Beeper Output, and Oven Display Output objects.
c) Because of the need to measure elapsed cooking time, there needs to be a software timer object, Oven Timer.
d) There also needs to be an entity object to store the cooking time, which is called Oven Data, and an entity object to store Oven Prompts.
e) Furthermore, to provide the overall control and sequencing for the microwave oven, there is a need for a control object, Microwave Oven Control. Since the actions of this control object depend on what happened previously, the control object needs to be state dependent and therefore execute a state machine.

By executing the Microwave Oven Control state machine, the state dependent control object, Microwave Oven Control, controls the execution of several objects. To fully understand and design the state dependent interactions, it is necessary to analyze how the interaction diagram and state machine work together. A message on the interaction diagram and its equivalent event on the state machine are given the same name and sequence number to emphasize how the diagrams work together. First, the main sequence is considered, followed by the alternative sequences.

9.7.1 Determine Main Sequence

Consider the main sequence of the Cook Food use case, which is described in Chapter 6, Section 6.6. It describes the user opening the microwave oven door, inserting the food into the oven, then entering the cooking time and pressing the Start button. The system sets the timer and starts cooking the food. When the timer elapses, the system stops cooking the food. The user then opens the door to remove the food.

This use case starts when the user opens the oven door, which is detected by the door sensor. The message sequence number starts at 1, which is the first external event initiated by the user actor, as described in the Cook Food use case. Subsequent numbering in sequence, representing the objects in the system reacting to the input event from the external object, is 1.1 and 1.2. The next input event from the external environment is the external event from the weight sensor numbered 2, and so on. The object interactions for the main sequence scenario are shown on the sequence diagrams in Figures 9.7 and continued on Figure 9.8, which depict external input and timer objects in addition to software objects, but for space reasons do not depict external output objects.

The message sequencing on the object interaction diagrams is faithful to the main sequence of the use case as given by the use case description. The message sequence from 1 to 1.2 starts with the door being opened by the user and detected by the hardware Door Sensor. Door Sensor then passes this input event to the software Door Sensor Input object, which consequently sends the Door Opened (message 1.1 on Figure 9.7) message to Microwave Oven Control. This state dependent control object executes the Microwave Oven Control state machine, shown in Figure 9.9. The Door Opened event (event 1.1 on Figure 9.9) causes the state machine to transition from the initial state, Door Shut, to Door Open. The resulting state machine action Switch On (event 1.2) leads to the Microwave Oven Control object sending the Switch On (message 1.2 on Figure 9.7) message to the Lamp Output object.

The message sequence from 2 to 2.1 follows a similar sequence involving the Weight Sensor Input object. Arrival of the Item Placed message (message 2.1 on Figure 9.7) causes the state machine to transition to the state Door Open with Item (event 2.1 on Figure 9.9). This sequence is followed by the message sequence from 3 to 3.2, which involves closing the oven door and again involves the Door Sensor Input object, which sends the Door Closed message (3.1) causing the state machine to transition to Door Shut Waiting for User and the action Switch Off.

The message sequence from 4 to 4.4 starts with the user pressing the Cooking Time button (message #4 on Figure 9.7), which is received by the Keypad Input, which sends the Cooking Time Selected message (#4.1) to Microwave Oven Control, which then transitions to Door Shut Waiting for Cooking Time. The resulting action is Prompt for Time (action #4.2on Figure 9.9), which is sent as a message to Oven Display Output, which then, given the prompt id, reads the time prompt from the Oven Prompts entity object (messages #4.3, 4.4 on Figure 9.7) and outputs it to the user. The user then enters the cooking time by pressing the appropriate number one or more times (message 5). For each digit, Keypad Input sends Cooking Time Entered (#5.1) message containing the digit to Microwave Oven Control. The state machine then transitions

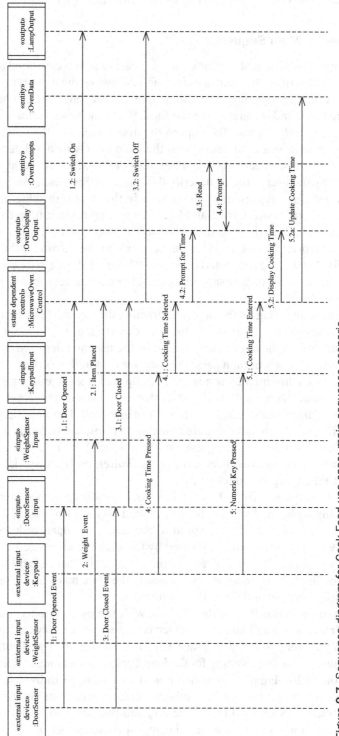

Figure 9.7. Sequence diagram for Cook Food use case: main sequence scenario.

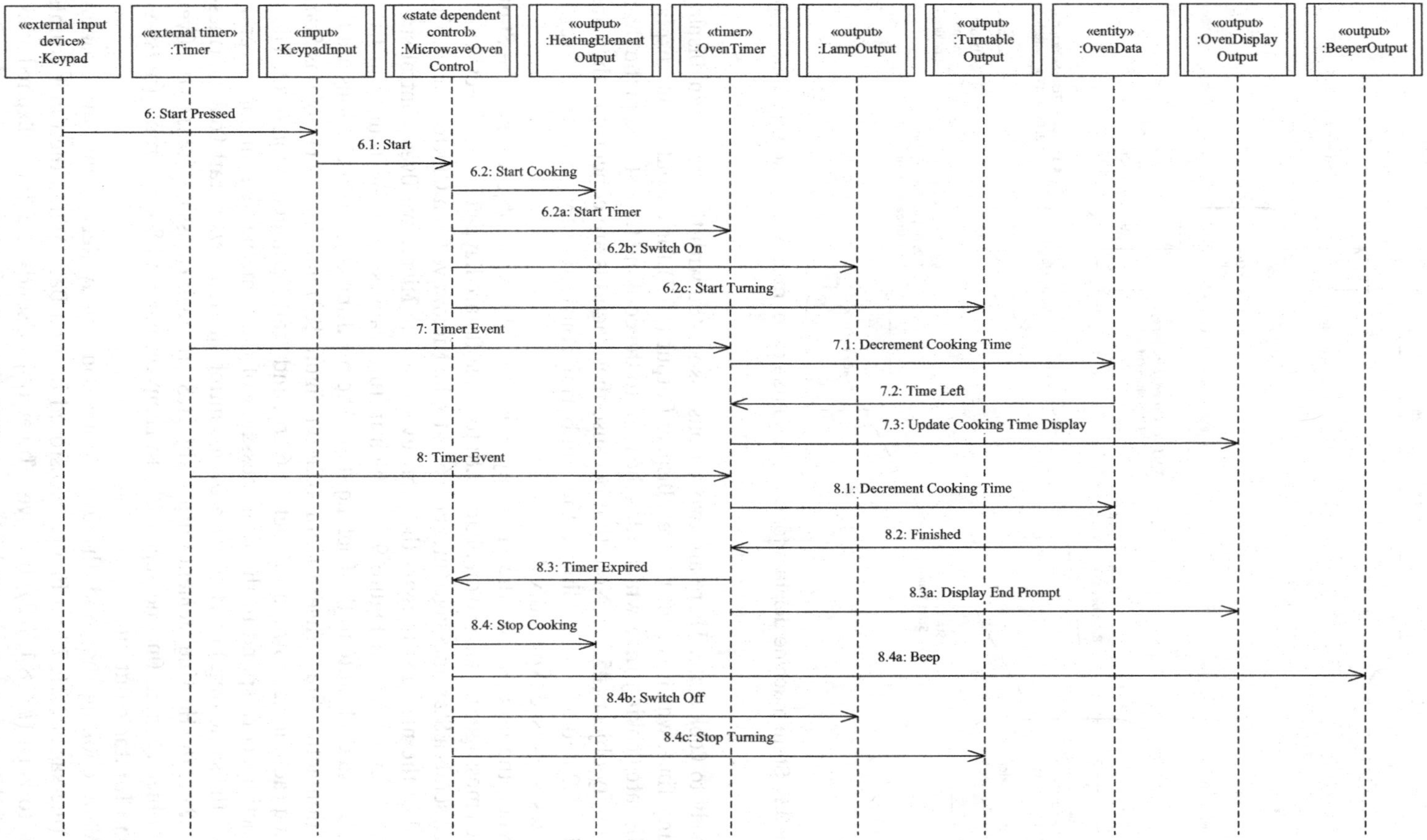

Figure 9.8. Sequence diagram for Cook Food use case: main sequence scenario (continued).

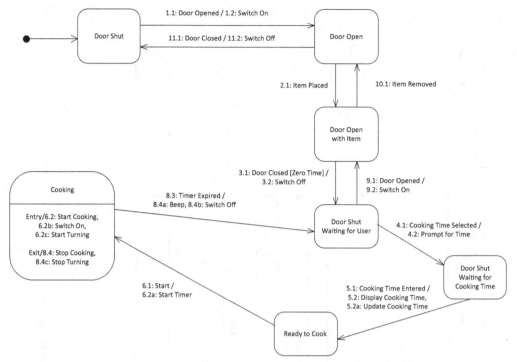

Figure 9.9. State machine diagram for Cook Food use case: main sequence scenario.

to Ready to Cook state. There are two actions associated with this transition, Display Cooking Time, which is sent to Oven Display Output (#5.2) for output to the display and Update Cooking Time, which adds the digit to the cooking time stored in the Oven Data entity object (#5.2a). Note that because these actions are concurrent, they are labeled 5.2 and 5.2a, according to the numbering convention for concurrent events and messages (see Appendix A).

When the user presses the **Start** key, the external Keypad object sends the Start Pressed message (message 6 on Figure 9.8) to the software Keypad Input object, which in turn sends a Start message (message 6.1) to the Microwave Oven Control object. The arrival of the message triggers the Start event on the Microwave Oven Control state machine (event 6.1 on Figure 9.9), which in turn causes the state transition from the Ready to Cook state to the Cooking state. The resulting concurrent actions are the transition action Start Timer (action 6.2a on Figure 9.9) and the entry actions Start Cooking (action 6.2), Switch On (action 6.2b), and Start Turning (action 6.2c). These four actions correspond to the four messages of the same name sent concurrently (i.e., at the same time) by Microwave Oven Control on Figure 9.8: Start Cooking (message 6.2) to the Heating Element Output object, Start Timer (message 6.2a) to the Oven Timer object, Switch On (message 6.2b) to Lamp Output, and Start Turning (message 6.2c) to Turntable Output.

While cooking the food, the Oven Timer continually decrements the cooking time (messages 7, 7.1, 7.2 on Figure 9.8) stored in Oven Data. When the timer counts down to zero (#8, 8.1, 8.2), the Oven Timer object sends the Timer Expired message (# 8.3 on Figures 9.8 and 9.9) to Microwave Oven Control and sends the Display End Prompt (#8.3a) to the Oven Display Output object. The Timer Expired event causes the state machine to transition to Door Shut Waiting for User state (Figure 9.9) and execute four concurrent actions, the two exit actions Stop Cooking (action 8.4) and Stop Turning (action 8.4c), as well as the two transition actions Beep (action 8.4a) and Switch Off (action 8.4b). These four actions correspond to the four messages of the same name sent concurrently by Microwave Oven Control on Figure 9.8: Stop Cooking (message 8.4) to the Heating Element Output object, Beep (message 8.4a) to Beeper Output, Switch Off (message 8.4b) to Lamp Output, and Stop Turning (message 8.4c) to Turntable Output.

Various concurrent sequences are shown in Figures 9.7 and 9.8. For example, Microwave Oven Control simultaneously sends messages to display the cooking time (#5.2) and update the cooking time in Oven Data (#5.2a); Microwave Timer sends the Timer Expired message to Microwave Oven Control (#8.3) and the Display End Prompt to Oven Display Output (#8.3a).

The message sequence description, which describes the messages on the sequence diagram (shown on Figures 9.7 and 9.8) and the events on the state machine diagram (shown in Figure 9.9), is described in detail in the Microwave Oven Control System case study in Section 19.6.

9.7.2 Determine Alternative Sequences

The interaction sequence described in the previous section follows the main sequence described in the use case. Next, consider the alternative sequences of the Cook Food use case, which are given in the Alternatives section of the use case (given in full in Chapter 6). Some alternatives have little impact on the system. However, there are three alternatives of note in the use case, which impact both the interaction diagrams and the state machine, two of which involve the user pressing the **Minute Plus** button and the third involves the user opening the door during cooking.

9.7.3 Alternative Minute Plus Scenarios

The Minute Plus alternative scenarios affect the Cook Food sequence diagram in different ways. If **Minute Plus** is pressed after cooking has started, then the cooking time is updated. If **Minute Plus** is pressed before cooking has started, then the cooking time is updated and cooking is started (assuming that the oven has the door shut and there is an item in the oven).

The two alternative Minute Plus scenarios are depicted inside the *alt* frame (drawn as a rectangle with an *alt* title in the top left corner) on the sequence diagram in Figure 9.10, in which an alternative sequence is identified by a [condition] that must be True for it to be executed. The conditions reflect whether the microwave oven is [Cooking] or [Not Cooking] at the start of each alternative sequence. A dashed line is the separator between the two alternative sequences.

Both **Minute Plus** scenarios start in the same way. The user presses the **Minute Plus** button on the keypad after pressing the **Start** button (message 6). This is depicted in Figure 9.10 as the Keypad external input device sending the Minute Plus Pressed message (6.10). Keypad Input sends the Minute Plus message (shown as message 6.11) to Microwave Oven Control. What follows is state dependent and depicted in the *alt* segment. If cooking is in progress, the alternative sequence for the [Cooking] condition is taken: Microwave Oven Control sends an Add Minute message (6.12)

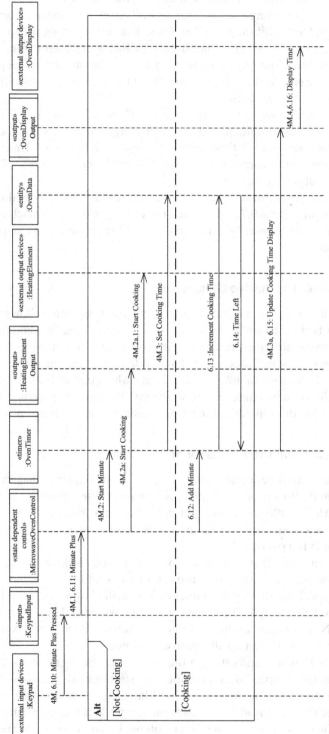

Figure 9.10. Sequence diagram for the Cook Food use case: impact of the Minute Plus alternative scenarios.

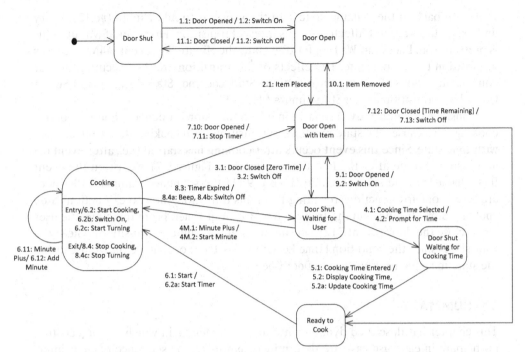

Figure 9.11. State machine diagram for Cook Food use case: Open Door while Cooking and Minute Plus scenarios.

to Oven Timer, which adds sixty seconds to the cooking time in Oven Data (messages 6.13 and 6.14). The scenario then exits the alternative sequence, rejoins the main sequence, and sends the new time to Oven Display Output (6.15), which in turn outputs the Display Time message (6.16) to the external display.

The alternative scenario of pressing **Minute Plus** when cooking is not in progress is depicted with an alternative message sequence starting with 4M. Keypad Input sends the Minute Plus message (4M.1) to Microwave Oven Control. Microwave Oven Control behaves differently in this situation, as depicted by the alternative sequence for the [Not Cooking] condition on Figure 9.10, by sending a Start Minute message (4M.2) to Oven Timer and a Start Cooking message (4M.2a) to Heating Element Output. Oven Timer then sets the cooking time to sixty seconds in Oven Data (message 4M.3). The scenario then rejoins the main sequence and sends the new time to Oven Display Output (message 4M.3a), which in turn outputs the Display Time message (4M.4) to the external display. To avoid clutter on the sequence diagram for the Not Cooking alternative scenario, the Lamp Output and Turntable Output objects are omitted, as well as the Switch On and Start Turning messages sent respectively to them by Microwave Oven Control. These interactions are similar to those for the Cook Food main sequence diagram in Figure 9.8.

9.7.4 Impact of Alternative Scenarios on State Machine

Consider the impact of the minute plus alternative scenarios on the Microwave Oven Control state machine, which is depicted in Figure 9.11. If the oven is in Cooking state when the Minute Plus button is pressed, the Minute Plus event (# 6.11) causes a transition back to the Cooking state, and the action is to Add Minute (#6.12). Entry and exit actions are not affected by this internal transition. However, if Minute Plus is pressed from Door Shut Waiting for User state, the Minute Plus event (#4M.1) causes a transition to Cooking state. The effects of this transition are the execution of four concurrent actions, the three entry actions Start Cooking, Start Turning, and Switch On and the transition action Start Minute (#4M.2).

Consider the alternative scenario in which the door is opened while the food is cooking. This causes the state machine to transition from Cooking state to Door Open with Item state. Since this event occurs after cooking has started (i.e., after event 6.3 and assumed to be after the first timer event 7 on Figure 9.7), we assign the event Door Opened on the state machine (Figure 9.11) the sequence number 7.10. There are three concurrent actions resulting from this transition, the two exit actions Stop Cooking, Stop Turning, and the transition action Stop Timer. From this state, the user could close the door (event 7.12), causing the state machine to transition to Ready to Cook state (since the condition [Time Remaining] is True) or remove the item, causing the state machine to transition to Door Open state.

9.8 SUMMARY

This chapter has described dynamic interaction modeling, in which the objects that participate in each use case are determined, as well as the sequence of their interactions. This chapter described the details of the **dynamic interaction modeling** approach for determining how objects collaborate with each other. **State dependent dynamic interaction modeling** involves a state dependent collaboration controlled by a state machine, and **stateless dynamic interaction modeling** does not.

During the transition from analysis to design described in Chapter 10, the interaction diagrams corresponding to each use case are synthesized into an integrated communication diagram, which represents the first step in developing the software architecture of the system. During analysis, all message interactions are depicted as asynchronous messages between concurrent objects and synchronous messages for communication with passive entity objects. During design, these decisions can be changed, as described in Chapter 13. Appendix A describes message sequence numbering conventions on interaction diagrams and state machines, as used in the examples in this chapter and in the case studies.

10

Software Architectures for Real-Time Embedded Systems

To address the complexity of large scale real-time embedded systems, it is necessary to provide an approach for decomposing the system into subsystems and components and designing the software architecture of the system. The software architecture separates the overall structure of the system, in terms of components and their interfaces, from the internal details of the individual components. This chapter presents an overview of software architecture for real-time embedded systems. Designing a software architecture, which is also referred to as a high level design, consists of structuring the system into subsystems (composite components) and subsystems into components, in addition to designing the interfaces between components.

Developing the software architecture is the first step in software design modeling. Whereas requirements modeling addresses analyzing and specifying software requirements, and analysis modeling considers the problem domain from static and dynamic modeling perspectives, the software architecture addresses the solution domain. During analysis modeling, dynamic interaction modeling considers the software system from a use case–based perspective, determining the software objects required to realize each use case and the interaction sequence of these objects. During software architecture, the use case–based interaction diagrams are synthesized into an initial software design, from which the software architecture can be developed.

An introduction to software architecture, components, and interfaces was given in Chapter 3. In this chapter, Section 10.1 describes the concepts of software architecture and component-based software architecture. Section 10.2 then describes how multiple, different views of a software architecture help with both its design and its understanding. Section 10.3 describes a systematic approach for the transition from analysis to design. Section 10.4 describes the important topic of separation of concerns in subsystem design, which leads into the description in Section 10.5 of how to use subsystem structuring criteria as a means of identifying software subsystems. Finally, Section 10.6 describes the decisions that need to be made in the design of message communication interfaces between subsystems. This chapter addresses subsystem design whereas Chapter 12 describes component-based design. Software architectural patterns are described in Chapter 11.

10.1 OVERVIEW OF SOFTWARE ARCHITECTURES

A software architecture is defined by Bass et al. (2013) as follows:

"The software architecture of a program or computing system is the structure or structures of the system, which comprise software elements, the externally visible properties of those elements, and the relationships among them."

The above definition considers a software architecture primarily from a structural perspective. However, in order to fully understand a software architecture, it is also necessary to study it from several perspectives, including both static and dynamic perspectives, as described in Section 10.2. It is also necessary to address the architecture from functional (i.e., functionality provided by the architecture) and nonfunctional perspectives (i.e., quality of service [QoS] provided). The software quality attributes of an architecture are described in Chapter 16.

A software architecture is structured into subsystems in which each subsystem has a well-defined interface to other subsystems. Applying the *separation of concerns* concept to subsystem design is described in Section 10.4. Structuring criteria for subsystem design are described in Section 10.5

10.1.1 Sequential Software Architectures

A **sequential software architecture** is designed as a sequential program with one thread of control. A sequential object-oriented software architecture is an object-oriented program designed using the concepts of information hiding, classes, and inheritance, a described in Chapter 3. Objects are instantiated from classes and are accessed through operations, which are also called methods. The program has one thread of control, and the internal objects are passive without a thread of control.

A sequential software architecture is a limitation for real-time design because it means that the design cannot take advantage of concurrent processing concepts. A sequential real-time design can be designed using a cyclic executive, in which there is a main cyclic loop that polls I/O devices on a regular basis to determine if there are any new inputs and takes the appropriate actions accordingly. However, this sequential design approach does not take advantage of concurrency, multiprocessing (using multicore systems), or the possibility of a distributed design. Thus, there are several disadvantages to restricting a modern embedded real-time system to a sequential design.

10.1.2 Concurrent Software Architectures

In a **concurrent software architecture**, there are several concurrent processes (tasks), each with its own thread of execution. In a concurrent object-oriented software architecture, there are multiple active classes. Each instance of an active class is an active object with its own thread of control. Each thread can execute on a processor in parallel with other tasks in a multiprocessor (e.g., multicore) environment.

A real-time system can be effectively designed using concurrent tasks for the reasons given in Chapter 3. In particular, a multitasking design permits a real-time system to manage multiple streams of input events in parallel (i.e., one stream per task). It also allows a real-time system to handle multiple periodic or aperiodic events concurrently, including external events that arrive from sources outside the system and internal events that arrive from other tasks. In concurrent designs, tasks can communicate with each other using different architectural communication patterns, as described in Chapter 11, including synchronous and asynchronous communication. A multitasking design can be deployed to multiple nodes in a distributed environment since each task can execute on a separate node. One approach for a distributed configuration is to preassign each task to a given node. However, greater flexibility in task deployment can be achieved using a component-based software architecture, as described next.

10.1.3 Component-Based Software Architectures

A **component-based software architecture** consists of multiple components that are each self-contained and encapsulate information. A component is either a composite component or a simple component. Unless explicitly stated, the term *component* refers to both a component type and a component instance.

A component provides an interface through which it communicates with other components. All information that is needed for one component to communicate with another component is contained in the interface, which is separate from the implementation. Thus, a component can be considered a black box since its implementation is hidden from other components. In a component-based software architecture, a *subsystem* is a composite component.

In a distributed design, component instances can be deployed to different nodes in a distributed environment and execute in parallel with component instances on the same or other nodes. The basic unit of component deployment is a simple component. In a concurrent and distributed design, components can communicate with each other using several different communication patterns, as described in Chapter 11, including synchronous, asynchronous, brokered, and group communication. An underlying middleware framework is typically provided to allow distributed components to communicate with each other, as described in Chapter 12.

Since real-time embedded systems can also be distributed, a distributed real-time design can be effectively designed using a component-based software architecture. With this approach, different instances of the same real-time component-based software architecture are capable of being deployed to different hardware configurations.

An important goal of both object-oriented design and component-based software architecture is the separation of the interface from the implementation. An **interface** specifies the externally visible operations of a class, service, or component without revealing the internal structure (i.e., implementation) of the operations. The interface can be considered a contract between the designer of the external view of the class and the implementer of the class internals. It is also a contract between a class that requires the interface (i.e., invokes the operations provided by the interface) and the class that provides the interface. The UML notation for depicting interfaces is described in Chapter 2. Defining component interfaces is described in more detail in Section 10.6 and Chapter 12.

Components are depicted on composite structure diagrams, as described in Section 10.2.1. Component instances are depicted on concurrent communication diagrams, as described in Section 10.2.2.

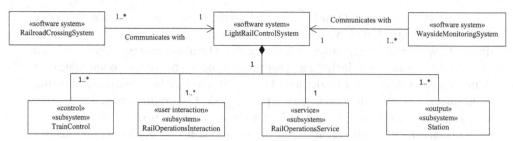

Figure 10.1. Structural view of software architecture: high level class diagram for Light Rail System.

10.1.4 Architecture Stereotypes

In UML 2, a modeling element can be described with more than one stereotype. During analysis modeling, a stereotype is used to represent the *role* characteristic of a modeling element (class or object). During design modeling, the *role stereotype* is carried over from analysis modeling to describe the *role* played by the modeling element, such as whether it is a «boundary» or «entity» class. A second stereotype, the *architecture stereotype*, is used in design modeling to represent the architectural characteristic of a modeling element, such as «subsystem» (as described in Sections 10.2 and 10.5), «component» (as described in Section 10.1.3 and Chapter 12), «service» (as described in Section 10.5.8), or concurrent task, which is depicted using the MARTE stereotype «swSchedulableResource» (as described in Chapter 13). It is important to realize that for a given class, the role stereotype and the architecture stereotype are orthogonal – that is, independent of each other.

10.2 MULTIPLE VIEWS OF A SOFTWARE ARCHITECTURE

The design of the software architecture can be depicted from different perspectives, referred to as different views. The structural view of the software architecture is depicted on class diagrams and composite structure diagrams, as described in Section 10.2.1. The dynamic view of the software architecture is depicted on communication diagrams, as described in Section 10.2.2. The deployment view of the software architecture is depicted on deployment diagrams, as described in Section 10.2.3.

10.2.1 Structural View of a Software Architecture

The structural view of a software architecture is a static view, which does not change with time. At the highest level, subsystems are depicted as concurrent subsystems or components on *subsystem class diagrams* or on *composite structure diagrams*. A *subsystem class diagram* depicts the static structural relationship between the subsystems, which are represented as composite classes, and the multiplicity of associations among them. The subsystem class diagram is useful for considering structural relationships between subsystem classes. However, for considering the interfaces between subsystems, the composite structure diagram is more useful.

As an example of the structural view of a software architecture, consider the design of the Light Rail System (Figure 10.1), which is depicted on a class diagram as a system of systems consisting of three software systems: Railroad Crossing System,

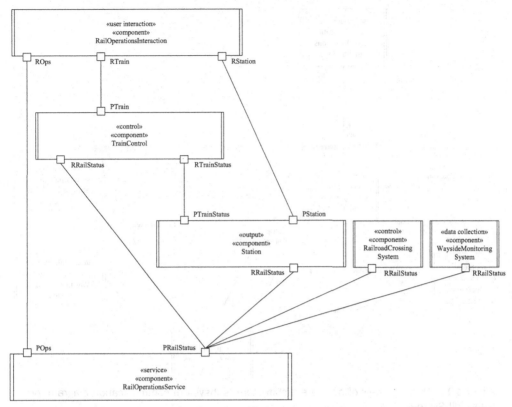

Figure 10.2. Structural view of software architecture: composite structure diagram for Light Rail System.

Wayside Monitoring System, and Light Rail Control System. Each of these classes is depicted with the architectural structuring stereotype of «software system» to clearly identify its role. The Light Rail Control System is modeled as a composite class, which is composed of four subsystem classes: Train Control, of which there are many instances, Station, of which there are many instances, Rail Operations Interaction, of which there are many instances, and Rail Operations Service, of which there is one instance.

A *composite structure diagram* (as described in Section 2.10) depicts the static structural relationship between components. The diagram depicts component types (and in some cases component instances), ports, and connectors that join the component ports together, as described in detail in Chapter 12. They also allow provided and required interfaces of each component to be explicitly specified, as described in Chapter 12.

An example of a composite structure diagram for the Light Rail System is given in Figure 10.2, which depicts the subsystems as concurrent component types and the connectors that join the components together. Four of the components constitute the parts of the Light Rail Control System (see Figure 10.1) and two represent the other software systems, Railroad Crossing System and Wayside Monitoring System. Several connectors are depicted, for example there is one connector between Rail Operations Interaction and Train Control, one connector between Rail Operations Interaction and Station, and one connector between Train Control and Station. Each component is depicted with both a role stereotype and an architecture stereotype. Thus, Train

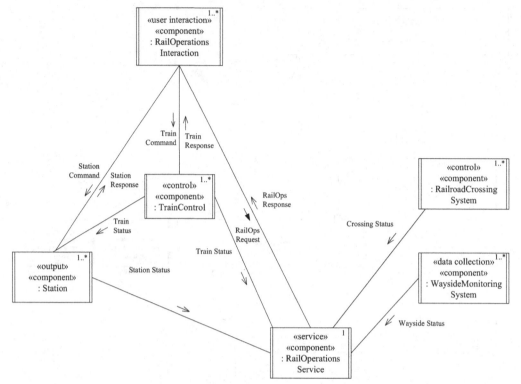

Figure 10.3. Dynamic view of software architecture: subsystem communication diagram for Light Rail System.

Control is depicted with the role stereotype «control» and the architecture stereotype «component». Five of the components are clients of Rail Operations Service. The composite structure diagram is described further in Chapter 12, and this example is described in more detail in Chapter 21.

10.2.2 Dynamic View of a Software Architecture

The dynamic view of a software architecture is a behavioral view, which is depicted on a communication diagram. A *subsystem communication diagram* shows the subsystems (depicted as composite objects or composite component instances) and the message communication between them. If the subsystems can be deployed to different nodes, they are depicted as concurrent component instances, since they execute in parallel and communicate with each other over a network. The *subsystem communication diagram* is also sometimes referred to as a high level communication diagram.

An example of the dynamic view of the software architecture for the Light Rail System depicts the six concurrent components (from Figure 10.2) on a subsystem communication diagram in Figure 10.3. Four of the six concurrent components are part of the Light Rail Control System, of which there are many instances of Train Control, Station, and Rail Operations Interaction and one instance of Rail Operations Service. Each instance of Train Control sends train arrival and departure status messages to each instance of Station. Rail Operations Interaction sends train command

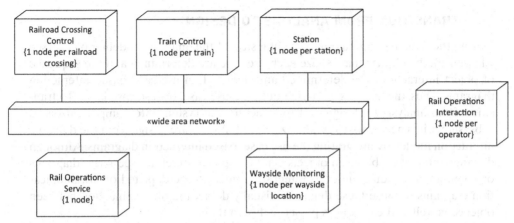

Figure 10.4. Deployment view of software architecture: deployment diagram for Light Rail System.

messages to a given instance of Train Control to transition into and out of service. All communication between the distributed components is asynchronous, except for the synchronous communication between Rail Operations Interaction and Rail Operations Service.

A subsystem communication diagram is a *generic* communication diagram because it depicts all possible interactions between objects (see Section 9.1.5). In particular, generic communication diagrams depict generic instances, that is, they depict potential instances rather than actual instances. In addition to being *generic*, a subsystem communication diagram is also *concurrent* because it depicts objects executing concurrently. Thus, Figure 10.3 depicts six concurrent subsystems, each of which is designed as a component.

10.2.3 Deployment View of a Software Architecture

The deployment view of the software architecture depicts the physical configuration of the software architecture. In particular, a deployment diagram depicts how the component-based subsystems of the architecture are allocated to physical nodes in a distributed configuration. A deployment diagram can depict a specific deployment with a fixed number of nodes. Alternatively, it can depict the overall structure of the deployment, for example identifying that a subsystem can have many instances, each deployable to a separate node, but not depicting the specific number of instances.

An example of the deployment view is given in Figure 10.4 for the software architecture of the Light Rail System. In this deployment diagram, each instance of Railroad Crossing Control is allocated to its own physical node, as is each instance of theWayside Monitoring. There are multiple instances of Train Control, Station, and Rail Operations Interaction, each of which is allocated to its own physical node. There is one instance of Rail Operations Service, which is assigned to a physical node. The nodes are geographically distributed and connected by a wide area network. Communication with a mobile component, such as Train Control, of which there is one instance for each train, needs to be by wireless communication.

10.3 TRANSITION FROM ANALYSIS TO DESIGN

During the dynamic interaction modeling step of the analysis modeling phase (see Chapter 9), the objects that realize each use case are determined and the sequence of object interactions are determined and depicted on use case–based interaction diagrams. Thus, the analysis is carried out on a use case–by–use case basis. To transition from analysis to design and to structure the system into component-based subsystems, it is necessary to synthesize an initial software design from the dynamic interaction model, by integrating the use case–based interaction diagrams. Although dynamic interaction between objects can be depicted on either sequence diagrams or communication diagrams, this integration needs to be depicted on communication diagrams because these diagrams visually depict the interconnection between objects, as well as the messages passed between them.

In the analysis model, at least one interaction diagram is developed for each use case. The **integrated communication diagram** is a synthesis of all the communication diagrams developed to realize the use cases and is developed as follows:

Frequently, there is a precedence order in which use cases are executed. The order of the synthesis of the communication diagrams should correspond to the order in which the use cases are executed. From a visual perspective, the integration is done as follows: Start with the communication diagram for the first use case and superimpose the communication diagram for the second use case on top of the first to form an integrated diagram. Next, superimpose the third diagram on top of the integrated diagram of the first two, and so on. In each case, add new objects and new message interactions from each subsequent diagram onto the integrated diagram, which gradually gets bigger as more objects and message interactions are added. Objects and message interactions that appear on more than one communication diagram are only shown once.

It is important to realize that the integrated communication diagram must show all message communication derived from the individual use case–based communication diagrams. Communication diagrams often show the main sequence through a use case, but not necessarily all the alternative sequences. In the integrated communication diagram, it is necessary to show the messages that are sent as a result of executing the alternative sequences in addition to the main sequence through each use case.

The **integrated communication diagram** is thus a synthesis of all relevant use case–based communication diagrams showing the realization of all use case scenarios, and all objects and their interactions. The integrated communication diagram is represented as a generic UML communication diagram (see Section 10.2.2), which means that it depicts all possible interactions between the objects. On the integrated communication diagram, objects and messages are shown, but the message sequence numbering is usually not shown because this would make the diagram too cluttered. As with the use case–based interaction diagrams, messages on the integrated communication diagram are depicted as asynchronous messages between concurrent objects and synchronous when communicating with a passive object. These initial decisions can later be reversed, when decisions about the type of message communication (synchronous or asynchronous) are finalized, as described in Section 10.6.

An example of an integrated communication diagram for the Railroad Crossing System is given in Figure 10.5, which integrates the object interaction diagrams that

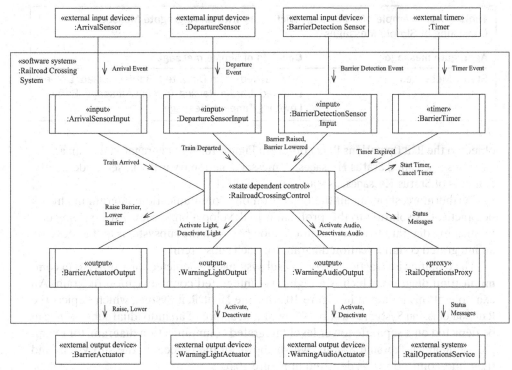

Figure 10.5. Integrated communication diagram for Railroad Crossing System.

realize the Arrive at Railroad Crossing and Depart from Railroad Crossing use cases. This consists of the integration of the communication diagrams that realize the two use cases of this system, including the main and alternative sequences for each use case. In this figure, most of the objects participate in both of the use case–based communication diagrams, except for the Arrival Sensor Input object, which only participates in the arrival use case, and the Departure Sensor Input object, which only participates in the departure use case. In addition, several messages are derived from one or the other of the use case–based communication diagrams. Thus, the Train Arrived, Lower Barrier, Activate Light, Activate Audio, and Barrier Lowered messages originate from the Arrive at Railroad Crossing use case, while the Train Departed, Raise Barrier, Deactivate Light, Deactivate Audio, and Barrier Raised messages originate from the Depart from Railroad Crossing use case. The messages Start Timer, Cancel Timer, and Status Messages originate from both use cases. The Timer Expired message originates from a timeout alternative sequence in each use case.

For a large system, the integrated communication diagram can get very complicated; it is therefore necessary to have ways to reduce the amount of information depicted. One way to reduce the amount of information on the diagram is to aggregate the messages – that is, if one object sends several individual messages to another, instead of showing all these messages on the diagram, use one aggregate message. The aggregate message is a useful way of grouping messages to reduce clutter on the diagram. It does not represent an actual message sent from one object to another; rather it represents the collection of messages sent at different times between the same pair of objects. For example, the messages sent by the Railroad Crossing Control

Table 10.1. Example of a Message Dictionary with an Aggregate Message Consisting of Simple Messages

Aggregate message	Consists of simple messages
Status Messages	Train Arrived, Train Departed, Barrier Raised, Barrier Lowered, Barrier Raising Timeout Message, Barrier Lowering Timeout Message

object to the Rail Operations Proxy object in Figure 10.5 are aggregated into an aggregate message called Status Messages. A message dictionary is then used to define the contents of Status Messages, as shown in Table 10.1.

Furthermore, showing all the objects on one communication diagram might not be practical. A solution to this problem is to develop a higher-level subsystem communication diagram to show the interaction between the subsystems and to develop an integrated communication diagram for each subsystem.

The dynamic interactions between subsystems are depicted on a **subsystem communication diagram**, which is a high-level integrated communication diagram. An example of this is shown in Figure 10.3 for the Light Rail System, which depicts the Railroad Crossing System as a subsystem. The structure of an individual subsystem can be depicted on a separate lower level integrated communication diagram, for example the Railroad Crossing System, which shows all the objects in the subsystem and their interconnections, as depicted in Figure 10.5.

10.4 SEPARATION OF CONCERNS IN SUBSYSTEM DESIGN

Some important structuring decisions need to be made when designing subsystems. The following design considerations addressing separation of concerns should be made when structuring the system into subsystems. The goal is to make subsystems more self-contained, so that different concerns are addressed by different subsystems.

10.4.1 Composite Object

Objects that are part of the same composite object should be in the same subsystem and separate from objects that are not part of the same composite object. As described in Chapter 5, both aggregation and composition are whole/part relationships; however, composition is a stronger form of aggregation. With composition, the composite object (the whole) and its constituent objects (the parts) are created together, live together, and die together. Thus, a subsystem consisting of a composite object and its constituent objects is more strongly coupled than one consisting of an aggregate object and its constituent objects.

A subsystem supports information hiding at a higher level of abstraction than an individual object does. A software object can be used to model a real-world object in the problem domain. A composite object models a composite real-world object in the problem domain. A composite object is typically composed of a group of related objects that work together in a coordinated fashion. This arrangement is analogous to the assembly structure in manufacturing. Often, multiple instances of a composite object (and hence multiple instances of each of its constituent objects) are needed in an application. The relationship between a composite class and its constituent classes

b) Composite component

a) Composite class

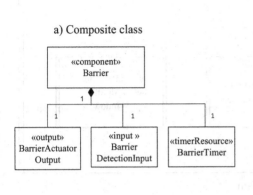

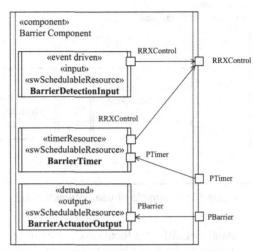

Figure 10.6. Example of a composite class: Barrier Component. (a) Barrier composite class. (b) Barrier composite component.

is best depicted in the static model because the class diagram depicts the multiplicity of the association between each constituent class and the composite class.

An example of a composite class from the Railroad Crossing System is the Barrier composite class, which is composed of three classes (see Figure 10.6a): Barrier Actuator Output, which sends commands to the physical barrier actuator; Barrier Detection Input, which receives inputs from the physical barrier detection sensor; and Barrier Timer, which detects if there is a delay in barrier raising or lowering. The Barrier composite class is designed as a composite component called Barrier Component that encapsulates three simple barrier related components (designed as concurrent tasks), as depicted in Figure 10.6b. Another example of a composite class is the Microwave Oven, which consists of a door, a weight sensor, a keyboard, a heating element, and a display.

10.4.2 Geographical Location

If two objects could potentially be physically separated in different geographical locations, mobile or stationary, they should be in different subsystems. In a distributed environment, component-based subsystems communicate only by means of messages that can be sent from one component to another. In the Light Rail System shown on the deployment diagram in Figure 10.4, there are several instances of each of the Railroad Crossing Control, Wayside Monitoring, Train Control, and Station components. Each instance of these mobile (Train Control) or stationary components physically resides on a separate node located in a different geographical location, connected by a wide area network.

10.4.3 Clients and Services

Clients and services should be in separate subsystems. This guideline can be viewed as a special case of the geographical location rule because clients and services are

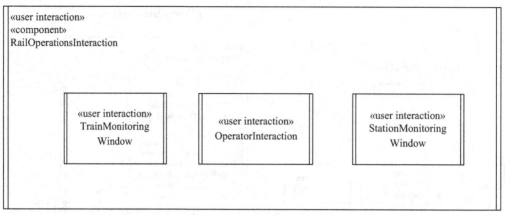

Figure 10.7. Example of user interaction subsystem.

usually at different locations. For example, the distributed light rail system, as shown in Figures 10.3 and 10.4, has many client subsystems of the same type, which reside at different locations, some static and some mobile, distributed around the region serviced by the system. Client subsystems include Train Control, for which there is one instance for each train, Railroad Crossing System, for which there is one instance for each railroad crossing, and Wayside Monitoring System, for which there is one instance for each wayside location. Rail Operations Service is a service subsystem located at a centralized location, and it is used for monitoring the progress of the whole light rail network.

10.4.4 User Interaction

Users often use their own PCs, laptops, tablets, or mobile phones as part of a larger distributed configuration, so the most flexible option is to keep user interaction objects in separate subsystems. Because user interaction objects are usually clients, this guideline can be viewed as a special case of the above client/service guideline. Furthermore, a user interaction object may be a composite user interaction object composed of several simpler user interaction objects. The Rail Operations Interaction component in Figure 10.7 is an example of a composite user interaction object, which contains three simple user interaction objects, an Operator Interaction object, a Train Monitoring Window object, and a Station Monitoring Window object, as described in more detail in Chapter 12. This subsystem is used for rail operators to interact with the Rail Operations Service Subsystem and other subsystems in the Light Rail Control System.

10.4.5 Interface to External Objects

A subsystem deals with a subset of the external real-world objects shown on the software context diagram. An external real-world object should interface to only one subsystem. An example is given for the Train Control Subsystem in Figure 10.8, in which the Train Control Subsystem interfaces to several external real-world entities, including several sensors including the Approaching Sensor, Arrival Sensor, Departure Sensor, Proximity Sensor, Door Sensor, Location Sensor, and Speed Sensor. There are

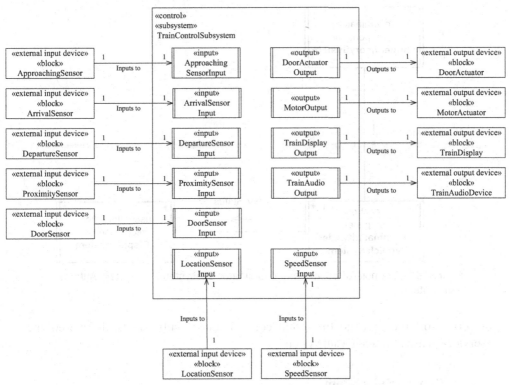

Figure 10.8. Example of interfacing to external classes.

also several external actuators, including Motor Actuator, Door Actuator, and other output devices such as Train Display and Train Audio Device. Each instance of the Train Control Subsystem interfaces to instances of these sensors and actuators. These external devices interface to software boundary classes, including input and output classes, as shown in Figure 10.8.

10.4.6 Scope of Control

A control object and all the entity and boundary (such as input/output) objects it directly controls should all be part of one subsystem and not split among subsystems. An example is the Railroad Crossing Control object within the Railroad Crossing Subsystem, shown in Figures 10.5, which provides the overall control of the objects in this subsystem, including several internal I/O objects (such as Arrival Sensor Input and Barrier Actuator Output) and proxy objects (such as Rail Operations Proxy).

10.5 SUBSYSTEM STRUCTURING CRITERIA

The design considerations described in the previous section can be formalized as subsystem structuring criteria, which help ensure that subsystems are designed effectively. The subsystem structuring criteria are described in this section with examples. Subsystems are depicted with the stereotype «subsystem». For certain software architectures consisting of distributed component-based subsystems, the stereotype «component» is used for such a subsystem and in component-based architectures

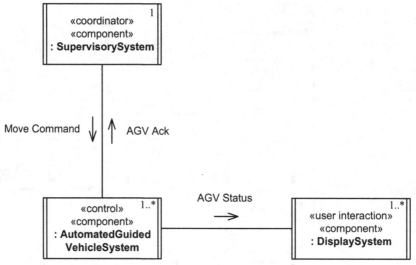

Figure 10.9. Example of control and coordinator subsystems in Factory Automation System.

or service-oriented architectures that contain service subsystems, the stereotype «service» is used for such a subsystem.

10.5.1 Control Subsystem

A **control subsystem** controls a given part of the system. The subsystem receives its inputs from the external environment and sends outputs to the external environment, usually without any human intervention. A control subsystem is usually state-dependent, in which case it includes at least one state dependent control object. In some cases, some input data might be gathered by some other subsystem(s) and used by this subsystem. Alternatively, this subsystem might provide some data for use by other subsystems.

A control subsystem might receive some high-level commands from another subsystem giving it overall direction, after which it provides the lower-level control. A control subsystem might also send status information to neighboring nodes, either on an ongoing basis or on demand.

An example of a control subsystem is the Railroad Crossing System, which is a control subsystem of the distributed Light Rail System, depicted in Figures 10.3 and 10.5. There are multiple instances of the Railroad Crossing System, one for each railroad crossing; however, each instance is independent of the others and only communicates with the Rail Operations Service subsystem (Figure 10.3). The control behavior of Railroad Crossing Control is to sequence the interactions with the various sensors and actuators and to control the I/O devices that raise and lower the barrier and start and stop the warning light and audio devices. The control behavior is explicitly depicted in the Railroad Crossing Control state machine (see case study in Chapter 20), in which the state machine actions trigger actions in the controlled objects.

Another example of a control subsystem is from the Factory Automation System given in Figure 10.9, in which the control subsystem is the Automated Guided Vehicle System, which receives move commands from a Supervisory System, commanding it to move to locations in the factory to load and unload parts. Automated Guided Vehicle System sends vehicle acknowledgments to the Supervisory System and vehicle status to the Display System.

10.5.2 Coordinator Subsystem

In software architectures with multiple control subsystems, it is sometimes necessary to have a **coordinator subsystem** that coordinates the control subsystems. If the multiple control subsystems are completely independent of each other, no coordination is required. In some real-time systems, the control subsystems can coordinate activities among themselves. Such distributed coordination is usually possible if the coordination is relatively simple. If the coordination activity is relatively complex, however, it is usually more advantageous to have a hierarchical control system with a separate coordinator subsystem overseeing the control subsystems. For example, the coordinator subsystem might decide what item of work a control subsystem should do next.

An example of a coordinator subsystem assigning jobs to control subsystems is given for the Factory Automation System, in which the Supervisory System (Figure 10.9) is a coordinator subsystem that assigns jobs to the individual instances of the Automated Guided Vehicle System to move to a factory station, pick up a part, and transport it to a different station, where it is unloaded.

10.5.3 User Interaction Subsystem

A **user interaction subsystem** provides the user interface and performs the role of a client in a client/server system, providing user access to services. There may be more than one user interaction subsystem – one for each category of user. A user interaction subsystem is usually a composite object that is composed of several simpler user interaction objects. It may also contain one or more entity objects for local storage and/or caching, as well as control objects for overall sequencing of user input and output.

With the proliferation of graphical workstations and personal computers, a subsystem providing a user interaction role might run on a separate node, interacting with subsystems on other nodes. This kind of subsystem can provide rapid responses to simple requests supported completely by the node, and relatively slower responses to requests requiring the cooperation of other nodes. This kind of subsystem usually needs to interface to specific user I/O devices, such as visual displays and keyboards.

A user interaction client subsystem could support a simple user interface, consisting of a command line interface or a graphical user interface, which contains multiple objects. A simple user interaction client subsystem would have a single thread of control.

A more complex user interaction subsystem would typically involve multiple windows and multiple threads of control. For example, a Windows client consists of multiple windows operating independently, each window supported by a concurrent object with its own separate thread of control. The concurrent objects might access some shared data. An example from the Light Rail System is given in Figure 10.7 where Rail Operations Interaction is a user interaction subsystem that has several windows and communicates with other components including Train Control, Station, and Rail Operations Service. An example of a user interaction subsystem interacting

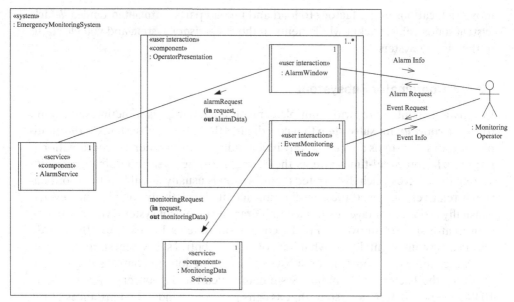

Figure 10.10. Example of user interaction subsystem with multiple windows.

with multiple services in an emergency monitoring system is given in Figure 10.10. Operator Presentation is a user interaction subsystem, which has several instances. The Operator Presentation subsystem has one internal user interaction object to display alarms in an Alarm Window and a second internal user interaction object to display monitoring status in an Event Monitoring Window. Alarm Window instance sends synchronous requests with reply to the Alarm Service subsystem, and Event Monitoring Window communicates in the same way with the Monitoring Data Service subsystem.

10.5.4 Input/Output Subsystem

An **input**, **output**, or **input/output subsystem** is a subsystem that performs input and/or output operations on behalf of other subsystems. It can be designed to be relatively autonomous. In particular, "smart" devices are given greater local autonomy and consist of the hardware plus the software that interfaces to and controls the device. An I/O subsystem typically consists of one or more input and/or output objects that interface to external I/O devices, and it may also contain control objects to provide localized control and entity objects to store local data.

An example of an input subsystem is the Monitoring Sensor Component in the emergency monitoring system depicted in Figure 10.12. There are several instances of this subsystem, each of which receive inputs from remote sensors that monitor a section of the external environment, and send sensory status information to the Monitoring Data Service subsystem and post alarms to the Alarm Service subsystem.

10.5.5 Data Collection Subsystem

A **data collection** subsystem collects data from the external environment. In some cases, it stores the data, possibly after collecting, analyzing, and reducing the data.

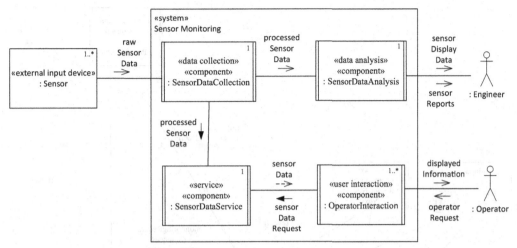

Figure 10.11. Examples of data collection and data analysis subsystems.

Depending on the application, the subsystem responds to requests for values of the data. Alternatively, the subsystem passes on the data in reduced form – for example, it might collect several raw sensor readings and pass on the average value, converted to engineering units. It should be noted that a data collection subsystem should do significantly more processing of the data it receives than an input/output subsystem.

An example of a data collection subsystem is the Sensor Data Collection subsystem in Figure 10.11, which collects raw data from a variety of digital and analog sensors in real time. The frequency with which the data is collected depends on the characteristics of the sensors. Data collected from analog sensors is converted to engineering units. Processed sensor data is sent to consumer subsystems such as the Sensor Data Analysis and Sensor Data Service subsystems.

10.5.6 Data Analysis Subsystem

A **data analysis** subsystem analyzes data and provides reports and/or displays for data collected by another subsystem. It is also possible for a subsystem to provide both data collection and data analysis. In some cases, data collection is done in real time, whereas data analysis is a non-real-time activity.

An example of a data analysis subsystem is the Sensor Data Analysis subsystem shown in Figure 10.11, which receives sensor data from the Sensor Data Collection subsystem. The Sensor Data Analysis subsystem analyzes current and historical sensor data, performs statistical analysis (such as computing means and standard deviations), produces trend reports, and generates alarms if disturbing trends are detected.

10.5.7 Client Subsystem

A **client subsystem** is a requester of one or more services. There are many different types of clients, some of which may be wholly dependent on a given service, while others are partially dependent. The former only communicate with one service while the latter might communicate with more than one service. Possible client subsystems include control subsystems, user interaction subsystems, I/O subsystems, and data

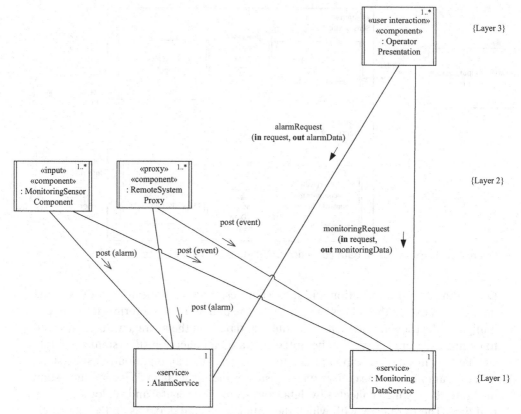

Figure 10.12. Examples of client and service subsystems in the emergency monitoring system.

collection subsystems, which are described in more detail in Sections 10.5.1, 10.5.3, 10.5.4, and 10.5.5, respectively.

In the Light Rail System shown in Figures 10.2 and 10.3, there is one service subsystem, Rail Operations Service. The Train Control, Station, Railroad Crossing System, Wayside Monitoring System, and Rail Operations Interaction components are all clients of Rail Operations Service. Examples of client subsystems from the emergency monitoring system, shown in Figure 10.12, are the Monitoring Sensor Component, Remote System Proxy and Operator Presentation subsystems, which are described in the next section.

10.5.8 Service Subsystem

A **service subsystem** is a subsystem that provides a service for client subsystems. It responds to requests from client subsystems, although it does not initiate any requests. Service subsystems are usually composite objects that are composed of two or more objects. These include entity objects, coordinator objects, which service client requests and determine what object should be assigned to handle them, and application logic objects, which encapsulate application specific logic, such as algorithms. Frequently, a service is associated with a data repository or a set of related data repositories, or it might provide access to a database or a file system.

A service subsystem may be designed as part of a service-oriented architecture (Gomaa 2011) or it may be designed as a service component within a component-based software architecture. A service subsystem is often allocated its own node. A data service supports remote access to a centralized database or file store. An I/O service processes requests for a physical resource that resides at that node.

An example of a system with one data service subsystem is the Light Rail System, which has a service subsystem, Rail Operations Service, to maintain the current status of the trains and stations in the system, as depicted in Figures 10.2 and 10.3. Examples of multiple data service subsystems are from the emergency monitoring system, in which the Alarm Service and the Monitoring Data Service subsystems, shown in Figure 10.12, store current and historical alarm and sensor data respectively. Monitoring Data Service receives new sensor data from the Monitoring Sensor Component and Remote System Proxy subsystems. Sensor data is requested by other client subsystems, such as the Operator Presentation subsystem, which displays the data.

Another example of a data service is the Sensor Data Service shown in Figure 10.11, which stores current and historical sensor data. It receives new sensor data from the Sensor Data Collection subsystem. Sensor data is requested by other subsystems, such as multiple instances of the Operator Interaction subsystem, which displays the data. The design of concurrent service subsystems is described in Chapter 12.

10.6 DECISIONS ABOUT MESSAGE COMMUNICATION BETWEEN SUBSYSTEMS

In the transition from analysis to design, one of the most important decisions relates to what type of message communication is needed between the subsystems. A second related decision is to determine more precisely the name and parameters of each message, that is, the interface specification. In the analysis model, an initial decision is made about the type of message communication. In addition, the emphasis is on the information passed between objects, rather than on precise message names and parameters. In design modeling, after the subsystem structure is determined (as described in Section 10.5), a decision has to be made about the precise semantics of message communication, such as whether message communication will be synchronous or asynchronous, introduced in Chapters 2 and 3, and the precise content of the message.

Message communication between two subsystems can be unidirectional or bidirectional. Figure 10.13a gives an analysis model example of unidirectional message communication between a producer and a consumer, as well as an example of bidirectional message communication between a client and a service. All messages between concurrent objects in the analysis model are depicted with one notation (the stick arrowhead) because it is assumed initially that message communication is asynchronous. During design modeling, this decision is either confirmed or changed, so the designer now needs to decide what type of message communication is required in both of these examples. (In UML 2, the stick arrowhead means asynchronous communication and the black arrowhead means synchronous communication. For an overview of the UML notation for message communication, see Chapter 2, Section 2.8.1.)

Figure 10.13b shows the result of message design decisions concerning the type of message communication between the subsystems. Figure 10.13b depicts the

a) Analysis Model – before decisions about type of message communication

(1) Unidirectional message communication between producer and consumer

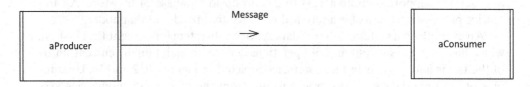

(2) Bidirectional message communication between client and service

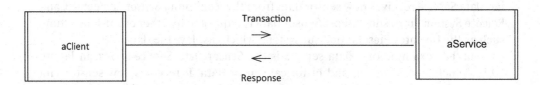

b) Design Model – after decisions about type of message communication

(3) Asynchronous message communication between producer and consumer

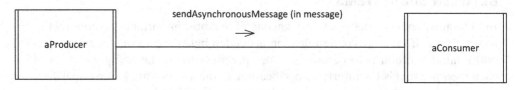

(4) Synchronous message communication with reply between client and service

Figure 10.13. Transition from analysis to design: decisions about type of message communication. (a) Analysis Model – before decisions about type of message communication. (b) Design Model – after decisions about type of message communication.

decision to use asynchronous message communication between the producer and consumer because this is one-way message communication with no reason to hold up the producer. By contrast, synchronous message communication is used between the client and service because the client needs to wait for the response from the service. In addition, the precise name and parameters of each message are determined. The asynchronous message has the name send Asynchronous Message and content called message. The synchronous message has the name send Asynchronous Message with Reply, with the input content called message and the service's reply called response.

The above decisions concerning asynchronous and synchronous communication are formalized into architectural communication patterns, as described in Chapter 11. Thus, the Asynchronous Message Communication pattern is applied to the unidirectional message between the producer and consumer and the Synchronous Message Communication with Reply pattern is applied to the message and response between the client and service.

10.7 SUMMARY

This chapter has given an overview of software architecture including different kinds of software architecture. It has described the multiple views of a software architecture, in particular the static, dynamic, and deployment views. After describing a systematic approach for the transition from analysis to design, this chapter described the separation of concerns in subsystem design and how to use subsystem structuring criteria as a means of identifying software subsystems. Finally, this chapter described the decisions that need to be made in the design of message communication interfaces between subsystems.

During software design modeling, design decisions are made relating to the characteristics of the software architecture. In designing the overall software architecture, it helps to consider applying the software architectural patterns, both architectural structure patterns and architectural communication patterns. Chapter 11 describes the software architectural design patterns and how they can be used in the design of real-time embedded systems. Chapter 12 describes the design of component-based software architectures, including the design of component interfaces, with component ports that have provided and required interfaces, and connectors that join compatible ports. Chapter 13 describes the design of real-time software architectures, which are concurrent architectures that frequently have to deal with multiple streams of input events. Chapter 14 describes the detailed design of software architectures. Chapter 15 describes the design of software product line architectures, which are architectures for families of products that need to capture both the commonality and variability in the family.

System and software quality issues in developing the software architecture of real-time embedded systems are described in Chapters 16 and 17. Chapter 16 describes the system and software quality attributes of a real-time system and how they are used to evaluate the quality of the software architecture. Chapters 17 and 18 describes performance analysis of software designs. Chapters 19 to 23 provide case study examples of applying COMET/RTE to the modeling and design of different real-time embedded software architectures.

11

Software Architectural Patterns for Real-Time Embedded Systems

In software design, designers frequently encounter a problem that they have solved before on a previous project. Often the context of the problem is different; it might be a different application, a different platform, or a different programming language. Because of the different context, a designer usually ends up redesigning and reimplementing the solution, thereby falling into the trap of "reinventing the wheel." The field of software patterns, including architectural and design patterns, is helping developers avoid unnecessary redesign and reimplementation.

In software development, the field of design patterns was popularized by Gamma, Helm, Johnson, and Vlissides in their book *Design Patterns* (1995), in which they described twenty-three design patterns. Later, Buschmann et al. (1996) described patterns that span different levels of abstraction, from high-level architectural patterns through design patterns to low-level idioms.

This chapter describes several software architectural patterns that can be used in the development of real-time embedded systems. Section 11.1 provides an overview of the different kinds of software patterns. Sections 11.2 through 11.7 describe the different software architectural patterns, with Sections 11.2 through 11.4 focusing on patterns that address the structure of the software architecture and Sections 11.5 through 11.7 discussing patterns that address the message communication among distributed components of the software architecture. Section 11.8 describes how to document software architectural patterns using a standard template. Section 11.9 describes how to apply software architectural patterns to build a new software architecture.

11.1 SOFTWARE DESIGN PATTERNS

A **design pattern** describes a recurring design problem to be solved, a solution to the problem, and the context in which that solution works (Buschmann et al. 1996, Gamma et al. 1995). The description is in terms of communicating objects and classes customized to solve a general design problem in a particular context. A design pattern is a larger-grained form of reuse than a class. A design pattern involves more than one class along with the interconnection among the different classes.

After the original success of the design pattern concept, other kinds of patterns were developed. The main kinds of reusable patterns are given below:

- **Design patterns.** In a widely cited book (Gamma et al. 1995), design patterns were described by four software designers – Erich Gamma, Richard Helm, Ralph Johnson, and John Vlissides – who were named in some quarters as the "gang of four." A design pattern is a small group of collaborating objects.
- **Architectural patterns.** This work was described by Buschmann et al. (1996) at Siemens. Architectural patterns are larger-grained than design patterns, addressing the structure of major subsystems of a system. This was followed by books describing architectural patterns in different application domains (Buschmann et al. (2007).
- **Analysis patterns.** Analysis patterns were described by Fowler (2002), who found similarities during analysis of different application domains. He described recurring patterns found in object-oriented analysis and described them with static models, expressed in class diagrams.
- **Domain-specific patterns.** These are patterns used in specific application areas, such as factory automation or electronic commerce. By concentrating on a specific application domain, design patterns can provide more tailored domain-specific solutions.
- **Idioms.** Idioms are low-level patterns that are specific to a given programming language and describe implementation solutions to a problem that use the features of the language – for example, Java or C++. These patterns are closest to code, but they can be used only by applications that are coded in the same programming language.
- **Design anti-patterns.** These are patterns that *should not* be used because they are incorrect or ineffective solutions to a recurring problems. For example, they lead to potential performance pitfalls. An example of this is for a component to use up CPU time unnecessarily by continually checking for message arrival, instead of waiting on a message arrival event.

11.1.1 Software Architectural Patterns

As introduced in the previous section, software **architectural patterns** provide the skeleton or template for the overall software architecture or high-level design of an application. Shaw and Garlan (1996) referred to *architectural styles* or patterns of software architecture, which are recurring architectures used in a variety of software applications (see also Bass et al. 2013). These include such widely used architectures as client/service and layered architectures.

This chapter groups software architectural patterns into two main categories, as described in the following sections: architectural structure patterns (which address the static structure of the architecture) and architectural communication patterns (which address the message communication among distributed components of the architecture). Furthermore, it is also possible for an architectural structure pattern to incorporate other architectural structure and/or communication patterns.

11.2 LAYERED SOFTWARE ARCHITECTURAL PATTERNS

This section describes layered software architectural structure patterns, which address the static structure of the architecture by organizing the architecture into hierarchical layers or levels of abstraction.

11.2.1 Layers of Abstraction Architectural Pattern

The **Layers of Abstraction** pattern (also known as the *Hierarchical Layers* or *Levels of Abstraction* pattern) is a common architectural pattern, which is applied in many different software domains (Buschmann et al. 1996). Operating systems, database management systems, and network communication software are examples of software systems that are often structured as hierarchies.

As Parnas (1979) pointed out in his seminal paper on designing software for ease of extension and contraction (see also Hoffman and Weiss 2001), if software is designed in the form of layers, it can be extended by the addition of upper layers that use services provided by lower layers and contracted by the removal of some or all the components in the upper layers.

With a *strict layered hierarchy*, each layer uses services in the layer immediately below it; for example, layer 3 can only invoke services provided by layer 2. With a *flexible layered hierarchy*, a layer does not have to invoke a service at the layer immediately below it but can instead invoke services at more than one layer below; for example, layer 3 could directly invoke services provided by layer 1.

The Layers of Abstraction architectural pattern is used in the TCP/IP protocol, which is the most widely used protocol on the Internet (Comer 2008). Each layer deals with a specific characteristic of network communication and provides an interface, as a set of operations, to the layer above it. This is an example of a strict layered hierarchy. For each layer on the sender node, there is an equivalent layer on the receiver node. TCP/IP is organized into five conceptual layers, as shown in Figure 11.1:

Layer 1: Physical layer. Corresponds to the basic network hardware, including electrical and mechanical interfaces, and the physical transmission medium.

Layer 2: Network interface layer. Specifies how data is organized into frames and how frames are transmitted over the network.

Layer 3: Internet Protocol (IP) layer. Specifies the format of packets sent over the Internet and the mechanisms for forwarding packets through one or more routers from a source to a destination (see Figure 11.2). The router node in Figure 11.2 is a gateway that interconnects a local area network to a wide area network.

Layer 4: Transport layer (TCP). Assembles packets into messages in the order they were originally sent. TCP is the Transmission Control Protocol, which uses the IP network protocol to send and receive messages. It provides a virtual connection from an application on one node to an application on a remote node, hence providing what is termed an *end-to-end protocol* (see Figure 11.2).

Layer 5: Application layer. Supports various network applications, such as file transfer (FTP), electronic mail, and the World Wide Web.

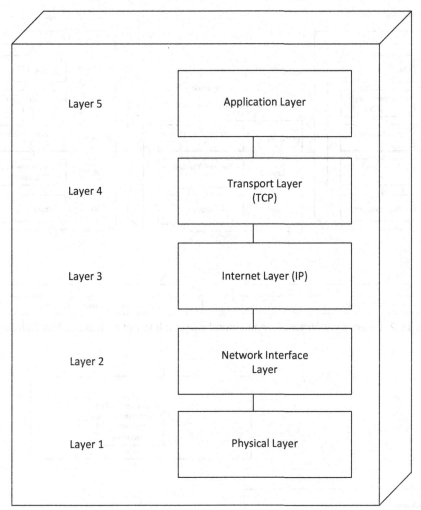

Figure 11.1. Layers of Abstraction architectural pattern: Example of the Internet (TCP/IP) reference model.

An interesting characteristic of the layered architecture is that it is possible to replace the upper layers of the architecture with different layers that use the unchanged services provided by the lower layers, as shown in Figure 11.2. The router node uses the lower three layers (layers 1-3) of the TCP/IP protocol, while the application nodes use all five layers. The Voice over IP application (VoIP) used for Internet telephony is an example of a real-time application that sits at the application layer (see Figure 11.2). Because VoIP has real-time constraints, it uses a faster but less reliable connectionless protocol at the transport layer, UDP (User Datagram Protocol) instead of TCP. However, like TCP, UDP uses the IP network protocol to carry messages (Comer 2008).

An example of the flexible Layers of Abstraction architectural pattern is the Emergency Monitoring System, as shown in Figure 11.3. Each layer contains one or more composite subsystems (components or services). At layer one is the service layer, which provides two services, **Alarm Service** and **Monitoring Data Service**, which

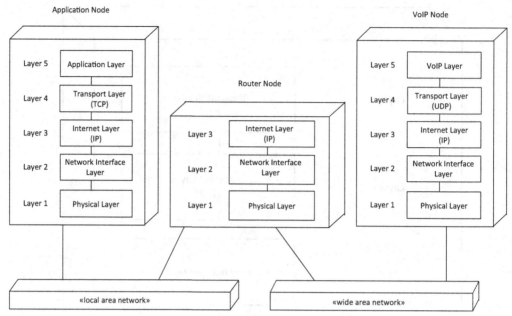

Figure 11.2. Layers of Abstraction architectural pattern: Internet communication with IP.

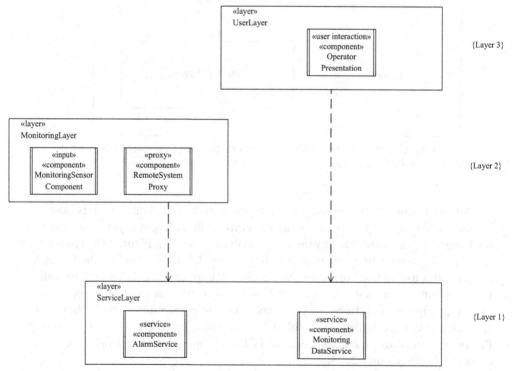

Figure 11.3. Example of the Layers of Abstraction architectural pattern: Emergency Monitoring System.

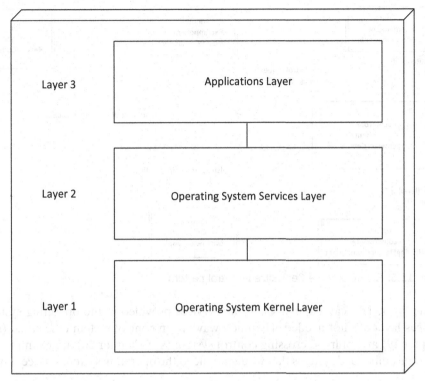

Figure 11.4. Example of the Kernel architectural pattern.

are used by higher layers. At layer two is the Monitoring layer, which has two components, Monitoring Sensor Component and Remote System Proxy. At layer three is a user layer consisting of a user interaction object, Operator Presentation.

11.2.2 Kernel Architectural Pattern

With the **Kernel** pattern, the core of a software system is encapsulated inside a kernel. If the kernel is very small, then this pattern is sometimes called the *Microkernel* pattern (Buschmann et al. 1996). The kernel provides a well-defined interface consisting of operations, in the form of procedures and/or functions, which can be called by other parts of the software system. This pattern is frequently used in operating systems in which the kernel or microkernel provides the minimal essential functionality that is needed for the operating system. Other services provided by the operating system use the core services provided by the kernel. The UNIX, Linux, and Windows operating systems all have a kernel. The kernel of an application can also be the lowest layer of a hierarchical architecture developed with the Layers of Abstraction pattern (described in Section 11.2.1).

Figure 11.4 shows the operating system kernel layer as layer one in a layered architecture. Typical services provided by an operating system kernel, such as task scheduling, are described in Chapter 3. Above the kernel layer is the operating system services layer, which provides additional services, such as file management and user account management. The third layer is the application layer, where applications consist of concurrent tasks that take advantage of the services of the lower layers. In some real-time-embedded systems, the application layer is built directly above the

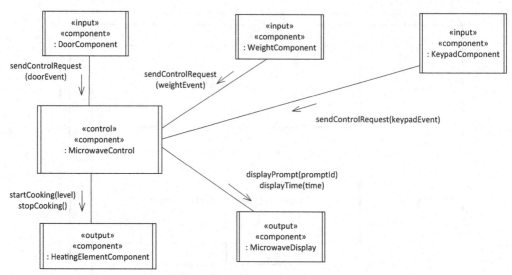

Figure 11.5. Example of the Centralized Control pattern.

kernel layer. This can happen when the services provided in the operating system services layer are not needed. The microwave oven control system case study (see Chapter 19) and railroad crossing control system (see Chapter 20) are examples of real-time embedded systems that would not need the operating system services layer.

11.3 CONTROL PATTERNS FOR REAL-TIME SOFTWARE ARCHITECTURES

Many real-time systems have an important control function. This section describes the different kind of control patterns that could be used for this purpose: centralized control patterns, distributed control patterns, and hierarchical control patterns. To make the patterns applicable to component-based software architectures in addition to real-time software architectures, the «component» stereotype is used in these patterns.

11.3.1 Centralized Control Architectural Pattern

In the **Centralized Control** pattern, there is one control component, which conceptually executes a state machine and provides the overall control and sequencing of the system or subsystem. The control component receives events from other components that it interacts with. These include events from various input components that interact with the external environment, for example, through sensors that detect changes in the environment. An input event to a control component usually causes a state transition on its encapsulated state machine, which results in one or more state dependent actions. The control component uses these actions to control other components, such as output components, which output to the external environment – for example, to switch actuators on and off. Entity objects are also used to store any temporary data needed by the other objects.

Examples of this pattern can be found in the railroad crossing control system (see Chapter 20) and the microwave oven control system case study (see Chapter 19). Figure 11.5 gives an example of the Centralized Control architectural

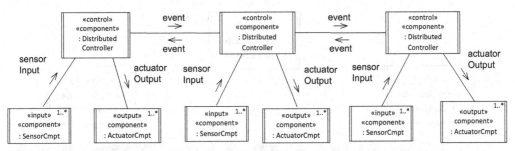

Figure 11.6. Example of the Distributed Collaborative Control architectural pattern.

pattern from the latter case study, in which the concurrent components are depicted on a concurrent communication diagram. The Microwave Control component is a centralized control component, which executes the state machine that provides the overall control and sequencing for the microwave oven. Microwave Control receives messages from three input components – Door Component, Weight Component, and Keypad Component – when they detect inputs from the external environment. Microwave Control actions are sent to two output components – Heating Element Component (to switch the heating element on or off) and Microwave Display (to display information and prompts to the user).

11.3.2 Distributed Collaborative Control Architectural Pattern

The **Distributed Collaborative Control** pattern contains several control components. Each of these components controls a given part of the system by conceptually executing a state machine. Control is distributed among the various control components, with no single component in overall control. To notify each other of important events, the components communicate through peer-to-peer communication. The components also interact with the external environment as in the Centralized Control pattern (see Section 11.3.1).

An example of the Distributed Collaborative Control pattern is given in Figure 11.6, in which control is distributed among several distributed controller components. Each Distributed Controller executes an encapsulated state machine, receiving inputs from the external environment through sensor components and controlling the external environment by sending outputs to actuator components. Each Distributed Controller communicates with the other Distributed Controller components by sending status messages containing events of interest.

11.3.3 Distributed Independent Control Architectural Pattern

The **Distributed Independent Control** pattern differs from the Distributed Collaborative Control pattern in that although control is also distributed among several control components with no single component in overall control, there is no communication among the control components. It is often the case with Distributed Independent Control that the components communicate asynchronously to send status information to another component, such as a service component. This pattern is also different from the Hierarchical Control pattern (see Section 11.3.4) because the service does not provide any coordination or control. It should also be noted that this

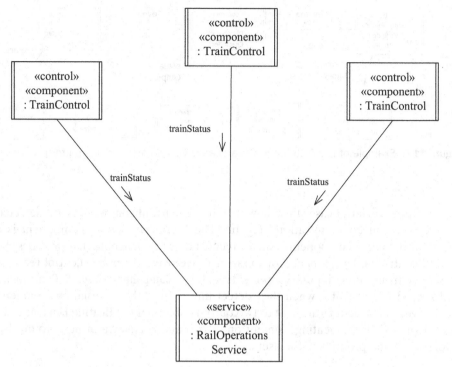

Figure 11.7. Example of the Distributed Independent Control pattern with unidirectional communication to a service.

pattern is different from the client/service pattern, in which a control component needs to wait for a response to a service request, as described in Section 11.4.

An example of distributed independent control with unidirectional communication to a service is from the Light Rail Control System (Chapter 21) and depicted in Figure 11.7. Each train is controlled by a Train Control component that sends train status information, such as arrival and departure from railroad stations, to a Rail Operations Service component. In this system, there are other independent control components that send status information to the service component, including the Railroad Crossing Control components (not shown) that send status information about raising and lowering of barriers at railroad crossings.

11.3.4 Hierarchical Control Architectural Pattern

The **Hierarchical Control** pattern (also known as the *Multilevel Control* pattern) contains several control components. Each component controls a given part of a system by conceptually executing a state machine. In addition, a coordinator component provides the overall system control by coordinating several control components. The coordinator provides high-level control by deciding the next job for each control component and communicating that information directly to the control component. The coordinator also receives status information from the control components.

One example of the Hierarchical Control pattern is given in Figure 11.8, in which a coordinator component, the Hierarchical Controller, sends high-level commands to each of the distributed controllers. The distributed controllers provide the low-level

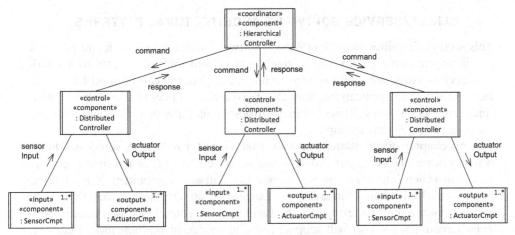

Figure 11.8. Example of the Hierarchical Control architectural pattern.

control, interacting with sensor and actuator components, and respond to the Hierarchical Controller when they have finished. They may also send progress messages to the Hierarchical Controller.

11.3.5 Master/Slave Architectural Pattern

In the **Master/Slave** pattern, there is one control component that provides the overall control and sequencing of several slave components. The Master component divides up the work to be performed and assigns each part to a slave. Each slave executes its assignment and, when it has finished, sends a response to the master. The master integrates the slave responses. This pattern takes advantage of concurrency and multiprocessing by allowing several slave components to execute in parallel. The slaves do not typically interact with each other and can therefore take advantage of executing in parallel on different processors on a multiprocessor system.

This pattern is different from the Hierarchical Control pattern in that the slaves, unlike a lower level controller, do not have any localized control. It is also different from the centralized control pattern, in which the controller typically interacts with multiple sensors and actuators. An example of this pattern is given in Figure 11.9, in which the Master sends assignment commands to each Slave. After completing the assignment, Slave sends its response to Master.

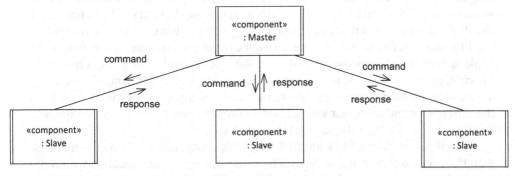

Figure 11.9. Example of the Master/Slave architectural pattern.

11.4 CLIENT/SERVICE SOFTWARE ARCHITECTURAL PATTERNS

This section describes two client/service software architectural structure patterns, specifically multiple clients with a single service and multiple clients with multiple services. Although client/service architectural patterns can be used for a wide range of software applications, they also have a role to play in the design of real-time embedded systems. This section describes the patterns that can be used for this purpose with real-time examples.

This chapter differentiates between a *server* and a *service*. A *server* is a hardware/software platform that provides one or more services for multiple clients. A *service* in a client/server system is an application software component that fulfills the needs of multiple clients. Since services execute on servers, there is sometimes confusion between the two terms, and the two terms are sometimes used interchangeably. Sometimes, a server will support just one service or perhaps more than one; other times, a large service might span more than one server node. In *client/server systems*, the service executes on a fixed server node(s), and the client has a fixed connection to the server. In *component-based systems*, a service is designed to be a component that can be instantiated and assigned to a separate node at deployment time, as described in Chapter 12. In a *service-oriented architecture*, services are autonomous and are typically accessed using brokering patterns, as described in Section 11.6.

11.4.1 Multiple Client/Single Service Architectural Pattern

The **Multiple Client/Single Service** pattern consists of **clients** that request services and a **service** that fulfills client requests. The simplest and most common client/service architecture has one service and many clients, and for this reason the Multiple Client/Single Service architectural pattern is also known as the *Client/Server* or *Client/Service* pattern. The Multiple Client/Single Service architectural pattern can be depicted on a deployment diagram, as in Figure 11.10, which shows multiple clients connected to a service that executes on a server node via a local area network.

An example of this pattern comes from a banking system (Gomaa 2011), which is depicted in Figure 11.11 and consists of multiple ATMs connected to a Banking Service component by means of a wide area network. Each ATM is controlled by an ATM Controller component. Each ATM Controller is independent of the other ATM Controllers, but all of them communicate with the Banking Service. A typical ATM control sequence consists of an ATM Controller reading a customer's ATM card, prompting for the PIN and cash amount, and communicating with the Banking Service to validate the PIN and determine that there is enough cash in the customer's account. If the Banking Service approves the request, then the ATM Controller component dispenses the cash, prints the receipt, and ejects the ATM card. Each ATM Controller executes a state machine that controls the above interaction sequence, receiving inputs from the card reader and customer keypad and controlling outputs to the cash dispenser, receipt printer, customer display, and card reader.

The clients in Figure 11.11 are ATM Controller components, which communicate with the Banking Service using the synchronous message communication with reply pattern (see Section 11.5.4) because a client sends a message to the service and then

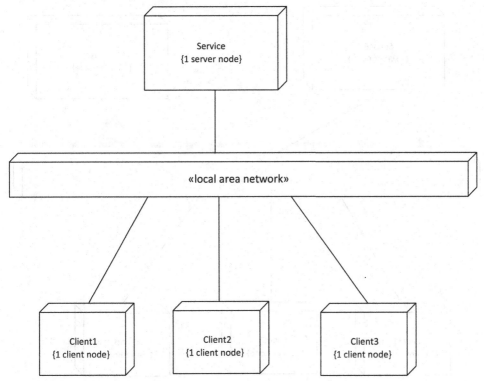

Figure 11.10. Multiple Client/Single Service architectural pattern.

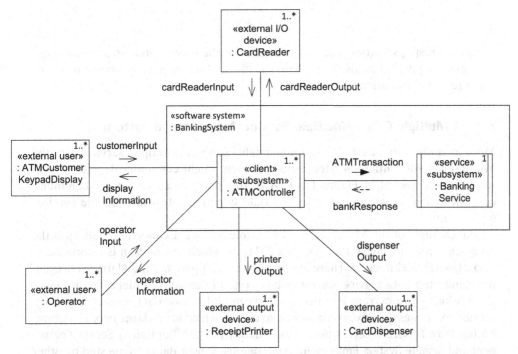

Figure 11.11. Example of Multiple Client/Single Service architectural pattern: Banking System.

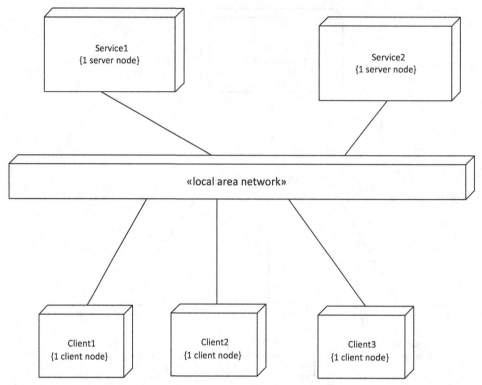

Figure 11.12. Multiple-Client/Multiple-Service architectural pattern.

waits for a response. After receiving the message, the service processes the message, prepares a reply, and sends the reply to the client. After receiving the response, the client resumes execution.

11.4.2 Multiple Client/Multiple Service Architectural Pattern

More complex client/service systems might support multiple services. In the **Multiple-Client/Multiple-Service** pattern, a client might communicate with several services, as depicted in Figure 11.12. With this pattern, a client could communicate with each service sequentially or could communicate with multiple services concurrently.

An example of the Multiple-Client/Multiple-Service architectural pattern is the emergency monitoring system (Gomaa 2011), in which this pattern is incorporated into a layered architecture. There are two service components, the Alarm Service and the Monitoring Data Service, shown at layer one of the layered hierarchy in Figure 11.13, which store current and historical alarm and sensor data respectively. Each service component receives data from two clients, which are at layer two. Thus, Monitoring Data Service receives new sensor data from the Monitoring Sensor Component and Remote System Proxy client components. Sensor data is requested by other clients, such as the Operator Presentation component at layer three, which displays the data.

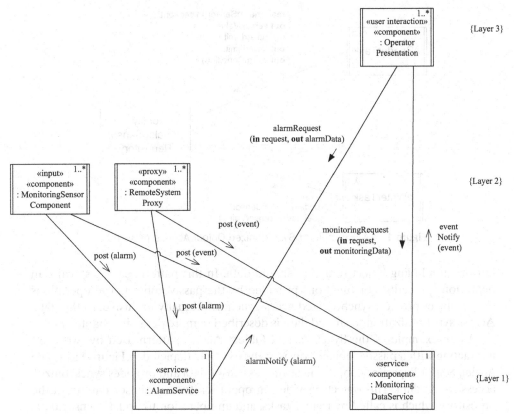

Figure 11.13. Example of Multiple-Client/Multiple-Service architectural pattern: emergency monitoring system.

11.5 BASIC SOFTWARE ARCHITECTURAL COMMUNICATION PATTERNS

Architectural communication patterns address the dynamic communication among concurrent and/or distributed components of the architecture. This section describes the basic communication patterns. The first pattern is the synchronized object access pattern, which is restricted to usage between concurrent components that execute on the same node. All the other patterns address message communication between either concurrent components that reside on the same node or distributed components that reside on different nodes. Communication patterns are frequently used sequences of interactions (also referred to as interaction protocols) by which concurrent and distributed components communicate with each other. Concurrent communication diagrams are the most effective way to depict patterns that address message communication between concurrent components. More advanced architectural communication patterns, namely brokered and group communication patterns are described in Sections 11.6 and 11.7 respectively.

11.5.1 Synchronized Object Access Pattern

The **Synchronized Object Access pattern** is used when two or more concurrent components (tasks) on the same node communicate with each through a passive

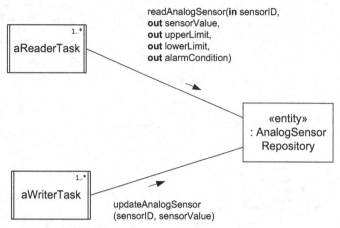

Figure 11.14. Example of Synchronized Object Access pattern.

information hiding object to access shared data. In this pattern, each task calls an operation (procedure or function) provided by the passive object. The operations of the object provide synchronized access, such as mutually exclusive, to the data. Access synchronization to shared data is described in more detail in Chapter 14.

As an example of the Synchronized Object Access pattern used by two tasks interacting with a passive object, consider the example depicted in Figure 11.14. The Analog Sensor Repository object encapsulates sensor data and provides synchronized access to the data. This object provides an operation to read sensor data from the repository, which is called by reader tasks, and an operation to update sensor data, which is called by writer tasks, as described in more detail in Chapter 14.

11.5.2 Asynchronous Message Communication Pattern

With the **Asynchronous Message Communication** pattern, the producer component sends a message to the consumer component (Figure 11.15) and does not wait for a reply. The producer continues because it either does not need a response or has other functions to perform before receiving a response (see the discussion of bidirectional asynchronous communication in Section 11.5.3). The consumer receives the message; if the consumer is busy when the message arrives, the message is queued. Because the producer and consumer components proceed asynchronously (i.e., at different speeds), a first-in, first-out (FIFO) message queue can build up between producer and consumer; that is, messages are queued in the order they are received. If a message is available when the consumer requests one, the consumer receives the message and continues executing. If no message is available, the consumer is suspended. When a message arrives, the consumer is reawakened. This pattern is also often used with

Figure 11.15. Asynchronous Message Communication pattern.

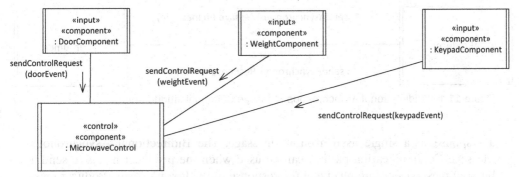

Figure 11.16. Example of the Asynchronous Message Communication pattern: microwave oven system.

multiple producers and one consumer. In distributed environments, asynchronous message communication is used wherever possible for greater flexibility. This pattern is particularly appropriate if the sender does not need a response from the receiver.

In a distributed environment, an additional requirement is that the producer needs to receive a positive or negative acknowledgment indicating whether or not the message has arrived at its destination. This is not an indication that the message has been received by the destination component – merely that it has safely arrived at the destination node. Thus, a significant additional amount of time might elapse before the message is actually received by the destination component. A timeout can be associated with sending a message so that a delay or failure in message transmission will result in a negative acknowledgment being returned to the source component. It is up to the source component to decide how to handle this situation.

An example of the Asynchronous Message Communication pattern is given in Figure 11.16 for the microwave control system, in which all communication between the components is asynchronous. The Asynchronous Message Communication pattern is used in the microwave oven software system because most communication is one-way, and this pattern has the advantage of not letting the consumers hold up the producers. The order in which messages are sent by the three producer components (Door Component, Weight Component, and Keypad Component) to the Microwave Control component (see Figure 11.16) is nondeterministic, because it is based on the user's actions. The Microwave Oven Control component needs to be able to receive a message from any of its three producers in any order. The best way to handle this requirement for flexibility is through asynchronous message communication, with one input message queue for the Microwave Control component in which incoming messages are queued in the order they are received.

11.5.3 Bidirectional Asynchronous Message Communication Pattern

The **Bidirectional Asynchronous Message Communication** pattern is used in situations in which the producer needs to send messages asynchronously to the consumer, and, although it does not need an immediate reply, it does need a reply later (as shown in Figure 11.17). This pattern is more flexible than the Asynchronous Message Communication with Callback pattern (see Section 11.5.5), which only addresses

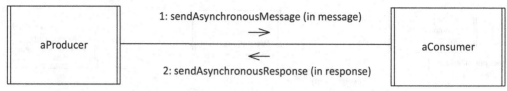

Figure 11.17. Bidirectional Asynchronous Message Communication pattern.

a response to a single asynchronous message. The Bidirectional Asynchronous Message Communication pattern can be used when the producer needs to send a burst of messages before receiving the response to the first message. Producer messages are queued up at the consumer. Consumer responses are queued up at the producer, which receives them when it needs to.

An example of the Bidirectional Asynchronous Message Communication pattern in a distributed environment is given in Figure 11.18 for the factory control system, in which all communication between the components is asynchronous. The Supervisory System component sends asynchronous messages containing move Command requests to the Automated Guided Vehicle (AGV) System component, requesting it to move to specific locations in the factory. The AGV System sends asynchronous response messages containing move Ack acknowledgments (indicating its current location, the direction it is taking, and its eventual arrival at the destination). In this example, Supervisory System could send several move requests to a given AGV to visit various factory locations. The AGV gradually services these requests as it moves around the factory, acknowledging the locations it is visiting.

11.5.4 Synchronous Message Communication with Reply Pattern

The **Synchronous Message Communication with Reply** pattern can be used between a producer and a consumer or alternatively between a client and a service. In either case, a sender (producer or client) component sends a message to a receiver (consumer or service) component and then waits for a reply. When the message arrives, the receiver accepts it, processes it, generates a reply, and then sends the reply to the sender. For a given producer/consumer pair, no message queue develops between them. The producer/consumer usage of the **Synchronous Message Communication with Reply** pattern is described in more detail in Chapter 13.

A client/service usage of the **Synchronous Message Communication with Reply** pattern typically involves multiple clients and one service. In typical client/service patterns, several clients send requests to a service and a message queue can build up at the service. The client uses synchronous message communication and waits for

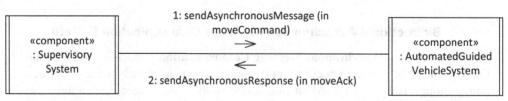

Figure 11.18. Example of the Bidirectional Asynchronous Message Communication pattern: factory control system.

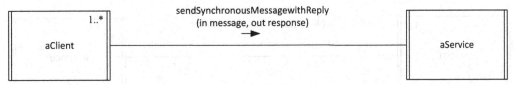

Figure 11.19. Synchronous Message Communication with Reply pattern between multiple clients and a service.

a response from the service, as depicted in Figure 11.19. The service processes each incoming message on a FIFO basis and sends a response to the client. Alternatively, a client can use asynchronous message communication with callback as described in Section 11.5.5.

Whether the client uses synchronous or asynchronous message communication with the service depends on the application and does not affect the design of the service. Indeed, some of a service's clients may communicate with it via synchronous message communication and others via asynchronous message communication. In distributed environments, synchronous message communication is typically provided by middleware technology such as the remote procedure call or remote method invocation.

An example of Multiple-Client/Single-Service message communication using synchronous communication is shown in Figure 11.20, where the service is Pump Status Service, which responds to service requests from multiple Operator Interaction clients. Pump Status Service has a message queue of incoming requests from the multiple user interaction clients. Pump Status Service processes each incoming status Request message on a FIFO basis and then sends the synchronous status Response to the client. Each Operator Interaction client sends a message to Pump Status Service and then waits for the response.

11.5.5 Asynchronous Message Communication with Callback Pattern

The **Asynchronous Message Communication with Callback** pattern is used between a client and a service when the client does not need to wait for the service response but does need the service response later (Figure 11.21). The callback is an asynchronous response to a message sent previously. This pattern allows the client to execute asynchronously but still follows the client/service paradigm in which a client sends only one message at a time to the service.

With the callback pattern, the client sends a remote reference or handle, which is then used by the service to respond to the client. A variation on the callback pattern is for the service to delegate the response to another component by forwarding to it the callback handle, as described in the examples in Section 12.7.

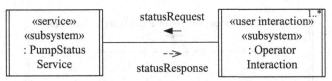

Figure 11.20. Example of the Synchronous Message Communication with Reply pattern between multiple clients and a service.

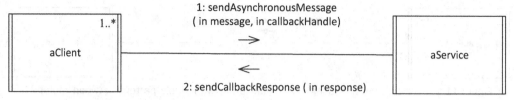

Figure 11.21. Asynchronous Message Communication with Callback pattern.

The Asynchronous Message Communication with Callback pattern is less flexible than the Bidirectional Asynchronous Message Communication pattern, since the latter allows a burst of messages before a response is sent.

11.5.6 Synchronous Message Communication without Reply Pattern

In the **Synchronous Message Communication without Reply** pattern, the producer sends a message to the consumer and then waits for acceptance of the message by the consumer (Figure 11.22). When the message arrives, the consumer accepts it, thereby releasing the producer. The producer and the consumer then both continue. The consumer is suspended if no message is available. For a given producer/consumer pair, no message queue develops between the producer and the consumer. The best time to use this pattern is when the producer is faster than the consumer and it is necessary to slow down the producer so that it does not get ahead of the consumer.

An example of the Synchronous Message Communication without Reply pattern is shown in Figure 11.23. The producer component, Sensor Statistics Algorithm, sends temperature and pressure statistics to the consumer component, Sensor Statistics Display Output, which then displays the information. In this example, the decision is made that there is no point in having the Sensor Statistics Algorithm component compute temperature and pressure statistics if the Sensor Statistics Display Output component cannot keep up with displaying them. Consequently, the communication between the two components uses the Synchronous Message Communication without Reply pattern, as depicted on the concurrent communication diagram in Figure 11.23.

The Sensor Statistics Algorithm component computes the statistics, sends the message, and then waits for the message to be accepted by Sensor Statistics Display Output before resuming execution. Sensor Statistics Algorithm is held up until Sensor Statistics Display Output finishes displaying the previous message. As soon as Sensor Statistics Display Output accepts the latest message, Sensor Statistics Algorithm is released from its wait and computes the next set of statistics while Sensor Statistics Display Output displays the previous set. This approach allows computation of the statistics

Figure 11.22. Synchronous Message Communication without Reply pattern.

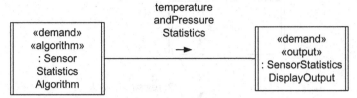

Figure 11.23. Example of the Synchronous Message Communication without Reply pattern.

(a compute-bound activity) to be overlapped with displaying of the statistics (an I/O-bound activity), while preventing an unnecessary message queue buildup of statistics at the display component. Thus, synchronous communication without reply between the two components acts as a brake on the producer component.

In distributed communication, synchronous message communication without reply is usually not necessary and should be used only in situations such as those described in this section. Communication between components should be asynchronous whenever possible; synchronous message communication should be used primarily when a response is required.

11.6 SOFTWARE ARCHITECTURAL BROKER PATTERNS

In a distributed component-based environment, clients and services are designed as distributed components. In brokered communication patterns (which are also known as *Object Broker* or *Object Request Broker* patterns), the **broker** acts as an intermediary between the clients and services. Services register with the broker. Clients locate services through the broker.

The broker provides both location transparency and platform transparency. **Location transparency** means that if the service is moved to a different location, clients are unaware of the move and only the broker needs to be notified. **Platform transparency** means that each service can execute on a different hardware/software platform and does not need to maintain information about the platforms that other services execute on.

With brokered communication, the service has to first register with a broker as described by the service registration pattern in Section 11.6.1. The pattern of communication, in which the client knows the service required but not the location, is referred to as **white page brokering**, analogous to the white pages of the telephone directory, and is described in Section 11.6.2. Yellow page brokering, in which the specific service is discovered, is described in Section 11.6.3.

Although brokering patterns are used widely in service-oriented architectures, as described in Gomaa (2011), they are also effectively used in distributed real-time embedded systems to allow dynamic binding of components at run time. Thus components can register their names with a name service, which acts as a broker for components, as described in Chapter 12.

11.6.1 Service Registration Pattern

In broker patterns, the service needs to register service information with the broker, including the service name, a description of the service, and the location at which the

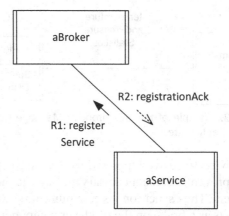

Figure 11.24. Service registration with Broker.

service is provided. Service registration is carried out the first time the service joins the brokering exchange (analogous to the stock exchange). On subsequent occasions, if the service relocates, it needs to re-register with the broker by providing its new location. The service registration pattern is illustrated in Figure 11.24, which depicts the service registering (or re-registering after a relocation) a service with the broker in the following message sequence:

R1: The Service sends a register Service request to the broker.

R2: The Broker registers the service in the service registry and sends a registration Ack acknowledgment to the service.

11.6.2 Broker Handle Pattern

With the *Broker Handle* pattern, the broker is an intermediary for establishing connections between clients and services. Once connected to a service, a client communicates with the service directly without involving the broker.

Most commercial object brokers use a Broker Handle design. This pattern is particularly useful when the client and service are likely to have a dialog and exchange several messages between them. The pattern is depicted in Figure 11.25 and consists of the following message sequence:

B1: The Service Requester client sends a service request to the Broker.

B2: The Broker looks up the location of the service and returns a service handle to the client.

B3: The Service Requester client uses the service handle to make the request to the appropriate Service.

B4: The Service executes the request and sends the reply directly to the Service Requester client.

An alternative brokering pattern is the Broker Forwarding pattern, in which the broker is an intermediary for every message sent between the client and service. Broker

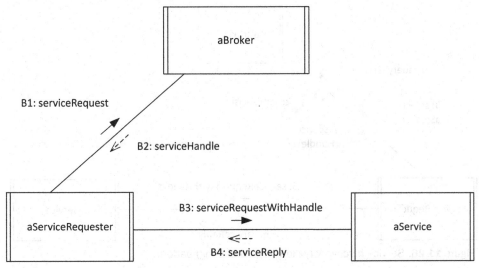

Figure 11.25. Broker Handle (white page brokering) pattern.

Forwarding is less efficient if the client/service dialog results in the exchange of several messages. The reason is that with Broker Handle, the interaction with the broker is only done once at the start of the dialog instead of every time, as with Broker Forwarding.

The message traffic using the Broker Handle pattern is equal to 2n+2, assuming that each request n has one response, and that two additional messages are needed for the client to communicate with the broker and receive a response. Compared with the Client/Service pattern (see Section 11.4.1) in which the message traffic is equal to 2n, the brokering overhead decreases as the value of n increases.

For a real time embedded system, the Broker Handle pattern can be used efficiently to establish a connection between client and service components at initialization time, and then during normal operation, communication between components is done efficiently without broker intervention.

11.6.3 Service Discovery Pattern

The brokered patterns of communication described earlier, in which the client knows the service required but not the location, are referred to as *white page brokering*. A different brokering pattern is **yellow page brokering**, analogous to the yellow pages of the telephone directory, in which the client knows the type of service required but not the specific service. This pattern, which is shown in Figure 11.26, is also known as the **Service Discovery** pattern because it allows the client to discover new services. The client sends a query request to the broker, requesting all services of a given type. The broker responds with a list of all services that match the client's request. The client selects a specific service. The broker returns the service handle, which the client uses for communicating directly with the service.

The pattern interactions, in which a yellow pages request is followed by a white pages request, are described in more detail as follows:

1: The Service Requester client sends a *yellow pages* request to the Broker requesting information about all services of a given type.

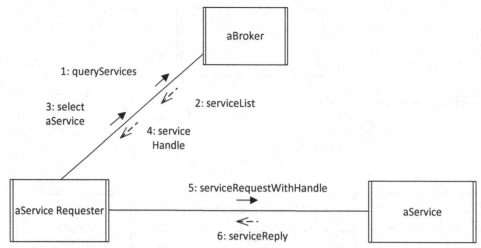

Figure 11.26. Service discovery (yellow page brokering) pattern.

2: The Broker looks up this information and returns a list of all services that satisfy the query criteria.

3: The Service Requester client selects one of the services and sends a *white pages* request to the Broker.

4: The Broker looks up the location of the service and returns a service handle to the Service Requester client.

5: The Service Requester client uses the service handle to send a request to the appropriate Service

6: The Service executes the request and sends the response directly to the Service Requester client.

The message traffic using yellow page brokering followed by white page brokering is equal to 2n+4. This assumes that each client request n has one response, two messages are needed for yellow page brokering, and two additional messages are needed for white page brokering. Compared with the Client/Service pattern (see Section 11.4.1) in which the message traffic is equal to 2n, the brokering overhead decreases as the value of n increases. For a real time embedded system, an efficient usage of these patterns is to establish a connection between client and service components at initialization time using the yellow pages service discovery pattern followed by the white pages brokering pattern, and then during subsequent operation, components can communicate efficiently with each other without any broker intervention.

11.7 GROUP MESSAGE COMMUNICATION PATTERNS

The message communication patterns described so far have involved one source and one destination component. A desirable property in some distributed applications is group communication. This is a form of one-to-many message communication in which a sender sends one message to many recipients. Two kinds of group message communication (sometimes referred to as *groupcast communication*) supported in distributed applications are broadcast and multicast communication.

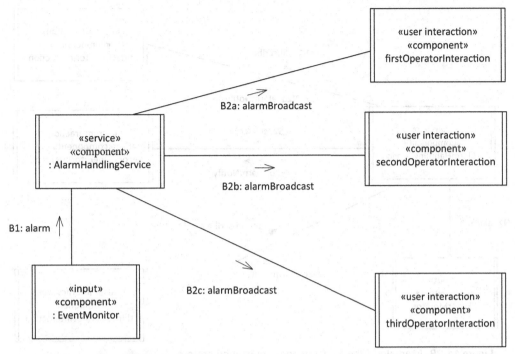

Figure 11.27. Broadcast pattern.

11.7.1 Broadcast Message Communication Pattern

With the **Broadcast** (or *Broadcast Communication*) pattern, an unsolicited message is sent to all recipients, perhaps informing them of a pending shutdown. Each recipient must then decide whether it wishes to process the message or discard it. An example of the Broadcast pattern is given in Figure 11.27. Alarm Handling Service sends alarm Broadcast messages to all instances of the Operator Interaction component. Each recipient must decide whether it wishes to take action in response to the alarm or to ignore the message. The pattern interactions are described in more detail as follows:

> **B1:** Event Monitor sends an alarm message to Alarm Handling Service.
> **B2a, B2b, B2c:** Alarm Handling Service broadcasts the alarm as an alarm Broadcast message to all instances of the Operator Interaction component. Each recipient decides whether to take action or discard the message.

11.7.2 Subscription/Notification Message Communication Pattern

Multicast communication provides a more selective form of group communication, in which the same message is sent to all members of a group. The **Subscription/ Notification** pattern (also called Publish/Subscribe pattern) uses a form of multicast communication in which components subscribe to a group and receive messages destined for all members of the group. A component can subscribe to (request to join) or unsubscribe from (leave) a group and can be a member of more than one group. A sender, also referred to as a *publisher*, sends a message to the group without having

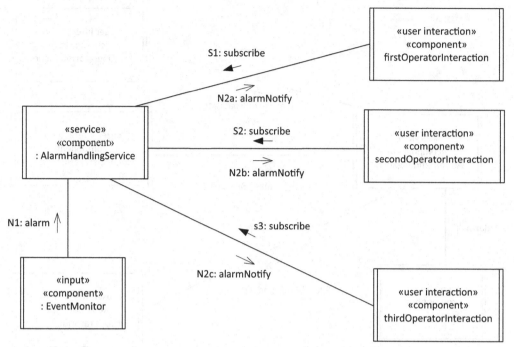

Figure 11.28. Example of the Subscription/Notification pattern.

to know who all the individual members are. The message is then sent to all members of the group. Sending the same message to all members of a group is referred to as *multicast communication*. A message sent to a subscriber is also referred to as an *event notification*. While on a subscription list, a member can receive several event notification messages. The Subscription/Notification pattern is widely used on the Internet.

Real-Time systems can use utilize the Subscription/Notification pattern by making subscriptions at initialization time and using event notifications during normal execution at run time. A variation on this pattern is the Multicast Notification pattern, in which multicast connections among components are made via a connection table (also called a name table, see Chapter 12) at initialization time. Thus the connection is implicit rather than through an explicit subscription and event notifications are handled as usual at run time.

An example of the Subscription/Notification pattern is shown in Figure 11.28. First, three instances of the Operator Interaction component send a subscribe message to Alarm Handling Service to receive alarms of a certain type. Every time the Alarm Handling Service component receives a new alarm message of this type, it multicasts the alarm Notify notification message to all subscriber Operator Interaction components. The pattern interactions are described in more detail as follows:

S1, S2, S3: Operator Interaction components subscribe to receive alarm notifications.

N1: Event Monitor sends an alarm message to Alarm Handling Service.

N2a, N2b, N2c: Alarm Handling Service looks up the list of subscribers who have requested to be notified of alarms of this type. It multicasts the alarm Notify message to all instances of the Operator Interaction component that are on the subscription list. Each recipient takes appropriate action in response to the alarm notification.

Another variation on the Subscription/Notification pattern is to have only one subscriber. This arrangement is useful in peer-to-peer situations in which the producer does not know who the consumer is and the consumer might change. The consumer can subscribe to the producer, sending it a handle, which the producer then uses for sending messages to the consumer. This is useful for reversing a dependency because, by virtue of the subscription, the consumer is dependent on the producer rather than vice versa.

11.8 DOCUMENTING SOFTWARE ARCHITECTURAL PATTERNS

Whatever the category of pattern, it is very useful to have a standard way of describing and documenting a pattern so that it can be easily referenced, compared with other patterns, and reused. Three important aspects of a pattern that need to be captured (Buschmann et al. 1996) are the context, problem, and solution. The *context* is the situation that gives rise to a problem. The *problem* refers to a recurring problem that arises in this context. The *solution* is a proven resolution to the problem. A template for describing a pattern usually also addresses its strengths, weaknesses, and related patterns. A typical template looks like this:

- **Pattern name**.
- **Aliases**. Other names by which this pattern is known.
- **Context**. The situation that gives rise to this problem.
- **Problem**. Brief description of the problem.
- **Summary of solution**. Brief description of the solution.
- **Strengths of solution**. Use to determine if the solution is right for your problem.
- **Weaknesses of solution**. Use to determine if the solution is wrong for your problem.
- **Applicability**. Situations in which you can use the pattern.
- **Related patterns**. Other patterns to consider for your solution.
- **Reference**. Where you can find more information about the pattern.

The patterns described in this chapter are documented with this standard template in Appendix B.

11.9 APPLYING SOFTWARE ARCHITECTURAL PATTERNS

This section describes how to develop a software architecture starting from software architectural patterns. A very important decision is to determine which architectural patterns – in particular, which architectural structure and communication patterns – are required. Architectural structure patterns can initially be identified during dynamic interaction modeling (see Chapter 9) because patterns can be recognized during development of the interaction diagrams. For example, any of the control patterns can first be used during dynamic modeling. Although architectural structure patterns can be identified during dynamic modeling, the real decisions are made during software architectural design. It is necessary to first decide what architectural structure patterns to apply in order to determine the organization of the components in the architecture, and then to apply the architectural communication patterns to determine how components communicate with each other.

The different architectural structure and communication patterns described in this chapter can be used together. Thus, a Layers of Abstraction architecture might incorporate the control, Kernel and Client/Service patterns. For example, the light rail control system (Chapter 21) incorporates various control patterns and client/service patterns within a layered architectural pattern. It also applies several communication patterns, including asynchronous and synchronous message communication, bidirectional message communication, and subscription/notification.

11.10 SUMMARY

This chapter has described several software architectural patterns. Architectural structure patterns are used to address the structure of a software architecture. Architectural communication patterns address how distributed components of the software architecture communicate with each other. Software architectural patterns can be combined to develop a new software architecture, starting with the architectural structure patterns and then incorporating architectural communication patterns.

This chapter has also described how to document software architectural patterns using a standard template. The software architectural patterns described in this chapter are documented with this template in Appendix B. Chapter 12 discusses several important topics in designing component-based software architectures. The case studies in Chapters 19 through 23 give several examples of applying the software architectural structure and communication patterns to real-time software designs.

12

Component-Based Software Architectures for Real-Time Embedded Systems

In earlier chapters, the term *component* has been used informally. This chapter describes the design of distributed component-based software architectures in which the architecture for a real-time embedded system is designed in terms of components that can be deployed to execute on different nodes in a distributed environment. It describes the component structuring criteria for designing components that can be deployed to execute in a distributed configuration. The design of component interfaces is described, with component ports that have provided and required interfaces and connectors that join compatible ports.

Components are initially designed using the subsystem structuring criteria described in Chapter 10. Additional component configuration criteria are used to ensure that components are configurable, in other words that they can be effectively deployed to distributed physical nodes in a distributed environment. Architectural structure and communication patterns described previously in Chapter 11 are also used in the design of component-based software architectures.

Components can be effectively modeled in UML with structured classes and depicted on composite structure diagrams. Structured classes have ports with provided and required interfaces. Structured classes can be interconnected through their ports via connectors that join the ports of communicating classes. Chapter 2, Section 2.10 and Chapter 10, Section 10.2.1 introduce the UML notation for composite structure diagrams. This chapter describes in detail how component-based software architectures are designed.

Section 12.1 describes concepts for distributed component-based software architectures. Section 12.2 describes the steps in designing distributed component-based software architectures. Section 12.3 describes how component interfaces are designed with provided and required interfaces. Section 12.4 describes the concepts and design of composite subsystems and components. Section 12.5 describes some examples of distributed component-based software architectures. Section 12.6 describes component structuring criteria for structuring a software architecture into configurable distributed components. Section 12.7 describes the design of sequential and concurrent service subsystems. Section 12.8 describes issues in the distribution of data in distributed systems. Section 12.9 describes component deployment to a distributed configuration. Finally, Section 12.10 describes the design of software connectors.

12.1 CONCEPTS FOR COMPONENT-BASED SOFTWARE ARCHITECTURES

A component integrates the concepts of encapsulation and concurrency. An important goal of a component-based software architecture is to provide a concurrent message-based design that is highly configurable. In other words, the objective is that the same software architecture should be capable of being deployed to many different distributed configurations. Thus, a given software system could be configured to have each component instance allocated to its own separate physical node, or alternatively to have all or some of its component instances allocated to the same physical node. To achieve this flexibility, it is necessary to design the software architecture in such a way that the decision about how component instances will be allocated to physical nodes is made not at design time but later, at system deployment time.

A component-based software development approach, in which each subsystem is designed as a distributed self-contained component, helps achieve the goal of a distributed, highly configurable, message-based design. A **distributed component** is a logical unit of distribution and deployment. A component can be either a composite component or a simple component. A **composite component** contains internal components, which are themselves either composite or simple components. A **simple component** has no constituent components within it. However, a simple component can encapsulate one or more objects, which could be active or passive, providing at least one object is active.

Because components can be deployed to different nodes in a geographically distributed environment, all communication between components must be restricted to message communication. Thus, a source component on one node sends a message over the network to a destination component on a different node. Components communicate with each other using the architectural communication patterns described in Chapter 11. The details of these patterns are encapsulated in connectors that interconnect the components.

12.2 DESIGNING DISTRIBUTED COMPONENT-BASED SOFTWARE ARCHITECTURES

A **distributed component-based software architecture** for a real-time embedded system consists of distributed components that can be configured to execute on distributed physical nodes. To successfully manage the inherent complexity of large-scale distributed real-time embedded systems, it is necessary to provide an approach for structuring the software architecture into components in which each component instance can potentially execute on its own node. After this design is performed and the interfaces between the components are carefully defined, each component can be designed independently.

The three main steps in designing a distributed component-based software architecture are:

1. **Design software architecture**. Structure the software architecture into constituent components that potentially could execute on separate nodes in a

distributed environment. Because component instances can reside on separate nodes, all communication between components must be restricted to message communication. The interfaces between components are defined. The subsystem structuring criteria, as described in Section 10.4, are used to initially determine the components. Additional component structuring criteria are used to ensure that the components are designed as configurable components that can be effectively deployed to physical nodes.

2. **Design constituent components as composite or simple components**. A composite component is designed as described in step 1. A simple component is structured into concurrent objects and passive information hiding objects, as described in Chapter 13. By definition, a simple component can execute on only one node

3. **Deploy the software components**. After the component-based software architecture has been designed and implemented, component instances can be deployed to a distributed configuration. During this stage, the component instances of the software are defined, instantiated, mapped to physical nodes, interconnected, and deployed to a hardware configuration consisting of distributed physical nodes.

12.3 COMPONENT INTERFACE DESIGN

This section describes the design of component interfaces, an important issue in software architecture. In particular, this section describes how interfaces are specified before describing provided and required interfaces, ports (and how they are specified in terms of provided and required interfaces), and connectors that interconnect components.

12.3.1 Component Interfaces

An important goal of both object-oriented design and component-based software architecture is the separation of the interface from the implementation. An **interface** specifies the externally visible operations of a class, service, or component without revealing the internal structure (implementation) of the operations, as described in Section 10.1.3. A given interface it provides is designed to consist of a selection of its operations, tailored to meet the needs of a subset of its client components.

Three interfaces from an emergency monitoring system will be used in the examples that follow. Each interface consists of one or more operations, as follows:

1. **Interface**: IAlarmService
   Operations provided:
   - alarmRequest (**in** request, **out** alarmData)
   - alarmSubscribe (**in** request, **in** notificationHandle, **out** ack)
2. **Interface**: IAlarmStatus
   Operation provided: post (**in** alarm)
3. **Interface**: IAlarmNotification
   Operation provided: alarmNotification (**in** alarm)

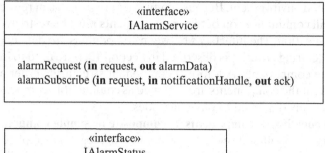

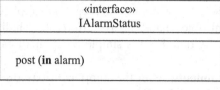

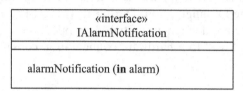

Figure 12.1. Example of component interfaces.

The interface of a component can be depicted with the static modeling notation (see Chapter 2), as shown in Figure 12.1, with the stereotype «interface».

12.3.2 Provided and Required Interfaces

To provide a complete definition of the component-based software architecture, it is necessary to specify the interface(s) provided by each component and the interface(s) required by each component. A **provided interface** specifies the operations that a component must fulfill. A **required interface** describes the operations that other components provide for this component to operate properly in a particular environment.

Although many components are designed to provide one interface, it is possible for a component to provide more than one interface. To do this, the component designer selects for each provided interface a subset of the component's operations that are required by some of its clients. An example of a component that provides more than one interface is the Alarm Service component, which provides two of the interfaces in Figure 12.1, IAlarmService and IAlarmStatus. IAlarmService is required by the Operator Alarm Presentation component and IAlarmStatus is required by the Monitoring Sensor Component, as shown in Figure 12.2.

12.3.3 Ports and Interfaces

A component has one or more *ports* through which it interacts with other components. Each component port is defined in terms of provided and/or required interfaces. A *provided* interface of a port specifies the requests that other components can make of this component. A *required* interface of a port specifies the requests

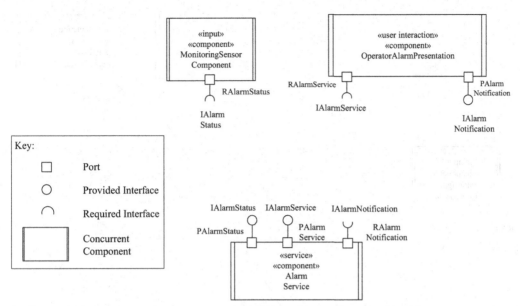

Figure 12.2. Examples of component ports, with provided and required interfaces.

that this component can make of other components. A **provided port** supports a provided interface. A **required port** supports a required interface. A **complex port** supports both a provided interface and a required interface. A component can have more than one port. In particular, if a component communicates with more than one component, it can use a different port for each component with which it communicates. Figure 12.2 shows an example of components with ports, as well as provided and required interfaces. Figure 12.2 depicts each component with two stereotypes: the first stereotype corresponding to its subsystem structuring criterion (Section 10.5), such as «service» or «user interaction», and the second stereotype is «component».

By convention, the name of a component's required port starts with the letter R to emphasize that the component has a *required* port. The name of a component's provided port starts with the letter P to emphasize that the component has a *provided* port. In Figure 12.2, the Monitoring Sensor Component has one required port, called RAlarmStatus, which supports a required interface called IAlarmStatus, as defined in Figure 12.1. The Operator Alarm Presentation component is a client component, which has a required port with a required interface (PAlarmService) and a provided port with a provided interface PAlarmNotification. The Alarm Service component has two provided ports, called PAlarmStatus and PAlarmService, and one required port, RAlarmNotification. The port PAlarmStatus provides an interface called IAlarmStatus, through which alarm status messages are sent. The port PAlarmService provides the main interface through which clients request alarm services (provided interface IAlarmService). The Alarm Service component sends alarm notifications through its RAlarmNotification port.

12.3.4 Connectors and Interconnecting Components

A **connector** joins the required port of one component to the provided port of another component. The connected ports must be compatible with each other. This

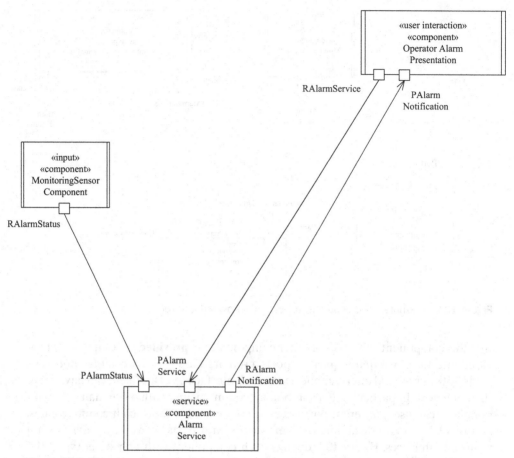

Figure 12.3. Example of components, ports, and connectors in a software architecture.

means that if two ports are connected, the required interface of one port must be compatible with the provided interface of the other port; that is, the operations required in one component's required interface must be the same as the operations provided in the other component's provided interface. In the case of a connector joining two complex ports (each with one provided interface and one required interface), the required interface of the first port must be compatible with the provided interface of the second port, and the required interface of the second port must be compatible with the provided interface of the first port.

Figure 12.3 shows how the three components (Monitoring Sensor Component, Operator Alarm Presentation, and Alarm Service) are interconnected. The first connector is unidirectional (as shown by the direction of the arrow representing the connector) and joins Monitoring Sensor Component's RAlarmStatus required port to Alarm Service's PAlarmStatus provided port. Figure 12.2 shows that these ports are compatible because it results in the IAlarmStatus required interface being connected to the IAlarmStatus provided interface. The second connector is also unidirectional and joins Operator Alarm Presentation's required port RAlarmService to Alarm Service's provided port PAlarmService. Examination of the port design in Figure 12.2 shows that these ports are also compatible, with the required IAlarmService interface connected to the provided interface of the same name. The third connector is also unidirectional

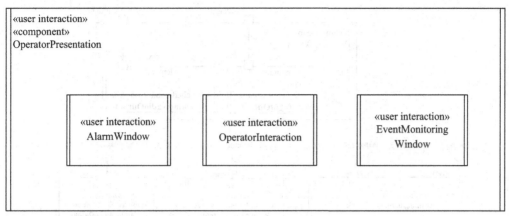

Figure 12.4. Example of composite component with nested simple components.

and joins Alarm Service's RAlarmNotification required port to Operator Alarm Presentation's PAlarmNotification provided port, and it is through this connector that alarm notifications are sent via the IAlarmNotification interface.

12.4 DESIGNING COMPOSITE COMPONENTS

A **composite component** is a component that encapsulates the internal components it contains. The component is both a logical and a physical container; however, it adds no further functionality. Thus, a component's functionality is provided entirely by the constituent components it contains. An example of a composite component with internal components is depicted in Figure 12.4, in which the composite Operator Presentation user interaction component contains three internal simple components, Operator Interaction, Alarm Window, and Event Monitoring Window.

Incoming messages to a composite component are passed through to the appropriate internal destination component, and outgoing messages from an internal component are passed through to the appropriate external (to the component) destination component. The exact pass-through mechanisms are implementation-dependent.

A composite component is structured into part components. A component with no internal components is referred to as a *simple component*. The part components within a composite component can be depicted as instances because it is possible to have more than one instance of the same part component within the composite component.

Figure 12.5 shows an example of a composite component, the Warning Alarm component from the Railroad Crossing Control System, which contains two simple components: Warning Light Output and Warning Audio Output. The composite component is depicted with the «component» stereotype. The simple components are designed as demand driven output tasks (see Chapter 13) and are therefore depicted with the stereotypes «demand» «output» «swSchedulableResource».

The provided port Plight of the composite Warning Alarm component is connected directly to the provided port Plight of the internal Warning Light Output component. The connector joining the two ports is called a **delegation connector**, which means that the outer delegating port provided by Warning Alarm forwards each message it

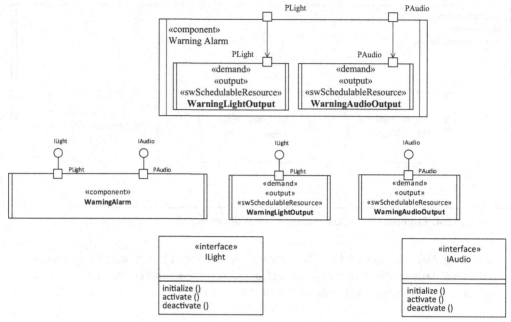

Figure 12.5. Design of composite component.

receives to the inner port provided by Warning Light Output. By convention, the two ports are given the same name, PLight, because they provide the same interface ILight, as shown in Figure 12.5. Delegation means that the operations of the outer component call the operations of the same name in the inner component. Thus, the **activate** and **deactivate** operations of the ILight interface of the Warning Alarm outer component respectively call the **activate** and **deactivate** operations of the ILight interface of the Warning Light Output inner component. The inner **activate** and **deactivate** operations are implemented differently since they send switch on and switch off commands respectively to the physical warning light. This discussion of connector delegation also applies to the PAudio ports and the IAudio interfaces of the outer component Warning Alarm and the inner component Warning Audio Output. Although the IAudio interfaces of the outer and inner components are the same, their implementation is different.

Only distributed components can be deployed to the physical nodes of a distributed configuration. Passive objects cannot be independently deployed, nor can any active object that directly invokes the operations of a passive object; in that situation, only the component (which contains the active and passive objects) can be deployed. By a COMET/RTE convention, only deployable components are depicted with the component stereotype.

12.5 EXAMPLES OF COMPONENT-BASED SOFTWARE ARCHITECTURE

As an example of a distributed component-based software architecture, consider the Factory Automation System, which is shown on the concurrent communication diagram in Figure 12.6. It depicts the three interacting distributed systems (designed as

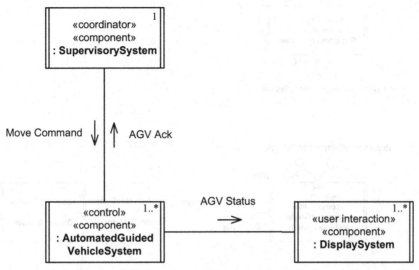

Figure 12.6. Concurrent communication diagram for Factory Automation System.

components), the Supervisory System, the Automated Guided Vehicle System, and the Display System. There is one instance of the Supervisory System and multiple instances of the Automated Guided Vehicle System and the Display System. All communication between the distributed components is asynchronous, allowing the greatest flexibility in message communication. Communication between the Supervisory System and the Automated Guided Vehicle System is an example of the bidirectional asynchronous communication pattern. This pattern is mapped to the component-based software architecture, as described below.

The component-based software architecture for the Factory Automation System is shown in Figure 12.7, in which the three systems are designed as distributed

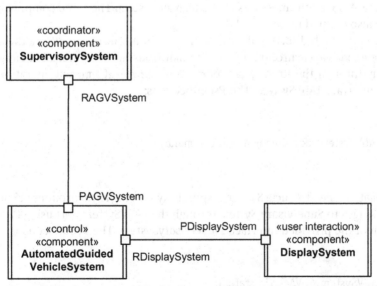

Figure 12.7. Component-based software architecture for Factory Automation System.

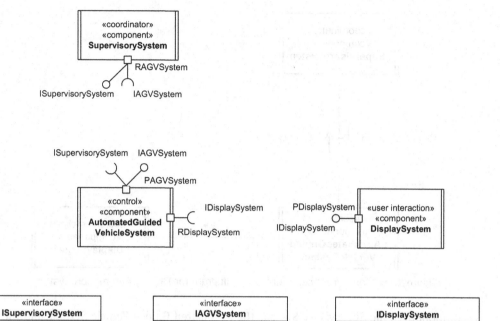

Figure 12.8. Composite component ports and interfaces for Factory Automation System.

components. The Automated Guided Vehicle System has a provided port for receiving messages from the Supervisory System and a required port for sending messages to the Display System. The provided port PAGVSystem is a complex port as it has both a provided interface IAGVSystem for receiving command messages and a required interface ISupervisorySystem for sending acknowledgment messages, as shown in Figure 12.8. The required port RDisplaySystem supports a required interface IDisplaySystem for sending AGV status messages to the Display System. The three component interfaces are also defined in Figure 12.8.

To support the bidirectional asynchronous communication pattern, the Supervisory System sends asynchronous move command messages to Automated Guided Vehicle System through the RAGVSystem port using the moveCommand operation of the required interface IAGVSystem. The Pseudocode is:

```
RAGVSystem.moveCommand (in command);
```

Automated Guided Vehicle System responds by sending asynchronous acknowledgment messages to Supervisory System through the PAGVSystem port using the AGVAck operation of the provided interface ISupervisorySystem. The Pseudocode is:

```
PAGVSystem.AGVAck (in status);
```

Note that each component sends a message by communicating through its own local port, which means that it need have no knowledge of the component that will actually receive the message.

12.6 COMPONENT STRUCTURING CRITERIA

A distributed software architecture must be designed with an understanding of the distributed environments in which it is likely to operate. The component structuring criteria provide guidelines on how to structure a software architecture into configurable distributed components, instances of which can be deployed to geographically distributed nodes. The actual assignment of component instances to physical nodes is done later, when an individual target system is instantiated and deployed. However, it is necessary to design the components as configurable components, instances of which are indeed capable of later being effectively deployed to distributed physical nodes. Consequently, the component structuring criteria must take into account the characteristics of distributed environments.

In a distributed environment, a component might be associated with a particular physical location or constrained to execute on a given hardware resource. In such a case, the component is constrained to execute on the node at that location.

12.6.1 Proximity to the Source of Physical Data and/or Physical Component

In a distributed environment, the sources of data and/or the physical components being controlled might be physically distant from each other. Designing a software component to be close to the source of physical data ensures fast access to the data, which is particularly important if data access rates are high. Proximity of a software component to a physical component permits a deployable software component to be physically located with the hardware component as one system (hardware/software) composite component, which is also referred to as a *smart device*.

An example of a software component designed to be in close proximity to a physical component that it controls is the Barrier Component in the Railroad Crossing Control System, as shown in Figure 12.9, which is designed to be in close proximity to the physical railroad barrier. The Barrier Component is a composite component that encapsulates three simple barrier-related components: Barrier Actuator Output, which sends commands to the physical barrier actuator; Barrier Detection Input, which receives inputs from the physical barrier detection sensor; and Barrier Timer, which detects if there is a delay in barrier raising or lowering. Each of the three simple components is designed as a concurrent task; for example, Barrier Detection Input is an event drive input task and is depicted with the stereotypes «event-driven» «input» «swSchedulableResource», as described in more detail in Chapter 13.

Another example of a component designed to be in close proximity to the physical component is the Warning Alarm component in Figure 12.5, which is designed to be close to the physical audio and visual warning alarms in the Railroad Crossing Control System.

12.6.2 Localized Autonomy

A distributed component often performs a specific site-related function, where the same function is performed at multiple sites. Each instance of the component resides

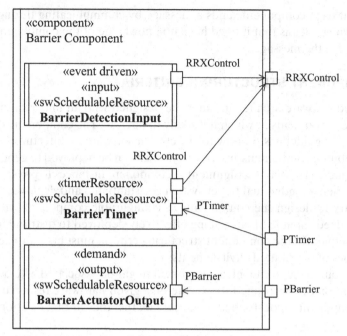

Figure 12.9. Example of component proximity to the source of physical data: Barrier Component.

on a separate node, thereby providing greater localized autonomy. Greater autonomy means that the component can execute on a given node independently of other nodes. Thus, it can be operational even if the other nodes are temporarily unavailable. Examples of autonomous components from the Light Rail System are the Train Control component, an instance of which is deployed to each physical train, Station component, an instance of which is deployed to each physical railroad station, and Railroad Crossing Control component, an instance of which is deployed to each physical railroad crossing, as depicted in the deployment diagram in Figure 12.10. Thus the execution of a Train Control component on a given train is not affected if other

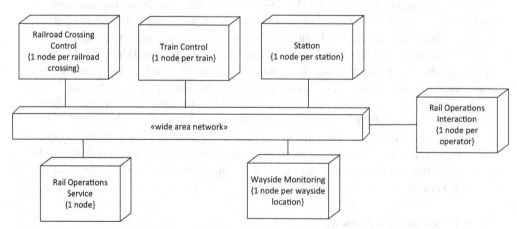

Figure 12.10. Examples of component localized autonomy and control in deployment of Light Rail System.

trains stop at stations or go out of service. An instance of Railroad Crossing Control is not affected if other railroad crossings are inoperable.

Another example of localized autonomy is from the Factory Automation System in which an instance of the Automated Guided Vehicle System component is deployed to each physical vehicle, as depicted in Figures 12.6 and 12.7.

12.6.3 Performance

If a time-critical function is executed entirely by a component on a given node without involving components on other nodes, better and more-predictable component performance can often be achieved. In a given distributed software architecture, a real-time component can perform a time-critical function at a given node, with less-time-critical functions performed elsewhere. Examples of components that satisfy this criterion are the Train Control and Railroad Crossing Control components in Figure 12.10 and the AGV System component in Figure 12.7.

12.6.4 Specialized Hardware

A component might need to reside on a particular node because it supports special-purpose hardware, such as interfacing to special-purpose peripherals, sensors, or actuators that are connected to a specific node. Both the Train Control component and the Railroad Crossing Control component (Figure 12.10) interface to special purpose sensors and actuators.

12.6.5 I/O Component

An I/O component can be designed to be execute on a separate node and in close proximity to the source of physical data. In particular, "smart" devices are typically given local autonomy, communicating with other components as needed, and consist of the hardware plus the software that interfaces to and controls the device. An I/O component typically consists of one or more input/output objects that interface to and communicate with external devices such as sensors and actuators, and it may also contain control objects to provide localized control and entity objects to store local data.

I/O component is a general name given to components that interact with the external environment; they include input components, output components, I/O components (which provide both input and output), network interface components, and system interface components.

Examples of I/O components are the Barrier Component (depicted in Figure 12.9) and the Warning Alarm (depicted in Figure 12.5) composite components from the Railroad Crossing Control System. The design of the Barrier Component is described in Section 12.6.1.

12.7 DESIGN OF SERVICE COMPONENTS

Service components play an important role in the design of distributed software architectures. Real-time embedded systems particularly need service components for storing and accessing status and alarm data, as well as for configuration data, which can be used during software initialization. A *service component* provides a service for multiple client components, as described by the client/service patterns in Chapter 11. Typical service components are file services and database services.

In distributed software architectures, a service component can encapsulate one or more entity objects. A simple service component does not initiate any requests for services; it only responds to requests from clients. There are two kinds of service components, sequential and concurrent, as described next.

12.7.1 Sequential Service Component

A sequential service component services client requests sequentially; that is, it completes one request before it starts servicing the next. A **sequential service** is designed as one active object (thread of control) that provides one or more services and responds to requests from client components to access the service. For example, a simple sequential service component responds to requests from client components to update or read data from a passive entity object. When the service component receives a message from a client component, it invokes the appropriate operation provided by the passive entity object – for example, to read or update the current value of a sensor. The Banking Service described in Chapter 11, Section 11.4 and Rail Operations Service in Figure 12.10 are both designed as sequential services. Sequential service components are described in more detail in chapters on the design of client/server software architectures and the Banking System case study in Gomaa (2011).

12.7.2 Concurrent Service Component with Multiple Readers and Writers

In a concurrent service design, the service functionality is shared among several concurrent (active) objects. If the client demand for services is high enough that the sequential service component could potentially become a bottleneck in the system, an alternative approach is for the services to be provided by a concurrent service component and hence shared among several concurrent objects.

A concurrent service can be designed as a multithreaded service component. Each incoming service request is assigned a new thread, such that each thread executes the same code. Such a design must ensure thread safety such that any access to shared data encapsulated in passive objects must be synchronized, as described in Chapter 14. With this approach, there could be a performance problem if too may requests are serviced concurrently. A solution to this problem is to provide a fixed number of threads such that there is a limit to the number of concurrent threads that could be concurrently executing at any one time. When a service request is received, a thread is assigned to execute the request. When the request is completed, the thread is released and is assigned the next service request or becomes idle if there are no outstanding requests. Requests that exceed the thread limit are placed in a waiting queue.

Another approach to providing concurrent service design using multiple readers and writers is described next. In a concurrent service component, several concurrent objects might wish to access a data repository at the same time, so access must be synchronized. Possible synchronization algorithms include the **mutual exclusion** algorithm and the **multiple readers and writers** algorithm. In the latter case, multiple readers are allowed to access a shared data repository concurrently; however, only one writer is allowed to update the data repository at any one time, and only after the readers have finished.

In the multiple readers and writers solution shown in Figure 12.11, each read and write service is performed by a concurrent object, either a reader or a writer. The Service Coordinator object keeps track of all service requests – those currently being serviced and those waiting to be serviced. When it receives a request from a client, Service Coordinator allocates the request to an appropriate reader or writer concurrent object to perform the service. For example, if the coordinator receives a read request from a client, it instantiates a Reader object and increments its count of the number of readers. The reader notifies the coordinator when it finishes, so that the coordinator can decrement the reader count. If a write request is received from a client, the coordinator allocates the request to a Writer object only when all readers have finished. This delay is to ensure that each writer has mutually exclusive access to the data. If the overhead of instantiating new concurrent objects is too high, the coordinator can maintain a pool of concurrent Reader objects and one concurrent Writer object and allocate new requests to concurrent objects that are free.

If new readers keep coming and are permitted to read, a writer could be indefinitely prevented from writing; this problem is referred to as *writer starvation*. The coordinator avoids writer starvation by queuing up new reader requests after receiving a writer request. After the current readers have finished reading, the waiting writer is then allowed to write before any new readers are permitted to read.

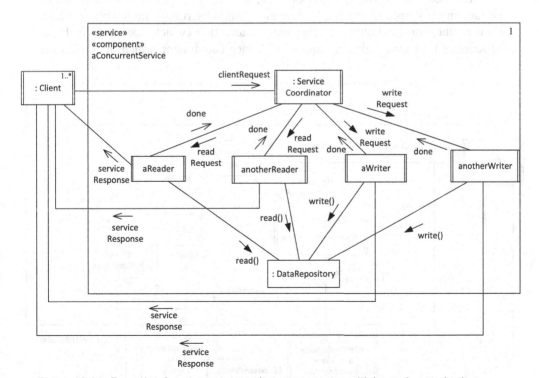

Figure 12.11. Example of a concurrent service component: multiple readers and writers.

In this example, the clients communicate with the service by using the Asynchronous Message Communication with Callback pattern (see Section 11.5.5). This means that the clients do not wait and can do other things before receiving the service response. In this case, the service response is handled as a **callback**. With the callback approach, the client sends an operation handle with the original request. The service uses the handle to remotely call the client operation (the callback) when it finishes servicing the client request. In the example illustrated in Figure 12.11, Service Coordinator passes the client's callback handle to the reader (or writer). On completion, the Reader concurrent object remotely invokes the callback, which is depicted on as the service Response message sent to the client.

12.7.3 Concurrent Service Component with Subscription and Notification

Another example of a concurrent service component is shown in Figure 12.12, which uses the Subscription/Notification Pattern (see Section 11.7.2). This service maintains an event archive and also provides a subscription/notification service to its clients. An example is given of a Real-Time Event Monitor concurrent component that monitors external events. The Subscription Service component maintains a subscription list of clients that wish to be notified of these events. When an external event occurs, Real-Time Event Monitor updates the event archive and informs Event Distributor of the event arrival. Event Distributor queries Subscription Service to determine the clients that have subscribed to receive events of this type and then notifies those clients of the new event.

The concurrent communication diagram in Figure 12.12 shows three separate interactions: a simple query interaction, an event subscription interaction, and an event notification interaction. In the query interaction (which does not involve a subscription) a client makes a request to Service Coordinator, which queries Event

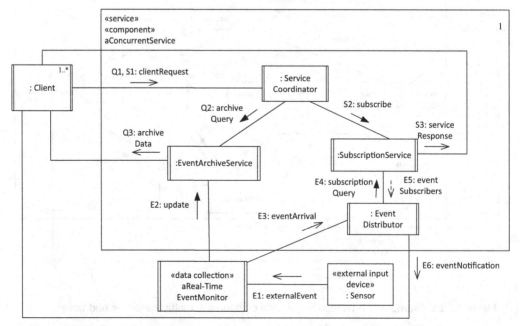

Figure 12.12. Example of a concurrent service component: subscription/notification.

Archive Service and sends the response directly to Client. The three event sequences are given different prefixes to differentiate them:

Query interaction (Q prefix):

Q1: A client sends a query to Service Coordinator – for example, requesting events over the past twenty-four hours.
Q2: Service Coordinator forwards the query to Event Archive Service.
Q3: Event Archive Service sends the appropriate archive data – for example, events over the past twenty-four hours – to the client.

Event subscription interaction (*S* prefix):

S1: Service Coordinator receives a subscription request from a client.
S2: Service Coordinator sends a subscribe message to Subscription Service.
S3: Subscription Service confirms the subscription by sending a service Response message to the client.

Event notification interaction (*E* prefix):

E1: An external event arrives at Real-Time Event Monitor.
E2: Real-Time Event Monitor determines that this is a significant event and sends an update message to Event Archive Service.
E3: Real-Time Event Monitor sends an event Arrival message to Event Distributor.
E4, E5: Event Distributor queries Subscription Service to get the list of event subscribers (i.e., clients that have subscribed to receive events of this type).
E6: Event Distributor multicasts an event Notification message to all clients that have subscribed for this event.

12.8 DISTRIBUTION OF DATA

Both sequential and concurrent service subsystems are single-service subsystems; thus, the data repositories they encapsulate are centralized. In distributed software architectures, the potential disadvantages of centralized services are that the service could become a bottleneck and that it is liable to be a single point of failure. A solution to these problems is data distribution. Two approaches to data distribution are the distributed service and data replication.

12.8.1 Distributed Service

With the **distributed service**, data that is collected at several locations is stored at those locations. Each location has a local service, which responds to client requests for that location's data. This approach is used in the distributed emergency response system (see Figure 12.13), where sensor monitoring status data is maintained at regional locations by a Monitoring Data Service component for each region, as described further in Section 12.9.2. Clients can request sensor status data from one or more regional data services.

12.8.2 Data Replication

With **data replication**, the same data is duplicated at more than one location to speed up access to it. Ensuring that procedures exist for updating the different copies of

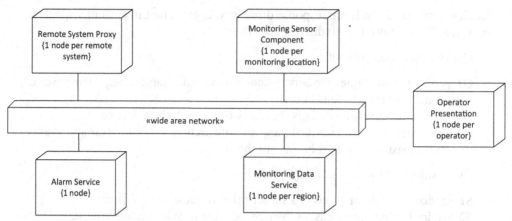

Figure 12.13. Example of a distributed software deployment: emergency monitoring system.

the replicated data is, of course, important so that the data does not become out-dated and/or inconsistent. This approach is used in the distributed Light Rail System example in Figure 12.10. Each instance of Train Control (one per train) maintains its own Train Data in an entity object to keep track of where the train is and which stations it stops at. Each instance of Train Control sends train status to Rail Operations Service, thereby allowing rail operations to monitor the status of all trains. For this purpose, Rail Operations Service maintains its own copy of each train's status in a Rail Operations Status entity object. See case study of Light Rail Control System in Chapter 21 for more detail.

12.9 SOFTWARE DEPLOYMENT

After the real-time software for a distributed embedded system has been designed and implemented, instances of it can be defined and deployed. During software deployment, an instance of the distributed software system – referred to as a *target system* – is defined and mapped to a distributed configuration consisting of multiple geographically distributed physical nodes connected by a network.

12.9.1 Software Deployment Issues

During software deployment, a decision is made about what component instances are required. In addition, it is necessary to determine how the component instances should be allocated to nodes, and how the component instances should be interconnected. Specifically, the following activities need to be performed:

■ **Define instances of the component**. For each component that can have multiple instances, it is necessary to define the instances desired. For example, in a distributed Light Rail system, it is necessary to define the number of instances of components required in the target system. It is thus necessary to define one Railroad Crossing Control instance for each railroad crossing, one Train Control instance for each train, one Station instance for each physical station, one instance of the Rail Operations Interaction component for each operator, and one instance of the service component, Rail Operations Service. Each component instance must have a unique name so that it can be uniquely identified. For components that are parameterized, the parameters for each instance need to be defined. Examples of component parameters are instance name (such as train ID, station ID, or operator ID), sensor names, sensor limits, and alarm names.

- **Map the component instances to physical nodes**. Each component instance is assigned to a node. For example, two component instances could be deployed such that each one could run on a separate physical node. Alternatively, they could both run on the same physical node. The physical configuration of the target system is depicted on a deployment diagram.
- **Interconnect component instances**. The component-based software architecture defines how components communicate with one another. At this stage, the component instances are connected to each other using software connectors, as described in Section 12.10. In the distributed Light Rail system in Figure 12.10, for example, each instance of the Train Control component is connected to each instance of the Station component as well as to the single instance of the Rail Operations Service. This interconnection can be done either at deployment time or at initialization time using a brokering service, as described in Section 12.10.

12.9.2 Examples of Software Deployment

An example of software deployment is given for the distributed Light Rail System in Section 12.6.2 and depicted in Figure 12.10. As another example of software deployment, consider the distributed emergency monitoring system. The distributed software configuration is depicted on a deployment diagram, as shown in Figure 12.13. Each instance of Monitoring Sensor Component (one per monitoring location) is allocated to a node to achieve localized autonomy and adequate performance. Thus, the failure of one sensor node will not affect other nodes. Each instance of Remote System Proxy (one per remote system) is allocated to a node because of proximity to the source of physical data. Loss of a remote system node means that the specific remote system will not be serviced, but other nodes will not be affected. Alarm Service and Monitoring Data Service are allocated to separate nodes for performance reasons, so that they can be responsive to service requests. For a large configuration, sensor monitoring status data can be maintained at regional locations by having multiple instances of Monitoring Data Service, with one instance for each region. Each operator has an instance of the Operator Presentation component, which is assigned to its own node, which is the operator's desktop node, laptop, or tablet.

12.10 DESIGN OF SOFTWARE CONNECTORS

This section describes how software connectors are designed in conjunction with distributed operating systems and middleware. Example of connectors for distributed message communication between producers and consumer components are provided.

Architectural communication patterns address different types of message communication among distributed components, as described in Chapter 11. These communication patterns can be used as the basis for designing distributed message connectors, which hide the communication details between components.

12.10.1 Distributed Message Communication

This section describes distributed message communication services provided by distributed real-time operating systems (RTOS) before describing the design of connectors that take advantage of these services. A distributed RTOS is an operating system that provides network communication services in addition to operating system services (see Chapter 3). As described in Chapter 1, distributed operating systems take advantage of middleware technology to integrate the middleware into the RTOS. Transparent message communication between distributed components can be handled by means of a distributed kernel of a distributed RTOS. There is one instance of the distributed kernel at each node.

In a distributed environment, it is desirable to have location transparency; that is, a component that wishes to send a message to another component should not need to know where that component resides. For a component A to explicitly refer to another component B by its location is inflexible. If component B is moved, then component A will need to be updated. Thus, it is desirable to have a name service with location-independent names. A *name service* in a distributed RTOS is a brokering service (as described in Chapter 11) that maintains the names and locations of all components registered with it. An example of a name service is the Domain Name System (DNS) used on the Internet (Comer 2008).

A distributed RTOS can provide communication among distributed components by using a name service. With this approach, each component registers its name and location with the name service, thereby allowing components to communicate with components on other nodes without knowing their location. Establishing the interconnection between components is done through the name service at run time, which is referred to as *dynamic binding*. If dynamic binding between components is done at initialization time and does not subsequently change, then the RTOS kernel at each node could (after dynamic binding is completed) keep a local copy of the name table for faster access during run time execution.

12.10.2 Connectors for Distributed Components

Using the services provided by a distributed RTOS, connectors are designed for transmitting messages among distributed components. Producer components sends messages to consumer components via message queue connectors (for asynchronous communication) or message and response buffer connectors (for synchronous communication). For this to work, the connector itself needs to be distributed with part of it servicing the producer component on the source node and part of it servicing the consumer component on the destination node. The connectors are active objects and use services of the distributed RTOS kernel to deliver messages. The local kernel on the source node is responsible for determining the location of the destination component and sending the message to the remote kernel on the destination node, from where it is passed on to the destination component via the connector.

Consider an example of a producer component sending an asynchronous message to a consumer component on a different node. To send a message, the producer sends the message by making a *send (in message)* request to the source connector (message 1 on Figure 12.14). The source connector then passes the message to the local RTOS kernel, which communicates with the name service (or a local name table)

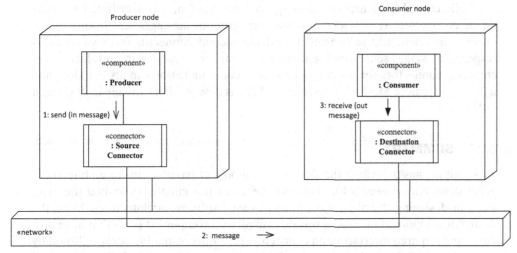

Figure 12.14. Example of software connector design.

to determine the destination node for the message. The local kernel then sends the message to its counterpart kernel on the remote node (message 2). On receiving the message, the remote kernel routes the message to the destination connector on that node. The connector adds the message to its FIFO queue. When the consumer needs a message, it makes a *receive (out message)* request (message 3) to the destination connector, which returns the first message on the queue, if one is available. Otherwise the component has to wait for a message to arrive.

12.10.3 Design of Distributed Message Connectors

The distributed message connectors are a distributed version of the three message connectors described in Chapter 14. Each distributed message connector consists of a source connector and a destination connector, as described next.

a) **Distributed message queue connector for asynchronous communication** (see Figure 12.14). The source connector provides a *send (in message)* operation and encapsulates an outgoing message queue. The destination connector provides a *receive (out message)* operation and encapsulates an incoming message queue.

b) **Distributed message buffer connector for synchronous message communication without reply**. The source connector provides a *send (in message)* operation and encapsulates an outgoing message buffer. The destination connector provides a *receive (out message)* operation and encapsulates an incoming message buffer.

c) **Distributed message buffer and response connector for synchronous message communication with reply**. The source connector provides a *send (in message, out response)* operation and encapsulates an outgoing message buffer and incoming response buffer. The destination connector provides *receive (out message)* and *reply (in response)* operations and encapsulates an incoming message buffer and outgoing response buffer.

For bidirectional asynchronous message communication, two distributed message queue connectors are provided, one for asynchronous messages sent from the producer component to the consumer, and the second connector for asynchronous response messages sent from the consumer component back to the producer. Synchronous connectors for distributed message communication can also be designed using Java Remote Method Invocation (RMI), as described in Chapter 15 of Gomaa (2011).

12.11 SUMMARY

This chapter has described the design of component-based software architectures. After describing concepts for these architectures, this chapter described the main steps in designing distributed component-based software architectures. Next, the design of component interfaces was described, with component ports that have provided and required interfaces and connectors that join compatible ports, followed by a description of the design of composite components. Next, this chapter described component structuring criteria for structuring a software architecture into configurable distributed components. This was followed by a description of the design of sequential and concurrent service subsystems, after which there was a discussion of issues in the distribution of data in distributed systems. Next, software deployment was described. Considerations and tradeoffs in component design were also discussed. Finally, the design of software connectors was described. The design of components as tasks is described in Chapter 13. Discussion of system and software quality attributes in the design of distributed component-based software architectures continues in Chapter 16. Examples of designing component-based software architectures are given in the case studies in Chapters 19 through 23.

13

Concurrent Real-Time Software Task Design

For a real-time embedded system, an important consideration in system or subsystem design is the design of the concurrent tasks it contains as well as the communication and synchronization between these tasks, as described in this chapter. A task type is an active class and a **task** is an active object with its own thread of control. A passive object is an instance of a passive class and has no thread of control.

During concurrent task design, a **task architecture** is developed in which the system is structured into concurrent tasks and the task interfaces and interconnections are designed. To help determine the concurrent tasks, task structuring criteria are provided to assist in mapping an object-oriented analysis model of the system to a concurrent tasking architecture. These criteria are a set of heuristics, also referred to as guidelines, which capture expert designer knowledge in the software design of concurrent real-time systems. Task structuring decisions are depicted using stereotypes. This chapter uses MARTE stereotypes (Selic 2014) to depict concurrent tasks, as introduced in Chapter 3. After task structuring, the task interfaces and interconnections are designed by applying the architectural communication patterns described in Chapter 11.

Real-time software architectures can also be distributed; for this reason they can be considered a special case of component-based software architectures. In this context, a *simple component* is either designed as one task or as a component that contains multiple active objects (tasks) and passive objects, as described in Chapter 12.

This chapter is organized as follows: Section 13.1 describes concurrent task structuring issues. Section 13.2 describes categorizing concurrent tasks using task structuring criteria. Section 13.3 describes I/O task structuring criteria, while Section 13.4 describes internal task structuring criteria. Section 13.6 describes task clustering structuring criteria. Section 13.7 describes design restructuring using task inversion. Section 13.8 describes the steps in developing the concurrent task architecture. Section 13.9 describes designing the task interfaces using task communication and synchronization. Section 13.10 describes documenting task interface and behavior specifications.

13.1 CONCURRENT TASK STRUCTURING ISSUES

A **concurrent task** is an active object, also referred to as a concurrent object, process or thread. In this chapter, the term *concurrent task* is used to refer to an active object with one thread of control. Concurrent tasking concepts are described in Chapter 3.

With the advent of relatively cheap multi-core processors, multitasking is even more important to consider with the need to structure a system into concurrent tasks in order to take advantage of executing multiple tasks concurrently on multiple processors. As described in Chapter 3, there are many advantages to having a concurrent tasking design; however, the designer must be careful in designing the task structure. Too many tasks in a system can unnecessarily increase complexity because of greater inter-task communication and synchronization and can lead to increased overhead because of additional context switching (see Section 3.10). The system designer must, therefore, make tradeoffs between, on the one hand, introducing tasks to simplify and clarify the design and, on the other hand, not introducing too many tasks, which could make the design overly complex. The task structuring criteria are intended to help the designer make these tradeoffs. They also enable the designer to analyze alternative task architectures.

The concurrent structure of a system is best understood by considering the dynamic characteristics of the system. In the analysis model interaction diagrams (Chapter 9) and the integrated communication diagrams (Chapter 10), the system is represented as a collection of collaborating objects that communicate by means of messages. As described in Chapter 8, during analysis, all objects are depicted as concurrent objects except for entity objects, which are depicted as passive objects. During the task structuring phase, the concurrent nature of the system is formalized by designing the concurrent tasks as well as the communication and synchronization interfaces between them.

13.2 CATEGORIZING CONCURRENT TASKS

Following the approach used in Chapter 8 for object structuring, stereotypes are used to differentiate among the different kinds of concurrent tasks. During concurrent task design, if an object is determined to be active, it is categorized further to show its concurrent task characteristics. A concurrent task is depicted using the MARTE stereotype of «swSchedulableResource», which identifies the task as a resource that is scheduled to execute on a CPU. Each task is depicted with two other stereotypes, the first is the object role criterion, determined during object structuring as described in Chapter 8, which is carried over to the task design and referred to as the *role stereotype*. The second stereotype is used to depict the type of concurrency, which is *periodic, event driven*, or *demand driven* and is referred to as the *concurrency stereotype*. Event driven and demand driven tasks are also known as *aperiodic tasks* to differentiate them from *periodic tasks*. The next section elaborates on the use of stereotypes to identify the different kinds of concurrent tasks, with examples of their use.

MARTE stereotypes are also used to depict the kinds of devices to which the concurrent tasks interface. Thus, an external hardware device is classified with the stereotype «hwDevice», and an interrupt-driven device is also classified with the stereotype «interruptResource».

The task structuring criteria are described next. In each case, a task structuring criterion is described followed by an example of a behavioral pattern in which an instance of a task of that type, such as an event driven I/O task, communicates with neighboring tasks in a typical interaction sequence.

13.2.1 Task Structuring Criteria

The task structuring criteria are organized into groups based on how they are used to assist in the task structuring activity. The following are the four task structuring groups:

1. **I/O task structuring criteria.** Address how I/O objects are mapped to I/O tasks as well as when and how an I/O task is activated.
2. **Internal task structuring criteria.** Address how internal objects are mapped to internal tasks as well as when and how an internal task is activated.
3. **Task priority criteria.** Address the importance of executing a given task relative to others.
4. **Task clustering criteria.** Address whether and how multiple objects should be grouped into a concurrent task. A form of task clustering is **task inversion,** which is used for merging tasks to reduce task overhead.

The task structuring criteria are applied in two stages. In the first stage, the I/O task structuring criteria, the internal task structuring criteria, and the task priority criteria are applied. This results in a one-to-one mapping of objects in the analysis model to tasks in the design model. In the second stage, the task clustering criteria are applied, with the objective of reducing the number of physical tasks. For an experienced designer, these two stages can be combined. After the tasks have been determined, the task interfaces are designed.

13.3 I/O TASK STRUCTURING CRITERIA

This section describes the various I/O task structuring criteria. An important factor in deciding on the characteristics of an I/O task is to determine the characteristics of the I/O device to which it has to interface.

13.3.1 Characteristics of I/O Devices

There is certain hardware-related information concerning I/O devices that interface to the embedded system, which is essential to determining the characteristics of tasks that interface to the devices. Before the I/O task structuring criteria can be applied, it is necessary to determine the hardware characteristics of the I/O devices that interface to the system. It is also necessary to determine the nature of the data being input to the system by these devices or being output by the system to these devices. In this section, the following I/O issues specific to task structuring are described:

- **Characteristics of I/O devices.** It is necessary to determine whether the I/O device is event driven (interrupt-driven), passive, or a smart device. Three major classes of I/O devices are

1. **Event driven I/O devices** (sometimes referred to as asynchronous I/O devices), which are interrupt-driven I/O devices. An event driven input device generates an interrupt when it has produced some input that requires processing by the system. An event driven output device generates an interrupt when it has finished processing an output operation and is ready to perform some new output. Stereotypes are used to depict the device as an input or output, interrupt-driven, hardware device, such as «input» «interruptResource» «hwDevice».

2. **Passive I/O devices**. A passive I/O device does not generate an interrupt on completion of the input or output operation. Thus, the input from a passive input device needs to be read either on a polled basis or on demand. Similarly, in the case of a passive output device, output needs to be provided on either a regular (i.e., periodic) basis or on demand. Stereotypes are used to depict the device as an input or output, passive, hardware device, such as «input» «passive» «hwDevice».

3. **Smart devices**. A smart device is a microprocessor-driven I/O device. It is usually connected to the embedded system by means of a communication link, which might be a point-to-point link or over a local area network. A communication protocol is used to specify how the embedded system and smart device communicate with each other (for example, TCP/IP). At the application level, tasks in the embedded system communicate with the smart device by means of messages, as described in this chapter.

■ **Characteristics of data**. It is necessary to determine whether the I/O device provides discrete data or continuous data. **Discrete data** either are Boolean or have a finite number of values. **Analog data** are continuous data and can in principle have an infinite number of values. An I/O device that provides analog data will almost certainly have to be polled or accessed on demand. If an analog device generated an I/O interrupt every time its value changed, it would be likely to flood the system with interrupts.

■ **Passive I/O device**. For a passive I/O device, it is necessary to determine whether:
  • Sampling the device on demand is sufficient, in particular when some consumer task needs the data.
  • The device needs to be polled on a periodic basis so that any change in value is sent to a consumer task without being explicitly requested, or the value is written to an entity object with sufficient frequency so that the data do not get out of date.

■ **Polling frequency**. If a passive I/O device is to be polled on a periodic basis, it is necessary to determine the polling frequency. The polling frequency depends on how critical the input is and how frequently it is expected to change. In the case of an output device, the polling frequency depends on how often the data should be output in order to prevent data previously generated from getting out of date.

13.3.2 Event Driven I/O Tasks

An *event driven* I/O task is needed when there is an interrupt-driven I/O device (also referred to as an event driven or asynchronous I/O device) to which the system has to interface. The event driven I/O task is activated by an interrupt from the event driven device. During task design, each device I/O object in the analysis model that interfaces to an interrupt-driven I/O device is designed as an event driven I/O task.

a) Analysis model – communication diagram

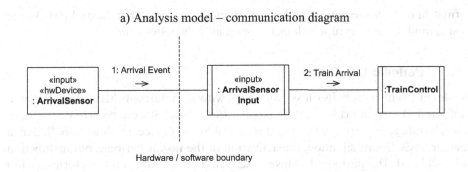

Hardware / software boundary

b) Design model – concurrent communication diagram

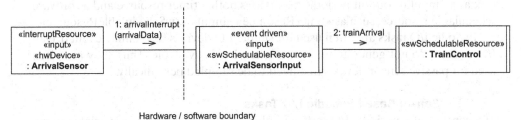

Hardware / software boundary

Figure 13.1. Example of event driven input task.

Stereotypes are used to depict an event driven I/O task as an input and/or output, event driven task, such as «event driven» «input» «swSchedulableResource».

An event driven I/O device interface task is often a device driver task. It is typically activated by a low-level interrupt handler or – in some cases – directly by the hardware. An event driven I/O task is constrained to execute at the speed of the I/O device with which it interacts. Thus, an input task might be suspended indefinitely awaiting an input. However, when activated by an interrupt, the input task typically has to respond to a subsequent interrupt within a few milliseconds to avoid any loss of data. After the input data is read, the input task might send the data to be processed by another task or update a passive object. This frees the input task to respond to another interrupt that might closely follow the first.

As an example of an event driven input task, consider the Arrival Sensor Input object shown on the analysis model communication diagram in Figure 13.1a. The Arrival Sensor Input object receives inputs from the real-world arrival sensor, which is depicted as an input hardware device. In preparation for task structuring, the Arrival Sensor is assigned the MARTE stereotypes «input» «hwDevice». The Arrival Sensor Input object then converts the input to an internal format and sends the train arrival message to the Train Control object. For task structuring, it is given that the arrival sensor is an *interrupt-driven input hardware device*, depicted on the design model concurrent communication diagram (see Figure 13.1b) with the stereotypes «interrupt-Resource» «input» «hwDevice», which generates an interrupt when the train arrival is detected. The Arrival Sensor Input object is designed as an *event driven input task* of the same name, depicted on the concurrent communication diagram with the stereotypes «event driven» «input» «swSchedulableResource». When the task is activated by the arrival Interrupt, it reads the arrival Data, converts the input data to an internal format, and sends the data as a train Arrival message to the Train Control task. In the design model, the interrupt is depicted as an asynchronous event.

13.3.3 Periodic I/O Tasks

While an event driven I/O task interfaces with an interrupt-driven I/O device, a periodic I/O task interfaces with a passive I/O device. Since a passive device does not generate an interrupt when input is available, the device needs to be polled on a regular basis. In this situation, the activation of the task is periodic, but its function is I/O-related. The periodic I/O task is activated by a timer event, performs an I/O operation (read or write), and then waits for the next timer event. The task's period is the time between successive activations. Stereotypes are used to depict a periodic I/O task as an input or output periodic task that is both a timer resource and a software schedulable resource, such as «timerResource» «input» «swSchedulableResource».

Periodic I/O tasks are often used for simple I/O devices that, unlike event driven I/O devices, do not generate interrupts when I/O is available. Thus, they are often used for passive sensor devices that need to be sampled periodically.

13.3.3.1 Sensor-Based Periodic I/O Tasks

The concept of a periodic I/O task is used in many sensor-based industrial systems. Such systems often have a large number of digital and analog sensors. A sensor-based periodic I/O task is activated on a regular basis, scans the sensors, and reads their values. A passive input device could be a digital or analog sensor. A digital sensor might be a passive device because it is cheaper than an interrupt-driven device, and if there are large numbers of sensors to interface to, the difference in price between interrupt-driven and passive devices could be significant. However, an analog sensor is often passive because the value of an analog sensor is usually changing continuously, in which case it is frequently more practical to sample it periodically.

Consider a passive digital input device – for example, a door sensor. This could be handled by a **periodic I/O task**. The task is activated by a timer event and then reads the status of the device. If the value of the digital sensor has changed since the previous time it was sampled, the task indicates the change in status. In the case of an analog sensor – a temperature or pressure sensor, for example – the device is sampled periodically and the current value of the sensor is read. As an example of a periodic input task, consider the Pressure Sensor Input object shown in Figure 13.2a. In the analysis model depicted on the communication diagram, the Pressure Sensor Input object is an «input» object that receives inputs from the real-world Pressure Sensor input hardware device, which in preparation for task structuring is depicted with the stereotype «input» «hwDevice». Because this analog sensor is a *passive input hardware device*, it is depicted on the design model concurrent communication diagram with the stereotype «passive» «input» «hwDevice» (see Figure 13.2b). Because a passive device does not generate an interrupt, an event driven input task cannot be used. Instead, this case is handled by a *periodic input task*, the Pressure Sensor Input task, which is activated periodically by an external timer to sample the value of the pressure sensor. Thus, the Pressure Sensor Input object is designed as the Pressure Sensor Input task, which is depicted as «timerResource» «input » «swSchedulableResource» on the concurrent communication diagram. To activate the Pressure Sensor Input task periodically, it is necessary to add an external timer object, the Digital Timer, which is

a) Analysis model – communication diagram

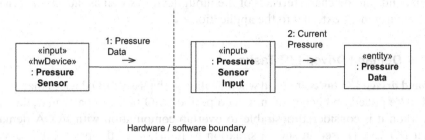

b) Design model – concurrent communication diagram

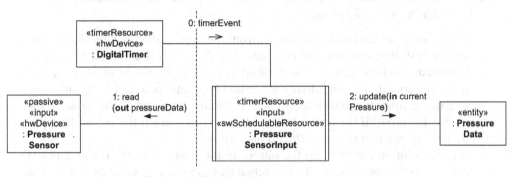

Figure 13.2. Example of a periodic input task.

depicted as a *hardware timer resource*, «timerResource» «hwDevice» in Figure 13.2b. When activated, the Pressure Sensor Input task samples the pressure sensor, updates the Pressure Data entity object with the new pressure reading and then waits for the next timer event. The timer event is depicted as an asynchronous event on the concurrent communication diagram.

13.3.3.2 Timing Considerations for Periodic I/O Tasks

The frequency with which a task samples a sensor depends on the frequency with which the sensor's value is expected to change. It also depends on the delay that can be tolerated in reporting this change. For example, ambient temperature varies slowly and so can be polled with a frequency in minutes. By contrast, to provide a fast response to the opening of a door, assuming the door is a passive input device, the door sensor might need to be polled every 100 milliseconds.

Although digital input can be supported by means of an interrupt-driven input device, analog input is rarely supported by means of an interrupt-driven input device. If an analog input device generated an interrupt every time its value changed, it would very probably impose a heavy interrupt load on the system.

The higher the sampling rate of a given task, the greater the overhead that will be generated. For a digital input device, a periodic input task is likely to consume more overhead than the equivalent event driven input task. This is because there will likely be times when the periodic input task is activated and the value of the sensor being monitored will not have changed. If the sampling rate chosen is too high, significant unnecessary overhead could be generated. The sampling rate selected for a given task depends on the characteristics of the input device as well as the characteristics of the environment external to the application.

13.3.4 Demand Driven I/O Tasks

Demand driven I/O tasks are used when dealing with passive I/O devices that do not need to be polled and hence do not need periodic I/O tasks. In particular, they are used when it is considered desirable to overlap computation with I/O. A demand driven I/O task is used in such a situation to interface to the passive I/O device. Stereotypes are used to depict a demand driven I/O task as an input or output demand driven task, such as «demand» «output» «swSchedulableResource».

Consider the following cases:

- In the case of input, overlap the input from the passive device with the computational task that receives and consumes the data. This is achieved by using a demand driven input task to read the data from the input device, when requested to do so. Separate demand driven input and computational tasks are only useful if the computational task has some computation to do while the input task is reading the input. If the computational task has to wait for the input, the input can be performed in the same thread of control.
- In the case of output, overlap the output to the device with the computational task that produces the data. This is achieved by using a demand driven output task to output to the device when requested to do so, usually via a message.

Demand driven I/O tasks are used more often with output devices than with input devices because the output can be overlapped with the computation more often, as shown in the following example. Usually, if the I/O and computation are to be overlapped for a passive input device, a periodic input task is used.

Consider a demand driven output task that receives a message from a producer task. Overlapping computation and output is achieved as follows: the consumer task outputs the data contained in the message to the passive output device, the display, while the producer is preparing the next message. This case is shown in Figure 13.3. Speed Display Output is a *demand driven output* task. It accepts a message containing the current speed from the Speed Computation Algorithm task and then formats and displays the speed while the Speed Computation Algorithm task is computing the next speed value to display. Thus, the computation is overlapped with the output. The Speed Display Output task is depicted on the concurrent communication diagram with the stereotypes «demand» «output» «swSchedulableResource». The Display *passive output hardware device* is depicted with the stereotypes «passive» «output» «hwDevice». This example is continued in Section 13.9.3.

13.3.5 Resource Monitor Tasks

A **resource monitor task** is a special case of the demand driven I/O task considered earlier. An input or output device that receives requests from multiple sources should have a resource monitor task to coordinate these requests, even if the device is passive. A resource monitor task has to sequence these requests so as to maintain data integrity and ensure that no data is corrupted or lost. A resource monitor task is

a) Analysis model – communication diagram

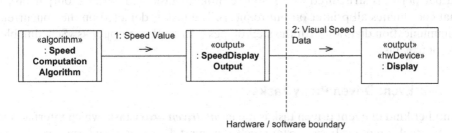

Hardware / software boundary

b) Design model – concurrent communication diagram

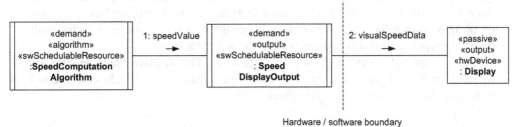

Hardware / software boundary

Figure 13.3. Example of a demand driven output task.

depicted with the same stereotypes as a demand driven I/O task, that is, «demand» «output» «swSchedulableResource».

For example, if two or more tasks are allowed to write to a printer simultaneously, output from the tasks will be randomly interleaved, and a garbled report will be produced. To avoid this problem, it is necessary to design a printer resource monitor task. This task receives output requests from multiple source tasks and has to deal with each request sequentially. Because the request from a second source task might arrive before the first task has finished, having a resource monitor task to handle the requests ensures that multiple requests are dealt with sequentially.

An example of a resource monitor task is given in Figure 13.4. Printer Output is an output object that receives requests from the multiple instances of Printer Client to print messages (Figure 13.4). The real-world printer is a passive output device.

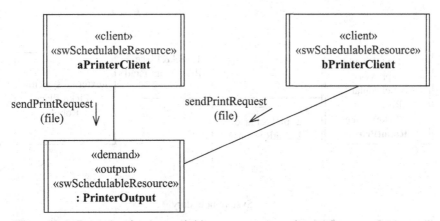

Figure 13.4. Example of a demand driven resource monitor task.

Because this output device can receive requests from multiple sources, the Printer Output object is structured as a resource monitor task – the Printer Output task – that coordinates all printer output requests. The task is depicted on the concurrent communication diagram with the stereotypes «demand» «output» «swSchedulable-Resource» task.

13.3.6 Event Driven Proxy Tasks

Another kind of event driven task is the *event driven proxy* task, which interfaces to an external computer-based system such as a smart device or an external system. An external system is outside the scope of the embedded system under development but typically communicates with it over a network as part of a larger distributed system. An *event driven proxy* task usually interacts with external computer-based systems by using messages, as described later in this chapter. A proxy task is depicted with the stereotypes «event driven» «proxy» «swSchedulableResource».

An example of an event driven proxy task is a Pick & Place Robot Proxy task, which communicates with and interfaces to a Pick & Place Robot, which is an external computer-based system, as given in Figure 13.5.

13.4 INTERNAL TASK STRUCTURING CRITERIA

Whereas the I/O task structuring criteria are used to determine I/O tasks, the internal task structuring criteria are used to determine internal (i.e., non I/O) tasks.

13.4.1 Periodic Tasks

Many real-time systems have activities that need to be executed on a periodic basis, such as counting down the microwave oven cooking time or measuring the time for raising and lowering the railroad crossing barrier. These periodic activities are typically handled by periodic tasks. Although periodic I/O activities are structured as periodic I/O tasks, periodic internal activities are structured as **periodic tasks**. In some cases, periodic activities are grouped into a temporally clustered task, as described in Section 13.6.1. Internal periodic tasks include *periodic algorithm tasks*. Stereotypes

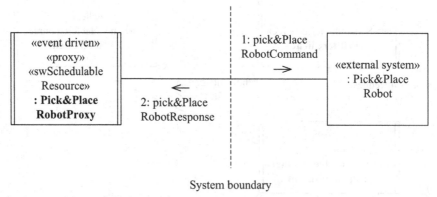

System boundary

Figure 13.5. Example of an event driven proxy task.

a) Analysis model – communication diagram

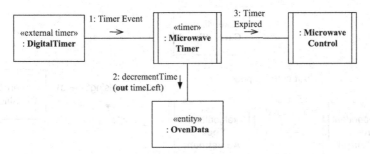

b) Design model – concurrent communication diagram

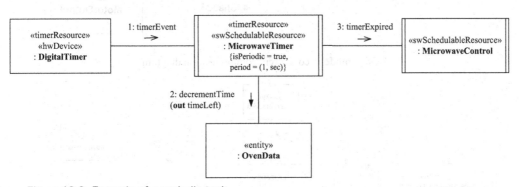

Figure 13.6. Example of a periodic task.

are used to depict a periodic task as both a timer resource and a software schedulable resource: «timerResource» «swSchedulableResource». An additional stereotype is used to depict the role of the periodic task, such as «algorithm».

An activity that needs to be executed periodically (i.e., at regular, equally spaced intervals of time) is structured as a separate periodic task. The task is activated by a timer event, performs the periodic activity, and then waits for the next timer event. The task's period is the time between successive activations. The «timerResource» stereotype has two attributes, a Boolean attribute *isPeriodic* and a *period* attribute in units of time. For example a periodic task with a period of 100 msecs is depicted with the tagged value {isPeriodic = true, period = (100, ms)}.

As an example of a periodic task, consider the Microwave Timer object shown in Figure 13.6a. The Microwave Timer object is activated by a timer event every second. It then requests the Oven Data object to decrement the cooking time by one second and return the time left. If the cooking time has expired, then the Microwave Timer object sends a Timer Expired message to Microwave Control. The Microwave Timer object is designed as a periodic task (Figure 13.6b) that is activated at regular intervals of 1 second, at which time it requests the Oven Data passive entity object to decrement the cooking time. The Microwave Timer task is depicted on the concurrent communication diagram with the stereotype «timerResource» «swSchedulableResource» task. The attributes of the «timerResource» stereotype are set to {isPeriodic = true, period = (1, sec)}, which means that the task is periodic and the length of the period is 1 second. The timer event is depicted as an asynchronous event.

a) Analysis model – communication diagram

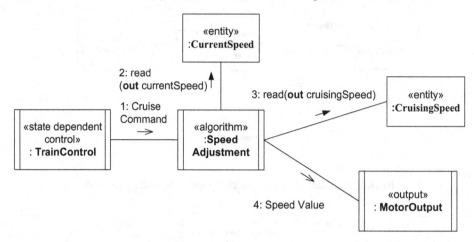

b) Design model – concurrent communication diagram

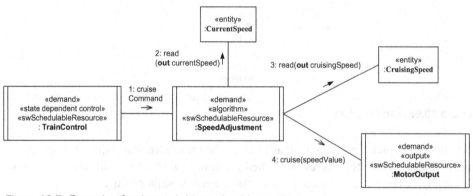

Figure 13.7. Example of a demand driven algorithm task.

13.4.2 Demand Driven Tasks

Many real-time and concurrent systems have activities that need to be executed on demand. These demand driven activities are typically handled by means of demand driven tasks. Whereas demand driven I/O tasks are activated by the arrival of external interrupts, demand driven internal tasks (also referred to as aperiodic tasks) are activated on demand by the arrival of internal messages or events.

An object that is activated on demand (i.e., when it receives an internal message or event sent by a different task) is structured as a separate **demand driven task**. The task is activated on demand by the arrival of the message or event sent by the requesting task, performs the demanded request, and then waits for the next message or event. Internal demand driven tasks include demand driven *algorithm* tasks. A demand driven task is depicted with the stereotypes «demand» «swSchedulableResource». An additional stereotype is used to depict the role of the demand driven task, such as «algorithm».

An example of a demand driven task is given in Figure 13.7. In the analysis model, the Speed Adjustment object is activated on demand by the arrival of a Cruise

Command message from the Train Control object, reads from the Current Speed and Cruising Speed entity objects, calculates the adjustment to the speed, and sends a Speed Value message with the speed adjustment to the Motor Output object (Figure 13.7a). In the design model, the Speed Adjustment object is structured as a *demand driven algorithm task* called Speed Adjustment, which is activated by the arrival of a cruise Command message. The Speed Adjustment task is depicted on the concurrent communication diagram with the stereotypes «demand» «algorithm» «swSchedulableResource» task (Figure 13.7b). The Train Control and Motor Output objects are also structured as demand driven tasks. The Current Speed and Cruising Speed objects are passive entity objects.

13.4.3 State Dependent Control Tasks

In the analysis model, a state dependent control object executes a state machine. Using the restricted form of state machines whereby concurrency within an object is not permitted, it follows that the execution of a state machine is strictly sequential. Hence, a task whose execution is also strictly sequential can perform the control activity. A task that executes a sequential state machine (typically implemented as a state transition table) is referred to as a **state dependent control task**. A control task is usually a demand driven task, which is activated on demand by the arrival of a message sent by another task. A state dependent control task is depicted with the stereotypes «demand» «state dependent control» «swSchedulableResource».

An example of a *demand driven state dependent control task* is shown in Figure 13.8. Train Control (Figure 13.8a) is structured as a state dependent control task because it executes the Train Control state machine, which is strictly sequential. The Train Control task (Figure 13.8b) receives train arrival events from an Arrival Sensor Input task and sends speed commands to a Speed Adjustment algorithm task. The Train Control *demand driven state dependent control* task is depicted on the concurrent communication diagram with the stereotypes «demand» « state dependent control» «swSchedulableResource».

Another example of a state dependent control task is the Character Control task, which executes the state machine for a computer game character, in which all characters are of the same type. There are multiple Character Control objects (depicted

a) Analysis model – communication diagram

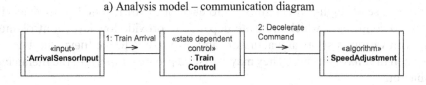

b) Design model – concurrent communication diagram

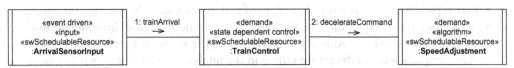

Figure 13.8. Example of a demand driven state dependent control task.

a) Analysis model – control object (multiple instances)

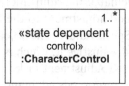

b) Design model – one task for each game character

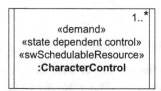

Figure 13.9. Example of multiple control tasks of same type.

by using the multiple instance 1..∗ notation in Figure 13.9a). Each Character Control instance is structured as a *demand driven state dependent control task*. Consequently, there is one Character Control task for each game character, which is also depicted by using the multiple instance notation in Figure 13.9b. The game character tasks are identical, and each task executes an instance of the same state machine. However, each character is likely to be in a different state on its state machine and either waiting for or executing a different event.

13.4.4 Coordinator Tasks

In addition to state dependent control objects, coordinator objects from the analysis model are mapped to *coordinator tasks*. A coordinator task is a decision-making task that is not state dependent. A coordinator task is demand driven and is activated on demand by the arrival of a message sent by another task. The decisions a coordinator task makes are based entirely on the content of the message it receives. A *demand driven coordinator task* is depicted with the stereotypes «demand» «coordinator» «swSchedulableResource».

An example of a coordinator task is the Hierarchical Coordinator task in Figure 13.10, which sends high-level commands to each of the distributed controllers. The distributed controllers, which are state dependent, provide low-level control, interacting with various sensors and actuators and responding to the Hierarchical Coordinator when they have finished. They may also send progress reports to the Hierarchical Coordinator.

13.4.5 User Interaction and Service Tasks

A user typically performs a set of sequential actions. Because the user's interaction with the system is a sequential activity, this can be handled by a **user interaction task**. The speed of this task is frequently constrained by the speed of user interaction. As its name implies, a **user interaction object** in the analysis model is mapped to a **user interaction** task. Because a user interaction task receives its inputs from an external

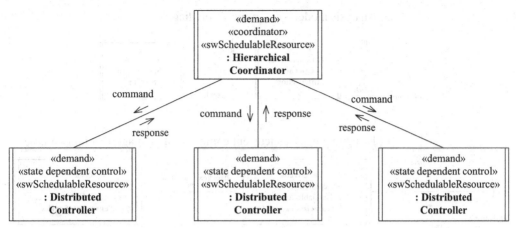

Figure 13.10. Example of a demand driven coordinator task.

user, it is considered event driven. An *event driven user interaction task* is depicted with the stereotypes «event driven» «user interaction» «swSchedulableResource».

A user interaction task usually interfaces with various standard I/O devices – such as the input keyboard, output display, and mouse – that are typically handled by the operating system. Because the operating system usually provides a standard interface to these devices, it is not necessary to develop special-purpose I/O tasks to handle them.

The concept of one task per sequential activity is used on modern workstations with multiple windows. Each window executes a sequential activity, so there is one task for each window. In the Windows operating system, it is possible for the user to have Word executing in one window, PowerPoint executing in another window, and the user browsing the Web in a third window. There is one user interaction task for each window, and each of these tasks can spawn other tasks (for example, to overlap printing with editing).

An example of a user interaction task is given in Figure 13.11. The Operator Interaction task accepts operator commands, requests sensor data from the Sensor Data Service task, and displays this data to the operator (Figure 13.11a). Because all operator interactions are sequential in this example, the Operator Interaction object is structured as an *event driven user interaction task* (Figure 13.11b). The task is depicted on the concurrent communication diagram with the stereotypes «event driven» «user interaction» «swSchedulableResource».

A service object that is designed as a *demand driven service task* is also depicted in Figure 13.11. The Sensor Data Service task is activated on demand by the arrival of sensor requests from its clients. The task is depicted on the concurrent communication diagram with the stereotypes «demand driven» «service» «swSchedulableResource». See Chapter 12 for a longer discussion on the design of service subsystems.

In a multiple window workstation environment, a factory operator might view factory status in one window (supported by one user interaction task) and acknowledge alarms in another window (supported by a different user interaction task). An example of this is given in Figure 13.11c. There are two *event driven user interaction tasks*, Factory Status Window and Factory Alarm Window, which are active concurrently. The Factory Status Window task interacts with the Factory Status Service

a) Analysis model – communication diagram

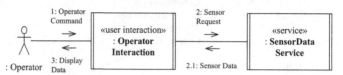

b) Design model – concurrent communication diagram with two tasks

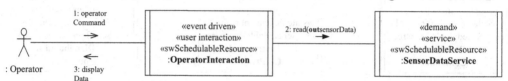

c) Design model – concurrent communication diagram with four tasks

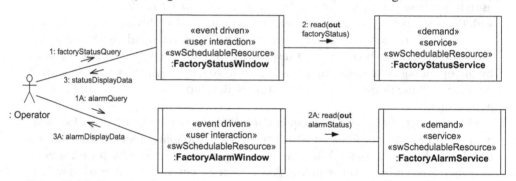

Figure 13.11. Example of event driven user interaction tasks and demand driven service tasks.

demand driven service task while the Factory Alarm Window task interacts with the Factory Alarm Service task.

13.4.6 Multiple Tasks of Same Type

As pointed out earlier, it is possible to have many objects of the same type. Each object is mapped to a task, where all the tasks are instances of the same task type. An example of multiple state dependent control tasks of the same type is given in Figure 13.9, in which there are multiple instances of the computer game Character Control task.

It might be that, for a given application, there are too many objects of the same type to allow each to be mapped to a separate task. This issue is addressed by using task inversion, as described in Section 13.7.

13.5 TASK PRIORITY CRITERIA

Task priority criteria take into account priority considerations in task structuring; in particular, high- and low-priority tasks are considered. Task priority is often addressed late in the development cycle. The main reason for considering it during the task structuring phase is to identify any time-critical or non-time-critical computationally intensive objects that need to be treated as separate tasks. Priorities for most tasks are determined based on real-time scheduling considerations, as described in Chapter 17.

13.5.1 Time-Critical Tasks

A **time-critical task** is a task that needs to meet a hard deadline. Such a task needs to run at a high priority. High-priority time-critical tasks are needed in most real-time systems.

Consider the case where the execution of a time-critical object is followed by a non-time-critical object. To ensure that the time-critical object gets serviced rapidly, it should be allocated to its own high-priority task.

As an example of a time-critical task, consider a Furnace Temperature Control object that monitors the temperature of a furnace. If the temperature is above 100 degrees Centigrade, the furnace must be switched off. Furnace Temperature Control is mapped to a high-priority task. It must execute within a predefined time; otherwise, the contents of the furnace could be damaged.

Other examples of time-critical tasks are control tasks and event driven I/O tasks. A control task executes a state machine and needs to execute at a high priority because state transitions must be executed rapidly. An event driven I/O task needs to have a high priority so it can service interrupts quickly; otherwise, there is a danger that it might miss interrupts. An example of a high-priority event driven input task is the Arrival Sensor Input task in Figure 13.1.

13.5.2 Non-Time-Critical Computationally Intensive Tasks

A **non-time-critical computationally intensive task** may run as a low-priority task consuming spare CPU cycles. A low-priority computationally intensive task executes as a background task that is preempted by higher-priority tasks that are more time critical.

An example of a non-time-critical computationally intensive task is given in Figure 13.3. The Speed Computation Algorithm object computes the next speed value to display and then passes this data to the Speed Display Output object (Figure 13.3a). Because the Sensor Computation Algorithm executes at a low priority, it is mapped to a low-priority background task (Figure 13.3b) that uses up spare CPU time. The Speed Computation Algorithm task, which is activated on demand, is depicted on the concurrent communication diagram with the stereotypes «demand» «algorithm» «swSchedulableResource».

A computationally intensive algorithm cannot always be mapped to a low-priority task. The priority of the algorithm is application-dependent. Hence, it is possible in some applications for a computationally intensive algorithm to be time-critical and thus need to be executed at a high priority.

13.6 TASK CLUSTERING CRITERIA

An analysis model can have a large number of objects, each of which is potentially concurrent and mapped to a candidate task. This high degree of concurrency in the analysis model provides considerable flexibility in the design. In fact, each object in the analysis model could be mapped to a task in the design model. However, if each object became a task, this could lead to a large number of small tasks, potentially resulting in increased system complexity and execution overhead.

The **task clustering criteria** are used to determine whether certain tasks, determined during the first stage of task structuring, could be consolidated further to reduce the overall number of tasks. The tasks determined during the first phase of task structuring (by using the I/O, internal, and priority task structuring criteria described in the previous subsections) are referred to as candidate tasks. Candidate tasks can actually be combined into physical tasks, based on the task clustering criteria described in this subsection.

The clustering criteria provide a means of analyzing the concurrent nature of the candidate tasks and hence provide a basis for determining whether two or more candidate tasks should be grouped into a single physical task and, if so, how. Thus, if two candidate tasks are constrained so they cannot execute concurrently and must instead execute sequentially, combining them into one physical task usually simplifies the design. There are exceptions to this general rule, as described later.

Although, task clustering is described as a second stage of task structuring, the experienced designer can combine the two stages.

This chapter describes task structuring by using the clustering criteria. However, the internal design of clustered tasks is described in Chapter 14.

13.6.1 Temporal Clustering

Certain candidate tasks may be activated by the same event, for example, a timer event. Each time the tasks are awakened, they execute some activity. If there is no sequential dependency between the candidate tasks – that is, no required sequential order in which the tasks must execute – the candidate tasks may be grouped into the same task, based on the **temporal clustering** criterion. When the task is activated, each of the clustered activities is executed in turn. Because there is no sequential dependency between these clustered activities, an arbitrary execution order needs to be selected by the designer.

Temporal clustering is usually applied to candidate tasks that are activated periodically. Thus, it is often the case that candidate tasks activated by the same periodic event and with the same frequency may be grouped into the same task, according to the temporal clustering criterion. In this case, a temporal clustered task is depicted with the stereotypes «timerResource» «temporal clustering» «swSchedulableResource».

13.6.1.1 Example of Temporal Clustering

An example of temporal clustering is given in Figure 13.12. Consider two I/O objects, one of which receives inputs from a temperature sensor while the other receives inputs from a pressure sensor. If these were event driven I/O devices, each device would be handled by a separate event driven I/O task, which would be activated by a device interrupt every time there was an input from the device. However, if the two sensors are passive, the only way for the system to be aware of a change in sensor status is for it to sample the sensors periodically. Figure 13.12a shows that each input object is structured as a periodic input task, depicted on the concurrent communication diagram with the stereotypes «timerResource» «input»

a) Example of temporal clustering
- periodic I/O tasks before temporal clustering

Design model – concurrent communication diagram

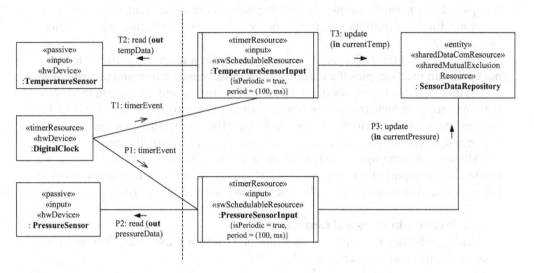

Hardware / software boundary

b) Example of temporal clustering
- After temporal clustering

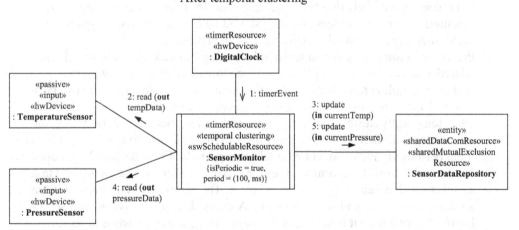

Figure 13.12. Example of temporal clustering.

«swSchedulableResource». The attributes of each «timerResource» stereotype are set to {isPeriodic = true, period = (100, ms)}.

In Figure 13.12a, the Temperature Sensor Input periodic input task periodically reads the current value of the temperature sensor and updates the current temperature in the Sensor Data Repository object. Similarly, the Pressure Sensor Input periodic input task periodically reads the current value of the pressure sensor and updates the current pressure in the Sensor Data Repository object.

Now, assume that the sensors are to be sampled with the same frequency, perhaps every 100 milliseconds. In this case, the Temperature Sensor Input and the Pressure Sensor Input tasks can be grouped into a task called Sensor Monitor, based on the temporal clustering criterion, as shown in Figure 13.12b. The Sensor Monitor task is depicted as a *periodic temporal clustering task* on the concurrent communication diagram with the stereotypes «timerResource» «temporal clustering» «swSchedulableResource».

The Sensor Monitor task is activated periodically by a timer event from the external timer and then samples the current values of the temperature and pressure sensors. It then updates the values of the current temperature and pressure in the Sensor Data Repository, which is a passive entity object. The attributes of the «timerResource» are set to {isPeriodic = true, period = (100, ms)}, which means that each sensor is sampled with a frequency given by the period value of 100 msec.

Although this example only has two sensors, the benefits of temporal clustering become more apparent if one considers 100 sensors sampled with the same period being clustered into one temporally cohesive task instead of into 100 periodic tasks.

13.6.1.2 Issues in Temporal Clustering

In deciding whether to combine candidate tasks into a temporally clustered task, some tradeoffs need to be considered:

- If one candidate task is more time-critical than a second candidate task, the tasks should not be combined; this gives the additional flexibility of allocating different priorities to the two tasks.
- If it is considered likely that two candidate tasks for temporal clustering could be executed on separate processors, they should be kept as separate tasks because each candidate task would execute on its own processor.
- Preference should be given in temporal clustering to tasks that are functionally related and likely to be of equal importance from a scheduling viewpoint.
- Period or sampling rate. Another issue is whether it is possible to group two periodic tasks that are functionally related to each other but have different periods into a temporally clustered task. This approach can be used if the periods are multiples of one another. However, this form of temporal clustering is weaker than if the periods are identical. For example, two periodic I/O tasks may be grouped into one task if one task samples a sensor (A) every 50 msec and the second task samples another sensor (B) every 100 msec. The temporally clustered task has a period of 50 msec and samples sensor A every time it is activated and sensor B every second time it is activated. However, there are cases when tasks should not be combined based on sampling rate. For example, if there are three periodic activities with periods of 15, 20, and 25 msec, the combined temporally clustered task would need to have a period of 5 msec (the highest common factor), resulting in a higher overhead than with three separate periodic tasks.

In short, the use of temporal clustering for related tasks is recommended in certain cases. However, grouping periodic tasks that are not functionally related into one task is not considered desirable from a design viewpoint, although it might be done for optimization purposes if the tasking overhead is considered too high.

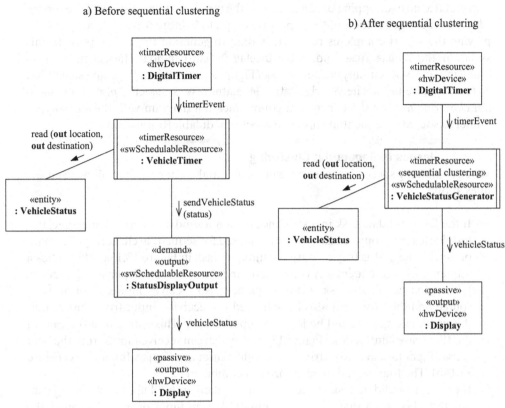

Figure 13.13. Example of sequential clustering.

13.6.2 Sequential Clustering

The execution of certain candidate tasks might be constrained by the needs of the application to be carried out in a sequential order. The first candidate task in the sequence is triggered by an aperiodic or periodic event. The other candidate tasks are then executed sequentially after it. These sequentially dependent candidate tasks may be grouped into a task based on the **sequential clustering** criterion. A sequentially clustered task is depicted with the stereotypes «sequential clustering» «swSchedulableResource».

Depending on the application, sequentially clustered tasks can be activated on demand or periodically, in which case an additional stereotype is used, «demand» for the former case and «timerResource» for the latter case.

13.6.2.1 Example of Sequential Clustering

As an example of sequential clustering, consider the two candidate tasks shown in Figure 13.13a. The Vehicle Timer task is a periodic task, activated periodically to prepare a report. When activated, it reads information from the entity object Vehicle Status, prepares the report, and then sends the report to the Status Display Output task, which outputs the report. The Status Display Output task is a demand driven output task, and the display is a passive output device dedicated to displaying this report. If the report is generated infrequently – perhaps once every 500 msec – there is in practice no overlapping of generation of the report with the display of the report. This is because generation of the report is completed before it is displayed, and displaying the report completes before it is time to generate the next report. In this situation, the Vehicle Timer and Status Display Output candidate tasks can be combined into one sequentially clustered task (Figure 13.13b) instead of being structured as two separate tasks. The Vehicle Status Generator task is depicted *periodic sequential clustering task* on the concurrent communication diagram with the stereotypes «timerResource» «sequential clustering» «swSchedulableResource».

13.6.2.2 Issues in Sequential Clustering

When combining successive tasks by using sequential clustering, the following guidelines apply:

- If the last candidate task in a sequence does not send an inter-task message, this terminates the group of tasks to be considered for sequential clustering. This happens with the Status Display Output candidate task in Figure 13.13a, which ends a sequence of two sequentially connected candidate tasks by displaying the report.
- If the next candidate task in the sequence also receives inputs from another source and therefore can also be activated by receiving input from that source, this candidate task should be left as a separate task. This happens in the case of the Microwave Control task (Figure 13.16b), which can receive inputs from the Door Sensor Input task as well as from the Weight Sensor and Keypad Input tasks (Figure 13.16b). The four candidate tasks are not combined.
- If the next candidate task in the sequence is likely to hold up the preceding candidate task(s) such that they could miss either an input or a state change, the next candidate task should be structured as a separate, lower-priority task. This is what happens with the Arrival Sensor Input task in Figure 13.1, which receives arrival events from the external arrival sensor, which it then passes on to the Train Control task. The Arrival Sensor Input task must not miss any external events, so it is structured as a higher-priority input task separate from the Train Control task.
- If the next candidate task in sequence is of a lower priority and follows a time-critical task, the two tasks should be kept as separate tasks. This is discussed in more detail in Task Priority Criteria in Section 13.5.

13.6.3 Control Clustering

A state dependent control object, which executes a sequential state machine, is mapped to a state dependent control task. In certain cases, the state dependent control task may be combined with other objects that execute actions triggered by the state machine. This is referred to as **control clustering**. A control clustered task is activated on demand by the arrival of a message from another task. *A demand driven control clustering task* is therefore depicted with the stereotypes «demand» «control clustering» «swSchedulableResource».

In the analysis model, a state dependent control object is defined by means of a sequential state machine. The control object should be structured as a separate state dependent control task (Section 13.4.3) because the execution of a state machine is defined to be strictly sequential. Furthermore, the control task might execute

a) Before control clustering

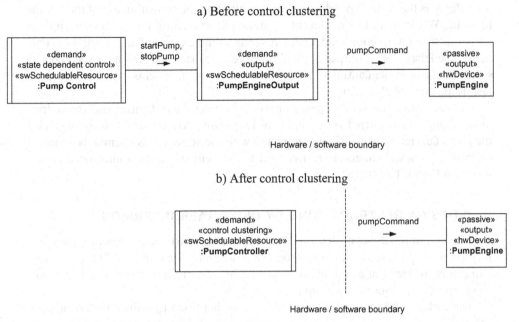

Hardware / software boundary

b) After control clustering

Hardware / software boundary

Figure 13.14. Example of control clustering.

other state dependent actions within its thread of control. Consider the following cases:

- **State dependent actions** that are triggered by the control object because of a state transition. Consider an action (designed as an operation provided by a separate object) that is triggered at the state transition and both starts and completes execution during the state transition. Such an action operation does not execute concurrently with the control object. When mapped to tasks, the operation is executed within the thread of control of the control task. If all the action operations of an object are executed within the thread of control of the control task, that object can be combined with the control task, based on the **control clustering** task structuring criterion.
- **State dependent activities** that are either enabled or disabled by the control object because of a state transition. Consider an activity (executed by a separate object) that is enabled at a state transition and then executes continuously until disabled at a subsequent state transition. This activity should be structured as a separate task, because both the control object and the activity will need to be active concurrently.

13.6.3.1 Example of Control Clustering

An example of control clustering is given from the Pump Control problem. Figure 13.14a shows a state dependent control task Pump Control that sends Start Pump and Stop Pump messages to a Pump Engine Output task. The messages sent by Pump Control are actually state dependent actions, which are triggered by incoming events that cause state transitions on Pump Control's internal state machine. Thus, Start Pump is the state dependent action executed on the transition into the Pumping state, and

Stop Pump is the state dependent action executed on the transition out of the Pumping state. When Pump Engine Output receives a Start or Stop Pump message, it converts this to a pump command, which it sends to the external Pump Engine without delay. The Pump Engine output device is passive. Because each action is executed at a state transition, Pump Control and Pump Engine Output can be clustered into the same task using control clustering.

Consequently, the state dependent control object Pump Control and the output object Pump Engine Output are grouped into a *demand driven control clustering task –* the Pump Controller task – which is depicted with the stereotypes «demand» «control clustering» «swSchedulableResource» on the concurrent communication diagram shown in Figure 13.14b.

13.7 DESIGN RESTRUCTURING BY USING TASK INVERSION

Task inversion is a concept that originated in Jackson Structured Programming and Jackson System Development (Jackson 1983), whereby the number of tasks in a system can be reduced in a systematic way. At one extreme, a concurrent solution can be mapped to a sequential solution.

The **task inversion** criteria are used for merging tasks to reduce task overhead. The task inversion criteria – and in particular multiple instance task inversion – may be used during initial task structuring if high task overhead is anticipated. Alternatively, they may be used for design restructuring in situations in which there are concerns about high tasking overhead. In particular, task inversion can be used if a performance analysis of the design indicates that the tasking overhead is too high.

13.7.1 Multiple Instance Task Inversion

Handling multiple control tasks of the same type was described in Section 13.4.6. With this approach, several objects of the same type can be modeled by using one task instance for each object, where all the tasks are of the same type. The problem is that, for a given application, the system overhead for modeling each object by means of a separate task might be too high.

With **multiple instance task inversion**, all identical tasks of the same type are replaced by one task that performs the same functionality. For example, instead of mapping each control object to a separate task, all control objects of the same type are mapped to the same task. Each object's state information is captured in a separate passive entity object. A multiple instance inversion task is typically activated on demand by the arrival of a message destined for one of the inverted tasks. A *demand driven multiple instance inversion task* is depicted with the stereotypes «demand» «multiple instance inversion» «swSchedulableResource».

As an example of multiple instance task inversion, consider the example described in Section 13.4.6, in which each computer game Character Control object is mapped to a separate game Character Control task. If there are a very large number of computer game characters and the system overhead is too high to allow this, an alternative solution is to have only one game Character Controller task. A separate passive entity object is designed for each game character called Character State Information, which contains the state machine information for a specific game character (see Figure 13.15). With task inversion, the main procedure of the task is a

a) Design model – one task for each game character

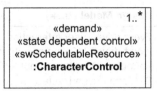

b) Design model – task inversion
one task for all game characters

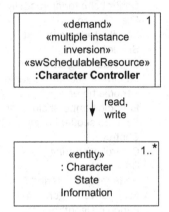

Figure 13.15. Example of multiple instance task inversion.

coordination procedure, which reads all inputs to the task and decides for which game character the data is intended, thereby ensuring that the appropriate game character entity object is used. There are other possible solutions such as having more than one Character Control task but applying multiple instance task inversion to assign a subset of the game characters (such as every ten or fifteen characters) to a task. This example is described in more detail in Albassam and Gomaa (2014).

13.8 DEVELOPING THE TASK ARCHITECTURE

The task structuring criteria can be applied to the analysis model in the following order. In each case, a decision must first be made whether the analysis model object should be mapped to an active object (task) or a passive object in the design model.

1. **I/O tasks.** Start with the I/O objects that interact with the outside world. Determine whether the object should be structured as an event driven I/O task, a periodic I/O task, a demand driven I/O task, a resource monitor task, or a temporally clustered periodic I/O task.
2. **Control tasks.** Analyze each control object (state dependent control object or coordinator object). Structure this object as a demand driven control task. Any object that executes an action (operation) triggered by the control task can potentially be combined with the control task based on the control clustering criterion (for a state dependent object) or sequential clustering criterion

Table 13.1 Mapping from Analysis Model to Design Model Tasks

Analysis Model (object)	Design Model (task)
User interaction	Event driven user interaction
Input/Output (input, output, I/O)	Event driven I/O (input, output, I/O)
	Periodic I/O (input, output, I/O)
	Demand driven I/O (usually output tasks)
	Demand driven resource monitor (usually output tasks)
	Periodic temporal clustering (usually input objects)
	Sequential clustering
	Control clustering (usually with output objects)
Proxy	Event driven proxy
	Any clustering criterion
Entity	Service
	Any clustering criterion
	Passive object (not a task)
Timer	Periodic timer
	Periodic temporal clustering
	Periodic sequential clustering
State dependent control	Control
	Control clustering
Coordinator	Coordinator
	Sequential clustering
Algorithm	Event driven algorithm
	Periodic algorithm
	Any clustering criterion

(for a coordinator object). Any activity that the control task enables and subsequently disables should be structured as a separate task.

3. **Periodic tasks.** Analyze the internal periodic activities, which are structured as periodic tasks. Determine if any candidate periodic tasks are triggered by the same event. If they are, they may be grouped into the same task, based on the temporal clustering criterion. Other candidate tasks that execute in sequence may be structured into the same task, according to the sequential clustering criterion.

4. **Other internal tasks.** For each internal candidate task activated by an internal event, identify whether any adjacent candidate tasks on the concurrent communication diagram may be grouped into the same task according to the *temporal, sequential,* or *multiple instance task inversion* clustering criteria.

The guidelines for mapping analysis model objects to design model tasks are summarized in Table 13.1. In cases in which the clustering criterion applies, this means that the analysis model object is designed as a passive object nested inside a clustered task, as described in more detail in Chapter 14.

Table 13.2 depicts the stereotypes for all the tasks described in this chapter.

13.9 TASK COMMUNICATION AND SYNCHRONIZATION

After structuring the system into concurrent tasks, the next step is to design the task interfaces. At this stage, the default interfaces between tasks are asynchronous

Table 13.2 Stereotypes for Concurrent Tasks

Task	Stereotypes
Event driven user interaction task	«event driven» «user interaction» «swSchedulableResource»
Event driven Input/Output (input, output, I/O) task	«event driven»«input»«swSchedulableResource» «event driven» «output» «swSchedulableResource» «event driven» «I/O» «swSchedulableResource»
Periodic I/O (input, output, I/O) task	«timerResource» «input» «swSchedulableResource» «timerResource» «output» «swSchedulableResource» «timerResource» «I/O» «swSchedulableResource»
Demand driven I/O (usually output) task	«demand» «output» «swSchedulableResource»
Demand driven resource monitor (usually output) task	«demand» «output» «swSchedulableResource»
Periodic temporal clustering task	«timerResource» «temporal clustering» «swSchedulableResource»
Demand driven sequential clustering task	«demand» «sequential clustering» «swSchedulableResource»
Periodic sequential clustering task	«timerResource» «sequential clustering» «swSchedulableResource»
Demand driven control clustering task	«demand» «control clustering» «swSchedulableResource»
Event driven proxy task	«event driven» «proxy» «swSchedulableResource»
Demand driven service task	«demand» «service» «swSchedulableResource»
Periodic (timer) task	«timerResource» «swSchedulableResource»
Demand driven state dependent control task	«demand» «state dependent control» «swSchedulableResource»
Demand driven coordinator task	«demand» «coordinator» «swSchedulableResource»
Demand driven algorithm task	«demand» « algorithm» «swSchedulableResource»
Periodic algorithm task	«timerResource» « algorithm» «swSchedulableResource»
Demand driven multiple instance inversion task	«demand» «multiple instance inversion» «swSchedulableResource».

messages and the interface to a passive object is through synchronous communication, as depicted on the analysis model interaction diagrams (Chapter 9) and the integrated communication diagrams (Chapter 10). It is now necessary to confirm or change these task interfaces, which need to be in the form of message communication, event synchronization, or access to information-hiding objects.

The UML notation for message communication is described in Chapter 2. Message interfaces between tasks are either asynchronous or synchronous, as introduced in Chapter 3 and described in Chapter 11 in the section on architectural communication patterns. For synchronous message communication, two possibilities exist: synchronous message communication with reply and synchronous message communication without reply. In this step of the design modeling, the task interfaces are designed and depicted on revised concurrent communication diagrams.

Various mechanisms for providing message communication services are described in Chapter 3. These include the operating system kernel, the constructs

a) Producer task communicating with Consumer task using
asynchronous message communication

b) 3 producer tasks communicating with one consumer task using
asynchronous message communication

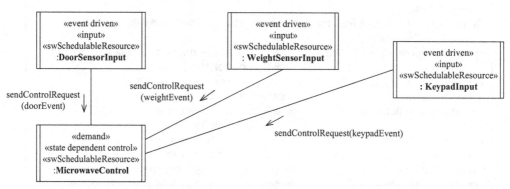

Figure 13.16. Examples of asynchronous message communication.

of a concurrent programming language, or a threads package. Alternatively, message communication connectors can be used, as described in Chapter 14. The various forms of inter-task communication are described next, with examples of their use.

13.9.1 Asynchronous Message Communication

With the **asynchronous message communication** pattern (Section 11.5.2) the producer sends a message to the consumer and continues without waiting for a response. Because the producer and consumer tasks proceed at different speeds, a first-in-first-out (FIFO) message queue can build up between producer and consumer. If no message is available when the consumer requests one, the consumer is suspended.

Consider the concurrent communication diagram (Figure 13.16a), which depicts the Door Sensor Input task sending a message to the Microwave Control task. The Door Sensor Input task sends the message and does not wait for it to be accepted by the Microwave Control task. This allows the Door Sensor Input task to quickly service any new external input that might arrive. Asynchronous message communication also provides the greatest flexibility for the Microwave Control task because it can wait on a queue of messages that arrive from multiple sources – in addition to the Door Sensor Input task, there are also the Weight Sensor Input and Keypad Input tasks that send control requests as messages to Microwave Control (Figure 13.16b). The messages from these producer tasks are queued FIFO in a message queue for Microwave Control. The Microwave Control task processes the requests in the order in which they arrive. This example is described in more detail in Chapter 19.

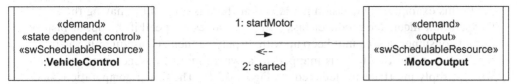

Figure 13.17. Example of synchronous message communication with reply.

13.9.2 Synchronous Message Communication with Reply

In the case of the **synchronous message communication with reply** pattern (Section 11.5.4), the producer sends a message to the consumer and then waits for a reply. When the message arrives, the consumer accepts the message, processes it, generates a reply, and sends the reply. The producer and consumer then both continue. The consumer is suspended if no message is available.

Although used in client/server systems (see Chapter 12), synchronous message communication with reply can also involve a single producer sending a message to a consumer and then waiting for a reply, in which case no message queue develops between the producer and the consumer. An example of synchronous message communication with reply involving a producer and consumer is a producer task, Vehicle Control, which sends start and stop messages to the consumer task, Motor Output, and waits for a reply, as depicted on the concurrent communication diagram (Figure 13.17). The producer must use synchronous communication with the consumer because it sends a message and then waits for a response. After receiving the message, the consumer processes the message, prepares a reply, and sends the reply to the producer. The notation for synchronous message communication with reply on the concurrent communication diagram (Figure 13.17) shows a synchronous message sent from the producer to the consumer with a dashed message, representing the response, sent by the consumer back to the producer.

13.9.3 Synchronous Message Communication without Reply

In the case of the **synchronous message communication without reply** pattern (Section 11.5.6), the producer sends a message to the consumer and then waits for acceptance of the message by the consumer. When the message arrives, the consumer accepts the message, thereby releasing the producer. The producer and consumer then both continue. The consumer is suspended if no message is available.

An example of synchronous message communication without reply is shown in Figure 13.18. The Speed Display Output is a demand driven output task. It displays the speed of the car while the Speed Computation Algorithm task is computing the next value of thecar speed. Thus, the computation is overlapped with the output.

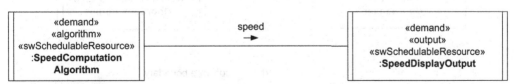

Figure 13.18. Example of synchronous message communication without reply.

In this example, the decision made is that there is no point in having the Speed Computation Algorithm producer task compute values of speed if the Speed Display Output consumer task cannot keep up with displaying them. Consequently, the interface between the two tasks is mapped to a synchronous message communication without reply interface, as depicted on Figure 13.18. The Speed Computation Algorithm computes the speed, sends the message, and then waits for the acceptance of the message by the Speed Display Output before resuming execution. The Speed Computation Algorithm is held up until the Speed Display Output finishes displaying the previous message. As soon as the Speed Display Output accepts the new message, the Speed Computation Algorithm is released from its wait and computes the next value of speed while the Speed Display Output displays the previous value. By this means, computation of the new value of speed (a compute-bound activity) can be overlapped with displaying of the previous value of speed (an I/O-bound activity), while preventing an unnecessary message queue build-up of speed messages at the display task. Thus, the synchronous message communication without reply between the two tasks acts as a brake on the producer task.

13.9.4 External and Timer Event Synchronization

Three types of **event synchronization** are possible: an external event, a timer event, and an internal event. This section describes event synchronization with external and timer events. The next section described internal event synchronization.

An *external event* is an event from an external entity, typically an interrupt from an external I/O device. A *timer event* represents a periodic activation of a task. Events are depicted in UML, using the asynchronous message notation to depict an event signal.

An example of an external event, typically a hardware interrupt from an input device, is given in Figure 13.19. The Door Sensor «interrupt Resource» «input» «hwDevice» generates an interrupt when it has door Input. The interrupt activates the Door Sensor Input «event driven» «input» «swSchedulableResource» task, which then reads the door Input. This interaction could be depicted as an event signal input from the device, followed by a read by the task. However, it is more concise to depict the interaction as an asynchronous event signal sent by the device, with the input data as a parameter, as depicted on the concurrent communication diagram (Figure 13.19).

An example of a timer event is given in Figure 13.20. The digital timer, which is a timer resource hardware device, generates a timer event to awaken the Microwave Timer «timerResource» «swSchedulableResource» task. The Microwave Timer task then

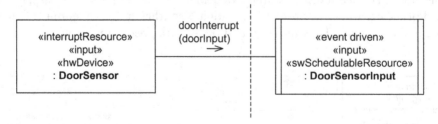

Hardware / software boundary

Figure 13.19. Example of external event.

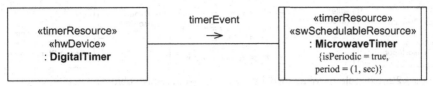

Figure 13.20. Example of timer event.

performs a periodic activity – in this case, decrementing the cooking time by one second and checking whether the cooking time has expired. The timer event is generated at fixed intervals of time.

13.9.5 Internal Event Synchronization

An *internal event* represents internal synchronization between a source task and a destination task. Internal event synchronization is used when two tasks need to synchronize their operations without communicating data between the tasks. The source task executes a *signal (event)* operation, which sends the event. The destination task executes a *wait (event)* operation, which suspends the task until the event is signaled. The destination task is not suspended if the event has previously been signaled. The event signal is depicted in UML by an asynchronous message that does not contain any data. An example of this is shown in Figure 13.21, in which the pick-and-place robot task signals the event part Ready. This awakens the drilling robot, which operates on the part and then signals the event part Completed, which the pick-and-place robot is waiting to receive. This example is described in more detail in Section 14.6.1.

13.9.5 Task Interaction via Information-Hiding Object

It is also possible for tasks to exchange information by means of a passive information-hiding object, as described in Section 3.7 and in Section 11.5.1 with the Synchronized Object Access Pattern. If two tasks are accessing the same passive entity object, and at least one of these tasks is writing to the object, then mutual exclusion must be enforced. A shared entity object is labeled with the MARTE stereotype «sharedDataComResource» because it is a resource for sharing data that is communicated between tasks. In addition, if access to the object is mutually exclusive, then the object is labeled with a second MARTE stereotype «sharedMutualExclusionResource» because it is a resource that ensures mutually exclusive access to the shared data. Thus, the full stereotype depiction for an entity object, which is both a mutually exclusive and shared data communication resource, is «entity» «sharedDataComResource» «swMutualExclusionResource».

An example of task access to a passive information-hiding object is given in Figure 13.22, in which the Sensor Statistics Algorithm task reads from the Sensor Data

Figure 13.21. Example of internal event synchronization between two tasks.

Figure 13.22. Example of tasks invoking operations of passive object.

Repository entity object, and the Sensor Input task updates the entity object. Because mutually exclusive access to the Sensor Data Repository needs to be enforced, the passive shared entity object is labeled with the stereotypes «entity» «sharedData-ComResource» «sharedMutualExclusionResource». This example of synchronized access to a passive object is described in more detail in Chapter 14.

It is important to realize how the synchronous message notation used between two concurrent tasks differs from that used between a task and a passive object. The notation looks the same in the UML: an arrow with a filled-in arrowhead. The semantics are different, however. The synchronous message notation between two concurrent tasks represents message communication between two tasks in which the producer task waits for the consumer task, as shown in Figures 13.17 and 13.18 using the synchronous communication with reply and without reply patterns respectively. However, the synchronous message notation between a task and a passive object represents an operation call (as shown in Figure 13.22) in which the task invokes an operation of the object, which executes in the thread of control of the task, using the Synchronized Object Access pattern (see Chapter 11).

13.10 TASK INTERFACE AND TASK BEHAVIOR SPECIFICATIONS

A **task interface specification (TIS)** describes a concurrent task's interface. It is an extension of the class interface specification (Gomaa 2011) with additional information specific to a task, including task structure, timing characteristics, relative priority, and errors detected. A **task behavior specification** (TBS) describes the task's event sequencing logic. The task's interface defines how it interfaces to other tasks. The task's structure describes how its structure is derived, using the task structuring criteria. The task's timing characteristics addresses frequency of activation and estimated execution time. This information is used for real-time scheduling purposes, as described in Chapter 17.

The TIS is introduced with the *task architecture* to specify the characteristics of each task. The TBS is defined later, during detailed software design (Chapter 14), and describes the **task event sequencing logic**, which is how the task responds to each of its message or event inputs, in particular, what output is generated as a result of each input.

A task (active class) differs from a passive class in that it should be designed with only one operation (in Java, this can be implemented as the *run* method). For this reason, the TIS only has a specification of one operation, instead of several for a typical passive class. The TIS is defined as follows, with the first five items identical to a class interface specification:

■ **Name.**
■ **Information hidden.**

- **Structuring criteria:** Both the role criterion (e.g., input) and concurrency criterion (e.g., event driven) need to be described.
- **Assumptions**
- **Anticipated Changes**
- **Task interface.** The task interface should include a definition of:
  a) Messages inputs and outputs. For each message interface (input or output) there should be a description of
    - Type of interface: asynchronous, synchronous with reply, or synchronous without reply
    - For each message type supported by this interface: message name and message parameters
  b) Events signaled (input and output), name of event, type of event: external, internal, timer
  c) External inputs or outputs. Define the inputs from and outputs to the external environment.
  d) Passive objects referenced
- **Errors detected.** This section describes the possible errors that could be detected during execution of this task.

Examples of task interface specifications for tasks in the Railroad Crossing Control System are described in Chapter 20.

13.11 SUMMARY

During the concurrent task design phase, the system is structured into concurrent tasks and the task interfaces are designed. To help determine the concurrent tasks, task structuring criteria are provided to assist in mapping an object-oriented analysis model of the system to a concurrent tasking architecture. Tasks are labeled using MARTE stereotypes. The task communication and synchronization interfaces are also designed.

Following concurrent task design, Chapter 14 describes the detailed software design, in which tasks that contain nested passive objects are designed, detailed task synchronization issues are addressed, connector classes are designed to encapsulate the details of inter-task communication, and each task's internal event sequencing logic is designed. Examples of task event sequencing logic for the different kinds of tasks described in this chapter are given in Appendix C. As soon as the task architecture has been designed, performance analysis of the concurrent real-time design can commence, as described in Chapter 17. Several examples of task structuring and designing task interfaces are described in the case studies in Chapters 19–23.

14

Detailed Real-Time Software Design

After structuring the system into tasks (in Chapter 13), this chapter describes the detailed software design. In this step, the internals of composite tasks that contain nested objects are designed, detailed synchronization issues of tasks accessing passive classes are addressed, connector classes are designed that encapsulate the details of inter-task communication, and each task's internal event sequencing logic is defined. Several examples are given in Pseudocode of the detailed design of task synchronization mechanisms, connector classes for inter-task communication, and task event sequencing logic.

The detailed software design is depicted on a detailed concurrent communication diagram, which adds more detail to the concurrent communication diagram developed during task structuring. It depicts the internal design of clustered tasks and the design of connector objects.

Section 14.1 describes the design of composite tasks, including the internal design of temporal and control clustering tasks. Section 14.2 describes the synchronization of access to classes using different synchronization mechanisms, including the mutual exclusion algorithm and the multiple readers and writers algorithm. Section 14.3 describes the synchronization of access to passive objects using the *monitor* concept. Section 14.4 describes the design of connectors for inter-task communication, in particular for synchronous and asynchronous message communication. Section 14.5 describes the detailed software design of tasks using task behavior specifications and event sequencing logic. Section 14.6 provides detailed software design examples of task communication and synchronization in real-time robot and vision systems. Finally, Section 14.7 briefly describes implementing concurrent tasks in Java using threads.

14.1 DESIGN OF COMPOSITE TASKS

A **composite task** is a task that encapsulates one or more nested objects. This section describes the detailed design of composite tasks, which includes tasks that were structured using the task clustering criteria. Such tasks are designed as composite active classes that contain nested passive classes. In a real-time design, typical nested classes are entity classes, input/output classes, and state machine classes.

266

After considering the relationship between tasks and classes, this section describes situations where it is useful to divide the responsibility between tasks and classes. Next, the design of two composite tasks is described in detail: a temporal clustering task and a control clustering task.

14.1.1 Separation of Concerns between Tasks and Nested Classes

The relationship between tasks and classes is handled as follows. The active object, the task, is activated by an external, internal, or timer event. It then calls an operation provided by a passive object, which might be nested inside the task, as described in this section, or external to the task, as described in Section 14.2.

Separation of concerns is applied to divide the responsibility between tasks and nested classes. Responsibility for control, sequencing, and communication is given to the task. Classes are designed using the information-hiding concept as described in Section 3.2 of Chapter 3. In real-time embedded software design, information hiding can be applied to the design of:

- Entity classes that encapsulate internal data structures (also referred to as *data abstraction* classes), as described initially in Section 3.2.2. Design of entity classes that are accessed by multiple tasks is described in Section 11.5.1, in Section 13.9.5, and in much more details in this chapter in Section 14.2.
- Device input or output classes that hide the details of how to interface to I/O devices, as described in Section 3.2.3 and in more detail in Section 14.1.2.
- State machine classes that hide the details of the encapsulated state transition table, as described in Section 14.1.3.

Consider how separation of concerns is used to interface to an input/output device: a composite task encapsulates one or more nested device I/O objects. The I/O object addresses the details of how to read from or write to the real-world device (as described in Section 14.1.2), and the task addresses issues of when and how the task is activated (which determines whether it is event driven, demand driven, or periodic) and communication with other active or passive objects. Consider how this works in the case of an input device. The task is activated by an interrupt or timer event, calls an operation provided by the passive object to read the input, and then either sends the data in a message to a consumer task or invokes an update operation of a passive entity object.

Another case of division of responsibility occurs between a composite task and a nested state machine object. The object encapsulates the state transition table and maintains the current state of the object, as described in Section 14.1.3. The control task (see Chapter 13) receives messages containing events from several producer tasks, extracts the event from the message, and calls the state machine object with the event as an input parameter. The object returns the action to be performed, and the task initiates the action by sending a message to a consumer task or invoking an operation on another object.

A composite task with several nested objects can be depicted on a detailed *concurrent communication diagram*. Each composite task has a coordinator object, which receives the task's incoming messages and can then invoke operations provided by other nested objects.

a) Example of passive input class

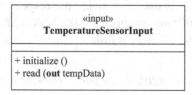

b) Example of passive output class

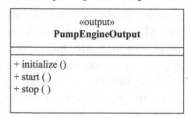

Figure 14.1. a. Example of passive input class. b. Example of passive output class.

14.1.2 Design of Device I/O Classes

A **device I/O class** provides a virtual interface that hides the actual interface to a real-world I/O device. The rationale for designing such classes using information hiding is described in Section 3.2.3. This section describes the design of the class operations.

A device I/O class interfaces to the real-world device and provides the operations that read from and/or write to the device. A device I/O class has an initialize operation. When an object is instantiated from the class, this operation is called at device initialization time to initialize the device and any internal variables used by the object. The other operations depend on the characteristics of the device. For example, a device input class is likely to have a read operation, and a device output class is likely to have a write or update operation. A device interface class that provides both input and output is likely to have both read and write operations.

An example of a passive input class for reading a temperature sensor is given in Figure 14.1a. The Temperature Sensor Input passive input class supports two operations: read (out tempData) and initialize. The read operation samples the current value of the temperature sensor and returns the value as an output parameter.

An example of a passive output class for starting and stopping an electric pump is given in Figure 14.1b. The Pump Engine Output passive output class provides an initialize operation as well as operations to start the pump and stop the pump.

14.1.3 Design of State Machine Classes

A **state machine class** encapsulates the information contained in a state machine. The state machine executed by the state machine object is encapsulated in a state transition table, in which the rows are indexed by event and the columns are indexed by state. Each element in the table is an intersection of event and state and contains the next state and the values of the action(s) to be executed. The state machine class

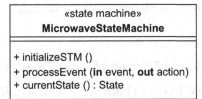

Figure 14.2. Example of passive state machine class.

hides the contents of the state transition table and maintains the current state of the machine.

The state machine class provides the operations that access the state transition table and change the state of the object. In particular, one or more operations are designed to process the incoming events that cause state changes. One way of designing the operations of a state machine class is to have one operation for each incoming event. This means that each state machine class is designed explicitly for a particular state machine. However, it is more desirable to design a state machine class that is application independent and hence more reusable.

A reusable state machine class hides the contents of the state transition table and the current state of the machine. It provides three reusable operations that are not application specific:

initializeSTM ()
processEvent (in event, out action)
currentState (): State

The processEvent operation is called when there is a new event to process, with the new event passed in as an input parameter. Given the current state of the machine and any specified conditions that must hold, the operation looks up the state transition table entry for Table (new event, current state). The information contained in that entry is the next state and action(s) to be performed. The *current state* is then updated to the new state and the action or action list is returned as an output parameter. The current State operation is optional; it returns the state of the machine and is only needed in applications where the current state needs to be known by tasks using the state machine class.

A state machine class is a reusable class in that it can be used to encapsulate any state transition table. The contents of the table are application-dependent and are defined at the time the state machine class is instantiated and/or initialized. At initialization time, the initializeSTM operation is called to populate the state machine (typically from a file) with the states, events, actions, and conditions, as well as setting the *current state* of the machine to the initial state.

An example of a state machine class from the Microwave Oven Control System is the Microwave State Machine state machine class, shown in Figure 14.2. The class encapsulates the microwave oven state transition table (which is mapped from the microwave oven state machine, as depicted in Chapters 7 and 19) and provides the initializeSTM, processEvent, and currentState operations. At initialization time, the *current state* of the state machine is set to Door Closed, which is the initial state of the microwave oven.

14.1.4 Temporal Clustering Task and Device Interface Objects

Consider the case of polled I/O from both the task structuring and class structuring perspectives. With polled I/O, structure the task according to either periodic I/O (for one I/O device) or temporal clustering (for two or more I/O devices) task structuring criteria. The details of how to interface to a given passive I/O device is encapsulated in a device interface class. Define the operations provided by the device interface class. Place the device interface class inside the task.

Consider the dynamic behavior. The task is first activated by a timer event. It then calls the operations provided by each device interface object to obtain the latest status of each device and then either sends the device status to a consumer task or writes it to a passive entity object.

An example of polled I/O is given in Figure 14.3. The initial design decision is to design two separate periodic input tasks, one for each input object, Temperature Sensor Input and Pressure Sensor Input (Figure 14.3a), which monitor the temperature and pressure sensors respectively. Given that the temperature and pressure sensors are sampled periodically and with the same frequency, an alternative design decision is to design one temporal clustering task, which samples both temperature and pressure, as described in Section 13.6.1 and shown in Figure 14.3b.

From a task structuring perspective, the Temperature Sensor Input and Pressure Sensor Input objects are grouped into a task called Sensor Monitor based on the temporal clustering criterion. The Sensor Monitor task (Figure 14.3b) is activated periodically by a timer event, at which time it reads the current values of the sensors. It then updates the Sensor Data Repository entity object with the latest sensor values.

From a class structuring perspective, two separate input classes are created for the temperature and pressure sensors (Figure 14.3c), namely the Temperature Sensor Input and Pressure Sensor Input classes. Each input class supports two operations: for Temperature Sensor Input, the operations are read (out tempData) and initialize. For Pressure Sensor Input, they are read (out pressureData) and initialize.

From a combined task and class perspective, the Sensor Monitor task is structured as a composite task, which contains three nested objects: a coordinator object, the Sensor Coordinator, and two input objects, Temperature Sensor Input and Pressure Sensor Input. The Sensor Data Repository entity class is outside the task and has operations to update and read the temperature and pressure sensor values, namely update (in currentPressure), update (in currentTemp), read (out pressureValue), and read (out temperatureValue).

Consider the dynamic behavior as depicted in Figure 14.3d. The Sensor Monitor task is activated periodically by a timer event. At this time, the coordinator object, Sensor Monitor Coordinator, reads the current values of the sensors by calling each of the operations, Temperature Sensor Input.read (out tempData) and Pressure Sensor Input.read (out pressureData). It then invokes the update operations of the Sensor Data Repository entity object, namely Sensor Data Repository.update (in currentTemp), and Sensor Data Repository.update (in currentPressure).

By separating the concern of **how** a device is accessed into the input class from the concern of **when** the device is accessed into the task, greater flexibility and

a) Periodic input tasks before temporal clustering

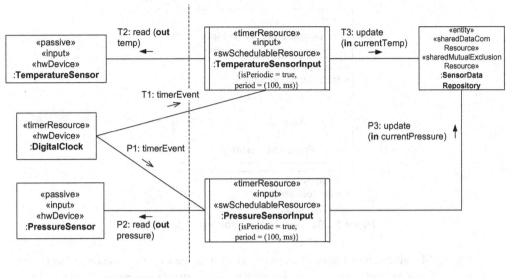

Hardware / software boundary

b) Periodic input with one temporal clustering task

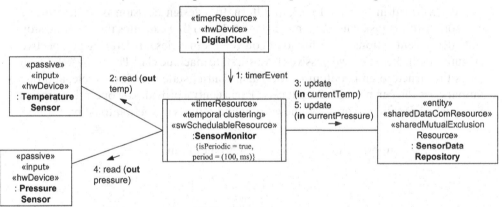

Figure 14.3. Example of temporal clustering and input objects. a. Periodic input tasks before temporal clustering. b. Periodic input with one temporal clustering task.

potential reuse is achieved. Thus, for example, the temperature input class could be used in different applications by an event driven input task, a periodic input task, or a temporally clustered periodic I/O task. Furthermore, the characteristics of different temperature sensors could be hidden inside the input class while preserving the same virtual device interface.

14.1.5 Control Clustering Task and Information-Hiding Objects

The next case to be considered is the design of a control clustering task with nested information-hiding objects. The task is activated on demand. It then calls operations provided by one or more passive objects.

c) Design of nested input classes

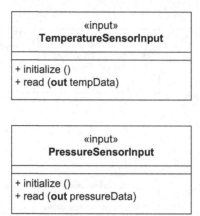

Figure 14.3c. Design of nested input classes.

Figure 14.4 gives an example of a control clustering task and the nested objects to which it interfaces. The initial design decision before control clustering (Figure 14.4a) is to have the control task Pump Control, which encapsulates a state machine, sends start and stop messages (at different state transitions) to the Pump Engine Output task.

As described in Section 13.6.3, an alternative design decision is to design one control clustering task Pump Controller (Figure 14.4b) that executes the start and stop state dependent actions in its thread of control. From a class structuring perspective (Figure 14.4c), there are two passive classes: a state machine class Pump Control, which hides the structure and content of the Pump Control state transition table, and one output class, the Pump Engine Output class. Pump Control provides an operation process Event, which is called to process a new event and returns the action to be performed.

d) Temporal clustering task with nested input objects

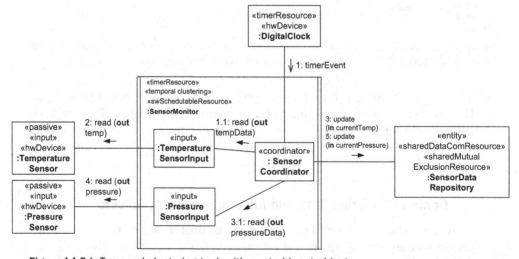

Figure 14.3d. Temporal clustering task with nested input objects.

a) Tasks before control clustering

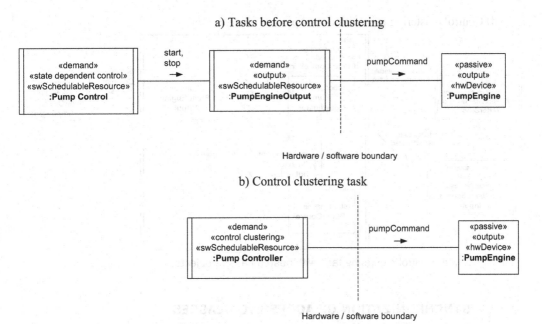

Hardware / software boundary

b) Control clustering task

Hardware / software boundary

Figure 14.4. Example of a control clustering task with passive objects. a. Tasks before control clustering. b. Control clustering task.

The start and stop actions are designed as the operations provided by the passive Pump Engine Output class, which start and stop the electric pump.

From a combined task- and class structuring perspective (Figure 14.4d), there is one task, the Pump Controller task, which is structured as a composite task. It contains three nested objects: a state machine object called Pump Control, a passive output object called Pump Engine Output, and a nested coordinator object called Pump Coordinator, which provides the overall internal coordination of the task. When a new message arrives at Pump Controller, it is received by Pump Coordinator, which extracts the specific event from the request and calls PumpControl.processEvent (in event, out action). Pump Control looks up the state transition table, given the current state and the new event. The entry in the table contains the new state and the action to be performed. Pump Control updates the current state and returns the action to be performed. Pump Coordinator then initiates the action. If the action is to start or stop the pump, it invokes the start or stop operation of Pump Engine Output.

c) Design of nested state machine and output classes

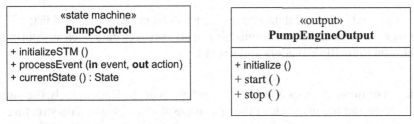

Figure 14.4c. Design of nested classes.

d) Control clustering task with nested passive objects

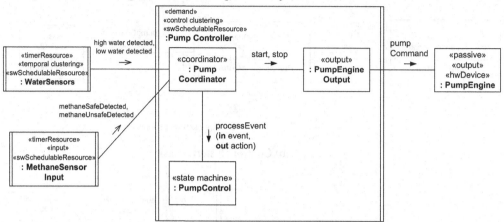

Figure 14.4d. Control clustering task with nested passive objects.

14.2 SYNCHRONIZATION OF ACCESS TO CLASSES

If a class is accessed by more than one task, the class's operations must synchronize the access to the data it encapsulates, as described in the Object Access Pattern in Section 11.5.1. This section describes mechanisms for providing this synchronization using the mutual exclusion algorithm and the multiple readers and writers algorithm.

14.2.1 Example of Synchronization of Access to Class

As an example of synchronization of access to a class, consider a passive entity class – the Analog Sensor Repository class, which encapsulates a sensor data repository. In designing this class, one design decision relates to whether the internal sensor data structure is to be designed as an array or a linked list. Another design decision relates to the nature of the synchronization required, whether an object of this class is to be accessed by more than one task concurrently, and – if so – whether mutual exclusion or the multiple readers and writers algorithm is required. These design decisions relate to the design of the class and need not concern users of the class.

By separating the concerns of **what** the class does – namely the specification of the operations – from **how** it does it – namely the internal design of the class – any changes to the internals of the class have no impact on users of the class. Possible changes are

- Changes to the internal data structure, such as from array to linked list;
- Changes to the internal synchronization of access to the data, such as from mutual exclusion to multiple readers and writers;

The impact of these changes is only on the internals of the class, namely, the internal data structure and the internals of the operations that access the data structure.

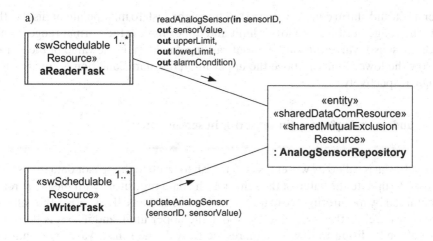

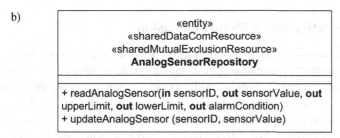

Figure 14.5. Example of concurrent access to passive entity object.

14.2.2 Operations Provided for Synchronized Access to Class

For the same external interface of the Analog Sensor Repository entity class, consider two different internal designs for the synchronization of access to the sensor data repository: mutual exclusion and multiple readers and writers. As described in Section 13.9.5 and depicted in Figure 14.5, a shared entity class is labeled with the MARTE stereotypes «sharedDataComResource» because it is a resource for sharing data that is communicated between tasks and «sharedMutualExclusionResource» because it is also a resource that ensures mutually exclusive access to the shared data. It should be pointed out that the mutual exclusion stereotype is interpreted as meaning that mutual exclusion is enforced when necessary and not that every access to the data is mutually exclusive.

In the sensor repository example, the Analog Sensor Repository entity class provides the following two operations (see Figure 14.5).

> readAnalogSensor (in sensorID, out sensorValue, out upperLimit, out lowerLimit, out alarmCondition)

This operation is called by reader tasks that wish to read from the sensor data repository. Given the sensor ID, this operation returns the current sensor value, upper limit, lower limit, and alarm condition to users who might wish to manipulate or display the data. The range between the lower limit and upper limit is the normal range within which the sensor value can vary without causing an alarm. If the value of the sensor is below the lower limit or above the upper limit, the alarmCondition is equal to low or high, respectively.

---

updateAnalogSensor (in sensorID, in sensorValue)

This operation is called by writer tasks that wish to write to the sensor data repository. It is used to update the value of the sensor in the data repository with the latest reading obtained by monitoring the external environment. It checks whether the value of the sensor is below the lower limit or above the upper limit, and if so sets the value of the alarmCondition to low or high, respectively. If the sensor value is within the normal range, the alarmCondition is set to normal.

14.2.3 Synchronization Using Mutual Exclusion

Consider first the mutual exclusion solution using a binary semaphore (see Section 3.6.1) in which the acquire and release operations on the semaphore are provided by the operating system. To ensure mutual exclusion in the sensor repository example, each task must execute an **acquire** operation on the semaphore readWriteSemaphore (initially set to 1) before it starts accessing the data repository. It must also execute a **release** operation on the semaphore after it has finished accessing the data repository. The Pseudocode for the read and update operations is as follows:

```
class AnalogSensorRepository
private readWriteSemaphore : Semaphore = 1
public readAnalogSensor (in sensorID, out sensorValue, out upperLimit, out
lowerLimit, out alarmCondition)
    -- Critical section for read operation.
      acquire (readWriteSemaphore);
      sensorValue := sensorDataRepository (sensorID, value);
      upperLimit := sensorDataRepository (sensorID, upLim);
      lowerLimit := sensorDataRepository (sensorID, loLim);
      alarmCondition := sensorDataRepository (sensorID, alarm);
      release(readWriteSemaphore);
    end readAnalogSensor;
```

In the case of the update operation, in addition to updating the value of the sensor in the data repository, it is also necessary to determine whether the sensor's alarm condition is high, low, or normal.

```
public updateAnalogSensor (in sensorID, in sensorValue)
    -- Critical section for write operation.
      acquire (readWriteSemaphore);
```

```
      sensorDataRepository (sensorID, value) := sensorValue;
      if sensorValue ≥ sensorDataRepository (sensorID, upLim)
         then sensorDataRepository (sensorID, alarm) := high;
      elseif sensorValue ≤ sensorDataRepository (sensorID, loLim)
         then sensorDataRepository (sensorID, alarm) := low;
         else sensorDataRepository (sensorID, alarm) := normal;
      end if;
      release (readWriteSemaphore);
   end updateAnalogSensor;
```

14.2.4 Synchronization of Multiple Readers and Writers

With the multiple readers and writers solution, multiple reader tasks may access the data repository concurrently, and writer tasks have mutually exclusive access to it. Two binary semaphores are used, readerSemaphore and readWriteSemaphore, which are both initially set to 1. A count of the number of readers, numberOfReaders, is also maintained, initially set to 0. The readerSemaphore is used by readers to ensure mutually exclusive updating of the reader count. Writers use the readWriteSemaphore to ensure mutually exclusive access to the sensor data repository. This semaphore is also accessed by readers. It is acquired by the first reader prior to reading from the data repository and released by the last reader after finishing reading from the data repository. The Pseudocode for the read and update operations is as follows:

```
   class AnalogSensorRepository
   private numberOfReaders : Integer = 0;
      readerSemaphore: Semaphore = 1;
      readWriteSemaphore: Semaphore = 1;
   public readAnalogSensor (in sensorID, out sensorValue, out upperLimit, out
   lowerLimit, out alarmCondition)
      -- Read operation called by reader tasks. Several readers are
      -- allowed to access the data repository providing there is no
      -- writer accessing it.
      acquire (readerSemaphore);
      Increment numberOfReaders;
      if numberOfReaders = 1 then acquire (readWriteSemaphore);
      release (readerSemaphore);
      sensorValue := sensorDataRepository (sensorID, value);
      upperLimit := sensorDataRepository (sensorID, upLim);
      lowerLimit := sensorDataRepository (sensorID, loLim);
      alarmCondition := sensorDataRepository (sensorID, alarm);
      acquire (readerSemaphore);
      Decrement numberOfReaders;
      if numberOfReaders = 0 then release (readWriteSemaphore);
      release (readerSemaphore);
   end readAnalogSensor;
```

The Pseudocode for the update operation is similar to that for the mutual exclusion example because it is necessary to ensure that writer tasks that call the update operation have mutually exclusive access to the sensor data repository.

```
public updateAnalogSensor (in sensorID, in sensorValue)
  -- critical section for write operation.
    acquire (readWriteSemaphore);
    sensorDataRepository (sensorID, value) := sensorValue;
    if sensorValue ≥ sensorDataRepository (sensorID, upLim)
      then sensorDataRepository (sensorID, alarm) := high;
    elseif sensorValue ≤ sensorDataRepository (sensorID, loLim)
      then sensorDataRepository (sensorID, alarm) := low;
      else sensorDataRepository (sensorID, alarm) := normal;
    end if;
    release (readWriteSemaphore);
  end updateAnalogSensor;
end AnalogSensorRepository;
```

This solution solves the problem; however, it intertwines the synchronization solution with the access to the data repository. It is possible to separate these two concerns, as described next.

14.3 DESIGNING MONITORS

Synchronization of access to passive objects can also be achieved using monitors, as described in this section. A monitor combines the concepts of information hiding and synchronization. A **monitor** is a data object that encapsulates data and has operations that are executed mutually exclusively. The critical section of each task is replaced by a call to a monitor operation. An implicit semaphore is associated with each monitor, referred to as the *monitor lock*. Thus, only one task is active in a monitor at any one time. A call to a monitor operation results in the calling task acquiring the associated semaphore. However, if the lock is already taken, the task blocks until the monitor lock is acquired. An exit from the monitor operation results in a release of the semaphore, that is, the monitor lock is released so that it can be acquired by a different task. The mutually exclusive operations of a monitor are also referred to as *guarded* operations or *synchronized* methods in Java.

14.3.1 Example of Mutual Exclusion with Monitor

An example of mutually exclusive access to the analog sensor repository using a monitor is described next. The monitor solution is to encapsulate the sensor data repository in an Analog Sensor Repository information-hiding object, which supports read and update operations. These operations are called by any task wishing to access the data repository. The details of how to synchronize access to the data repository are hidden from the calling tasks.

The monitor provides for mutually exclusive access to the analog sensor repository. There are two mutually exclusive operations, one to read from and one to update the contents of the analog repository. The specification of the two operations is given in Section 14.2.2 and depicted in Figure 14.5. The Pseudocode for the mutually exclusive operations is as follows:

```
monitor AnalogSensorRepository

public readAnalogSensor (in sensorID, out sensorValue, out upperLimit, out
lowerLimit, out alarmCondition)
    sensorValue := sensorDataRepository (sensorID, value);
    upperLimit := sensorDataRepository (sensorID, upLim);
    lowerLimit := sensorDataRepository (sensorID, loLim);
    alarmCondition := sensorDataRepository (sensorID, alarm);
end readAnalogSensor;

public updateAnalogSensor (in sensorID, in sensorValue)
    sensorDataRepository (sensorID, value) := sensorValue;
    if sensorValue ≥ sensorDataRepository (sensorID, upLim)
        then sensorDataRepository (sensorID, alarm) := high;
    elseif sensorValue ≤ sensorDataRepository (sensorID, loLim)
        then sensorDataRepository (sensorID, alarm) := low;
        else sensorDataRepository (sensorID, alarm) := normal;
    end if;
end updateAnalogSensor;
end AnalogSensorRepository;
```

14.3.2 Monitors and Condition Synchronization

In addition to providing synchronized operations, monitors support *condition synchronization*. This allows a task executing the monitor's mutually exclusive operation to block by executing a *wait* operation until a particular condition is true, for example, waiting for a buffer to become full or empty. When a task in a monitor blocks, it releases the monitor lock, allowing a different task to acquire the monitor lock. A task that blocks in a monitor is awakened by some other task executing a *signal* operation (referred to as *notify* in Java). For example, if a reader task needs to read an item from a buffer and the buffer is empty, it executes a *wait* operation. The reader remains blocked until a writer task places an item in the buffer and executes a *notify* operation.

If semaphore support is unavailable, mutually exclusive access to a resource may be provided by means of a monitor with condition synchronization, as described next. The Boolean variable busy is encapsulated by the monitor to represent the state of the resource. A task that wishes to acquire the resource calls the acquire operation. The task is suspended on the wait operation if the resource is busy. On exiting from the wait, the task will set busy equal to true, thereby taking possession of the resource.

When the task finishes with the resource, it calls the release operation, which sets busy to false and calls the notify operation to awaken a waiting task.

The following is the monitor design for mutually exclusive access to a resource:

```
monitor Semaphore
        -- Declare Boolean variable called busy, initialized to false.
private busy : Boolean = false;

        -- acquire is called to take possession of the resource
        -- the calling task is suspended if the resource is busy
public acquire ()
                while busy = true do wait;
                busy := true;
                end acquire;

        -- release is called to relinquish possession of the resource
        -- if a task is waiting for the resource, it will be awakened
public release ()
                busy := false;
                notify;
end release;
end Semaphore;
```

14.3.3 Synchronization of Multiple Readers and Writers Using a Monitor

This section describes a monitor solution to the multiple readers and writers problem. Because the operations of a monitor are executed mutually exclusively, a mutual exclusion solution to the sensor repository problem can easily be achieved using monitors, as described in Section 14.3.1. However, a multiple readers and writers solution cannot use a monitor solution for the design of the Analog Sensor Repository class because the readAnalogSensor operation needs to be executed by several readers concurrently. Instead, the synchronization parts of the multiple readers and writers algorithm are encapsulated in a monitor, which is then used by a redesigned Analog Sensor Repository class. Two solutions to this problem are presented, the first providing the same functionality as the previous section. The second solution provides an added capability, that of preventing writer starvation.

A ReadWrite monitor is declared that uses two semaphore monitors and provides four mutually exclusive operations. The semaphores are the readerSemaphore and the readWriteSemaphore. The four mutually exclusive operations are the startRead, endRead, startWrite, and endWrite operations. A reader task calls the startRead operation before it starts reading and the endRead operation after it has finished reading. A writer task calls the startWrite operation before it starts writing and the endWrite operation after it has finished writing. A semaphore monitor (Section 14.3.2) provides an acquire operation – which is called to first get hold of the resource and involves a possible delay if the resource is initially busy – and a release operation to free up the resource.

The startRead operation has to first acquire the readerSemaphore, increment the number of readers, and then release the semaphore. If the reader count was zero before incrementing, then startRead also has to acquire the readWriteSemaphore, which is acquired by the first reader and released by the last reader. Although monitor operations are executed mutually exclusively, the readerSemaphore is still needed. This is because it is possible for the reader to be suspended, waiting for the readWriteSemaphore semaphore, and hence release the ReadWrite monitor lock. If another reader now acquires the monitor lock by calling startRead or endRead, it is suspended, waiting for the readerSemaphore.

The design of the ReadWrite monitor is described next:

---

monitor ReadWrite
   -- Design for multiple readers/single writer access to resource
   -- Declare an integer counter for the number of readers.
   -- Declare semaphore for accessing count of number of readers
   -- Declare a semaphore for mutually exclusive access to buffer
private numberOfReaders : Integer = 0;
     readerSemaphore: Semaphore = 1;
     readWriteSemaphore: Semaphore = 1;

public startRead ()
   -- A reader calls this operation before it starts to read
     readerSemaphore.acquire;
     if numberOfReaders = 0 **then** readWriteSemaphore.acquire ();
     Increment numberOfReaders;
     readerSemaphore.release;
end startRead;

public endRead ()
   -- A reader calls this operation after it has finished reading
     readerSemaphore.acquire;
     Decrement numberOfReaders;
     if numberOfReaders = 0 **then** readWriteSemaphore.release ();
     readerSemaphore.release;
end endRead;

public startWrite ()
   -- A writer calls this operation before it starts to write
     readWriteSemaphore.acquire ();
end startRead;

public endWrite ()
   -- A writer calls this operation after it has finished writing
     readWriteSemaphore.release ();
end endWrite;
end ReadWrite;

To take advantage of the ReadWrite monitor, the Analog Sensor Repository is now redesigned to declare its own private instance of the ReadWrite monitor called multiReadSingleWrite. The readAnalogSensor operation now calls the startRead operation of the monitor before reading from the repository and calls the endRead operation after finishing reading. The updateAnalogSensor operation calls the startWrite operation of the monitor before updating the repository and calls the endWrite operation after completing the update.

```
class AnalogSensorRepository
private multiReadSingleWrite : ReadWrite
public readAnalogSensor (in sensorID, out sensorValue, out upperLimit, out
lowerLimit, out alarmCondition)
    multiReadSingleWrite.startRead();
    sensorValue := sensorDataRepository (sensorID, value);
    upperLimit := sensorDataRepository (sensorID, upLim);
    lowerLimit := sensorDataRepository (sensorID, loLim);
    alarmCondition := sensorDataRepository (sensorID, alarm);
    multiReadSingleWrite.endRead();
end readAnalogSensor;

public updateAnalogSensor (in sensorID, in sensorValue)
    -- Critical section for write operation.
    multiReadSingleWrite.startWrite();
    sensorDataRepository (sensorID, value) := sensorValue;
    if sensorValue ≥ sensorDataRepository (sensorID, upLim)
        then sensorDataRepository (sensorID, alarm) := high;
    elseif sensorValue ≤ sensorDataRepository (sensorID, loLim)
        then sensorDataRepository (sensorID, alarm) := low;
        else sensorDataRepository (sensorID, alarm) := normal;
    end if;
    multiReadSingleWrite.endWrite();
end updateAnalogSensor;
end AnalogSensorRepository;
```

14.3.4 Synchronization of Multiple Readers and Writers without Writer Starvation

The previous solution to this problem has a limitation in that a busy reader population could indefinitely prevent a writer from accessing the buffer, a problem referred to as writer starvation. The following monitor solution prevents this problem by adding a writerWaitingSemaphore. The startWrite operation must now acquire the writerWaitingSemaphore before acquiring the readWriteSemaphore. The startRead operation must acquire (and then release) the writerWaitingSemaphore before acquiring the readerSemaphore.

The reason for these changes is explained in the following scenario. Assume that several readers are reading and a writer now attempts to write. It successfully acquires the writerWaitingSemaphore but is then suspended while trying to acquire the readWriteSemaphore, which is held by the readers. If a new reader tries to read from the buffer, it calls startRead and is then suspended, waiting to acquire the writer-WaitingSemaphore. Gradually, the current readers will finish reading until the last reader reduces the reader count to zero and releases the readWriteSemaphore. The semaphore is now acquired by the waiting writer, which releases the writerWait-ingSemaphore, thereby allowing a reader or writer to acquire the semaphore. The monitor solution is given next – compared with the previous solution, the startRead and startWrite operations have changed.

```
monitor ReadWrite
    -- Prevent writer starvation by adding new semaphore.
    -- Design for multiple readers/single writer access to resource.
    -- Declare an integer counter for the number of readers.
    -- Declare semaphore for accessing count of number of readers
    -- Declare a semaphore for mutually exclusive access to buffer
    -- Declare a semaphore for writer waiting
private numberOfReaders : Integer = 0;
    readerSemaphore: Semaphore = 1;
    readWriteSemaphore: Semaphore = 1;
    writerWaitingSemaphore: Semaphore = 1;

public startRead ()
    -- A reader calls this operation before it starts to read
    writerWaitingSemaphore.acquire
    writerWaitingSemaphore.release
    readerSemaphore.acquire;
    if numberOfReaders = 0 then readWriteSemaphore.acquire ();
    Increment numberOfReaders;
    readerSemaphore.release;
end startRead;

public endRead ()
    -- A reader calls this operation after it has finished reading
    readerSemaphore.acquire;
    Decrement numberOfReaders;
    if numberOfReaders = 0 then readWriteSemaphore.release ();
    readerSemaphore.release;
end endRead;

public startWrite ()
    -- A writer calls this operation before it starts to write
    writerWaitingSemaphore.acquire();
    readWriteSemaphore.acquire ();
    writerWaitingSemaphore.release();
end startRead;

public endWrite ()
```

```
       -- A writer calls this operation after it has finished writing
          readWriteSemaphore.release ();
   end endWrite;
   end ReadWrite;
```

No change is required in the design of the Analog Sensor Repository class to take advantage of this variant.

14.4 DESIGNING CONNECTORS FOR INTER-TASK COMMUNICATION

As described in Chapter 3, a multitasking kernel can provide services for inter-task communication and synchronization. Some concurrent programming languages, such as Ada and Java, also provide mechanisms for inter-task communication and synchronization. An alternative approach is to use a **connector** that encapsulate the details of inter-task communication and synchronization.

This section describes the design of three connectors to handle asynchronous message communication, synchronous message communication without reply, and synchronous message communication with reply. Each connector is designed as a monitor, which combines the concepts of information hiding and task synchronization as described in the previous section. These monitors can be used on a single processor system or a multiprocessor system with shared memory.

Each connector is depicted with the stereotypes «connector» «sharedDataCom-Resource» «sharedMutualExclusionResource» because it stores data (the messages) that are communicated from the sender task to the receiver task and ensures mutually exclusive access to the tasks so that they can store and remove messages.

14.4.1 Design of Message Queue Connector

A **message queue connector** is used to encapsulate the communication mechanism for *asynchronous message communication*. The connector is designed as a monitor that encapsulates a message queue, usually implemented as a linked list. The connector provides synchronized operations to send a message, which is called by a producer task, and receive a message, which is called by a consumer task (see Figure 14.6). Figure 14.6a depicts asynchronous message communication between producer and consumer tasks. Figure 14.6b depicts the Producer and Consumer tasks interacting via a Message Queue connector. Figure 14.6c depicts the specification of the Message Queue connector with the public send and receive operations and the encapsulated data structure for the message queue.

To send a message, the producer calls the send operation and is suspended if the queue is full ($messageCount = maxCount$). The producer is reactivated when a slot becomes available to accept the message. After adding the message to the queue, the producer continues executing and might send additional messages. To receive a message, the consumer calls the receive operation and is suspended if the message queue is empty ($messageCount = 0$). When a new message arrives, the consumer is activated and given the message. The consumer is not suspended if there is a message on the queue. It is assumed that there can be several producers and one consumer. The Pseudocode for the connector is described next.

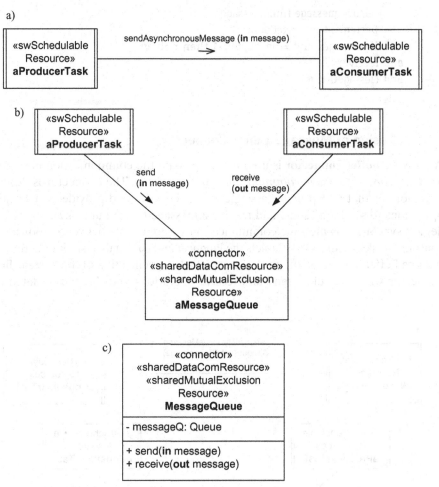

Figure 14.6. Design of a message queue connector.

```
monitor MessageQueue
    -- Encapsulate message queue that holds max of maxCount messages
    -- Monitor operations are executed mutually exclusively;
private messageQ : Queue;
private maxCount : Integer;
private messageCount : Integer = 0;

public send (in message)
    while messageCount = maxCount do wait;
    place message in messageQ;
    Increment messageCount;
    if messageCount = 1 then notify;
end send;

public receive (out message)
    while messageCount = 0 do wait;
```

```
        remove message from messageQ;
        Decrement messageCount;
        if messageCount = maxCount-1 then notify;
    end receive;
    end MessageQueue;
```

14.4.2 Design of Message Buffer Connector

A **message buffer connector** is used to encapsulate the communication mechanism for *synchronous message communication without reply*. The connector is designed as a monitor that encapsulates a single message buffer and provides synchronized operations to send a message and receive a message (see Figure 14.7). Figure 14.7a depicts synchronous message communication without reply between producer and consumer tasks. Figure 14.7b depicts the Producer and Consumer tasks interacting via a Message Buffer connector. Figure 14.7c depicts the specification of the Message Buffer connector with the public send and receive operations and the encapsulated data

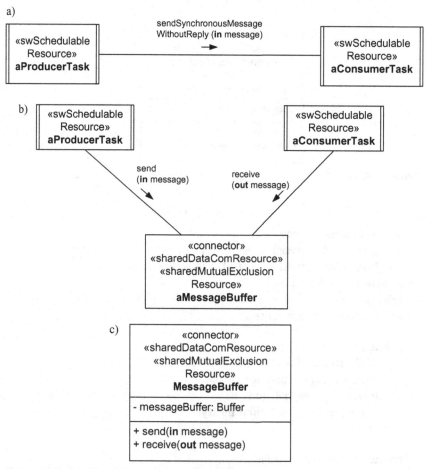

Figure 14.7. Design of a message buffer connector.

structure for the message buffer. The producer task calls the send operation and the consumer task calls the receive operation in Figure 14.7b.

To send a message, the producer calls the send operation. After it has written the message into the buffer, the producer is suspended until the consumer receives the message. The consumer calls the receive operation and is suspended if the message buffer is empty. It is assumed that there is only one producer and one consumer. The Pseudocode for the connector is described next.

```
monitor MessageBuffer
    -- Encapsulate a message buffer that holds at most one message.
    -- Monitor operations are executed mutually exclusively
private messageBuffer : Buffer;
private messageBufferFull : Boolean = false;

public send (in message)
    place message in messageBuffer;
    messageBufferFull := true;
    notify;
    while messageBufferFull = true do wait;
end send;

public receive (out message)
    while messageBufferFull = false do wait;
    remove message from messageBuffer;
    messageBufferFull := false;
    notify;
end receive;
end MessageBuffer;
```

14.4.3 Design of Message Buffer and Response Connector

A **message buffer and response connector** is used to encapsulate the communication mechanism for *synchronous message communication with reply*. The connector is designed as a monitor that encapsulates a single message buffer and a single response buffer. It provides synchronized operations to send a message, receive a message, and send a reply (see Figure 14.8). Figure 14.8a depicts synchronous message communication with reply between producer and consumer tasks. Figure 14.8b depicts the Producer and Consumer tasks interacting via a Message Buffer & Response connector. Figure 14.8c depicts the specification of the connector with the public send, receive, and reply operations and the encapsulated data structures for the message and response buffers.

The producer calls the send message operation (S1 in Figure 14.8b). After it has written the message into the message buffer, the producer is suspended until the response is received from the consumer. The consumer calls the receive message operation (R1) and is suspended if the message buffer is empty. When a message is available, the consumer processes the message, prepares the response, and calls

a)

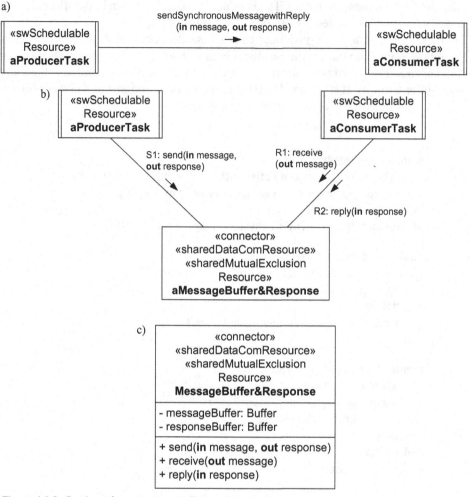

Figure 14.8. Design of a message buffer and response connector.

the reply operation (R2) to place the response in the response buffer. It is assumed that there is only one producer and one consumer. The Pseudocode for the connector is described next.

```
monitor MessageBuffer&Response
    -- Encapsulates a message buffer that holds at most one message
    -- and a response buffer that holds at most one response.
    -- Monitor operations are executed mutually exclusively.
private messageBuffer : Buffer;
private responseBuffer : Buffer;
private messageBufferFull : Boolean = false;
private responseBufferFull : Boolean = false;

public send (in message, out response)
    place message in messageBuffer;
```

```
        messageBufferFull := true;
        notify;
        while responseBufferFull = false do wait;
        remove response from responseBuffer;
        responseBufferFull := false;
    end send;

    public receive (out message)
        while messageBufferFull = false do wait;
        remove message from messageBuffer;
        messageBufferFull := false;
    end receive;

    public reply (in response)
        Place response in responseBuffer;
        responseBufferFull := true;
        notify;
    end reply;
    end MessageBuffer&Response;
```

14.4.4 Design of Cooperating Tasks Using Connectors

Next, consider the design of a group of cooperating tasks that communicate by means of connector objects. This is illustrated by means of an example taken from the Microwave Oven Control System case study in which four producer tasks send asynchronous messages to the Microwave Oven Control consumer task, as depicted in Figure 14.9a. In addition, Microwave Oven Control is a producer task that sends asynchronous messages to the Oven Timer consumer task. Thus, the asynchronous communication between Microwave Oven Control and Oven Timer is bidirectional.

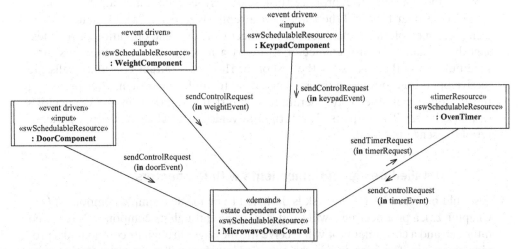

Figure 14.9a. Example of cooperating tasks using asynchronous message communication and bidirectional asynchronous message communication.

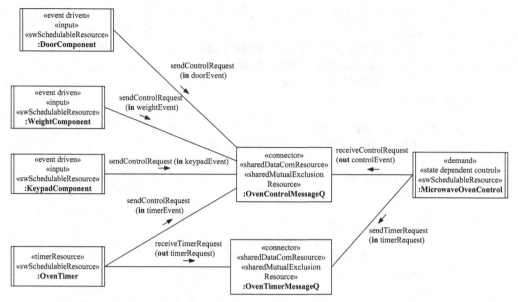

Figure 14.9b. Example of cooperating tasks using message queue connectors.

The connectors for the Microwave Oven Control task are depicted on Figure 14.9b. The Oven Control Message Q encapsulates the queue of incoming messages to the Microwave Oven Control consumer task, for which there are four producers. In each case, a producer calls the sendControlRequest operation of the message queue connector object to insert a message in the connector queue, and the consumer calls the receiveControlRequest operation to remove a message from the queue. There is also an Oven Timer Message Q message queue connector object to encapsulate the asynchronous communication between the Microwave Oven Control producer task and the Oven Timer consumer task, in which the producer calls the sendTimerRequest operation of the connector and the consumer calls the receiveTimerRequest operation.

An example of a message buffer and response connector is given in Figure 14.10, in which the Vehicle Control producer task sends a synchronous message to the Motor Output consumer task and then waits for a reply (Figure 14.10a). In Figure 14.10b using a connector, the Vehicle Control producer calls the send operation of the message buffer and response connector to insert a message in the connector's message buffer and then waits for the response. The Motor Output consumer calls the receive operation to remove the message from the buffer and then, after preparing the response, calls the reply operation to insert the response in the connector's response buffer. The response is returned to Vehicle Control as the output parameter of the send operation.

14.4.5 Detailed Design of Components with Connectors

It should be noted that if the task is designed to be inside a simple component (see Chapter 12), a producer task will send a message through its component's required interface and a consumer task will receive the message through its component's provided interface. The operation in the provided interface will place the incoming message in a message buffer (for synchronous communication) or a message queue (for asynchronous communication) from which the consumer task removes the message.

a)

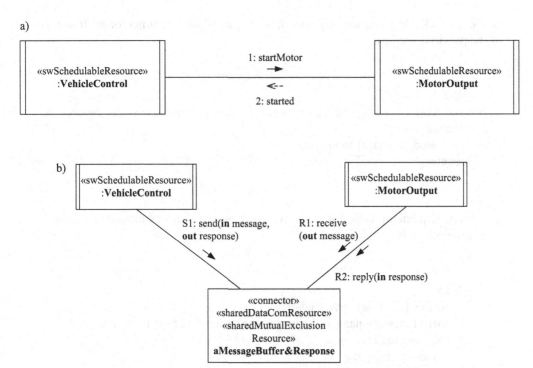

Figure 14.10. Example of synchronous message communication using a message buffer and response connector.

With this approach, the connector is designed to be inside the consumer component. As before, the operations of the connector are designed to have synchronized access to the encapsulated buffer or queue. Examples of this approach are given in the Microwave Oven case study in Chapter 19.

14.5 TASK EVENT SEQUENCING LOGIC

During the detailed software design, the task event sequencing logic of the Task Behavior Specification, as described in Chapter 13, is specified. The task's **event sequencing logic** describes how the task responds to each of its message or event inputs – in particular, what output is generated as a result of each input. The event sequencing logic is described informally in Pseudocode or in Precise English and may be supplemented by a diagram – for example, to depict a state machine diagram or state transition table for a control task.

For a composite task with several nested objects, a nested coordinator object receives the task's incoming messages and then invokes operations provided by other nested objects. In such cases, the coordinator object executes the task's event sequencing logic.

14.5.1 Example of Event Sequencing Logic for Sender and Receiver Tasks

The event sequencing logic for a sender task, which sends messages to other tasks, is given next. The exact form of the send (message) will depend on whether this is a service provided by the operating system or whether it uses a connector, as described in the previous section.

```
loop
      Prepare message containing message name (type) and optional message
parameters;
      send (message) to receiver;
endloop;
```

The event sequencing logic for a receiver task, which receives incoming messages from other tasks, is

```
loop
    receive (message) from sender;
    Extract message name and any message parameters from message
    case message of
       message type 1:
          objectA.operationX (optional parameters);
          ....
       message type 2:
          objectB.operationY (optional parameters);
          .....
       endcase;
    endloop;
```

If a connector called aConnector is used, the send message becomes

```
    aConnector.send (message)
```

and the receive message becomes

```
    aConnector.receive (message)
```

Templates in Pseudocode for the task event sequencing logic for the different kinds of tasks described in Chapter 13 are given in Appendix C. Examples of task event sequencing logic for task communication and synchronization are given next, and in the Microwave Oven Control case study described in Chapter 19.

Figure 14.11. Example of event synchronization between Robot Tasks.

14.6 DETAILED REAL-TIME SOFTWARE DESIGN IN ROBOT AND VISION SYSTEMS

Consider the following detailed software design examples of task communication and synchronization in real-time robot and vision systems. Each robot and vision system is designed as a real-time embedded system. In each robot system, a task controls a robot arm that performs factory operations such as picking up a part, placing down a part, or welding two parts together. Each vision system has a task that analyzes images of factory parts and extracts important properties, such as the type and location of the part. In these examples, the interaction between tasks is explained in detail by providing the task event sequencing logic for each task's behavior.

14.6.1 Example of Event Synchronization between Robot Tasks

The first example is of event synchronization (see Section 13.9.4) between two robot tasks, in which a pick-and-place robot brings a part to the work location so that a drilling robot can drill four holes in the part. On completion of the drilling operation, the pick-and-place robot moves the part away.

Several synchronization problems need to be solved. First, there is a collision zone where the pick-and-place and drilling robot arms could potentially collide. Second, the pick-and-place robot must deposit the part before the drilling robot can start drilling the holes. Third, the drilling robot must finish drilling before the pick-and-place robot can remove the part. The solution is to use event synchronization, as described next.

The pick-and-place robot moves the part to the work location, moves out of the collision zone, and then signals the event part Ready, as depicted in Figure 14.11. This awakens the drilling robot, which moves to the work location and drills the holes. After completing the drilling operation, it moves out of the collision zone and then signals a second event, part Completed, which the pick-and-place robot is waiting to receive. After being awakened, the pick-and-place robot removes the part. Each robot task executes a loop, because the robots repetitively perform their operations, as described in the task event sequencing logic below.

Pick & Place Robot:

```
loop
    while workAvailable do
    Pick up part;
    Move part to work location;
    Release part;
```

```
        Move to safe position;
        signal (partReady);
        wait (partCompleted);
        Pick up part;
        Remove part from work location;
        Place part;
        end while;
    end loop;
```

Drilling Robot:

```
    loop
        while workAvailable do
        wait (partReady);
        Move to work location;
        Drill four holes in part;
        Move to safe position;
        signal (partCompleted);
        end while;
    end loop;
```

14.6.2 Example of Message Communication between Vision and Robot Tasks

Consider next an example of task communication, in particular synchronous message communication with reply (see Section 13.9.2), between a vision task and a robot task. The vision task has to inform the robot of the type of part coming down a conveyor, for example, whether the car body frame is a sedan or station wagon. The robot has a different welding program for each car body type. In addition, the vision task has to send the robot information about the location and orientation of a part on a conveyor. Usually this information is sent as an offset (i.e., relative position) from a point known to both systems. The vision task sends the robot a synchronous message, the carIDMessage, which contains the carModelID and carBodyOffset, and then waits for a reply from the robot. The robot indicates that it has completed the welding operation by sending the doneReply. This message exchange is illustrated in Figure 14.12.

Figure 14.12. Example of message communication between Vision and Robot Tasks.

In addition, the following event synchronization is needed. Initially, a sensor signals the external event carArrived to notify the vision task. Finally, the vision task signals the actuator moveCar, which results in the taking away of the car by the conveyor. The task event sequencing logic is described next.

Vision Task:

```
loop
    while workAvailable do
    wait (carArrived) from arrival sensor;
    Take image of car body;
    Identify the model of car;
    Determine location and orientation of car body;
    send carIdMessage (carModelId, carBodyOffset) to Robot Task;
    wait for reply from Robot Task;
    signal (moveCar) to conveyor actuator;
    end while;
end loop;
```

Robot Task:

```
loop
    while
    workAvailable do
    wait for message from Vision Task;
    receive carIDMessage (carModelId, carBodyOffset);
    Select welding program for carModelId;
    Execute welding program using carBodyOffset for car position;
    send (doneReply) to Vision Task;
    end while;
end loop;
```

14.7 IMPLEMENTING CONCURRENT TASKS IN JAVA

In Java, tasks are implemented as threads. The simplest way to design a thread class in Java is to inherit from the Java Thread class, which has one method, called *run*. The new thread class must then implement the run method, which, when invoked, will execute independently with its own thread of control. In the following example, the Railroad Crossing Control class is designed to be a thread. The body of the thread is contained in the run method. Typically, the body of the task is a loop, in which the task would wait for either an external event (from an external device or timer) or a message from a producer task.

```
public class RailroadCrossingControl extendsThread{}
public void run ()
while (true) {//task body/}
```

More information about implementing tasks in Java is given in textbooks on concurrency and multithreading in Java (Carver 2006, Goetz 2006) and real-time programming in Java (Bruno and Bollella 2009, Wellings 2004).

In Java, it is possible for an object to encapsulate a thread but also to have operations (methods in Java) that may be invoked by other threads. These operations do not necessarily need to be synchronized with the internal thread. In this case, the object has both active and passive characteristics. In this book, however, we will maintain a distinction between active and passive objects. Thus, an object is defined as active or passive, but not both.

14.8 SUMMARY

After structuring the system into tasks in Chapter 13, this chapter has described the detailed software design. In this step, the internals of composite tasks that contain nested objects are designed, detailed task synchronization issues are addressed using semaphores and monitors, connector classes are designed that encapsulate the details of inter-task communication, and each task's internal event sequencing logic is defined. Several examples were given in Pseudocode of the detailed design of task synchronization mechanisms, connector classes for inter-task communication, and task event sequencing logic. Detailed software design examples were given of task communication and synchronization in real-time robot and vision systems. Templates in Pseudocode for the task event sequencing logic for the different kinds of tasks are given in Appendix C. Finally, a brief overview was given of implementing concurrent tasks in Java using threads.

15

Designing Real-Time Software Product Line Architectures

A **software product line** (SPL) consists of a family of software systems that have some common functionality and some variable functionality (Parnas 1979, Clements 2002, Weiss 1999). Software product line engineering involves developing the requirements, architecture, and component implementations for a family of systems, from which products (family members) are derived and configured. The problems of developing individual software systems are scaled upward when developing software product lines because of the increased complexity due to variability management. This chapter gives an overview of designing software product line architectures using the PLUS (Product Line UML-based Software engineering) method. The topic is covered in considerable detail in the author's book on this topic (Gomaa 2005a).

SPL technology is particularly valuable for developing real-time embedded product families, in which some external devices, such as sensors and actuators, may be optional (such as light or turntable in a microwave oven SPL) in some family members or there may be variants (one-level on/off heating element or multi-level high/medium/low/off heating element) that are used by different family members. To manage the variability of SPL architectures and implementations necessitates developing feature models to determine *what* the variability is and developing variable software architectures consisting of kernel, optional, and variant components to determine *how* the variability is mapped to the design.

As with single systems, a better understanding of a software product line can be obtained by considering the multiple views, such as requirements models, static models, and dynamic models of the product line. A visual modeling language such as UML helps in developing, understanding, and communicating the different views. A key view in the multiple views of a software product line is the feature modeling view. The feature model is crucial for managing variability and product derivation as it describes the product line requirements in terms of commonality and variability, as well as defining the product line dependencies. Furthermore, it is necessary to have a development approach that promotes software evolution, such that original development and subsequent maintenance are both treated using feature-driven evolution.

Section 15.1 describes the software process model for SPL Engineering. Section 15.2 presents the problem description for the SPL example used in this chapter.

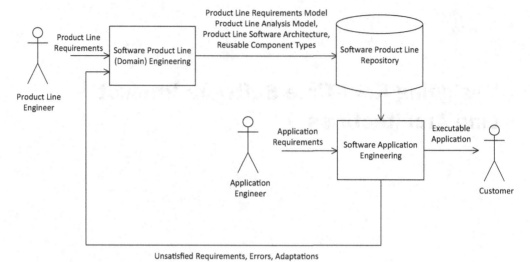

Figure 15.1. Software process model for software product line engineering.

Section 15.3 describes requirements modeling for SPLs, in particular use case modeling and feature modeling for SPLs. Section 15.4 describes analysis modeling for SPLs, in particular how variability is handled in static models, dynamic interaction models, and dynamic state machine models for SPLs. Section 15.5 describes how variability is addressed in design models of SPLs.

15.1 SOFTWARE PRODUCT LINE ENGINEERING

The software process model for SPL Engineering is a highly iterative software process that eliminates the traditional distinction between software development and maintenance. Furthermore, because new software systems are outgrowths of existing ones, the process takes a software product line perspective; it consists of two main processes (see Figure 15.1):

a) **Software Product Line Engineering** (also referred to as **Domain Engineering**). A product line multiple-view model, which addresses the multiple views of a software product line, is developed. The product line requirements model, product line analysis model, product line architecture, and reusable component types (referred to as core assets in Clements [2002]) are developed and stored in the product line repository.

b) **Software Application Engineering**. A software application is an individual product line member derived from the software product line models and architecture in the SPL repository. The user selects the required features for the individual product line member. Given the features, the product line models and architecture are adapted and tailored to derive the application models and architecture. The architecture determines which of the reusable component types are needed for deriving and configuring the executable application.

15.2 PROBLEM DESCRIPTION OF MICROWAVE OVEN SPL

The manufacturer of the microwave oven product line is an original equipment manufacturer with an international market. The microwave oven will form the basis of this product line, which will offer options from basic to top-of-the-line.

The basic microwave oven system has input buttons for selecting **Cooking Time**, **Start**, and **Cancel**, as well as a numeric keypad. It also has a display to show the cooking time left. In addition, the oven has a microwave heating element for cooking the food, a door sensor to sense when the door is open, and a weight sensor to detect if there is an object in the oven.

Options available for more advanced ovens are a beeper to indicate when cooking is finished, a light that is switched on when the door is open and when food is being cooked, and a turntable that turns during cooking. The microwave oven displays messages to the user such as prompts and warning messages. Because the oven is to be sold around the world, it must be able to vary the display language. The default language is English, but other possible languages are French, Spanish, German, and Italian. The basic oven has a one-line display; more-advanced ovens can have multi-line displays. Other options include a time-of-day clock, which needs the multi-line display option.

The top-of-the-line oven has a recipe cooking feature, which needs an analog weight sensor in place of the basic Boolean weight sensor, the multi-line display feature, and a multi-power level feature (high, medium, low) in place of the basic on/off power feature. Vendors can configure their microwave oven systems of choice from a wealth of optional and alternative features, although feature dependency constraints must be obeyed.

15.3 REQUIREMENTS MODELING FOR SOFTWARE PRODUCT LINES

For single systems, use case modeling (see Chapter 6) is the primary vehicle for describing software functional requirements. For software product lines, feature modeling is an additional important part of requirements modeling. The strength of feature modeling is in differentiating between the functionality provided by the different family members of the product line in terms of common functionality, optional functionality, and alternative functionality.

15.3.1 Use Case Modeling for Software Product Lines

The functional requirements of a system are defined in terms of use cases and actors. For a single system, all use cases are required. In a software product line, only some of the use cases, which are referred to as kernel use cases, are required by all members of the family. Other use cases are optional, in that they are required by some but not all members of the family. Some use cases may be alternative; that is, different versions of the use case are required by different members of the family. In UML, the use cases are labeled with the stereotype «kernel», «optional», or «alternative» (Gomaa 2005a). In addition, variability can be incorporated into a use case by means of variation points, which specify where in the use case description variability can be introduced (Jacobson 1997, Webber and Gomaa 2004, Gomaa 2005a).

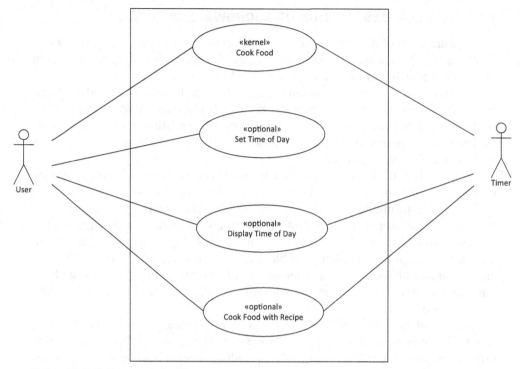

Figure 15.2. Software product line use cases.

Analyzing the commonality and variability in the functionality of the microwave oven SPL indicates that commonality can be captured by one kernel use case, Cook Food, which all members of the product line must provide. Some of the variability in the product line can be captured by variation points in the kernel use case, reflecting small variations. However, the large variations need to be addressed by different use cases, which are the three optional use cases Set Time of Day, Display Time of Day, and Cook Food with Recipe. Only some members of the product line realize these use cases. The use case model is depicted on the use case diagram in Figure 15.2.

Variation points are provided for both the kernel and optional use cases. One variation point concerns the display prompt language. Since the Microwave System family members will be deployed in different countries, the appropriate prompt language can be selected for a given microwave oven product. The default language is English, with alternative languages being French, Spanish, Italian, and German. An example of a variation point is for all steps that involve displaying information to the customer in the Cook Food use case. *Mandatory alternative* means that a selection among the alternative choices must be made.

> **Variation point** in Cook Food use case:
> **Name**: Display Language.
> **Type of functionality**: Mandatory alternative.
> **Use case step number(s)**: 3, 8.
> **Description of functionality**: There is a choice of language for displaying messages. The default is English. Alternative mutually exclusive languages are French, Spanish, Italian, and German.

15.3.2 Feature Modeling

Feature modeling is an important modeling view for product line engineering (Kang et al. 1990), as it addresses SPL variability. Features are analyzed and categorized as common features (must be supported in all product line members), optional features (only required in some product line members), alternative features (a choice of feature is available), and prerequisite features (dependent on other features). There may also be dependencies among features, such as mutually exclusive features. The emphasis in feature modeling is capturing the product line variability, as given by optional and alternative features, since these features differentiate one member of the product family from the others.

Features are used widely in product line engineering but are not typically used in UML. In order to effectively model product lines, it is necessary to incorporate feature modeling concepts into UML. Features are incorporated into UML in the PLUS method using the meta-class concept, in which features are modeled using the UML static modeling notation and given stereotypes to differentiate between «common feature», «optional feature», and «alternative feature» (Gomaa 2005a). Feature dependencies are depicted as associations with the name *requires*; for example, the TOD Clock feature *requires* the Multi-Line Display feature. Furthermore, feature groups, which place a constraint on how certain features can be selected for a product line member, such as mutually exclusive features, are also modeled using meta-classes and given stereotypes, such as «zero-or-one-of feature group» or «exactly-one-of feature group» (Gomaa 2005a). A feature group is modeled as an aggregation of features, since a feature *is part of* a feature group.

The common features identify the common functionality in the SPL, as specified by the kernel use case; the optional and alternative features represent the variability in the product line as specified by the optional use cases and the variation points. The common feature in the Microwave SPL is the Microwave Oven Kernel, which corresponds to the core functionality described in the Cook Food kernel use case.

The variable features correspond to optional or alternative functional requirements, which are determined from the use case model. A number of features are determined from the kernel use case, Cook Food. Some of these (e.g., Light, Turntable, and Beeper) are optional features that can be added to the kernel functionality. Two features correspond to the optional use cases. The TOD Clock feature corresponds to a use case package containing the Set Time of Day and Display Time of Day use cases. The Recipe feature corresponds to the Cook Food with Recipe use case. The feature model for the Microwave Oven is depicted in Figure 15.3.

Some features have prerequisite features, meaning that for the feature to be selected, the prerequisite feature must also be selected. Some features are alternative features; that is, one out of a group of alternatives must be chosen. If an alternative is not chosen, then the default is used. Feature groups, such as Display Unit and Heating Element, use alternative features to specify alternative I/O devices (both the hardware and software support) that can be chosen for the oven display and oven heating unit respectively.

In single systems, use cases are used to determine the functional requirements of a system; they can also serve this purpose in product families. Griss (1998) has pointed out that the goal of the use case analysis is to get a good understanding of the functional requirements, whereas the goal of feature analysis is to enable reuse.

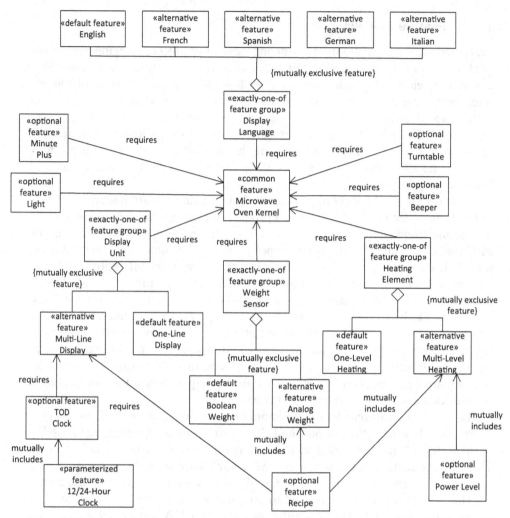

Figure 15.3. Features and feature groups in Microwave Oven feature model.

Use cases and features complement each other. Thus, optional and alternative use cases are mapped to optional and alternative features respectively, while use cases variation points are also mapped to features (Gomaa 2005a).

The relationship between use cases and features can be explicitly depicted in a feature/use case relationship table, as shown in Table 15.1. For each feature, the use case it relates to is depicted. In the case of a feature derived from a variation point, the variation point name is listed.

Three features correspond to use cases, and the remaining features correspond to variation points in the use cases. For example, Microwave Oven Kernel is a common feature determined from the kernel use case, Cook Food. Light is an optional feature determined from the Cook Food use case; however, it represents a use case variation point also called Light. TOD Clock is an optional feature that corresponds to the two optional time-of-day use cases. Language is an exactly-one-of feature group, which corresponds to the Language variation point in the use case model. This feature group

Table 15.1. Feature/Use Case Relationship Table for Microwave Oven SPL

Feature Name	Feature Category	Use Case Name	Use Case Category/ Variation Point (vp)	Variation Point Name
Microwave Oven Kernel	common	Cook Food	kernel	
Light	optional	Cook Food	vp	Light
Turntable	optional	Cook Food	vp	Turntable
Beeper	optional	Cook Food	vp	Beeper
Minute Plus	optional	Cook Food	vp	Minute Plus
One-Line Display	default	Cook Food	vp	Display Unit
Multi-Line Display	alternative	Cook Food	vp	Display Unit
English	default	Cook Food	vp	Display Language
French	alternative	Cook Food	vp	Display Language
Spanish	alternative	Cook Food	vp	Display Language
German	alternative	Cook Food	vp	Display Language
Italian	alternative	Cook Food	vp	Display Language
Boolean Weight	default	Cook Food	vp	Weight Sensor
Analog Weight	alternative	Cook Food	vp	Weight Sensor
One-Level Heating	default	Cook Food	vp	Heating Element
Multi-Level Heating	alternative	Cook Food	vp	Heating Element
Power Level	optional	Cook Food	vp	Power Level
TOD Clock	optional	Set Time of Day	optional	
		Display Time of Day	optional	
12/24 Hour Clock	parameterized	Set Time of Day	vp	12/24 Hour Clock
		Display Time of Day		
Recipe	optional	Cook Food with Recipe	optional	

consists of the default feature English and the alternative features of Spanish, French, Italian, or German.

15.4. ANALYSIS MODELING FOR SOFTWARE PRODUCT LINES

As with single systems, analysis modeling consists of both static and dynamic modeling. However, both modeling approaches need to address modeling SPL variability.

15.4.1 Static Modeling for Software Product Lines

In single systems, a class is categorized by the role it plays. Application classes are classified according to their role in the application using stereotypes, such as «entity», «control», and «boundary» (see Chapter 8). In modeling software product lines, each class can be categorized according to its reuse characteristic using the stereotypes «kernel», «optional», and «variant». In UML, a modeling element can be described with more than one stereotype. Thus, one stereotype can be used to represent the

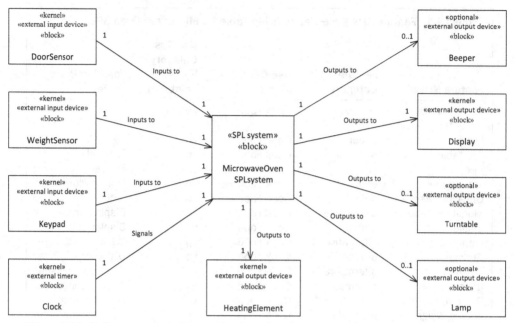

Figure 15.4. Software context diagram for the microwave oven software product line.

reuse characteristic, while a different stereotype is used to represent the role of the modeling element. The role of a class and the reuse characteristic are orthogonal.

After developing the use case and feature models, the next step is to develop a structural model of the problem domain (see Chapter 5), from which the product line software context diagram is developed. This diagram defines the boundary between a product line system (i.e., any member of the product line) and the external environment (i.e., the external entities (depicted using SysML blocks) to which members of the product line have to interface). The product line software context model is depicted on a block definition diagram (Figure 15.4) and shows the multiplicity of the associations between the external blocks and the product line system, which is depicted as one aggregate block.

Each external block is depicted with three stereotypes: The first stereotype represents the reuse category, whether the external block is a kernel or optional block in the product line. The second stereotype represents the role of the external block; for example, Door Sensor is an external input device. The third stereotype is the SysML notation for «block», as described in Chapter 5. In this case study, Door Sensor, Weight Sensor, and Keypad are all external input devices; they are also kernel blocks. Heating Element and Display are external output devices that are also kernel. Clock is an external timer that is kernel. However, Beeper, Turntable, and Lamp are external output devices that are optional. Kernel external blocks have a one-to-one association with the product line system; optional external blocks have a zero-to-one association with the product line system.

15.4.2 Dynamic Interaction Modeling for Software Product Lines

Dynamic interaction modeling for software product lines uses an iterative strategy called **evolutionary dynamic analysis** to help determine the dynamic impact of each

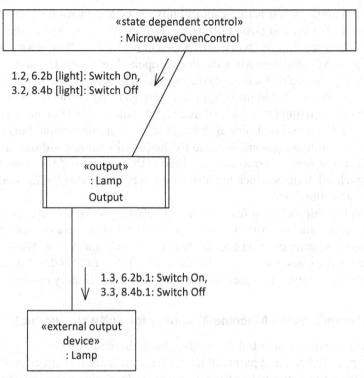

Figure 15.5. Evolutionary dynamic analysis of Light feature on Cook Food communication diagram.

feature on the software architecture. This results in new components being added or existing components having to be adapted. The **kernel system** is a minimal member of the product line. In some product lines, the kernel system consists of only the kernel objects. For other product lines, some default objects may be needed in addition to the kernel objects. The kernel system is developed by considering the kernel use cases, which are required by every member for the product line. For each kernel use case, an interaction diagram is developed depicting the objects needed to realize the use case. The kernel system consists of the integration of all these objects and the classes from which they are instantiated.

The **software product line evolution approach** starts with the kernel system and considers the impact of optional and/or alternative features (Gomaa 2005a). This results in the addition of optional or variant components to the product line architecture. This analysis is done by considering the variable (optional and alternative) use cases, as well as any variation points in the kernel or variable use cases. For each optional or alternative use case, an interaction diagram is developed consisting of new optional or variant objects – the variant objects are kernel or optional objects that are impacted by the variable scenarios and must therefore be adapted.

An example of evolutionary dynamic analysis for the Microwave SPL is given in Figure 15.5, which depicts the impact of the Light feature on the use case–based communication diagram for Cook Food. The impact of the Light feature is that the lamp is switched on whenever the door is opened or whenever food is cooking. The lamp is switched off whenever the door is closed or whenever cooking is stopped. The first impact is the need for the Lamp external output device and the Lamp Output object, as shown in Figure 15.5. It is the responsibility of the Microwave Oven Control object to send the Switch On and Switch Off messages (which correspond to state machine actions) to the Lamp Output object, as depicted in Figure 15.5. Microwave Oven Control sends the Switch On message when the door is opened (message 1.2) and when cooking is started (message 6.2b). It sends the Switch Off message when the door is closed (message 3.2) and when cooking is stopped (message 8.4b). Lamp Output in turn sends the Switch On command (messages 1.3 and 6.2b.1,) and Switch Off command (3.3 and 8.4b.1) to the Lamp external output device. On the communication diagram, Switch On and Switch Off messages are guarded by the [light] feature condition. The impact on the Microwave Oven Control state machine is the addition of the optional Switch On and Switch Off actions, which are also guarded by the [light] feature condition, as described in Section 15.5.

The relationship between features and the classes can be depicted on a feature/class table, which shows for each feature the classes that realize the feature, as well as the class reuse category (kernel, optional, or variant) and, in the case of a parameterized class, the class parameter. This table (see Table 15.2) is developed after the dynamic impact analysis has been carried out using evolutionary dynamic analysis.

15.4.3 Dynamic State Machine Modeling for Software Product Lines

When components are adapted for product lines, there are two main approaches to consider, specialization and parameterization. Specialization is effective when there are a relatively small number of changes to be made, so that the number of specialized classes is manageable. However, in product lines, there can be a large degree of variability. Consider the key issue for real-time product lines of variability in state machines, which can be handled either by using parameterized state machines or specialized state machines. Depending on whether the product line uses a centralized or decentralized approach, it is likely that there will be several different state dependent control components, each modeled by its own state machine. The following discussion relates to variability within a given state dependent component.

To capture state machine variability, it is necessary to specify optional states, events and transitions, and actions. A further decision that needs to be made is whether to use state machine inheritance or parameterization. The problem with using inheritance is that a different state machine is needed to model each alternative or optional feature, or feature combination, which rapidly leads to a combinatorial explosion of inherited state machines. For example, with only three features that could impact the state machine, there would be eight possible feature and feature combinations, resulting in eight variant state machines. With ten features, there would be over 1,000 variant state machines. However, ten features can be easily modeled on a parameterized state machine as ten feature-dependent transitions, states, or actions.

It is often more effective to design a parameterized state machine, in which there are feature-dependent states, events, and transitions. Optional transitions are specified by having an event qualified by a Boolean feature condition, which guards entry into the state. Optional actions are also guarded by a Boolean feature condition, which is set to True if the feature is selected and False if the feature is not selected for a given SPL member.

Table 15.2. Feature/Class Dependency Table for Microwave Oven SPL

Feature Name	Feature Category	Class Name	Class Category	Class Parameter
Microwave Oven Kernel	common	Door Sensor Interface	kernel	
		Weight Sensor Interface	kernel-abstract-vp	
		Keypad Interface	kernel-param-vp	
		Heating Element Interface	kernel-abstract-vp	
		Display Interface	kernel-abstract-vp	
		Microwave Oven Control	kernel-param-vp	
		Oven Timer	kernel-param-vp	
		Oven Data	kernel-param-vp	
		Display Prompts	kernel-abstract-vp	
Light	optional	Lamp Interface	optional	
		Microwave Oven Control	kernel-param-vp	light : Boolean
Turntable	optional	Turntable Interface	optional	
		Microwave Oven Control	kernel-param-vp	turntable : Boolean
Beeper	optional	Beeper Interface	optional	
		Microwave Oven Control	kernel-param-vp	beeper : Boolean
Minute Plus	optional	Keypad Interface	kernel-param-vp	minuteplus : Boolean
		Microwave Oven Control	kernel-param-vp	minuteplus : Boolean
		Oven Timer	kernel-param-vp	minuteplus : Boolean
		Oven Data	kernel-param-vp	minuteplus : Boolean
One-Line Display	default	One-Line Display Interface	default	
Multi-Line Display	alternative	Multi-Line Display Interface	variant	
English	default	English Display Prompts	default	
French	alternative	French Display Prompts	variant	
Spanish	alternative	Spanish Display Prompts	variant	
German	alternative	German Display Prompts	variant	
Italian	alternative	Italian Display Prompts	variant	
Boolean Weight	default	Boolean Weight Sensor Interface	default	
Analog Weight	alternative	Analog Weight Sensor Interface	variant	
		Oven Data	kernel-param-vp	itemWeight : Real
One-Level Heating	default	One-Level Heating Element Interface	default	
Multi-Level Heating	alternative	Multi-Level Heating Element Interface	variant	
		Microwave Oven Control	kernel-param-vp	multi-levelHeating : Boolean
		Oven Data	kernel-param-vp	selectedPowerLevel : Integer
Power Level	optional	Keypad Interface	kernel-param-VP	powerLevel : Boolean
		Microwave Oven Control	kernel-param-VP	powerLevel : Boolean
TOD Clock	optional	TOD Timer	optional	
		Keypad Interface	kernel-param-VP	TODClock : Boolean
		Microwave Oven Control	kernel-param-VP	TODClock : Boolean
		Oven Data	kernel-param-VP	TODvalue : Real
12/24 Hour Clock	parameter-ized	Oven Data	kernel-param-vp	TODmaxHour : Integer
Recipe	optional	Recipes	optional	
		Recipe	optional	
		Keypad Interface	kernel-param-vp	recipe : Boolean
		Microwave Oven Control	kernel-param-vp	recipe : Boolean
		Oven Data	kernel-param-vp	selectedRecipe : Integer
		Oven Timer	kernel-param-vp	recipe : Boolean

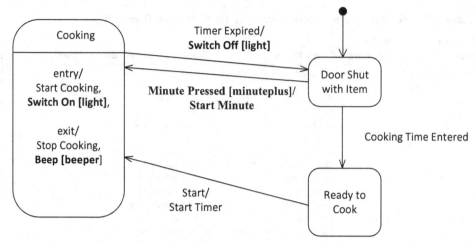

Figure 15.6. Feature-dependent transitions and actions.

Examples of feature-dependent events and actions are given for an extract from a Microwave Oven product line. Minute Plus is an optional microwave oven feature that cooks food for a minute. In the state machine, Minute Pressed is a feature-dependent transition guarded by the feature condition minuteplus in Figure 15.6, which is True if the feature is selected. There are feature-dependent actions, such as Switch On and Switch Off in Figure 15.6, which are only enabled if the light feature condition is True, and the Beep action, which is only enabled if the beeper feature condition is True. Thus, the feature condition is True if the optional feature is selected for a given product line member, and false if the feature is not selected. The impact of feature interactions can be modeled very precisely using state machines through the introduction of alternative states or transitions. Designing parameterized state machines is often more manageable than designing specialized state machines.

15.5 DESIGN MODELING FOR SOFTWARE PRODUCT LINES

In design modeling, variability is handled by developing variant and parameterized components. Certain software architectural patterns (see Chapter 11) are particularly appropriate for SPLs because they encourage variability and evolution.

15.5.1 Modeling Component-Based Software Architectures

A software component's interface is specified separately from its implementation and, unlike a class, the component's required interface is designed explicitly in addition to the provided interface, as described in Chapter 12. This is particularly important for architecture-centric adaptation, since it is necessary to know the impact of a change to a component on all components that interface to it.

This capability for modeling component-based software architectures is particularly valuable in product line engineering, to allow the development of kernel, optional, and variant components, "plug-compatible" components, and component interface inheritance. There are various ways to design components. It is highly desirable, where possible, to design components that are **plug-compatible**, so that the

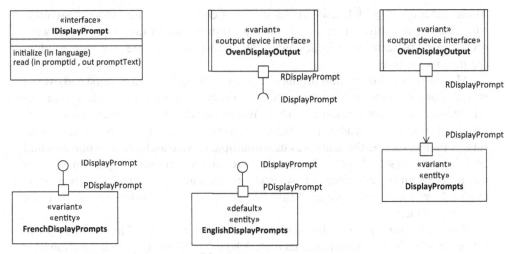

Figure 15.7. Design of plug-compatible variant components.

required port of one component is compatible with the provided ports of other components to which it needs to connect (see Chapter 12). Consider the case in which a producer component must be able to connect to different alternative consumer components in different product line members, as shown in Figure 15.7. The most desirable approach, if possible, is to design all the consumer components with the same provided interface, so that the producer can be connected to any consumer without changing its required interface. In Figure 15.7, Oven Display Output can be connected to any variant version of the Display Prompts component (which correspond to the default and alternative features in Figure 15.3). The component interface is shown in Figure 15.7, which specifies two operations, to initialize the component and read prompt text given the prompt ID. Each default or variant component, such as English Display Prompts or French Display Prompts, which realizes the interface inherits the component interface from the variant Display Prompts component and provides the language-specific implementation.

It is possible for a component to connect to different components and have different interconnections such that in one case it communicates with one component and in a different case it communicates with two different components. This flexibility helps in providing variability in the software architecture. When plug-compatible components are not practical, an alternative component design approach is **component interface inheritance**. Consider a component architecture that is modified in such a way that the interface through which the two components communicate must be specialized to allow for additional functionality. In this case, both the component that provides the interface and the component that requires the interface have to be modified – the former to realize the new functionality, and the latter to request it. These approaches can be used to complement compositional approaches for developing component-based software architectures.

15.5.2 Software Architectural Patterns

Software architectural patterns (described in Chapter 11) provide the skeleton or template for the overall software architecture or high-level design of an application.

These include such widely used architectures as client/service and layered architectures. Basing the software architecture of a product line on one or more software architectural patterns helps in designing the original architecture as well as modifying the architecture.

Most software systems and product lines can be based on well-understood overall software architectures. For example, the client/server software architecture is prevalent in many software applications. There is the basic client/service architectural pattern, with one service and many clients. However, there are also many variations on this theme, such as the multiple client/multiple service architectural patterns and broker patterns (see Chapter 11). Furthermore, with a client/service pattern, services can evolve with the addition of new services, which are discovered and invoked by clients. New clients can be added that discover services provided by one or more service providers.

An architectural pattern that is worth considering because of its desirable properties for SPLs is the layered architecture. A layered architectural pattern allows for ease of extension and contraction (Parnas 1979) because components can be added to or removed from higher layers, which use the services provided by components at lower layers of the architecture.

In addition to these architectural structure patterns, certain architectural communication patterns also encourage evolution. In software product lines, it is often desirable to decouple components. The Broker, Discovery, and Subscription/Notification patterns (see Chapter 11) encourage such decoupling. With the broker patterns, services register with brokers, and clients can then discover new services. Thus, a product line can evolve with the addition of new clients and services. A new version of a service can replace an older version and register itself with the broker. Clients communicating via the broker are automatically connected to the new version of the service. The Subscription/Notification pattern also decouples the original sender of the message from the recipients of the message.

15.6 SUMMARY

This chapter has given an overview of designing software product line architectures. The requirements, analysis, and design modeling steps of COMET/RTE are extended and applied to modeling commonality and variability in SPLs as follows:

a) Requirements modeling – develop use case model and feature model.
b) Analysis modeling – develop static model, dynamic interaction model, and dynamic state machine model; analyze feature/class dependencies.
c) Design modeling – develop component-based software architecture by applying software architectural patterns.

The feature model is the unifying model for relating variability in requirements to variability in the SPL architecture. For more information on these topics, considerable detail is provided in the author's book on designing software product lines with UML (Gomaa 2005a).

PART III

Analysis of Real-Time Software Designs

16

System and Software Quality Attributes for Real-Time Embedded Systems

Software quality attributes (Bass et al. 2013) refer to nonfunctional requirements of software, which can have a profound effect on the quality of a real-time embedded system. During requirements specification, software quality requirements are specified as nonfunctional requirements. Many software quality attributes can be addressed and evaluated at the time the software architecture is developed.

Some quality attributes are actually system quality attributes because both hardware and software considerations are needed to achieve high quality. These system quality attributes include scalability, performance, availability, safety, and security. Other quality attributes are purely software in nature because they rely entirely on the quality of the software. These software quality attributes include maintainability, modifiability, testability, traceability, and reusability. This chapter provides an overview of system and software quality attributes, and discusses how they are supported by the COMET/RTE software design method.

16.1 SCALABILITY

Scalability is the extent to which the system is capable of growing after its initial deployment. There are system and software factors to consider in scalability. From a system perspective, there are issues of adding further hardware to increase the capacity of the system. In a centralized system, the scope for scalability is limited, such as adding more memory, more disk capacity, or an additional CPU. A distributed system offers much more scope for scalability by adding more nodes to the configuration.

From a software perspective, the system needs to be designed in such a way that it is capable of growth. A distributed component-based software architecture is much more capable of scaling upward than a centralized design. Components are designed such that multiple instances of each component can be deployed to different nodes in a distributed configuration. A light rail control system that supports multiple trains and multiple stations can have a component-based software design, such that there is one instance of a train component for each train and one instance of a station component for each station. Such a software architecture can be deployed to execute

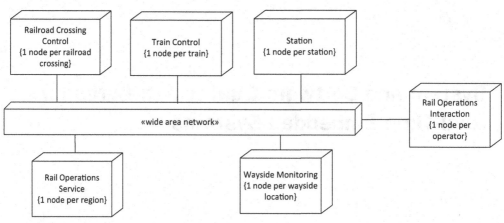

Figure 16.1. Scale-up in emergency monitoring system.

in a small town, in a large city, or in a wide geographical region. A service-oriented architecture can be scaled up by adding more services or additional instances of existing services. New clients can be added to the system as needed. Clients can discover new services and take advantage of their offerings.

COMET/RTE addresses scalability by providing the capability of designing distributed component-based software architectures and service-oriented architectures that can be scaled up after deployment. For example, the Light Rail Control System can be expanded by adding more instances of Train Control (one for each added train), and if the railway system is expanded, more instances of Station (one for each new station), more instances of Railroad Crossing Control and Wayside Monitoring (for additional railroad crossings and sensor monitoring clusters respectively), and more instances of Rail Operations Interaction (for additional operators). It would also be possible to add more instances of the Rail Operations Service component, one for each region to accommodate the expansion of the light rail system over a wider geographical area. The deployment diagram for the expanded Light Rail Control System (Figure 16.1) shows how the component-based software architecture could be scaled up.

Scalability can also be achieved by hierarchical layering. This is frequently used in factory automation systems in which at the lowest layer are the individual robots, automated guided vehicles, programmable logic controllers, etc. At the next level are factory workstations consisting for example of a pick and place robot and an assembly robot. Next is a factory cell consisting of a cluster of factory workstations or an assembly line consisting of factory workstations connected in sequence. Each area in the factory is controlled by an area controller. The different area controllers are connected to a factory management system, which sets and tracks overall production goals for each factory area. In a multi-national company, each of the factories reports to the corporate level management system. There are different levels of networks at several levels, including the Internet for general communication and intranets for internal communication. Architectural patterns used to support this hierarchy include the layered pattern, hierarchical control, client/service, and brokered patterns.

16.2 PERFORMANCE

Performance is also an important consideration in many systems (Menascé et al. 2004). For real-time embedded systems, **performance analysis** during design is a quantitative analysis of a real-time software design conceptually executing on a given hardware configuration with a given external workload applied to it. **Performance modeling** is an abstraction of the real computer system behavior developed for the purpose of gaining greater insight into the performance of the system, whether or not the system actually exists. Performance modeling of a system during design is important to determine whether the system will meet its performance goals, such as throughput and response times. Performance modeling methods include queuing modeling (Gomaa and Menascé 2001, Menascé and Gomaa 2000) and simulation modeling (Jain 2015). Performance modeling is particularly important in real-time systems, in which failing to meet a deadline could be catastrophic.

In COMET/RTE, performance analysis of software designs is achieved by applying **real-time scheduling** theory. **Real-time scheduling** (Buttazzo 2011) is an approach that is particularly appropriate for hard real-time systems that have deadlines that must be met. With this approach, the real-time design executing on a given hardware configuration is analyzed to determine whether it can meet its deadlines. A second approach for analyzing the performance of a design is to use **event sequence analysis** and to integrate this with the **real-time scheduling** theory. Event sequence analysis is used to analyze scenarios of communicating tasks and annotate them with the timing parameters for each of the participating tasks, in addition to considering system overhead for inter-object communication and context switching. Performance analysis of real-time designs using real-time scheduling is described in considerable detail in Chapters 17 and 18.

16.3 AVAILABILITY

Availability is the extent to which the system is available for operational usage. Availability addresses system failure and its impact on users or other systems (Bass et al. 2013). There are times when the system is not available due to scheduled system maintenance; this planned unavailability is not usually counted in measures of availability. However, unplanned system maintenance due to system failure is always counted. Some real-time systems need to be operational at all times; thus, the effect of a system failure on a system controlling an airplane or spacecraft could be catastrophic.

Fault-tolerant systems have recovery built into them so that the system can recover from failure automatically. However, such systems are typically very expensive, requiring such capabilities as triple redundancy and voting systems. Other less expensive solutions are possible, such as a hot standby, which is a machine ready for usage very soon after the failure of the system. The hot standby could be for a server in a client/server system. It is possible to design a distributed system without a single point of failure, such that the failure of one node results in reduced service with the system operational in a degraded mode. This is usually preferable to having no service whatever.

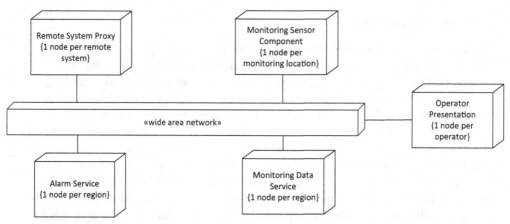

Figure 16.2. Example of system with no single hardware point of failure.

From a software design perspective, support for availability necessitates the design of systems without single points of failure. COMET/RTE supports availability by providing an approach for designing distributed component-based software architectures that can be deployed to multiple nodes with distributed control, data, and services, so that the system does not fail if a single node goes down but can operate in a degraded mode.

For the case study examples, the hot standby could be used for a Banking System, which is a centralized client/server system in which the Bank Server is a single point of failure. A hot standby is a backup server that can be rapidly deployed if the main server goes down. An example of a distributed system without a single hardware point of failure is the Emergency Monitoring System (Figure 16.2), in which the remote system and sensor monitoring components, the monitoring and alarm services, and the operator interaction components can all be replicated. There are several instances of each of the client components, so if a component goes down, the system can still operate. The services can be replicated so that there are multiple instances of Monitoring Data Service and Alarm Service. This is illustrated in the deployment diagram in Figure 16.2. It is assumed that the network used is the Internet, in which there might be local failures but not a global failure, so that individual nodes or even regional subnets might be unavailable at times but other regions would still be operational.

16.4 SAFETY

The Federal Aviation Administration (FAA) describes *system safety* as: "The primary objective of system safety is accident prevention. Proactively identifying, assessing, and eliminating or controlling safety-related hazards, to acceptable levels, can achieve accident prevention." According to the FAA, "A *hazard* is a present condition, event, or circumstance that could lead to or contribute to an unplanned or undesired event" (FAA 2000).

For a real-time system, safety is a critically important consideration. In an industrial furnace control system, an important safety requirement is that the temperature of the furnace shall not exceed a pre-specified maximum temperature, and if it does, then the furnace must be switched off so that it can cool down. In the Railroad

Crossing Control System (Chapter 20), a safety requirement is that the barrier must be lowered within a pre-specified time. In addition, the system must keep track of the number of trains at the railroad crossing, such that the barrier is lowered when the first train arrives and only raised after the last train departs. In the Light Rail Control System (Chapter 21), there is a safety requirement that the train must slow down to a stop if an obstacle is detected on the rail track ahead.

A safety critical system must be designed in such a way that safety-related hazards are identified during requirements specification and documented as nonfunctional safety requirements. The software design must then ensure that these hazards will be detected and that safety mechanisms are designed into the system to avoid undesirable events that might be caused by these hazards.

16.5 SECURITY

Security is an important consideration in many systems. There are many potential threats to distributed application systems, such as electronic commerce and banking systems. There are several textbooks that address computer and network security, including Bishop (2004) and Pfleeger et al. (2015). Some of the potential threats are:

- System penetration – An unauthorized person tries to gain access to an application system and execute unauthorized transactions.
- Authorization violation – A person authorized to use an application system misuses or abuses it.
- Confidentiality disclosure – Secret information such as card numbers and bank accounts are disclosed to an unauthorized person.
- Integrity compromise – An unauthorized person changes application data in database or communication data.
- Repudiation – A person who performs some transaction or communication activity later falsely denies that the transaction or activity occurred.
- Denial of service – Legitimate access to application systems is deliberately disturbed.

COMET/RTE extends the use case descriptions to allow the description of nonfunctional requirements, which include security requirements. An example of the extension of use cases to allow nonfunctional requirements is given in Chapter 6.

These potential threats can be addressed in the following ways for a Banking System, not all of which can be addressed by software means:

- System penetration –Messages must be encrypted at the source, in particular transactions originating at the ATM Client and the responses sent by the Banking Service, and then decrypted at the destination.
- Authorization violation – A person authorized to use an application system misuses or abuses it. A log of all access to the system must be maintained, so that cases of misuse or abuse can be tracked down and any abuse can be corrected.
- Confidentiality disclosure – Secret information such as card numbers and bank accounts must be protected by an access control method that only allows users with the appropriate privileges to access the data.

- Integrity compromise – An access control method must be enforced to ensure that unauthorized persons are prevented from making changes to application data in the database or communication data.
- Repudiation – A log must be maintained of all transactions so that a claim that the transaction or activity did not occur can be verified by analyzing the log.
- Denial of service – An intrusion detection capability is required so that the system can detect unauthorized intrusions and act to reject them.

As cybersecurity threats become more dangerous and widespread, including malware, security risks, vulnerabilities, and spam, the security response must also become more sophisticated. This cyber warfare between security attacks and security defense is likely to continue to be waged for the foreseeable future.

16.6 MAINTAINABILITY

Maintainability is the extent to which software is capable of being changed after deployment. Reasons why the software may need to be modified are:

- Fix remaining errors. These are errors that were not detected during testing of the software prior to deployment.
- Address performance issues. Performance problems may not become apparent until after the software application has been deployed and is operational in the field.
- Changes in software requirements. The biggest agent for software change is frequently due to changes in software requirements.

In many cases, software maintenance is actually a misnomer for software evolution. In particular, unanticipated changes in software requirements necessitate modifications to the software that could be extensive. To cope with future evolution, software should be designed for change and adaptability. Quality must be built into the original product to make it maintainable, which means using a good software development process and providing comprehensive documentation of the product. The documentation should be kept up to date as the software is modified. Design rationale should be provided to explain the design decisions that were made. Otherwise, maintainers will have no option but to work with undocumented code, which might well be poorly structured.

COMET/RTE supports maintainability by providing comprehensive documentation of the design. Design decisions are actually captured in the design through the use of stereotypes, which allows design structuring decisions to be included in the design. Textual documentation of tasks in task interface and behavior specifications (Chapters 13 and 14), and classes with class interface specifications, can be included with the task and class code, thereby facilitating updating the documentation at the same time the code is modified.

With the use case–based development approach, the effect of a change to a requirement can be traced from use case to software design and implementation (Section 16.9). In addition the COMET/RTE support for modifiability (Section 16.7) and testability (Section 16.8) greatly assists in the maintainability of the product.

Table 16.1. Example of Modifiability – Prompt Table with Language-Specific Prompts

Prompt ID	Prompt Text
time-prompt	Please enter cooking time:
end-Prompt	Cooking food complete
door-prompt	Close door and press Start to resume cooking.

16.7 MODIFIABILITY

Modifiability is the extent to which software is capable of being modified during and after initial development. A modular design consisting of modules with well-defined interfaces is essential. Parnas et al. (1984) advocated *design for change* based on the information-hiding concept, in which change is anticipated and managed by each information-hiding module hiding a *secret* that could change independently of other parts of the software. Information Hiding is a fundamental concept and forms the basis of OOD.

COMET/RTE supports modifiability by providing support for information hiding at the class and component level and providing support for separation of concerns at the subsystem level. Decisions such as encapsulating each finite state machine within a separate state machine class, each interface to a separate external device, system, or user within a separate boundary class, and each separate data structure within a separate data abstraction class, assist with modifiability. At the architecture level, the COMET/RTE component-based software architectural design approach leads to the design of components that can be deployed to different distributed nodes at software deployment time, so that the same architecture can be deployed to many different configurations in support of different instances of the application.

As an example of how modifiability is provided in COMET/RTE, consider a change in requirements that necessitates that the Microwave Oven System shall become available in South America, Europe, Asia, and Africa. In particular, this requires that prompts be displayed in different languages. Every use case that provides prompts to the customer is potentially affected by this change. An analysis of the design reveals that the only object that interfaces to the customer is Oven Display Output. A good design solution would attempt to limit the design change to a minimum. A change to achieve this goal is that all prompts sent by the Microwave Control object to the Oven Display Output object have a prompt ID instead of the prompt text. If Oven Display Output already has the prompt messages hardcoded, the prompts need to be removed and placed in a prompt table. The prompt table will have one column for prompt IDs and a second column for the corresponding prompt text. A simple table lookup will, given the prompt ID, return the prompt text. At system initialization time, the prompt table for the desired language will be loaded. The default prompt table will be in English. For the South American market (apart from Brazil) and for the Spanish market, the Spanish prompt table will be loaded. For France, Quebec, and large parts of West Africa, the French prompt table will be loaded at initialization time. An example of the prompt table with English prompts is given in Table 16.1.

By applying the information-hiding concept, the prompt table should be encapsulated in a prompt class. Because support for different languages is required, a good

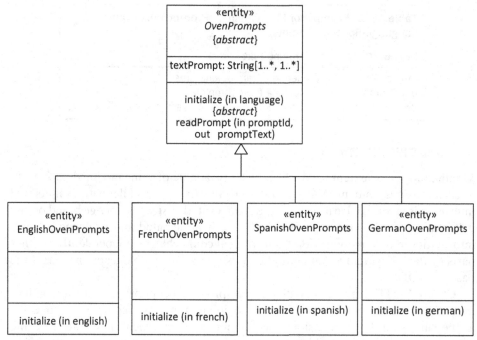

Figure 16.3. Example of modifiability – abstract Oven Prompts superclass and language-specific subclasses.

approach is to design a superclass called Oven Prompts and design subclasses for each language, the initial requirement is for English (default), French, Italian, Spanish, and German language prompts (see Figure 16.3). However, the design should allow for extension to other languages. The solution is to design the Oven Prompts class as an abstract class with the encapsulated data structure for the prompt table and a common interface consisting of a readPrompt operation, which reads a prompt from the prompt table given the prompt ID, and an abstract initializeLanguage operation. The language-specific prompt subclass inherits the data structure and interface unchanged and then provides the language-specific implementation of the initialize-Language operation, which populates the prompt table with prompts in the appropriate language. An alternative solution to this problem using software product line technology is described in Chapter 15.

16.8 TESTABILITY

Testability is the extent to which software is capable of being tested during and after its initial development (Bass et al. 2013). It is important to develop a software test plan early in the software life cycle and to plan on developing test cases in parallel with software development. The following paragraphs describe how the different stages of software testing can be integrated with the COMET/RTE method. A comprehensive introduction to software testing is given by Ammann and Offutt (2008).

During the Requirements Phase, it is necessary to develop functional (black box) test cases. These test cases can be developed from the use case model, in particular the use case descriptions. Because the use case descriptions describe the sequence of user interactions with the system, they describe the user inputs that must be captured for the test cases and the expected system output. A test case must be developed for each use case scenario, one of the main sequence and one for each alternative sequence of the use case. Using this approach, a test suite can be developed to test the functional requirements of the system.

During Software Architectural Design, it is necessary to develop integration test cases, which test the interfaces between the components that communicate with each other. A testing approach called scenario-based testing can be used to test the software using a sequence of scenarios that correspond to the realization of the use case scenarios on interaction models (diagrams), which show the sequence of objects communicating with each other and messages passed between the objects. Thus, an integration test case(s) would be developed for each object communication scenario.

During detailed design and coding, in which the internal algorithms for each component are developed, white box test cases can be developed that test the component internals using well-known coverage criteria, such as executing every line of code and the outcome of every decision. By this means, it is possible to develop unit test cases to test the individual units, such as components.

An example of a black box test case based on the Cook Food use case in the Microwave Oven System would consist of opening the oven door, placing the food in the oven, closing the door, entering the cooking time, and pressing the Start button. Initially a test stub object could be developed, which simulates the customer going through the earlier-discussed sequence. The system prompts for the cooking time and after the cooking time has expired, outputs the end of cooking prompt. A test environment could be set up with an external environment simulator simulating the door and weight sensors inputting events to the system, and the oven starting and stopping cooking. This would allow the main sequence of the Cook Food use case as well as all the alternative sequences to be tested (door opened after cooking has started, customer pressing cancel, pressing Minute Plus before and after cooking has started, etc.).

16.9 TRACEABILITY

Traceability is the extent to which artifacts of each phase can be traced back to products of previous phases. Requirements traceability is used to ensure that each software requirement has been designed and implemented. Each requirement is traced to the software architecture and to the implemented code modules. Requirements traceability tables are a useful tool during software architecture reviews for analyzing whether the software architecture has addressed all the software requirements.

It is possible to build traceability into software development method, as is the case with the COMET/RTE method. COMET/RTE is a use case–based development approach, which starts with use cases and then determines the objects required to realize each use case. Each use case described in the software requirements is elaborated into a use case–based interaction diagram, which describes the sequence of object communication resulting from an external input described in the use case through to system output. These interaction diagrams are integrated into the software architecture. This means that each requirement can be traced from use case to software design and implementation. The impact of a change to a requirement can therefore be determined by following the trace from requirement through to design.

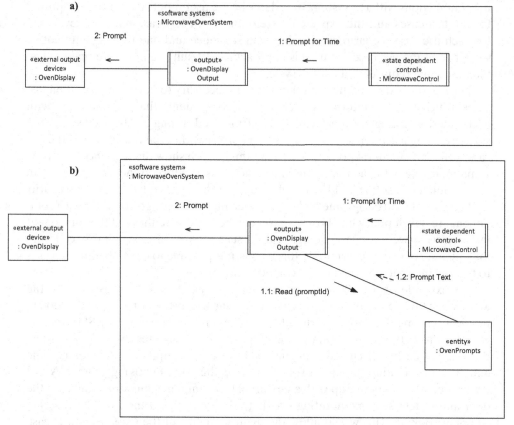

Figure 16.4. Traceability analysis before and after change to introduce Oven Prompts object.

As an example of traceability, consider the Cook Food use case from the Microwave Oven System. This use case is realized in the dynamic interaction model by the Cook Food communication diagram. The change required by the addition of the prompt language requirement can be determined by an impact analysis, which reveals that the prompt object would need to be accessed by the Oven Display Output object prior to displaying the prompt, as shown in Figure 16.4a. Figure 16.4a shows the original design with Oven Display Output outputting directly to the display, and Figure 16.4b shows the modified design with Oven Display Output reading the prompt text from the Oven Prompts object before outputting to the display. A solution to this problem using product line concepts is described in Chapter 15.

16.10 REUSABILITY

Software reusability is the extent to which software is capable of being reused. In traditional software reuse, a library of reusable code components is developed, such as a statistical subroutine library. This approach requires the establishment of a library of reusable components and of an approach for indexing, locating, and distinguishing between similar components (Jacobson et al. 1997). Problems with this approach include managing the large number of components that such a reuse library is likely to contain and distinguishing among similar though not identical components.

When a new design is being developed, the designer is responsible for designing the software architecture – that is, the overall structure of the program and the overall flow of control. Having located and selected a reusable component from the library, the designer must then determine how this component fits into the new architecture.

Instead of reusing an individual component, it is much more advantageous to reuse a whole design or subsystem, consisting of the components and their interconnections. This means reuse of the control structure of the application. Architecture reuse has much greater potential than component reuse because it is large-grained reuse, which focuses on reuse of requirements and design. The most promising approach for architecture reuse is to develop a software product line (SPL) architecture, which explicitly captures the commonality and variability in the family of systems that constitutes the product line.

COMET/PLUS is an extension of COMET to design software product line architectures. An overview of COMET/PLUS is given in Chapter 15, with a complete and detailed description of how it can be applied to develop reusable SPL architectures given in Gomaa (2005a). The example of how the Oven Prompts superclass and language-specific subclasses could be designed using a software product line approach is described in Chapter 15.

16.11 SUMMARY

This chapter has provided an overview of system and software quality attributes of a software architecture and how they are used to evaluate the quality of the software architecture. The system quality attributes described in this chapter include scalability, performance, availability, safety, and security. The software quality attributes described in this chapter include maintainability, modifiability, testability, traceability, and reusability. Software quality attributes are described in more detail in Bass et al. (2013) and Taylor et al. (2009).

17

Performance Analysis of Real-Time Software Designs

Performance analysis of software designs is particularly important for real-time systems. The consequences of a real-time system failing to meet a deadline can be catastrophic. It is therefore necessary to analyze the performance of a real-time software design before it is implemented. Since the performance analysis is for a concurrent design, it can be carried out as soon as the task architecture has been designed, as described in Chapter 13.

Quantitative analysis of a real-time system design allows the early detection of potential performance problems. The analysis is for the concurrent software design conceptually executing on a given hardware configuration with a given external workload applied to it. Early detection of potential performance problems allows alternative software designs and hardware configurations to be investigated, including single-processor and multiprocessor systems.

This chapter describes performance analysis of software designs by applying real-time scheduling theory to software designs. Real-time scheduling is a particularly appropriate approach for hard real-time systems that have deadlines that must be met (Sha and Goodenough 1990). With this approach, the real-time design is analyzed to determine whether it can meet its deadlines.

This chapter describes two approaches for analyzing the performance of a design. The first approach uses **real-time scheduling theory**, and the second uses **event sequence analysis**. The two approaches are then combined. Both real-time scheduling theory and event sequence analysis are applied to a design consisting of a set of concurrent tasks. Section 17.1 provides an introduction to real-time scheduling theory, in particular the rate-monotonic algorithm and two of its theorems, the utilization bound theorem, and the completion time theorem. Section 17.2 describes how real-time scheduling theory can be extended to address aperiodic tasks and task synchronization. Section 17.3 describes the generalized real-time scheduling theory, which can be applied in cases in which the rate-monotonic assumptions do not hold. Section 17.4 describes performance analysis of real-time software designs using event sequence analysis. Section 17.5 then describes how real-time scheduling theory and event sequence analysis can be combined to analyze the performance of real-time software designs. Section 17.6 describes advanced real-time scheduling algorithms, including deadline-monotonic scheduling, dynamic priority scheduling, and scheduling for multiprocessor systems. Section 17.7 describes performance analysis of multiprocessor systems, including multicore systems. Finally, Section 17.8 describes the estimation and measurement of performance parameters.

17.1 REAL-TIME SCHEDULING THEORY

Real-time scheduling theory addresses the issues of priority-based scheduling of concurrent tasks with hard deadlines. The theory addresses how to determine whether a group of tasks, whose individual CPU utilization is known, will meet their deadlines. The theory assumes a priority preemption scheduling algorithm, as described in Chapter 3. This section is based on the reports and book on real-time scheduling produced at the Software Engineering Institute (Sha and Goodenough 1990, SEI 1993), which should be referenced for more information on this topic.

As real-time scheduling theory has evolved, it has gradually been applied to more complicated scheduling problems. Problems that have been addressed include scheduling independent periodic tasks, scheduling in situations in which there are both periodic and aperiodic (i.e., event driven and demand driven) tasks, and scheduling in cases in which task synchronization is required.

17.1.1 Scheduling Periodic Tasks

Initially, real-time scheduling algorithms were developed for independent periodic tasks – that is, periodic tasks that do not communicate or synchronize with each other (Liu and Layland 1973). Since then, the theory has been developed considerably so it can now be applied to other practical problems, as will be illustrated in the examples. In this chapter, it is necessary to start with the basic rate-monotonic theory for independent periodic tasks for us to understand how it has been extended to address more complex situations.

A periodic task has a period T (the frequency with which it executes) and an execution time C (the CPU time required during the period). Its CPU utilization U is the ratio C/T. A task is schedulable if all its deadlines are met, that is, if the task completes its execution before its period elapses. A group of tasks is considered schedulable if each task can meet its deadlines.

For a set of independent periodic tasks, the **rate-monotonic algorithm** assigns each task a fixed priority based on its period, such that the shorter the period of a task, the higher its priority. Consider three tasks t_a, t_b, and t_c, with periods 10, 20, and 30, respectively. The highest priority is given to t_a, the task with the shortest period; the medium priority is given to task t_b; and the lowest priority is given to t_c, the task with the longest period.

In Liu and Layland (1973), it is formally proven that for a set of independent periodic real-time tasks, the rate-monotonic priority assignment is optimal among all schemes that assign unique and fixed priorities to individual tasks, when the tasks have to complete their execution by their respective periods.

17.1.2 Utilization Bound Theorem

According to the rate-monotonic scheduling theory (RMS), a group of n-independent periodic tasks can be shown to always meet their deadlines, providing

Table 17.1. Utilization Bound Theorem

Number of Tasks n	Utilization Bound U(n)
1	1.000
2	0.828
3	0.779
4	0.756
5	0.743
6	0.734
7	0.728
8	0.724
9	0.720
Infinity	ln 2 (0.69)

the sum of the ratios C/T for each task is below an upper bound of overall CPU utilization.

The **Utilization Bound Theorem** (Liu and Layland 1973) states that:
Utilization Bound Theorem (Theorem 1):
A set of n-independent periodic tasks scheduled by the rate-monotonic algorithm will always meet its deadlines for all task phasings, if:

$$\frac{C_1}{T_1} + \cdots\cdots + \frac{C_n}{T_n} \le n(2^{1/n} - 1) = U(n)$$

where C_i and T_i are the execution time and period of task t_i respectively.

The upper bound $U(n)$ converges to 69 percent (ln 2) as the number of tasks approaches infinity. The utilization bounds for up to nine tasks, according to the Utilization Bound Theorem, are given in Table 17.1. This is a worst-case approximation, and for a randomly chosen group of tasks, Lehoczky, Sha, and Ding (1989) show that the likely upper bound is 88 percent. For tasks with harmonic periods – that is, with periods that are multiples of each other – the upper bound is even higher and could reach 100 percent if all the tasks have harmonic periods.

The rate-monotonic algorithm has the advantage of being stable in conditions in which there is a transient overload. In other words, a subset of the total number of tasks – namely, those with the highest priorities (and hence, shortest periods) – will still meet their deadlines if the system is overloaded for a relatively short time. The lower priority tasks, namely those with longer periods, might occasionally miss their deadlines as the processor load increases.

17.1.3 Example of Applying Utilization Bound Theorem

As an example of applying the Utilization Bound Theorem, consider three tasks with the following characteristics, where all times are in milliseconds and the utilization $U_i = C_i/T_i$:

Task t_1: $C_1 = 20$; $T_1 = 100$; $U_1 = 0.2$
Task t_2: $C_2 = 30$; $T_2 = 150$; $U_2 = 0.2$
Task t_3: $C_3 = 60$; $T_3 = 200$; $U_3 = 0.3$

It is assumed that the context-switching overhead, once at the start of the task's execution and once at the end of its execution, is included in the CPU times.

The total utilization of the three tasks is 0.7, which is below 0.779, the Utilization Bound Theorem's upper bound for three tasks. Thus, the three tasks can meet their deadlines in all cases.

However, consider that the task t_3's characteristics are instead as follows:

Task t_3: $C_3 = 90$; $T_3 = 200$; $U_3 = 0.45$

In this case, the total utilization of the three tasks is 0.85, which is higher than 0.779, the Utilization Bound Theorem's upper bound for three tasks. Thus, the Utilization Bound Theorem indicates that the tasks may not meet their deadlines. Next, a check is made to determine whether the first two tasks can meet their deadlines.

Given that the rate-monotonic algorithm is stable, the first two tasks can be checked by using the Utilization Bound Theorem. The utilization of these two tasks is 0.4, well below the Utilization Bound Theorem's upper bound for two tasks of 0.828. Thus, the first two tasks always meet their deadlines. Given that the Utilization Bound Theorem is a pessimistic theorem, a further check can be made to determine whether Task t_3 can meet its deadlines by applying the more exact Completion Time Theorem.

17.1.4 Completion Time Theorem

If a set of tasks have a utilization greater than the Utilization Bound Theorem's upper bound, the Completion Time Theorem, which gives a more exact schedulability criterion (Lehoczky, Sha, and Ding 1989), can be checked. For a set of independent periodic tasks, the Completion Time Theorem provides an exact determination of whether the tasks are schedulable. The theorem assumes a worst case of all the periodic tasks ready to execute at the same time, which is sometimes referred to as the *critical instant*. It has been shown that in this worst case, if a task completes execution before the end of its first period, it will never miss a deadline (Liu and Layland 1973; Lehoczky, Sha, and Ding 1989). The Completion Time Theorem therefore checks whether each task can complete execution before the end of its first period.

> **Completion Time Theorem (Theorem 2):**
> For a set of independent periodic tasks, if each task meets its first deadline when all tasks are started at the same time, the deadlines will be met for any combination of start times.

To do this, it is necessary to check the end of the first period of a given task t_i, as well as the end of all periods of higher priority tasks in interval $[0, T_i]$. Following the rate-monotonic theory, these tasks will have shorter periods than t_i. These periods are referred to as scheduling points. Task t_i will execute once for a total CPU amount of C_i during its period T_i. However, higher priority tasks will execute more often and can preempt t_i at least once. It is therefore necessary to consider the CPU time used up by the higher priority tasks as well.

The Completion Time Theorem can be illustrated graphically with a timing diagram. A **timing diagram** is a **time-annotated sequence diagram**, based on the UML sequence diagram, which is a sequence diagram that explicitly depicts the passage

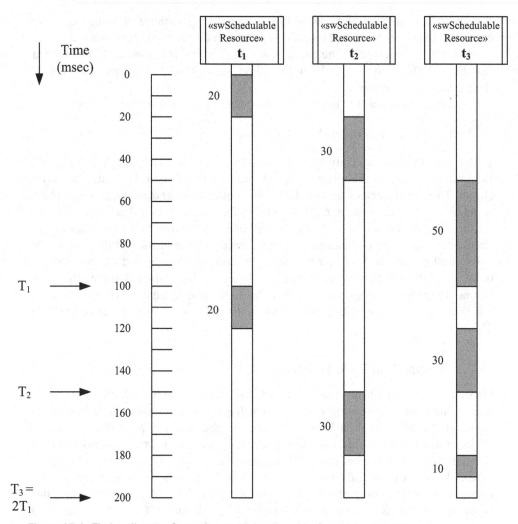

Figure 17.1. Timing diagram for tasks executing on a single-processor system.

of time in a time-ordered execution sequence of a group of concurrent tasks. See Section 2.14 for more details of the timing diagram.

17.1.5 Example of Applying Completion Time Theorem

Consider the example described in Section 17.1.3 of three tasks with the following characteristics:

Task t_1: $C_1 = 20$; $T_1 = 100$; $U_1 = 0.2$
Task t_2: $C_2 = 30$; $T_2 = 150$; $U_2 = 0.2$
Task t_3: $C_3 = 90$; $T_3 = 200$; $U_3 = 0.45$

The execution of the three tasks is illustrated by the timing diagram shown in Figure 17.1. The tasks are shown as active throughout, with the shaded portions identifying when tasks are executing. Because there is one CPU in this example, only one task can execute at any one time.

Given the worst case of the three tasks being ready to execute at the same time, t_1 executes first because it has the shortest period and hence the highest priority. It completes after 20 msec, after which the task t_2 executes for 30 msec. On completion of t_2, t_3 executes. At the end of the first scheduling point, $T_1 = 100$, which corresponds to t_1's deadline; t_1 has already completed execution and thus met its deadline. Task t_2 has also completed execution and easily met its deadline of 150 msec, and t_3 has executed for 50 msec out of the necessary 90.

At the start of task t_1's second period, t_3 is preempted by task t_1. After executing for 20 msec, t_1 completes and relinquishes the CPU to task t_3 again. Task t_3 executes until the end of period T_2 (150 msec), which represents the second scheduling point due to t_2's deadline. Because t_2 completed before T_1 (which is less than T_2) elapsed, it easily met its deadline. At this time, t_3 has used up 80 msec out of the necessary 90.

Task t_3 is preempted by task t_2 at the start of t_2's second period. After executing for 30 msec, t_2 completes, relinquishing the CPU to task t_3 again. Task t_3 executes for another 10 msec, at which time it has used up all its CPU time of 90 msec, thereby completing before its deadline. Figure 17.1 shows the third scheduling point, which is both the end of t_1's second period ($2T_1 = 200$) and the end of t_3's first period ($T_3 = 200$). Figure 17.1 also shows that each of the three tasks completes execution before the end of its first period, and thus they successfully meet their deadlines.

Figure 17.1 shows that the CPU is idle for 10 msec before the start of t_1's third period (also the start of t_3's second period). It should be noted that a total CPU time of 190 msec was used up over the 200 msec period, giving a CPU utilization for this 200 msec period of 0.95, although the overall utilization is 0.85. After an elapsed time equal to the least common multiple of the three periods (600 msec in this example) the utilization averages out to 0.85.

17.1.6 Mathematical Formulation of Completion Time Theorem

The Completion Time Theorem for single-processor systems can be expressed mathematically in Theorem 3 (Sha and Goodenough 1990) as follows:

Mathematical Formulation of Completion Time Theorem (Theorem 3):
A set of n-independent periodic tasks scheduled by the rate-monotonic algorithm will always meet its deadlines for all task phasings, if and only if:

$$\forall i, \ 1 \le i \le n, \ \min \sum_{j=1}^{i} C_j \frac{1}{pT_k} \left\lceil \frac{pT_k}{T_j} \right\rceil \le 1$$
$$(k, p) \in R_i$$

where C_j and T_j are the execution time and period of task t_j respectively and $R_i = \{(k, p) | 1 \le k \le i, p = 1, \ldots, \lfloor T_i / T_k \rfloor\}$.

In the formula, t_i denotes the task to be checked, and t_k denotes each of the higher priority tasks that impact the completion time of task t_i. For a given task t_i and a given task t_k, each value of p represents a scheduling point of task t_k. At each scheduling point, it is necessary to consider task t_i's CPU time C_i once, as well as the CPU time used by the higher priority tasks. Hence, you can determine whether t_i can complete its execution by that scheduling point.

Consider Theorem 3 applied to the three tasks, which were illustrated with the timing diagram in Figure 17.1. The timing diagram is a graphical representation of what Theorem 3 computes. Again, the worst case is considered of the three tasks being ready to execute at the same time. The inequality for the first scheduling point, $T_1 = 100$, is given from Theorem 3:

$$C_1 + C_2 + C_3 \leq T_1 \quad 20 + 30 + 90 > 100 \quad p = 1, k = 1$$

For this inequality to be satisfied, all three tasks would need to complete execution within the first task t_1's period T_1. This is not the case because before t_3 completes, it is preempted by t_1 at the start of t_1's second period.

The inequality for the second scheduling point, $T_2 = 150$, is given from Theorem 3:

$$2C_1 + C_2 + C_3 \leq T_2 \quad 40 + 30 + 90 > 150 \quad p = 1, k = 2$$

For this inequality to be satisfied, task t_1 would need to complete execution twice and tasks t_2 and t_3 would each need to complete execution once within the second task t_2's period T_2. This is not the case, because t_3 is preempted by task t_2 at the start of t_2's second period.

The inequality for the third scheduling point, which is both the end of t_1's second period ($2T_1 = 200$) and the end of t_3's first period ($T_3 = 200$), is given from Theorem 3:

$$2C_1 + 2C_2 + C_3 \leq 2T_1 = T_3 \quad 40 + 60 + 90 < 200 \quad p = 2, k = 1 \quad \text{or} \quad p = 1, k = 3$$

This time the inequality is satisfied and all three tasks meet their deadlines. As long as all three tasks meet at least one of the scheduling point deadlines, the tasks are schedulable.

17.2 REAL-TIME SCHEDULING FOR APERIODIC TASKS AND TASK SYNCHRONIZATION

Real-time scheduling theory can be extended to address aperiodic tasks, which do not execute periodically, and to situations in which task synchronization is needed, as described in this section.

17.2.1 Scheduling Periodic and Aperiodic Tasks

To address aperiodic tasks as well as periodic tasks, the rate-monotonic theory must be extended. An aperiodic task is assumed to arrive randomly and execute once within some period T_a, which represents the minimum inter-arrival time of the event that activates the task. The CPU time C_a used by the aperiodic task to process the event is reserved as a ticket of value C_a for each period T_a. When the event arrives, the aperiodic task is activated, claims its ticket, and consumes up to C_a units of CPU time. If the task is not activated during the period T_a, the ticket is discarded. Thus, based on these assumptions, the CPU utilization of the aperiodic task is C_a/T_a. However, this represents the worst-case CPU utilization because, in general, reserved tickets are not always claimed.

If there are many aperiodic tasks in the application, the *sporadic server algorithm* (Sprunt, Lehoczy, and Sha 1989) can be used. From a schedulability analysis viewpoint, an aperiodic task (referred to as the sporadic server) is equivalent to a periodic task whose period is equal to the minimum inter-arrival time of the events that activate the aperiodic task. Hence T_a, the minimum inter-arrival time for an aperiodic task t_a, can be considered the period of an equivalent periodic task. Each aperiodic task is also allocated a budget of C_a units of CPU time, which can be used up at any time during its equivalent period T_a. In this way, aperiodic tasks can be placed at different priority levels according to their equivalent periods and treated as periodic tasks.

17.2.2 Scheduling with Task Synchronization

Real-time scheduling theory has also been extended to address task synchronization. The problem here is that a task that enters a critical section can block other, higher priority tasks that wish to enter the critical section. The term **priority inversion** is used to refer to the case where a low priority task prevents a higher priority task from executing, typically by acquiring a resource needed by the latter.

Unbounded priority inversion can occur because the lower priority task, while in its critical section, could itself be blocked by other medium priority tasks, thereby prolonging the total delay experienced by the higher priority task. One solution to this problem is to prevent preemption of tasks while in their critical sections. This is acceptable only if tasks have very short critical sections. For long critical sections, lower priority tasks could block higher priority tasks that do need to access the shared resource.

The **priority ceiling protocol** (Sha and Goodenough 1990) avoids mutual deadlock and provides bounded priority inversion; that is, one lower priority task, at most, can block a higher priority task. Only the simplest case of one critical section is considered here.

Adjustable priorities are used to prevent lower priority tasks from holding up higher priority tasks for an arbitrarily long time. While a low priority task t_l is in its critical section, higher priority tasks can become blocked by it because they wish to acquire the same resource. If that happens, t_l's priority is increased to the highest priority of all the tasks blocked by it. The goal is to speed up the execution of the lower priority task so blocking time for higher priority tasks is reduced.

The priority ceiling P of a **binary semaphore** S is the highest priority of all tasks that may acquire the semaphore. Thus, a low priority task that acquires S can have its priority increased up to P, depending on what higher priority tasks it blocks.

Another case that could occur is **deadlock**, in which two tasks each need to acquire two resources before they can complete. If each task acquires one resource, neither will be able to complete, because each one is waiting for the other to release its resource – a deadlock situation. The priority ceiling protocol overcomes this problem (Sha and Goodenough 1990).

The rate-monotonic scheduling theorems need to be extended to address the priority inversion problem, as described in the next section.

17.3 GENERALIZED REAL-TIME SCHEDULING THEORY

In real-world problems, situations often arise in which the rate-monotonic assumptions do not hold. There are many practical cases in which tasks have to execute at actual priorities different from their rate-monotonic priorities. It is therefore necessary to extend the basic rate-monotonic scheduling theory to address these cases. One case is given in the previous section concerning lower priority tasks blocking higher priority tasks from entering critical sections.

A second case often happens when there are aperiodic tasks. As discussed in Section 17.2.1, aperiodic tasks can be treated as periodic tasks, with the worst-case inter-arrival time considered the equivalent periodic task's period. Following the rate-monotonic scheduling algorithm, if the aperiodic task has a longer period than a periodic task, it should execute at a lower priority than the periodic task. However, if the aperiodic task is interrupt-driven, it will need to execute as soon as the interrupt arrives, even if its worst-case inter-arrival time, and hence equivalent period, is longer than that of the periodic task.

17.3.1 Priority Inversion

The term **priority inversion** is given to any case in which a task cannot execute because it is blocked by a lower priority task. In the case of rate-monotonic priority inversion, the term "priority" refers to the *rate-monotonic priority*; that is, the priority assigned to a task based entirely on the length of its period and not on its relative importance. A task may be assigned an actual priority that is different from the rate-monotonic priority. *Rate-monotonic priority inversion* refers to a task A preempted by a higher priority task B, when in fact task B's rate-monotonic priority is lower than A's (i.e., B's period is longer than A's).

This is illustrated by the following example of rate-monotonic priority inversion, in which there is a periodic task with a period of 25 msec and an interrupt-driven task with a worst-case inter-arrival time of 50 msec. The periodic task has the higher rate-monotonic priority because it has the shorter period; however, in practice, giving the interrupt-driven task the higher actual priority is preferable so it can service the interrupt as soon as it arrives. Whenever the interrupt-driven task preempts the periodic task, this is considered a case of priority inversion relative to the rate-monotonic priority assignment, because if the interrupt-driven task had been given its rate-monotonic priority, it would not have preempted the periodic task.

It is necessary to extend the basic rate-monotonic scheduling theory to address these practical cases of rate-monotonic priority inversion. This has been achieved by extending the basic algorithms to take into account the blocking effect from lower priority tasks as well as preemption by higher priority tasks that do not observe rate-monotonic priorities (SEI 1993). Because rate-monotonic scheduling theory assumes rate-monotonic priorities, preemption by higher priority tasks that do not observe the rate-monotonic priorities is treated in a similar way to blocking by lower priority tasks.

Consider a task t_i with a period T_i during which it consumes C_i units of CPU time. The extensions to Theorems 1, 2, and 3 mean it is necessary to consider explicitly each task t_i to determine whether it can meet its first deadline. In particular, four factors must be considered for each task:

a. **Preemption time by higher priority tasks with periods less than t_i.** These tasks can preempt t_i many times. Call this set H_n and let there be j tasks in this set. Let C_j be the CPU time for task j and T_j the period of task j, where $T_j < T_i$, the period of task t_i. The utilization of a task j in the H_n set is given by C_j/T_j.

b. **Execution time for the task t_i.** Task t_i executes once during its period T_i and consumes C_i units of CPU time.

c. **Preemption by higher priority tasks with longer periods.** These are tasks with non-rate-monotonic priorities. They can only preempt t_i once because they have longer periods than t_i. Call this set H_1 and let there be k tasks in this set. Let the CPU time used by a task in this set be C_k. The worst-case utilization of a task k in the H_1 set is given by C_k/T_i, because this means k preempts t_i and uses up all its CPU time C_k during the period T_i.

d. **Blocking time by lower priority tasks, as described in the previous section.** These tasks can also execute only once because they have longer periods. Blocking delays have to be analyzed on an individual basis for each task to determine its worst-case blocking situation as given by the priority ceiling protocol. If B_i is the worst-case blocking time for a given task t_i, the worst-case blocking utilization for the period T_i is B_i/T_i.

17.3.2 Generalized Utilization Bound Theorem

Because for any given task t_i factors a and b of the preceding paragraph are taken care of by Theorems 1, 2, and 3, the generalization of these theorems is necessary to take into account factors c and d. Theorem 1, the **Utilization Bound Theorem**, is extended to address all four factors described in the preceding paragraph as follows:

Generalized Utilization Bound Theorem (Theorem 4):

$$U_i = \left(\sum_{j \in H_n} \frac{C_j}{T_j} \right) + \frac{1}{T_i} \left(C_i + B_i + \sum_{k \in H_1} C_k \right)$$

U_i is the utilization bound during a period T_i for task t_i. The first term in the Generalized Utilization Bound Theorem is the total preemption utilization by higher priority tasks with periods of less than t_i. The second term is the CPU utilization by task t_i. The third term is the worst-case blocking utilization experienced by t_i. The fourth term is the total preemption utilization by higher priority tasks with longer periods than t_i.

By substituting in the equation for Theorem 4, the utilization U_i can be determined for a given task. If U_i is less than the worst-case upper bound, this means the task t_i will meet its deadline. It is important to realize that the utilization bound test needs to be applied to each task because in this generalized theory, in which rate-monotonic priorities are not necessarily observed, the fact that a given task meets its deadline is no guarantee that a higher priority task will meet its deadline.

17.3.3 Generalized Completion Time Theorem

As before, if the generalized utilization bound theorem fails, a more precise test is available that verifies whether each task can complete execution during its period. This is a generalization of the **Completion Time Theorem**. The **Generalized Completion Time Theorem** determines whether t_i can complete execution by the end of its period, given preemption by higher priority tasks and blocking by lower priority tasks. The theorem assumes the worst case that all tasks are ready for execution at the start of the task t_i's period. Pictorially, the **Generalized Completion Time Theorem** can be illustrated by drawing a timing diagram for all the tasks up to the end of task t_i's period T_i. An example of this is given in Section 17.3.6.

17.3.4 Real-Time Scheduling and Design

Real-time scheduling theory can be applied to a set of concurrent tasks at the design stage or after the tasks have been implemented. In this book, the emphasis is on applying real-time scheduling theory at the design stage. During design, because all CPU times are estimates, it is best to err on the side of caution. For real-time tasks with hard deadlines, it is therefore safer to rely on the more pessimistic **Utilization Bound Theorem**. This theorem has a worst-case upper bound utilization of 0.69. If this worst-case upper bound cannot be satisfied, alternative solutions should be investigated. From a pessimistic designer's perspective, a predicted upper bound utilization of higher than 0.69 is acceptable, providing the utilization above 0.69 is entirely due to lower priority soft real-time or non-real-time tasks. For these tasks to miss their deadlines occasionally is not serious.

It is also the case at design time that the designer has the freedom to choose the priorities to be assigned to the tasks. In general, wherever possible, priorities should be assigned according to the rate-monotonic theory. This is most easily applied to the periodic tasks. Estimate the worst-case inter-arrival times for the aperiodic tasks and attempt to assign the rate-monotonic priorities to these tasks. Interrupt-driven tasks will often need to be given the highest priorities to allow them to quickly service interrupts. This means that an interrupt-driven task may need to be allocated a priority that is higher than its rate-monotonic priority. If two tasks have the same period and hence the same rate-monotonic priority, it is up to the designer to resolve the tie. In general, assign the higher priority to the task that is more important from an application perspective.

The Generalized Utilization Bound Theorem described in this chapter can be applied to analyzing the performance of software designs executing on a single-processor system. As described previously, for time-critical tasks that miss their deadlines according to the Utilization Bound Theorem, the Generalized Completion Time Theorem can be applied for a more precise analysis.

17.3.5 Example of Applying Generalized Utilization Bound Theorem

As an example of applying the generalized real-time scheduling theory with the **Generalized Utilization Bound Theorem** (Section 17.3.2), consider the following case. There are four tasks, of which two are periodic and two are aperiodic. One of the aperiodic tasks, t_a, is interrupt-driven and must execute within 200 msec of the arrival of its interrupt or data will be lost. The other aperiodic task, t_2, has a worst-case inter-arrival time of T_2, which is taken to be the period of the equivalent periodic task. The detailed characteristics are as follows, where all times are in msec and the utilization $U_i = C_i / T_i$:

Periodic task t_1: $C_1 = 20$; $T_1 = 100$; $U_1 = 0.2$
Aperiodic task t_2: $C_2 = 15$; $T_2 = 150$; $U_2 = 0.1$
Interrupt-driven aperiodic task t_a: $C_a = 4$; $T_a = 200$, $U_a = 0.02$
Periodic task t_3: $C_3 = 30$; $T_3 = 300$; $U_3 = 0.1$

In addition, t_1, t_2, and t_3 all access the same data store, which is protected by a semaphore s. It is assumed that the context-switching overhead, once at the start of a task's execution and once at the end of its execution, is included in the CPU times.

If tasks were allocated priorities strictly according to their rate-monotonic priorities, t_1 would have the highest priority, followed respectively by t_2, t_a, and t_3. However, because of t_a's stringent response time need, it is given the highest priority. The priority assignment is therefore t_a highest, followed respectively by t_1, t_2, and t_3.

The overall CPU utilization is 0.42, which is below the worst-case utilization bound of 0.69. However, it is necessary to investigate each task individually because rate-monotonic priorities have not been assigned. First consider the interrupt-driven task t_a. Task t_a is the highest priority task, which always gets the CPU when it needs it. Its utilization is 0.04, so it will have no difficulty meeting its deadline.

Next consider the task t_1, which executes for 20 msec during its period T_1 of duration 100 msec. Applying the **Generalized Utilization Bound Theorem**, it is necessary to consider the following four factors:

a. **Preemption time by higher priority tasks with periods less than T_1.** There are no tasks with periods less than T_1.

b. **Execution time C_1 for the task t_1** = 20. Execution utilization = U_1 = 0.2.

c. **Preemption by higher priority tasks with longer periods.** The task t_a falls into this category. Preemption utilization during the period $T_1 = C_a/T_1 = 4/100 = 0.04$.

d. **Blocking time by lower priority tasks.** Both t_2 and t_3 can potentially block t_1. Based on the priority ceiling algorithm, at most, one lower priority task can actually block t_1. The worst case is t_3, because it has a longer CPU time of 30 msec. Blocking utilization during the period $T_1 = B_3/T_1 = 30/100 = 0.3$.

Worst-case utilization = preemption utilization + execution utilization + blocking utilization = $0.04 + 0.2 + 0.3 = 0.54$ < worst-case upper bound of 0.69. Consequently, t_1 will meet its deadline.

Next consider task t_2, which executes for 15 msec during its period T_2 of duration 150 msec. Again, applying the **Generalized Utilization Bound Theorem**, it is necessary to consider the following four factors:

a. **Preemption time by higher priority tasks with periods less than T_2.** Only one task, t_1, has a period less than T_2. Its preemption utilization during the period $T_2 = U_1 = 0.2$.

b. **Execution time C_2 for the task t_2** = 15. Execution utilization = U_2 = 0.1.

c. **Preemption by higher priority tasks with longer periods.** The interrupt-driven task t_a falls into this category. Preemption utilization during the period $T_2 = C_a/T_2 = 4/150 = 0.03$. Total preemption utilization by t_1 and $t_a = 0.2 + 0.03 = 0.23$.

d. **Blocking time by lower priority tasks.** The task t_3 can block t_2. In the worst case, it blocks t_2 for its total CPU time of 30 msec. Blocking utilization during the period $T_2 = B_3/T_2 = 30/150 = 0.2$.

Worst-case utilization = preemption utilization + execution utilization + blocking utilization = $0.23 + 0.1 + 0.2 = 0.53$ < worst-case upper bound of 0.69. Consequently, t_2 will meet its deadline.

Finally, consider task t_3, which executes for 30 msec during its period T_3 of duration 300 msec. Once again, applying the **Generalized Utilization Bound Theorem**, it is necessary to consider the following four factors:

a.   **Preemption time by higher priority tasks with periods less than t_3.** All three higher priority tasks fall into this category, so total preemption utilization = $U_1 + U_2 + U_a = 0.2 + 0.1 + 0.02 = 0.32$.

b.   **Execution time C_3 for the task t_3.** Execution utilization = $U_3 = 0.1$

c.   **Preemption by higher priority tasks with longer periods.** No tasks fall into this category.

d.   **Blocking time by lower priority tasks.** No tasks fall into this category.

Worst-case utilization = preemption utilization + execution utilization = $0.32 + 0.1 = 0.42 <$ worst-case upper bound of 0.69. Consequently, t_3 will meet its deadline.

In conclusion, all four tasks will meet their deadlines.

17.3.6 Example of Applying Generalized Completion Time Theorem

Consider how the **Generalized Completion Time Theorem** (Section 17.3.3) is applied to the example given in the previous section, in which there are two periodic tasks (t_1 and t_3)and two aperiodic tasks (t_a and t_3). Three of the tasks (t_1, t_2, and t_3) have mutually exclusive access to a critical section. Given that one of the aperiodic tasks, t_a, needs to be assigned the highest priority, which is different from its rate-monotonic priority, the priority assignment is t_a highest, followed respectively by the t_1, t_2, and t_3. The execution of these four tasks on a single-processor system is depicted on Figure 17.2, which considers the worst case of the four tasks being ready to execute at the same time. The highest priority task t_a executes first for 4 msec, followed by the task with the next highest priority t_1 for its execution time of 20 msec. The next two tasks, t_2, and t_3, also execute in order of priority and all tasks meet their deadlines. In this example, mutual exclusion is ensured by the tasks executing in sequence.

17.4 PERFORMANCE ANALYSIS USING EVENT SEQUENCE ANALYSIS

During the requirements phase of the project, the system's required response times to external events are specified. After task structuring, a first attempt at allocating time budgets to the concurrent tasks in the system can be made. Event sequence analysis is used to determine the sequence of tasks that need to be executed to service a given external event. The first task in an event sequence waits for the event that initiates the sequence (such as an external event) while the other tasks in the event sequence execute in a strict sequence because each task is activated by a message sent by its predecessor. It is also possible for an event sequence to divide into more than one event sequence, if a given task sends messages to more than one waiting task. A **timing diagram** is used to depict the sequence of internal events and tasks activated after the arrival of the external event. The approach is described next.

Consider an external event. Determine which I/O task is activated by this event and then determine the sequence of internal events that follow. This necessitates identifying the tasks that are activated and the I/O tasks that generate the system response to the external event. Estimate the CPU time for each task. Estimate the

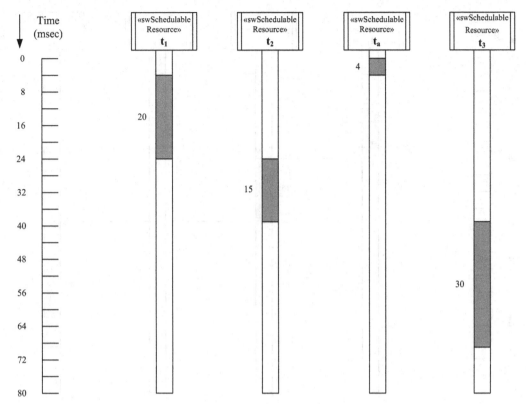

Figure 17.2. Timing diagram for tasks executing on a single-processor system with mutual exclusion.

CPU overhead, which consists of context-switching overhead, interrupt-handling overhead, and inter-task communication and synchronization overhead. It is also necessary to consider any other tasks that execute during this period. The sum of the CPU times for the tasks that participate in the event sequence, plus any additional tasks that execute, plus CPU overhead, must be less than or equal to the specified system response time. If there is some uncertainty over the CPU time for each task, allocate a worst-case upper bound.

To estimate overall CPU utilization, it is necessary to estimate, for a given time interval, the CPU time for each task. If there is more than one path through the task, estimate the CPU time for each path. Next, estimate the frequency of activation of tasks. This is easily computed for periodic tasks. For aperiodic tasks, consider the average and maximum activation rates. Multiply each task's CPU time by its activation rate. Sum all the task CPU times and then compute CPU utilization.

An example of applying the event sequence analysis approach is given next. A more detailed example is given in Chapter 18.

17.4.1 Example of Performance Analysis Using Event Sequence Analysis

For an example of applying the event sequence analysis approach, consider four tasks with the same CPU times and periods as those described in Section 17.3.5. However, this time consider the situation where three of these tasks are involved in an event

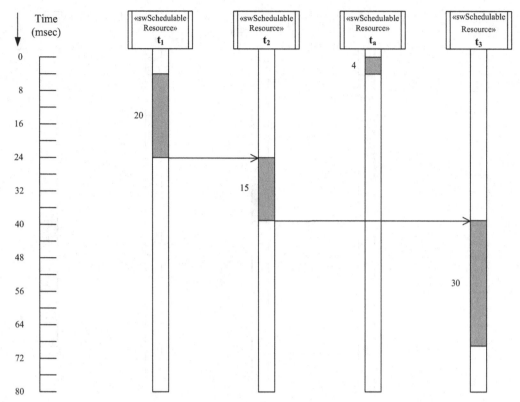

Figure 17.3. Timing diagram for tasks in an event sequence executing on a single-processor system.

sequence in which the tasks execute in the order t_1, t_2, and t_3, such that task t_1 is awakened by an external event, and tasks t_2 and t_3 each wait for a message from their predecessor task in the event sequence. As before, the priority assignment is t_a highest, followed respectively by the tasks t_1, t_2, and t_3. The execution of these four tasks on a single-processor system is depicted on Figure 17.3 with the worst-case scenario of all tasks being ready to execute at the same time.

In this situation, the highest priority task t_a executes first for 4 msec, followed by the task with the next highest priority t_1 for its execution time of 20 msec. Task t_1 sends a message to task t_2 just before completing execution. Task t_2 is then unblocked and starts executing. However the lower priority task t_3 remains blocked waiting for a message from t_2. When task t_2 sends the message to task t_3, t_3 is unblocked, and when t_2 completes execution, t_3 starts executing to completion.

17.5 PERFORMANCE ANALYSIS USING REAL-TIME SCHEDULING THEORY AND EVENT SEQUENCE ANALYSIS

This section describes how the real-time scheduling theory can be combined with the event sequence analysis approach. Instead of considering individual tasks, it is necessary to consider all the tasks in an event sequence. The task activated by the external event executes first and then initiates a series of internal events, resulting in activation and execution of other internal tasks. It is necessary to determine whether all the tasks in the event sequence can be executed before the deadline.

Initially attempt to allocate all the tasks in the event sequence the same priority. These tasks can then collectively be considered one equivalent task from a real-time scheduling viewpoint. This equivalent task has a CPU time equal to the sum of the CPU times of the tasks in the event sequence, plus context-switching overhead, plus message communication or event synchronization overhead. The worst-case inter-arrival time of the external event that initiates the event sequence is then made the period of this equivalent task.

To determine whether the equivalent task can meet its deadline, it is necessary to apply the real-time scheduling theorems. In particular, it is necessary to consider preemption by higher priority tasks, blocking by lower priority tasks, and execution time of this equivalent task. An example of combining event sequence analysis with real-time scheduling using the equivalent task approach is given in Chapter 18, for the Light Rail Control System.

In some cases, you cannot assume that all the tasks in the event sequence can be replaced by an equivalent task. This happens if one of the tasks is used in more than one event sequence or if executing the equivalent task at that priority would prevent other tasks from meeting their deadlines. In such cases, the tasks in the event sequence need to be analyzed separately and assigned different priorities. In determining whether the tasks in the event sequence will meet their deadlines, it is necessary to consider preemption and blocking on a per task basis; however, it is still necessary to determine whether all tasks in the event sequence will complete before the deadline. An example of this case is also described in Chapter 18.

17.6 ADVANCED REAL-TIME SCHEDULING ALGORITHMS

The scheduling theory for performance analysis of real-time designs described so far in this chapter has considered *implicit deadline* task sets, where the relative deadline of each task coincides with its next arrival time. While this represents many real-time applications, there are cases when the deadlines can be less than the periods. For such cases, the *deadline-monotonic* algorithm, which assigns fixed priorities according to the relative deadlines, is known to be optimal among all fixed-priority scheduling algorithms (Leung and Whitehead 1982).

The rate-monotonic and deadline-monotonic priority assignments fall within the general class of fixed-priority scheduling algorithms, in which all tasks are assigned a static priority before execution. This has the advantage of supporting directly most of the existing real-time embedded systems with limited priority levels. However, in *dynamic priority* systems, the relative priorities of tasks can change during execution. For instance, with the preemptive Earliest-Deadline-First (EDF) scheduling algorithm, which assigns the priorities to the current active jobs by considering their absolute deadlines, the utilization bound is 100 percent on a single-processor system (Liu and Layland 1973).

This chapter has focused so far on single-processor systems. For multiprocessor systems, there are two general approaches in real-time scheduling. With *partitioned scheduling*, tasks are first partitioned on individual processors and then the schedulability is analyzed on each processor separately. However, in general, making optimal partitioning decisions is an NP-Hard problem. With *global scheduling*, tasks are allowed to migrate; that is, at any time, a ready task may be assigned to any of the idle processors. However, the fact that a given task can only execute on one processor at a time in a multiprocessor system creates significant difficulties for the schedulability analysis. For instance, it is known that for fixed-priority assignments (such as RMS), the worst-case response time for tasks is not necessarily obtained when tasks are activated simultaneously (Lauzac et al. 1998). Moreover, the general utilization bound for RMS on a real-time system consisting of m processors is only m/3, as long as the largest task utilization in the workload does not exceed 1/3 (Baruah and Goossens 2003). The reader is referred to a comprehensive survey (Davis and Burns 2011) for recent results on multiprocessor schedulability theory including partitioned and global scheduling approaches.

Given the issues with applying real-time scheduling theory to tasks executing on multiprocessor systems, one approach is to consider using *partitioned scheduling*, such that a subset of the task set is exclusively assigned to each processor. The real-time scheduling theory for a single processor can then be applied to analyze the performance of those tasks assigned to execute on each individual processor in turn. Thus, for two CPUs, the partitioned scheduling algorithm would consider the tasks assigned to CPU A independently of those assigned to CPU B. An advantage of this approach on multicore systems is that there is likely to be less cache flushing at context-switching time than in global scheduling approaches, which negatively impacts performance.

17.7 PERFORMANCE ANALYSIS OF MULTIPROCESSOR SYSTEMS

To analyze the performance of tasks executing on a multiprocessor system using global scheduling, a practical approach is to use timing diagrams. This section describes three examples of analyzing the performance of concurrent tasks on a dual-processor system using timing diagrams. However the approach can easily be extended to multiprocessor systems with more than two processors, as described in the case studies in Chapters 19 and 20.

17.7.1 Performance Analysis of Independent Tasks on Multiprocessor Systems

Consider the example of the three tasks described in Section 17.1.5 (and depicted on Figure 17.1) executing on a dual-processor system, which can execute two tasks in parallel on CPU A and CPU B. The execution of the three tasks is illustrated by the timing diagram shown in Figure 17.4. The execution of the tasks is depicted with the shaded portions identifying when tasks are executing on CPU A or CPU B. Because there are two CPUs in this example, two tasks can execute at any one time, providing they are ready to execute.

Consider the worst case of the three tasks being ready to execute at the same time when there are two CPUs available. This scenario starts with t_1 executing on CPU A and t_2 executing on CPU B, because both t_1 and t_2 have shorter periods and hence higher priorities than t_3. Task t_1 completes execution on CPU A after 20 msec and thus meets its deadline. Task t_3 then starts executing on CPU A while task t_2 continues executing on CPU B. After a further 10 msec, task t_2 completes execution (easily meeting its deadline) on CPU B, which then becomes idle, as task t_1 is not yet

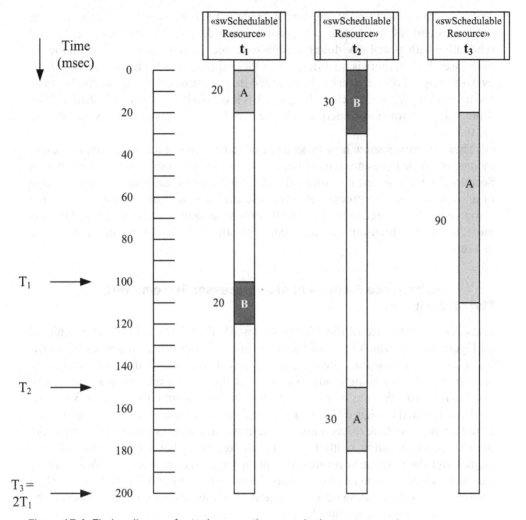

Figure 17.4. Timing diagram for tasks executing on a dual-processor system.

ready to resume execution. At the start of task t_1's second period, $T_1 = 100$, task t_1 resumes executing but this time on CPU B.

After executing for 90 msec, t_3 completes, which after a total elapsed time of 110 msec is less than its deadline of 200 msec. As there is no ready task, CPU A becomes idle. After executing for 20 msec, t_1 completes and, since there are no ready tasks, CPU B becomes idle again. At this time, both CPUs are idle. Task t_2 resumes executing again at the start of its second period, $T_2 = 150$, on CPU A and finishes 30 msec later.

Now consider the same tasks executing with partitioned scheduling instead of global scheduling. Assume tasks are partitioned such that tasks t_1 and t_3 are assigned CPU A and task t_2 is assigned CPU B. There is no difference in execution until the start of t_1's second period, $T_1 = 100$. With partitioned scheduling, task t_1 resumes execution on CPU A (instead of CPU B) by preempting task t_3, which by then has been executing for 80 msec. Task t_1 completes execution after 20 msec, at which time task t_3 resumes executing on CPU A and completes execution after a further 10 msec.

Task t_2 resumes executing at the start of its second period, $T_2 = 150$, but this time on CPU B instead of CPU A. Thus all tasks meet their deadlines. Comparing partitioned scheduling with global scheduling for this example, all tasks meet their deadlines in both cases. In fact, there is no difference in the elapsed times for tasks t_1 and t_2. However, the elapsed time for task t_3 is extended from 110 msec with global scheduling to 130 msec with partitioned scheduling, which is less than its deadline of 200 msec. (The timing diagram for partitioned scheduling is not depicted and is left as an exercise for the reader).

These examples show how tasks can take advantage of an additional processor by meeting their deadlines earlier than on the single-processor system described in Section 17.1.5. However, it is often the case that tasks cannot take full advantage of a second (or more) processor(s) because they are held up waiting for a scarce resource (such as shared memory or I/O) or for a message from another task. Furthermore, memory contention can also negatively affect the performance of multicore systems.

17.7.2 Performance Analysis of Multiprocessor Systems with Mutual Exclusion

Consider next the case of the four tasks described in Section 17.3.6 (and depicted on Figure 17.2), in which three of the tasks have mutually exclusive access to a critical section, executing on a dual-processor system. We assume the same worst-case scenario of all tasks being ready to execute at the same time. In this situation, the two highest priority tasks, t_a and t_1, execute in parallel on CPUs A and B respectively, as depicted in Figure 17.5. Task t_a completes execution on CPU A after 4 msec. However, because task t_1 has mutually exclusive access to its critical section for the duration of its execution, neither t_2 nor t_3 can execute as they are both blocked waiting to enter their critical sections; consequently, CPU A becomes idle. When task t_1 leaves its critical section just before completing execution on CPU B, task t_2 is then unblocked, starts executing on CPU A, and enters its critical section. However, the lowest priority task, t_3, remains blocked and cannot take advantage of a free CPU. When task t_2 leaves its critical section before completing execution on CPU A, t_3 is then unblocked, starts executing on CPU B, and enters its critical section.

This example shows that, with multiprocessor systems, there can be situations when concurrent tasks are unable to take full advantage of available CPUs because the tasks are blocked waiting for scarce resources.

17.7.3 Performance Analysis of Multiprocessor Systems with Event Sequence Analysis

Consider next applying the event sequence analysis approach to tasks executing on a dual-processor system. This example uses the same four tasks with the same CPU times and periods as those described in Section 17.3.6 and depicted in Figure 17.3. However, this time consider the situation where three of these tasks are involved in an event sequence in which the tasks execute in the order t_1, t_2, and t_3, such that task t_1 is awakened by an external event, and tasks t_2 and t_3 each wait for a message from their predecessor task in the event sequence. As before, the priority assignment is t_a highest, followed respectively by the tasks t_1, t_2, and t_3. The execution of these

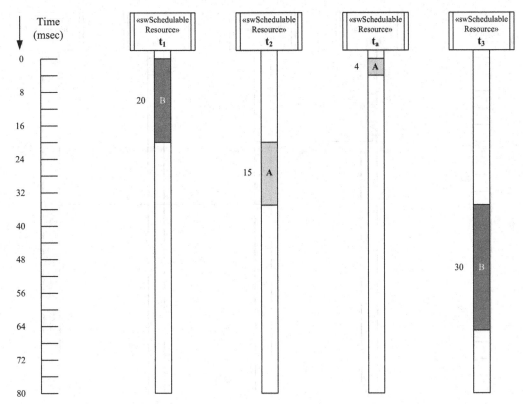

Figure 17.5. Timing diagram for tasks executing on a dual-processor system with mutual exclusion.

four tasks on a dual-processor system is depicted on Figure 17.6 with the worst-case scenario of all tasks being ready to execute at the same time.

In this situation, the two highest priority tasks, t_a and t_1, start executing in parallel on CPUs A and B respectively. Task t_a completes execution on CPU A after 4 msec. However, because tasks t_2 and t_3 are blocked waiting for messages, neither of these tasks can execute, and consequently CPU A becomes idle. Just before completing execution on CPU B, task t_1 sends a message to task t_2. Task t_2 is then unblocked and executes on CPU A. However, the lower priority task, t_3, remains blocked waiting for a message from t_2 and cannot take advantage of a free CPU. When task t_2 sends the message to task t_3, t_3 is then unblocked and executes on CPU B.

As with the example in the previous section, this example of applying event sequence analysis shows that, with multiprocessor systems, there are situations when concurrent tasks are unable to take full advantage of available CPUs, in this case because they are blocked waiting for messages from other tasks.

17.8 ESTIMATION AND MEASUREMENT OF PERFORMANCE PARAMETERS

Several performance parameters must be determined through estimation or measurement before a real-time performance analysis can be carried out. These are

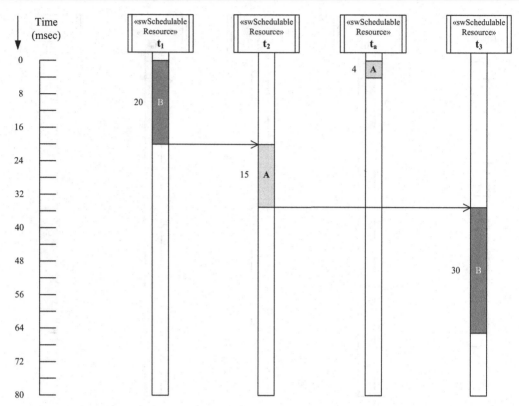

Figure 17.6. Timing diagram for tasks in an event sequence executing on a dual-processor system.

independent variables whose values are inputs to the performance analysis. Dependent variables are variables whose values are estimated by the real-time scheduling theory.

A major assumption made for the real-time scheduling is that all tasks are locked in main memory so there is no paging overhead. Paging overhead adds another degree of uncertainty and delay that cannot be tolerated in hard real-time systems.

The following parameters must be estimated for each task involved in the performance analysis:

a. **The task's period T_i, which is the frequency with which it executes.** For a periodic task, the period is fixed (refer to Chapter 13 for more details on periodic tasks). For an aperiodic task, use the worst-case (i.e., minimum) external event inter-arrival time for an input task and then extrapolate from this for downstream internal tasks that participate in the same event sequence.

b. **The execution time C_i, which is the CPU time required for the period.** At design time, this figure is an estimate. Estimate the number of source lines of code for the task, and then estimate the number of compiled lines of code. Use benchmarks of programs developed in the selected source language executing on the selected hardware with the selected operating system. Compare benchmark results with the size of the task to estimate compiled code execution time.

When the task has been implemented, substitute performance measurements of the task executing on the hardware for the task estimates.

CPU system overhead parameters are also needed for the performance analysis. These parameters can be determined by performance measurements of benchmark programs. These programs need to be developed in the programming language selected for the real-time system, executing on the hardware platform selected for the RT system, and with the multitasking operating system or kernel selected for the RT system. The following system overhead parameters must be measured:

a. **Context-switching overhead**. The CPU time for the operating system to switch the CPU allocation from one task to another (see Chapter 3).
b. **Interrupt-handling overhead**. The CPU time required to handle an interrupt.
c. **Inter-task communication and synchronization overhead**. The CPU time to send a message or signal an event from a source task to a destination task. This will depend on the communication and synchronization primitives used by the tasks in the real-time application.
d. **Memory contention in multicore systems**. The system overhead due to memory contention between tasks executing in parallel on different processors needs to be measured.

These overhead parameters must be factored into the computation of task CPU time, as described in this chapter and applied in the next chapter.

17.9 SUMMARY

This chapter has described the performance analysis of software designs by applying real-time scheduling theory to a concurrent tasking design executing on single-processor or multiprocessor systems. This approach is particularly appropriate for hard real-time systems with deadlines that must be met. This chapter has described two approaches for analyzing the performance of a design: **real-time scheduling theory** and **event sequence analysis**. The two approaches were then combined. This chapter also briefly described advanced real-time scheduling algorithms, including deadline-monotonic scheduling, dynamic priority scheduling, and scheduling for multiprocessor systems. Because the performance analysis is applied to a design consisting of a set of concurrent tasks, the analysis can start as soon as the task architecture has been designed, as described in Chapter 13. It can then be refined as the real-time application development progresses through detailed software design and implementation. A detailed example of performance analysis of a real-time software design is described in Chapter 18. Other examples of performance analysis are described in the case studies of real-time embedded systems in Chapters 19 and 20.

18

Applying Performance Analysis to Real-Time Software Designs

This chapter applies the real-time performance analysis concepts and theory described in Chapter 17 to a real-time embedded system, namely the Light Rail Control System. The complete case study is described in Chapter 21. This chapter focuses on the real-time performance analysis using real-time scheduling theory and event sequence analysis.

Sections 18.1 through 18.3 provide a detailed example of analyzing the performance of the Light Rail Control System. Section 18.1 describes a performance analysis using event sequence analysis. Section 18.2 describes a performance analysis using real-time scheduling theory. Section 18.3 describes a performance analysis using both real-time scheduling theory and event sequence analysis. Section 18.4 describes design restructuring to meet performance goals.

18.1 EXAMPLE OF PERFORMANCE ANALYSIS USING EVENT SEQUENCE ANALYSIS

The example of performance analysis using event sequence analysis describes three time-critical event sequences for a train approaching a station, arriving at a station, and detecting a hazard. Assume that the first case to be analyzed is that of the Approaching Sensor detecting that the train is approaching a station at which it must stop, followed by the Arrival Sensor detecting that the train has arrived at the station. Assume also that the train is operating at the cruising speed. A performance requirement is that the system must respond to each of the approaching sensor and arrival sensor input events within 200 msec. The sequence of internal events following the approaching sensor input is depicted by the event sequence on the timing diagram in Figure 18.1, in which there are two hardware devices and four software tasks shown with their appropriate stereotypes (see Chapter 13). Tasks that are not involved in this scenario are excluded from the figure.

Assume that the Train Control state machine is in Cruising state. Consider the case of input from the approaching sensor. The event sequence is as follows, with the CPU time to process each event given in parentheses (where C_i is the CPU time required to process event i).

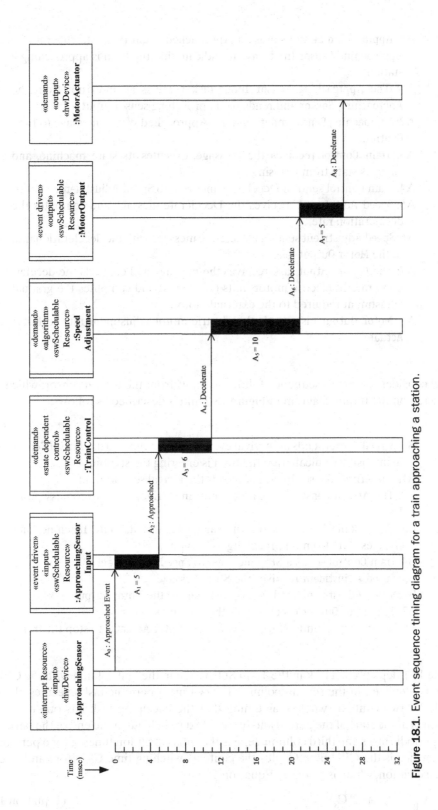

Figure 18.1. Event sequence timing diagram for a train approaching a station.

A0: Approaching Sensor sends an Approached event (i.e., interrupt) to the Approaching Sensor Input task to indicate that the train is approaching a station.

A1: The Approaching Sensor Input task receives an interrupt from the Approaching Sensor and reads the approaching sensor input.

A2: Approaching Sensor Input sends an Approached station message to Train Control.

A3: Train Control receives the message, executes its state machine, and changes state from Cruising to Approaching.

A4: Train Control sends a Decelerate message to Speed Adjustment.

A5: Speed Adjustment receives the Decelerate message and computes the deceleration rate.

A6: Speed Adjustment sends a Decelerate message with the deceleration rate to the Motor Output task.

A7: The Motor Output task receives the message and converts the deceleration rate to electric motor units (e.g., volts) and computes the gradual adjustment required to the external motor.

A8: Motor Output task sends the electric motor adjustment rate to Motor Actuator.

Now consider the event sequence following input from the arrival sensor, which is depicted on the timing diagram in Figure 18.2 and is described as follows:

B0: Arrival Sensor sends an Arrival event (i.e., interrupt) to the Arrival Sensor Input task to indicate that the train is entering the station.

B1: The Arrival Sensor Input task reads the arrival sensor input.

B2: The Arrival Sensor Input task sends an Arrived at station message to Train Control.

B3: Train Control receives the message, executes its state machine, and changes state from Approaching to Stopping.

B4: Train Control sends a Stop message to Speed Adjustment.

B5: Speed Adjustment receives the Stop message.

B6: Speed Adjustment sends a Stop message to the Motor Output task.

B7: The Motor Output task receives the Stop message.

B8: Motor Output sends a Stop command to Motor Actuator to stop the train.

Table 18.1 depicts each task in the Train Subsystem in the first column with the CPU time C_i depicted in the second column. Every time a periodic task executes, there could be two context switches, assuming that the executing task has one context switch in at the start of the period and one context switch out at the end of the period. For periodic tasks, the third column depicts the total execution time C_p for a periodic task, which is the CPU time C_i plus the context-switching time C_x before and after task execution, which is given by Equation 1:

$$C_p = C_i + 2^*C_x \qquad \text{(Equation 1)}$$

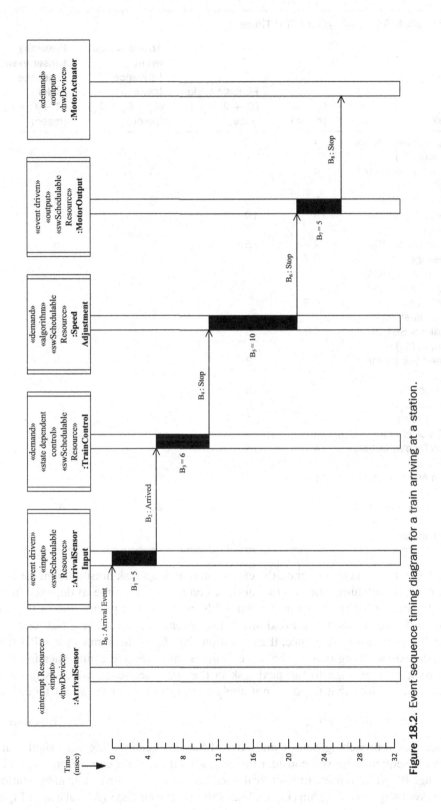

Figure 18.2. Event sequence timing diagram for a train arriving at a station.

Table 18.1. Train Subsystem CPU Times

Task	C_i (msec)	Periodic tasks $(C_i + 2^* C_x)$ (msec)	Arrival sensor event sequence tasks $(C_i + C_x + C_m)$ (msec)	Proximity sensor event sequence tasks $(C_i + C_x + C_m)$ (msec)
Approaching Sensor Input (C_0)	4	5		
Arrival Sensor Input (C_1)	4	5	5	
Train Control (C_3)	5	6	6	6
Speed Adjustment (C_5)	9	10	10	10
Motor Output (C_7)	4	5	5	5
Message communication overhead (C_m)	0.7			
Context-switching overhead (C_x)	0.3			
Proximity Sensor Input (C_8)	4	5		5
Speed Sensor Input (C_9)	2	3		
Location Sensor Input (C_{10})	5	6		
Train Status Dispatcher (C_{11})	10	11		
Train Display Output (C_{12})	14	15		
Train Audio Output (C_{13})	11	12		
Total CPU time used by tasks in event sequence			26	26

For tasks in the event sequence, the execution time for a task must account for both the context-switching time and the message communication time, as depicted in the fourth column for the tasks in the Arrival Sensor event sequence and in the fifth column for the tasks in the Proximity Sensor event sequence. For a task that participates in an event sequence, the execution time C_e is the sum of the CPU time C_i, context-switching time C_x before execution, and message communication time C_m to send a message to the next task in the event sequence, which is given by Equation 2. (Note that C_m does not apply to the last task in the event sequence).

$$C_e = C_i + C_x + C_m \qquad \text{(Equation 2)}$$

Since the Approaching Sensor and Arrival Sensor scenarios are very similar and occur in sequence, we will consider the train arrival event sequence from events B1 through B8, which is more time-critical since it requires the train to stop at the station. The event sequence diagram (Figure 18.2) shows that four tasks (Arrival Sensor Input,

Train Control, Speed Adjustment, and Motor Output) are required to support the arrival sensor external event. Assume that the CPU time to execute event B_i is C_i. There is also a minimum of four context switches required, $4{*}C_x$, where C_x is the context-switching overhead, as well as three message transfers.

The total CPU time for the tasks in the arrival event sequence (C_e) is the sum of CPU time for the four tasks in the event sequence (C_1, C_3, C_5, C_7), plus CPU time for message communication (C_2, C_4, C_6) and context-switching overhead ($4{*}C_x$):

$$C_e = C_1 + C_2 + C_3 + C_4 + C_5 + C_6 + C_7 + 4{*}C_x$$

Assume that message communication overhead C_m is the same in all cases. The times C_2, C_4, and C_6 for message communication should therefore be equal to C_m. The execution time C_e is thus equal to:

$$C_e = C_1 + C_3 + C_5 + C_7 + 3{*}C_m + 4{*}C_x \qquad \text{(Equation 3)}$$

A second event sequence of note is depicted in the fifth column of Table 18.1 and is for the tasks in the Proximity Sensor event sequence, which detects hazards ahead on the rail track such as approaching too close to an earlier train, a hazard signal indicating a problem with the rail track, or a vehicle stopped on a railroad crossing. The total CPU time for the tasks in the proximity event sequence is based on the four tasks in the event sequence, which are Proximity Sensor Input, Train Control, Speed Adjustment, and Motor Output, three of which are also in the arrival event sequence. The execution time C_p is thus equal to:

$$C_p = C_8 + C_3 + C_5 + C_7 + 3{*}C_m + 4{*}C_x \qquad \text{(Equation 4)}$$

This event sequence consists of the following events, as depicted in Figure 18.3:

P1, P2: The Proximity Sensor Input task receives an interrupt from the Proximity Sensor and reads the proximity sensor input, which indicates that a hazard has been detected ahead of the train.

P3: The Proximity Sensor Input task sends a Hazard Detected message to Train Control.

P4: Train Control receives the message, executes its state machine, and changes state from Cruising to Emergency Stopping.

P5: Train Control sends an Emergency Stop message to Speed Adjustment.

P6, P7: Speed Adjustment receives the Emergency Stop message and sends it to the Motor Output task.

P8, P9: The Motor Output task receives the Emergency Stop message and outputs the Stop command to Motor Actuator to stop the train.

18.2 EXAMPLE OF PERFORMANCE ANALYSIS USING REAL-TIME SCHEDULING THEORY

This section applies the real-time scheduling theory to the Light Rail Control System. The performance analysis starts by considering the worst-case steady state in which the train is in motion and cruising at the maximum speed. In this state, several periodic tasks execute as well as some aperiodic tasks. In the case of an aperiodic

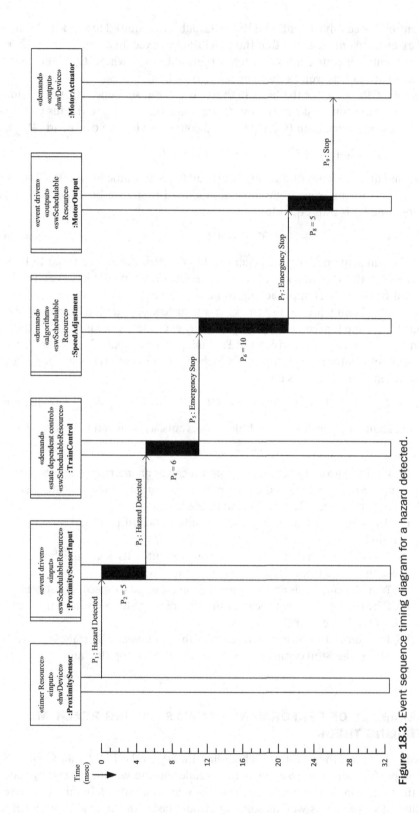

Figure 18.3. Event sequence timing diagram for a hazard detected.

Table 18.2. Real-Time Scheduling Parameters: Steady-State Periodic and Aperiodic Task Parameters

Task	CPU time C_i	Period T_i	Utilization U_i	Priority
Speed Sensor Input	3	10	0.30	1
Location Sensor Input	6	50	0.12	2
Proximity Sensor Input	5	100	0.05	3
Motor Output	5	100	0.05	4
Speed Adjustment	10	100	0.10	5
Train Status Dispatcher	11	600	0.02	6
Train Display Output	15	600	0.03	7
Train Audio Output	12	600	0.02	8
Total Utilization for all tasks			0.68	

task, an equivalent period is assigned, which is the minimum inter-arrival time of the event that activates the task.

Table 18.2 depicts the real-time scheduling parameters for the steady state periodic and aperiodic tasks. Table 18.2 depicts the period of each task T_i in Column 3 and the CPU time required by the task C_i in Column 2. The CPU time for each periodic task includes the CPU time for two context switches, as depicted in Table 18.1. Each task's CPU utilization U_i, which is the ratio $U_i = C_i/T_i$, is depicted in Column 4 of Table 18.2. There are some rounding errors in the computation of CPU utilization U_i in this and subsequent tables. The periodic and aperiodic tasks are described next.

- **Speed Sensor Input**. It is assumed that this task is a periodic task. It is actually aperiodic because it is activated by a shaft interrupt. However, the interrupt arrives on a regular basis, every shaft rotation, so the task is assumed to behave as a periodic task. Assume a worst case of 6,000 rpm, meaning there will be an interrupt every 10 msec, which therefore represents the minimum period of the equivalent periodic task. Because this task has the shortest period, it is assigned the highest priority. Its CPU time is 3 msec.
- **Proximity Sensor Input**. This task has a period of 100 msec and a CPU time of 5 msec.
- **Train Status Dispatcher**. This task has a period of 600 msec and a CPU time of 11 msec.
- **Speed Adjustment**. When activated under automated control, this task executes periodically every 100 msec to compute the required speed value and has a CPU time of 10 msec.
- **Motor Output**. This task is activated by a message from the periodic Speed Adjustment task. It is therefore assumed that the Motor Output task has period equal to that of Speed Adjustment, namely 100 msec, and executes for 5 msec.
- **Location Sensor Input**. This task executes aperiodically with an equivalent period of 50 msec and has a CPU time of 6 msec. It executes on a regular basis to determine the location of the train.
- **Train Display Output**. This task is activated by, and therefore has the same period (600 msec) as Train Status Dispatcher. Its CPU time is 15 msec.
- **Train Audio Output**. This task is also activated by, and therefore has the same period (600 msec) as Train Status Dispatcher. Its CPU time is 12 msec.

The rate-monotonic priorities of the tasks are assigned in inverse proportion to their periods (as depicted in Column 5 of Table 2), such that higher priorities are allocated to tasks with shorter periods. Thus, the highest priority task is Speed Sensor Input, which has a period of 10 msec. The next highest priority task is Location Sensor Input, which has a period of 50 msec. Next highest priority is Proximity Sensor Input, which has a period of 100 msec. Two other tasks have a period of 100 msec: Speed Adjustment and Motor Output. Even though Speed Adjustment sends messages that are consumed by Motor Output, the higher priority is given to Motor Output because it interfaces to the external motor. Priorities are next assigned to Train Status Dispatcher, Train Display Output, and Train Audio Output tasks. Since these tasks all have the same priority, higher priority is given to Train Status Dispatcher, which is the producer of the messages consumed by the other two tasks.

From Table 18.2, the total utilization of the steady-state periodic and aperiodic tasks is 0.68, which is below the theoretical worst-case upper bound of 0.69 given by the **Utilization Bound Theorem**. Therefore, according to the rate-monotonic algorithm, all the tasks are able to meet their deadlines.

18.3 EXAMPLE OF PERFORMANCE ANALYSIS USING REAL-TIME SCHEDULING THEORY AND EVENT SEQUENCE ANALYSIS

Next, consider the case of an external event, such as that from the approaching sensor, arrival sensor, or proximity sensor, triggering an event sequence. Since the approaching sensor event occurs a significant time before the arrival sensor event, the approaching sensor event sequence and the arrival sensor event sequence do not overlap in time. Because the two event sequences are very similar in behavior, only one of them needs to be considered. This analysis must consider the tasks in the event sequence, in addition to the steady-state periodic and aperiodic tasks described in the previous section. The first solution uses an equivalent event sequence task to replace the tasks in the event sequence.

18.3.1 Equivalent Event Sequence Tasks

It is necessary to consider the impact of the additional load imposed by the arrival sensor event sequence or the proximity sensor event sequence on the steady-state load of the periodic and aperiodic tasks. This is done by considering the impact of the tasks in each event sequence on the steady-state analysis described in Section 18.1. For the four aperiodic tasks participating in the arrival sensor event sequence (namely Arrival Sensor Input, Train Control, Speed Adjustment, and Motor Output) consider the equivalent aperiodic task, which is referred to as the *event sequence task*.

First consider an input from the arrival sensor. As described in the event sequence analysis and shown in the event sequence diagram, the tasks required to process this input are Arrival Sensor Input, Train Control, Speed Adjustment, and Motor Output. Although four tasks are involved in the event sequence, they have to execute in strict sequence because each task is activated by a message sent by its predecessor in the sequence. We can therefore assume, to a first approximation, that the four tasks are equivalent to one aperiodic task whose CPU time is C_e. C_e is the sum of the CPU times of the four individual tasks plus message communication overhead and context-switching overhead, as given by Equation 3. The equivalent aperiodic task is referred to as the *arrival event sequence task*. From Equation 3 and Table 18.1, C_e is equal to 26 msec.

From the real-time scheduling theory, an aperiodic task can be treated as a periodic task whose period is given by the minimum inter-arrival time of the aperiodic requests. Let the period for the equivalent periodic event sequence task be T_e. Assume that T_e is also the necessary response time to the arrival sensor input. For example, if T_e is 200 msec, the desired response to the external event from the arrival sensor is 200 msec.

Now consider the second event sequence task, which is the *proximity event sequence task*. This event sequence is initiated by the proximity sensor detecting a hazard on the track. However, an event sequence will only occur if the Proximity Sensor Input task actually detects a hazard ahead; if it does not, then it just completes executing and waits for the next timer event. If a hazard is detected, then an input from the proximity sensor can be treated in a similar way to the arrival event sequence. In the proximity sensor case, the tasks in the event sequence are Proximity Sensor Input, Train Control, Speed Adjustment, and Motor Output, with the last three identical to those for the arrival sensor. The main difference is that the Proximity Sensor Input task is periodic, with a period of 100 msec, and hence is activated more frequently. From Table 18.1, the estimated CPU time for Proximity Sensor Input of 5 msec. Thus, from Equation 4 and Table 18.1, the CPU time to process input from the proximity sensor is 26 msec. However, the period for Proximity Sensor Input is 100 msec, which is lower than the arrival sensor. The higher sampling rate for the proximity sensor is to ensure the quick detection of hazards, which are unexpected, in comparison to train arrival at a station, which is expected. This allows approaching sensors to be placed at a preplanned distance from each station to allow the train to decelerate to a slower speed and allows the arrival sensors to be placed near the entrance to the station to allow the train to stop at the station.

18.3.2 Assigning Rate-Monotonic Priorities

Next, consider the real-time scheduling impact of adding each event sequence task in turn on the steady-state situation previously considered. Table 18.3 provides the real-time scheduling parameters in which the two event sequence tasks are added to the steady state tasks from Table 18.2. Besides the CPU time and period for each periodic task and event sequence task, in columns 2 and 3 respectively, the data for three scenarios are provided. Columns 4 and 5 respectively depict the CPU utilization and priorities for tasks participating in the *arrival event sequence*. Columns 6 and 7 provide the same information for tasks in the *proximity event sequence*, while columns 8 and 9 provide this information for tasks when the *arrival* and *proximity event sequences* occur simultaneously.

When assigning a priority to the event sequence task, the task is initially assigned its rate-monotonic priority, which is based on its period. First consider the periodic proximity event sequence task. When an obstacle is detected, this event sequence task, consisting of the four tasks starting with the Proximity Sensor Input task (in Table 18.3), which replaces the Proximity Sensor Input task executing alone. The

Table 18.3. Real-Time Scheduling Parameters with Event Sequencing Tasks

Task	CPU time C_i	Period T_i	Arrival event sequence utilization U_a	Arrival event sequence priority	Proximity event sequence utilization U_p	Proximity event sequence priority	Arrival & proximity event sequences utilization U_q	Arrival & proximity event sequences priority
Speed Sensor Input	3	10	0.30	1	0.30	1	0.30	1
Location Sensor Input	6	50	0.12	2	0.12	2	0.12	2
Proximity Sensor Input	5	100	0.05	3				
Motor Output	5	100	0.05	4	0.05	4	0.05	4
Speed Adjustment	10	100	0.10	5	0.10	5	0.10	5
Train Status Dispatcher	11	600	0.02	7	0.02	6	0.02	7
Train Display Output	15	600	0.03	8	0.03	7	0.03	8
Train Audio Output	12	600	0.02	9	0.02	8	0.02	9
Arrival Event Sequence Task	26	200	0.13	6			0.13	6
Proximity Event Sequence Task	26	100			0.26	3	0.26	3
Total Utilization for all tasks			0.81		0.89		1.02	

proximity event sequence task has the same period and therefore is assigned the same rate-monotonic priority as Proximity Sensor Input (the third highest after Speed Sensor Input) and has a CPU time of 26 msec. Given that the period is 100 msec, the CPU utilization for this event sequence task is 0.26. The total CPU utilization of the steady-state tasks and the proximity event sequence task is 0.89 (column 6 in Table 18.3), which is well above the worst-case upper bound of 0.69 given by the **Utilization Bound Theorem**. Consequently, the proximity event sequence task is likely to miss its deadline.

Next consider the *arrival event sequence task*, which is aperiodic. Because this task has a longer period than five other steady-state tasks, namely Speed Sensor Input, Proximity Sensor Input, Location Sensor Input, Speed Adjustment, and Motor Output, it is given a lower rate-monotonic priority than these five tasks. The real-time scheduling parameters for this case, as well as the assigned task priorities, are given in Table 18.3. Given that the *arrival event sequence task* has a CPU time C_e of 26 msec and an equivalent period T_e of 200 sec, the task CPU utilization is 0.13. The total CPU utilization of the steady-state tasks (column 4 in Table 18.3) and the arrival event sequence task is 0.81, which is also above the worst-case upper bound of 0.69 given by the **Utilization Bound Theorem**. Consequently, the arrival event sequence task could also miss its deadline in addition to all the periodic tasks.

It should be noted that the impact of each event sequence task on the steady-state periodic tasks was considered separately. What would the impact be if both event sequence tasks were triggered in quick succession? This analysis is depicted in columns 8 and 9 of Table 18.3. The total CPU utilization is 1.02, which is obviously an impossible number (more than 100%) and well above the utilization bound upper limit of 0.69. Since rapid successive inputs from the arrival and proximity sensors would be interleaved, this impact needs a more detailed analysis. A more detailed rate-monotonic analysis is given in the next section.

18.3.3 Detailed Rate-Monotonic Analysis

A more comprehensive analysis of the light rail control problem is obtained by treating each of the tasks in the event sequences separately rather than together. The CPU parameters for each task, including the individual tasks in the proximity and arrival event sequences, are shown in Table 18.4, in which each task has its context-switching and message communication overhead added to its CPU time. Table 18.4 provides the CPU time, period, and utilization (in columns 2, 3, and 4 respectively) for all periodic and aperiodic tasks. All the tasks in the event sequence are treated as periodic tasks with a period equal to the minimum inter-arrival time of 200 msec for the tasks in the arrival event sequence and 100 msec for the tasks in the proximity event sequence. However, since three of the tasks (Train Control, Speed Adjustment, and Motor Output) are in both event sequences, this worst-case analysis assigns all three tasks the lower period of 100 msecs.

The detailed analysis initially assigns the rate-monotonic priority to each task (case 1 in Table 18.4). As before, Speed Sensor Input is given the highest rate-monotonic priority because it has the shortest period of 10 msec, followed by Location Sensor Input. The third highest rate-monotonic priority is Proximity Sensor Input (which initiates the proximity event sequence) since it has the next shortest period of 100 msec. Next are the three other tasks in the proximity event sequence, namely

Table 18.4. Real-Time Scheduling: Periodic and Aperiodic Task Parameters (*tasks in event sequence)

Task	CPU time C_i	Period T_i	Utilization U_i	Rate-monotonic priorities (Case 1)	Non-rate-monotonic priorities (Case 2)
Speed Sensor Input	3	10	0.30	1	1
Location Sensor Input	6	50	0.12	2	2
Proximity Sensor Input*	5	100	0.05	3	4
Motor Output*	5	100	0.05	4	5
Speed Adjustment*	10	100	0.10	6	7
Train Status Dispatcher	11	600	0.02	8	8
Train Display Output	15	600	0.03	9	9
Train Audio Output	12	600	0.02	10	10
Arrival Sensor Input*	5	200	0.03	7	3
Train Control*	6	100	0.06	5	6
Total Utilization for all tasks			0.77		

Train Control, Speed Adjustment, and Motor Output. Because these three tasks participate in both the arrival and proximity event sequences, which have different periods, for a worst-case analysis, the three tasks are assumed to have the shorter proximity sensor period of 100 msec. In addition, Speed Adjustment and Motor Output also execute in the steady-state situation when the train is accelerating or cruising with a period of 100 msec. Because all three tasks have the same period of 100 msec as Proximity Sensor Input, they are assigned the same rate-monotonic priority. The decision is made to give Motor Output the highest priority of the three tasks because it outputs to the motor, followed by Train Control, because it is the control task, and then Speed Adjustment, which is an algorithm task with the longest CPU time of the three. Rate-monotonic priorities are then assigned to the remaining tasks, namely Arrival Sensor Input with a period of 200 msec, Train Status Dispatcher, Train Display Output, and Train Audio Output tasks, all three of which have a period of 600 msec.

From column 4 in Table 18.4, the total utilization of these tasks is 0.77, which is above the theoretical worst-case upper bound of 0.69 given by the **Utilization Bound Theorem**. Therefore, according to the rate-monotonic algorithm, not all the tasks will be able to meet their deadlines in the worst case with the execution of the tasks in both the proximity and arrival event sequences.

18.3.4 Assigning Non-Rate-Monotonic Priorities

The detailed analysis described in the previous section assumed that each task was assigned its rate-monotonic priority, that is, priority in inverse proportion to its period. The major concern is that Arrival Sensor Input, which should be a high-priority input task to respond to the arrival sensor interrupt in a timely manner, is assigned a relatively low rate-monotonic priority because of its relatively long period of 200 msec. A problem with giving the Arrival Sensor Input task its rate-monotonic priority is that the task could potentially miss the arrival sensor interrupt if it has to wait for six higher-priority tasks (Speed Sensor Input, Proximity Sensor Input, Speed Adjustment, Train Control, Location Sensor Input, and Motor Output) to execute.

Because of the risk of missing the arrival interrupt, it is therefore decided to raise the priority of the Arrival Sensor Input task above its rate-monotonic priority. Assigning the Arrival Sensor Input task the highest priority could lead to Speed Sensor Input missing its deadlines because it is also interrupt-driven and has a much shorter period of 10 msec. In addition, the Location Sensor Input is also an input task that receives time-critical external inputs. To avoid delaying these two input tasks, the Arrival Sensor Input task is given a lower priority than these tasks but a higher priority than all the other tasks, which is therefore the third highest priority. This means the Arrival Sensor Input task is given a higher priority than its rate-monotonic priority, as shown in Table 18.4 (case 2). The assignment of non-rate-monotonic priorities is described next.

18.3.5 Applying Generalized Real-Time Scheduling Theory to Tasks with Non-Rate-Monotonic Priorities

To carry out a full analysis of tasks assigned non-rate-monotonic priorities, it is necessary to apply the *Generalized Real-Time Scheduling Theory*, as described in Section 17.3. Because of the assignment of non-rate-monotonic priorities, each task must be checked explicitly against its upper bound to determine whether it meets its deadline. This section analyzes the performance of the tasks shown in Table 18.4 (case 2).

In this analysis, Proximity Sensor Input is considered with the other tasks in the proximity event sequence because it is important to determine that all four tasks complete before the 100 msec deadline. Similarly, Arrival Sensor Input is considered with the other tasks in the arrival event sequence in order to determine that all four tasks complete before the 200 msec deadline. Note that even though we are considering the four tasks together, this analysis is different from the equivalent event sequence task analysis given in Section 18.3.2 because the tasks are considered separately in all other cases.

Performance Analysis of Tasks in Proximity Event Sequence

Consider the four tasks in the *proximity event sequence* (Proximity Sensor Input, Train Control, Speed Adjustment, and Motor Output) over the period T_e of 100 msec. The objective is to determine that the four tasks will complete execution before the 100 msec deadline. It is necessary to apply the Generalized Utilization Bound Theorem, and if necessary the Generalized Completion Time Theorem, to consider the following four factors:

a. **Execution time for the tasks in the event sequence**. The total execution time for the four tasks in the event sequence, $C_e = 26$ msec and $T_e = 100$ msec. Execution utilization = 0.26.

b. **Preemption time by higher-priority tasks with shorter periods**, i.e., less than 100 msec, the period of the tasks in the event sequence. There are two tasks in this set.
   - Speed Sensor Input, with a period of 10 msec, can preempt any of the four tasks a maximum of ten times over 100 msec for a total preemption time of 10*3 msec = 30 msec and preemption utilization of 0.3.

- The other task is Location Sensor Input, with a period of 50 msec, can pre-empt any of the four tasks a maximum of twice over 100 msec for a total preemption time of 2*6 msec = 12 msec and preemption utilization of 0.12.
- Total preemption time of these two higher-priority tasks = 30 + 12 = 42 msec.
- Total preemption utilization of these two higher-priority tasks in the 100 msec period = 0.3 + 0.12 = 0.42.

c. **Preemption by higher-priority tasks with longer periods**. There is one task in this set, namely the Arrival Sensor Input, which could preempt once all four tasks in the proximity event sequence, namely Proximity Sensor Input, Train Control, Speed Adjustment, and Motor Output.
  - Total preemption time = 5 msec.
  - Total preemption utilization during the 100 msec period = 0.05.
  - Total preemption time by higher-priority tasks with both shorter and longer periods = 42 +5 = 47 msec.
  - Total preemption utilization by higher-priority tasks with both shorter and longer periods during the 100 msec period = 0.42 + 0.05 = 0.47.

d. **Blocking time by lower-priority tasks**. Possible blocking of Speed Adjustment task by tasks that access the shared passive entity object Train Data, namely Speed Sensor Input, Location Sensor Input, and Train Status Dispatcher. The first two of these tasks have already been accounted for in factor b.
  - Worst-case blocking time of Train Status Dispatcher = 11 msec
  - Worst-case blocking utilization during the 100 msec period = 0.11

After considering these four factors, we now determine the total elapsed time and total utilization:

- Total elapsed time = total execution time + total preemption time + worst-case blocking time = 26 + 47 + 11 = 84 < 100
- Total utilization = execution utilization + preemption utilization + worst-case blocking utilization = 0.26 + 0.47 + 0.11 = 0.84 > 0.69

The total utilization of 0.84 is greater than the Generalized Utilization Bound Theorem's upper bound of 0.69. However, the more accurate timing analysis using the Generalized Completion Time Theorem, which considers the actual execution time of the tasks, determines that the four tasks in the proximity event sequence all meet their deadlines because the total elapsed time of 84 msec is less than the period of 100 msec.

Performance Analysis of Tasks in Arrival Event Sequence

The analysis for the tasks in the *arrival event sequence* (Arrival Sensor Input, Train Control, Speed Adjustment, and Motor Output) is also carried out using the Generalized Utilization Bound Theorem, as described next. Consider the four tasks in the arrival event sequence over the period T_e of 200 msec. Because the Arrival Sensor Input is assigned a higher priority than its rate-monotonic priority, in order to respond to the arrival sensor interrupt in a timely manner, a detailed rate-monotonic analysis is needed.

As before, the objective is to determine that the four tasks in the arrival event sequence will complete execution before the 200 msec deadline. It is necessary to apply the Generalized Utilization Bound Theorem and consider the following four factors:

a. **Execution time for the tasks in the event sequence**. The total execution time for the four tasks in the event sequence, $C_e = 26$ msec and $T_e = 200$ msec. Execution time = 26 msec. Execution utilization = 0.13.

b. **Preemption time by higher-priority tasks with shorter periods**, i.e., less than 200 msec, the period of the tasks in the event sequence. There are three tasks in this set.
   - Speed Sensor Input, with a period of 10 msec, can preempt any of the four tasks a maximum of twenty times for a total of 20*3 msec = 60 msec and preemption utilization of 60/200 = 0.3.
   - Location Sensor Input, with a period of 50 msec, can preempt any of the four tasks a maximum of four times over 200 msec for a total preemption time of 4*6 msec = 24 msec and preemption utilization of 24/200 = 0.12.
   - Proximity Sensor Input, with a period of 100 msec, can preempt three of the four tasks a maximum of twice over 200 msec for a total preemption time of 2*5 msec = 10 msec and preemption utilization of 10/200 = 0.05.
   - Total preemption time by higher-priority tasks with shorter periods = 60 + 24 + 10 = 94 msec.
   - Total preemption utilization by higher-priority tasks with shorter periods = 0.3 + 0.12 + 0.05 = 0.47

c. **Preemption by higher-priority tasks with longer periods**. There are no such tasks.

d. **Blocking time by lower-priority tasks**. Possible blocking of Speed Adjustment task by tasks that access the shared passive entity object Train Data, namely Speed Sensor Input, Location Sensor Input, and Train Status Dispatcher. The first two of these tasks have already been accounted for in factor b.
   - Worst-case blocking time of Train Status Dispatcher = 11 msec;
   - Worst-case blocking utilization during the 200 msec period = 0.06.

After considering these four factors, we now determine the total elapsed time and total utilization:

- Total elapsed time = total execution time + total preemption time + worst-case blocking time = 26 + 94 + 11 = 131 < 200;
- Total utilization = execution utilization + preemption utilization + worst-case blocking utilization = 0.13 + 0.47 + 0.06 = 0.66 < 0.69.

The total utilization of 0.66 is less than the Generalized Utilization Bound Theorem's upper bound of 0.69, so the four tasks in the event sequence all meet their deadlines. This result is confirmed by the Generalized Completion Time Theorem.

Performance Analysis of Highest Priority Tasks

To determine whether the two highest priority tasks (Speed Sensor Input and Location Sensor Input) with the shorter periods of 10 and 50 msec respectively meet their deadlines, it is necessary to check preemption and execution times during the 50 msec period.

a. **Execution time for the two tasks.** In the 50 msec period, Speed Sensor Input will execute 5 times for 3 msec each time while Location Sensor Input will execute once for 6 msec. Total execution time = 5*3 + 6 = 21 msec. Execution utilization = 0.3 + 0.12 = 0.42.

b. **Preemption time by higher-priority tasks with shorter periods,** i.e., less than 50 msec. There are no such tasks.

c. **Preemption by higher-priority tasks with longer periods.** There are no such tasks.

d. **Blocking time by lower-priority tasks.** Possible blocking of both Speed Sensor Input and Location Sensor Input tasks by tasks that access the shared passive entity object Train Data, namely Speed Adjustment and Train Status Dispatcher.
   - Worst-case blocking time of Speed Adjustment and Train Status Dispatcher = 10 + 11 = 21 msec; assuming each task executes once in a 50 msec period.
   - Worst-case blocking utilization during the 50 msec period = 21/50 = 0.42.

After considering these four factors, we now determine the total elapsed time and total utilization:

- Total elapsed time = total execution time + total preemption time + worst-case blocking time = 21 + 0 + 21 = 42 < 50;
- Total utilization = execution utilization + preemption utilization + worst-case blocking utilization = 0.42 + 0.0 + 0.42 = 0.84 > 0.69.

The total utilization of 0.84 is greater than the Generalized Utilization Bound Theorem's upper bound of 0.69. However, the more accurate timing analysis using the Generalized Completion Time Theorem determines that the two high-priority tasks with the shorter periods will meet their deadlines because the total elapsed time of 42 msec is less than the period of 50 msec.

Performance Analysis of Lowest Priority Tasks

The remaining tasks that need to be analyzed are the three lowest priority tasks that execute with a 600 msec period, namely Train Status Dispatcher, Train Display Output, and Train Audio Output tasks. Consider these three tasks. These three tasks are the lowest-priority tasks and so will be preempted by all the other tasks:

a. **Execution time for the three tasks.** In the 600 msec period, each task will execute once.
   - Total execution time = 11 + 15 +12 = 38 msec.
   - Execution utilization = 0.02 + 0.03 + 0.02 = 0.07.

b. **Preemption time by higher-priority tasks with periods less than 600 msec.** There are seven tasks with higher priorities that will preempt these tasks. Speed Sensor Input will execute sixty times while Location Sensor Input will execute twelve times. Proximity Sensor Input, Train Control, Speed Adjustment, and Motor Output will each execute six times, and Arrival Sensor Input will execute three times.
   - Total utilization is = 0.30 + 0.12 + 0.05 + 0.06 + 0.10 + 0.05 + 0.03 = 0.71.
   - Total preemption time = 60*3 + 12*6 + 6*5 + 6*6 + 6*10 + 6*5 + 3*5 = 423 msec.

c. **Preemption by higher-priority tasks with longer periods.** There are no such tasks.

d. **Blocking time by lower-priority tasks**. Possible blocking of Train Status Dispatcher task by tasks that access the shared passive entity object Train Data, namely Speed Sensor Input, Location Sensor Input, and Speed Adjustment. However, all three of these tasks have already been accounted for in factor b.

After considering these four factors, we now determine the total elapsed time and total utilization:

- Total utilization = execution utilization + preemption utilization = 0.07 + 0.71 = 0.78 > 0.69
- Total elapsed time = total execution time + total preemption time = 38 + 423 = 461 < 600

The total utilization of 0.78 is greater than the Generalized Utilization Bound Theorem's upper bound of 0.69, so according to this theorem, the three tasks could miss their deadlines. However, the Generalized Completion Time Theorem, which considers the actual execution time of the tasks, shows that 461 msec out of 600 msec are used, so that the three tasks do meet their deadlines.

18.3.6 Applying the Generalized Completion Time Theorem to Tasks with Non-Rate-Monotonic Priorities

The Generalized Completion Time Theorem, as described in Section 17.3.6, was also applied to evaluate the performance of the multitasking design described in the previous section. The results of this performance analysis are depicted on the timing diagram in Figure 18.4, which shows the execution of the seven highest-priority tasks in Table 18.4 on a single processor.

The scenario depicted in Figure 18.4 is for train arrival at a station with the Arrival Sensor Input task initiating an arrival event sequence (which also consists of Train Control, Speed Adjustment, and Motor Output) in addition to the tasks Speed Sensor Input, Location Sensor Input, and Proximity Sensor Input (not detecting a hazard). Assume a worst case that all tasks are ready to execute at the start of this scenario, except that the tasks in the *arrival event sequence* must execute according to that sequence.

Speed Sensor Input is the highest-priority task, with a period of 10 msec. Consequently, it executes first for 3 msec, as depicted in Figure 18.4. When Speed Sensor Input needs to execute, it preempts all other tasks and thus always meets its deadline. On completion, next to execute is the second highest-priority task, Location Sensor Input, which executes for 6 msec. The next highest-priority task to execute is Arrival Sensor Input, which is the first task in the arrival event sequence. It start executing for 1 msec before it is preempted by Speed Sensor Input (at the start of its second period) for 3 msec, after which Arrival Sensor Input resumes execution for the remaining 4 msec and sends a message to Train Control before terminating. The next highest-priority task, Proximity Sensor Input, then executes for 3 msec before it is in turn preempted by Speed Sensor Input (third period) for 3 msec, after which Proximity Sensor Input resumes execution for the remaining 2 msec. After this, Train Control (second task in the arrival event sequence) executes for 5 msec before being preempted by Speed Sensor Input (fourth period) for 3 msec. Train Control then

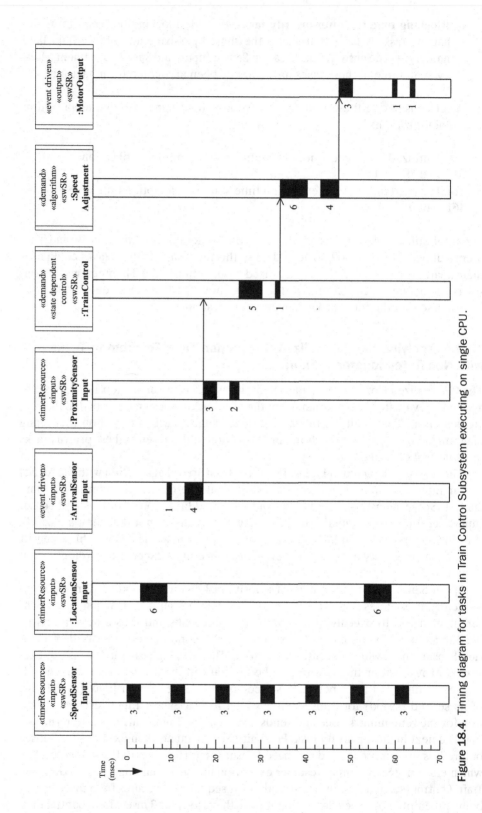

Figure 18.4. Timing diagram for tasks in Train Control Subsystem executing on single CPU.

resumes execution for the remaining 1 msec and sends a message to Speed Adjustment before terminating. Next to execute is Speed Adjustment (third task in the arrival event sequence), which executes for 6 msec before being preempted by Speed Sensor Input (fifth period) for 3 msec. Speed Adjustment then resumes execution for the remaining 4 msec and sends a message to Motor Output before terminating. Motor Output (fourth and last task in the arrival event sequence) is next to execute for 3 msec before being preempted by both Speed Sensor Input (for its sixth period) and Location Sensor Input (for its second period) for 3 msec and 6 msec respectively. After this, Motor Output resumes execution for 1 msec, before being preempted again by Speed Sensor Input (seventh period) after which it completes the last msec.

In conclusion, in this scenario the total elapsed time (from the start of the scenario) for tasks in the arrival event sequence to complete execution is 64 msec, during which time Speed Sensor Input executes seven times, Location Sensor Input executes twice, and Proximity Sensor Input executes once. Thus, all four tasks in the arrival event sequence complete before the 200 msec deadline. Similarly, if Proximity Sensor Input detected a hazard it would initiate the hazard detected event sequence, which would also complete execution before the 100 msec deadline. Note that the timing analysis described in this section only considers the scenario over 70 msec whereas the real-time scheduling analysis in the previous section considered the elapsed time over a 200 msec period.

18.3.7 Performance Analysis of Tasks Executing on a Multiprocessor System

If the concurrent tasks in the software design are to execute on a multiprocessor system, then the performance can be analyzed using timing diagrams to evaluate the impact of increasing the number of processors, as described in Section 17.7.

Consider the task in the event sequence described in Section 18.3.6 executing on a dual-processor system, as depicted on the timing diagram in Figure 18.5, using *global scheduling*. The scenario is for train arrival at a station with the Arrival Sensor Input initiating an arrival event sequence, which also consists of Train Control, Speed Adjustment, and Motor Output, and Proximity Sensor Input not detecting a hazard. As before, a worst-case scenario is assumed in which all tasks are ready to execute at the start of the scenario, except that the tasks in the arrival event sequence must execute according to that sequence.

With a dual-processor system, the two highest-priority tasks can execute in parallel. Thus, this scenario starts with both Speed Sensor Input and Location Sensor Input executing in parallel on CPU A and CPU B respectively. Speed Sensor Input completes execution after 3 msec and releases CPU A for the highest-priority ready task, which is Arrival Sensor Input. After executing for 6 msec, Location Sensor Input completes execution and releases CPU B for the highest-priority ready task, which is Proximity Sensor Input. Arrival Sensor Input sends a message to Train Control before completing execution after 5 msec and releasing CPU A. Train Control is next to execute on CPU A for 2 msec before being preempted by Speed Sensor Input at the start of its second period (elapsed time of 10 msec). Proximity Sensor Input completes executing after 6 msec and releases CPU B. Train Control can now resume execution for its remaining 4 msec on CPU B. Speed Sensor Input completes its second execution cycle of 3 msec and releases CPU A, which becomes idle because the other tasks

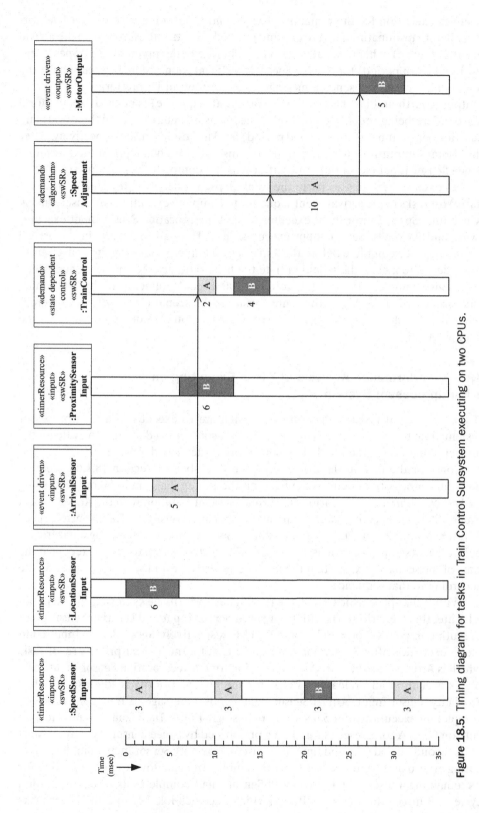

Figure 18.5. Timing diagram for tasks in Train Control Subsystem executing on two CPUs.

are blocked waiting for a message or for their period to elapse. Train Control sends a message to the next task in the event sequence, Speed Adjustment, before completing execution and releasing CPU B. The arrival of the message unblocks Speed Adjustment, which starts executing on CPU A for 10 msec. Speed Sensor Input is ready to execute at the start of its third period (elapsed time of 20 msec) and is assigned to the free CPU B, on which it executes for a further 3 msec before releasing the CPU. Just before completing execution for 10 msec, Speed Adjustment sends a message to the last task in the event sequence, Motor Output, which immediately starts executing on the free CPU B for 5 msec. At elapsed time of 30 msec, Speed Sensor Input is ready to execute at the start of its fourth period on the free CPU A for a further 3 msec. At elapsed time of 31 msec, Motor Output completes its execution time of 5 msec.

In conclusion, in this scenario the total elapsed time of the four tasks in the arrival event sequence to complete execution is 31 msec. At this time, Speed Sensor Input is executing for the fourth time, while Location Sensor Input and Proximity Sensor Input have both completed execution once. Thus, all four tasks in the arrival event sequence complete long before the 200 msec deadline, and the tasks that execute periodically also all meet their deadlines. Similarly, if Proximity Sensor Input detected a hazard it would initiate the hazard detected event sequence, which would also complete execution before the 100 msec deadline.

A different multiprocessing performance analysis could also be carried out using *partitioned scheduling*, as described in Chapter 17. A caveat, as pointed out in Section 17.7, is that memory contention can negatively affect the performance of multicore systems.

18.4 DESIGN RESTRUCTURING

If the performance analysis determines that the real-time design does not meet its performance goals, the design needs to be restructured. This can be achieved by applying the **task clustering criteria**, in which two or more tasks are combined to execute in the same task. In particular, **temporal task clustering**, **sequential task clustering**, and **multiple instance task inversion** can be applied. This could potentially reduce the task overhead.

If there is a performance problem in the Light Rail Control System example, one attempt at design restructuring is to apply sequential clustering. Consider the case of the Train Control task sending a speed command message to the Speed Adjustment task, which in turn sends speed messages to the Motor Output task. These three tasks could be combined into one task using sequential clustering, the clustered Train Control task with passive objects for Speed Adjustment and Motor Output. This eliminates the message communication overhead between these tasks, as well as the context-switching overhead. Let the CPU time for the clustered task be C_v. Then, referring to Table 18.1:

$$C_v = C_3 + C_5 + C_7 \qquad \text{(Equation 5)}$$

The CPU time for the two tasks in the new event sequence C_{ee} is now given by

$$C_{ee} = C_1 + C_v + C_m + 2^*C_x \qquad \text{(Equation 6)}$$

It is interesting to compare Equation 6 (with two tasks in the event sequence) with Equation 3 in Section 18.1 (with four tasks in the event sequence): the message communication overhead is reduced from 3^*C_m to C_m, and the context-switching overhead is reduced from 4^*C_x to 2^*C_x. Given the estimated timing parameters in Table 18.1 and substituting for them in Equations 3 and 6 results in a reduction of total CPU time from 26 msec to 24 msec. If the message communication and context-switching overhead times were larger, the savings would be more substantial. However, if the overhead times were shorter, the savings would be less.

A performance study measuring performance of multitasking on multicore systems (Albassam and Gomaa 2014) showed that, although less necessary than in earlier systems, there are still multitasking situations, when there are potentially a large number of tasks, where task clustering is useful with multicore systems.

18.5 SUMMARY

This chapter has described a detailed example of how to analyze the performance of a real-time software design by applying real-time scheduling theory and event sequence analysis. A detailed performance analysis was described of the Train Control subsystem of the Light Rail Control System, showing a progressively more detailed analysis. The case study of the design of this real-time embedded system is given in Chapter 21. Other case studies that have examples of analyzing the performance of concurrent real-time designs are the Microwave Oven Control System, described in Chapter 19, and the Railroad Crossing Control System, described in Chapter 20.

PART IV

Real-Time Software Design Case Studies for Embedded Systems

19

Microwave Oven Control System
Case Study

This chapter describes a case study for a microwave oven control system. The software design for this embedded system is typical of many consumer products. Thus, the microwave oven embedded system interfaces with the external environment by means of several sensors and actuators, supports a simple user interface, keeps track of time, and provides centralized control that necessitates the design of a state machine. As the microwave oven is an embedded system, the design approach benefits from starting with a systems engineering perspective of the total hardware/software system before the software modeling and design.

The problem is described in Section 19.1. Section 19.2 describes structural modeling of the microwave oven embedded system, in which the system and software context block definition diagrams are developed. Section 19.3 describes the use case model for the microwave oven system. Section 19.4 describes how the object and class structuring criteria are applied to this system. Section 19.5 describes the design of the state machines for controlling the microwave oven. Section 19.6 describes how dynamic interaction modeling is used to develop sequence diagrams from the use cases. Section 19.7 describes the design modeling for the microwave oven software system, which is designed as a concurrent component-based software architecture based on architectural structure and communication patterns. Section 19.8 describes the performance analysis of the real-time design. Section 19.9 describes the design of components, interfaces, and connectors of the component-based software architecture. Section 19.10 describes detailed software design and Section 19.11 describes system deployment.

19.1 PROBLEM DESCRIPTION

The microwave oven has input buttons for selecting **Cooking Time**, **Start**, **Minute Plus**, **Time of Day**, and **Cancel**, as well as a numeric keypad. It also has a display to show the cooking time left and time of day. In addition, the oven has a microwave heating element for cooking the food, a door sensor to sense when the door is open, and a weight sensor to detect if there is an item in the oven. Cooking is only permitted when the door is closed and when there is something in the oven. The oven has

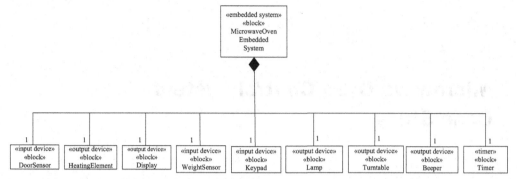

Figure 19.1. Conceptual structural model for the microwave oven embedded system – SysML block definition diagram.

several actuators. Besides the heating element, there are light, beeper, and turntable actuators. The microwave oven displays the cooking time, the time-of-day clock, as well as messages to the user such as prompts and warning messages.

To allow for international sales, the microwave oven system needs to be configurable. In particular, the display language and the type of time-of-day clock, twelve- or twenty-four-hour clock, must be selected at system configuration (generation) time.

19.2 STRUCTURAL MODELING

An important step in system and software modeling is to determine the boundary of the system. Using a system engineering modeling approach, the first step is to develop a conceptual structural model of the problem domain, from which the system and software context block definition diagrams are developed. These diagrams define the boundary of the total (hardware/software) system and software system respectively. SysML block definition diagrams are used for this structural modeling of the system.

19.2.1 Conceptual Structural Model of Problem Domain

The real-world entities that compose the Microwave Oven Embedded System are determined by structural modeling of the problem domain. The microwave oven contains many real-world devices, including several sensors and actuators, which interact with the external environment. The conceptual structural model of the problem domain is depicted on a block definition diagram in Figure 19.1.

The Microwave Oven Embedded System is modeled as a composite block with the stereotype «embedded system», which is composed of several blocks including sensors and actuators. The oven is composed of three input devices: a door sensor, which senses when the door is opened and closed by the user, a weight sensor to weigh food, and a keypad for entering user commands. There are five output devices: a heating element for cooking food, a lamp that is switched on during cooking and when the door is open, a turntable that turns during cooking, a beeper that beeps when the food is cooked, and an oven display for displaying information and prompts to the user. There is also a timer block, namely the real-time timer.

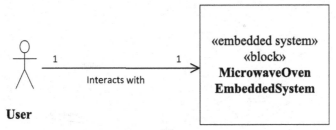

Figure 19.2. System context diagram for the microwave oven embedded system – SysML block definition diagram.

19.2.2 System Context Model

The system context model, which is also referred to as a system context diagram, is determined from the structural model of the problem domain. The system context diagram defines the boundary between the total hardware/software system and the external environment, which is modeled as external blocks to which the system has to interface. The context model is depicted on a SysML block definition diagram (Figure 19.2), which shows the embedded system, the external blocks, and multiplicity of the associations between the external blocks and the system. The Microwave Oven Embedded System is modeled as a single composite block and is labelled with the stereotypes «embedded system» «block». The system context diagram for the Microwave Oven Embedded System is quite simple, as there is only one external entity, the microwave oven user (depicted as an actor), which has a one-to-one association with the embedded system block Microwave Oven Embedded System. The reason is that the embedded system is a hardware/software system, which contains all the hardware microwave sensors and actuators, and the physical timer.

19.2.3 Software System Context Model

The software system context diagram for the software system, namely the Microwave Oven System, is depicted in Figure 19.3. The user from the system context diagram is replaced on the software system context diagram by the external input devices through which the user interacts with the system, the external output devices that are controlled by the software system, and the external timer that provides timer events for the system.

Each external block on the software context diagram is depicted with a stereotype that represents the role of the external device. In this case study, Door Sensor, Weight Sensor, and Keypad are all external input devices. Heating Element, Lamp, Turntable, Beeper, and Display are external output devices. There is also an external timer called Timer. The external blocks all have a one-to-one association with the software system aggregate block.

19.3 USE CASE MODELING

As described in Chapter 6, use case modeling can be applied at the systems or software engineering level. In the former case, the user is the primary actor, whereas in the latter case, the various I/O devices are the actors. For this problem, we decide to use a combination of the systems engineering and software engineering approach

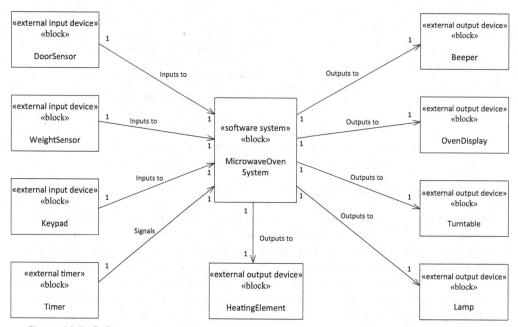

Figure 19.3. Software context diagram for the microwave oven software system.

for the use case model. In particular, from a systems engineering perspective, we consider the user as an actor and not the various input devices (in particular the door and weight sensors, and keypad) he or she uses. From a software engineering perspective, the timer is also considered an actor. This is because the timer plays a very important role in the use case model as it counts down the cooking time and notifies the system when the cooking time has elapsed.

The functionality of the microwave oven system is captured by three use cases, Cook Food, Set Time of Day, and Display Time of Day. The use case model is depicted on the use case diagram in Figure 19.4. The User is the primary actor for the Cook

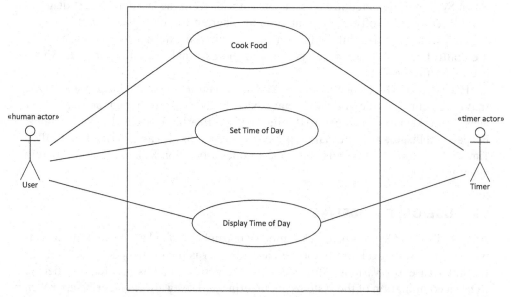

Figure 19.4. Use case model for the microwave oven software system.

Food and Set Time of Day use cases, and a secondary actor for the Display Time of Day use case. The Timer is the primary actor for the Display Time of Day use case and a secondary actor for the Cook Food use case.

19.3.1 Cook Food Use Case

The Cook Food use case is the primary use case of the system, because the description of the main and alternative sequences of the use case address the different scenarios for cooking food in the oven. The user is the primary actor because this actor initiates the use case by opening the door and putting the food in the oven. The timer is a secondary actor because it counts down the cooking time and notifies the system when the time has elapsed. In addition, there is a nonfunctional configuration requirement, namely the choice of display language.

Use case: Cook Food.
Summary: User puts food in oven, and microwave oven cooks food.
Actors: User (primary), Timer (secondary).
Precondition: Microwave oven is idle.
Main sequence:
1. User opens the door.
2. System switches on the oven light.
3. User puts food in the oven and closes the door.
4. System switches off the oven light.
5. User presses the **Cooking Time** button.
6. System prompts for cooking time.
7. User enters cooking time on the numeric keypad and presses **Start**.
8. System starts cooking the food, starts the turntable, and switches on the light.
9. System continually displays the cooking time remaining.
10. Timer notifies the system when the cooking time has elapsed.
11. System stops cooking the food, switches off the light, stops the turntable, sounds the beeper, and displays the end message.
12. User opens the door.
13. System switches on the oven light.
14. User removes the food from the oven and closes the door.
15. System switches off the oven light and clears the display.

Alternative sequences:
Step 3: User presses **Start** when the door is open. System does not start cooking.
Step 5: User presses **Start** when the door is closed and the oven is empty. System does not start cooking.
Step 5: User presses **Start** when the door is closed and the cooking time is equal to zero. System does not start cooking.
Step 5: User presses **Minute Plus**, which results in the system adding one minute to the cooking time. If the cooking time was previously zero, **System** starts cooking, starts the timer, starts the turntable, and switches on the light.
Step 7: User opens door before pressing the **Start** button. System switches on the light.

Step 9: User presses **Minute Plus**, which results in the system adding one minute to the cooking time.

Step 9: User opens door during cooking. System stops cooking, stops the turntable, and stops the timer. The user closes the door (system then switches off the light) and presses **Start**; **System** resumes cooking, resumes the timer, starts the turntable, and switches on the light.

Step 9: User presses **Cancel**. System stops cooking, stops the timer, switches off the light, and stops the turntable. User may press **Start** to resume cooking. Alternatively, user may press **Cancel** again; system then cancels timer and clears display.

Configuration requirement:
Name: Display Language.
Description: There is a choice of language for displaying messages. The default is English. Alternative mutually exclusive languages are French, Spanish, German, and Italian.
Postcondition: Microwave oven has cooked the food.

19.3.2 Set Time of Day Use Case

Set Time of Day and Display Time of Day are separate use cases because they have different primary actors and separate sequences of interactions. The user is the only actor for the Set Time of Day use case. The Set Time of Day use case also has a configuration requirement relating to the type of clock: twelve-hour or twenty-four-hour.

Use case: Set Time of Day.
Summary: User sets time-of-day clock.
Actor: User.
Precondition: Microwave oven is idle.
Main sequence:
1. User presses **Time of Day** (**TOD**) button.
2. System prompts for time of day.
3. User enters the time of day (in hours and minutes) on the numeric keypad.
4. System stores and displays the entered time of day.
5. User presses **Start**.
6. System starts the time-of-day timer.

Alternative sequences:
Lines 1, 3: If the oven is busy, the system will not accept the user input.
Line 5: The user may press **Cancel** if the incorrect time was entered. The system clears the display.

Configuration requirement:
Name: Twelve-/Twenty-Four-Hour Clock.
Description: There is a choice of whether the TOD clock display is a twelve-hour clock (U.S. civilian style) or a twenty-four-hour clock (U.S. military and

European style). The default of these two alternatives is the twelve-hour clock.

Postcondition: TOD clock has been set.

19.3.3 Display Time of Day Use Case

The timer is the primary actor for the Display Time of Day use case, and the user is the secondary actor. This use case executes periodically, every second, when triggered by the timer actor.

Use case: Display Time of Day.
Summary: System displays time of day.
Actors: Timer (primary actor), User (secondary actor).
Precondition: TOD clock has been set (by Set Time of Day use case).
Main sequence:
   1. Timer notifies system that one second has elapsed.
   2. System increments TOD clock every second, adjusting for minutes and hours.
   3. System updates the display with time of day every minute.

Postcondition: TOD clock has been updated (every second) and time of day displayed (every minute).

19.4 OBJECT AND CLASS STRUCTURING

The next step is to determine the software classes and objects needed to realize the use cases. The software system context diagram for an embedded system also helps with this step as the type of each external device helps determine the software class that needs to interface to it. The software classes are primarily determined by consideration of the Cook Food use case. The classes are categorized according to the object and class structuring criteria. As described in Chapter 8, it is assumed that all classes except for entity classes are concurrent and are therefore modeled as active (i.e., concurrent) classes.

The software input classes are determined by consideration of the external device classes on the software system context diagram. In this case study, Door Sensor Input, Weight Sensor Input, and Keypad Input are all software input classes that communicate with the corresponding external device classes. Heating Element Output, Lamp Output, Turntable Output, Beeper Output, and Oven Display Output are software output classes that communicate with the corresponding external output devices. Clock is an external timer that appears on the context diagram. A software timer object, namely Oven Timer, receives timer events from Clock. Oven Timer needs to keep track of the cooking time remaining and when the cooking time expires, as well as the time of day.

There is also a need for an entity class to store microwave oven data, such as the cooking time, which is called Oven Data. In addition, because there is a need to

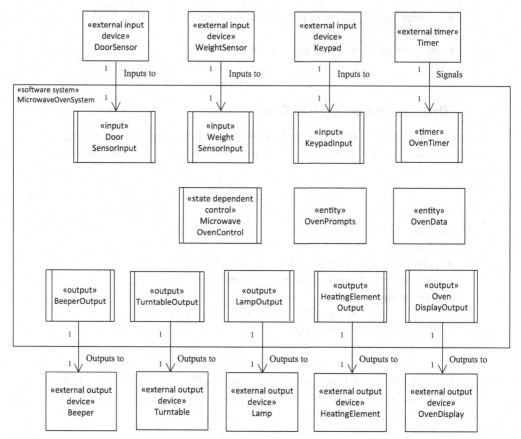

Figure 19.5. Software classes in the microwave oven software system.

provide display prompts to the user, configurable in different languages, the decision is made to separate the textual prompts from the Oven Display Output object. The prompts are stored in an entity class called Oven Prompts. Finally, because of the complex sequencing and control required for the oven, a state dependent control class is required – Microwave Oven Control – which executes the state machine for the oven. The software classes are therefore categorized as follows:

- Input classes:
  - Door Sensor Input
  - Weight Sensor Input
  - Keypad Input
- Output classes:
  - Heating Element Output
  - Lamp Output
  - Turntable Output
  - Beeper Output
  - Oven Display Output
- State Dependent Control classes:
  - Microwave Oven Control

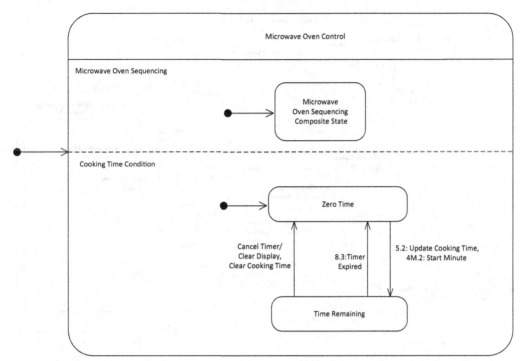

Figure 19.6. State machine for Microwave Oven Control: top-level state machine.

- Timer classes:
  - Oven Timer (it should be noted that this class is a timer because it is activated by timer events from the hardware timer, but it is also state dependent and is therefore designed using a state machine as described in the next section).
- Entity classes:
  - Oven Data
  - Oven Prompts

The software classes are depicted on a class diagram, as shown in Figure 19.5.

19.5 DYNAMIC STATE MACHINE MODELING

This section describes the state machines for the Microwave Oven Control System. Two state machines are developed, one for Microwave Oven Control and the other for Oven Timer. Chapter 7 describes how the Microwave Oven Control state machine can be developed from the Cook Food use case.

19.5.1 State Machine Model for Microwave Oven Control

The state machine for Microwave Oven Control (Figure 19.6) is composed of two orthogonal finite state machines. One is Microwave Oven Sequencing (which is decomposed into substates as shown in Figure 19.7); the other is Cooking Time Condition, which consists of two sequential substates: Zero Time and Time Remaining. The reason for this design is to explicitly model the time condition, without which Microwave

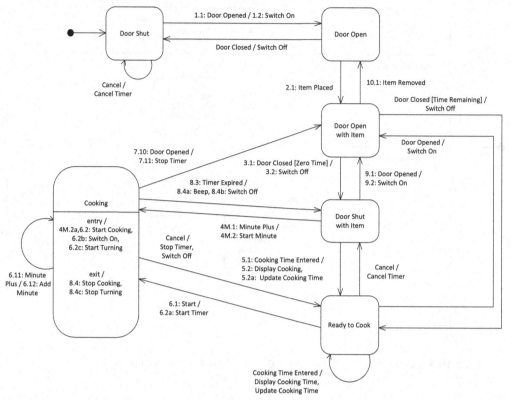

Figure 19.7. State machine for Microwave Oven Control: decomposition of the Microwave Oven Sequencing Composite State.

Oven Control would be a lot more complicated. Thus, the Zero Time and Time Remaining substates of Cooking Time Condition are guard conditions on the Microwave Oven Sequencing state machine (Figure 19.6). The sequence numbers for the main Cook Food scenario are also shown on the figures. This state machine is also used as an example in Chapter 7.

Microwave Oven Sequencing is hierarchically structured and consists of the following substates (see Figure 19.7):

- Door Shut. This is the initial state, in which the oven is idle with the door shut and there is no food in the oven.
- Door Open. In this state the door is open and there is no food in the oven.
- Door Open with Item. This state is entered after an item has been placed in the oven.
- Door Shut with Item. This state is entered after the door has been closed with an item in the oven. This state is a composite state consisting of the following substates (see Figure 19.8):
  • Waiting for User. Waiting for user to press the **Cooking Time** button.
  • Waiting for Cooking Time. Waiting for user to enter the cooking time.
  Because of the effect of opening and closing the door, two substates of the Door Shut with Item composite state are entered via a history state H, as described in Chapter 7. This mechanism is used to ensure that when the door is opened

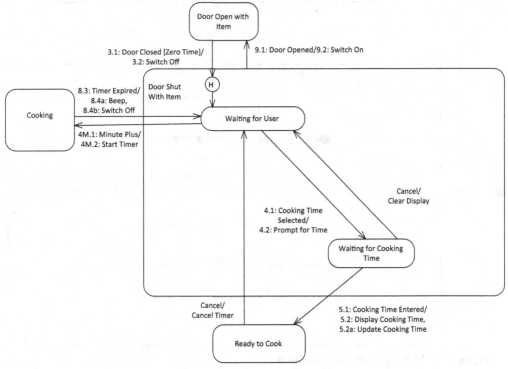

Figure 19.8. State machine for Microwave Oven Control: decomposition of the Door Shut with Item composite state.

(e.g., while in the Waiting for Cooking Time substate) and then closed again, the previously active substate (in this example Waiting for Cooking Time) is reentered.

- Ready to Cook. The oven is ready to start cooking food.
- Cooking. The food is cooking. This state is entered from the Ready to Cook state when the **Start** button is pressed. This state is exited if the timer expires, the door is opened, or **Cancel** is pressed.

19.5.2 State Machines for Oven Timer and Cooking Timer

Timing decisions in the microwave oven are state dependent, and for this reason the Oven Timer object is designed to contain a state machine. Because two different times need to be controlled in the microwave oven, the Oven Timer object is composed of two orthogonal timer state machines, one to keep track of cooking time (after cooking has started) and the other to keep track of the time of day. For this reason, the Oven Timer is designed as an orthogonal state machine with two orthogonal regions, one for the Cooking Timer state machine and the other for the TOD Timer, as depicted in Figure 19.9. This section describes the Cooking Timer state machine, and the TOD Timer state machine is described in Section 19.6.2.

Because time plays such an important and wide-ranging role in the operation of the microwave oven, it is advantageous to consider the different states that the oven timer needs to go through. The state machine for Cooking Timer has the following states for cooking food (Figure 19.10):

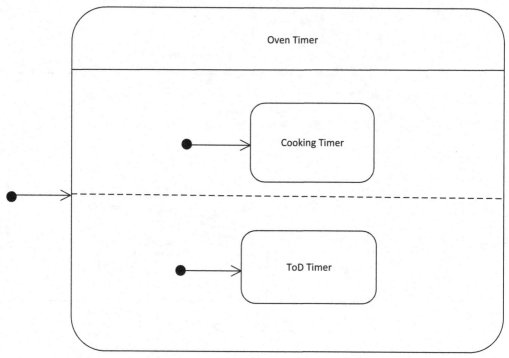

Figure 19.9. State machine for Oven Timer.

- Cooking Time Idle. This is the initial state, in which the oven is idle.
- Cooking Food. The timer is keeping track of the cooking time. This state is entered when the timer is started.
- Updating Cooking Time. This state is entered every time a timer event is received, which is every second. It is an interim state from which either Cooking Food is reentered if the timer has not yet expired or Cooking Time Idle is entered if the timer has expired.

The sequence numbers on the state transitions of the Cooking Timer state machine (depicted on Figure 19.10) correspond to the Cook Food scenario described in Section 19.6.1, in particular the Start Timer, Timer Event, Time Left, and Finished state transitions. Additional state transitions for Start minute and Add Minute correspond to the Minute Plus scenarios described in the next section.

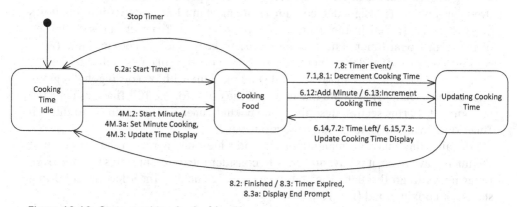

Figure 19.10. State machine for Cooking Timer.

19.5.3 Impact of Minute Plus Alternative Scenarios

The **Minute Plus** button on the oven keypad provides a fast way for the user to add a minute to the cooking time. However, the system behaves differently depending on whether food is being cooked or not when the button is pressed. This necessitates two alternative scenarios on state machine diagrams and sequence diagrams to be considered, as described in detail in Sections 7.7 and 9.7 respectively.

The impact of the **Minute Plus** alternative scenarios feature is state dependent and results in additional transitions on the Microwave Oven Control state machine (Figure 19.7). **Minute Plus** can be pressed when the oven is in the state Door Shut with Item, in which case the Cooking state is entered and the output action is Start Minute in addition to the entry actions of Cooking state. **Minute Plus** can also be pressed while the oven is in the Cooking state, in which case the state is not changed and an internal transition causes the Add Minute action. These output actions are sent to Oven Timer, as described next.

The impact of the **Minute Plus** alternative scenarios results in two additional state transitions on the Cooking Timer state machine, as depicted in Figure 19.10. If the timer is in the Cooking Time Idle state when **Minute Plus** is pressed, the input event (sent by Microwave Oven Control) is Start Minute, and the timer transitions to the Cooking Food state. However, if the state machine is in the Cooking Food state when **Minute Plus** is pressed, the input event is Add Minute and the timer transitions to the Updating Cooking Time state. The actions corresponding to each transition are depicted in Figure 19.10.

19.6 DYNAMIC INTERACTION MODELING

With the dynamic interaction modeling approach, a sequence diagram is developed for each use case. For state dependent scenarios, the state machines for the state dependent objects are also developed. This section describes the sequence diagrams developed for the three use cases depicted in Figure 19.4, namely the Cook Food, Set Time of Day, and Display Time of Day use cases.

19.6.1 Dynamic Interaction Modeling of Cook Food use case

First consider the Cook Food use case. Because of the amount of detail, three sequence diagrams are developed to depict the event sequencing among the objects that realize the use case. The first sequence diagram (Figure 19.11) provides a black box perspective, which depicts the sequence of interactions between the external input and output devices with the Microwave Oven software System (depicted as a composite concurrent object). The second and third sequence diagrams (Figures 19.12 and 19.13) depict the interactions among the software objects that realize the Cook Food use case, in addition to the external input devices. Because these interactions are state dependent, the scenario is also shown on the state machines for the state dependent objects: Microwave Oven Control and Oven Timer (Figures 19.7, 19.8, and 19.10 respectively) as described in the previous section. For more information on how to develop the object interaction sequence from the Cook Food use case in conjunction with the Microwave Oven Control state machine, see the description in Chapter 9, Section 9.7.

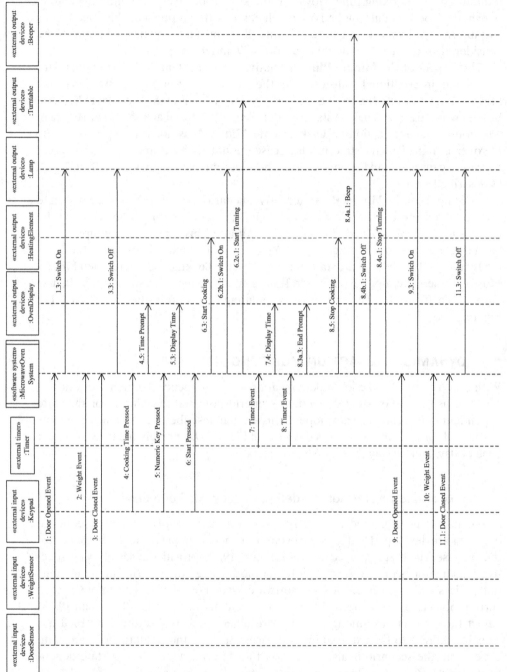

Figure 19.11. Sequence diagram for Cook Food use case depicting external input and output devices interacting with software system.

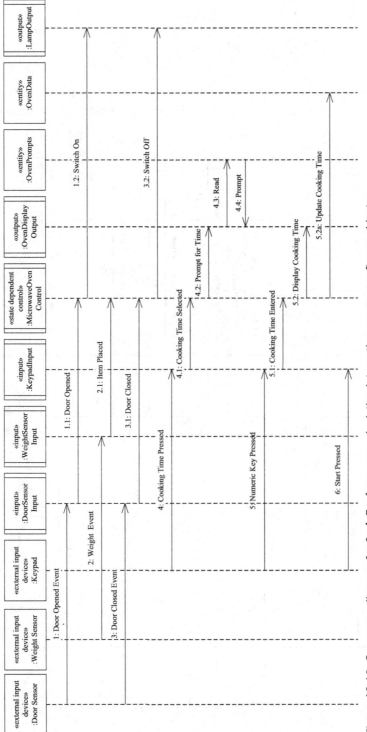

Figure 19.12. Sequence diagram for Cook Food use case depicting interactions among software objects.

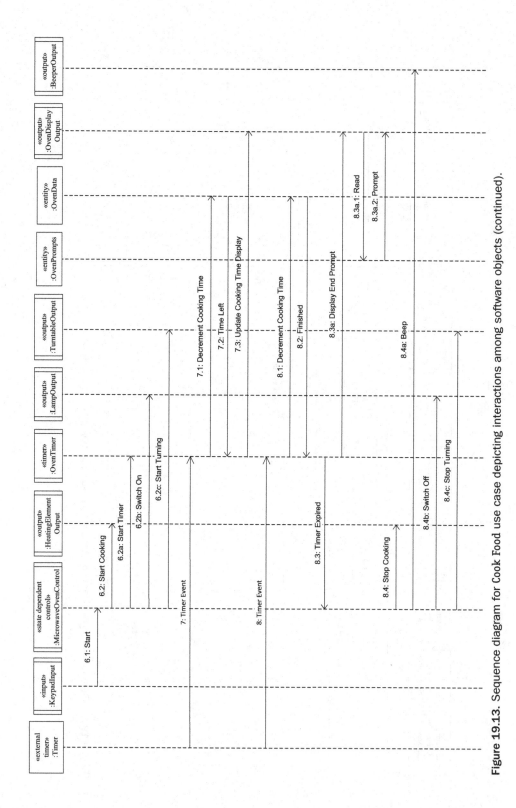

Figure 19.13. Sequence diagram for Cook Food use case depicting interactions among software objects (continued).

The following is the sequence of messages for the sequence diagram and state machines based on the main sequence through the Cook Food use case, as described in Section 19.2.1. The sequence numbers correspond to the messages on the sequence diagrams depicted in Figures 19.11 through 19.13, and to the events and actions depicted on the state machines in Figures 19.7 through 19.10.

1: Door Opened Event. The user opens the door. The external Door Sensor object sends this input to the Door Sensor Input object.

1.1: Door Opened. Door Sensor Input sends the Door Opened message to the Microwave Oven Control object, which changes state.

1.2, 1.3: Switch On. Microwave Oven Control sends Switch On message to the Lamp Output object, which in turn sends the Switch On message to the external Lamp.

2: Weight Event. The user places an item to be cooked into the oven. The external Weight Sensor object sends this input to the Weight Sensor Input object.

2.1: Item Placed. Weight Sensor Input sends the Item Placed message to the Microwave Oven Control object, which changes state.

3: Door Closed Event. The user closes the door. The external Door Sensor object sends this input to the Door Sensor Input object.

3.1: Door Closed. Door Sensor Input sends the Door Closed message to the Microwave Oven Control object, which changes state.

3.2, 3.3: Switch Off. Microwave Oven Control sends Switch Off message to the Lamp Output object, which in turn sends the Switch Off message to the external Lamp.

4: Cooking Time Pressed. The user presses the **Cooking Time** button on the keypad. The external Keypad object sends this input to the Keypad Input object.

4.1: Cooking Time Selected. Keypad Input sends the Cooking Time Selected message to the Microwave Oven Control object, which changes state.

4.2: Prompt for Time. As a result of changing state, Microwave Oven Control sends the Prompt for Time message to the Oven Display Output object.

4.3: Read. The message arriving at Oven Display Output contains a prompt ID, so Oven Display Output sends a Read message to Oven Prompts to get the corresponding prompt message.

4.4: Prompt. Oven Prompts returns the text for the Time Prompt message.

4.5: Time Prompt. Oven Display Output sends the Time Prompt output to the external Display object.

5: Numeric Key Pressed. The user enters the numeric value of the time on the keypad. Keypad sends the value of the numeric key(s) input to Keypad Input.

5.1: Cooking Time Entered. Keypad Input sends the internal value of each numeric key to Microwave Oven Control.

5.2: Display Cooking Time. Microwave Oven Control sends the value of each numeric key to Oven Display Output, to ensure that these values are sent only in the appropriate state.

5.2a: Update Cooking Time. Microwave Oven Control concurrently sends the numeric value of each numeric key to Oven Data to update the cooking time.

5.3: Display Time. Oven Display Output shifts the previous digit to the left and adds the new digit. It then sends the new value of cooking time to the external Display object.

6: Start Pressed. The user presses the **Start** button. The external Keypad object sends this input to the Keypad Input object.

6.1: Start. Keypad Input sends the Start message to Microwave Oven Control, which changes state.

6.2: Start Cooking. As a result of changing state, Microwave Oven Control sends the Start Cooking message to the Heating Element Output object.

6.2a: Start Timer. Microwave Oven Control concurrently notifies the Oven Timer to start the oven timer.

6.2b, 6.2b.1: Switch On. Microwave Oven Control concurrently sends the Switch On message to Lamp Output, which in turn sends the Switch On message to the external Lamp.

6.2c, 6.2c.1: Start Turning. Microwave Oven Control concurrently sends the Start Turning message to Turntable Output, which in turn sends the Start Turning message to the external Turntable.

6.3: Start Cooking. Heating Element Output sends this output to Heating Element to start cooking the food.

7: Timer Event. The external Clock object sends a timer event every second to Oven Timer.

7.1: Decrement Cooking Time. As Oven Timer is counting, it sends this message to the Oven Data object, which maintains the cooking time.

7.2: Time Left. After decrementing the cooking time, which is assumed to be greater than zero at this step of the scenario, Oven Data sends the Time Left message to Oven Timer.

7.3: Update Cooking Time Display. Oven Timer sends the cooking time left to Oven Display Output.

7.4: Display Time. Oven Display Output sends the new cooking time value to the external Display object.

8: Timer Event. The external Clock object sends a timer event every second to Oven Timer.

8.1: Decrement Cooking Time. As Oven Timer is counting, it sends this message to the Oven Data object, which maintains the cooking time.

8.2: Finished. After decrementing the cooking time, which is assumed to be equal to zero at this step of the scenario, Oven Data sends the Finished message to Oven Timer.

8.3: Timer Expired. Oven Timer sends the Timer Expired message to Microwave Oven Control, which changes state.

8.3a: Display End Prompt. Oven Timer concurrently sends the Display End Prompt message to Oven Display Output.

8.3a.1: Read. The message arriving at Oven Display Output contains a prompt ID, so Oven Display Output sends a Read message to Oven Prompts to get the corresponding prompt message.

8.3a.2: Prompt. Oven Prompts returns the text for the End Prompt message.

8.3a.3: End Prompt. Oven Display Output sends the End Prompt message to the external Display object.

8.4, 8.5: Stop Cooking. As a result of changing state (in step 8.3), Microwave Oven Control sends the Stop Cooking message to Heating Element Output object, which in turn sends this message to the Heating Element object to stop cooking the food.

8.4a, 8.4a.1: Beep. Microwave Oven Control sends the Beep message to Beeper Output object, which in turn sends this message to the external Beeper.

8.4b, 8.4b.1: Switch Off. Microwave Oven Control sends Switch Off message to the Lamp Output object, which in turn sends the Switch Off message to the external Lamp.

8.4c, 8.4c.1: Stop Turning. Microwave Oven Control sends the Stop Turning message to Turntable Output object, which in turn sends this message to the external Turntable.

8.5: Stop Cooking. Heating Element Output sends this message to the Heating Element object to stop cooking the food.

Because of lack of space, the remaining messages are only depicted on the sequence diagram depicting external objects (Figure 19.11) and as events and actions on the state machine (Figure 19.7):

9: Door Opened Event. The user opens the door. The external Door Sensor object sends this input to the Door Sensor Input object.

9.1: Door Opened. Door Sensor Input sends the Door Opened message to the Microwave Oven Control object, which changes state.

9.2, 9.3: Switch On. Microwave Oven Control sends Switch On message to the Lamp Output object, which in turn sends the Switch On message to the external Lamp.

10: Weight Event. The user removes the cooked item from the oven. The external Weight Sensor object sends this message to the Weight Sensor Input object.

10.1: Item Removed. Weight Sensor Input sends the Item Removed message to the Microwave Oven Control object, which changes state.

11.1: Door Closed Event. Door Sensor Input sends the Door Closed message to the Microwave Oven Control object, which changes state.

11.2, 11.3: Switch Off. Microwave Oven Control sends Switch Off message to the Lamp Output object, which in turn sends the Switch Off message to the external Lamp.

19.6.2 Dynamic Modeling for the TOD Clock Use Cases

The TOD Clock use cases are Set Time of Day and Display Time of Day. Because these are different use cases, it is necessary to determine the objects needed to support each of them and to develop new sequence diagrams to depict the dynamic execution of the objects for these use cases.

For the Set Time of Day use case, the objects needed are Keypad Input (to receive inputs from the **TOD Clock** button), Microwave Oven Control (because the time of day can be set only when the oven is idle), Oven Data (to store the current time of day),

Oven Display Output (to display the TOD), and Oven Timer (in particular the orthogonal state machine within it (see Figure 19.9), the TOD Timer).

For the Display Time of Day use case, the objects needed are Oven Timer (to receive timer events), Oven Data (to store the time of day that must be incremented), and Oven Display Output (to display the new time).

Figures 19.14 and 19.15 respectively depict the sequence diagrams for the Set Time of Day and the Display Time of Day use cases. The following is the sequence of messages for the sequence diagrams and state machines developed for these use cases. The sequence numbers correspond to the messages on the sequence diagrams depicted in Figures 19.14 and 19.15 and to the events and actions depicted on the state machine for TOD Timer in Figure 19.16 and state machine for the Door Shut composite state in Figure 19.17, which is in turn a substate of the Microwave Oven Control state machine depicted in Figure 19.7 and described in Section 19.5.1.

The message sequence for the Set Time of Day use case is as follows:

C1: TOD Clock Key. The user presses the **TOD Clock** button on the keypad. The external Keypad object sends this input to the Keypad Input object.

C1.1: TOD Clock Selected. Keypad Input sends the TOD Clock Selected message to the Microwave Oven Control object, which changes state.

C1.2: Prompt for TOD. As a result of changing state, one action is for Microwave Oven Control to send the Prompt for TOD message to the Oven Display Output object.

C1.2a: Stop TOD Timer. As a result of changing state, a second concurrent action is for Microwave Oven Control to send the Stop TOD Timer message to the TOD Timer object (within Oven Timer).

C1.2b: Clear TOD. As a result of changing state, a third concurrent action is for Microwave Oven Control to send the Clear TOD message to the Oven Data object.

C1.3: Read. The message arriving at Oven Display Output contains a prompt ID, so Oven Display Output sends a Read message to Oven Prompts to get the corresponding prompt message.

C1.4: Prompt. Oven Prompts returns the text for the Enter TOD Prompt message.

C1.5: Enter TOD Prompt. Oven Display Output sends the Enter TOD Prompt message to the external Display object.

C2: Numeric Key Input. The user enters the numeric value of the time on the keypad. Keypad sends the value of the numeric key(s) input to Keypad Input.

C2.1: Time Entered. Keypad Input sends the internal value of each numeric key to Microwave Oven Control.

C2.2: Display TOD. Microwave Oven Control sends the value of each numeric key to Oven Display Output, to ensure that these values are sent only in the appropriate state.

C2.2a: Update TOD. Microwave Oven Control concurrently sends the numeric value of each numeric key to Oven Data to update the time of day.

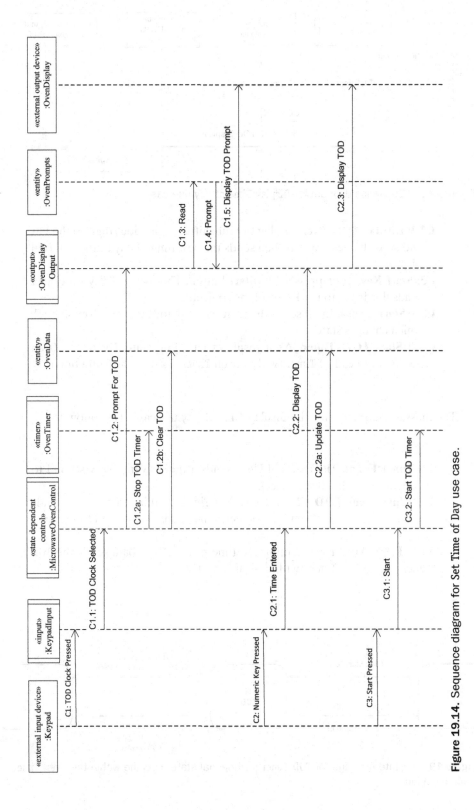

Figure 19.14. Sequence diagram for Set Time of Day use case.

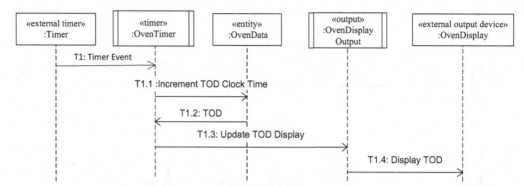

Figure 19.15. Sequence diagram for Display Time of Day use case.

C2.3: Display TOD. Oven Display Output shifts the previous digit to the left and adds the new digit. It then sends the new time of day to the external Display.

C3: Start Key. User presses the **Start** button. The external Keypad object sends this input to the Keypad Input object.

C3.1: Start. Keypad Input sends the Start message to Microwave Oven Control, which changes state.

C3.2: Start TOD Timer. As a result of changing state, Microwave Oven Control notifies TOD Timer (within Oven Timer) to start the TOD timer.

The message sequence for the Display Time of Day use case is as follows:

T1: Timer Event. The external Clock sends a timer event every second to TOD Timer (within Oven Timer).

T1.1: Increment TOD Clock Time. TOD Timer (within Oven Timer) sends this message to the Oven Data object, which adds one second to the time of day.

T1.2: TOD. After incrementing the time of day, Oven Data sends the TOD message to TOD Timer (within Oven Timer).

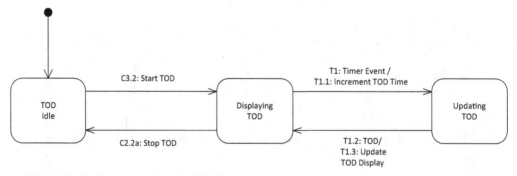

Figure 19.16. State machine for TOD Timer (orthogonal state machine within the Oven Timer state machine).

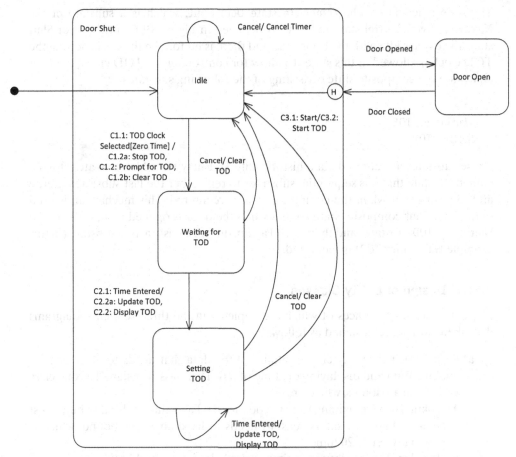

Figure 19.17. State machine for Door Shut (substate of Microwave Oven Control) composite state.

> **T1.3: Update TOD Display**. TOD Timer (within Oven Timer) sends the current time of day to Oven Display Output.
>
> **T1.4: Display TOD**. Oven Display Output sends the new TOD value to the external Multi-line Display.

19.6.3 State Machines for TOD Timer and Door Shut

TOD Timer is an orthogonal state machine within the Oven Timer state machine as depicted in Figure 19.10. The state machine for TOD Timer, which is depicted in Figure 19.16, has three states:

- **TOD Idle.**
- **Displaying TOD.** The TOD clock is active. This state is entered when the TOD clock receives the Start TOD event,
- **Updating TOD.** This is a transient state, which is entered when a Timer Event is received, which results in incrementing the TOD Time (stored in Oven data).

The state machine for the composite state Door Shut, which is a substate of the Microwave Oven Control state machine, is depicted in Figure 19.17. In the Door Shut state, the oven is idle with the door shut, and there is no food in the oven. Setting the TOD clock is allowed in this state. To allow for controlling the TOD clock, the Door Shut state is a composite state consisting of the following substates:

- Idle,
- Waiting for TOD,
- Setting TOD.

These substates are entered via a history state H. Entry via a history state allows a composite state that has sequential substates to remember the last substate entered and to return to it when the composite state is reentered. This mechanism is used in the Door Shut composite state so that when the door is opened (e.g., while in the Waiting for TOD substate) and then closed again, the previously active substate (in this example Waiting for TOD) is reentered.

19.6.4 Design of Entity Classes

The entity classes, instances of which are depicted in the three sequence diagrams described earlier, are designed as follows:

a) Oven Data. This entity class contains all the data that needs to be stored for cooking food and displaying the time of day. This class is designed as one class with three attributes, which are:
   - cookingTime (remaining time to cook food). The value of this attribute must be $> = 0$ and for safety reasons needs to have an upper bound, which is nominally set to 20 mins.
   - TODvalue. This attribute is a time variable initialized to 12:00.
   - TODmaxHour. This attribute is a parameterized constant set at system configuration to 12:00 or 24:00 to indicate the maximum hour on the clock.

   The attributes held by the Oven Data class are depicted in Figure 19.18, which shows the variable name, the type of variable, the range for the variable, and permitted values. Configuration parameters, such as TODmaxHour, are depicted as static variables because once the value of the parameter is set at configuration time, it cannot be changed. When TODvalue is incremented every minute,

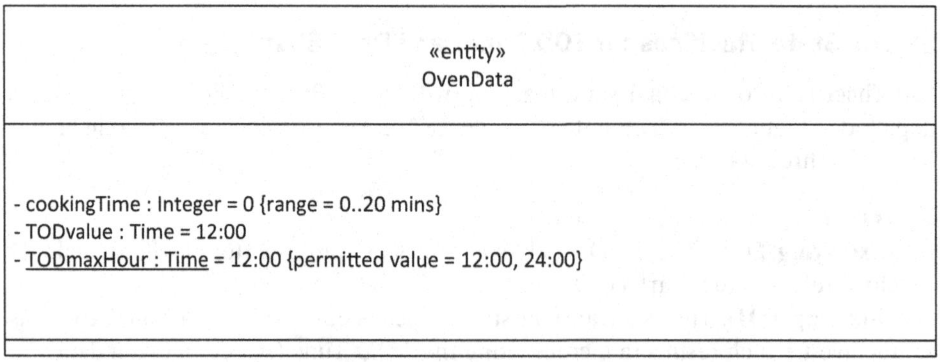

«entity»
OvenData

- cookingTime : Integer = 0 {range = 0..20 mins}
- TODvalue : Time = 12:00
- TODmaxHour : Time = 12:00 {permitted value = 12:00, 24:00}

Figure 19.18. Oven Data entity class.

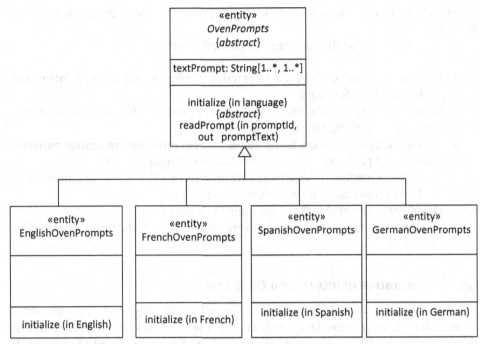

Figure 19.19. Oven Prompts class and subclasses.

this parameter is checked to determine whether after 12:59, the clock should be set to 1:00 or 13:00.

b) Oven Prompts. This class is needed because the prompt language is selected at system configuration time. Each set of language prompts is stored in a separate subclass, as depicted in Figure 19.19:

- **Abstract class**: «entity» Oven Prompts
- **Default subclass**: «entity» English Oven Prompts
- **Variant subclasses:**
  - «entity» French Oven Prompts,
  - «entity» Spanish Oven Prompts,
  - «entity» German Oven Prompts,
  - «entity» Italian Oven Prompts.

Each prompt is identified by a prompt ID, which is an index into a prompt table encapsulated in Oven Prompts class that contains the prompt text corresponding to each prompt ID. Each subclass has an initialize operation, which is used at initialization to populate the prompt table with the text prompts for the selected language.

19.7 DESIGN MODELING

The microwave oven software system is designed as a component-based software architecture, in which simple components are designed as concurrent tasks and depicted using COMET and MARTE stereotypes. The architecture is based on the Centralized Control pattern (see Chapter 11). Thus, there is one control task that provides the overall control of the system, receiving messages from other tasks that contain events causing the control task to change state and send action messages to other tasks.

The steps to develop the software design model are:

1. Integrate the use case–based interaction diagrams and develop integrated communication diagrams.
2. Design the concurrent software architecture (based on the centralized control pattern) by applying the task structuring criteria.
3. Design the task interfaces based on the architectural communication patterns.
4. Analyze the performance of the concurrent real-time software design.
5. Design the component-based software architecture that allows components to be deployed to different system configurations.
6. Develop the detailed task design using Pseudocode.
7. Deploy the component-based software architecture to the target system configuration.

19.7.1 Integration of Interaction Diagrams

The initial attempt at design modeling is to develop the integrated communication diagram for the Microwave Oven System, which necessitates the integration of the three use case–based interaction diagrams for Cook Food (Figures 19.12 and 19.13), Set Time of Day (Figure 19.14) and Display Time of Day (Figure 19.15). Since these diagrams are sequence diagrams, the objects and object interactions must be depicted on the integrated communication diagram as in Figure 19.20. Figure 19.20 depicts 12 objects, which are instances of the 12 classes depicted in Figure 19.5, as well as the interactions between them as determined from the sequence diagrams. Since the sequence diagrams realize the main sequence of each use case, it is also necessary to consider the alternative sequences that are not depicted on the three use case–based sequence diagrams. This includes the interaction sequences for **Minute Plus** (depicted in Figure 9.10 in Chapter 9) as well as other alternative sequences, such as opening the door while cooking. The integrated communication diagram depicts all possible interactions between the objects.

19.7.2 Concurrent Software Architecture

In this concurrent real-time design, the task structuring criteria are applied to determine the concurrent tasks in the Microwave Oven System. The concurrent software architecture (Figure 19.21) is developed by starting from the integrated communication diagram in Figure 19.20, which shows all the objects in the system. Apart from the passive entity objects, all the objects are active and designed as tasks, because they need to operate asynchronously. Each task is depicted with the MARTE stereotype for task: «swSchedulableResource».

This paragraph describes the mapping from the integrated communication diagram of Figure 19.20 to the concurrent component-based software architecture depicted in Figure 19.21. There are two simple components, the Microwave Control and Microwave Display components, which contain tasks and passive objects. All the other components are simple components designed as tasks.

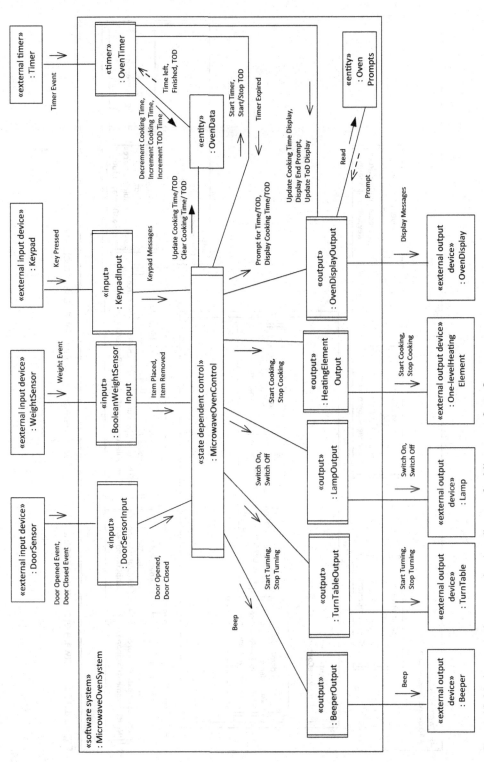

Figure 19.20. Integrated communication diagram for Microwave Oven System.

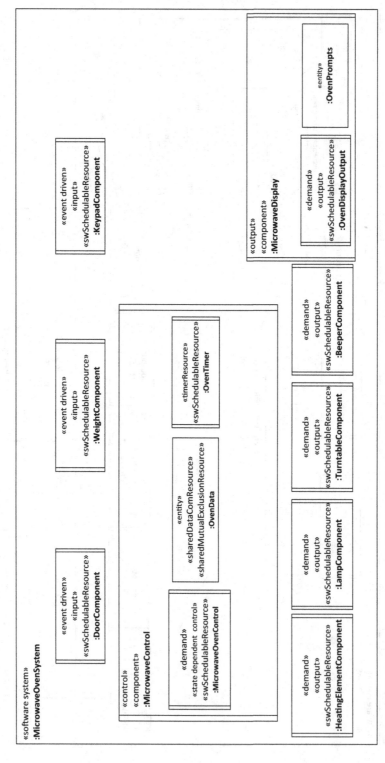

Figure 19.21. Software architecture for the Microwave Oven System: component and task structuring.

- **Input components designed as tasks**. Each input components is designed as a concurrent task that receives inputs from an external input device and sends corresponding messages to the control component. Door Component, Weight Component, and Keypad Component (see Figure 19.21) are simple components determined from the input objects depicted in integrated communication diagram (see Figure 19.20): Door Sensor Input, Weight Sensor Input, and Keypad Sensor Input, respectively. Each input component is designed as an event driven input task, which is awakened by the arrival of a sensor or keypad input event. The three input tasks are each depicted with the stereotypes «event driven» «input» «swSchedulableResource».

- **Control component containing two tasks and a passive object**. The Microwave Control component is the centralized control component for the system. It contains two concurrent tasks, Microwave Oven Control and Oven Timer, and the Oven Data passive entity object, as shown in Figure 19.21. All three internal objects are determined from the integrated communication diagram (see Figure 19.20). These three objects are grouped into the Microwave Control component because the overall control of the microwave oven needs both the state dependent control task Microwave Oven Control and the timer task, Oven Timer, as well as the entity object Oven Data, which stores essential data. Microwave Oven Control is a demand-driven state dependent control task and is hence depicted with the stereotypes «demand» «state dependent control» «swSchedulableResource». Oven Timer is a software periodic (i.e., timer) task and is hence depicted with the MARTE stereotypes «timerResource» «swSchedulableResource». Oven Data is an entity object that is both shared (hence given the MARTE stereotype «sharedData-ComResource») and accessed mutually exclusively by two tasks (hence given the MARTE stereotype «sharedMutualExclusionResource»). Thus, the full stereotype depiction for an entity object, which is a mutually exclusive shared data communication resource, is «entity» «sharedDataComResource» «sharedMutual-ExclusionResource».

- **Output components designed as tasks**. The Heating Element Component is designed as a concurrent task that interfaces to the external Heating Element. The Heating Element Output object (Figure 19.20) is designed as a simple output component, Heating Element Component (see Figure 19.21). Other output components are designed in the same way, namely Turntable Component, Beeper Component, and Lamp Component, which interface respectively with the external Turntable, Beeper, and Lamp output devices. The output components are designed as demand driven output tasks, which are awakened by the arrival of messages from Microwave Oven Control. The four output tasks are each depicted with the stereotypes «demand» «output» «swSchedulableResource».

- **Output component containing a task and a passive object**. The Microwave Display component contains the Oven Display Output task and the Oven Prompts passive entity object, as shown in Figure 19.21. These two objects are grouped together because they must always be used together. Oven Display Output receives commands to display prompts, in which each prompt is identified by a prompt ID. The text for the prompts is maintained by the Oven Prompts entity object. This separation of concerns means that the prompt language and prompt text can be changed independently of the other objects. The output task is depicted with the stereotypes «demand» «output» «swSchedulableResource», and since it is only accessed by one task and thus not shared, the entity object is only depicted with the stereotype «entity».

19.7.3 Architectural Communication Patterns

The messages to be sent between the components in the microwave oven system are determined from the integrated communication diagram in Figure 19.20. The actual type of message communication – synchronous or asynchronous – still needs to be determined. To handle the variety of communication between the components in the architecture, three communication patterns are applied:

- **Asynchronous Message Communication**. The Asynchronous Message Communication pattern is widely used in the microwave oven software system because most communication is one-way, and this pattern has the advantage of not letting the consumers hold up the producers. The order in which messages are sent by the four producer (three input and one timer) components to the Microwave Oven Control component (see Figures 19.22 and 19.23) is nondeterministic because it is based on the user's actions. The Microwave Oven Control component needs to be able to receive a message from any of its four producers in any order. The best way to handle this requirement for flexibility is through asynchronous message communication, with one input message queue for the Microwave Oven Control component. The Microwave Oven Control component receives messages from each of the three input components and the Oven Timer component (see Figure 19.23), which arrive on the same message queue.

  The Microwave Display component also receives messages from two producers: the Microwave Oven Control component and the Oven Timer component (see Figures 19.23 and 19.24), which are displayed on one line of the display. To avoid race conditions, the two producer components are designed to send display Time messages in different states. The Microwave Oven Control component sends display Time messages only when the oven is not cooking. The Oven Timer component sends display Time messages when the oven is cooking. The Oven Timer component also sends display TOD messages to Microwave Display whether the oven is cooking or not. However, these messages are displayed on a separate line of the display and so do not interfere with the other messages. The Oven Display Output component (Figure 19.24) receives all display messages on a message queue and determines from the message, which line it should be displayed on.

- **Bidirectional Asynchronous Message Communication**. This pattern is used when the producer sends asynchronous messages to a consumer and requires an eventual response but does not need to wait for it. This pattern is used between the Microwave Oven Control and Oven Timer components (see Figure 19.23), both of which are within the Microwave Control component. The Microwave Oven Control component sends Start Timer and Cancel Timer messages as timer requests to the Oven Timer component. After sending the Start Timer request, the Microwave Oven Control component needs to continue executing because a relatively long time is likely to elapse before Oven Timer responds with the timer expiration response, during which time the user might open the door or cancel the timer. At timer expiration, Oven Timer sends an asynchronous timer expiration message as a control request to Microwave Oven Control.

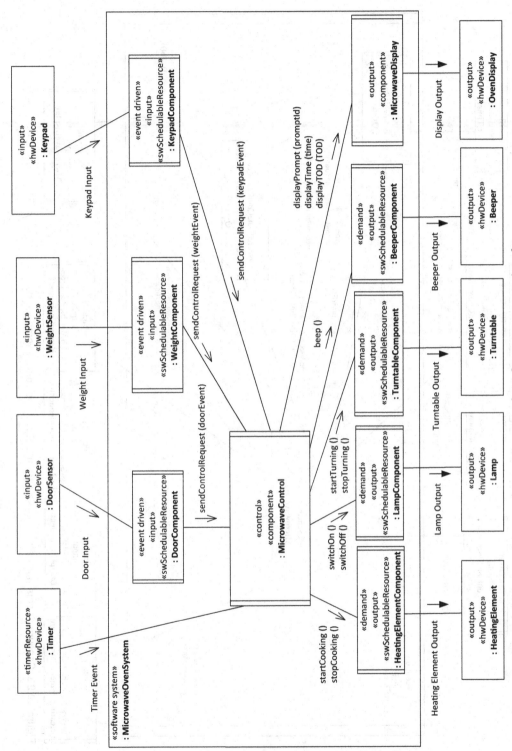

Figure 19.22. Distributed software architecture for the Microwave Oven System: message interfaces.

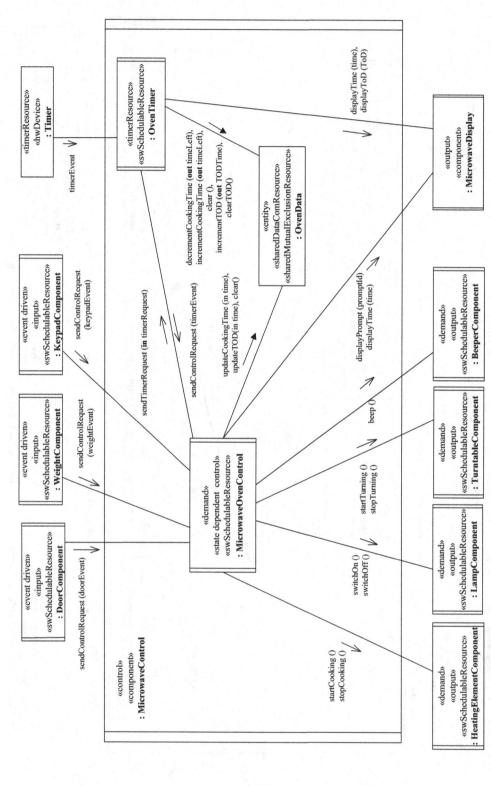

Figure 19.23. Concurrent communication diagram for the Microwave Control component.

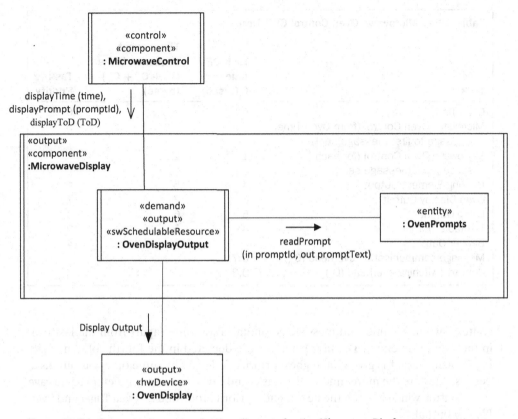

Figure 19.24. Concurrent communication diagram for the Microwave Display component.

- **Synchronized Object Access**. This pattern is used for the invocation of operations on shared passive entity objects accessed by more than one task – in particular, the Oven Data (see Figure 19.23) entity object. Access to this shared object by the Microwave Oven Control and Oven Timer tasks must be mutually exclusive.

19.8 PERFORMANCE ANALYSIS OF REAL-TIME SOFTWARE DESIGN

This section describes the real-time performance analysis of the Microwave Oven Control System. The software system is both event driven (because it reacts to external events) and periodic (because certain events happen on a regular basis). To analyze the performance, it is necessary to consider the time-critical scenarios using an event sequence analysis for each scenario with the help of timing diagrams, as described in Chapters 17 and 18.

A time-critical scenario is the Oven Timer counting down the cooking time and alerting Microwave Oven Control when the cooking time has expired. This event sequence is fully described in Section 19.6. The seven tasks that participate in this scenario are depicted in the first column of Table 19.1, with the CPU time C_i depicted in the second column, and the task execution time depicted in the third column. The execution time for each task in the event sequence is the sum of its CPU time,

Table 19.1. Microwave Oven Control CPU Times

Task	Task CPU time C_i(msec)	Timer event sequence tasks $(C_i + C_x + C_m)$ (msec)	Task Priority
Oven Timer	6	7	6
Microwave Oven Control (from Oven Timer message to first message sent)	5	6	5
Microwave Oven Control (for each subsequent message sent)	1	2	
Heating Element Output	4	5	1
Oven Display Output	6	7	7
Lamp Output	5	6	3
Turntable Output	4	5	2
Beeper Output	3	4	4
Message communication overhead (C_m)	0.7		
Context-switching overhead (C_x)	0.3		

context-switching time, and message communication time (apart from the last task in the event sequence). The task priorities are depicted in the fourth column. Heating Element Output is given the highest priority, followed by three other output tasks because they are the more time-critical tasks and can, if necessary, preempt Microwave Oven Control, which is given the next highest priority followed by Oven Timer and Oven Display Output.

19.8.1 Performance Analysis on Single Processor System

The task execution for the event sequence on a single processor is depicted on the timing diagram in Figure 19.25. In this timer-driven scenario, the event sequence starts with the external Timer sending a timer event that activates the Oven Timer task, which then executes for 7 msec, during which it decrements the cooking time. In this scenario, Oven Timer determines that the remaining time is zero, and therefore it sends a timer expired message to the Microwave Oven Control task. At this time, all other tasks are blocked, so that even though Microwave Oven Control has a lower priority than the output tasks, it is the highest priority task ready to execute when the message arrives, and it preempts Oven Timer.

The Timer Expired event causes a state transition on the internal Microwave Oven Control state machine from Cooking state to Door Shut with Item state (Figure 19.7). The effect of the state transition is to trigger four concurrent actions to Stop Cooking, Stop Turning, Switch Off Light, and Beep. On the timing diagram, this is depicted as follows: after executing for 6 msec, Microwave Oven Control sends the Stop Cooking message to Heating Element Component. Because this output task has a higher priority than Microwave Oven Control, when it receives the message, it unblocks and preempts Microwave Oven Control. After executing for 5 msec it sends the Stop Cooking command to the external heating element and terminates.

Microwave Oven Control then resumes execution for 2 msec before sending the Beep message to Beeper Component. Because it has a higher priority, upon receiving

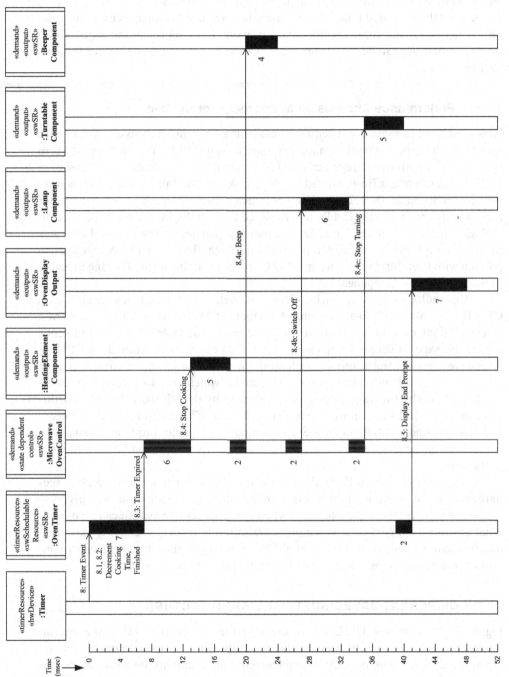

Figure 19.25. Timing diagram for Microwave Oven System tasks executing on a single processor system. (Note that «swSchedulableResource» is abbreviated to «swSR» for space reasons).

the message, Beeper Component preempts Microwave Oven Control, executes for 4 msec, sends the Beep command to the external beeper device, and terminates. The same procedure is then followed with Microwave Oven Control resuming execution and sending messages to Lamp Component and Turntable Component, which in turn execute for their allotted times. After Turntable Component completes execution, the only ready task, Oven Timer, resumes execution and sends a prompt message to Oven Display Output. As can be seen from Figure 19.25, the total elapsed time for this scenario is 48 msec.

19.8.2 Performance Analysis on Multiprocessor System

Now consider the same event sequence executing on a multiprocessor system with four CPUs, as depicted on the timing diagram in Figure 19.26. This scenario starts in the same way with Oven Timer activated by a timer event, executing for 7 msec on CPU A and sending a Timer Expired message to Microwave Oven Control. In this multiprocessor scenario, Oven Timer then continues executing on CPU A for a further 2 msec and sends a Display End Prompt message to Oven Display Output before terminating. Upon receiving the Timer Expired message, Microwave Oven Control executes for 6 msec on CPU B (initially in parallel with Oven Timer on CPU A and later in parallel with Oven Display Output on CPU C) before sending a Stop Cooking message to Heating Element Component.

In this multiprocessor scenario, Microwave Oven Control continues executing on CPU B in parallel with Heating Element Component executing on CPU D and Oven Display Output on CPU C. After a further 2 msec, Microwave Oven Control sends a Beep message to Beeper Component, which then executes in parallel on CPU A. Microwave Oven Control continues executing on CPU B and after a further 2 msec sends a Switch Off message to Lamp Component, which starts executing in parallel on CPU C (by this time having been released by Oven Display Output). At this time, there are tasks executing in parallel on all four CPUs. After a further 2 msec, Railroad Crossing Control sends a Stop Turning message to Turntable Component, which then executes on CPU D, replacing the recently terminated Heating Element Component.

As depicted on Figure 19.26, the total elapsed time for this multiprocessor scenario is 23 msec, which is 25 msec less than the single processor scenario. This comparison shows that there are situations when a multiprocessor system can be used to great advantage, in particular when there are multiple tasks concurrently executing independent actions. However, it should be pointed out that due to memory contention, the actual elapsed time could be longer on a multicore system.

19.9 COMPONENT-BASED SOFTWARE ARCHITECTURE

Figure 19.27 depicts a UML composite structure diagram showing the overall microwave oven component-based software architecture, component interfaces, and connectors. All the components are concurrent and communicate with other components through ports. The composite structure of the component architecture and connectivity among components depicted in Figure 19.27 is determined from the concurrent communication design depicted in Figure 19.22.

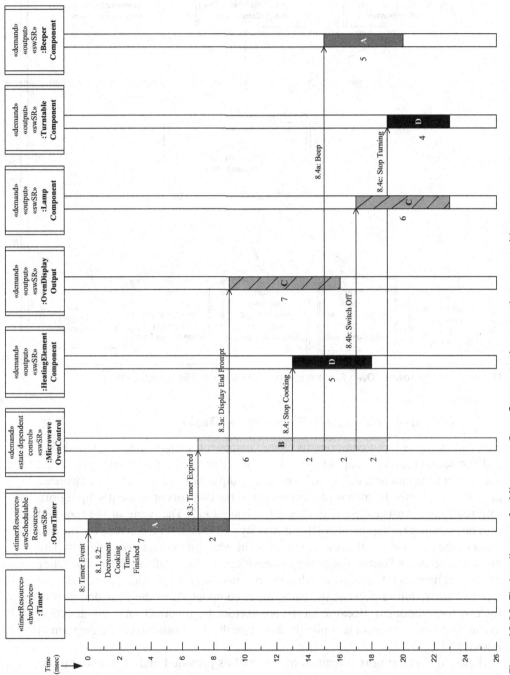

Figure 19.26. Timing diagram for Microwave Oven System tasks executing on a multiprocessor system. (Note that «swSchedulableResource» is abbreviated to «swSR» for space reasons).

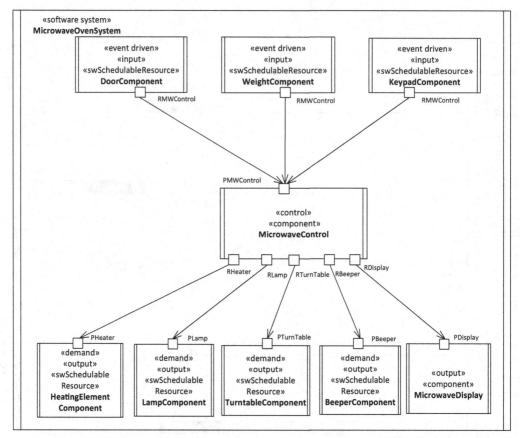

Figure 19.27. Microwave Oven System component-based software architecture.

19.9.1 Design of Components Structured as Tasks

Because the three input components (Door Component, Weight Component, and Keypad Component) send messages to the Microwave Control component in Figure 19.22, each input component is designed to have an output port, referred to as a *required port*, which is joined by means of a connector to the control component's input port, referred to as a *provided port*, as shown in Figure 19.27. The name of the required port on each input component is RMWControl; by a COMET/RTE convention, the first letter of the port name is R to emphasize that the component has a *required* port. The name of Microwave Control Component's provided port is PMWControl; the first letter of the port name is P to emphasize that the component has a provided port. Connectors join the required ports of the three input components to the provided port of the control component. Because all the connectors are unidirectional, the direction in which messages are sent is explicitly shown on the composite structure diagram in Figure 19.27.

Each component port is defined in terms of its provided and/or required interfaces. Some producer components – in particular, the input components – do not provide a software interface because they receive their inputs directly from the external hardware input devices. However, they require an interface provided by the control component in order to send messages to the control component. Figure 19.28

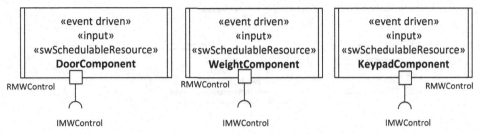

Figure 19.28. Ports and required interfaces of input components.

depicts the ports and required interfaces for the three input components of Figure 19.27: Door Component, Weight Component, and Keypad Component. Each of the three input components has the same required interface – IMWControl – which is provided by the Microwave Control component.

The Microwave Control component has several required ports from which it sends messages to the provided ports of the five output components depicted in Figure 19.27 (Heating Element Component, Lamp Component, Turntable Component, Beeper Component, and Microwave Display).

The output components do not require a software interface, because their outputs go directly to external hardware output devices. However, they need to provide an interface to receive messages sent by the control component. Figure 19.29 depicts the ports and provided interfaces for all the output components of the system. Figure 19.29 also shows the specifications of the interfaces in terms of the operations they provide. Lamp Component, Turntable Component, and Beeper Component are output components, each of which has a provided port – for example, PLamp for Lamp Component, which provides an interface (e.g., ILamp).

Consider next Heating Element Component, which has a provided port called PHeater, which in turn provides an interface called IHeatingElement. The provided interface (IHeatingElement) has one provided port (PHeater). The interface specifies three operations called initialize, start Cooking, and stop Cooking.

The Microwave Display component has a provided port called PDisplay, which in turn provides an interface called IDisplay. This interface specifies four operations, display Prompt, display Time, clear Screen, and display TOD. Figure 19.29 shows the specification of the interface.

Some components, such as control components, need to provide interfaces for the input components to use and require interfaces that are provided by output components. The Microwave Control component has several ports – one provided port and five required ports – as shown in Figure 19.30. Each required port is used to interface to a different output component and is given the prefix R – for example, RLamp. The provided port, which is called PMWControl, provides the interface IMWControl, which is required by the input components. This interface is specified in Figure 19.30. It is kept simple by having only one operation (send Control Request), with a parameter for the type of request instead of one operation for each type of request. Designing each control request as a separate operation would make the interface more complicated. It also makes it easier to modify the design of the Microwave Control component, since an additional request type only requires a new value for the request type parameter instead of necessitating a change to the interface to add a new operation.

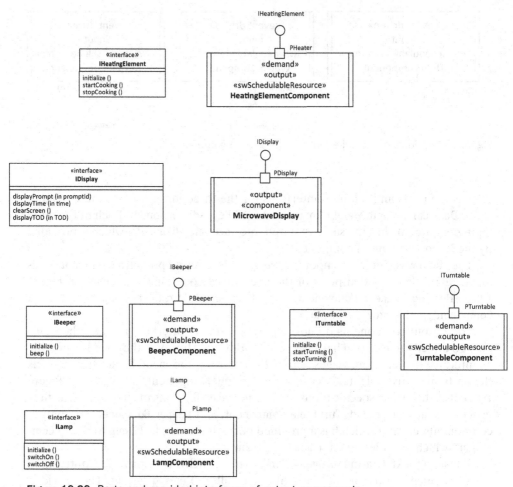

Figure 19.29. Ports and provided interfaces of output components.

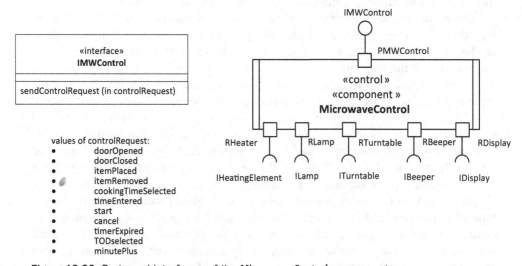

Figure 19.30. Ports and interfaces of the Microwave Control component.

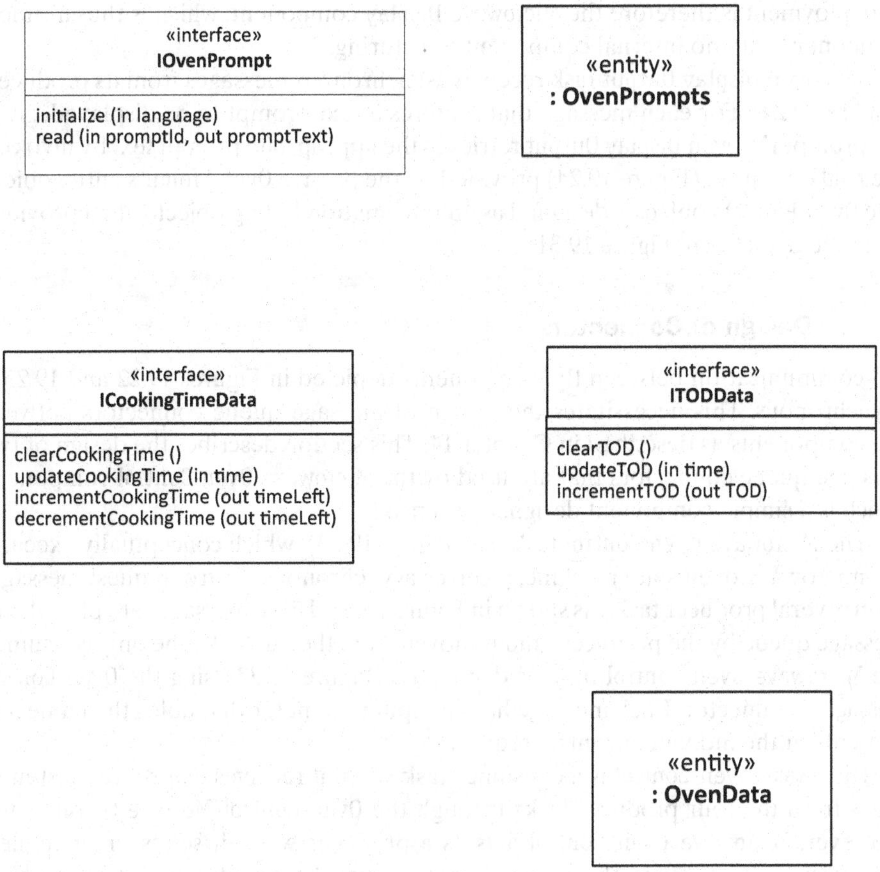

```
«interface»
IOvenPrompt

initialize (in language)
read (in promptId, out promptText)
```

```
«entity»
: OvenPrompts
```

```
«interface»
ICookingTimeData

clearCookingTime ()
updateCookingTime (in time)
incrementCookingTime (out timeLeft)
decrementCookingTime (out timeLeft)
```

```
«interface»
ITODData

clearTOD ()
updateTOD (in time)
incrementTOD (out TOD)
```

```
«entity»
: OvenData
```

Figure 19.31. Interfaces of passive objects.

19.9.2 Design of Components Containing Multiple Objects

The Microwave Control component is designed to contain two concurrent tasks (Microwave Oven Control and Oven Timer) and a passive entity object (Oven Data). Because the entity object is passive, as depicted in Figure 19.23, the two concurrent tasks that access it directly, Microwave Oven Control and Oven Timer, cannot be deployed to different nodes as separate components. The unit of deployment is therefore the Microwave Control component, which for this reason is a simple component with no internal component structuring.

The passive object Oven Data is designed as an information hiding object with two provided interfaces, one to specify operations relating to updating the cooking time, ICookingTimeData , and the other to specify operations related to updating the time-of-day clock, ITODData, as depicted in Figure 19.31.

The Microwave Display component is designed to contain one task and one passive entity object, as shown in Figure 19.24: a concurrent task called Oven Display Output and a passive entity object called Oven Prompts. As with the Microwave Control component, because the entity object is passive, the Oven Display Output task that accesses it directly cannot be deployed to its own node as a separate component. The unit of deployment is therefore the Microwave Display component, which is thus a simple component with no internal component structuring.

The Oven Display Output task receives asynchronous messages from its producers (Figure 19.24). For each message that requires a text prompt to be displayed, given the prompt ID, Oven Display Output retrieves the appropriate prompt text by invoking the read operation (Figure 19.24) provided by the passive Oven Prompts entity object. The Oven Prompts object is designed as an information hiding object with a provided interface depicted in Figure 19.31.

19.9.3 Design of Connectors

All communication between the components depicted in Figures 19.22 and 19.23 is asynchronous. This necessitates the design of message queue connectors between the components as described in Chapter 14. This section describes the design of two message queue connectors that are used by the Microwave Oven Control component, which is a simple component designed as a task.

The Microwave Oven Control task (see Figure 19.23), which conceptually executes the microwave oven state machine, receives asynchronous control request messages from several producer tasks, as shown in Figure 19.23. These messages are placed on a message queue by the producers and removed from the queue by the only consumer, the Microwave Oven Control task, as depicted in Figure 19.32 using the Oven Control Message Q connector. Each message has an input parameter that holds the name and contents of the individual control request.

Microwave Oven Control is a consumer task when it receives control request messages from the four producer tasks through the Oven Control Message Q connector. However, Microwave Oven Control acts as a producer when it sends timer request messages to Oven Timer through a message queue connector called Oven Timer Message Q.

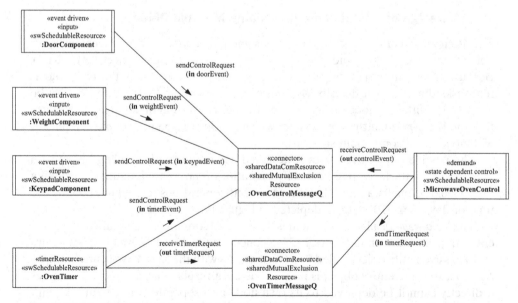

Figure 19.32. Microwave Oven tasks communicating through message queue connectors.

Oven Timer is a producer task when it sends control request messages to Microwave Oven Control in the same way as the input components through the Oven Control Message Q connector. However, Oven Timer is a consumer task when it receives asynchronous timer request messages from the producer Microwave Oven Control task. This necessitates the design of a different connector, the Oven Timer Message Q connector (as depicted in Figure 19.32) to hold the timer request messages. Each message has an parameter called timerRequest that holds the name of the individual message – for example, startOven Timer, stopOvenTimer, addMinute, and startMinute.

19.10 DETAILED SOFTWARE DESIGN

The detailed software design involves developing the Pseudocode for the single threaded components, such as Door Component, and tasks inside the components that contain multiple objects, such as the Microwave Oven Control and Oven Timer tasks that are inside the Microwave Control component, as shown in Figure 19.23.

Door Component is designed as a producer task that sends door opened and door closed control request messages to Microwave Oven Control through a message queue connector called Oven Control Message Q, as depicted in Figure 19.32. However, this connector is inside the Microwave Control component and is therefore accessed via the required port RMWControl of DoorComponent, which invokes the sendControlRequest operation provided by the IMWControl interface. The task event sequencing logic described in Pseudocode for DoorComponent is as follows.

```
Initialize door sensor;
loop
-- Wait for external asynchronous event from door sensor;
wait (inputEvent);
Read door event;
if event = doorOpened
      then
          -- send message to Microwave Oven Control task through connector;
          RMWControl.sendControlRequest (in doorOpened);
elseif event = doorClosed;
      then
          -- send message to Microwave Oven Control task through connector;
          RMWControl.sendControlRequest (in doorClosed);
      else
          Handle error case;
end if;
end loop;
```

The task event sequencing logic for Microwave Oven Control task is as follows. Note that the actions are determined by the Microwave Oven Control state machine (depicted in Figures 19.7 and 19.8), which is encapsulated as a state transition table inside the MOCStateMachine object, as described in Chapter 14. Note also that Microwave Oven Control receives control request messages from its four producers through the Oven Control Message Q connector and sends timer messages to Oven Timer through the Oven Timer Message Q connector; both these connectors are inside the Microwave Control component. However, Microwave Oven Control sends messages to the output components, such Heating Element Component, by invoking an operation in the Microwave Control component's required port interface for connecting to that component (depicted in Figures 19.27 and 19.30). For example, to start cooking food, Microwave Control invokes the startCooking operation (from the IHeatingElement interface provided by Heating Element Component in Figure 19.29), through the requiredRHeater port (see Figure 19.30), as described next.

```
loop
    -- Messages from all senders are received on Oven Control Message Q
    OvenControlMessageQ.receiveControlRequest (out controlEvent);
    -- Extract the event name and any message parameters
    newEvent = controlEvent
    -- Assume state machine is encapsulated in object MOCStateMachine;
    -- Given the incoming event, lookup state transition table;
    -- change state if required; return action to be performed;
    MOCStateMachine.processEvent (in newEvent, out action);
    -- Execute state dependent action(s) given by MOC state machine;
    case action of
        Start Actions:
            OvenTimerMessageQ.sendTimerRequest (in startTimer);
            RHeater.startCooking ();
            RLamp.switchOn ();
            RTurntable.startTurning ();
            exit;
        Timer Expired Actions:
            RHeater.stopCooking ();
            RTurntable.stopTurning ();
            RLamp.switchOff ();
            RBeeper.beep ();
            exit;
        Door Opened while Cooking Actions:
            RHeater.stopCooking ();
            RTurntable.stopTurning ();
            OvenTimerMessageQ.sendTimerRequest (in stopTimer);
            exit;
        Switch On Action:
            RLamp.switchOn ();
            exit;
        Switch Off Action:
            RLamp.switchOff ();
            exit;
        Cancel Timer Action:
            OvenTimerMessageQ.sendTimerRequest (in cancelTimer);
            exit;
```

```
        Add Minute:
          OvenTimerMessageQ.sendTimerRequest (in addMinute);
          exit;
        Start Minute:
          OvenTimerMessageQ.sendTimerRequest (in startMinute);
          exit;
        Display Cooking Time Actions:
          RDisplay.displayTime (in time);
          OvenData.updateCookingTime (in time)
          exit;
  -- other actions not shown
      end case;
   end loop;
```

The task event sequencing logic for Heating Element Component task is given next. It is assumed that incoming messages arrive on its message queue, where they are placed by the startCooking and stopCooking operations of the Heating Element Component.

```
   Initialize heating element actuator;
   loop
   -- Wait for message from Microwave Oven Control task arriving via
   connector;
   heatingElementMessageQ.receive (in message);
   Extract action event from message;
   -- Process message;
   if action = startCooking
      then
          Send startCookingCommand to heating element actuator;
   elseif action = stopCooking
      then
          Send stopCookingCommand to heating element actuator
      else error condition;
   end if;
   end loop;
```

19.11 SYSTEM CONFIGURATION AND DEPLOYMENT

At system deployment time, the type of configuration required – centralized or distributed – is determined. Figure 19.33 shows one possible configuration, in which each of the component-based subsystems is allocated to a separate node in a distributed configuration. The nodes are physically connected by means of a high-speed bus.

Only distributable components can be deployed to the physical nodes of a distributed configuration. Passive objects (such as Oven Data in Figure 19.31) cannot be

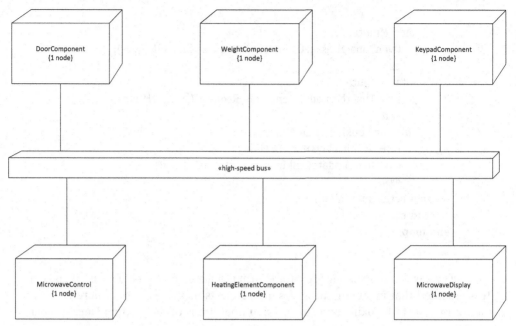

Figure 19.33. Distributed system configuration.

independently deployed, nor can any task that directly invokes the operations of a passive component (such as Microwave Oven Control and Oven Timer in Figure 19.23). In this situation, only the distributable component (which contains the passive object and concurrent tasks that invoke operations of the passive object) can be deployed. Thus, only the Microwave Control composite component can be deployed, as depicted in Figure 19.33. Note that this figure depicts a reduced configuration with only two output components, Heating Element Component and Microwave Display.

20

Railroad Crossing Control System Case Study

This chapter describes a case study for a railroad crossing control embedded system. This software design is for a safety-critical system, in which the raising and lowering of railroad barriers must be done safely and in a timely manner. As is typical of embedded systems, the system interfaces with the external environment by means of several sensors and actuators. It also must send status messages to a Rail Operations Service. Control of the railroad crossing is state dependent, which necessitates the design of a state machine to provide overall control of the software system. As the Railroad Crossing Control System (RXCS) is an embedded system, the design approach benefits from starting with a systems engineering perspective of the total hardware/software system, the Railroad Crossing Embedded System.

The problem is described in Section 20.1. Section 20.2 describes the structural modeling of the system, consisting of the structural model of the problem domain, followed by the system and software system context models, and the hardware/software boundary model. Section 20.3 describes the use case model from a software engineering perspective, describing both the functional and nonfunctional requirements of the safety-critical system. Section 20.4 describes the dynamic state machine modeling, which is particularly important to model the state dependent intricacies of this embedded system. Section 20.5 describes how the object and class structuring criteria are applied to this system. Section 20.6 describes how dynamic interaction modeling is used to develop sequence diagrams from the use cases. Section 20.7 describes the design model for the software system, which is designed as a concurrent software architecture that is based on software architectural patterns. Section 20.8 describes the performance analysis of the real-time design executing on single and multiprocessor systems. Section 20.9 describes the design of the RXCS component-based software architecture that is part of the distributed Light Rail System described in Chapter 21. Section 20.10 describes system configuration and deployment.

20.1 PROBLEM DESCRIPTION

A railroad crossing consists of two barriers, each with a flashing warning light and an audio warning signal. The barriers are normally raised. When a train approaches,

417

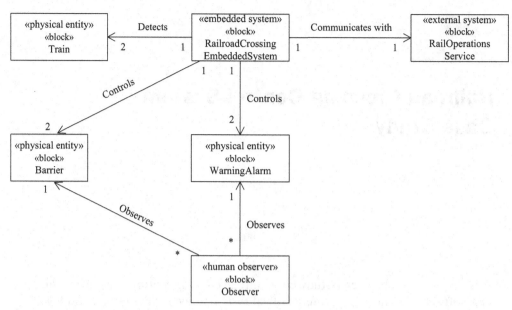

Figure 20.1. Conceptual structural model of the problem domain.

the barriers are lowered, the warning lights start flashing, and the audio warnings are sounded. When the train departs, the barriers are raised, the warning lights stop flashing, and the audio warnings are stopped. Since there are two sets of rails, it is possible for two trains to be at the railroad crossing simultaneously, in which case the barriers are lowered when the first train arrives and only raised when the second train has departed.

20.2 STRUCTURAL MODELING

From a structural modeling perspective, four diagrams are developed and depicted on SysML block definition diagrams. First there is a conceptual static model of the problem domain, which views the system in its real-world perspective. A structural model is then developed of the total hardware/software system. From these two diagrams, the system context block definition diagram is developed depicting the external entities to the total hardware/software system. Finally, the software system context block definition diagram is developed depicting the software system and the external entities that interface to it.

20.2.1 Structural Model of the Problem Domain

The conceptual structural model of the problem domain is depicted on a SysML block definition diagram in Figure 20.1. From a total system perspective, the problem domain for Railroad Crossing Embedded System consists of the following blocks:

- Railroad Crossing Embedded System, which is the *embedded system* to be developed.
- Train, which is a *physical entity* detected by the system.

- Barrier, which is a *physical entity* controlled by the system and which consists of a barrier actuator and a barrier sensor.
- Warning Alarm, which consists of Warning Lights and Warning Audio and which is a *physical entity* controlled by the system.
- Observer, who is a driver, cyclist, or pedestrian who stops at the railroad crossing and who is a *human observer* of the system.
- Rail Operations Service, which is an *external system* that is notified of the status of the railroad crossing.

20.2.2 Structural Model of the Total System

Using the SysML notation, the structural model of the total system is depicted on a block definition diagram in Figure 20.2. The Railroad Crossing Embedded System is depicted as a composite block, which is composed of the following part blocks:

- Two barriers, which are commanded by the system to move up and down. Each Barrier is composed of a Barrier Actuator, a Barrier Detection Sensor, and a Timer.
  - Barrier Actuator is commanded to lower and raise the barrier.
  - Barrier Detection Sensor detects when the barrier has been lowered and raised and sends barrier lowered and barrier raised messages.
  - Barrier Timer times out if a barrier exceeds pre-specified lowering and raising times.
- Two warning signals. Each Warning Signal is composed of a Warning Light Actuator and Warning Audio Actuator:
  - Warning Light Actuator is commanded by the system to switch and switch off the warning light.
  - Warning Audio Actuator is commanded by the system to switch on and switch off the audio warning.
- Train arrival at and departure from the railroad crossing is detected by two sets of sensors. Train Sensor is specialized into Arrival Sensor and Departure Sensor.
  - Arrival Sensor detects when a train is approaching the railroad crossing.
  - Departure Sensor detects when a train has departed from the railroad crossing.
- In addition, the system sends notification and safety messages to Rail Operations Service, which is an external system.

20.2.3 System Context Model

The system context model depicts the Railroad Crossing Embedded System from a total system perspective, as depicted on a SysML block definition diagram in Figure 20.3. It is derived from the conceptual static model of the problem domain. There are five external blocks:

- The Train, which is an external physical entity detected by the system.
- Barrier, which is an external physical entity controlled by the system (barrier actuator + barrier sensor).
- Warning Alarm, which consists of Warning Lights and Warning Audio, is an external physical entity controlled by the system.
- The Rail Operations Service, which is an external system that is notified by the system of the status of the railroad crossing.

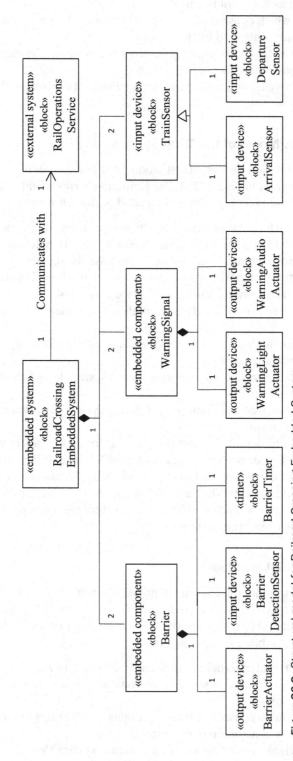

Figure 20.2. Structural model for Railroad Crossing Embedded System.

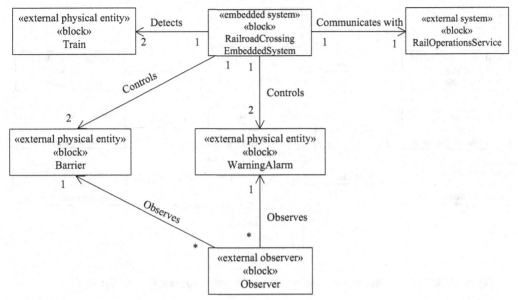

Figure 20.3. System context model for Railroad Crossing Embedded System.

- The Observer (who stops at the railroad crossing), who is an external observer of the system.

In the system context model, the train is depicted (Figure 20.3) as an external physical entity, which is detected by the system. The observer, in particular the vehicle driver, is an external observer of the system. It is worth noting that two of the external blocks on the system context diagram, namely the train and the observer, do not physically interact with the system. The arrival and departure of the train are detected by arrival and departure sensors. The observer is alerted of an imminent train arrival by the closing of the barrier, the warning lights, and the warning audio alarm.

20.2.4 Software System Context Model

The software system context model for RXCS is depicted on a SysML block definition diagram in Figure 20.4. As is typical for an embedded system, there are several external input and output devices, which are depicted by means of SysML blocks. These I/O devices are part of the embedded hardware/software system and hence not depicted in Figure 20.3. However, they are external to the software system and therefore need to be depicted on the software system context model.

Since train arrival and departure are detected by arrival and departure sensors, the Train external physical entity block on the system context model (Figure 20.3) is replaced by Arrival Sensor and Departure Sensor external input device blocks on the software system context model (Figure 20.4). Since the raising and lowering of the Barrier external physical entity is controlled by an actuator and detected by a sensor, it is replaced by the Barrier Actuator external output device and the Barrier Detection Sensor external input device. In addition, there is a Timer to help determine if there are delays in lowering or raising the barrier. Since the Warning Alarm external physical entity is activated by switching actuators on and off, it is replaced by the Warning

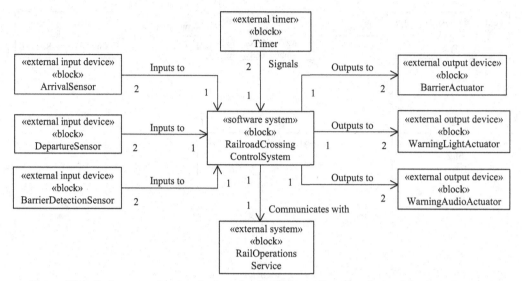

Figure 20.4. Software system context model for Railroad Crossing Control System.

Light Actuator and Warning Audio Actuator external output devices. Since the Observer on the system context diagram does not interact with the software system, it is not needed on the software system context diagram. Finally, the external Rail Operations Service on the system context diagram is also depicted on the software system context diagram.

Consider next the multiplicity between the software system and the external devices. The software system interfaces to two instances of each of the arrival and departure sensors, one pair for each railroad track, and two barriers. Each barrier consists of a barrier actuator, barrier detection sensor, barrier timer, warning light actuator and warning audio actuator. Thus, as depicted in Figure 20.4, the software system interfaces to two instances of each external device and one instance of the external system.

20.2.5 Hardware/Software Boundary Model

The specification of the I/O devices, in particular the three input sensors and three output actuators, are given in Table 20.1. The inputs to the software system from the three input sensors and the outputs from the software system to the three output actuators are specified. An example of an input device is the Barrier Detection Sensor, which sends Barrier Raised and Barrier Lowered input events to the software system. An example of an output device is the Barrier Actuator, which receives Raise Barrier and Lower Barrier commands from the software system.

The hardware characteristics of the I/O devices are that all sensors are event driven; that is, an interrupt is generated when there is an input from one of these devices. The output devices are passive; that is, they do not generate interrupts.

20.3 USE CASE MODELING

For an embedded system such as the RXCS, there are no human external actors. The use cases reflect the requirements of the system, namely Arrive at Railroad Crossing

Table 20.1. I/O Device Boundary Specification

Device name	Device type	Device function	Inputs from device	Outputs to device
Arrival Sensor	Input	Signals when train arrives	Arrival Event	
Departure Sensor	Input	Signals when train departs	Departure Event	
Barrier Detection Sensor	Input	Signals when barrier has been raised or lowered	Barrier Lowered Event, Barrier Raised Event	
Barrier Actuator	Output	Raises and lowers barrier		Raise Barrier, Lower Barrier
Warning Light Actuator	Output	Switches warning lights on and off		Switch On, Switch Off
Warning Audio Actuator	Output	Switches audio warning on and off		Switch On, Switch Off

and Depart from Railroad Crossing. The use case model can be developed from a systems engineering perspective or a software engineering perspective. From a systems engineering perspective, the train is the primary actor of both use cases, since it is the arrival of the train that triggers the Arrive at Railroad Crossing use case and the departure of the train that triggers the Depart from Railroad Crossing use case. However, from a software engineering perspective, the train is replaced in the software level use cases by the sensors that detect the arrival and departure of the train. The actors in the software engineering view are therefore input device actors (corresponding to the sensors), output device actors (corresponding to the actuators), a timer, and an external system. The arrival sensor is the primary actor of the Arrive at Railroad Crossing use case (Figure 20.5a) because it is the arrival of the train that initiates this use case. Similarly, the departure sensor is the primary actor of the Depart from Railroad Crossing use case (Figure 20.5b). The use case specifications are as follows, which include both functional requirements and nonfunctional requirements. The use cases are modeled from a software engineering perspective to allow full consideration of the sensors and actuators.

20.3.1 Arrive at Railroad Crossing Use Case

The Arrive at Railroad Crossing use case starts with an input from the Arrival Sensor actor:

Use case: Arrive at Railroad Crossing.
Summary: Train approaches railroad crossing. The system lowers the barriers, switches on the warning lights, and switches on the audio warning alarm.
Actors:
- Primary actor: Arrival Sensor
- Secondary actors: Barrier Detection Sensor, Barrier Actuator, Warning Light Actuator, Warning Audio Actuator, Rail Operations Service, Barrier Timer.

Precondition: There is either no train or one train in the railroad crossing.

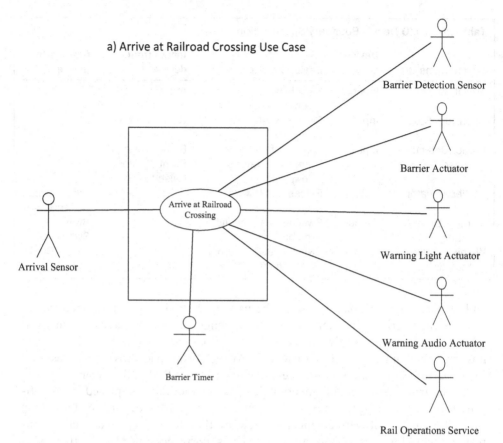

a) Arrive at Railroad Crossing Use Case

Figure 20.5. Use case model for Railroad Crossing Control System.

Main sequence:
1. Arrival Sensor detects the train arrival and informs the system.
2. System commands each Barrier Actuator to lower a barrier, each Warning Light Actuator to switch on the flashing lights, and each Warning Audio Actuator to switch on the audio warning.
3. Barrier Detection Sensor detects that a barrier has been lowered and informs the system.
4. System sends a train arrival message to Rail Operations Service.

Alternative sequences:

Step 2: If there is another train already at the railroad crossing, skip steps 2 and 3.

Step 3: If a barrier lowering timer times out, the system sends a safety warning message to the Rail Operations Service.

Nonfunctional requirements:
- Safety requirements:
  - Barrier lowering time shall not exceed a pre-specified time. If a barrier timer times out, the system shall notify Rail Operations Service.
  - System shall keep track of the number of trains at the railroad crossing, such that the barrier shall only be lowered when the first train arrives.

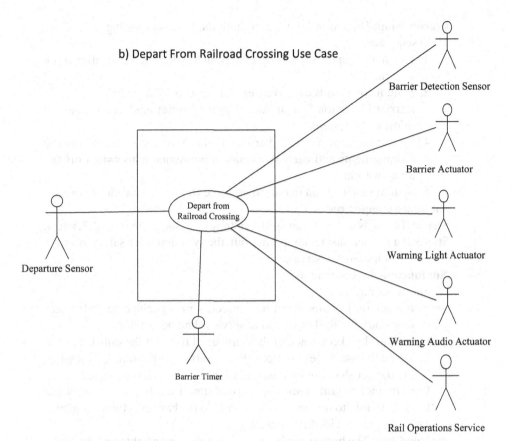

b) Depart From Railroad Crossing Use Case

Barrier Detection Sensor

Barrier Actuator

Depart from
Railroad Crossing

Warning Light Actuator

Departure Sensor

Warning Audio Actuator

Barrier Timer

Rail Operations Service

Figure 20.5 Use case model for Railroad Crossing Control System *(continued)*.

- **Performance requirement**: The elapsed time from the detection of the train arrival to sending the command to the barrier actuator shall not exceed a pre-specified response time.
Postcondition: The barriers have been closed, the warning lights are flashing and the audio warning is sounding.

20.3.2 Depart from Railroad Crossing Use Case

The Depart from Railroad Crossing use case starts with an input from the Departure Sensor actor:

Use case: Depart from Railroad Crossing.
Summary: Train departs from railroad crossing. The system raises the barriers, switches off the warning lights, and switches off the audio warning alarm.
Actors:
- Primary actor: Departure Sensor
- Secondary actors: Barrier Detection Sensor, Barrier Actuator, Warning Light Actuator, Warning Audio Actuator, Rail Operations Service, Barrier Timer.

Precondition: There is at least one train in the railroad crossing.

Main sequence:

1. Departure Sensor detects that the train has departed and informs the system.
2. System commands each Barrier Actuator to raise a barrier.
3. Barrier Detection Sensor detects that a barrier has been raised and informs the system.
4. System commands each Warning Light Actuator to switch off the flashing lights and each Warning Audio Actuator to switch off the audio warning.
5. System sends a train departed message to Rail Operations Service.

Alternative sequences:

Step 2: If there is another train at the railroad crossing, skip steps 2, 3, and 4.

Step 3: If a barrier raising timer times out, the system sends a safety message to the Rail Operations Service.

Nonfunctional requirements:

- Safety requirement:
  - Barrier raising time must not exceed a pre-specified time. If timer times out, the Rail Operations Service shall be notified.
  - System shall keep track of the number of trains at the railroad crossing, such that, if there is more than one train at the railroad crossing, the barrier shall not be raised until the last train has departed.
- **Performance requirement**: The elapsed time from the detection of the train departure to sending the command to the barrier actuator shall not exceed a pre-specified response time.

Postcondition: The barrier has been raised, the warning lights and the audio warning signal have been switched off.

20.4 DYNAMIC STATE MACHINE MODELING

The state machine for RXCS is an orthogonal state machine that consists of two orthogonal regions, Barrier Control and Train Count, as depicted in Figure 20.6a. The reason for this is because barrier control actions depend on whether there are one or two trains in the railroad crossing. The state machine for Barrier Control is depicted in Figure 20.6b and the state machine for Train Count in Figure 20.6c. There are four states in Barrier Control as follows:

- Up – This is the initial state in which the railroad crossing is open. This state is also entered when the barrier sensor detects that the second barrier has been raised. The associated transition (into this state) actions are to switch off both the warning lights and the audio warnings, send a departed message, and cancel the barrier timer.
- Lowering – This state is entered when the first train arrives. The associated transition actions are to lower the barriers, sound the audio warning signals, switch on the flashing lights, and start the barrier timers. If the timer elapses while in this state, which indicates that lowering a physical barrier is too slow, a warning message is sent.

a) State machine for Railroad Crossing Control

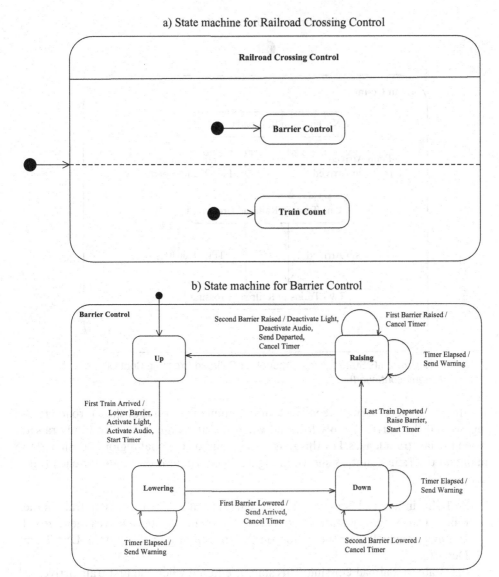

Figure 20.6. State Machine model for Railroad Crossing Control System.

- Down – This state is entered when the barrier sensor detects that the first barrier has been lowered. The associated transition actions are to send the arrived message and cancel the barrier timer. There is no change of state if a barrier lowered event indicates that the second barrier has been lowered or a timer elapsed event indicates that lowering the second physical barrier is too slow.

- Raising – This state is entered when the last train has departed. The associated transition actions are to raise the barrier and to start the barrier timers. There is no change of state if a barrier raised event indicates that the first barrier has been raised or a timer elapsed event indicates that raising a physical barrier is too slow, in which case, a warning message is sent.

Since, it is possible for two trains to be passing the railroad crossing at the same time, it is vital to ensure that the barrier is not raised until the second train has left.

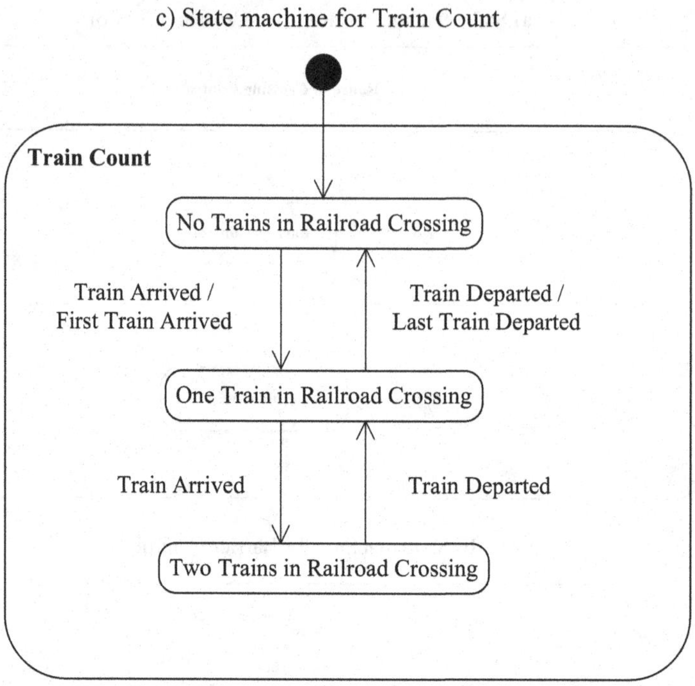

c) State machine for Train Count

Figure 20.6 State Machine model for Railroad Crossing Control System *(continued)*.

It is therefore necessary to keep track of the number of trains at the railroad crossing, so that the barrier is only lowered when the first train arrives and only raised when the last train leaves. For this reason, a second orthogonal region is designed to maintain the Train Count, as shown in Figure 20.6c. There is one state for each train count.

- No Trains in Railroad Crossing. This is the initial state when there is no train in the railroad crossing. This state is also entered when the last train leaves the railroad crossing, in which case the action on the transition into the state is Last Train Departed.
- One Train in Railroad Crossing. This state is entered when the first train arrives at the railroad crossing. The action on the transition is First Train Arrived.
- Two Trains in Railroad Crossing. This state is entered when the second train arrives at the railroad crossing. When the first of two trains leaves the railroad crossing, the state machine transitions out of this state.

To avoid race conditions in the two orthogonal regions, the Train Arrived and Train Departed sensor inputs come to the Train Count state machine. The first Train Arrived input causes a transition from No Trains in Railroad Crossing to One Train in Railroad Crossing state. The action on this transition is First Train Arrived. This action is propagated as an input event to the Barrier Control state machine (Figure 20.6b), which causes the transition from Up state to Lowering state, thereby triggering the Lower Barrier and related actions. The second Train Arrived event causes a transition to Two Trains in Railroad Crossing state in the Train Count state machine but has no effect on the Barrier Control state machine. A similar approach is used on train departure. The first Train Departed input causes a transition from Two Trains in Railroad Crossing state to One Train in Railroad Crossing state in the Train Count state machine but has no effect on the Barrier Control state machine. The second Train Departed input causes a transition from One Train in Railroad Crossing state to No Trains in Railroad Crossing state in the Train Count state machine. The action on this transition is Last Train Departed, which is propagated as an input event to the Barrier Control state machine (Figure 20.6b) and causes a transition from Down state to Raising state, thereby triggering the Raise Barrier and Start Timer actions.

20.5 OBJECT AND CLASS STRUCTURING

Software class structuring is carried out in preparation for dynamic interaction modeling. Given that the system to be developed is a real-time embedded system, it is assumed that all classes, except for entity classes, are concurrent and will therefore be modeled as active (i.e., concurrent) classes.

The software boundary classes in the system can be determined by careful consideration of the external classes on the software context diagram. There must be a software input class to interface to and communicate with each external input device depicted on the software context diagram. Since there are three external input devices, the corresponding input classes are the Arrival Sensor Input, Departure Sensor Input, and Barrier Detection Sensor Input classes. Similarly, there needs to be a software output class to interface to and communicate with each external output device on the software context diagram. Since there are three external output devices, the corresponding output classes are the Barrier Actuator Output, Warning Light Output, and Warning Audio Output classes. There is also a need for a state dependent control class, namely Railroad Crossing Control, which executes its encapsulated state machine to control the other classes. There is also a proxy class, Rail Operations Proxy, to interface to and communicate with the external Rail Operations Service. Since there are no entity classes, these software classes are all considered to be active, meaning each object is instantiated from an active class, has its own thread of control, and can execute concurrently with the other active objects.

The software classes in the system are depicted in Figure 20.7 inside the outer box that represents the software system. The external blocks that interface to and communicate with the boundary classes (input, output, and proxy) are also depicted outside the box representing the software system in Figure 20.7. Because there are two instances of each of the external sensors and each of the external actuators, there are correspondingly two instances of each of the software input classes and output classes that interface to these external devices.

20.6 DYNAMIC INTERACTION MODELING

Next, the dynamic interaction model is developed to depict the interaction among the objects that realize the two use cases, Arrive at Railroad Crossing and Depart from Railroad Crossing. Because of the large number of objects that realize each use case, it is clearer to show the object interaction sequence on two sequence diagrams

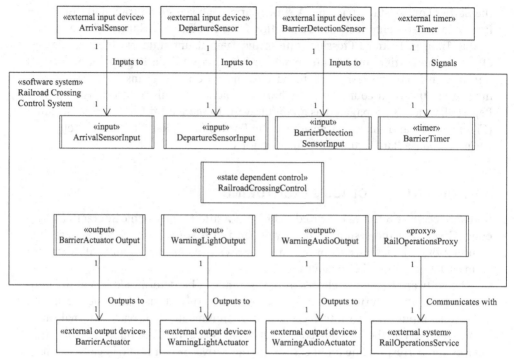

Figure 20.7. Software classes in Railroad Crossing Control System.

for each use case instead of one, the first depicting interaction between the external objects and the software system, and the second depicting the interaction among the external input objects and the software objects. The sequence diagrams depict the realization of the main sequence of each use case.

20.6.1 Sequence Diagrams for Arrive at Railroad Crossing

The first sequence diagram depicts the interaction of the external objects with the software system, as shown in Figure 20.8 for Arrive at Railroad Crossing. On this sequence diagram, there are two external input devices, three external output devices and one external system in addition to the RXCS software system, which is depicted as one composite object. This sequence diagram faithfully follows the interaction sequence described in the Arrive at Railroad Crossing software level use case. The sequence starts with the arrival input event from the Arrival Sensor external input device (message #1), which results in the system lowering the barrier, switching on the warning lights, and switching on the warning audio. When the barrier has been lowered, the Barrier Detection Sensor sends a Barrier Lowered event to the system (message #2), which causes the system to send a status message to the external Rail Operations Service.

The second sequence diagram depicts the interaction among the external input objects and the software objects within the software system, as shown in Figure 20.9 for Arrive at Railroad Crossing. The first object in this sequence is the external Arrival Sensor. The interaction sequence (for all messages depicted on Figure 20.9

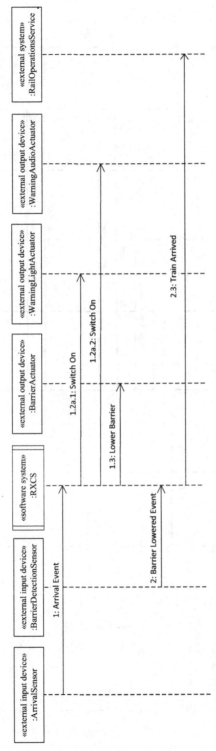

Figure 20.8. Sequence diagram for Arrive at Railroad Crossing use case (external objects).

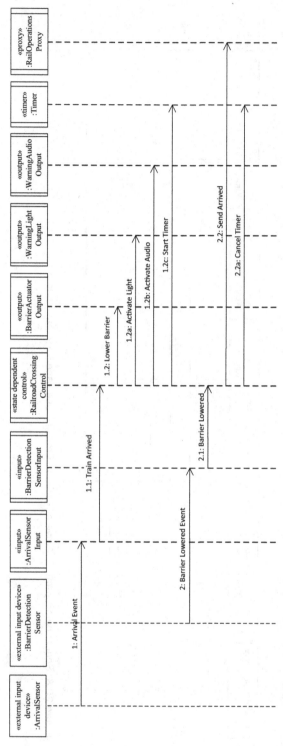

Figure 20.9. Sequence diagram for Arrive at Railroad Crossing use case (external input objects and software objects).

and messages to external output objects depicted on Figure 20.8) is described as follows:

1: Arrival Sensor detects train arrival and sends the Arrival Event to Arrival Sensor Input object.

1.1: Arrival Sensor Input sends Train Arrived message to Railroad Crossing Control.

1.2: Railroad Crossing Control commands the Barrier Actuator Output object to lower the barrier.

1.2a: Railroad Crossing Control commands the Warning Light Output object to activate (i.e., switch on) the warning lights.

1.2b: Railroad Crossing Control commands the Warning Audio Output object to activate the audio warning signal.

1.2c: Railroad Crossing Control commands the Timer to start the barrier lowering timer.

1.2a.1: Warning Light Output sends the Switch On message to the external Warning Light Actuator (see Figure 20.8).

1.2a.2: Warning Audio Output sends the Switch On message to the external Warning Audio Actuator (see Figure 20.8).

1.3: Barrier Actuator Output sends the Lower Barrier message to the external Barrier Actuator (see Figure 20.8).

2: Barrier Detection Sensor detects that the barrier has been lowered and sends the Barrier Lowered Event to the Barrier Detection Sensor Input object.

2.1: Barrier Detection Sensor Input sends Barrier Lowered message to Railroad Crossing Control.

2.2: Railroad Crossing Control sends a train arrived message to Rail Operations Proxy.

2.2a: Railroad Crossing Control cancels the barrier lowering timer.

2.3: Rail Operations Proxy sends the train arrival message to the external Rail Operations Service (see Figure 20.8).

It should be noted that in Figures 20.8 through 20.11, Railroad Crossing Control sends concurrent messages (corresponding to concurrent actions on its encapsulated state machine) such as messages 1.2, 1.2a, 1.2b, and 1.2c. The subsequent message for #1.2 is #1.3, for #1.2a is #1.2a.1, and so on (see Appendix A for conventions on message sequence numbering).

20.6.2 Sequence Diagrams for Depart from Railroad Crossing

The Depart from Railroad Crossing interaction sequence is also depicted on two sequence diagrams. Figure 20.10 depicts the interaction of the external objects with the software system, which starts with the Departure Event from the external Departure Sensor (message #1), which results in the system raising the barrier. When the Barrier Detection Sensor detects that the barrier has been raised, it sends a Barrier Raised Event (message #2) to the system. The system then switches off the warning lights, switches off the warning audio signal, and sends a train departed status message to Rail Operations Service.

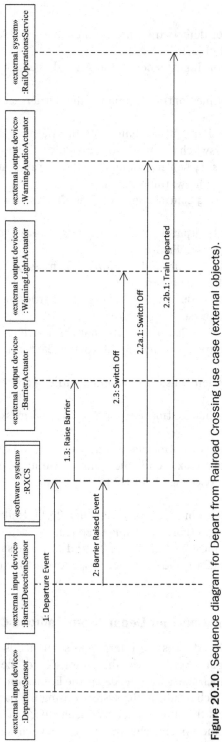

Figure 20.10. Sequence diagram for Depart from Railroad Crossing use case (external objects).

The second sequence diagram depicts the interaction among the external input objects and the software objects within the software system, as shown in Figure 20.11 for Depart from Railroad Crossing. The first object in this sequence is the Departure Sensor. The interaction sequence (for all messages depicted on Figure 20.11 and messages to external output objects depicted on Figure 20.10) is described as follows:

1: Departure Sensor sends Departure Event to Departure Sensor Input.

1.1: Departure Sensor Input sends Train Departed message to Railroad Crossing Control.

1.2: Railroad Crossing Control sends Raise Barrier command to Barrier Actuator Output.

1.2a: Railroad Crossing Control commands the Timer to start the barrier raising timer.

1.3: Barrier Actuator Output sends the Raise Barrier message to the external Barrier Actuator (see Figure 20.10).

2: Barrier Detection Sensor detects the raising of the barrier and sends the Barrier Raised Event to the Barrier Detection Sensor Input object.

2.1: Barrier Detection Sensor Input sends Barrier Raised message to Railroad Crossing Control.

2.2: Railroad Crossing Control commands Warning Light Output to deactivate (i.e., switch off) the warning lights.

2.2a: Railroad Crossing Control commands Warning Audio Output to deactivate the audio warning signal.

2.2b: Railroad Crossing Control sends a train departed message to Rail Operations Proxy.

2.2c: Railroad Crossing Control cancels the barrier raising timer.

2.3: Warning Light Output sends the switch off message to the Warning Light Actuator (see Figure 20.10).

2.2a.1: Warning Audio Output sends the switch off message to the Warning Audio Actuator (see Figure 20.10).

2.2b.1: Rail Operations Proxy sends the train departed message to Rail Operations Service(see Figure 20.10).

20.7 DESIGN MODELING

The software architecture of the Railroad Crossing Control System is designed around a Centralized Control Pattern. Centralized control is provided by the Railroad Crossing Control component receiving inputs from the arrival, departure, and barrier detection sensors via input objects and controlling the external environment by means of the barrier, warning light, and warning audio actuators via output objects. However, viewed from the larger distributed Light Rail System (Chapter 21), the Railroad Crossing Control System is also an example of a Distributed Independent Control pattern, because each instance of the control system is independent of the other instances and sends status messages to Rail Operations Service. The initial software architecture is designed by integrating the use case–based sequence diagrams.

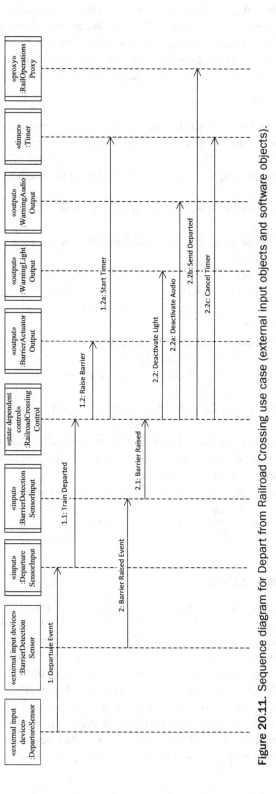

Figure 20.11. Sequence diagram for Depart from Railroad Crossing use case (external input objects and software objects).

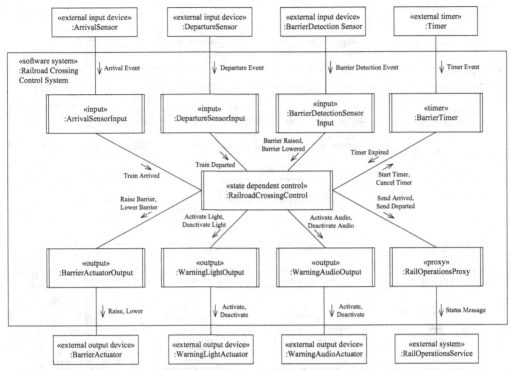

Figure 20.12. Integrated communication diagram for Railroad Crossing Control System.

20.7.1 Integrated Communication Diagram

The initial attempt at design modeling is to develop the integrated communication diagram for the Railroad Crossing Control System, which necessitates the integration of the use case–based interaction diagrams shown in Figures 20.8 through 20.11. Since these diagrams are sequence diagrams, the objects and object interactions must be mapped to an integrated communication diagram as depicted in Figure 20.12. In addition, it is necessary to address alternative sequences that are not depicted on the sequence diagrams, in particular for the barrier lowering and raising timers. The integration is quite straightforward because most of the objects support both use cases. However, the Arrival Sensor Input object only supports the Arrival use case, and the Departure Sensor Input object only supports the Departure use case. The integrated communication diagram is a *generic* concurrent communication diagram in that it depicts all possible communications between the objects.

20.7.2 Concurrent Software Architecture

In this concurrent real-time design, the concurrent task structuring criteria are applied to determine the tasks in the Railroad Crossing Control System. The concurrent communication diagram for the Railroad Crossing Control System is shown in Figure 20.13, which depicts the concurrent tasks in the software architecture. The concurrent task design is developed by starting from the integrated communication diagram in Figure 20.12, which depicts all the objects in the system. The most flexible

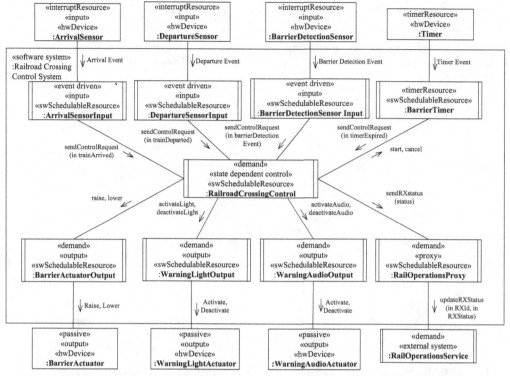

Figure 20.13. Concurrent communication diagram for Railroad Crossing Control System.

design is for all the objects to be designed as tasks that execute concurrently. Each task is depicted with the MARTE stereotype for task: «swSchedulableResource». The concurrent tasks are described as follows:

- **Input tasks.** Concurrent input tasks receive inputs from the external environment and send corresponding messages to the control task. There are three input tasks – Arrival Sensor Input, Departure Sensor Input, and Barrier Detection Sensor Input – each of which is designed as an event driven input task that is awakened by the arrival of the corresponding sensor input. Thus, the three input tasks are all depicted with the stereotypes «event driven» «input» «swSchedulableResource».
- **Control task.** Railroad Crossing Control is the centralized state dependent control task for the Railroad Crossing Control System. It executes the Railroad Crossing Control state machine, receiving messages from the input and timer tasks, and sends action messages to the output, proxy, and timer tasks. Railroad Crossing Control is designed as a demand driven task awakened by the arrival of a message from any of the input tasks or timer task. The control task is depicted with the stereotypes «demand» «state dependent control» «swSchedulableResource».
- **Output tasks.** There are three output objects, each of which is designed as a demand driven task awakened on demand by the arrival of a message from the Railroad Crossing Control task and then outputs to an external actuator. The three demand driven output tasks are Barrier Actuator Output, which interfaces to the external barrier actuator, Warning Light Output, which interfaces to the external warning light actuator, and Warning Audio Output, which interfaces to the external

warning audio actuator. The three output tasks are all depicted with the stereo-types «demand» «output» «swSchedulableResource».

- **Proxy task**. Rail Operations Proxy is the proxy task that sends railroad crossing status message to the Rail Operations Service. Rail Operations Proxy is designed as a demand driven task awakened by messages from Railroad Crossing Control. The proxy task is depicted with the stereotypes «demand» «proxy» «swSchedulableResource».
- **Timer task**. Barrier Timer is designed as a periodic task awakened by timer events from the external timer. Its timing is initiated by a start timer message from Railroad Crossing Control, which can later be cancelled. When it does time out, it sends a timeout message to Railroad Crossing Control to warn it that the barrier raising or lowering is slower than expected. The periodic task is depicted with the stereotypes «timerResource» «swSchedulableResource».

20.7.3 Architectural Communication Patterns

Next the communication patterns between the tasks are considered. The messages to be sent between the tasks in the RXCS system (Figure 20.13) are determined from the integrated communication diagram (Figure 20.12) in which all messages between tasks are assumed to be asynchronous. The actual type of message communication – synchronous or asynchronous – is now determined. To handle the communication between the tasks in the Railroad Crossing Control System, two communication patterns are applied:

Asynchronous Message Communication. The Asynchronous Message Communication pattern is widely used in the RXCS system because most communication is one-way, and this pattern has the advantage of preventing the consumers from holding up the producers. The Railroad Crossing Control consumer task needs to be able to receive messages from any of its four producers, Arrival Sensor Input, Departure Sensor Input, Barrier Detection Sensor Input, and Barrier Timer, in whatever order they arrive. The best way to handle this requirement for flexibility is through asynchronous message communication, with one input message queue for the Railroad Crossing Control task, so that the control task will receive whichever message is sent first. Asynchronous message communication is also used between Railroad Crossing Control as a producer to four consumers, the three output tasks, and the proxy task. The reason is that the producer in this case frequently sends messages concurrently to several consumers and does not need a response. Message communication between the Rail Operations Proxy task and Rail Operations Service subsystem is also asynchronous because the former sends status messages to the latter and does not need a response.

Bidirectional asynchronous communication. This communication pattern is used between the Railroad Crossing Control and Barrier Timer. After Railroad Crossing Control sends a start timer message to the Barrier Timer, it waits for a message from either Barrier Detection Sensor Input (either a barrier lowered or barrier raised message) or a timer expiration message from Barrier Timer (indicating a timeout) and accepts the first message to arrive.

20.7.4 Examples of Task Interface Specification

This section provides two examples of task interface specifications (see Chapter 13). The first TIS is for the Railroad Crossing Control task as described next:

Name: Railroad Crossing Control.

Information hidden: Details of the encapsulated Railroad Crossing Control state machine.

Structuring criteria: Role criterion: state dependent control; concurrency criterion: demand driven.

Assumptions: At most two trains can be simultaneously in the railroad crossing.

Anticipated changes: Possible addition of further sensors and actuators, requiring changes to the encapsulated state machine and communication with additional tasks.

Task interface:

Task inputs:

Asynchronous message communication: sendControlRequest (eventRX) – values of eventRX: trainArrived, trainDeparted, barrierRaised, barrierLowered, timerExpired

Task outputs:

Asynchronous message communication: raise, lower, activateLight, deactivateLight, activateAudio, deactivateAudio, start, cancel, sendRXstatus (status).

Errors detected: Unrecognized message.

The second task interface specification is for the Arrival Sensor Input task:

Name: Arrival Sensor Input.

Information hidden: Details of processing input from the hardware arrival sensor.

Structuring criteria: Role criterion: input; concurrency criterion: event driven

Assumptions: Only one arrival sensor input is handled at one time.

Anticipated changes: Possible additional information will be sent by the arrival sensor.

Task interface:

Task inputs:

Event input: Arrival sensor external interrupt to indicate that train arrival has been detected.

External input: Arrival Event.

Task outputs:

Asynchronous message communication: sendControlRequest (train Arrived)

Errors detected: Unrecognized input event; sensor malfunction.

Table 20.2. Railroad Crossing Control CPU Times

Task	Task CPU time C_i (msec)	Arrival sensor event sequence tasks $(C_i + C_x + C_m)$ (msec)	Task priority
Arrival Sensor Input	4	5	1
Railroad Crossing Control – from Oven Timer message to first message sent	5	6	6
Railroad Crossing Control – for each subsequent message sent	1	2	
Barrier Actuator Output	4	5	2
Warning Light Output	6	7	4
Warning Audio Output	5	6	5
Timer	3	4	7
Barrier Sensor Input	4		3
Rail Operations Proxy	5		8
Message communication overhead (C_m)	0.7		
Context switching overhead (C_x)	0.3		

The development of task behavior specifications, which describe the event sequencing logic for these tasks, is left as an exercise for the reader.

20.8 PERFORMANCE ANALYSIS OF REAL-TIME SOFTWARE DESIGN

This section describes the real-time performance analysis of the Railroad Crossing Control System. The system is event driven because it reacts to the external events arriving at the system. Consequently, a combination of event sequence analysis and timing diagrams, as described in Chapters 17 and 18, is applied.

A time-critical scenario is the arrival of a train at the railroad crossing, which is detected by the arrival sensor and results in the system lowering the barrier. This barrier lowering event sequence is fully described in Section 20.6. The tasks that participate in this scenario are depicted in Table 20.2, with the CPU time C_i depicted in the second column. The execution times for the six tasks that participate in the arrival event sequence are depicted in the third column. The execution time for each task in the event sequence is the sum of its CPU time, context-switching time, and message communication time. The task priorities are depicted in the fourth column. Arrival Sensor Input and Barrier Actuator Output are given the highest priorities because they are the most time-critical tasks. The other input and output tasks are given the next highest priorities so that they can, if necessary, preempt Railroad Crossing Control, which is given a lower priority.

20.8.1 Performance Analysis on Single Processor System

The task execution for the event sequence on a single processor is depicted on the timing diagram in Figure 20.14. In this event driven scenario, at the start of the analysis, the system is idle, waiting for an external event. The event sequence starts with the Arrival Sensor sending an Arrival Event to Arrival Sensor Input, which is activated by the interrupt, executes for 5 msec, sends a Train Arrived message to Railroad Crossing

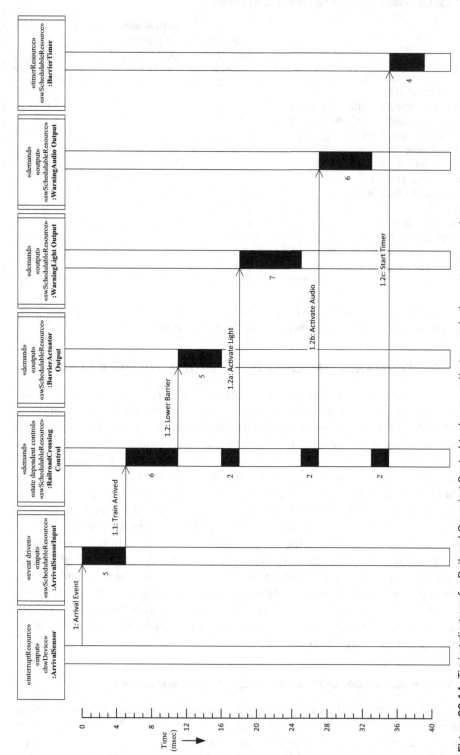

Figure 20.14. Timing diagram for Railroad Crossing Control tasks executing on a single-processor system.

Control, and terminates. When the message arrives at Railroad Crossing Control, even though it has a lower priority than most of the other tasks, it is the only task available to execute because all other tasks are blocked. Assuming that this is the only train at the railroad crossing, the Train Arrived event causes a state transition from Up state to Lowering state on the internal Barrier Control state machine (Figure 20.6). The effect of the state transition is to trigger four concurrent actions to Lower Barrier, Activate Light, Activate Audio, and Start Timer.

On the timing diagram, after executing for 6 msec, Railroad Crossing Control sends the Lower Barrier message to Barrier Actuator Output. When it receives the message, because Barrier Actuator Output has a higher priority than Railroad Crossing Control, it unblocks and preempts Railroad Crossing Control. After executing for 5 msec, Barrier Actuator Output sends the lower barrier command to the external barrier actuator and terminates. Railroad Crossing Control then resumes execution for 2 msec before sending the Activate Light message to Warning Light Output. Because the latter task has a higher priority, upon receiving the message, Warning Light Output preempts Railroad Crossing Control, executes for 7 msec, sends the activate command to the warning light, and then terminates. The same procedure is then followed with Railroad Crossing Control resuming execution and sending messages to Warning Audio Actuator and Barrier Timer respectively. As can be seen from Figure 20.14, the total elapsed time for this scenario is 39 msec.

20.8.2 Performance Analysis on Multiprocessor System

Now consider the same event sequence executing on a multiprocessor system with four CPUs, as depicted on the timing diagram in Figure 20.15. This scenario starts with Arrival Sensor Input activated by an interrupt, executing for 5 msec on CPU A and sending a Train Arrived message. Railroad Crossing Control receives the message and executes for 6 msec on CPU B before sending a lower barrier message to Barrier Actuator Output. However, in this multiprocessor scenario, Railroad Crossing Control continues executing on CPU B in parallel with Barrier Actuator Output executing on CPU C. After a further 2 msec, Railroad Crossing Control sends an activate message to Warning Light Output, which then starts executing on CPU D. Railroad Crossing Control continues executing on CPU B and, after a further 2 msec, sends an activate message to Warning Audio Output, which starts executing on CPU A. At this time, there are tasks executing in parallel on all four CPUs.

After a further 2 msec, Railroad Crossing Control sends a start timer message to Barrier Timer, which then executes on CPU C, replacing the recently terminated Barrier Actuator Output. As depicted on Figure 20.15, the total elapsed time for this multiprocessor scenario is 21 msec, which is 18 msec less than the single-processor scenario. This comparison shows that there are situations when a multiprocessor system can be used to significant advantage, in particular when there are multiple tasks concurrently executing independent actions. However, it should be pointed out that memory contention negatively affects performance, and therefore elapsed times, in multicore systems.

20.9 COMPONENT-BASED SOFTWARE ARCHITECTURE

The design for the component-based software architecture for the Railroad Crossing Control System is given on Figure 20.16, which depicts a UML composite structure

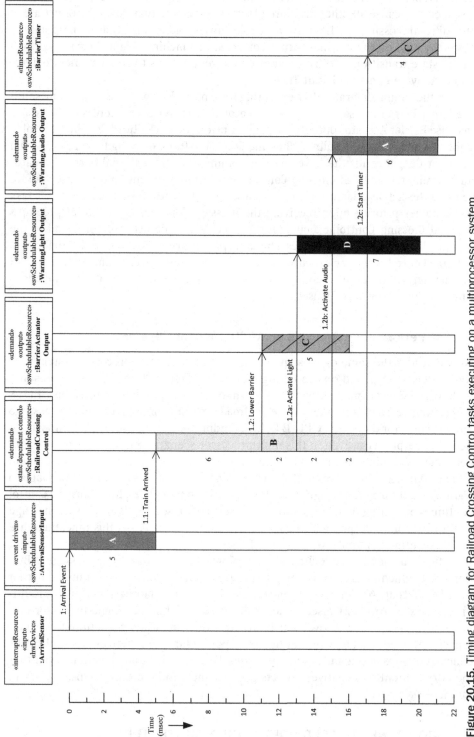

Figure 20.15. Timing diagram for Railroad Crossing Control tasks executing on a multiprocessor system.

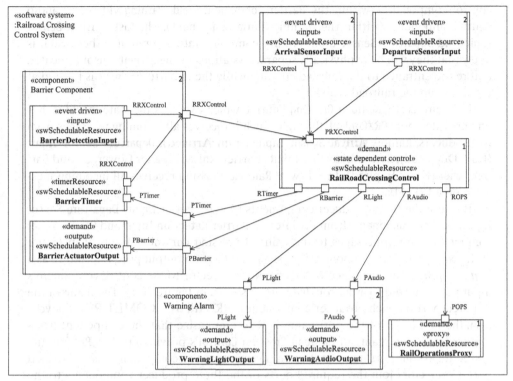

Figure 20.16. Railroad Crossing Control System component-based software architecture.

diagram showing the RXCS components, ports, and connectors. All the components are concurrent and communicate with other components through ports. The overall architecture and connectivity among components is initially determined from the RXCS concurrent communication diagram shown in Figure 20.13. However, there are other factors to consider concerning the creation of composite components. In particular, composite components are created such that they could be deployed to execute on different nodes in a distributed configuration.

20.9.1 Design of Components

RXCS is designed as a composite component that contains six components, four of which are simple components and two of which are in turn composite components, as depicted in Figure 20.16. Each simple component has a single thread of control (Arrival Sensor Input, Departure Sensor Input, Railroad Crossing Control, and Rail Operations Proxy). These simple components correspond to the concurrent tasks determined in the concurrent communication diagram of Figure 20.13 and are depicted with the MARTE stereotype «swSchedulableResource». The two composite components are Barrier Component (which contains the simple components Barrier Actuator Output, Barrier Detection Input, and Barrier Timer) and Warning Alarm Component (which contains the simple components Warning Light Output and Warning Audio Output). The composite components are depicted with the component stereotype. This design allows components to be deployed to be in close proximity to the devices they monitor or control, in particular the barrier sensor monitoring and barrier actuator control components (within the Barrier Component) and warning video and audio alarm components (within the Warning Alarm Component). The tasks Arrival Sensor Input and Departure Sensor Input are not combined into a component because it is likely that they will be in physically separate locations, as the arrival sensor is located before the entrance to the railroad crossing while the departure sensor is located at the exit from the railroad crossing.

In Figure 20.16, Railroad Crossing Control, which executes the state machine, has one provided port PRXControl, through which it receives all incoming messages from its producers, namely Arrival Sensor Input (train Arrived), Departure Sensor Input (train Departed), Barrier Detection Input (barrier Raised, barrier Lowered), and Barrier Timer (timer Expired). In this way, Railroad Crossing receives all incoming messages on a FIFO basis.

Because the three producer components (Arrival Sensor Input, Departure Sensor Input, Barrier Component (from the internal Barrier Detection Input and Barrier Timer components) send messages to the Railroad Crossing Control component in Figure 20.13, each producer component is designed to have an output port, referred to as a *required port*, which is joined by means of a connector to the control component's input port, referred to as a *provided port*, as shown in Figure 20.16. The name of the required port on each producer component is RRXCtrl; by a COMET/RTE convention, the first letter of the port name is R to emphasize that the component has a *required* port. The name of Railroad Crossing Control's provided port is PRXCtrl; the first letter of the port name is P to emphasize that the component has a provided port. Connectors join the required ports of the three producer components to the provided port of the control component.

Railroad Crossing Control also has five required ports through which it communicates with Rail Operations Proxy, Barrier Component (in particular the internal Barrier Actuator Output and Barrier Timer components), and Warning Alarm (in particular the internal Warning Light Output and Warning Audio Output simple components). For example, the RLight and RAudio required ports of Railroad Crossing Control are respectively connected to the PLight and PAudio ports of the Warning Alarm composite component.

It should be noted that delegation connectors join the RRXCtrl ports of the Barrier Detection Input and Barrier Timer internal components to the port of the same name in the composite component Barrier Component. Note also that delegation connectors join the PLight and PAudio ports of the composite component Warning Alarm respectively to the ports of the same name in the two internal components Warning Light Output and Warning Audio Output. This means that the outer port for PLight forwards the messages it receives to the inner PLight port. The two ports have the same name because they provide the same interface.

20.9.2 Design of Component Interfaces

Each component port is defined in terms of its provided and/or required interfaces. Some producer components – in particular, the input components – do not provide a software interface because they receive their inputs directly from the external hardware input device. However, they require an interface (which is provided by the control component) in order to send messages to the control component. Figure 20.17

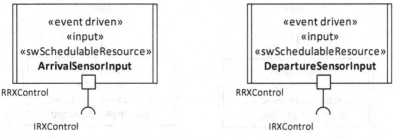

Figure 20.17. Component ports and interfaces for input components.

depicts the port and required interfaces for the input components Arrival Sensor Input and Departure Sensor Input. These input components, as well as the Barrier Component (in addition to the internal Barrier Detection Input and Barrier Timer component) have the same required interface – IRXControl – which is provided by the Railroad Crossing Control component.

Control components need to provide interfaces for the producer components to use and require interfaces that are provided by output components. The Railroad Crossing Control component (see Figure 20.16 and 20.18), which conceptually executes the Railroad Crossing Control state machine, receives asynchronous control request messages from its producer components, as depicted in Figure 20.13. The provided interface IRXControl, which is specified in Figure 20.18, is kept simple by having only one operation (sendcontrolRequest), which has an input parameter (eventRX) that holds the name and contents of the individual message. Having each control

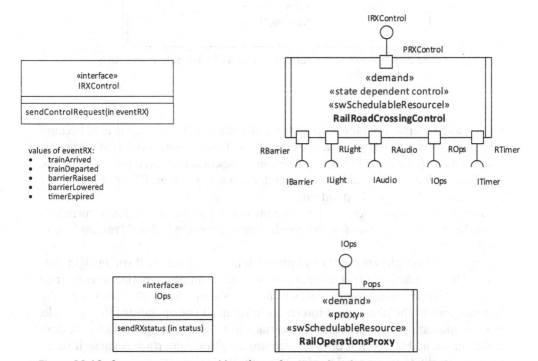

Figure 20.18. Component ports and interfaces for control and proxy components.

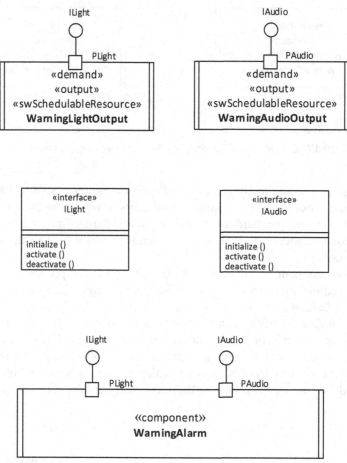

Figure 20.19. Component ports and interfaces for output and composite components.

request as a separate operation would make the interface more complicated because it would consist of five operations instead of one. Furthermore, evolution of the system would require the addition or deletion of operations rather than leaving the interface unchanged and adding a parameter value to the eventRX input parameter of the send controlRequest operation.

Figure 20.18 also depicts the port and provided interface for the Rail Operations Proxy. The provided interface IOps is a required interface of the Railroad Crossing Control component.

Figure 20.19 depicts the ports and provided interfaces for the Warning Light Output and Warning Audio Output components, which are simple components contained within the Warning Alarm component, which is also shown. Figure 20.19 also shows the specifications of the component interfaces in terms of the operations they provide. Each output component provides an interface to receive messages sent by the control component. However, it does not require a software interface because it sends outputs directly to an external hardware output device.

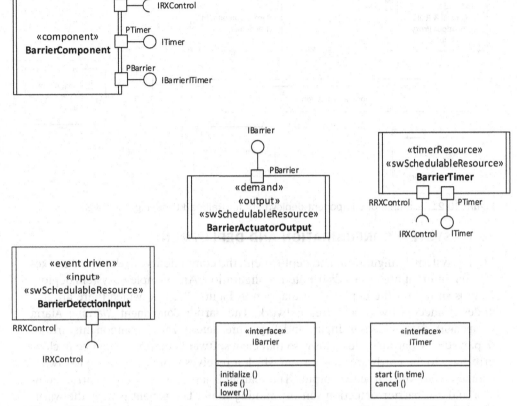

Figure 20.20. Component ports and interfaces for Barrier composite component and simple components it contains.

The output components each have a provided port:

- PLight for Warning Light Output, which provides the interface ILight. The provided operations are to activate and deactivate the warning lights.
- PAudio for Warning Audio Output, which provides the interface IAudio. The provided operations are to activate and deactivate the audio warning device.

The Barrier Component composite component and simple components it contains are depicted in Figure 20.20. The ports and interfaces of the periodic timer inner component are also shown in Figure 20.20. The encapsulated Barrier Timer simple component has one provided port with a provided interface and one required port with a required interface. The provided interface is ITimer, which allows it to receive start and cancel timer requests from Railroad Crossing Control via a delegation connector from the composite Barrier Component. The required interface is IRXControl, which allows Barrier Timer to send timer expired messages to Railroad Crossing Control via a delegation connector to the composite Barrier Component. The Barrier Detection Input inner component communicates with Railroad Crossing Control via the IRXControl required interface in the same way. The Barrier Actuator Output inner component has a port PBarrier, which provides the interface IBarrier. The provided operations are to raise and lower the barrier.

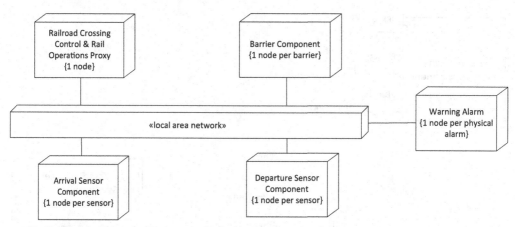

Figure 20.21. Example of component deployment for Railroad Crossing Control System.

20.10 SYSTEM CONFIGURATION AND DEPLOYMENT

During system configuration and deployment, the components are deployed to execute on different nodes in a distributed configuration. An example of system deployment is shown on the deployment diagram in Figure 20.21, in which there are five nodes connected by a local area network. The Barrier Component, Warning Alarm Component, Arrival Sensor Input, and Departure Sensor Input components are all deployed to separate nodes. This is so that each software component can be in close proximity to the hardware sensor from which it receives inputs and/or the hardware actuator(s) to which it sends outputs. Thus Barrier Component is near the barrier actuator and the barrier detection sensor; Warning Alarm Component is near the warning light and audio actuators; Arrival Sensor Input and Departure Sensor Input are respectively near the arrival and departure sensors. The remaining components, the Railroad Crossing Control and Rail Operations Proxy components, are deployed to the same node.

The performance requirement that the elapsed times from detection of train arrival/departure to sending a command to the barrier actuator do not exceed predetermined response times is addressed by the performance analysis in Section 20.8. The safety requirement that the system keep track of the number of trains at the railroad crossing, such that the barrier is lowered when the first train arrives and raised when the last train departs, is addressed by the design of the Railroad Crossing Control state machine. The safety requirement that the system measure the barrier lowering and raising times and raise a warning if predetermined elapsed times are exceeded is addressed by the design of the Barrier Timer object and the Railroad Crossing Control state machine.

21

Light Rail Control System Case Study

This chapter describes a case study for an embedded **Light Rail Control System**. This design is for a safety-critical system, in which the automated control of driverless trains must be done safely and in a timely manner. As is typical of embedded systems, the system interfaces with the external environment by means of several sensors and actuators. Control of each train is state dependent, which necessitates the design of a state machine to provide control of the train. As this system is an embedded system, the design approach benefits from starting with a systems engineering perspective of the total hardware/software system before the real-time software modeling and design. The **Light Rail Embedded System** refers to the total hardware/software system, while **Light Rail Control System** refers to the software system.

The problem is described in Section 21.1. Section 21.2 describes the structural modeling of the system, consisting of the structural model of the problem domain, followed by the system and software system context models. Section 21.3 describes the use case model from a software engineering perspective, describing both the functional and nonfunctional requirements of the safety-critical system. Section 21.4 describes the dynamic state machine modeling, which is particularly important to model the state dependent intricacies of this embedded system. Section 21.5 describes how the system structuring criteria are applied to this system, followed by Section 21.6, which describes how the object and class structuring criteria are applied to each subsystem. Section 21.7 describes how dynamic interaction modeling is used to develop sequence diagrams from the use cases. Section 21.8 provides an overview of the design model for the software system. Section 21.9 describes developing integrated communication diagrams, which leads to the design of the distributed software architecture in Section 21.10, and the component-based software architecture in Section 21.11. Section 21.12 describes system configuration and deployment.

21.1 PROBLEM DESCRIPTION

The **Light Rail Control System** consists of several trains that travel between stations along a track in both directions with a semi-circular loop at each end. Trains have to stop at each station. If a proximity sensor detects a hazard ahead, the train decelerates before stopping. If taken out of service, a train stops at the next station to discharge passengers, after which it goes out of service with doors closed.

For each **train**, there are the following I/O devices:

■ **A motor actuator.** Controlled by commands to accelerate, cruise, decelerate, and stop.
■ **Door actuators.** Each door actuator is controlled by commands to open and close a door.
■ **Door sensors.** For each door actuator, there is also a door sensor to detect when the door is open.
■ **Approaching Sensor** Detects when train is approaching station. Used to start deceleration of train.
■ **Arrival Sensor.** Detects when train arrives at station. Used to stop train.
■ **Departure Sensor.** Detects when train has left the station.
■ **Proximity Sensor.** Detects when a hazard is on or crossing the railroad track ahead of the train and when the hazard is removed.
■ **A GPS location sensor**, which determines the coordinates of the train at regular intervals.
■ **A speed sensor**, which determines the current speed of the train.
■ **Train displays.** Display the next stations to be visited by the train.
■ **Train audio devices.** Broadcast audio messages to the train passengers, informing them of arrival at station.

For each **station**, there are the following I/O devices

■ **A station display.** Displays the next trains in sequence to arrive and expected times of arrival.
■ **A station audio device.** Broadcasts audio messages to the station passengers.

There are several **railroad crossings** that cross the track, the operation of which is described in Chapter 20.

The hardware characteristics of the I/O devices are that all sensors except for the proximity sensor are event driven; that is, an interrupt is generated when there is an input from one of these devices. The proximity sensor and all output devices are passive.

21.2 STRUCTURAL MODELING

The static structural model of the problem domain captures the structural entities (modeled as SysML blocks) and relationships in the **Light Rail Embedded System,** as depicted in Figure 21.1. The **Light Rail Embedded System** is modeled as an embedded system composite block, which is composed of several Train and Station blocks. The Train is a modeled as an embedded subsystem composite block composed of input and output device blocks. Thus, there are several output device blocks: one Motor, many Door Actuators, many Train Displays, and many Train Audio Device blocks. There are also several train sensors, which are generalized into a Sensor input device block. The specialized sensor blocks are the Approaching Sensor, Arrival Sensor, Departure Sensor, Proximity Sensor, Location Sensor, Speed Sensor, and Door Sensor. Station is also modeled as an embedded subsystem composite block, composed of Station

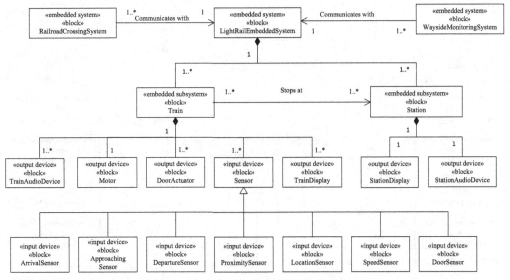

Figure 21.1. Conceptual structural model for Light Rail Embedded System.

Display and Station Audio Device blocks. The Train block has a many-to-many association with the Station block, as any train can stop at any station. The embedded systems Railroad Crossing System and Wayside Monitoring System communicate with the **Light Rail Embedded System**.

Next, the system context block diagram is developed for the **Light Rail Embedded System**, which models the external entities to the hardware/software system and is depicted in Figure 21.2. From a system point of view, all sensors and actuators are part of the system. The external entities are the Train (which is an external physical entity block that is detected and controlled by the system), Hazard (which is an external physical entity block such as train or vehicle ahead that is detected by the system),

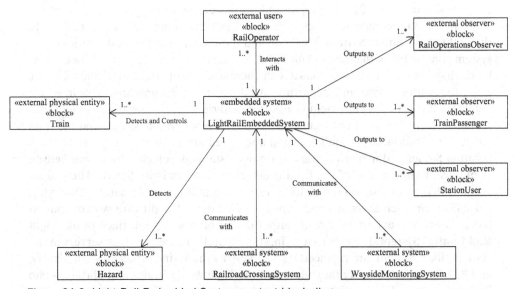

Figure 21.2. Light Rail Embedded System context block diagram.

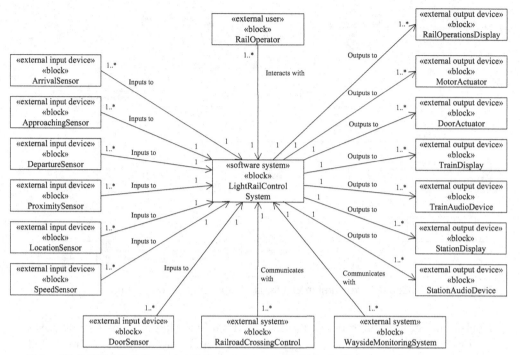

Figure 21.3. Light Rail Control software system context block diagram.

the Rail Operator (an external user block that interacts with the system), the external observer blocks Train Passenger, Station User, and Rail Operations Observer, and the external system blocks Railroad Crossing System and Wayside Monitoring System.

After modeling the system context, the next step is to develop the software system context block diagram, which depicts in Figure 21.3 the **Light Rail Control System** as a software system block that interfaces to several external input and output device blocks, two external system blocks, and an external user block. From the conceptual static model in Figure 21.1, the input and output device blocks that are part of the Train and Station composite blocks are in fact external input and output devices to the **Light Rail Control System**. The Train and Hazard external physical entities in the system context block diagram (Figure 21.2) are represented on the software context block diagram by the sensors that detect them and/or actuators that control them. Thus, the train's arrival and departure are detected by Approaching Sensor, which detects that the train is approaching a station, Arrival Sensor, which detects the train's imminent arrival at a station, and Departure Sensor block which detects that the train has left the station. The train's location and speed are measured respectively by a Location Sensor and a Speed Sensor. Train door status is detected by a Door Sensor. A physical hazard ahead of the train is detected by a Proximity Sensor. The system is controlled by outputs to the Motor Actuator and many Door Actuators. The external sensors and actuators are respectively depicted on the software system context block diagram as external input or output device blocks that interface to the **Light Rail Control System**. The external train, station, and rail operations observers in the system block diagram are replaced respectively by the Train Display, Station Display, and Rail Operations Display they view and the Train Audio Device and Station Audio Device they hear. The remaining external blocks carry over from the system context diagram, namely a human external user, the Rail Operator and two external systems, Railroad Crossing System and Wayside Monitoring System.

21.3 USE CASE MODELING

The next step is to develop the use case model for the **Light Rail Control System**. Because this is an embedded system with many external sensors and actuators, it is desirable to develop a more detailed use case model from a software engineering perspective, in which there will be many actors. There is one human actor, namely the Rail Operator, several I/O device actors, and two external system actors. There are nine input and/or output device actors, which are the Approaching Sensor, Arrival Sensor, Departure Sensor, Proximity Sensor, Motor, Door Actuator, Door Sensor, Location Sensor, and Speed Sensor. The input and output actors correspond to the external input and output device blocks on the software context block diagram. There is one generalized actor representing the Railroad Media. There are two external system actors, Railroad Crossing System and Wayside Monitoring System.

Because the use case model for the **Light Rail Control System** has many use cases and actors, it is preferable to structure the use case model into use case packages, which group together related use cases. Thus, the use cases are grouped into four use case packages based on their functionality. Because of the number of use cases and actors, each of the four use case packages with its corresponding use cases and actors is shown on a separate use case diagram. From the problem definition, the use case packages and use cases in each package are identified and described next.

21.3.1 Use Case Package for Light Rail Operations

Use cases that address the train arriving and leaving a station during normal operation. These use cases are grouped into a use case package called Light Rail Operations, as depicted in Figure 21.4:

- Arrive at Station. A train arrives at the station. The actors are Approaching Sensor (primary actor), Arrival Sensor, Motor, and Door Actuator.
- Control Train at Station. Addresses opening and closing of train doors at the station. The actors are Door Sensor (primary actor) and Door Actuator.
- Depart from Station. A train leaves the station. The actors are Door Sensor (primary actor), Departure Sensor, and Motor.
- Control Train Operation, which is a high level use case that includes the Arrive at Station, Control Train at Station, and Depart from Station use cases. It describes the sequence of use cases for normal train operation. The actor for this use case is Railroad Media, which is also an actor of the inclusion use cases.

The use case descriptions are given next. The Arrive at Station use case starts with an input from the Approaching Sensor actor.

Use case: Arrive at Station.
Actors: Approaching Sensor (primary), Arrival Sensor, Motor, Door Actuator.
Precondition: Train is moving toward next station.

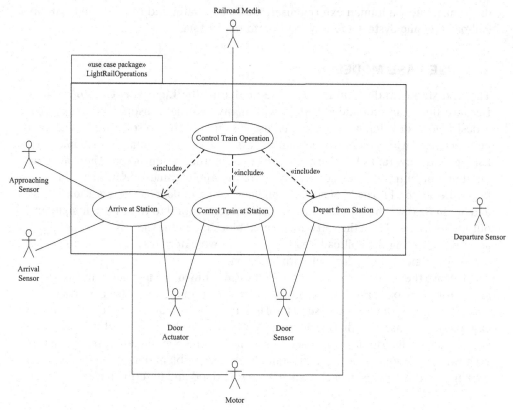

Figure 21.4. Light Rail Control System actors and use cases: Light Rail Operations use case package.

Main sequence:
1) Approaching Sensor signals that train is approaching station
2) System sends Decelerate command to Motor.
3) System sends Train Approaching message to Railroad Media.
4) System continues decelerating and monitoring speed of train.
5) Arrival Sensor signals that train is entering the station.
6) System sends Stop Motor command to Motor.
7) Motor responds that train has stopped.
8) System sends Open Doors command to Door Actuator.
9) System sends Train Arrival message to Railroad Media.

Alternative sequences:
Steps 1 to 4: If hazard is detected, extend with Detect Hazard Presence use case. When hazard is removed and train is stationary, extend with Detect Hazard Removal use case.

Postcondition: Train has stopped at station with doors opening.

The Control Train at Station use case starts with an input from the Door Sensor actor.

Use case: Control Train at Station.
Actors: Door Sensor (primary), Door Actuator.

Precondition: Train is stopped at station with doors opening.
Main sequence:
1) Door Sensor sends Doors Opened message.
2) After time interval, System sends Close Doors command to Door Actuator.
3) System sends Train Departing message to Railroad Media

Alternative:
Step 2: If there is a hazard ahead, train remains at station with doors open until the hazard has been removed.
Postcondition: Train is stopped at station with doors closing.

The Depart from Station use case starts with an input from the Door Sensor actor.

Use case: Depart from Station.
Actor: Door Sensor (primary), Departure Sensor, Motor.
Precondition: Train is stopped at station with doors closing.
Main sequence:
1) Door Sensor sends doors have closed message to System.
2) System commands Motor to accelerate train to cruising speed.
3) Departure Sensor detects that the train has left the station and notifies System.
4) System sends Train Departed message to Railroad Media.
5) System continues accelerating and monitoring speed of train.
6) When train has reached cruising speed, System commands Motor to stop accelerating and start cruising at a constant speed.
7) System maintains the train's speed at the predefined cruising speed.

Alternative sequences:
Steps 5 to 7: If a hazard is detected, extend with Detect Hazard Presence use case. When hazard is removed and train is stationary, extend with Detect Hazard Removal use case.
Postcondition: Train is moving toward next station at cruising speed.

The Control Train Operation is a high level use case that includes three use cases.

Use case: Control Train Operation.
Actor: Railroad Media.
Dependency: Includes Arrive at Station use case, Control Train at Station use case, Depart from Station use case.
Precondition: Train is moving toward next station.
Main sequence:
1) Include Arrive at Station use case.
2) Include Control Train at Station use case.
3) Include Depart from Station use case.
Postcondition: Train is moving toward next station at cruising speed.

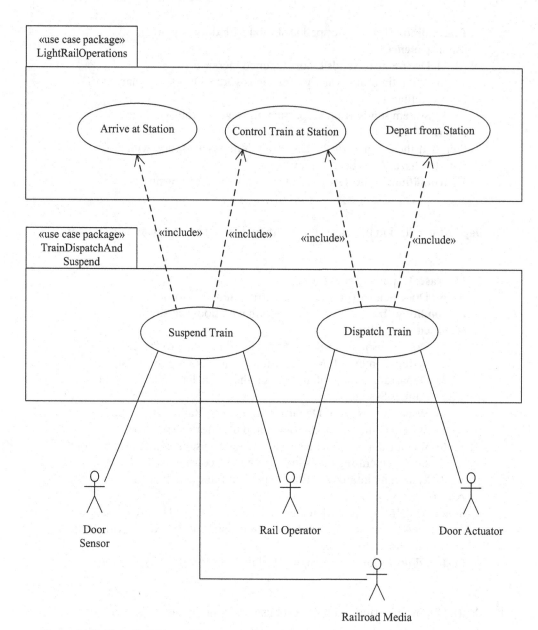

Figure 21.5. Light Rail Control System: Train Dispatch and Suspend use case package.

21.3.2 Use Case Package for Train Dispatch and Suspend

Use cases that address the train going out of service and going back into service are grouped into Train Dispatch and Suspend use case package, which also include use cases from the Light Rail Operations use case package, as depicted in Figure 21.5. A train is dispatched into service using the Dispatch Train use case and then continues normal operation as described in the Control Train Operation use case. It can then be suspended from service using the Suspend Train use case.

- Dispatch Train. The Rail Operator commands a train to start or resume service. This use case includes the Control Train at Station and Depart from Station use cases. Actors of this use case are the Rail Operator (primary actor), Door Actuator, and Railroad Media.
- Suspend Train. The Rail Operator commands a train to go out of service. This use case includes the Arrive at Station and Control Train at Station use cases. Actors of this use case are the Rail Operator (primary actor), Door Sensor, and Railroad Media.

The use case descriptions are given next. The Suspend Train use case starts with an input from the Rail Operator actor.

Use case: Suspend Train.
Actor: Rail Operator (primary), Door Sensor, Railroad Media.
Dependency: Includes Arrive at Station use case, Control Train at Station use case.
Precondition: Train is operational and moving toward next station.
Main sequence:
1) Rail Operator sends suspend train operation command to System.
2) System sends arriving train is going out of service message to Railroad Media.
3) Include Arrive at Station use case.
4) Include Control Train at Station use case.
5) Door Sensor sends doors have closed message to system.
6) System confirms that the train is out of service.
Alternative sequence:
Step 3: If the train is already at the station with doors open, then, after the time interval, the system sends a close doors message to the door actuator and resumes at step 5.
Postcondition: Selected Train has been commanded to go out of service.

The Dispatch Train use case starts with an input from the Rail Operator actor.

Use case: Dispatch Train.
Actor: Rail Operator (primary), Door Actuator, Railroad Media.
Dependency: Include Control Train at Station and Depart from Station use cases.
Precondition: Train is out of service, stopped at station with doors closed.
Main sequence:
1) Rail Operator sends a command for the train to resume service.
2) System sends open doors command to Door Actuator.
3) System sends Train in Service message to Railroad Media.
4) Include Control Train at Station use case.
5) Include Depart from Station use case.
Postcondition: Train has resumed service.

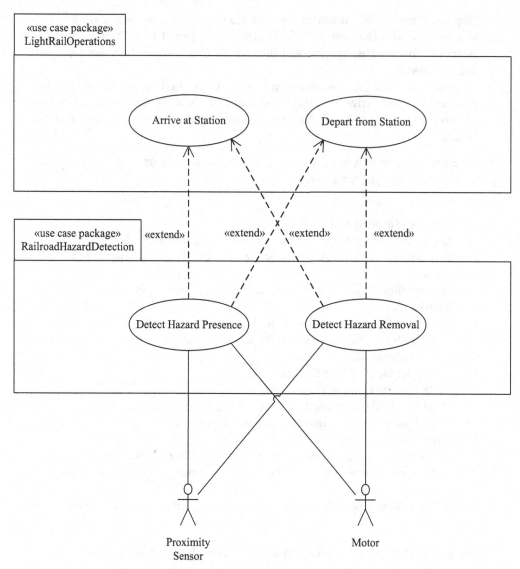

Figure 21.6. Light Rail Control System: Railroad Hazard Detection use case package.

21.3.3 Use Case Package for Railroad Hazard Detection

Use cases that address the train detecting the presence of a hazard and removal of the hazard are grouped into the Railroad Hazard Detection use case package as depicted in Figure 21.6. These use cases extend use cases from the Light Rail Operations use case package. Actors of both use cases are the Proximity Sensor (primary actor) and Motor:

- Detect Hazard Presence. When a hazard ahead is detected, the train slows down to a stop. This use case is an extension use case that extends the Arrive at Station and Depart from Station use cases when they encounter a hazard.
- Detect Hazard Removal. When the hazard is removed, the train starts moving. This use case is an extension use case that extends the Arrive at Station and Depart from Station use cases when a hazard they previously encountered is removed.

The use case descriptions are given next. The Detect Hazard Presence use case starts with an input from the Proximity Sensor actor.

Use case: Detect Hazard Presence.
Actors: Proximity Sensor (primary), Motor.
Dependency: Extends Arrive at Station use case, Depart from Station use cases.
Precondition: Train is moving toward next station.
Main sequence:
1) Proximity sensor detects a hazard ahead and sends message to System.
2) System sends decelerate to stop command to Motor.
3) Motor responds to System when train has stopped.
4) Exit use case and return to base use case.
Alternative sequence:
Step 3: If proximity changes to clear (>100 meters) before train has stopped, system commands motor to start accelerating. Exit use case and return to base use case.
Postcondition: Train has stopped because of hazard ahead.

The Detect Hazard Removal use case starts with an input from the Proximity Sensor actor.

Use case: Detect Hazard Removal.
Actors: Proximity Sensor (primary), Motor.
Dependency: Extends Arrive at Station use case, Depart from Station use cases.
Precondition: Train has stopped because of hazard.
Main sequence:
1) Proximity sensor detects hazard removal and sends message to System.
2) System commands Motor to start accelerating.
3) Exit use case and return to base use case.
Postcondition: Train has resumed operation following removal of hazard.

21.3.4 Use Case Package for Railroad Monitoring

Use cases that monitor the progress of the train and the light rail system are grouped into the Railroad Monitoring use case package, as depicted in Figure 21.7:

- Monitor Train Location. GPS Location Sensor actor informs train of its current location.
- Monitor Train Speed. Speed Sensor actor informs train of its current speed.

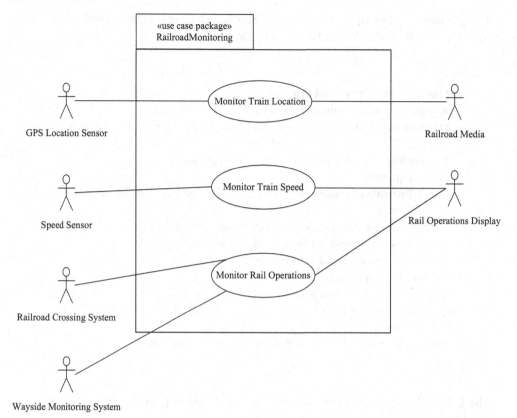

Figure 21.7. Light Rail Control System: Railroad Monitoring use case package.

■ Monitor Rail Operations. The external Railroad Crossing System and Wayside Monitoring System (modeled as actors) send status information, such as status of rail track and railroad crossing, to the system.

In addition, the actor Railroad Media is specialized to the five actors that receive railroad status messages, as depicted in Figure 21.8. These are Train Display, Train Audio Device, Station Display, Station Audio Device, and Rail Operations Display.

The use case descriptions are given next. The Monitor Train Speed use case starts with an input from the Speed Sensor actor.

Use case: Monitor Train Speed.
Actors: Speed Sensor (primary), Rail Operations Display.
Precondition: Train is moving.
Main sequence:
1) Speed Sensor notifies System of current speed of Train.
2) System converts current speed to engineering units and stores the current value.
3) System outputs current speed to Rail Operations Display.
Postcondition: Current Speed has been updated and displayed.

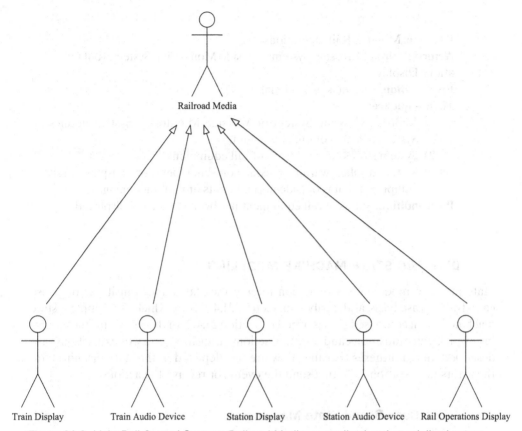

Figure 21.8. Light Rail Control System: Railroad Media generalized and specialized actors.

The Monitor Train Location use case starts with an input from the GPS Location Sensor actor.

Use case: Monitor Train Location.
Actors: GPS Location Sensor (primary), Railroad Media.
Precondition: Train is moving.
Main sequence:
  1) GPS Location Sensor sends physical location of Train.
  2) System uses train location and current speed to estimate arrival times at Train stations
  3) System sends train location to Railroad Media.
Postcondition: Location and speed information has been stored and distributed.

The Monitor Rail Operations use case starts with an input from the Railroad Crossing System or Wayside Monitoring System actor.

Use case: Monitor Rail Operations.
Actors: Railroad Crossing System, Wayside Monitoring System, Rail Operations Display.
Precondition: System is operational.
Main sequence:
1) Railroad Crossing System or Wayside Monitoring System notifies System of status of rail equipment.
2) System stores current status of rail equipment.
3) System displays warning message on Rail Operations Display of rail equipment that is outside normal limits or malfunctioning.

Postcondition: Status of rail equipment has been stored and displayed.

21.4 DYNAMIC STATE MACHINE MODELING

State machine modeling starts by considering the states and transitions on a use case–by–use case basis, as described in Section 21.4.1, from which the complete state machine is then composed, as described in Section 21.4.2. In the following, the incoming events, state transitions, and resulting actions (transition, entry, or exit actions) are described. In parentheses (because they are not depicted in the state machine) are the actors (see Section 21.3) that send the events or receive the actions.

21.4.1 Use Case-Based State Machines

The state machine for the Arrive at Station use case starts with the train in Cruising state, as depicted in Figure 21.9. The Approached event (originating from the Approaching Sensor) causes the state machine to transition to Approaching state, with a resulting Decelerate transition action (sent to Motor) and an entry action to Send Approaching message (to Railroad Media). The next event is the Arrived event (from the Arrival Sensor), which causes a state transition to Stopping state, with a resulting action of a Stop command (to Motor). This is followed by the Stopped event (from Motor), which causes a state change to Doors Opening state, an entry action to Open Doors, and a transition action to Send Arrived message (to Railroad Media).

The state machine for the Control Train at Station use case starts with the train in Doors Opening state, as depicted in Figure 21.10. The Opened event (originating from the Door Sensor) causes the state machine to transition to Doors Open state, with a resulting Start Timer transition action (to the local timer). After the timeout event, and assuming no hazards ahead (i.e., [All Clear] guard condition is True), the state machine transitions state to Doors Closing state from Doors Open state, with a resulting exit action to send a command to Close Doors (to Door Actuator) and a transition action to Send Departing message (to Railroad Media).

The state machine for the Depart from Station use case starts with the train in Doors Closing state as depicted in Figure 21.11. The Closed event (originating from the Door Sensor) causes the state machine to transition to Accelerating state, with a resulting entry action to send an Accelerate command (to Motor). The Departed event (originating from the Departure Sensor) causes a transition to the Accelerating state and

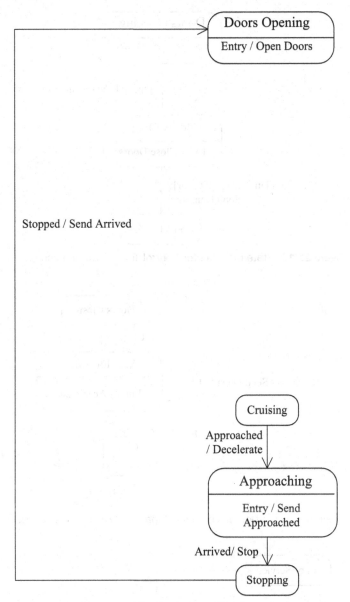

Figure 21.9. State machine for Arrive at Station use case.

the transition action to Send Departed message (to Railroad Media). When the system detects that the train has reached the cruising speed, the state machine transitions to Cruising state and sends a Cruise command (to Motor).

The state machine for the Suspend Train use case starts with the train in Doors Open state, when the timeout expires. If the train has been commanded to go out of service (i.e., [Suspending] guard condition is True), the state machine will transition to Out of Service state, which results in an exit action to Close Doors (sent to Door Actuator) and a transition action to Send Out of Service message (to Railroad Media) as depicted in Figure 21.12.

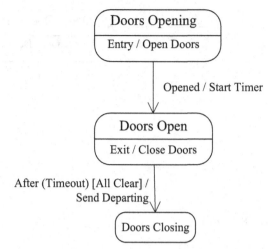

Figure 21.10. State machine for Control Train at Station use case.

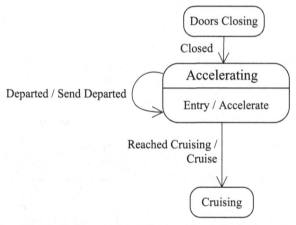

Figure 21.11. State machine for Depart from Station use case.

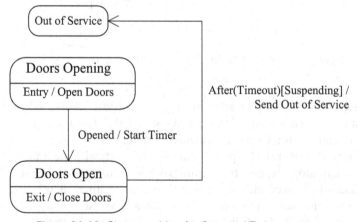

Figure 21.12. State machine for Suspend Train use case.

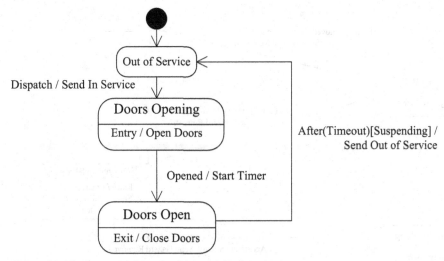

Figure 21.13. State machine for Dispatch Train use case.

The state machine for the Dispatch Train use case starts with the train in Out of Service state when a Dispatch message arrives (from the Rail Operator). The state machine transitions to Doors Opening state, which results in an entry action to send an Open Doors command to the Door Actuator and a transition action to Send In Service message (to Railroad Media), as depicted in Figure 21.13.

The state machine for the Detect Hazard Presence use case starts with the train in any of the Accelerating, Cruising, or Approaching states. When the proximity sensor sends a Hazard Detected message, the state machine transitions to Emergency Stopping state, leading to entry actions to send an Emergency Stop message (to Motor) and to Send Hazard Detected message (to Railroad Media), as depicted in Figure 21.14. If the

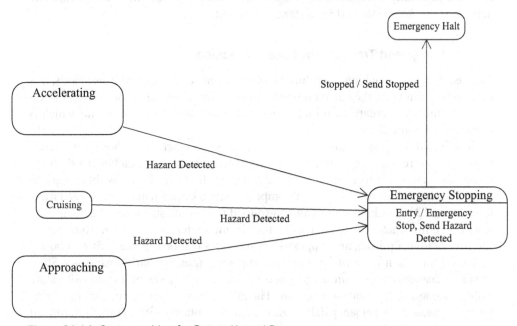

Figure 21.14. State machine for Detect Hazard Presence use case.

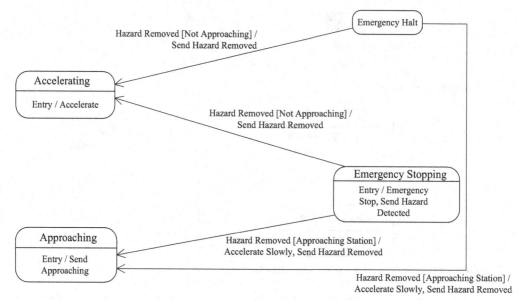

Figure 21.15. State machine for Detect Hazard Removal use case.

Motor sends a Stopped event, the state machine transitions to Emergency Halt state, which results in a transition action to Send Stopped message (to Railroad Media).

The state machine for the Detect Hazard Removal use case starts with the train in either Emergency Stopping or Emergency Halt states. If the proximity sensor sends a Hazard Removed message (as depicted in Figure 21.15), this causes the state machine to transition to: (a) Approaching state if the train is approaching a station, in which case the transition actions are to Accelerate Slowly and Send Hazard Removed message or (b) Accelerating state if the train is not approaching a station, in which case the actions are to Accelerate and Send Hazard Removed message.

21.4.2 Integrated Train Control State Machine

Because the state machine modeling involves seven state dependent use cases, it is necessary to integrate the partial state machines of these use cases and consider alternative branches to create an initial integrated Train Control state machine, which is depicted in Figure 21.16.

The initial integrated state machine is a flat state machine without any hierarchy; hence, there is an opportunity to design a hierarchical state machine by defining composite states to represent the major states of the train. It is possible to group certain states in Figure 21.16 into a composite state. In particular, the Accelerating, Cruising, and Approaching states can be grouped to become substates of a composite state called In Motion. The reason is that the Hazard Detected transition from each of the Accelerating, Cruising, and Approaching substates can be replaced with a Hazard Detected transition from the In Motion composite state. Similarly, Emergency Stopping and Emergency Halt can be grouped to become substates of a composite state called Emergency. The reason is that the Hazard Removed transition from the Emergency Stopping and Emergency Halt substates can be replaced with a Hazard Removed transition from the Emergency composite state.

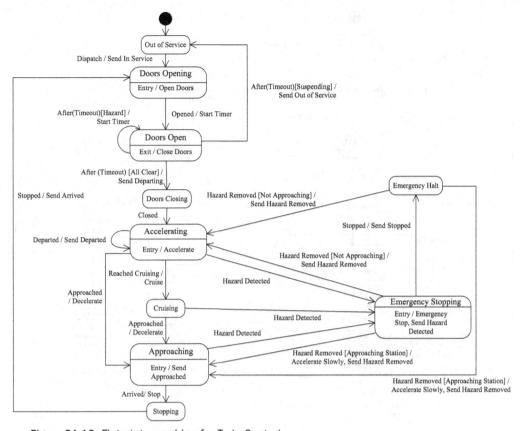

Figure 21.16. Flat state machine for Train Control.

The composite states and substates of the Train Control hierarchical state machine are described next and depicted in Figure 21.17. The initial state is Out of Service:

- Out of Service. The train is stationary at a station with doors closed.
- Doors Opening. This state is entered when the train has stopped at a station and the doors are opening. It is also entered when a train is dispatched into service. On the state machine, the Open Doors action is shown as an entry action because the transition to Doors Opening state can arrive from either the Out of Service state or the Stopping state. It is more concise to depict one entry action on the state machine instead of transition actions on each of the two incoming state transitions.
- Doors Open. This state is entered when the train doors have completed opening. There is an action to start a timer on transition into the state. When the timeout expires, there are three possible transitions. If the Hazard condition is True, this state is re-entered. If the Suspending condition is True, the state machine transitions to Out of Service state. If the All Clear condition is True, the state machine transitions to Doors Closing state. On exit from this state to either Doors Closing or Out of Service state, there is an exit action to Close Doors. It should be noted that the All Clear condition is defined in terms of the Hazard and Suspending conditions using the following Boolean expression:
  - All Clear = NOT Hazard AND NOT Suspending

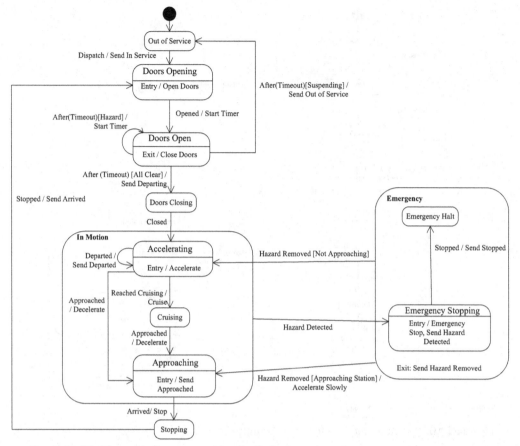

Figure 21.17. Hierarchical state machine for Train Control.

- **Doors Closing.** This state is entered when the train doors start closing to satisfy a request to move to the next station.
- **In Motion.** This is a composite state, which is entered when the train is moving and consists of the following substates:
  - **Accelerating.** A train is increasing speed until it reaches the cruising state.
  - **Cruising.** A train is moving at a constant speed.
  - **Approaching.** A train is approaching a station.
- **Stopping.** This state is entered when the train is arriving at a station.
- **Emergency.** This is a composite state, which is entered when a hazard is detected and consists of the following substates:
  - **Emergency Stopping.** If a hazard is detected ahead, the train slows down, eventually to an emergency stop if the hazard is not removed. This substate can be entered from any of the In Motion substates: Accelerating, Cruising, or Approaching. If the hazard is removed, the train transitions to Approaching substate (if it is near a station) or Accelerating substate (if it is not).
  - **Emergency Halt.** The train has stopped because of the emergency with doors closed. This substate is entered from Emergency Stopping substate.

21.5 SUBSYSTEM STRUCTURING

As the **Light Rail Control System** is a large system with many objects, it is necessary to considering how the system is structured into subsystems. Because this is a distributed application, the geographical location and aggregation/composition considerations take precedence. From a geographical perspective, train and stations are distinct distributed entities. The conceptual static model in Figure 21.1 shows that there are multiple trains and multiple stations, each of which is composed of several parts. Thus, trains and stations can be modeled structurally as geographically distributed subsystems.

Because the primary purpose of the train subsystem is to control the physical train, the subsystem is named the Train Control Subsystem, of which there is one instance for each train. There is also a Station Subsystem, of which there is one instance for each station in the system. This subsystem is an output subsystem, as its main function is to output train status information to station visual displays and audio devices.

Because the system needs an operator to view train and station status, as well as to command trains to go into and out of service and to notify stations of delays, a user interaction subsystem is designed called Rail Operations Interaction. Finally, Rail Operations Service is a service subsystem of which there is only one instance. It is independent of the number of trains and stations and is responsible for maintaining the status of the system, as well as dynamically outputting real-time train and station statuses on large screens in the rail operations center.

Thus, the **Light Rail Control System** consists of four subsystems, as depicted in Figure 21.18. They are the Train Control Subsystem, the Station Subsystem, the Rail Operations Services subsystem, and the Rail Operations Interaction subsystem. Starting from the software context diagram depicted in Figure 21.3, Figure 21.18 depicts these four subsystems as well as the external entities to which they interface.

21.6 OBJECT AND CLASS STRUCTURING

Because this is a real-time embedded system, there are many external devices and consequently many software boundary classes. The COMET/RTE object and class structuring criteria are applied to determine the objects and classes in each subsystem. The behavior of these objects is described in detail in Section 21.7.

All train-related classes, such as the train's proximity sensor and motor, are part of the Train Control Subsystem. Boundary classes are determined by considering the software classes that interface to and communicate with the external entities. Input classes are needed to receive inputs from the seven external input devices shown in Figures 21.18. As depicted in Figure 21.19, the corresponding seven input classes, which are all in the Train Control Subsystem, are Approaching Sensor Input, Arrival Sensor Input, Departure Sensor Input, Proximity Sensor Input, Door Sensor Input, Location Sensor Input, and Speed Sensor Input.

Next, the output classes that output to the external output devices are determined. Figure 21.3 shows that there are seven external output devices. Four of the corresponding output classes are in the Train Control Subsystem, as depicted in

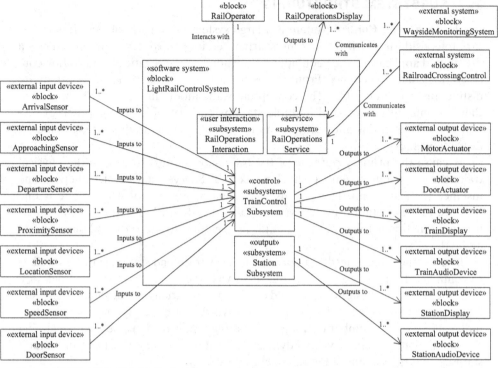

Figure 21.18. Light Rail Control software subsystems.

Figure 21.19. These are Door Actuator Output, Motor Output, Train Display Output, and Train Audio Output.

Now consider the control objects needed by the Train Control Subsystem. A Train Control object is needed for each train. This must be a state dependent control object that executes the state machine described in Section 21.4. Since controlling the speed of the train is an important factor in this system, there needs to be a separate Speed Adjustment algorithm object, which sends speed commands to the Motor Output object, which in turn interfaces to the external motor. There also must be a Train Timer for periodic events, such as the time that train doors need to be kept open at a station.

An entity object is needed to hold Train Data, including the current speed and location of the train. Because train status needs to be sent to various train and station objects on a regular basis, a coordinator object, the Train Status Dispatcher, is designed for this purpose.

Next consider the classes needed by the Station Subsystem. Two output classes are in the Station Subsystem, namely Station Display Output and Station Audio Output, as depicted in Figure 21.20. For each station, there is also a need for a coordinator object, the Station Coordinator, and an entity object, Station Status.

The Rail Operations Interaction subsystem consists of one user interaction object, Operator Interaction, which interacts with an external user, the Rail Operator.

The Rail Operations Service subsystem consists of a coordinator object, Rail Ops Coordinator, a passive entity object, Rail Operations Status, and an output object, Rail Operations Display Output, which outputs to the external Rail Operations

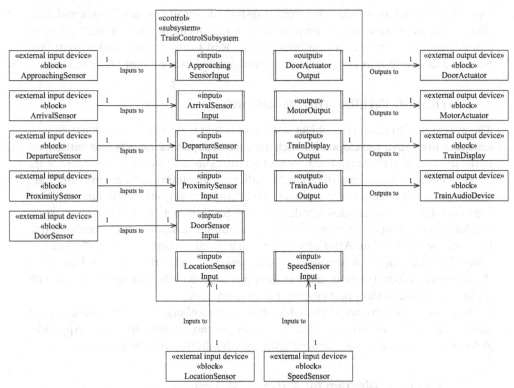

Figure 21.19. Input and output classes for Train Control Subsystem.

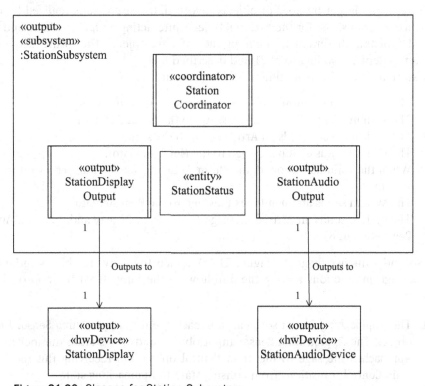

Figure 21.20. Classes for Station Subsystem.

Display. Although there are two external systems, Railroad Crossing System and Wayside Monitoring System, that communicate with Rail Operations Service, they are actually designed as subsystems of a larger Light Rail Component-based System (see Section 21.11), and thus proxy objects are not needed to communicate with them.

21.7 DYNAMIC INTERACTION MODELING

The next step is to design the object interactions that correspond to each use case. A sequence diagram is developed for each use case to depict the objects that participate in the use case and the sequence of object interactions. The message descriptions are also given for each sequence diagram. In addition, if the interaction involves the Train Control state dependent control object, the events and actions on the internal Train Control state machine are described. Note that Section 21.4 described how the state machine receives inputs from actors and sends outputs to actors, which correspond to the use case description. After object structuring, this section describes the interactions of the state dependent control object (which executes the state machine) with the software objects (such as input and output objects), which in turn interact with input and output devices that correspond to the actors.

Sequence numbers are depicted with whole numbers. For some use cases, an optional letter (a use case identifier) precedes the sequence number. See Appendix A for more information on message sequence numbering conventions.

21.7.1 Sequence Diagram for Arrive at Station

Because of the larger number of objects involved, this use case is realized by two sequence diagrams, one for the external objects interacting with the system, and the second depicting the interaction among the software objects. The former sequence diagram is depicted in Figure 21.21 and described first:

External objects participating in this use case are

1: The Approaching Sensor sends an Approach event to the system.
2: The system sends a Decelerate message to the Motor Actuator.
3: The Arrival Sensor sends an Arrive event to the system.
4: The system sends a Stop message to the Motor Actuator.
5: When the train has stopped, the Motor Actuator sends a Stopped event to the system.
6: The system sends an Open Doors message to the Door Actuator.
7: The system sends an Arrived message to the Train Display and the Train Audio Device (event 8).

The second sequence diagram (Figure 21.22) depicts the software objects and internal message interactions among them, following the input from the approaching sensor:

1: The Approaching Sensor sends an Approach event to Approaching Sensor Input object. The Approaching Sensor Input object sends the station number in the Approached message to the Train Control object. On receiving this message, Train Control transitions from Cruising state to Approaching state.
2: As a result of the transition to Approaching state, the Train Control object sends a Decelerate command to Speed Adjustment object.

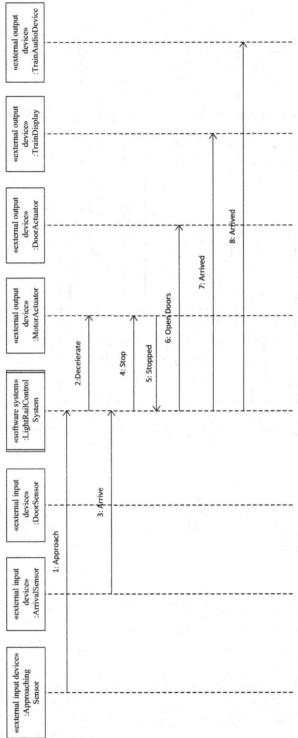

Figure 21.21. Sequence diagram for Arrive at Station use case (external objects).

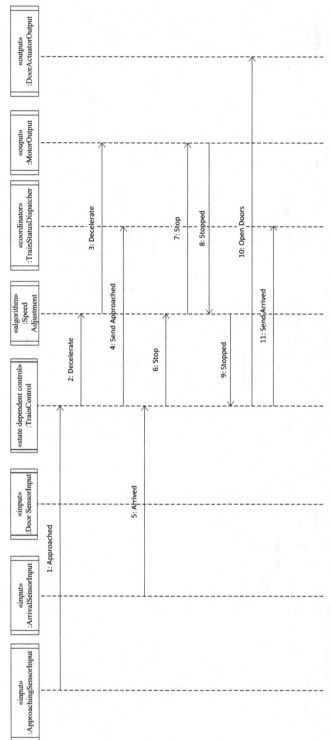

Figure 21.22. Sequence diagram for Arrive at Station use case (software objects).

3: By reading current speed and cruising speed, Speed Adjustment object computes the deceleration rate and sends a Decelerate message with the deceleration rate as a parameter to Motor Output. The Motor Output object converts the deceleration rate to electrical units and sends the voltage to be applied to the real-world motor.

4: (parallel sequence with event 2 because both are actions associated with the state transition): Train Control sends a Send Approached message to Train Status Dispatcher.

5: Arrival Sensor Input object receives an arrival event from the external Arrival Sensor indicating that the train has arrived at the station. The Arrival Sensor Input object sends the Arrived message to the Train Control object. On receiving this message, Train Control transitions from Approaching state to Stopping state.

6: Train Control sends Stop message to Speed Adjustment object.

7: Speed Adjustment object sends Stop message to Motor Output, which in turn sends Stop message to the real-world motor.

8: When the train has stopped, the motor sends a stopped response to the Motor Output object. Motor Output object sends a Stopped message to the Speed Adjustment object.

9: Speed Adjustment object sends a Stopped message to Train Control object, which then transitions to Doors Opening state.

10: (parallel sequence because there are two actions associated with the state transition) On transitioning to Doors Opening state, the Train Control object sends the Door Actuator Output object a command to Open Doors. On the state machine, the Open Doors event is shown as an entry action, because the transition to Doors Opening state can arrive from either the Out of Service state or the Stopping state. It is more concise to depict one entry action on the state machine instead of two actions, one on each of the incoming state transitions.

11: (parallel sequence because there are two actions associated with the state transition) The Train Control object sends a Send Arrived message to the Train Status Dispatcher.

21.7.2 Sequence Diagram for Train Status Dispatcher

The Train Status Dispatcher sends multicast status messages to all the Railroad Media actors depicted in Figure 21.23. The corresponding objects that received status messages are: Train Display Output, Train Audio Output, Station Subsystem (for Station

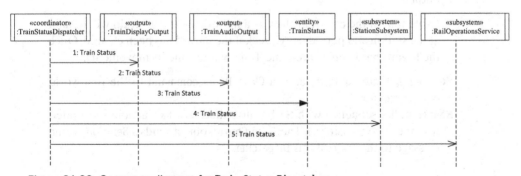

Figure 21.23. Sequence diagram for Train Status Dispatcher.

Display Output and Station Audio Output), Rail Operations Service (for Rail Operations Display), and also the Train Status entity object, as shown in Figure 21.23.

1: Train Status Dispatcher sends a train status message to the Train Display Output, which updates the train display.
2: Train Status Dispatcher sends a train status message to the Train Audio Output, which sends the message to the train audio device.
3: Train Status Dispatcher updates the Train Status entity object with the arrival status.
4: Train Status Dispatcher sends the multicast message Arrived Station n message to all instances of the Station Subsystem object. The Station Manager object in the Station subsystem receives the multicast station arrived message and updates the station display and the audio device via the objects Station Display Output and Station Audio Output, as well as updating the Station Status entity object.
5: Train Status Dispatcher sends a train status message to the Rail Operations Service subsystem.

21.7.3 Sequence Diagram for Control Train at Station

This sequence diagram (Figure 21.24) depicts the software objects and internal message interactions among them following the door sensor detecting train doors have opened:

S1: The Door Sensor sends the Opened message to the Door Sensor Input object.
S2: The Door Sensor Input object sends an Opened message to the Train Control object, which then transitions to Doors Open state.
S3: The Train Control object sends a Start Timer message to the Train Timer to start a timer.
S4: A timer event is generated after a period of time equal to timeout. Timer object sends Timer Elapsed event to Train Control.
S5: If the track condition is All Clear, then Train Control object transitions to Doors Closing state and sends a Close Doors command to Door Actuator Output.

(Note that in the case that there is a hazard ahead, the Train will remain at the station and periodically check if the hazard has been cleared. Once the hazard has been cleared, the Train will resume its movement).

S6: Door Actuator Output sends a Close Doors command to the real-world doors actuator.
S5a: (parallel sequence with S5 because there are two actions associated with the state transition): The Train Control object sends a Send Departing message to the Train Status Dispatcher.

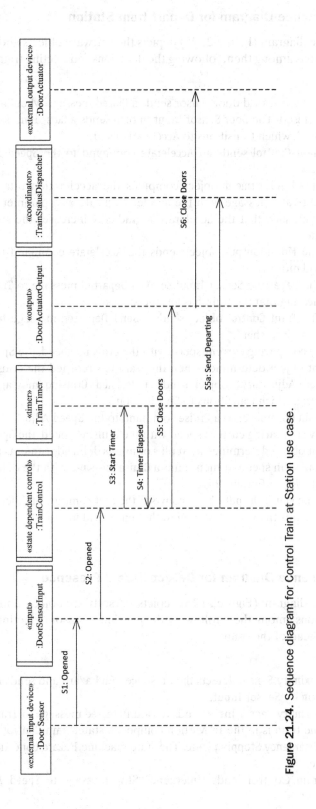

Figure 21.24. Sequence diagram for Control Train at Station use case.

21.7.4 Sequence Diagram for Depart from Station

This sequence diagram (Figure 21.25) depicts the software objects and internal message interactions among them following the door sensor detecting train doors closed:

> **D1**: The real-world door sensor sends a Closed message when all the doors are closed. The Door Sensor Input in turn sends a Closed message to Train Control, which transitions to Accelerating state.
>
> **D2**: Train Control sends an Accelerate command to the Speed Adjustment object.
>
> **D3**: Speed Adjustment object computes the acceleration rate and sends Accelerate message with the acceleration rate as a parameter to Motor Output, such that the acceleration gradually increases the speed of the train.
>
> **D4**: The Motor Output object sends the Accelerate command to the real-world motor.
>
> **D5**: The Departure Sensor Input sends a Departed message to Train Control, indicating that the train has left the station.
>
> **D6**: The Train Control object sends a Send Departed message to the Train Status Dispatcher.
>
> **D7**: By comparing current speed with the cruising speed, the Speed Adjustment object determines when the train has reached the cruising speed. Speed Adjustment object sends a Reached Cruising message to Train Control, which transitions to Cruising state.
>
> **D8**: Train Control sends a Cruise command to the Speed Adjustment object.
>
> **D9**: By comparing current speed with the cruising speed, the Speed Adjustment object determines what plus or minus delta adjustments are needed to the train speed. It then sends a Cruise message with the delta amounts to the Motor Output object.
>
> **D10**: The Motor Output object converts the delta amounts to electrical units and sends the voltage setting to the real-world motor.

21.7.5 Sequence Diagram for Detect Hazard Presence

This sequence diagram (Figure 21.26) depicts the software objects and internal message interactions among them following the proximity sensor detecting the presence of a hazard ahead of the train:

> **P1**: Proximity Sensor detects the presence of a hazard and sends message to Proximity Sensor Input.
>
> **P2**: Proximity Sensor Input sends Hazard Detected message to Train Control. If the train is in the In Motion composite state, Train Control transitions to Emergency Stopping state. The state machine Hazard condition is set to True.
>
> **P3**: Train Control sends Emergency Stop message to Speed Adjustment object.

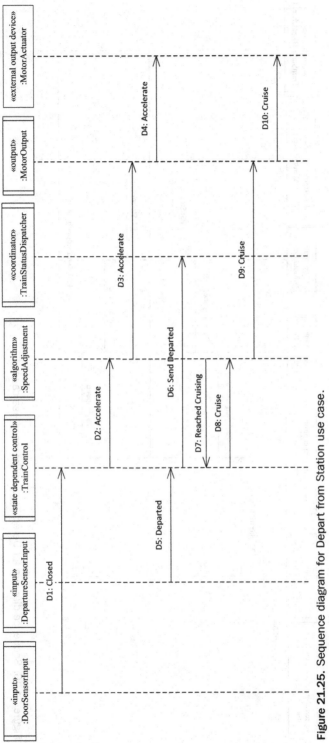

Figure 21.25. Sequence diagram for Depart from Station use case.

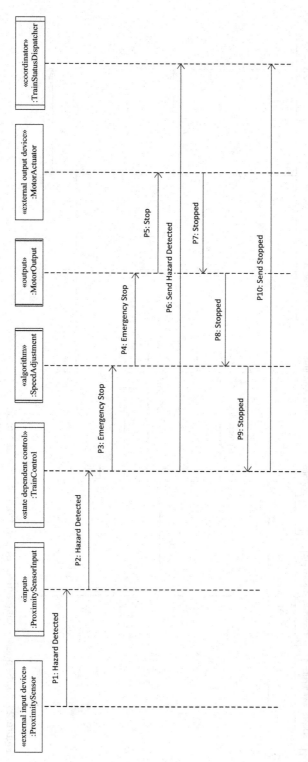

Figure 21.26. Sequence diagram for Detect Hazard Presence use case.

P4: Speed Adjustment object computes fast deceleration value for motor and sends Emergency Stop message with the deceleration rate as a parameter to Motor Output.

P5: Motor Output converts deceleration amount to electrical units and sends Stop message to Motor.

P6 (parallel sequence with P3 because there are two actions associated with the state transition): The Train Control object sends a Hazard Detected message to the Train Status Dispatcher.

P7: Motor responds that train has stopped.

P8, P9: Motor Output sends Stopped message to Speed Adjustment, which forwards the Stopped message to Train Control. Train Control transitions to Emergency Halt state.

P10: The Train Control action is to send the Send Stopped message to the Train Status Dispatcher.

21.7.6 Sequence Diagram for Detect Hazard Removal

This sequence diagram (Figure 21.27) depicts the software objects and internal message interactions among them following the proximity sensor detecting the removal of the hazard:

R1: Proximity Sensor detects the removal of the hazard and sends message to Proximity Sensor Input.

R2: Proximity Sensor Input sends Hazard Removed message to Train Control. Train Control transitions from its current state (Emergency Stopping or Emergency Halt) to Accelerating or Approaching state. Train Control state machine's Hazard condition is set to False.

R3: Assuming Train Control transitions to Accelerating state, the resulting action is for Train Control to send the Accelerate message to Speed Adjustment object.

R4: Speed Adjustment object computes the acceleration rate and sends Accelerate message with the acceleration rate as a parameter to Motor Output, such that acceleration gradually increases the speed of the train.

R5: The Motor Output object sends the accelerate command to the real-world motor.

R6: (parallel sequence with R3 because there are two actions associated with the state transition): The Train Control action is to Send Hazard Removed message to the Train Status Dispatcher.

21.7.7 Sequence Diagram for Dispatch Train

This sequence diagram (Figure 21.28) depicts the software objects and internal message interactions among them following the operator sending a dispatch message to the train:

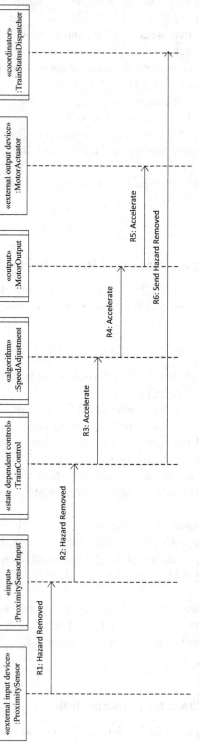

Figure 21.27. Sequence diagram for Detect Hazard Removal use case.

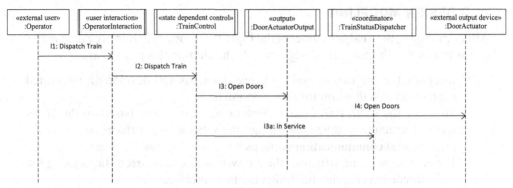

Figure 21.28. Sequence diagram for Dispatch Train use case.

I1: Operator sends Dispatch Train message to Operator Interaction object.

I2: Operator Interaction object sends Dispatch Train message to selected Train Control object. Train Control transitions from Out of Service state to Doors Opening state. Train Control state machine's Suspending condition is set to False.

I3: On transitioning to Doors Opening state, the Train Control object sends the Door Actuator Output object a command to Open Doors.

I3a (parallel sequence with I3): The Train Control object sends an In Service message to the Train Status Dispatcher.

I4: The Door Actuator Output object sends the Open Doors command to the real-world Door Actuator.

21.7.8 Other Event Sequences

The following event sequences are very simple; consequently sequence diagrams are not provided.

Event sequence for Suspend Train:

1: Operator sends Suspend Train message to Operator Interaction object.

2: Operator Interaction object sends Suspend Train message to designated Train Control object. Train Control state machine's Suspending condition is set to True.

3: Timeout arrives at Train Control when the state machine is in Doors Open state AND the Suspending condition is True. As a result, the state machine transitions to Out of Service state.

Event sequence for Monitor Train Speed:

1: Speed Sensor object sends current train speed to Speed Sensor Input object.

2: Speed Sensor Input object converts speed to engineering units and updates Train Data object.

21.8 DESIGN MODELING

After developing the analysis model of the Light Rail Control System, the next major step is to develop the software design model. The steps in this process are:

1. Integrate the use case–based sequence diagrams and develop an integrated communication diagram for each subsystem.
2. Structure the Light Rail Control System into subsystems based on the architectural structure patterns and design the subsystem interfaces based on the architectural communication patterns.
3. For each subsystem, structure the subsystem into concurrent tasks using the task structuring criteria and design the task interfaces.
4. Analyze the performance of the concurrent real-time software design. This step is described in detail in Chapter 18 for the Light Rail Control System.
5. Design a distributed component-based software architecture that allows components to be deployed to a distributed system configuration.

21.9 SUBSYSTEM INTEGRATED COMMUNICATION DIAGRAMS

The first step in software design modeling involves developing integrated communication diagrams for each subsystem; subsystems were first determined in Section 21.6. This necessitates the integration of the objects and interactions from the use case-based sequence diagrams and assigning them to subsystems. The integrated communication diagram for the Train Control Subsystem is depicted on Figure 21.29. Because of the large number of objects in this subsystem, the figure focuses on the software objects and the interaction among these objects and with other subsystems.

Figure 21.29 depicts the state dependent control object Train Control, which receives messages from several input objects including Approaching Sensor Input, Arrival Sensor Input, Proximity Sensor Input, Departure Sensor Input, and Door Sensor Input. The events contained in these messages cause state transitions in the state machine encapsulated by Train Control (Figure 21.17). The resulting state machine actions are sent as speed command messages to Speed Adjustment, door command messages to Door Actuator Output, and train status messages to Train Status Dispatcher. Train location and speed data is stored in the Train Data entity object, which is updated periodically by the Location Sensor Input and Speed Sensor Input objects. Train Status Dispatcher reads and combines this data with the train status messages that it sends to the Train Display Output and Train Audio Output objects as well as the Station Subsystem and Rail Operations Service.

The integrated communication diagram for the Station Subsystem is depicted in Figure 21.30. The Station Subsystem consists of a coordinator object, the Station Coordinator, which receives train status from Train Status Dispatcher in the Train Control Subsystem and forwards this status to Station Display Output and Station Audio Output, in addition to updating the Station Status entity object. Station Coordinator also receives station commands from Operator Interaction in the Rail Operations Interaction subsystem, which are commands to output station status information (such as train delays) to the Station Display Output and Station Audio Output objects, in addition to updating the Station Status entity object.

The integrated communication diagram for the Rail Operations Interaction and Rail Operations Service subsystems is depicted in Figure 21.31. The Rail Operations

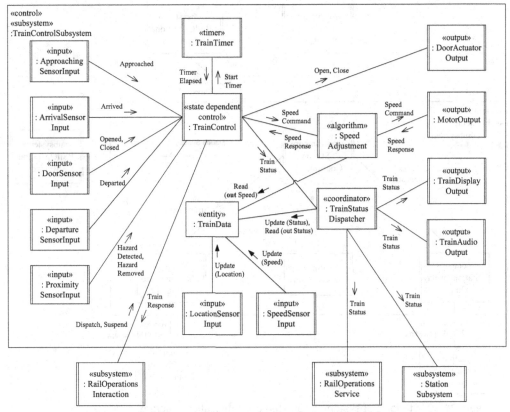

Figure 21.29. Train Control Subsystem: integrated communication diagram.

Interaction subsystem consists of the user interaction object called Operations Inter-action, which sends train commands to dispatch and suspend trains to the Train Con-trol Subsystem and station commands to the Station Subsystem. The Rail Operations Service consists of three objects. The coordinator object Rail Ops Coordinator receives rail status messages from Train Control Subsystem and Station Subsystem, as well as the external systems Railroad Crossing System and Wayside Monitoring System. It updates the Rail Operations Status entity object with this rail status and sends rail status to the output object Rail Operations Display Output, which dynamically outputs real-time train and station status on large screens in the rail operations center.

21.10 DESIGN OF DISTRIBUTED LIGHT RAIL SYSTEM

The overall software design of the distributed Light Rail System consists of the four subsystems of the Light Rail Control System (Train Control Subsystem, Station Subsys-tem, Rail Operations Interaction, and Rail Operations Service) in addition to the Railroad Crossing System (described as a separate case study in Chapter 20) and the Wayside Monitoring System, which monitors rail sensors inserted in the rail track. The Railroad Crossing System and the Wayside Monitoring System are both embedded systems that send status messages to the Rail Operations Service. This section describes the over-all distributed software architecture before describing the task architecture for each subsystem in the Light Rail Control System. The starting point for this design are

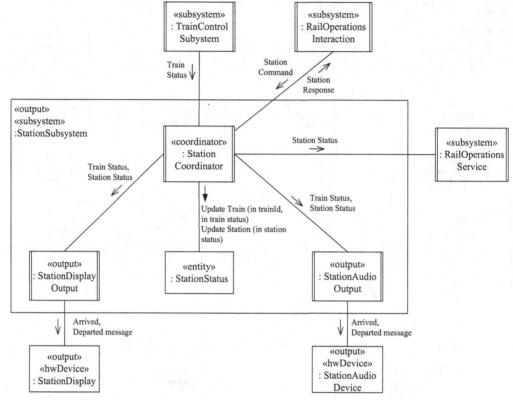

Figure 21.30. Station Subsystem: integrated communication diagram.

the integrated communication diagrams for the four subsystems depicted in Figures 21.29 through 21.31.

21.10.1 Design of Distributed Software Architecture

Applying the subsystem structuring criteria described in Chapter 10, the Train Control Subsystem is a control subsystem because each instance automatically controls a driverless train; the Station Subsystem is an output subsystem because it receives status information from other subsystems that it outputs to audio devices and visual displays; Rail Operations Interaction is a user interaction subsystem because it allows a rail operator to sends train commands to Train Control Subsystem and station commands to Station Subsystem; and the Rail Operations Service is a service subsystem that maintains the rail status it receives from other subsystems and responds to rail status requests from Rail Operations Interaction. From the perspective of the distributed Light Rail System, the Railroad Crossing System is a control subsystem because it controls a railroad crossing, and the Wayside Monitoring System is a data collection subsystem because it gathers data from several rail track sensors, tracks their status and sends summary status information and warnings of malfunction to Rail Operations Service.

In a distributed software architecture, it is necessary to enforce the rule that all communication between distributed subsystems is only by means of messages. The overall distributed software architecture is depicted in Figure 21.32 on a concurrent

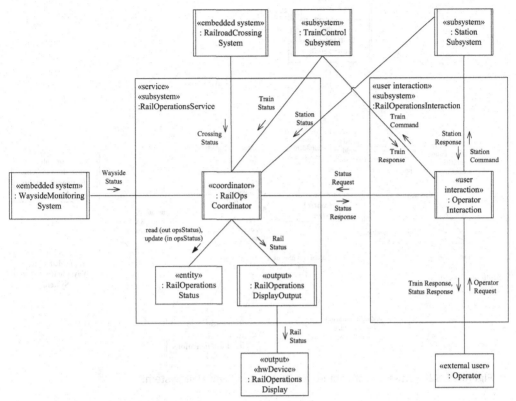

Figure 21.31. Rail Operations Interaction and Rail Operations Service Subsystems: integrated communication diagram.

communication diagram, which shows multiple instances of the Train Control Subsystem (one instance per train), multiple instances of the Station Subsystem (one instance per station), multiple instances of Rail Operations Interaction (one per operator), multiple instances of Railroad Crossing System (one for each railroad crossing), multiple instances of Wayside Monitoring System (one for each monitoring area), and one instance of the Rail Operations Service subsystem.

The architectural structure patterns used by the distributed Light Rail System are

a) **Centralized Control pattern.** Used by each instance of Train Control Subsystem and Railroad Crossing System.

b) **Distributed Independent Control pattern.** Each control subsystem is independent of the other control subsystems but sends status data as asynchronous messages to Rail Operations Service.

c) **Client/Service pattern.** The Rail Operations Interaction subsystem requests data from Rail Operations Service.

21.10.2 Design of Subsystem Message Communication

All communication between the subsystems is (with one exception) via asynchronous message communication. The Asynchronous Message Communication pattern is used for all unidirectional communication, such as for all status messages

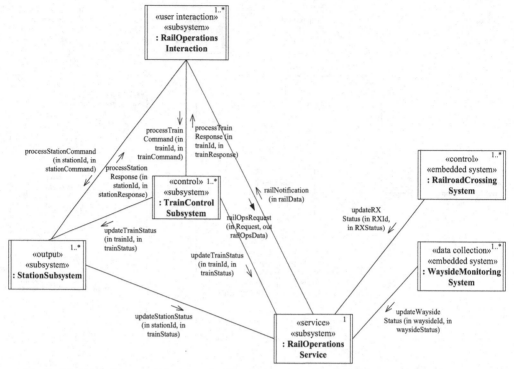

Figure 21.32. Software architecture for Distributed Light Rail System.

sent from multiple instances of the four producers (Train Control Subsystem, Station Subsystem, Railroad Crossing System, and Wayside Monitoring System) to the Rail Operations Service consumer. Asynchronous communication is also used for messages sent from multiple instances of the Train Control Subsystem to multiple instances of the Station Subsystem. The Bidirectional Asynchronous Message Communication pattern is applied between Rail Operations Interaction in its respective interactions with Train Control Subsystem and Station Subsystem.

There are two reasons for the emphasis on asynchronous message communication: firstly, the producer task is not delayed by a consumer task. Secondly, the design of the consumer task is less complex if it receives incoming asynchronous messages from multiple producers on a single FIFO message queue, which it then services in the order of messages received. The Synchronous Message Communication with Reply pattern is applied between Rail Operations Interaction and Rail Operations Service for requests that need a response. The Subscription/Notification pattern is also used between Rail Operations Interaction (which subscribes to receive rail notifications) and Rail Operations Service, which responds with a notification every time it receives a rail status update.

Because there is no shared memory in a distributed configuration, information about train and station status cannot be shared by the different subsystems through a passive entity object. Instead, train and station status needs to be sent to other subsystems through message communication. The most effective way to achieve this is by using a variation on the Subscription/Notification pattern, namely the Multicast Notification pattern, which involves sending asynchronous notification messages to

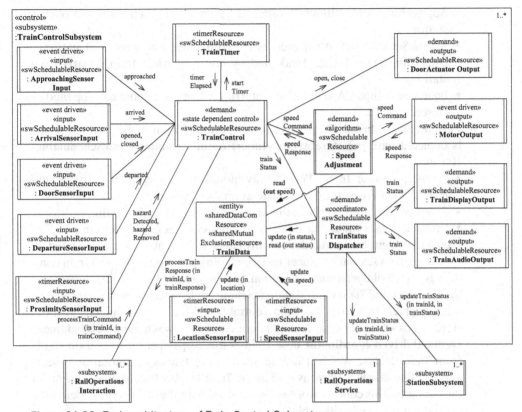

Figure 21.33. Task architecture of Train Control Subsystem.

multiple recipients during system operation without explicit subscription; essentially the recipients are determined at initialization time. This pattern is used by Train Status Dispatcher in the Train Control Subsystem to send train status to multiple recipients, as described in Section 21.7.2.

21.10.3 Concurrent Task Design of Train Control Subsystem

In the distributed design, there is one instance of the Train Control Subsystem for each train. Each task in this subsystem is depicted with the MARTE stereotype for a task: «swSchedulableResource». The task architecture for the Train Control Subsystem is shown in Figure 21.33. During target system configuration (as described in Section 21.12), each instance of the Train Subsystem is deployed to a separate train node. Thus, each train node can execute autonomously on its own node independently of the other nodes.

Each instance of this subsystem is composed of one instance of each of the following tasks:

a) **Event driven input tasks**. There are several event driven input tasks, each of which is depicted with the stereotypes «event driven» «input» «swSchedulableResource».

- Approaching Sensor Input. Awakened by interrupt when train approaches station.
- Arrival Sensor Input. Awakened by interrupt when train arrives at station.
- Departure Sensor Input. Awakened by interrupt when train departs from station.
- Door Sensor Input. Awakened by interrupt when train doors have opened or closed.

b) **Periodic input tasks**. There are several periodic input tasks, each of which is depicted with the stereotypes «timerResource» «input» «swSchedulable-Resource».

- Proximity Sensor Input. Periodically monitors distance between train and hazard ahead (e.g., train or vehicle at railroad crossing).
- Speed Sensor Input. Periodically monitors current speed of train.
- Location Sensor Input. Periodically monitors GPS location of train.

c) **Demand driven state dependent control task**. Train Control task is activated by messages from several producer tasks including five input tasks and train commands from Rail Operations Interaction. Incoming messages are input events on the encapsulated Train Control state machine. State machine actions are sent as outgoing messages from the Train Control task. This task is depicted with the stereotypes «demand» «state dependent control» «swSchedulableResource».

d) **Demand driven coordinator task**. Train Status Dispatcher receives train status from Train Control, which it multicasts to all instances of Station Subsystem and Rail Operations Service, as well as the Train Display Output and Train Audio Output tasks. This coordinator task is depicted with the stereotypes «demand» «coordinator» «swSchedulableResource».

e) **Demand driven algorithm task**. Speed Adjustment is initially activated by a speed command message on demand from Train Control and then executes periodically to adjust train speed by sending messages to Motor Output when the train is in motion. This task is depicted with the stereotypes «demand» «algorithm» «swSchedulableResource». This task is categorized as a demand driven task because it is initially activated on demand.

f) **Event driven output task**. Motor Output is activated by messages from Speed Adjustment, which then sends motor commands to the external electric motor and receives an interrupt when the motor has completed the command. This output task is depicted with the stereotypes «event driven» «output» «swSchedulableResource». This task is categorized as an event driven output task because it receives interrupts from the output device, whereas a demand driven output task interfaces to a passive output device that does not generate interrupts.

g) **Demand driven output tasks**. These output tasks are activated on demand by messages from other tasks in the Train Control Subsystem. Each task is depicted with the stereotypes «demand» «output» «swSchedulableResource».

- Door Actuator Output. Activated on demand by messages from Train Control and interfaces to external door actuator.
- Train Display Output. Activated on demand by messages from Train Status Dispatcher and interfaces to external train display.
- Train Audio Output. Activated on demand by messages from Train Status Dispatcher and interfaces to external train audio device.

Passive Objects in Station Subsystem

Each instance of the Train Control Subsystem also maintains its own local instance of the Train Data passive entity object, which stores the current GPS location (updated periodically by Location Sensor Input), current speed (updated periodically by Speed Sensor Input), and status (in motion, arriving, at station, departing) of train (updated by Train Status Dispatcher). Since this passive object is accessed mutually exclusively by multiple tasks, it is depicted with the stereotypes «entity» «sharedDataComResource» «sharedMutualExclusionResource».

Design of Message Communication Interfaces

The Train Control task is at the heart of the Train Control subsystem. Because of this, it is essential that all communication with it is asynchronous. It receives messages from several input tasks, such as the Arrival Sensor Input and Proximity Sensor Input tasks. Train Control sends speed control messages to Speed Adjustment (which in turn sends messages to Motor Output), door control messages to Door Actuator Output, and status messages to Train Status Dispatcher. Train Control Subsystem receives Dispatch and Suspend messages from the Rail Operations Interaction subsystem to enter and leave normal operation. The Train Status Dispatcher sends train status messages to Train Display Output and Train Audio Output, the Station Subsystem, and Rail Operations Service.

21.10.4 Concurrent Task Design of Station Subsystem

In the distributed design, there is one instance of the Station Subsystem for each station. Each instance of the Station Subsystem has one instance each of the Station Coordinator, Station Display Output, and Station Audio Output tasks, and one instance of the Station Status passive object. The task architecture for the Station Subsystem is shown in Figure 21.34.

The Station Coordinator task receives train status from the multiple instances of Train Control Subsystem and uses this to update the Station Status passive entity object and to send status messages to Station Display Output and Station Audio Output. The tasks in the Station Subsystem are:

- Station Coordinator. Demand driven coordinator task. A coordinator task is depicted with the stereotypes «demand» «coordinator» «swSchedulableResource».
- Station Display Output. Demand driven output task sends messages to station displays concerning train arrival at station and departure from station, as well as estimated time-of-arrival (ETA) of forthcoming trains at this station. The output tasks are all depicted with the stereotypes «demand» «output» «swSchedulableResource».
- Station Audio Output. Demand driven output task sends messages to station audio device concerning train arrival at station and departure from station.

Passive object in Station Subsystem:

- Station Data. Because this passive entity object is not shared, it is only labeled with the stereotype «entity».

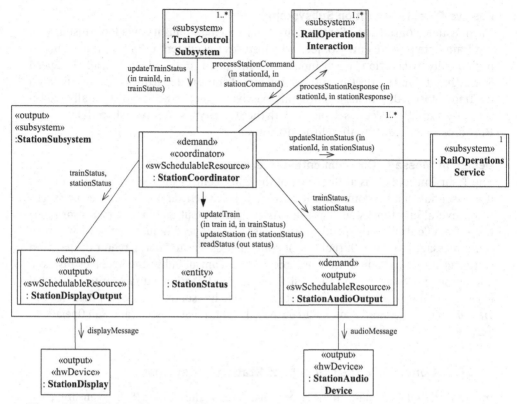

Figure 21.34. Task architecture of Station Subsystem.

21.10.5 Concurrent Task Design of Rail Operations Interaction and Service Subsystems

The task architecture for the Rail Operations Service and Rail Operations Interaction subsystems is shown in Figure 21.35, which depicts the tasks and task interfaces in these subsystems.

There is only one instance of the Rail Operations Service Subsystem, which consists of two tasks and one passive information-hiding object. The information-hiding object is the Rail Operations Status entity object, which contains the current status of each train and station. The tasks are the Rail Ops Coordinator task (a coordinator task) and the Rail Operations Display Output task (an output task). The Rail Ops Coordinator task receives status messages from each instance of Train Control Subsystem and Station Subsystem, in addition to each instance of Railroad Crossing System and Wayside Monitoring System; and updates the Rail Operations Status entity object. The Rail Operations Display Output task receives status data from Rail Ops Coordinator and then displays the status of all trains and stations on the large rail operations display.

The Rail Operations Interaction subsystem consists of one user interaction task. The Operator Interaction task views the status of trains, but more importantly it commands trains to enter and leave operational service.

Tasks in Rail Operations Service Subsystem:

- Rail Ops Coordinator. Demand driven coordinator task. Receives train and station status and updates Rail Operations Status object. This task is depicted with the stereotypes «demand» «coordinator «swSchedulableResource».

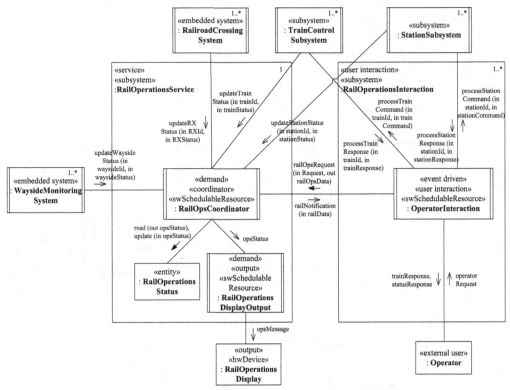

Figure 21.35. Task architecture of Rail Operations Service and Rail Operations Interaction Subsystems.

- Rail Operations Display Output. Demand driven output task. Outputs status of all trains and stations to rail operations display. The output task is depicted with the stereotypes «demand» «output» «swSchedulableResource».

Passive object in Rail Operations Service subsystem:

- Rail Operations Status. Because this passive entity object is not shared, it is only labeled with the stereotype «entity».

Tasks in Rail Operations Interaction Subsystem. There is only one task in this subsystem:

- Operator Interaction. Event driven user interaction task. Sends train commands to Train Control and Station Subsystems, and requests status from Rail Operations Service subsystem. A user interaction task is depicted with the stereotypes «event driven» «user interaction» «swSchedulableResource».

21.11 COMPONENT-BASED SOFTWARE ARCHITECTURE

Because this is a software design for a distributed real-time embedded system, the system is structured into component-based subsystems, such that each component instance can be deployed to execute on a separate node in a distributed configuration. The component-based software architecture for the distributed Light Rail System is depicted on Figure 21.36, which depicts a UML composite structure diagram

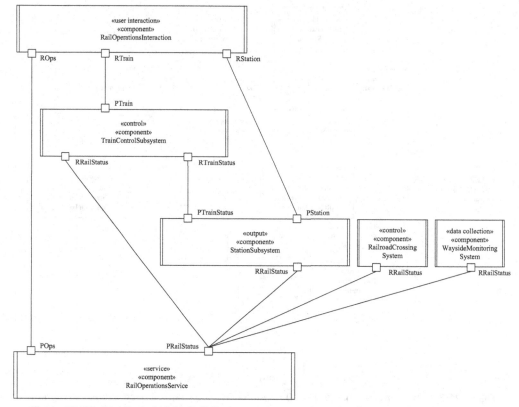

Figure 21.36. Distributed Light Rail System component-based software architecture.

showing the components, ports, and connectors. All the components are concurrent and communicate with other components through ports. The overall architecture and connectivity among components is initially determined from the Light Rail System concurrent communication diagram depicted in Figure 21.32. Figure 21.36 depicts the four subsystems of the Light Rail Control System, as well as the external Railroad Crossing System and the Wayside Monitoring System. The latter two systems send status messages to the Rail Operations Service. Each subsystem of the LRCS (Train Control Subsystem, Station Subsystem, Rail Operations Interaction, and Rail Operations Service) and each external embedded system (Railroad Crossing System and Wayside Monitoring System) is designed as a separate component.

21.11.1 Software Component Structuring

There are five client components of the Rail Operations Service (see Figure 21.36), four of which have required ports called RRailStatus that are connected to the PRailStatus provided port of Rail Operations Service to allow them to send their status at regular intervals. Rail Operations Interaction is also a client of Rail Operations Service, which has a required port called ROps that are connected to the POps provided port of Rail Operations Service. In addition, Rail Operations Interaction also has connectors to Train Control Subsystem (RTrain connected to PTrain) and Station Subsystem (RStation connected to PStation), through which it sends train and station commands

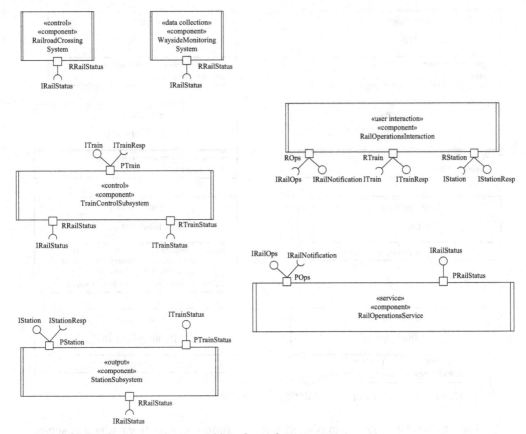

Figure 21.37. Component ports and interfaces for components.

respectively. Train Control Subsystem also has a connector to Station Subsystem (RTrainStatus connected to PTrainStatus), through which it sends train status. There are multiple instances of all components except for Rail Operations Service.

21.11.2 Design of Component Interfaces

Each component port is defined in terms of its provided and/or required interfaces. Figure 21.37 depicts the provided and required interfaces for the six components. The four client components (Train Control Subsystem, Station Subsystem, Railroad Crossing, and Wayside Monitoring) that send status messages to Rail Operations Service all have the same required interface – IRailStatus – which is provided by the Rail Operations Service component, as depicted in Figure 21.37.

The Train Control Subsystem component has two required ports from which it sends messages to the provided ports of two components depicted in Figure 21.36 (Station Subsystem and Rail Operations Service). It sends train status messages to both components using the ITrainStatus and IRailStatus required interfaces respectively depicted in Figure 21.37. Train Control also has one complex port PTrain, with both a provided and a required interface, to allow it to receive asynchronous commands from Rail Operations Interaction on the ITrain provided interface and send asynchronous responses on the ITrainResp required interface.

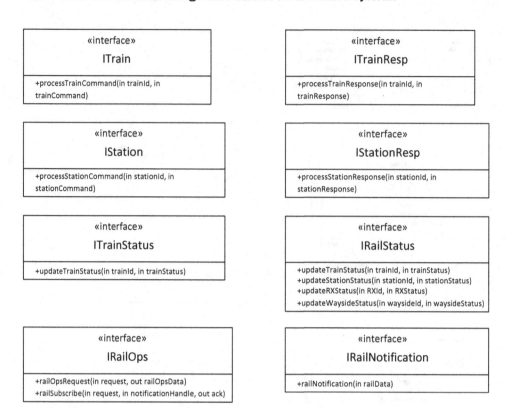

Figure 21.38. Design of component interface specifications.

The Station Subsystem component has one required port from which it sends messages to the provided port of Rail Operations Service using the IRailStatus interface. It receives status messages from Train ControlSubsystem on the PTrainStatus port through the ITrain Status provided interface. It also has a complex port PStation through which it receives asynchronous commands on the IStation provided interface and sends asynchronous responses on the IStationResp required interface, as depicted in Figure 21.37.

The Rail Operations Interaction component has three complex ports, which allow it to be a client of each of the Train Control Subsystem, Station Subsystem, and Rail Operations Service components, sending requests on its required interface and receiving responses on its provided interface. For example, it sends asynchronous train commands (such as Suspend Train x) on the ITrain required interface and receives asynchronous train responses (such as Train x Suspended) on the ITrainResp provided interface. For communication with Rail Operations Service, the complex port between them supports the IRailOps interface through which Rail Operations Service provides synchronous communication with response for status and subscription requests, as well as an IRailNotification interface provided by Rail Operations Interaction through which it receives asynchronous notifications.

Finally, the components Railroad Crossing System and Wayside Monitoring System each have one required port with a required interface IRailStatus through which they send asynchronous status messages to the Rail Operations Service component.

The component interface specifications, which describe the operations provided by each interface, are depicted in Figure 21.38. These operation names of the provided interfaces correspond to the incoming messages that arrive at the destination

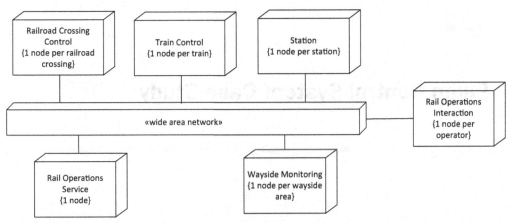

Figure 21.39. Example of component deployment for Distributed Light Rail System.

tasks depicted in Figure 21.37. For example the incoming messages from Train Control Subsystem to Rail Operations Service on Figure 21.32 are defined by the interface depicted in Figure 21.38, namely updateTrainStatus (in trainId, in trainStatus).

21.12 SYSTEM CONFIGURATION AND DEPLOYMENT

During system configuration and deployment, the components are deployed to execute on different nodes in a distributed configuration. In the Distributed Light Rail System, the physical configuration consists of multiple nodes interconnected by a wide area network. An example of system deployment is shown on the deployment diagram in Figure 21.39, in which there are six node types interconnected by a wide area network. Communication with a mobile component, such as Train Control, of which there is one instance for each train, needs to be by wireless communication.

Each instance of Train Control (one per train) is allocated to a node to achieve localized autonomy and adequate performance. Thus, the failure of one train node does not affect other nodes. For the same reason, each instance of Railroad Crossing Control (one per crossing) is assigned its own node. Station Subsystem (one per station) is allocated to a node for localized autonomy. Loss of a station node means that the station is temporarily out of service but does not affect other nodes. Wayside Monitoring is also allocated to a separate node for each wayside area to be in close proximity to the sensors that it is monitoring. Rail Operations Interaction is assigned a separate node so that it can be both dedicated and responsive to its local user. Rail Operations Service is assigned a separate node so that it can be responsive to service requests. There is only one instance of this node. However, a backup hot standby node could be provided, which would receive all status information sent to the primary Rail Operations Service node and would therefore be available to be immediately switched into service should there be a failure on the primary node.

The performance analysis in Chapter 18 confirms that the real-time design addresses performance requirements that the elapsed times for detection of a train approaching a station, stopping on arrival at a station, and stopping on detection of a hazard, do not exceed predetermined response times. The safety requirement that a train respond to a hazard ahead is provided by the Train Control state machine reacting to input from the hazard detection sensor and commanding the electric motor to stop the train.

22

Pump Control System Case Study

This chapter describes a concise case study of a real-time embedded system, namely a Pump Control System. Of particular interest are several periodic activities necessitating the design of periodic tasks, in addition to examples of task design with temporal and control clustering. There is also a need for a state machine that is designed with three separate orthogonal regions in order to separate three different but interrelated control concerns. This is one of the shorter case studies in which the details of dynamic interaction modeling (covered in detail in other case studies) are left as an exercise for the reader. The end product of dynamic interaction modeling is an integrated communication diagram, which is used to transition into design modeling.

The problem description is given in Section 22.1. Section 22.2 describes the structural modeling, and Section 22.3 describes the use case model. Section 22.4 describes the object and class structuring. Section 22.5 describes the state machine model. Section 22.6 describes the integrated interaction model, which is an outcome of dynamic interaction modeling. Section 22.7 describes the design modeling, which consists of the distributed software design and distributed software deployment. This is followed by the design of the concurrent task architecture and detailed software design.

22.1 PROBLEM DESCRIPTION

A Pump Control System for a mineral mine has several pumps situated underground, which are used to pump out water that has collected at the bottom of the mine. Each pump has an engine, which is controlled automatically by the system. The system uses Boolean high- and low-level water sensors, in addition to an analog methane sensor, to monitor the environment inside the mineral mine. Detection of the high water level causes the system to pump water out of the mine until the low water level is detected. For safety reasons, the system must switch off the pump when the level of methane in the atmosphere exceeds a preset safety limit. Once the pump has been switched off, five minutes must elapse before it can be switched on again. For each pump, status information on the methane and water level sensors, as well as the pump engine, is sent to a central server. Human operators can view the status of the various pumps.

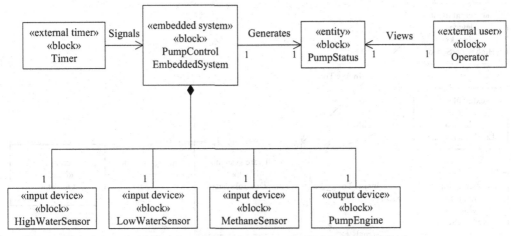

Figure 22.1. Conceptual Structural Model for Pump Control Embedded System.

For the design of the system, it is assumed that all I/O devices are passive (do not generate interrupts) and that an external timer is used to generate periodic timer events.

22.2 STRUCTURAL MODELING

Structural modeling starts with the development of a conceptual structural model, which is depicted as a block definition diagram. Each structural element is modeled as a SysML block with a stereotype identifying its role. The Pump Control Embedded System in Figure 22.1 is modeled as a composite block with the stereotype «embedded system», which contains four part blocks, the High Water Sensor «input device», the Low Water Sensor «input device», the Methane Sensor «input device», and the Pump Engine «output device». The system generates Pump Status, which is stored in an «entity» block and viewed by the Operator «external user». An external Timer signals the system at regular intervals.

From the conceptual static model, a software system context block definition diagram for the Pump Control System is developed, as shown in Figure 22.2, in which the software system and external entities are depicted as SysML blocks. There are three external input device blocks, namely the High and Low Water Sensors and the Methane Sensor, one external output device block, namely the Pump Engine, one external Timer block, and one external user block, the Operator. There are multiple instances of each external block.

22.3 USE CASE MODELING

The use case model for the Pump Control System is depicted in Figure 22.3, in which there are two use cases, Control Pump and View Pump Status. The use cases are depicted at the software engineering level, which is the reason for having six actors that correspond to the external classes on the software context class diagram: three representing the three external sensors (High Water Sensor, Low Water Sensor, and Methane Sensor), one for the Pump Engine, one Timer actor, and an external user actor, the Operator. The external Timer signals timer events to the system every second.

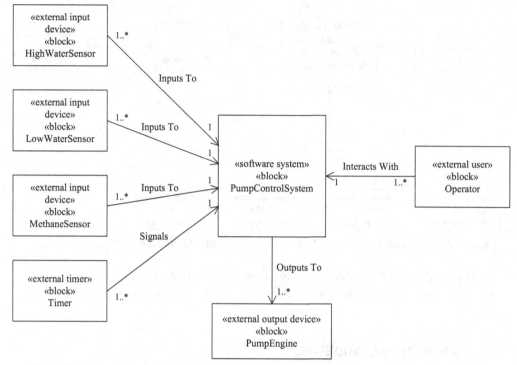

Figure 22.2. Pump Control System software system context diagram.

The use case descriptions are as follows. The Control Pump use case is started with an input from the High Water Sensor actor.

Use case: Control Pump.

Summary: Based on inputs from the water and methane sensors, the system determines when to switch the pump engine on and off.

Actors: High Water Sensor (primary actor), Low Water Sensor, Methane Sensor, Pump Engine, Timer.

Preconditions: Water level is low, methane is at a safe level, pump engine is switched off.

Main sequence:

1. High water sensor indicates that the water level is high.
2. System switches on pump engine.
3. Low water sensor indicates that the water level is low.
4. System switches off pump engine.

Alternative sequences:

Step 2: If the methane sensor detects that the methane level is unsafe when the high water level is detected, the system does not switch on the pump engine.

Step 2: If the methane sensor detects that the methane level becomes unsafe while the pump engine is operational, the system switches off the pump engine.

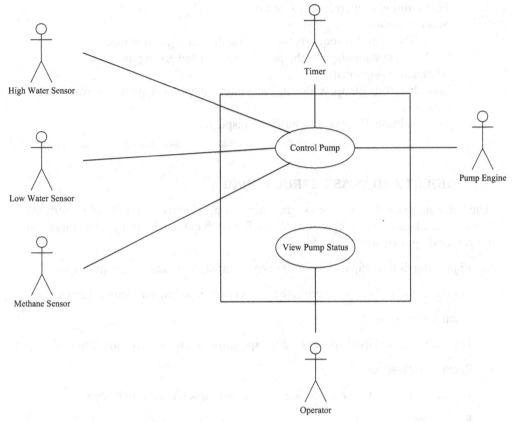

Figure 22.3. Use case model for Pump Control System.

Step 2: If the methane sensor detects that the methane level has become safe when the water level is high, the system switches on the pump engine, providing it has been off for at least five minutes.

Step 4: After switching off the pump engine, five minutes must elapse before the system can switch on the engine again.

Step 4: After the five minutes elapsed time, the system switches on the pump engine, if the water level is high and the methane level is safe.

Nonfunctional requirements:

Safety requirement: System must not switch on the Pump Engine when the methane level is unsafe.

Performance requirement: After switching off the pump engine, the system must not switch on the Pump Engine until at least five minutes have elapsed.

Postcondition. The pump engine has been switched off.

The View Pump Status use case is started with an input from the Operator actor.

Use case: View Pump Status.
Summary: Operator views pump status.
Actor: Operator.

Preconditions. Operator is logged on.

Main sequence:

1. The operator requests the pump status for a given pump.
2. The system displays the pump status for the given pump.

Alternative sequence:

Step 2: If the pump is down, the system displays a pump unavailable message.

Postcondition. Pump status has been displayed

22.4 OBJECT AND CLASS STRUCTURING

The software system context class diagram is a good starting point for identifying the software boundary objects and classes. For each external input device, there is a corresponding software input object:

■ High Water Sensor Input, Low Water Sensor Input, Methane Sensor Input.

For each external output device, there is a corresponding software output object:

■ Pump Engine Output.

For each external user, there is a corresponding software user interaction object:

■ Operator Interaction.

For each external timer, there is a corresponding software timer object:

■ Pump Timer.

In addition, because this is a real-time control system, there is a need for a state dependent control object to execute an encapsulated state machine:

■ Pump Control.

Furthermore, since the pump controller and the user interaction object need to be on separate nodes in a distributed configuration, the pump status needs to be maintained by a service object:

■ Pump Status Service.

22.5 DYNAMIC STATE MACHINE MODELING

Next, the Pump Control state machine is designed. Since it is necessary to track three orthogonal but interrelated states, namely the Pump State, Water State, and Methane State, it is more effective to design the Pump Control state machine to consist of three orthogonal state machines for Pump State (substates are Pump Idle, Pumping, and Resetting Pump), Water State (substates are Initial Water, High Water, and Low Water), and Methane State (substates are Initial Methane, Methane Safe, and Methane Unsafe), as depicted in Figure 22.4. The High Water and Low Water substates on the Water State machine are guard conditions on the Pump State machine. The Methane Safe and Methane Unsafe substates on the Methane State machine are also guard conditions on the Pump State machine.

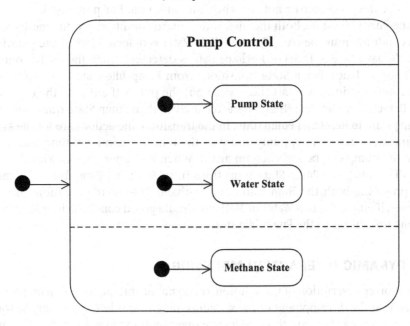

a) Pump Control State Machine

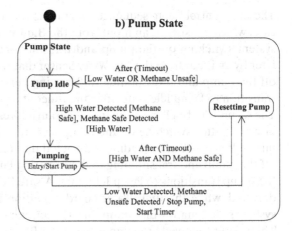

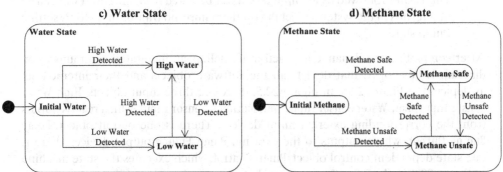

Figure 22.4. Pump Control state machine.

In the Pump State machine, the water and methane conditions need to be checked before deciding whether or not to switch the pump on. For pumping to be started from the Pump Idle state, both the high water guard condition and the methane safe guard condition must be true. If either High Water is detected (when the guard condition Methane Safe is True) or Methane Safe is detected (when the guard condition High Water is True), Pump State transitions from Pump Idle state to Pumping state, and the entry action is to start (i.e., switch on) the pump. If either of the events Low Water Detected or Methane Unsafe Detected arrives, then Pump State transitions from Pumping state to Resetting Pump state. In the transition, the actions are for the system to stop (i.e., switch off) the pump and start the timer. A minimum time must elapse before the pump can be switched on again. When the timer elapses with the event After (Timeout), the Pump State transitions from Resetting Pump back to Pumping state, providing both the High Water and Methane Safe guard conditions are True. However, if either the Low Water or Methane Unsafe guard condition is True, the state machine transitions to the Pump Idle state.

22.6 DYNAMIC INTERACTION MODELING

In this shorter description of the solution, the dynamic interaction modeling is shortened, so that the development of the sequence diagrams is left as an exercise for the reader. Assuming there are three sequence diagrams developed, two for the Control Pump use case and one for the View Pump Status use case:

a) The first Control Pump sequence diagram is for the main sequence of the use case, which consists of an input from the High Water Sensor that results in the system switching on the pump and transitioning to Pumping state, followed later by an input from the Low Water Sensor that results in the system switching off the pump and transitioning to Resetting Pump state. This is followed by a transition to Pump Idle state after the timeout.

b) The second Control Pump sequence diagram addresses the alternative sequence in which, after switching on the pump and transitioning to Pumping state, an unsafe Methane Sensor reading is detected that results in the system switching off the pump and transitioning to the Resetting Pump state. After five minutes, the pump transitions to Pump Idle state. A safe Methane Sensor reading is then detected, when the High Water guard condition is True, which results in the system switching on the pump and transitioning back to the Pumping state. This is later followed by an input Low Water Detected from the Low Water Sensor that results in the system switching off the pump and transitioning to Resetting Pump state.

After completing the dynamic interaction modeling, an integrated communication diagram is developed that depicts all the software objects and their interactions, as depicted in Figure 22.5. In Figure 22.5, there are three input objects, High Water Sensor Input, Low Water Sensor Input, and Methane Sensor Input, which receive inputs from the corresponding external input devices. There is one output object, Pump Engine Output, which outputs to the external Pump Engine output device. There is one state dependent control object, Pump Control, which executes the state machine in Figure 22.4, and a Pump Timer object that receives timer events from the external timer. All these objects are active objects.

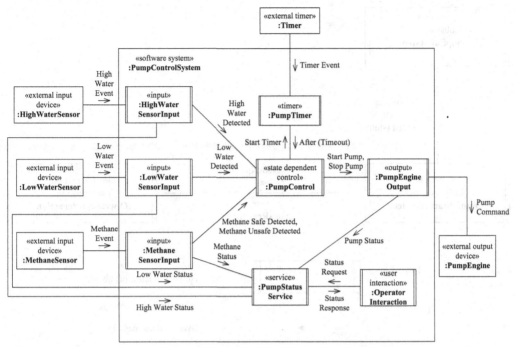

Figure 22.5. Integrated Communication diagram for Pump Control System.

Messages sent to the Pump Control object, such as High Water Detected and Low Water Detected from the High Water Sensor Input and Low Water Sensor Input objects respectively in Figure 22.5, are the events that cause state changes on the state machine in Figure 22.4. Actions in Figure 22.4, such as Start Pump and Stop Pump, correspond to output messages from the Pump Control object to the Pump Engine Output object in Figure 22.5.

The three input objects also send water and methane sensor status information to the Pump Status Service object. The Operator Interaction object requests status information from the Pump Status Service.

22.7 DESIGN MODELING

22.7.1 Distributed Software Architecture

The Pump Control System is structured into three distributed subsystems, as depicted on Figure 22.6. The three subsystems are Pump Subsystem (a control subsystem of which there is one instance for each pump), Pump Status Service (a service subsystem of which there is one instance), and Operator Interaction (a user interaction subsystem of which there is one instance for each operator).

Figure 22.6 also depicts the message communication between the three subsystems. The Pump Subsystem sends asynchronous pump control status messages to the Pump Status Service subsystem. The Operator Interaction subsystem communicates with the Pump Status Service using synchronous communication with response, requesting and receiving pump status data.

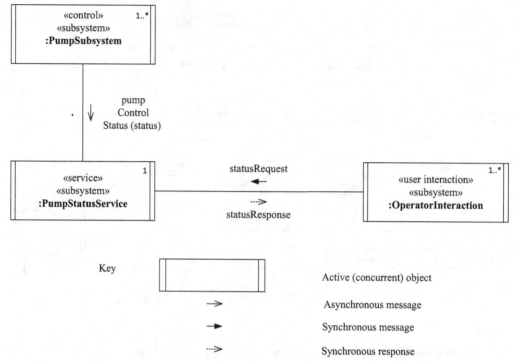

Figure 22.6. Distributed software architecture.

22.7.2 Distributed System Deployment

Each subsystem is designed as a configurable component so that instances of the three subsystems can be deployed to a distributed configuration. The configuration of the distributed real-time system is depicted on a deployment diagram, an example of which is depicted in Figure 22.7, with the subsystem instances deployed to distributed nodes communicating over a local area network.

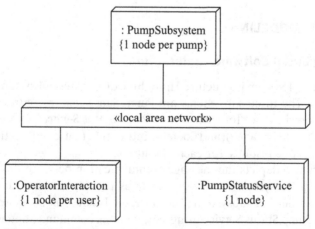

Figure 22.7. Distributed system deployment.

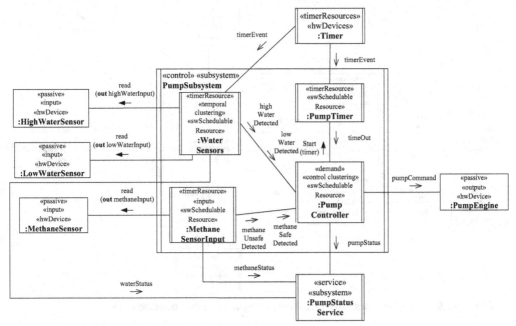

Figure 22.8. Pump Subsystem – task architecture.

22.7.3 Concurrent Task Architecture

The task architecture for the Pump Control System is given in Figure 22.8. There are four tasks in the Pump Subsystem:

- A periodic input task, Methane Sensor Input, to monitor the status of a passive methane sensor. The MARTE stereotypes for this task, which correspond to it being a periodic input task, are «timerResource» «input» «swSchedulableResource».
- A periodic temporal clustering task, Water Sensors, to monitor the status of the high and low water sensors. These sensors need to be monitored with the same frequency and are therefore grouped into the same task. The stereotypes for this task, which correspond to it being a periodic temporal clustering task, are «timerResource» «temporal clustering» «swSchedulableResource».
- A demand driven control clustering task, Pump Controller, in which the Pump Control task is clustered with Pump Engine Output, since the start and stop pump commands are executed at state transitions. The stereotypes for this task, which correspond to it being a demand driven control clustering task, are «demand» «control clustering» «swSchedulableResource».
- A periodic timer task, Pump Timer, to receive the timer events from the clock. The MARTE stereotypes for this task, which correspond to it being a periodic task, are «timerResource» «swSchedulableResource».

22.7.4 Detailed Software Design

The detailed design of a periodic temporal clustering task is given in Figure 22.9. The Water Sensors task of Figure 22.8 is a composite task that contains three passive

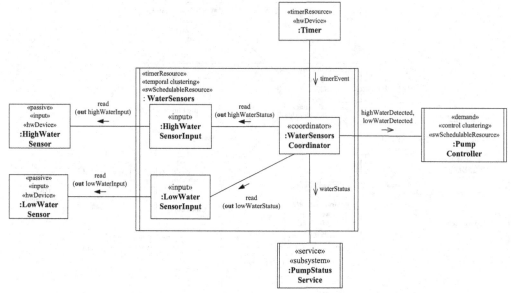

Figure 22.9. Water Sensors – temporal clustering with nested passive objects.

objects, a coordinator object called the Water Sensors Coordinator, two input objects called the High Water Sensor Input and Low Water Sensor Input objects.

The detailed design of a demand driven control clustering task is given in Figure 22.10. The Pump Controller is a composite task that contains three passive objects, a coordinator object called the Pump Coordinator, an output object called Pump Engine Output, and a state machine object called Pump Control.

The design of the passive information-hiding classes, instances of which are nested in the two clustered tasks, are depicted in Figure 22.11. The classes are High Water Sensor Input and Low Water Sensor Input (instances of which are nested in the

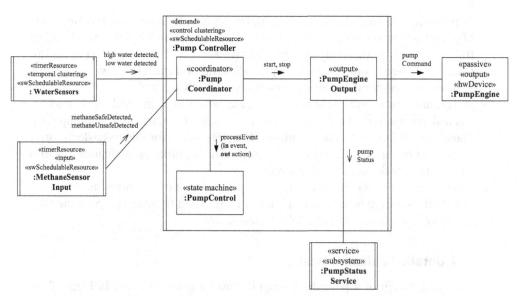

Figure 22.10. Pump Controller – control clustering with nested passive objects.

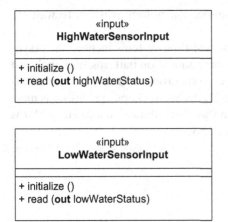

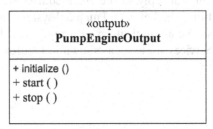

Figure 22.11. Design of passive information-hiding classes.

Water Sensors task), and Pump Engine Output and Pump Control (instances of which nested in the Pump Controller task).

22.7.5 Applying Software Architectural Patterns

The Pump Control System uses several software architectural structure and communication patterns. The Centralized Control pattern is used because for a given Pump Subsystem, there is one control task, which executes a state machine. It receives sensor input from input tasks and controls the external environment via an output task, as shown in Figure 22.8 for the Pump Controller task. In a Centralized Control pattern, the control task executes a state machine, which for Pump Controller is depicted in Figure 22.4. A second architectural structure pattern used in the Pump Control System is the Distributed Independent Control pattern because the system has several instances of the Pump Subsystem, each of which is a control subsystem that executes independently of the other control subsystems and sends pump status to the Pump Status Service subsystem. Note that each instance of the Pump Subsystem is independent of the service subsystem because it sends unidirectional asynchronous messages to the service and therefore never has to wait for a response. The third architectural structure pattern is the Multiple Client/Single Service pattern, as shown in Figure 22.6, in which the multiple instances of the Operator Interaction subsystem are clients of the Pump Status Service subsystem, because each client sends status requests to and receives status responses from the service subsystem. The difference between the second and third architectural structure patterns is that the Pump Subsystem is independent of the Pump Status Service subsystem whereas the Operator

Interaction subsystem is dependent on the service subsystem as it has to wait for responses from it.

Architectural communication patterns for real-time systems include the Asynchronous Communication and Synchronous Communication patterns, both with and without reply. In the Pump Control System, both asynchronous message communication (e.g., between Pump Subsystem and Pump Status Service) and synchronous message communication with reply (e.g., between Operator Interaction and Pump Status Service) are used, as shown in Figures 22.6 and 22.8.

23

Highway Toll Control System Case Study

This chapter describes a concise case study of a Highway Toll Control System in which there are several entry and exit toll booths. Each toll booth is controlled by a real-time embedded subsystem that communicates with a Highway Toll Service subsystem, which receives entry and exit transactions from the toll booths and charges customer accounts. At each toll booth there are multiple sensors and actuators, requiring state dependent entry and exit control. Because entry and exit toll booths are similarly configured and behave in a similar way, this shorter case study concentrates on the design of the entry toll booth. There is less emphasis on the structural modeling in this case study, which has been covered in detail in other case studies.

The problem description is given in Section 23.1. Section 23.2 describes the use case model, and Section 23.3 describes the software system context modeling. Section 23.4 describes the object and class structuring. Section 23.5 describes the state machine model, and Section 23.6 describes the dynamic interaction modeling. Section 23.7 describes the design modeling, which consists of the distributed software design and distributed software deployment, followed by the design of the concurrent task architecture and detailed software design.

23.1 PROBLEM DESCRIPTION

A highway toll road has several entry and exit points, at each of which, there is a toll plaza with one or more tollbooths. To use the system, a customer purchases a RFID (radio frequency ID) transponder, which holds the encoded customer account number, from the Highway Toll Service and mounts the transponder on the windshield of the vehicle. The Highway Toll Service maintains customer accounts in a database including owner and vehicle information, and account balance. Customers purchasing a transponder must pay in advance for toll fees by credit card. Accounts are reduced by the toll charge incurred at the end of each trip. The toll charge to be paid depends on the length of the trip and category of the vehicle.

All tollbooths consist of a vehicle arrival sensor (placed fifty feet in front of the tollbooth), a vehicle departure sensor, a traffic light to indicate whether the vehicle has been authorized to pass through the tollbooth, a transponder detector, and a camera.

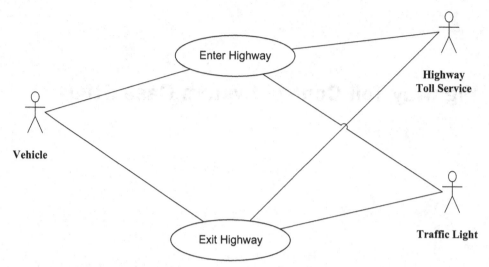

Figure 23.1. Use case model for Highway Toll Control System.

The traffic light at each tollbooth is initially red. When a vehicle approaches the tollbooth, the vehicle sensor detects the vehicle's presence. If the transponder detector detects a valid transponder (i.e., the transponder holds a valid customer account) in the approaching vehicle, the system switches the light to green. If there is no transponder or the account is low on funds, the system switches the light to yellow. In addition, the video camera photographs the license plate, and the image is sent to Highway Toll Service. After the car departs, the system switches the light to red.

23.2 USE CASE MODELING

The use case model for the Highway Toll Control System is depicted in Figure 23.1, in which there are two use cases, Enter Highway and Exit Highway. The use cases are depicted at the system engineering level, which is the reason for having only three actors: the Vehicle actor, movement of which is tracked by four input devices, Traffic Light actor, which corresponds to the output device of the same name, and the external system actor, the Highway Toll Service. The timer is assumed to be internal to the system.

The use case descriptions are as follows. The Enter Highway use case is started with an input from the Vehicle actor.

Use case: Enter Highway
Actor: Vehicle (primary), Traffic Light, Highway Toll Service
Summary: Vehicle enters highway through a toll booth
Precondition: Tollbooth is open, and the traffic light at the tollbooth is set to red.
Main sequence:
   1. Vehicle approaches the tollbooth.
   2. System detects vehicle's presence.
   3. System reads the account RFID in the approaching vehicle.

4. System sends a vehicle entry transaction consisting of time of entry, day, location, and transponder ID, to Highway Toll Service.
5. System switches traffic light to green.
6. Vehicle passes through the tollbooth.
7. System detects that the vehicle has departed.
8. System switches traffic light to red.

Alternative sequences:

Step 3: Unrecognized or missing account RFID. If the system detects a vehicle with an unrecognized or missing account RFID, System switches the traffic light to yellow. System commands video camera to photograph the vehicle's license plate. System sends the license plate image to the Highway Toll Service.

Step 3: Account is low in funds. If the system determines that the account is low in funds, System switches traffic light to yellow.

Postcondition: The vehicle has departed from the toll booth.

The Exit Highway use case is started with an input from the Vehicle actor. For information purposes, this use case describes functionality performed by the Highway Toll Service actor.

Use case: Exit Highway
Actor: Vehicle (primary), Traffic Light, Highway Toll Service
Summary: Vehicle exits highway through a toll booth.
Precondition: Tollbooth is open and the traffic light at the tollbooth is red
Main sequence:

1. Vehicle approaches toll booth.
2. System detects vehicle's presence.
3. System reads the account RFID in the approaching vehicle.
4. System sends a vehicle exit transaction consisting of time of exit, day, location, vehicle type, and transponder ID, to Highway Toll Service.
5. Highway Toll Service calculates toll based on start time and day, exit time and day, start location, exit location, and vehicle type.
6. Highway Toll Service deducts toll amount from customer's account.
7. System switches traffic light to green.
8. Vehicle leaves the tollbooth.
9. System detects that the vehicle has departed and switches traffic light to red.

Alternative sequences:

Step 3: Unrecognized or missing account RFID. If the system detects a vehicle with an unrecognized or missing account RFID, System switches the traffic light to yellow. System commands video camera to photograph the vehicle's license plate. System sends the license plate image to the Highway Toll Service.

Step 3: Insufficient funds. If the system determines that there are insufficient funds in the account, System switches traffic light to yellow.

Postcondition: The vehicle has departed from the toll booth.

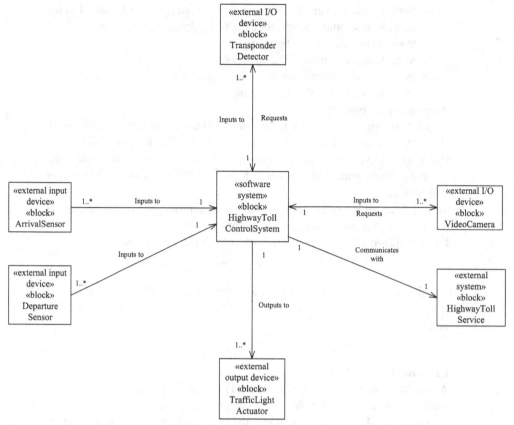

Figure 23.2. Highway Toll Control software system context diagram.

23.3 SOFTWARE SYSTEM CONTEXT MODELING

The software system context diagram for the Highway Toll Control System, which is shown in Figure 23.2, depicts the software system and external entities as SysML blocks. The Vehicle actor from the use case model is replaced by two external input devices, namely the Arrival Sensor and Departure Sensor, and two external input/output devices, the Video Camera and the Transponder Detector. There is one external output device, namely the Traffic Light Actuator, which corresponds to the Traffic Light actor, and one external system, the Highway Toll Service, which corresponds to the actor of the same name.

The association between Highway Toll Control System and Transponder Detector is bidirectional because the software system requests the transponder to provide input and the transponder responds with the input. The association between Highway Toll Control System and Video Camera is bidirectional for the same reason.

23.4 OBJECT AND CLASS STRUCTURING

Analysis Modeling is based around the Enter Highway use case. Next, the software objects and classes are determined that realize this use case. All objects, except for entity objects, are assumed to be concurrent. The software system context class diagram is a good starting point for identifying the software boundary objects and classes. For each external input device, there is a corresponding software input object:

- Arrival Sensor Input, Departure Sensor Input.

For each external input/output device, there is a corresponding software input/output object:

- Video Camera I/O and Transponder Detector I/O.

For each external output device, there is a corresponding software output object:

- Traffic Light Output.

For each external system, there is a corresponding software proxy object:

- Highway Toll Service Proxy.

In addition, because the behavior of this control system is state dependent, there will need to be a state dependent control object to execute an encapsulated state machine:

- Entry Control.

Furthermore, there needs to be a passive entity object to store the entry transaction, before it is sent to the Highway Toll Service:

- Entry Transaction.

23.5 DYNAMIC STATE MACHINE MODELING

Next the Entry Control state machine is designed, as depicted in Figure 23.3. The states are:

- Waiting for Arrival. In this state, the tollbooth is idle.
- Detecting Transponder. This state is entered upon receipt of the Vehicle Arrives event. The system attempts to detect the transponder in this state.
- Creating Transaction. After the transponder is detected and the transponder ID read, a transaction is created.
- Validating Account. The entry transaction is sent to the Highway Toll Service for validation.
- Waiting for Departure. If the account is valid, this state is entered.
- Waiting for Photo. This state is entered if no transponder is detected or if the account is invalid.
- Taking Photo. This state is entered after a vehicle with no transponder or an invalid account has departed.

23.6 DYNAMIC INTERACTION MODELING

This section describes the dynamic modeling interaction sequence, which is depicted on both the sequence diagram for the Enter Highway use case (Figure 23.4) and the state machine (Figure 23.3). Messages arriving at the Entry Control object on Figure 23.4 correspond to events on the encapsulated Entry Control state machine (Figure 23.3), while actions on the state machine correspond to messages leaving the Entry

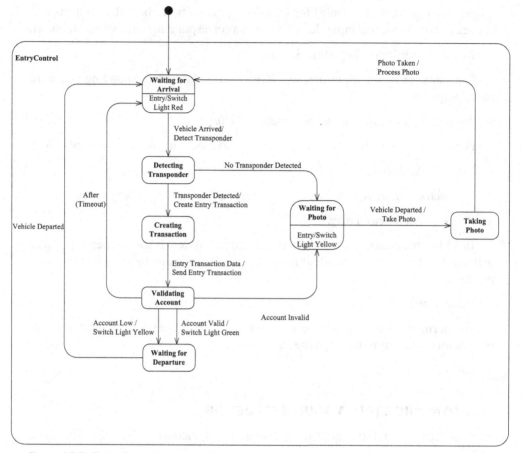

Figure 23.3. Entry Control state machine.

Control object. The sequence diagram starts when the Arrival Sensor Input object (after receiving an arrival event from the arrival sensor) sends a Vehicle Arrived message to the Entry Control object. This event causes the Entry Control state machine to transition from Waiting for Arrival state to Detecting Transponder state. The resulting action is Detect Transponder, which is sent as a message of the same name from Entry Control to Transponder Detector I/O. The latter object responds with the Transponder Detected message, which arrives at Entry Control, causing it to transition to Creating Transaction state; the resulting action is to send a create entry transaction request to the Entry Transaction object, which responds with the entry transaction data containing the transaction ID and transponder ID. Entry Control then sends the entry transaction to the Highway Toll Service Proxy, which in turn sends it to the Highway Toll Service to validate the vehicle account. Highway Toll Service Proxy sends the service response (whether the transponder account is valid or not) to Entry Control. If the account is valid, Entry Control sends a Switch Light Green message to Traffic Light Output. Alternatively, if the account is invalid or low in funds or if no transponder is detected, Entry Control sends a Switch Light Yellow message to Traffic Light Output. When the Vehicle Departed message is received by Entry Control, and if the account is invalid or no transponder is detected, Entry Control sends a Take Photo message

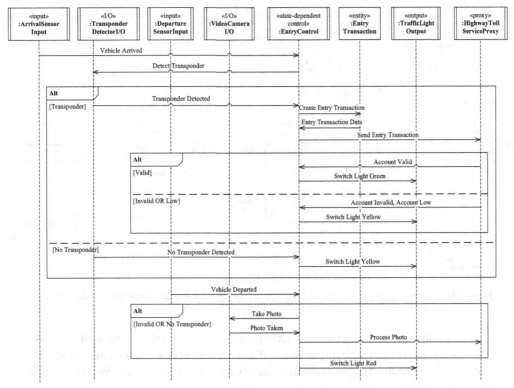

Figure 23.4. Sequence diagram for Enter Highway use case.

to Video Camera I/O. When the Photo Taken response is received, Entry Control sends a Process Photo message to the Highway Toll Service Proxy, which in turn sends the message to the Highway Toll Service. For all scenarios, when the Vehicle Departed message is received, Entry Control sends a Switch Light Red message to Traffic Light Output.

The objects in the Entry Tollbooth Controller subsystem are also depicted on an integrated communication diagram in Figure 23.5, which depicts all the objects in this subsystem as well as all the messages passed between them.

23.7 DESIGN MODELING

23.7.1 Distributed Software Architecture

The Highway Toll System (which consists of the Highway Toll Control System and the Highway Toll Service) is structured into three distributed subsystems, as depicted on Figure 23.6. The three subsystems are Entry Tollbooth Controller subsystem (a control subsystem of which there is one instance for each entry tollbooth), Exit Tollbooth Controller subsystem (a control subsystem of which there is one instance for each exit tollbooth), and Highway Toll Service (a service subsystem of which there is one instance).

Figure 23.6 also depicts the message communication between the three subsystems. The Entry Tollbooth Controller and Exit Tollbooth Controller subsystems send

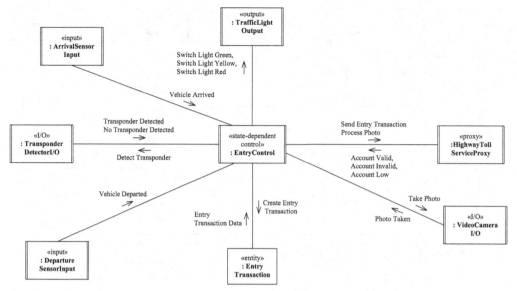

Figure 23.5. Integrated Communication diagram for Entry Tollbooth Controller subsystem.

asynchronous entry and exit transaction messages respectively, as well as asynchronous process photo messages, to the Highway Toll Service subsystem. The service subsystem responds to entry and exit transactions with asynchronous valid or invalid account status messages.

23.7.2 Distributed System Deployment

Each subsystem is designed as a configurable component so that instances of the three subsystems can be deployed to a distributed configuration. The configuration of the distributed real-time system is depicted on a deployment diagram, an example of

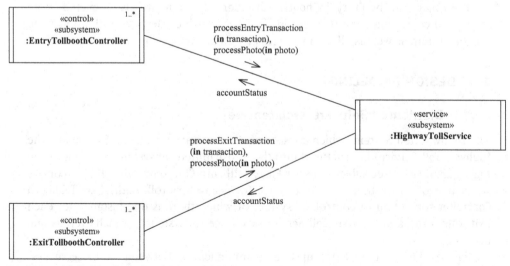

Figure 23.6. Distributed software architecture.

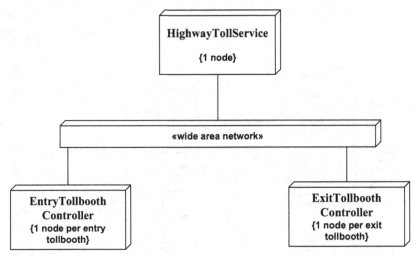

Figure 23.7. Distributed system deployment for Highway Toll Control System.

which is depicted in Figure 23.7, with the subsystem instances deployed to distributed nodes communicating over a wide area network. Each instance of the Entry Tollbooth Controller and Exit Tollbooth Controller is assigned to its own node and the single instance of the Highway Toll Service is assigned to a separate node.

23.7.3 Concurrent Task Architecture

The task architecture for the Entry Booth Controller subsystem is given in Figure 23.8. Tasks are depicted using MARTE stereotypes. There are seven tasks in this subsystem:

- An event driven input task, Arrival Sensor Input, which receives inputs from the arrival sensor. The stereotypes for this task, which correspond to it being an event driven input task, are «event driven» «input» «swSchedulableResource».
- A second event driven input task, Departure Sensor Input, which receives inputs from the departure sensor. The stereotypes for this task are also «event driven» «input» «swSchedulableResource».
- An event driven input/output task, Transponder Detector I/O, which receives the transponder ID from the transponder detector. The stereotypes for this task are «event driven» «I/O» «swSchedulableResource».
- A demand driven control clustering task, Entry Controller, in which the Entry Control task is clustered with the Entry Transaction entity object to create a control clustering task. The stereotypes for this task, which correspond to it being a demand driven control clustering task, are «demand» «control clustering» «swSchedulableResource».
- A demand driven input/output task, Video Camera I/O, which sends a command to the external video camera to take a photo of the car before it departs. The stereotypes for this task are «demand» «I/O» «swSchedulableResource».
- A demand driven output task, Traffic Light Output, which sends commands to the external traffic light to change the color of the light to red, green, or yellow. The stereotypes for this task are «demand» «output» «swSchedulableResource».

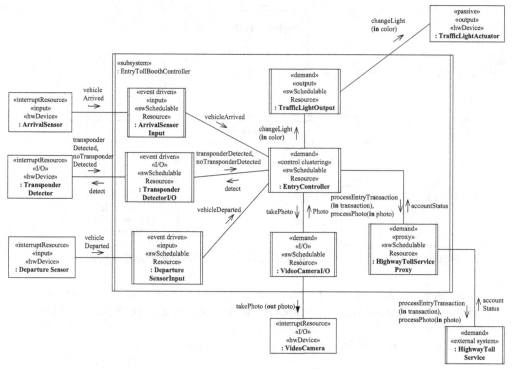

Figure 23.8. Entry Tollbooth Controller Subsystem – task architecture.

- Finally, there is a demand driven proxy task, Highway Toll Service Proxy, which sends requests to the external Highway Toll Service to process entry and exit transactions for cars with valid transponders or to process photos of cars with invalid or no transponders. The stereotypes for this task are «demand» «proxy» «swSchedulableResource».

23.7.4 Detailed Software Design

The detailed design of a demand driven control clustering task is given in Figure 23.9. The Entry Controller is a composite task that contains three passive objects, a coordinator called the Entry Coordinator, an entity object called Entry Transaction, and a state machine object called Entry Control. Entry Coordinator receives messages from the three producer tasks, Arrival Sensor Input, Departure Sensor Input, and Transponder Detector I/O on a FIFO queue, and invokes the operations of the Entry Control and Entry Transaction passive objects.

23.7.5 Architectural Pattern Usage

The Highway Toll Control System uses several software architectural structure and communication patterns. The Centralized Control pattern is used in the Entry Tollbooth Controller and Exit Tollbooth Controller subsystems because in each case, there is one control task, which executes a state machine. It receives sensor input from multiple input and I/O tasks and controls the external environment via output and I/O tasks, as shown in Figure 23.8 for the Entry Tollbooth Controller subsystem. In

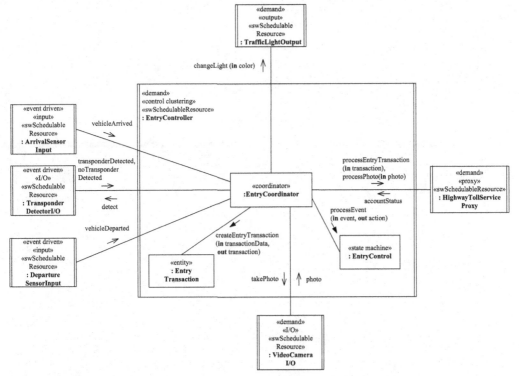

Figure 23.9. Entry Controller – control clustering with nested passive objects.

a Centralized Control pattern, the control task executes a state machine, which for Entry Tollbooth Controller is depicted in Figure 23.3. Another architectural pattern used in the Highway Toll Control System is the Multiple-Client/Single-Service pattern, as shown in Figure 23.6, in which the multiple instances of the Entry Tollbooth Controller and Exit Tollbooth Controller subsystems are clients of the service subsystem, the Highway Toll Service.

Architectural communication patterns used in the Highway Toll Control System are the Asynchronous Message Communication and Bidirectional Asynchronous Message Communication patterns, as shown in Figures 23.6 and 23.8.

APPENDIX A

Conventions Used in This Textbook

For improved readability, certain conventions are used in this book. These are the naming conventions used in this book and the conventions for message sequence numbering on interaction diagrams.

A.1 NAMING CONVENTIONS USED IN THIS BOOK

For improved readability, the conventions used for depicting names of classes, objects, and so on in the figures are sometimes different from the conventions used for the same names in the text. In the figures, examples are shown in Times New Roman font. In the body of the text, however, examples are shown in a different font to distinguish them from the regular Cambria Math font. Some specific additional conventions used in the book vary depending on the phase of the project. For example, the conventions for capitalization are different in the analysis model (which is less formal) than in the design model (which is more formal).

A.1.1 Requirements Modeling

In both figures and text, use cases are shown with initial uppercase and spaces in multiword names – for example, Cook Food.

A.1.2 Analysis Modeling

The naming conventions for the analysis model are as follows.

Classes

Classes are shown with an uppercase initial letter. In the figures, there are no spaces in multiword names – for example, HeatingElement. In the text, however, spacing is introduced to improve the readability – for example, Heating Element.

Attributes are shown with a lowercase initial letter – for example, weight. For multiword attributes, there are no spaces between the words in figures, but spaces are introduced in the text. The first word of the multiword name has an initial lowercase letter; subsequent words have an initial uppercase letter – for example, sensorValue in figures and sensor Value in text.

The type of the attribute has an initial uppercase letter – for example, Boolean, Integer, or Real.

Objects

An object may be depicted in various ways, in particular as:

- **An individual named object**. In this case, the first letter of the first word is lower-case, and subsequent words have an uppercase first letter. In figures, the objects appear as, for example, aWarningAlarm and anotherWarningAlarm. In the text, these objects appear as a Warning Alarm and another Warning Alarm.
- **An individual unnamed object**. Some objects are shown in the figures as class instances without a given object name – for example : WarningAlarm. In the text, this object is referred to as Warning Alarm. For improved readability, the colon is removed, and a space is introduced between the individual words of a multiword name.

This means that, depending on how the object is depicted in a figure, it will appear in the text sometimes with a first word initial letter uppercase and sometimes with a first word initial letter lowercase.

Messages

In the analysis model, messages are depicted with an uppercase initial letter. Multi-word messages are shown with spaces in both figures and text – for example, Simple Message Name.

State Machines

In both figures and text, states, events, conditions, actions, and activities are all shown with initial letter uppercase and spaces in multiword names – for example, the state Emergency Stopping, the event Timer Event, and the action Open Doors.

A.1.3 Design Modeling

The naming conventions for the design model are as follows.

Active and Passive Classes

The naming conventions for active classes (concurrent classes) and passive classes are the same as for classes in the analysis model (see Section A.1.2).

Active and Passive Objects

The naming conventions for active objects (concurrent objects) and passive objects are the same as for objects in the analysis model (see Section A.1.2).

Messages

In the design model, the first letter of the first word of the message is lowercase, and subsequent words have an uppercase first letter. In both the figures and text, there is no space between words, as in alarmMessage.

Message parameters are shown with a lowercase initial letter – for example, speed. For multiword attributes, there are no spaces between the words in both the figures and the text. The first word of the multiword name has a lowercase initial letter, and subsequent words have an uppercase initial letter – for example, cumulativeDistance in both figures and text.

Operations

The naming conventions for operations (a.k.a. methods) follow the conventions for messages in both figures and text. Thus, the first letter of the first word of both the operation and the parameter is lowercase, and subsequent words have an upper-case first letter. There is no space between words – for example, validatePassword (userPassword).

A.2 MESSAGE SEQUENCE NUMBERING ON INTERACTION DIAGRAMS

Messages on a communication diagram or sequence diagram are given message sequence numbers. This section provides some guidelines for numbering message sequences. These guidelines follow the general UML conventions; however, they have been extended to address concurrency, alternatives, and large message sequences better. These conventions are followed in the examples given in this book, including the case studies in Chapters 19 through 23.

A.2.1 Message Labels on Interaction Diagrams

A message label on a communication or sequence diagram has the following syntax (only those parts of the message label that are relevant in the analysis phase are described here):

[sequence expression]: Message Name (argument list)

where the sequence expression consists of the message sequence number and an indicator of recurrence.

- **Message sequence number**. The message sequence number is described as follows: The first message sequence number represents the event that initiates the message sequence depicted on the communication diagram. Typical message sequences are 1, 2, 3, …; A1, A2, A3, …

    A more elaborate message sequence can be depicted with the Dewey classification system, such that A1.1 precedes A1.1.1, which in turn precedes A1.2. In the Dewey system, a typical message numbering sequence would be A1, A1.1, A1.1.1, A1.2.
- **Recurrence**. The recurrence term is optional and represents conditional or iterative execution. The recurrence term represents zero or more messages that are sent, depending on the conditions being met.
  1. *** [iteration-clause]**. An asterisk (*) is added after the message sequence number to indicate that more than one message is sent. The optional iteration clause is used to specify repeated execution, such as [j : = 1,n]. An example of an iteration by putting an asterisk after the message sequence number is 3*.

2. **[condition-clause]**. A condition is specified in square brackets to indicate a branch condition. The optional condition clause is used for specifying branches – for example, [x < n] – meaning that the message is sent only if the condition is true. Examples of conditional message passing by showing a condition after the message sequence number are 4[x < n] and 5[Normal]. In each case, the message is sent only if the condition is true.

- **Message name**. The message name is specified.
- **Argument list**. The argument list of the message is optional and specifies any parameters sent as part of the message.

There can also be optional return values from the message sent.

A.2.2 Message Sequence Numbering on Interaction Diagrams

On a sequence or communication diagram supporting a use case, the sequence in which the objects participate in each use case is described and depicted by message sequence numbers. A message sequence number for a use case takes the following form:

[first optional letter sequence] [numeric sequence] [second optional letter sequence]

The first optional letter sequence is an optional use case ID and identifies a specific use case. The first letter is an uppercase letter and might be followed by one or more upper- or lowercase letters if a more descriptive use case ID is desired.

The simplest form of message sequencing is to use a sequence of whole numbers, such as M1, M2, and M3. However, in a real-time system with several external inputs from the actor(s), it is often helpful to include a numeric sequence that includes decimal numbers – that is, to number the external events as whole numbers followed by decimal numbers for the ensuing internal events. For example, if the actor's inputs were designated as A1, A2, and A3, the full message sequence depicted on the communication diagram would be A1, A1.1, A1.2, A1.3,..., A2, A2.1, A2.2,..., and A3, A3.1, A3.2,....

An example is V1, where the letter V identifies the use case, and the number identifies the message sequence within the communication diagram supporting the use case. The object sending the first message – V1 – is the initiator of the use case–based communication. Subsequent message numbers following this input message are V1.1, V1.2, and V1.3. If the dialog were to continue, the next input from the actor would be V2.

A.2.3 Concurrent and Alternative Message Sequences

The second optional letter sequence is used to depict special cases of branches – either concurrent or alternative – in the message sequence numbering.

Concurrent message sequences may also be depicted on a communication diagram. A lowercase letter represents a concurrent sequence; in other words, sequences designated as A3 and A3a would be concurrent sequences. For example, the arrival of message A2 at an object X might result in the sending of two messages from object

X to two objects Y and Z, which could then execute in parallel. To indicate the concurrency in this case, the message sent to object Y would be designated as A3, and the one to object Z as A3a. Subsequent messages in the A3 sequence would be A4, A5, A6, ..., and subsequent messages in the independent A3a sequence would be A3a.1, A3a.2, A3a.3, and so on. Because the sequence numbering is more cumbersome for the A3a sequence, use A3 for the main message sequence and A3a and A3b for the supporting message sequences. An alternative way to show two concurrent sequences is to avoid A3 altogether and use the sequence numbers A3a and A3b; however, this can lead to a more cumbersome numbering scheme if A3a initiates another concurrent sequence, so the former approach is preferred.

Alternative message sequences are depicted with the condition indicated after the message. An uppercase letter is used to name the alternative branch. For example, the main branch may be labeled 1.4[Normal], and the other, less frequently used branch could be named 1.4A[Error]. The message sequence numbers for the normal branch would be 1.4[Normal], 1.5, 1.6, and so on. The message sequence numbers for the alternative branch would be 1.4A[Error], 1.4A.1, 1.4A.2, and so on.

APPENDIX B

Catalog of Software Architectural Patterns

The architectural structure patterns and architectural communication patterns are documented with the template described in Chapter 11, Section 11.8, in Sections B.1 and B.2, respectively. The patterns are summarized in the following tables.

Table B.1. Software Architectural Structure Patterns

Software architectural structure patterns	Section of Chapter 11	Appendix B
Centralized Control	Section 11.3.1	B.1.1
Distributed Collaborative Control	Section 11.3.2	B.1.2
Distributed Independent Control	Section 11.3.3	B.1.3
Hierarchical Control	Section 11.3.4	B.1.4
Layers of Abstraction	Section 11.2.1	B.1.5
Kernel	Section 11.2.2	B.1.6
Master/Slave	Section 11.3.5	B.1.7
Multiple Client/Multiple Service	Section 11.4.2	B.1.8
Multiple Client/Single Service	Section 11.4.1	B.1.9

Table B.2. Software Architectural Communication Patterns

Software architectural communication patterns	Section of Chapter 11	Appendix B
Asynchronous Message Communication	Section 11.5.2	B.2.1
Asynchronous Message Communication with Callback	Section 11.5.5	B.2.2
Bidirectional Asynchronous Message Communication	Section 11.5.3	B.2.3
Broadcast	Section 11.7.1	B.2.4
Broker Handle	Section 11.6.2	B.2.5
Service Discovery	Section 11.6.3	B.2.6
Service Registration	Section 11.6.1	B.2.7
Subscription/Notification	Section 11.7.2	B.2.8
Synchronized Object Access	Section 11.5.1	B.2.9
Synchronous Message Communication with Reply	Section 11.5.4	B.2.10
Synchronous Message Communication without Reply	Section 11.5.6	B.2.11

B.1 SOFTWARE ARCHITECTURAL STRUCTURE PATTERNS

This section describes the architectural structure patterns, which address the static structure of the architecture, in alphabetical order, using the standard template.

B.1.1 Centralized Control Pattern

Pattern name	Centralized Control.
Aliases	Centralized Controller, System Controller.
Context	Centralized application for which overall control is needed.
Problem	Several actions and activities are state dependent and need to be controlled and sequenced.
Summary of solution	There is one control component, which conceptually executes a state machine and provides the overall control and sequencing of the system or subsystem.
Strengths of solution	Encapsulates all state dependent control in one component.
Weaknesses of solution	Could lead to overcentralized control, in which case decentralized control should be considered.
Applicability	Real-time control systems, state dependent applications.
Related patterns	Distributed Collaborative Control, Distributed Independent Control, Hierarchical Control.
Reference	Chapter 11, Section 11.3.1.

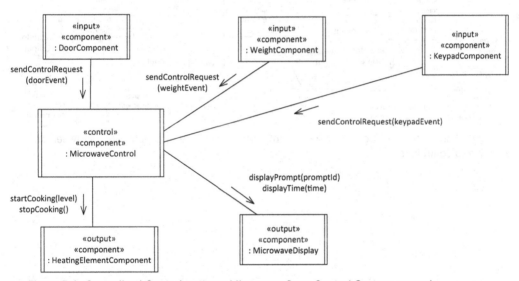

Figure B.1. Centralized Control pattern: Microwave Oven Control System example.

B.1.2 Distributed Collaborative Control Pattern

Pattern name	Distributed Collaborative Control.
Aliases	Distributed Control, Decentralized Collaborative Control.
Context	Distributed application with real-time control requirement.
Problem	Distributed application with multiple locations for which real-time localized control is needed at several locations and control components communicate with each other.
Summary of solution	There are several control components, such that each component controls a given part of the system by conceptually executing a state machine. Control is distributed among the various control components, which communicate with each other. No single component has overall control.
Strengths of solution	Overcomes potential problem of over-centralized control.
Weaknesses of solution	Does not have an overall coordinator. If this is needed, consider using Hierarchical Control pattern.
Applicability	Distributed real-time control systems, distributed state dependent applications.
Related patterns	Distributed Independent Control, Hierarchical Control, Centralized Control.
Reference	Chapter 11, Section 11.3.2.

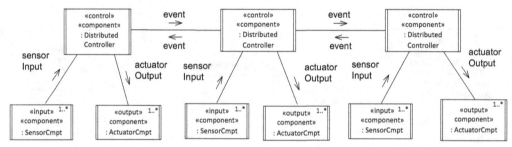

Figure B.2. Distributed Collaborative Control pattern: example of collaboration between distributed controllers.

B.1.3 Distributed Independent Control Pattern

Pattern name	Distributed Independent Control.
Aliases	Distributed Independent Controller, Decentralized Independent Control.
Context	Distributed application with real-time control requirement.
Problem	Distributed application with multiple locations for which real-time localized control is needed at several locations; control components do not communicate with each other.
Summary of solution	There are several control components, such that each component controls a given part of the system by conceptually executing a state machine. Control is distributed among the various control components, which do not communicate with each other but might communicate asynchronously with a service component. No single component has overall control.
Strengths of solution	Overcomes potential problem of over-centralized control.
Weaknesses of solution	Does not have an overall coordinator. If this is needed, consider using Hierarchical Control pattern.
Applicability	Distributed real-time control systems, distributed state dependent applications.
Related patterns	Distributed Collaborative Control, Hierarchical Control, Centralized Control, Multiple Client/Single Service.
Reference	Chapter 11, Section 11.3.3.

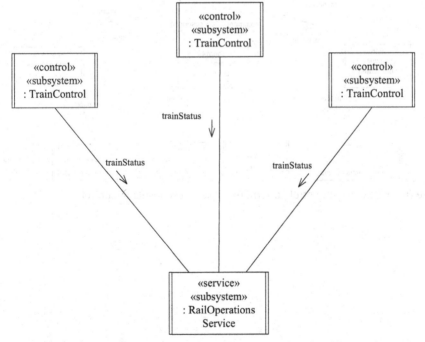

Figure B.3. Distributed Independent Control pattern: example with asynchronous communication to service.

B.1.4 Hierarchical Control Pattern

Pattern name	Hierarchical Control.
Aliases	Multilevel Control; Hierarchical Coordination.
Context	Distributed application with real-time control requirement.
Problem	Distributed application with multiple locations for which both real-time localized control and overall control are needed.
Summary of solution	There are several control components, each controlling a given part of a system by conceptually executing a state machine. There is also a coordinator component, which provides high-level control by deciding the next job for each control component and communicating that information directly to the control component.
Strengths of solution	Overcomes potential problem with Distributed Control pattern by providing high-level control and coordination.
Weaknesses of solution	Coordinator may become a bottleneck when the load is high.
Applicability	Distributed real-time control systems, distributed state dependent applications.
Related patterns	Distributed Collaborative Control, Distributed Independent Control, Centralized Control.
Reference	Chapter 11, Section 11.3.4.

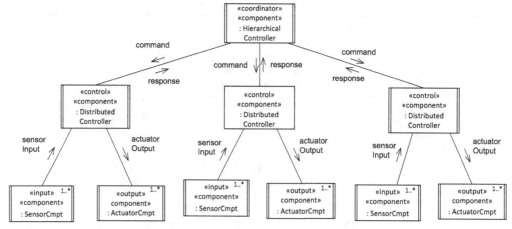

Figure B.4. Hierarchical Control pattern: example of two levels of control.

B.1.5 Layers of Abstraction Pattern

Pattern name	Layers of Abstraction.
Aliases	Hierarchical Layers, Levels of Abstraction.
Context	Software architectural design.
Problem	A software architecture that encourages design for ease of extension and contraction is needed.
Summary of solution	Components at lower layers provide services for components at higher layers. Components may use only services provided by components at lower layers.
Strengths of solution	Promotes extension and contraction of software design.
Weaknesses of solution	Could lead to inefficiency if too many layers need to be traversed.
Applicability	Operating systems, communication protocols, real-time systems, software product lines.
Related patterns	Kernel can be lowest layer of Layers of Abstraction architecture. Variations of this pattern include Flexible Layers of Abstraction.
Reference	Chapter 11, Section 11.2.1; Hoffman and Weiss 2001; Parnas 1979.

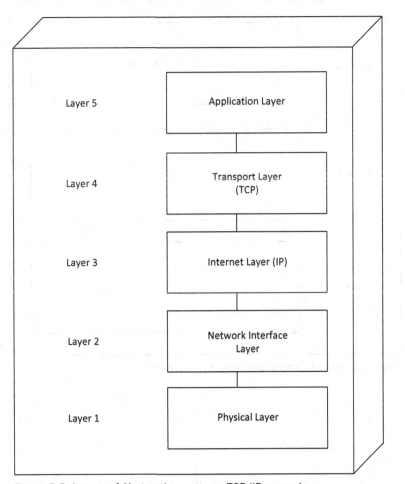

Figure B.5. Layers of Abstraction pattern: TCP/IP example.

B.1.6 Kernel Pattern

Pattern name	Kernel.
Aliases	Microkernel.
Context	Software architectural design; real-time software design.
Problem	A small core of essential functionality that can be used by other components is needed.
Summary of solution	Kernel provides a well-defined interface consisting of operations (procedures or functions) that can be called by other parts of the software system.
Strengths of solution	Kernel can be designed to be highly efficient.
Weaknesses of solution	If care is not taken, kernel can become too large and bloated. Alternatively, essential functionality could be left out in error.
Applicability	Operating systems, real-time systems, software product lines.
Related patterns	Can be lowest layer of Layers of Abstraction architecture.
Reference	Chapter 11, Section 11.2.2; Buschmann et al. 1996.

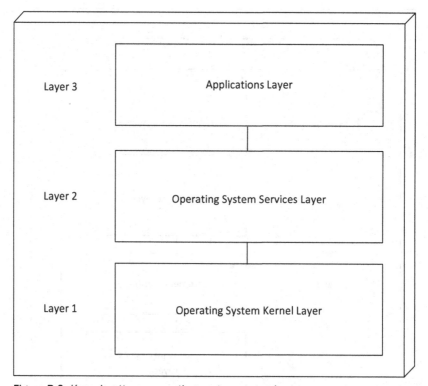

Figure B.6. Kernel pattern: operating system example.

B.1.7 Master/Slave Pattern

Pattern name	Master/Slave.
Aliases	None.
Context	Software architectural design; real-time applications.
Problem	Several computations need to be executed in parallel.
Summary of solution	Master divides up the work to be performed and assigns each part to a slave. Each slave executes its assignment and, when it has finished, sends a response to the master. The master integrates the slave responses.
Strengths of solution	Divides up work to be done so that it can be done in parallel.
Weaknesses of solution	Could have situations where the work is not divided evenly between slaves, which results in less efficient master/slave operation. A slave might be held up or fail and hence slow down the entire master/slave operation.
Applicability	Real-time applications, computationally intensive applications.
Related patterns	Centralized Control, Hierarchical Control.
Reference	Chapter 11, Section 11.3.5.

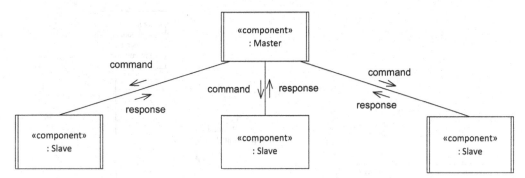

Figure B.7. Master/Slave pattern: Example of Master assigning work to slaves.

B.1.8 Multiple Client/Multiple Service Pattern

Pattern name	Multiple Client/Multiple Service.
Aliases	Client/Service, Client/Server.
Context	Software architectural design, distributed real-time systems.
Problem	Distributed real-time application in which multiple clients require services from multiple services.
Summary of solution	Client communicates with multiple services, usually sequentially but could also be in parallel. Each service responds to client requests. Each service handles multiple client requests. A service may delegate a client request to a different service.
Strengths of solution	Good way for client to communicate with multiple services when it needs different information from each service.
Weaknesses of solution	Client can be held up indefinitely if there is a heavy load at any server.
Applicability	Distributed processing: client/service and distributed real-time applications with multiple services.
Related patterns	Multiple Client/Single Service.
Reference	Chapter 11, Section 11.4.2.

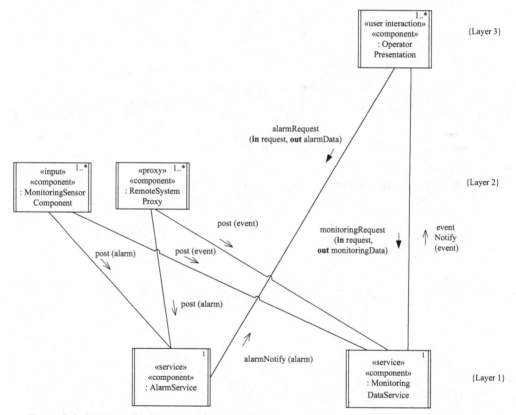

Figure B.8. Multiple Client/Multiple Service Pattern: Example of Emergency Monitoring System.

B.1.9 Multiple Client/Single Service Pattern

Pattern name	Multiple Client/Single Service.
Aliases	Client/Service, Client/Server.
Context	Software architectural design, distributed real-time systems.
Problem	Distributed real-time application in which multiple clients require services from a single service.
Summary of solution	Client requests service. Service responds to client requests and does not initiate requests. Service handles multiple client requests.
Strengths of solution	Good way for client to communicate with service when it needs a reply from service. Very common form of communication in client/service applications.
Weaknesses of solution	Client can be held up indefinitely if there is a heavy load at the server.
Applicability	Distributed processing: client/service and distributed real-time applications.
Related patterns	Multiple Client/Multiple Service, Distributed Independent Control.
Reference	Chapter 11, Section 11.4.1.

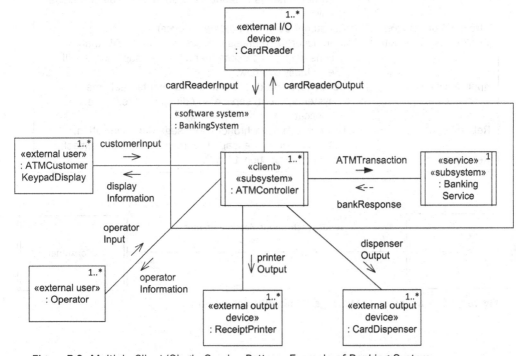

Figure B.9. Multiple Client/Single Service Pattern: Example of Banking System.

B.2 SOFTWARE ARCHITECTURAL COMMUNICATION PATTERNS

This section describes the architectural communication patterns, which address the dynamic communication among distributed components of the architecture, in alphabetical order, using the standard template.

B.2.1 Asynchronous Message Communication Pattern

Pattern name	Asynchronous Message Communication.
Aliases	Loosely Coupled Message Communication.
Context	Concurrent or distributed real-time systems.
Problem	Concurrent or distributed application has concurrent components that need to communicate with each other. Producer does not need to wait for consumer. Producer does not need a reply.
Summary of solution	Use message queue between producer component(s) and consumer component. Producer sends message to consumer and continues. Consumer receives message. Messages are queued FIFO if consumer is busy. Consumer is suspended if no message is available. Producer needs timeout notification if consumer node is down.
Strengths of solution	Consumer does not hold up producer.
Weaknesses of solution	If producer(s) produces messages more quickly than consumer can process them, the message queue will eventually overflow.
Applicability	Centralized and distributed environments: real-time systems, client/service and distributed real-time applications.
Related patterns	Bidirectional Asynchronous Message Communication, Asynchronous Message Communication with Callback.
Reference	Chapter 11, Section 11.5.2.

Figure B.10. Asynchronous Message Communication pattern.

B.2.2 Asynchronous Message Communication with Callback Pattern

Pattern name	Asynchronous Message Communication with Callback.
Aliases	Loosely Coupled Communication with Callback.
Context	Concurrent or distributed real-time systems.
Problem	Concurrent or distributed application in which concurrent components need to communicate with each other. Client does not need to wait for service but does need to receive a reply later.
Summary of solution	Use asynchronous communication between client components and service component. Client sends service request to service, which includes client operation (callback) handle. Client does not wait for reply. After service processes the client request, it uses the handle to call the client operation remotely (the callback).
Strengths of solution	Good way for client to communicate with service when it needs a reply but can continue executing and receive reply later.
Weaknesses of solution	Suitable only if the client does not need to send multiple requests before receiving the first reply.
Applicability	Distributed environments: client/service and distributed real-time applications with multiple services.
Related patterns	Consider Bidirectional Asynchronous Message Communication as alternative pattern.
Reference	Chapter 11, Section 11.5.5.

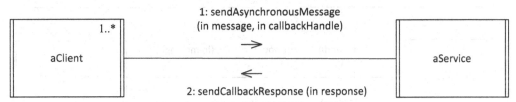

Figure B.11. Asynchronous Message Communication with Callback pattern.

B.2.3 Bidirectional Asynchronous Message Communication Pattern

Pattern name	Bidirectional Asynchronous Message Communication.
Aliases	Bidirectional Loosely Coupled Message Communication.
Context	Concurrent or distributed real-time systems.
Problem	Concurrent or distributed application in which concurrent components need to communicate with each other. Producer does not need to wait for consumer, although it does need to receive replies later. Producer can send several requests before receiving first reply.
Summary of solution	Use two message queues between producer component and consumer component: one for messages from producer to consumer and one for messages from consumer to producer. Producer sends message to consumer on P→C queue and continues. Consumer receives message. Messages are queued if consumer is busy. Consumer sends replies on C→P queue.
Strengths of solution	Producer does not get held up by consumer. Producer receives replies later, when it needs them.
Weaknesses of solution	If producer produces messages more quickly than consumer can process them, the message (P→C) queue will eventually overflow. If producer does not service replies quickly enough, the reply (C→P) queue will overflow.
Applicability	Centralized and distributed environments: real-time systems, client/service and distributed applications.
Related patterns	Asynchronous Message Communication with Callback.
Reference	Chapter 11, Section 11.5.3.

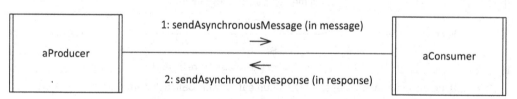

Figure B.12. Bidirectional Asynchronous Message Communication pattern.

B.2.4 Broadcast Pattern

Pattern name	Broadcast.
Aliases	Broadcast Communication.
Context	Distributed real-time systems.
Problem	Distributed application with multiple clients and services. At times, a service needs to send the same message to several clients.
Summary of solution	Crude form of group communication in which a service sends a message to all clients, regardless of whether clients want the message or not. Client decides whether it wants to process or discard the message.
Strengths of solution	Simple form of group communication.
Weaknesses of solution	Places an additional load on the client because the client may not want the message.
Applicability	Distributed environments: client/service and distributed real-time applications with multiple services.
Related patterns	Similar to Subscription/Notification, except that it is not selective.
Reference	Chapter 11, Section 11.7.1.

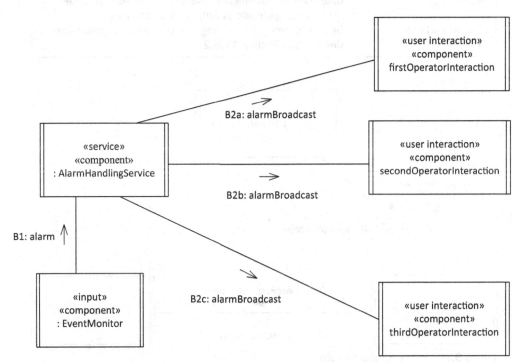

Figure B.13. Broadcast pattern: alarm broadcast example.

B.2.5 Broker Handle Pattern

Pattern name	Broker Handle.
Aliases	White Pages Broker Handle, Broker with Handle-Driven Design.
Context	Distributed real-time systems.
Problem	Distributed application in which multiple clients communicate with multiple services. Clients do not know locations of services.
Summary of solution	Use broker. Services register with broker. Client sends service request to broker. Broker returns service handle to client. Client uses service handle to make request to service. Service processes request and sends reply directly to client. Client can make multiple requests to service without broker involvement.
Strengths of solution	Location transparency: services may relocate easily. Clients do not need to know locations of services.
Weaknesses of solution	Additional overhead because broker is involved in initial message communication. Broker can become a bottleneck if there is a heavy load at the broker. Client may keep outdated service handle instead of discarding.
Applicability	Distributed environments: client/service and distributed real-time applications with multiple services.
Related patterns	Similar to Broker Forwarding but with better performance.
Reference	Chapter 11, Section 11.6.2.

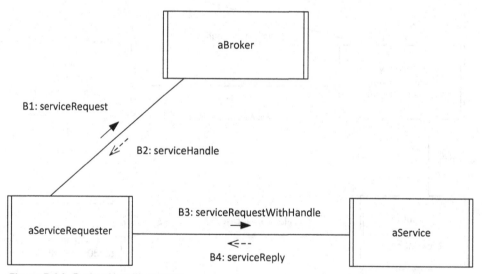

Figure B.14. Broker Handle pattern.

B.2.6 Service Discovery Pattern

Pattern name	Service Discovery.
Aliases	Yellow Pages Broker, Broker Trader, Discovery.
Context	Distributed real-time systems.
Problem	Distributed application in which multiple clients communicate with multiple services. Client knows the type of service required but not the specific service.
Summary of solution	Use broker's discovery service. Services register with broker. Client sends discovery service request to broker. Broker returns names of all services that match discovery service request. Client selects a service and uses broker handle service to communicate with service.
Strengths of solution	Location transparency: Services may relocate easily. Clients do not need to know specific service, only the service type.
Weaknesses of solution	Additional overhead because broker is involved in initial message communication. Broker can become a bottleneck if there is a heavy load at the broker.
Applicability	Distributed environments: client/service and distributed real-time applications with multiple services.
Related patterns	Broker Handle, Service Registration.
Reference	Chapter 11, Section 11.6.3.

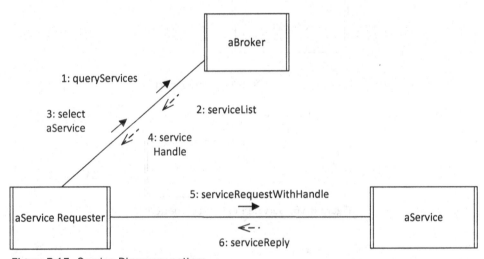

Figure B.15. Service Discovery pattern.

B.2.7 **Service Registration Pattern**

Pattern name	Service Registration.
Aliases	Broker Registration.
Context	Distributed real-time systems.
Problem	Distributed application in which multiple clients communicate with multiple services. Clients do not know locations of services.
Summary of solution	Service registers service information with broker, including service name, service description, and location. Clients send service requests to broker. Broker acts as intermediary between clients and services. If service relocates, it needs to re-register with the broker.
Strengths of solution	Location transparency: services may relocate easily. Clients do not need to know locations of services.
Weaknesses of solution	Additional overhead because broker is involved in message communication. Broker can become a bottleneck if there is a heavy load at the broker.
Applicability	Distributed environments: client/service and distributed real-time applications with multiple services.
Related patterns	Broker Handle, Service Registration.
Reference	Chapter 11, Section 11.6.1.

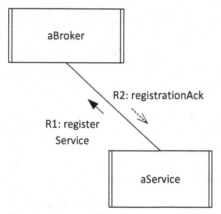

Figure B.16. Service Registration pattern.

B.2.8 Subscription/Notification Pattern

Pattern name	Subscription/Notification.
Aliases	Multicast.
Context	Distributed real-time systems.
Problem	Distributed application with multiple clients and services. Clients want to receive messages of a given type.
Summary of solution	Selective form of group communication. Clients subscribe to receive messages of a given type. When service receives message of this type, it notifies all clients who have subscribed to it.
Strengths of solution	Selective form of group communication. Widely used on the Internet and in World Wide Web applications.
Weaknesses of solution	If client subscribes to too many services, it may unexpectedly receive a large number of messages.
Applicability	Distributed environments: client/service and distributed real-time applications with multiple services.
Related patterns	Similar to Broadcast, except that it is more selective. Variation on this pattern is Multicast Notification, in which connections between components are established at initialization time without explicit component subscription.
Reference	Chapter 11, Section 11.7.2.

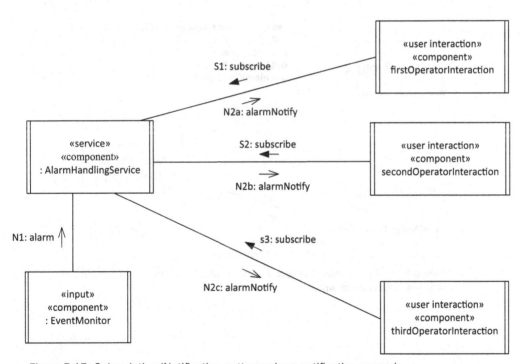

Figure B.17. Subscription/Notification pattern: alarm notification example.

B.2.9 Synchronized Object Access Pattern

Pattern name	Synchronized Object Access.
Aliases	Synchronized Operation Invocation, Synchronized Method Invocation; Synchronized Class Access.
Context	Object-oriented and real-time systems.
Problem	Concurrent components or tasks need to access shared data, which is encapsulated in a passive object.
Summary of solution	Two or more concurrent components (tasks) on the same node communicate with each through a passive information-hiding object to access (read and write) shared data. A task calls an operation provided by the passive object. The operations of the object provide synchronized access, such as mutually exclusive, to the data.
Strengths of solution	This pattern allows concurrent components or tasks to access shared data on the same node.
Weaknesses of solution	This pattern cannot be used if the tasks need to execute on separate nodes.
Applicability	Real-time systems with tasks that access shared data.
Related patterns	Software Architectural Communication patterns in which message passing is used instead of operation invocation.
Reference	Chapter 11, Section 11.5.1.

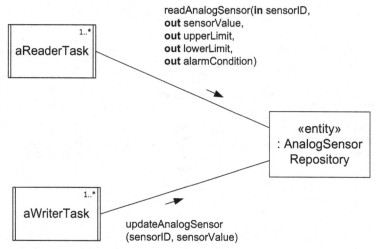

Figure B.18. Synchronized Object Access pattern: example of multiple readers and multiple writers.

B.2.10 Synchronous Message Communication with Reply Pattern

Pattern name	Synchronous Message Communication with Reply.
Aliases	Tightly Coupled Message Communication with Reply.
Context	Concurrent or distributed real-time systems.
Problem	Concurrent or distributed application in which multiple clients communicate with a single service or a producer communicates with a consumer. Client (or producer) needs to wait for reply from service (or consumer).
Summary of solution	Use synchronous communication between client (producer) component and service (consumer) component. Client (producer) sends message to service (consumer) and waits for reply. Use message queue at service when there are many clients. Service processes message FIFO. Service (consumer) sends reply to client. Client (producer) is activated when it receives reply from service (consumer).
Strengths of solution	Good way for client (producer) to communicate with service (consumer) when it needs a reply. Very common form of communication in client/service and producer/consumer applications.
Weaknesses of solution	Client (producer) can be held up indefinitely if there is a heavy load at the service (consumer).
Applicability	Concurrent or distributed environments, client/service and distributed real-time applications with multiple services.
Related patterns	Asynchronous Message Communication with Callback.
Reference	Chapter 11, Section 11.5.4.

Figure B.19. Synchronous Message Communication with Reply pattern.

B.2.11 Synchronous Message Communication without Reply Pattern

Pattern name	Synchronous Message Communication without Reply.
Aliases	Tightly Coupled Message Communication without Reply.
Context	Concurrent or distributed real-time systems.
Problem	Concurrent or distributed application in which concurrent components need to communicate with each other. Producer needs to wait for consumer to accept message. Producer does not want to get ahead of consumer. There is no queue between producer and consumer.
Summary of solution	Use synchronous communication between producer and consumer. Producer sends message to consumer and waits for consumer to accept message. Consumer receives message. Consumer is suspended if no message is available. Consumer accepts message, thereby releasing producer.
Strengths of solution	Good way for producer to communicate with consumer when it wants confirmation that consumer received the message and producer does not want to get ahead of consumer.
Weaknesses of solution	Producer can be held up indefinitely if consumer is busy doing something else.
Applicability	Concurrent and distributed environments, client/service and distributed real-time applications with multiple services.
Related patterns	Consider Synchronous Message Communication with Reply as alternative pattern.
Reference	Chapter 11, Section 11.5.6.

Figure B.20. Synchronous Message Communication without Reply pattern.

APPENDIX C

Pseudocode Templates for Concurrent Tasks

This appendix provides pseudocode templates of the event sequencing logic for the different kinds of concurrent tasks described in Chapter 13 of this textbook. These templates include event driven input tasks; periodic input and algorithm tasks; and demand driven general purpose, coordinator, output, user interaction, and state dependent control tasks.

C.1 PSEUDOCODE FOR EVENT DRIVEN INPUT TASK

An **event driven input task** is needed when there is an event driven (also referred to as interrupt-driven) input device to which the system has to interface (Section 13.3.2). The event driven I/O task is activated by an external event (such as an interrupt) from the device, reads the input data, does any necessary processing of the data, including sending a message to a consumer or updating a passive entity object, and then waits for the next external event.

```
Initialize input device, if needed;
loop
-- Wait for external event from input device;
wait (inputEvent);
read input data;
if data is recognized
then -- Process data;
    convert data to internal format if needed,
        e.g., convert analog data to engineering units;
    process data, if needed;
    prepare message containing message name and optional parameters
    -- send message to consumer task via connector;
    aConnector.send (message);
else -- input was not recognized;
    Handle error case;
end if;
end loop;
```

C.2 PSEUDOCODE FOR PERIODIC INPUT TASK

A **periodic input task** interfaces with a passive input device, where the device is polled on a regular basis (Section 13.3.3). The periodic input task is activated by a timer event, reads the sampled input data, does any necessary processing of the data, and then waits for the next timer event. The task's period is the time between successive activations.

```
Initialize input device, if needed;
loop
-- Wait for timer event;
wait (timerEvent);
read input data sample;
if data is recognized
then -- Process input data;
    convert data to internal format if needed,
        e.g., convert analog data to engineering units;
    If Boolean data, check if data has changed from previous reading;
    process data, if needed;
    prepare message containing message name and optional parameters
    -- send message to consumer or write to data repository;
    dataRepository.update(newData);
else -- input was not recognized;
    Handle error case;
end if;
end loop;
```

C.3 PSEUDOCODE FOR DEMAND DRIVEN OUTPUT TASK

A **demand driven output task** is used to interface to a passive output device that does not need to be polled and hence does not need a periodic output task (Section 13.3.4). In particular, it is used when it is desirable to overlap computation with output. The demand driven output task is activated on demand by the arrival of a message from a producer task, reads the message, prepares the data for output, outputs the data, and then waits for the next message.

```
Initialize output device, if needed;
loop
-- wait for message from producer task arriving via connector;
aConnector.receive (message);
extract message name and any message parameters from message;
-- process message;
convert data to output format if needed,
output data to output device;
```

```
if output device error;
    Handle error case;
end if;
end loop;
```

C.4 PSEUDOCODE FOR DEMAND DRIVEN COORDINATOR TASK

A **demand driven coordinator task** is a control task that is not state dependent; that is, the action it takes is based entirely on the contents of the input message it receives (Section 13.4.4). The coordinator task is activated on demand by the arrival of a message from a producer task, reads the message, executes the appropriate action (such as sending a message to a consumer task), and then waits for the next message.

```
loop
    -- Wait for message from another task arriving via message connector;
    aConnector.receive (message);
    extract message name and any message parameters from message;
    -- perform coordination action (assumed to be not state dependent)
    case message of
        message type 1:
            objectA.methodX (optional parameters);
            ....
        message type 2:
            objectB.methodY (optional parameters);
            .....
    endcase;
    prepare output message containing message name and parameters
    -- send output message;
    aConnector.send (message);
    end if;
    end loop;
```

C.5 PSEUDOCODE FOR PERIODIC ALGORITHM TASK

A **periodic algorithm task** is a task that executes an algorithm periodically, that is, at regular, equally spaced intervals of time (Section 13.4.1). The task is activated by a timer event, executes the periodic algorithm, and then waits for the next timer event. The task's period is the time between successive activations.

```
loop
    -- Wait for timer event;
    wait (timerEvent);
```

```
execute periodic algorithm;
prepare output message containing message name and parameters
-- send output message;
aConnector.send (message);
end if;
end loop;
```

C.6 PSEUDOCODE FOR DEMAND DRIVEN TASK

A **demand driven task** is a task that is activated on demand by the arrival of a message or event sent by a producer task (Section 13.4.2). The action the demand driven task takes is based entirely on the contents of the input message it receives. The task reads the incoming message, performs the demanded action, and then communicates the result, such as by sending a message to a consumer task, by sending a response to the original producer task, or by updating a passive entity object. The task then loops back and waits for the next message.

```
loop
-- wait for message or event from producer task arriving via message
connector;
aConnector.receive (message);
extract message name and any message parameters from message;
perform requested action on demand
-     Read data from passive entity object(s) if needed
-     Execute action
-     Update data in passive entity object(s) if needed
prepare output message or response containing message name and parameters
-- send output message or event;
aConnector.send (message);
end loop;
```

C.7 PSEUDOCODE FOR USER INTERACTION TASK

A **user interaction task** is a demand driven task that interacts with a human user. It typically outputs a prompt to a user (either on initialization or on arrival of a message from another task) and then waits for the input from the user (Section 13.4.5). It will read the input, possibly following this up with further prompts and user inputs, determine the desired user action, and send a message to a consumer object (which could be a passive entity object, service task or control task). It typically receives a response from the consumer. It then formats the response in textual and/or graphical form, and outputs this response to the user. The task then loops back and waits for the next user interaction.

```
loop
   output menu or prompt to user;
   wait (user response);
   read user input;
   process user input and have further interactions with user if necessary;
   -- send message with user request to consumer task
   aConnector.send (user request);
   -- wait for response from consumer task arriving via message connector;
   aConnector.receive (consumer response);
   extract and process consumer response;
   prepare textual and/or graphical output for user;
   output response to user
end loop;
```

C.8 PSEUDOCODE FOR DEMAND DRIVEN STATE DEPENDENT CONTROL TASK

A **state dependent control task** is a demand driven task (Section 13.4.3) that executes a sequential state machine. The task receives messages from its producers on a message queue. Given the next message, the task extracts the event from the message and uses this event as an input parameter to invoke the processEvent method of a passive STM (Section 14.1.3) object, which encapsulates a state transition table. Given the new event and current state, the method looks up the state transition table entry for Table (new event, current state) and reads the next state and action(s) to be performed. It then sets the current state to the next state and returns the action(s) to be performed. The task then executes each action, such as by sending a message to another task, and then loops back to receive the next message.

```
loop
   -- messages from all senders are received on Message Queue
   Receive (messageQ, message);
   -- extract the event name and any message parameters
   newEvent = message.event
   -- assume state machine is encapsulated in object aSTM;
   -- given the incoming event, lookup state transition table;
   -- change state if required; return action to be performed;
   aSTM.processEvent (in newEvent, out action);
   -- execute statedependent action(s) as given on state machine;
      case state_dependent_action of
        action_1:
          execute state_dependent_action 1;
          exit;
        action_2
          execute state_dependent_action 1;
```

```
        exit;
    ...
    action_n
      execute state_dependent_action n;
      exit;
  end case;
end loop;
```

APPENDIX D

Teaching Considerations

D.1 OVERVIEW

The material in this book may be taught in different ways depending on the time available and the knowledge level of the students. This appendix describes possible academic and industrial courses that could be based on this book.

A prerequisite of these courses is an introductory course on software engineering covering the software life cycle, and the main activities in each phase of the life cycle. This prerequisite course would cover the material described in introductory books on Software Engineering such as Pressman (2009) or Sommerville (2010).

In each of these courses, there are three components: description of the method, presentation of at least one case study using the method, and hands-on design exercise for students to apply the method to a real world problem.

D.2 SUGGESTED ACADEMIC COURSES

The following academic courses could be could be taught in graduate and advanced undergraduate courses in Computer Science, Software Engineering, Systems Engineering, and Computer Engineering programs, and are based on the material covered in this textbook.

1. A senior undergraduate or graduate level course on real-time software modeling and design.
2. A Design Lab course is held as a follow-up course or as an alternative to the real-time software modeling and design course (course 1) in which the students work in teams to develop a solution to a substantial real-time software problem. In this case, students could also implement all or part of the system.

D.3 SUGGESTED INDUSTRIAL COURSES

The following industrial courses could be based on the material covered in this book:

1. A course on real-time software modeling and design. Concepts are presented briefly from Part I, and then the course would concentrate on Part II and,

depending on the length of the course, performance analysis from Part III, together with a case study from Part IV. The design lab would concentrate on working on a real-time software problem. This course could be run at any length from two to five days, depending on the level of detail covered.

2. A practical hands-on course in which each stage of the real-time software design method is followed by a hands-on design lab. The design lab could be on a problem of the company's choice, assuming an in-house course.

D4. DESIGN EXERCISES

The following discussion applies to both academic and industrial courses:

As part of the course, students should also work on one or more real-time problems, either individually or in teams. Whether one or more problems are tackled depends on the size of the problem and the length of the course. However sufficient time should be allocated for students to work on the problems since this is the best way for the students to really understand the method.

Software problems that may be used are:

a. Consumer product such as a dishwasher system,
b. Space Flight System,
c. Factory automation system,
d. House-cleaning robot,
e. Driverless car,
f. Air traffic control system.

Possible teaching approaches are:

1. Work on one problem throughout the course using COMET/RTE. This has the advantage that students get an in-depth appreciation of the method.
2. Divide the class up into teams. Each group solves a different problem using COMET/RTE. Time is allocated at the end of the course for each group to present their solution. A class discussion is held on the strengths and weaknesses of each solution.
3. A Design Lab course is held as a follow-up course to the course on real-time software modeling and design, in which the students work in teams to develop a substantial real-time software architecture. In this case, students could also implement all or part of the system.

Glossary

abstract class   A *class* that cannot be directly instantiated (Booch, Rumbaugh, and Jacobson 2005). Compare *concrete class*.

abstract data type   A data type that is defined by the *operations* that manipulate it and thus has its representation details hidden.

abstract interface specification   A specification that defines the external view of the *information hiding class* – that is, all the information required by the user of the *class*.

abstract operation   An *operation* that is declared in an *abstract class* but not implemented.

action   A computation that executes as a result of a *state transition*.

active object   See *concurrent object*.

activity   A computation that executes for the duration of a *state*.

actor   An outside user or related set of users who interact with the system (Rumbaugh, Booch, and Jacobson 2005).

actuator   The means by which a real-time computer system can control an external device or mechanism

aggregate class   A *class* that represents the whole in an *aggregation* relationship (Booch, Rumbaugh, and Jacobson 2005).

aggregation   A weak form of *whole/part relationship*. Compare *composition*.

algorithm object   An object that encapsulates an algorithm used in the problem domain.

analog data   Continuous data that can, in principle, have an infinite number of values.

analysis modeling   A phase of the COMET/RTE system and software life cycle in which *static modeling* and *dynamic modeling* are performed. Compare *design modeling* and *requirements modeling*.

aperiodic task   A task that is activated on demand. See event driven or demand driven task.

application deployment   A process for deciding which *component* instances are required, how component instances should be allocated to physical *nodes* in a *distributed* environment, and how component instances should be interconnected.

application logic object   An *object* that hides the details of the application logic separately from the data being manipulated.

architectural pattern   See *software architectural pattern*.

association   A relationship between two or more *classes*.

asynchronous message communication   A form of communication in which a *concurrent* producer component (or task) sends a message to a concurrent consumer component (or task) and does not wait for a response; a message queue could potentially build up between the concurrent components (or tasks). Compare *synchronous message communication*.

availability   The extent to which the system is available for operational usage.

behavioral model   A model that describes the responses of the system to the inputs that the system receives from the external environment. Also referred to as *dynamic model*.

binary semaphore   A Boolean variable used to enforce *mutual exclusion*. Also referred to simply as *semaphore*.

black box specification   A specification that describes the externally visible characteristics of the system.

block   A *class* that has the *stereotype* «block».

block definition diagram   A *SysML* diagram that is a *class diagram* in which each *class* has the *stereotype* «block».

boundary object   A software *object* that interfaces to and communicates with the external environment.

broadcast communication   A form of group communication in which unsolicited messages are sent to all recipients.

broker   An intermediary in interactions between *clients* and *services*. Also referred to as *object broker* or *object request broker*.

brokered communication   Message communication in a *distributed* object environment in which *clients* and *services* interact via a *broker*.

callback   An *operation* handle sent by a *client* in an asynchronous request to a *service* and used by the *service* to respond to the client request.

CASE   See *Computer-Aided Software Engineering*.

category   A specifically defined division in a system of classification.

class   An *object* type; hence, a template for objects. An implementation of an *abstract data type*.

class diagram   A *UML* diagram that depicts a static view of a system in terms of *classes* and the relationships between classes. Compare *interaction diagram*.

class interface specification   A specification that defines the externally visible view of a *class*, including the specification of the *operations* provided by the class.

class structuring criteria   See *object structuring criteria*.

client   A requester of *services* in a *client/server system*. Compare *server*.

client/server system   A system that consists of *clients* that request *services* and one or more *servers* that provide *services*.

Collaborative Object Modeling and Architectural Design Method (COMET)   An iterative use case-driven and object-oriented method that addresses the requirements, analysis, and design modeling phases of the software development life cycle.

COMET   See *Collaborative Object Modeling and Architectural Design Method*.

COMET/RTE See Concurrent Object Modeling and architectural design mEThodfor Real-Time Embedded Systems.

Concurrent Object Modeling and architectural design mEThod for Real-Time Embedded Systems A software design method for real-time embedded systems. See COMET/RTE.

commonality The functionality that is common to all members of a *software product line*. Compare *variability*.

commonality/variability analysis An approach for examining the functionality of a *software product line* to determine which functionality is common to all product line members and which is not.

communication diagram A *UML 2 interaction diagram* that depicts a dynamic view of a system in which *objects* interact by using messages.

complex port A *port* that supports both a *provided interface* and a *required interface*.

Completion Time Theorem A real-time scheduling theorem that states that for a set of independent periodic tasks, if each task meets its first deadline, when all tasks are started at the same time, then the deadlines will be met for any combination of start times.

component A *concurrent* self-contained *object* with a well-defined *interface*, capable of being used in different applications from that for which it was originally designed. Also referred to as *distributed component*.

component-based software architecture A software architecture in which an infrastructure is provided that is specifically intended to accommodate preexisting *components*.

component-based system A system in which an infrastructure is provided that is specifically intended to accommodate preexisting *components*.

component structuring criteria A set of heuristics for assisting a designer in structuring a system into *components*.

composite component A *component* that contains nested components. Compare *simple component*.

composite state A *state* on a *statechart* that is decomposed into two or more *substates*. Also referred to as a *superstate*.

composite structure diagram A *UML 2* diagram that depicts the structure and interconnections of composite *classes*; specifically used to depict *components*, *ports*, and *connectors*.

composite subsystem A subsystem designed as a *composite component*.

composite task A task that contains nested objects.

composition A form of *whole/part relationship* that is stronger than an *aggregation*; the part *objects* are created, live, and die together with the composite (whole) object.

Computer-Aided Software Engineering (CASE) tool A software tool that supports a software engineering method or notation.

concrete class A *class* that can be directly instantiated (Booch, Rumbaugh, and Jacobson 2005). Compare *abstract class*.

concurrent Referring to a problem, process, system, or application in which many activities happen in parallel, where the order of incoming *events* is not usually predictable and is often overlapping. A concurrent system or application has many threads of control. Compare *sequential*.

concurrent communication diagram   A *communication diagram* that depicts *concurrent* objects and their interactions in the form of *asynchronous* and *synchronous message communication*.

concurrent object   An autonomous *object* that has its own thread of control. Also referred to as an *active object, process, task, thread, concurrent process*, or *concurrent task*.

concurrent process   See *concurrent object*.

concurrent sequence diagram   A *sequence diagram* that depicts *concurrent* objects and their interactions in the form of *asynchronous* and *synchronous message communication*.

concurrent service   A *service* that services multiple *client* requests in parallel. Compare *sequential service*.

concurrent task   See *concurrent object*.

condition   The value of a Boolean variable that can be true or false over a finite interval of time.

connector   An *object* that encapsulates the interconnection protocol between two or more *components*.

constraint   A *condition* that must be true.

continuous data   Data that flows without interruption.

control clustering   A task structuring criterion by which a control object is combined into a task with the objects it controls.

control object   An *object* that provides overall coordination for other objects.

coordinator object   An overall decision-making *object* that determines the overall sequencing for a collection of objects and is not *state dependent*.

critical section   The section of a *concurrent task*'s internal logic that is *mutually exclusive*.

data abstraction   An approach for defining a data structure or data type by the set of *operations* that manipulate it, thus separating and hiding the representation details.

data abstraction class   A *class* that encapsulates a data structure or data type, thereby hiding the representation details; *operations* provided by the class manipulate the hidden data.

data replication   Duplication of data in more than one location in a *distributed application* to speed up access to the data.

database wrapper class   A *class* that hides how to access data stored in a database.

deadlock   A situation in which two or more *concurrent tasks* are suspended indefinitely because each task is waiting for a resource acquired by another task.

delegation connector   A *connector* that joins the outer *port* of a *composite component* to the inner port of a *part component* such that messages arriving at the outer port are forwarded to the inner port.

demand driven task   A *task* that is activated on demand by the arrival of a message or internal event from another task.

deployment diagram   A *UML* diagram that shows the physical configuration of the system in terms of physical *nodes* and physical connections between the nodes, such as network connections.

design concept   A fundamental idea that can be applied to designing a system.

design method   A systematic approach for creating a design. The design method helps identify the design decisions to be made, the order in which to make them, and the criteria used in making them.

design modeling A phase of the *COMET/RTE* system and software life cycle in which the *software architecture* of the system is designed. Compare *analysis modeling* and *requirements modeling*.

design notation A graphical, symbolic, or textual means of describing a design.

design pattern A description of a recurring design problem to be solved, a solution to the problem, and the context in which that solution works.

design strategy An overall plan and direction for developing a design.

device interface object An *information hiding object* that hides the characteristics of an I/O device and presents a virtual device *interface* to its users.

device I/O boundary object A software *object* that receives input from and/or outputs to a hardware I/O device.

discrete data Data that arrive at specific time intervals.

distributed A system or application that is *concurrent* in nature and executes in an environment consisting of multiple *nodes*, which are in geographically different locations.

distributed application An application that executes in a *distributed* environment.

distributed component See *component*.

distributed processing environment A system configuration in which several geographically dispersed *nodes* are interconnected by means of a local area or wide area network.

distributed service A *service* with functionality that is spread over several server *nodes*.

domain-specific pattern A software pattern that is specific to a given application domain.

duration An interval of time between two *events*.

dynamic interaction model A view of a problem or system in which control and sequencing are considered by the sequence of interaction among objects.

dynamic interaction modeling The process of developing the *dynamic interaction model*.

dynamic model A view of a problem or system in which control and sequencing are considered, either within an *object* by means of a *finite state machine* or by consideration of the sequence of interaction among objects. Also referred to as *behavioral model*.

dynamic state machine model A view of a problem or system in which control and sequencing are considered by means of a *finite state machine*.

encapsulation See *information hiding*.

entity class A class, in many cases persistent, whose instances are *objects* that encapsulate information.

entity object A software *object*, in many cases persistent, which encapsulates information.

entry action An *action* that is performed on entry into a *state*. Compare *exit action*.

environment simulator A tool that models the inputs arriving from the external entities that interface to the system, and feeds them to the systems being tested.

event (1) In *concurrent* processing, an external or internal stimulus used for synchronization purposes; it can be an external interrupt, a timer expiration, an internal signal, or an internal message. (2) On an *interaction diagram*, a stimulus that arrives at an *object* at a point in time. (3) On a *state machine*, the occurrence of a stimulus that can cause a *state transition* on a state machine.

event driven I/O device   An input/output device that generates an interrupt when it has produced some input or when it has finished processing an output operation.

event driven task   A *task* that is activated by an external event, such as an interrupt.

event sequence   A time-ordered description of events and/or messages sent between objects.

event sequence analysis   Performance analysis of the sequence of tasks that need to be executed to service a given external event.

event sequencing logic   A description of how a task responds to each of its message or event inputs – in particular, what output is generated as a result of each input.

event synchronization   Control of *concurrent task* activation by means of signals. Three types of event synchronization are possible: external interrupts, timer expiration, and internal signals from other concurrent tasks.

event trace   A time-ordered description of each external input and the time at which it occurred.

exit action   An *action* that is performed on exit from a *state*. Compare *entry action*.

external block   A *block* that is outside the system and part of the external environment.

external event   An *event* from an external object, typically an interrupt from an external I/O device. Compare *internal event*.

family of systems   See *software product line*.

feature   A functional requirement; a reusable product line requirement or characteristic. A requirement or characteristic that is provided by one or more members of the *software product line*.

feature/class dependency   The relationship in which one or more *classes* support a *feature* of a *software product line* (i.e., realize the functionality defined by the feature).

feature group   A group of *features* with a particular *constraint* on their usage in a *software product line* member.

feature modeling   The process of analyzing and specifying the *features* and *feature groups* of a *software product line*.

finite state machine   A conceptual machine with a finite number of *states* and *state transitions* that are caused by input *events*. The notation used to represent a finite state machine is a *state transition diagram*, *statechart*, or *state transition table*. Also referred to simply as *state machine*.

formal method   A software engineering method that uses a formal specification language – that is, a language with mathematically defined syntax and semantics.

generalization/specialization   A relationship in which common attributes and *operations* are abstracted into a superclass (generalized class) and are then inherited by subclasses (specialized classes).

idiom   A low-level pattern that describes an implementation solution specific to a given programming language.

incremental software development   See *iterative software development*.

information hiding   The concept of encapsulating software design decisions in *objects* in such a way that the object's *interface* reveals only what its users need to know. Also referred to as *encapsulation*.

information hiding class   A *class* that is structured according to the *information hiding* concept. The class hides a design decision and is accessed by means of *operations*.

information hiding class specification   A specification of the external view of an information hiding class, including its operations.

Information hiding object   An instance of an *information hiding class*.

inheritance   A mechanism for sharing and reusing code between *classes*.

input object   A software device I/O boundary object that receives input from an external input device.

input/output (I/O) object   A software device I/O boundary object that receives input from and sends output to an external I/O device.

integrated communication diagram   A synthesis of several *communication diagrams* depicting all the *objects* and interactions shown on the individual diagrams.

interaction diagram   A *UML* diagram that depicts a dynamic view of a system in terms of *objects* and the sequence of messages passed between them. *Communication diagrams* and *sequence diagrams* are the two main types of interaction diagrams. Compare *class diagram*.

interface   Specifies the externally visible *operations* of a *class, service,* or *component* without revealing the internal structure (implementation) of the operations.

internal event   A means of synchronization between two *concurrent objects*. Compare *external event*.

I/O task structuring criteria   A category of the *task structuring criteria* that addresses how device I/O objects are mapped to I/O tasks and when an I/O task is activated.

iterative software development   An incremental approach to developing software in stages. Also referred to as *incremental software development*.

maintainability   The extent to which software is capable of being changed after deployment.

MARTE   (Modeling and Analysis of Real-Time Embedded Systems) A UML *profile* developed explicitly for real-time embedded systems.

mathematical model   A mathematical representation of a system.

message buffer and response connector   A connector object that encapsulates the communication mechanism for *synchronous message communication with reply*. See *Connector*.

message buffer connector   A connector object that encapsulates the communication mechanism for *synchronous message communication without reply*. See *Connector*.

message dictionary   A collection of definitions of all aggregate messages depicted on *interaction diagrams* that consist of several individual messages.

message queue connector   A connector object that encapsulates the communication mechanism for *asynchronous message communication*. See *Connector*.

message sequence description   A narrative description of the sequence of messages sent from source objects to destination objects, as depicted on a *communication diagram* or *sequence diagram*, describing what happens when each message arrives at a destination object.

middleware   A layer of software that sits above the heterogeneous operating system to provide a uniform platform above which *distributed applications* can run (Bacon 2003).

modifiability   The extent to which software is capable of being modified during and after initial development.

monitor   A data *object* that encapsulates data and has operations that are executed *mutually exclusively*.

multicast communication   See *subscription/notification*.

multiple instance task inversion   A *task clustering* technique where all identical tasks of the same type are replaced by one task that performs the same functionality.

multiple readers and writers   An algorithm that allows multiple readers to access a shared data repository concurrently; however, writers must have mutually exclusive access to update the data repository. Compare *mutual exclusion*.

mutual exclusion   An algorithm that allows only one *concurrent task* to have access to shared data at a time, which can be enforced by means of *binary semaphores* or through the use of *monitors*. Compare *multiple readers and writers*.

node   In a *distributed* environment, a unit of deployment, usually consisting of one or more processors with shared memory.

non-time-critical computationally intensive task   A low-priority compute-bound task that consumes spare CPU cycles.

object   An instance of a *class* that contains both hidden data and *operations* on that data.

object broker   See *broker*.

object-oriented analysis   An analysis method that emphasizes identifying real-world objects in the problem domain and mapping them to software *objects*.

object-oriented design   A software *design method* based on the concept of *objects*, *classes*, and *inheritance*.

object request broker   See *broker*.

object structuring criteria   A set of heuristics for assisting a designer in structuring a system into *objects*. Also referred to as *class structuring criteria*.

operation   A specification of a function performed by a *class*. An access procedure or function provided by a class.

output object   A software device I/O boundary object that sends output to an external output device.

package   A grouping of *UML* model elements.

part component   A *component* within a *composite component*.

passive I/O device   A device that does not generate an interrupt on completion of an input or output operation. The input from a passive input device needs to be read either on a polled basis or on demand.

passive object   An *object* that has no thread of control; an object with *operations* that are invoked directly or indirectly by *concurrent objects*.

performance analysis   A quantitative analysis of a *real-time* software design conceptually executing on a given hardware configuration with a given external workload applied to it.

performance model   An abstraction of the real computer system behavior, developed for the purpose of gaining greater insight into the performance of the system, whether or not the system actually exists.

period   A measurement of recurring intervals of the same *duration*.

periodic task   A *concurrent task* that is activated periodically (i.e., at regular, equally spaced intervals of time) by a *timer event*.

Petri net   A dynamic mathematical model with a graphical notation consisting of places and transitions, used for modeling concurrent systems.

port   A connection point through which a *component* communicates with other components.

primary actor   An *actor* that initiates a *use case*. Compare *secondary actor*.

priority ceiling protocol   An algorithm that provides bounded priority inversion; that is, at most one lower-priority task can block a higher priority task. See *Priority inversion*.

priority inversion   A case where a task cannot execute because it is blocked by a lower-priority task.

priority message queue   A queue in which each message has an associated priority. The consumer always accepts higher-priority messages before lower-priority messages.

process   See *concurrent object*.

Product Line UML-Based Software Engineering (PLUS)   A *design method* for *software product lines* that describes how to conduct *requirements modeling, analysis modeling*, and *design modeling* for software product lines in *UML*.

profile   In *UML*, a "coherent set of extensions applicable to a given domain or purpose" (Rumbaugh et al. 2005).

provided interface   Specifies the *operations* that a *component* (or *class*) must fulfill. Compare *required interface*.

provided port   A *port* that supports a *provided interface*. Compare *required port*.

proxy object   A software object that interfaces to and communicates with an external system or subsystem.

pseudocode   A form of structured English used to describe the algorithmic details of an *object*.

queuing model   A mathematical representation of a computer system that analyzes contention for limited resources.

rate monotonic algorithm   A real-time scheduling algorithm that assigns higher priorities to tasks with shorter periods.

rate monotonic analysis   A performance analysis using *rate monotonic algorithm*.

real-time   Referring to a problem, system, or application that is *concurrent* in nature and has timing *constraints* whereby incoming *events* must be processed within a given time frame.

real-time scheduling theory   A theory for priority-based scheduling of concurrent tasks with hard deadlines. It addresses how to determine whether a group of tasks, whose individual CPU utilization is known, will meet their deadlines.

remote method invocation (RMI)   A *middleware* technology that allows *distributed* Java *objects* to communicate with each other.

required interface   The operations that another *component* (or *class*) provides for a given component (or class) to operate properly in a particular environment. Compare *provided interface*.

required port   A *port* that supports a *required interface*. Compare *provided port*.

requirements modeling   A phase of the *COMET/RTE* system and software software life cycle in which the functional requirements of the system are determined through the development of *use case models*. Compare *analysis modeling* and *design modeling*.

reuse category   A classification of a modeling element (*use case, feature, class*, etc.) in a *software product line* by its reuse properties, such as *kernel* or *optional*. Compare *role category*.

reuse stereotype   A *UML* notation for depicting the *reuse category* of a modeling element.

RMI   See *remote method invocation*.

role category   A classification of a modeling element (*class*, *object*, *component*) by the role it plays in an application, such as *control* or *entity*. Compare *reuse category*.

role stereotype   A *UML* notation for depicting the *role category* of a modeling element.

scalability   The extent to which the system is capable of growing after its initial deployment.

scenario   A specific path through a *use case* or *object interaction diagram*.

secondary actor   An *actor* that participates in (but does not initiate) a *use case*. Compare *primary actor*.

semaphore   See *binary semaphore*.

sequence diagram   A *UML interaction diagram* that depicts a dynamic view of a system in which the objects participating in the interaction are depicted horizontally, time is represented by the vertical dimension, and the sequence of message interactions is depicted from top to bottom.

sequential   Referring to a problem, process, system, or application in which activities happen in strict sequence; a sequential system or application has only one thread of control. Compare *concurrent*.

sequential clustering   A task structuring criterion in which objects that are constrained to execute sequentially are mapped to a task.

sequential service   A *service* that completes one *client* request before it starts servicing the next. Compare *concurrent service*.

sensor   A device that detects events or changes in a physical property or entity and converts the measurement or event into an electrical signal.

server   A system *node* that executes one or more services.

service   Software functionality that is distributed, autonomous, heterogeneous, loosely coupled, discoverable, and reusable.

service object   A software object that provides a *service* for other objects.

service-oriented architecture (SOA)   A software architecture composed of services that are distributed, autonomous, heterogeneous, loosely coupled, discoverable, and reusable.

simple component   A *component* that has no components within it. Compare *composite component*.

simulation model   An algorithmic representation of a system, reflecting system structure and behavior, that explicitly recognizes the passage of time, hence providing a means of analyzing the behavior of the system over time.

software application engineering   A process within *software product line engineering* in which the *software product line architecture* is adapted and configured to produce a given software application, which is a member of the *software product line*. Also referred to as *application engineering*.

software architectural communication pattern   A *software architectural pattern* that addresses the dynamic communication among *distributed components* of the *software architecture*.

software architectural structure pattern   A *software architectural pattern* that addresses the static structure of the *software architecture*.

software architectural pattern   A recurring architecture used in a variety of software applications. Also referred to simply as *architectural pattern*.

software architecture   A high-level design that describes the overall structure of a system in terms of *components* and their interconnections, separately from the internal details of the individual components.

software product family   See *software product line*.

software product family engineering   See *software product line engineering*.

software product line   A family of software systems that have some common functionality and some variable functionality. Also referred to as *family of systems*, *software product family*, *product family*, or *product line*.

software product line architecture   The architecture for a family of products, which describes the kernel, optional, and variable *components* in the *software product line*, and their interconnections.

software product line engineering   A process for analyzing the *commonality* and *variability* in a *software product line* and developing a product line *use case model*, product line *analysis model*, *software product line architecture*, and reusable *components*. Also referred to as *software product family engineering*, *product family engineering*, or *product line engineering*.

software system context diagram   A *block definition diagram* that depicts the relationships between the software system and the *external blocks* outside the software system. Compare *system context diagram*.

software system context model   A model of a software system boundary that is depicted on a *software system context diagram*. Compare *system context model*.

spiral model   A risk-driven software process model.

state   A recognizable situation that exists over an interval of time.

statechart   A *UML* hierarchical *state transition diagram* in which the *nodes* represent *states* and the arcs represent *state transitions*.

state dependent control object   An *object* that hides the details of a *finite state machine*; that is, the object encapsulates a *statechart*, a *state transition diagram*, or the contents of a *state transition table*.

state machine   See *finite state machine*.

state machine diagram   See *statechart*.

state transition   A change in *state* that is caused by an input *event*.

state transition diagram   A graphical representation of a *finite state machine* in which the *nodes* represent *states* and the arcs represent transitions between states.

state transition table   A tabular representation of a *finite state machine*.

static modeling   The process of developing a static, structural view of a problem or system.

stereotype   A classification that defines a new building block that is derived from an existing *UML* modeling element but is tailored to the modeler's problem (Booch, Rumbaugh, and Jacobson 2005).

structural modeling   See *static modeling*.

subscription/notification   A form of group communication in which subscribers receive *event* notifications. Also referred to as *multicast communication*.

substate   A *state* that is part of a *composite state*.

subsystem   A significant part of the whole system; a subsystem provides a subset of the overall system functionality.

subsystem communication diagram   A high-level *communication diagram* depicting the *subsystems* and their interactions.

superstate   A *composite state*.

synchronous message communication   A form of communication in which a producer *component* (or *concurrent task*) sends a message to a consumer component (or concurrent task) and then immediately waits for an acknowledgment. Compare *asynchronous message communication*.

synchronous message communication with reply   A form of communication in which a client *component* (or producer *task*) sends a message to a service component (or consumer task) and then waits for a reply.

synchronous message communication without reply   A form of communication in which a producer *component* (or *task*) sends a message to a consumer component (or task) and then waits for acceptance of the message by the consumer.

SysML (Systems Modeling Language)   A visual modeling language based on UML 2 for modeling systems requirements and designs.

system context diagram   A *block definition diagram* that depicts the relationships between the system and the *external blocks* outside the system. Compare *software system context diagram*.

system context model   A model of a system (hardware and software) boundary that is depicted on a *system context diagram*. Compare *software system context model*.

task   A task represents the execution of a sequential program or a sequential component of a concurrent program. Each task deals with a sequential thread of execution; there is no concurrency within a task. See *concurrent object*.

task architecture   A description of the *concurrent tasks* in a system or *subsystem* in terms of their *interfaces* and interconnections.

task behavior specification (TBS)   A specification that describes the concurrent *task event sequencing logic*.

task clustering criteria   A category of the *task structuring criteria* that addresses whether and how objects should be grouped into concurrent tasks.

task event sequencing logic   A description of how a task responds to each of its message or event inputs; in particular, what output is generated as a result of each input.

task interface specification (TIS)   A specification that describes a concurrent task's interface, structure, timing characteristics, relative priority, and errors detected.

task inversion   A *task clustering* concept that originated in Jackson Structured Programming and Jackson System Development, whereby the tasks in a system can be merged in a systematic way.

task priority criteria   A category of the *task structuring criteria* that addresses the importance of executing a given task relative to others.

task structuring   A stage in software design where the objective is to structure a concurrent application into concurrent tasks and define the task interfaces.

task structuring criteria   A set of heuristics for assisting a designer in structuring a system into concurrent tasks.

temporal clustering   A *task structuring* criterion by which activities that are not sequentially dependent but are activated by the same event are grouped into a task.

testability   The extent to which software is capable of being tested during and after its initial development.

thread   See *concurrent object, task.*

time-critical task   A task that needs to meet a hard deadline.

timed Petri net   A *Petri net* that allows finite times to be associated with the firing of transitions.

timer event   A stimulus used for the periodic activation of a *concurrent task.*

timer object   A *control object* that is activated by an external timer.

timing diagram   A *sequence diagram* that shows the time-ordered execution sequence of a group of *concurrent tasks.*

traceability   The extent to which products of each phase can be traced back to products of previous phases.

UML   See *Unified Modeling Language.*

Unified Modeling Language (UML)   A language for visualizing, specifying, constructing, and documenting the artifacts of a software-intensive system (Booch, Rumbaugh, and Jacobson 2005).

Unified Software Development Process (USDP)   An iterative *use case*-driven software process that uses the *UML* notation.

use case   A description of a sequence of interactions between one or more *actors* and the system.

use case diagram   A *UML* diagram that shows a set of *use cases* and *actors* and their relationships (Booch, Rumbaugh, and Jacobson 2005).

use case model   A description of the functional requirements of the system in terms of *actors* and *use cases.*

use case modeling   The process of developing the *use cases* of a system or *software product line.*

use case package   A group of related *use cases.*

user interaction object   A software *object* that interacts with and interfaces to a human user.

user interaction task   A task that interacts sequentially with a human user.

utilization bound theorem   A real-time scheduling theorem that states the conditions under which a set of n independent periodic tasks scheduled by the *rate monotonic algorithm* will always meet their deadlines.

variability   The functionality that is provided by some, but not all, members of the *software product line.* Compare *commonality.*

variation point   A location at which change can occur in a *software product line* artifact (e.g., in a *use case* or *class*).

visibility   The characteristic that defines whether an element of a *class* is visible from outside the class.

white page brokering   A pattern of communication between a *client* and a *broker* in which the client knows the service required but not the location. Compare *yellow page brokering.*

whole/part relationship   A *composition* or *aggregation* relationship in which a whole class is composed of part classes.

yellow page brokering   A pattern of communication between a *client* and a *broker* in which the client knows the type of service required but not the specific service. Compare *white page brokering.*

Bibliography

Albassam E., H. Gomaa, and R. Pettit. 2014. Experimental Analysis of Real-Time Multitasking on Multicore Systems, Proc. 17th IEEE Symposium on Object/Component/Service-oriented Real-time Distributed Computing (ISORC), June 2014.

Ammann, P. and J. Offutt. 2008. *Introduction to Software Testing*. New York: Cambridge University Press.

Ambler, S. 2005. *The Elements of UML 2.0 Style*. New York: Cambridge University Press.

Atkinson, C., J. Bayer, O. Laitenberger, et al. 2002. *Component-Based Product Line Engineering with UML*. Boston: Addison-Wesley.

Awad, M., J. Kuusela, and J. Ziegler. 1996. *Object-Oriented Technology for Real-Time Systems: A Practical Approach Using OMT and Fusion*. Upper Saddle River, NJ: Prentice Hall.

Bacon, J. 2003. *Concurrent Systems: An Integrated Approach to Operating Systems, Database, and Distributed Systems*, 3rd ed. Reading, MA: Addison-Wesley.

Baruah, S. K. and Goossens, J. 2003. Rate-monotonic Scheduling on Uniform Multiprocessors. IEEE Transactions Computing. 52, 7, 966–970.

Bass, L., P. Clements, and R. Kazman. 2013. *Software Architecture in Practice*, 3rd ed. Boston: Addison-Wesley.

Beck, K. and C. Andres. 2005. *Extreme Programming Explained: Embrace Change*, 2nd ed. Boston: Addison-Wesley.

Bishop, M. 2005. *Introduction to Computer Security*. Boston: Addison-Wesley.

Bjorkander, M. and C. Kobryn. 2003. "Architecting Systems with UML 2.0." *IEEE Software* 20(4): 57–61.

Blaha, J. and J. Rumbaugh. 2005. *Object-Oriented Modeling and Design*, 2nd ed. Upper Saddle River, NJ: Pearson Prentice Hall.

Boehm, B. 1988. "A Spiral Model of Software Development and Enhancement." *IEEE Computer* 21(5): 61–72.

Boehm, B. 2006. "A View of 20th and 21st Century Software Engineering." In *Proceedings of the International Conference on Software Engineering, May 20–26, 2006, Shanghai, China*, pp. 12–29. Los Alamitos, CA: IEEE Computer Society Press.

Booch G. 1994. "Object-Oriented Design with Applications," Second Edition, Addison Wesley, Reading MA.

Booch, G., R. A. Maksimchuk, and M. W. Engel. 2007. *Object-Oriented Analysis and Design with Applications*, 3rd ed. Boston: Addison-Wesley.

Booch, G., J. Rumbaugh, and I. Jacobson. 2005. *The Unified Modeling Language User Guide*, 2nd ed. Boston: Addison-Wesley.

Bosch, J. 2000. *Design & Use of Software Architectures: Adopting and Evolving a Product-Line Approach*. Boston: Addison-Wesley.

Brooks, F. 1995. *The Mythical Man-Month: Essays on Software Engineering*, anniversary ed. Boston: Addison-Wesley.

Brown, A. 2000. *Large-Scale, Component-Based Development*. Upper Saddle River, NJ: Prentice Hall.

Bruno, E. and G. Bollella. 2009. *Real-Time Java Programming: With Java RTS*. Upper Saddle River, NJ: Prentice Hall

Budgen, D. 2003. *Software Design*, 2nd ed. Boston: Addison-Wesley.

Buede, D. M. 2009. *The Engineering Design of Systems: Methods and Models*. 2nd ed. New York: Wiley.

Buhr, R. J. A. and R. S. Casselman, 1996. *Use Case Maps for Object-Oriented Systems*. Upper Saddle River, NJ: Prentice Hall.

Burns, A. and A. Wellings, 2009. *Real-Time Systems and Programming Languages*, 4th ed. Boston: Addison Wesley.

Buschmann, F., R. Meunier, H. Rohnert, et al. 1996. *Pattern-Oriented Software Architecture: A System of Patterns*. New York: Wiley.

Buschmann, F., M. Henney, and D. Schmidt, 2007. *Pattern Oriented Software Architecture*, Volume 3: A Pattern Language for Distributed Computing. New York: John Wiley & Sons.

Buttazzo, G. 2011. *Hard Real-Time Computing Systems: Predictable Scheduling Algorithms and Applications*, 2nd ed. New York: Springer.

Carver, R., and K. Tai. 2006. *Modern Multithreading:Implementing, Testing, and Debugging Multithreaded Java and C++/Pthreads/Win32 Programs* New York: Wiley-Interscience

Clements, P. and L. Northrop. 2002. *Software Product Lines: Practices and Patterns*. Boston: Addison-Wesley.

Cockburn, A. 2006. *Agile Software Development: The Cooperative Game*, 2nd ed. Boston: Addison-Wesley.

Cohn, M. 2006. *Agile Estimating and Planning*. Upper Saddle River, NJ: Pearson Prentice Hall.

Comer, D. E. 2008. *Computer Networks and Internets*, 5th ed. Upper Saddle River, NJ: Pearson Prentice Hall.

Cooling, J. 2003. *Software Engineering for Real-Time Systems*. Harlow: Addison Wesley.

Davis, R. I. and Burns, A. 2011. A Survey of Hard Real-Time Scheduling for Multiprocessor Systems. ACM Computer Surveys. 43, 4, Article 35 (October 2011), 44 pages.

Dollimore J., T. Kindberg, and G. Coulouris. 2005. *Distributed Systems: Concepts and Design*, 4th ed. Boston: Addison-Wesley.

Dahl, O. and C. A. R. Hoare. 1972. "Hierarchical Program Structures." In *Structured Programming*, O. Dahl, E. W. Dijkstra, and C. A. R. Hoare (eds.), pp. 175–220. London: Academic Press.

Davis, A. 1993. *Software Requirements: Objects, Functions, and States*, 2nd ed. Upper Saddle River, NJ: Prentice Hall.

Dijkstra, E. W. 1968. "The Structure of T.H.E. Multiprogramming System." *Communications of the ACM* 11: 341–346.

Douglass, B. P. 1999. *Doing Hard Time: Developing Real-Time Systems with UML, Objects, Frameworks, and Patterns*. Reading, MA: Addison-Wesley.

Douglass, B. P. 2002. *Real-Time Design Patterns: Robust Scalable Architecture for Real-Time Systems*. Boston: Addison-Wesley.

Douglass, B. P. 2004. *Real Time UML: Advances in the UML for Real-Time Systems*, 3rd ed. Boston: Addison-Wesley.

Eeles, P., K. Houston, and W. Kozaczynski. 2002. *Building J2EE Applications with the Rational Unified Process*. Boston: Addison-Wesley.

Eriksson, H. E., M. Penker, B. Lyons, et al. 2004. *UML 2 Toolkit*. Indianapolis, IN: Wiley.

Erl, T. 2006. *Service-Oriented Architecture (SOA): Concepts, Technology, and Design.* Upper Saddle River, NJ: Prentice Hall.

Espinoza H., D. Cancila, B. Selic, and S. Gérard, 2009. "Challenges in Combining SysML and MARTE for Model-Based Design of Embedded Systems." *Lecture Notes in Computer Science* 5562, pp. 98–113. Berlin: Springer.

FAA. 2000. *System Safety Handbook*. https://www.faa.gov/regulations_policies/ handbooks_manuals/aviation/risk_management/ss_handbook/

Fowler, M. 2002. *Patterns of Enterprise Application Architecture*. Boston: Addison-Wesley.

Fowler, M. 2004. *UML Distilled: Applying the Standard Object Modeling Language*, 3rd ed. Boston: Addison-Wesley.

Friedenthal S, A. Moore, and R. Steiner, 2015. *A Practical Guide to SysML: The Systems Modeling Language*, 3rd ed. San Francisco: Morgan Kaufmann.

Gamma, E., R. Helm, R. Johnson, and J. Vlissides. 1995. *Design Patterns: Elements of Reusable Object-Oriented Software*. Reading, MA: Addison-Wesley.

Goetz, B. et al. 2006. *Java Concurrency in Practice*. Boston: Addison-Wesley.

Gomaa, H. 1984. "A Software Design Method for Real Time Systems." *Communications of the ACM* 27(9): 938–949.

Gomaa, H. 1986. "Software Development of Real Time Systems." *Communications of the ACM* 29(7): 657–668.

Gomaa, H. 1989a. "A Software Design Method for Distributed Real-Time Applications." *Journal of Systems and Software* 9: 81–94.

Gomaa, H. 1989b. "Structuring Criteria for Real Time System Design." In *Proceedings of the 11th International Conference on Software Engineering, May 15–18, 1989, Pittsburgh, PA, USA*, pp. 290–301. Los Alamitos, CA: IEEE Computer Society Press.

Gomaa, H. 1990. "The Impact of Prototyping on Software System Engineering." In *Systems and Software Requirements Engineering*, pp. 431–440. Los Alamitos, CA: IEEE Computer Society Press.

Gomaa, H. 1993. *Software Design Methods for Concurrent and Real-Time Systems*. Reading, MA: Addison-Wesley.

Gomaa, H. 2001. "Use Cases for Distributed Real-Time Software Architectures." In *Engineering of Distributed Control Systems*, L. R. Welch and D. K. Hammer (eds.), pp. 1–18. Commack, NY: Nova Science.

Gomaa, H. 2000. *Designing Concurrent, Distributed, and Real-Time Applications with UML*. Boston: Addison-Wesley.

Gomaa, H. 2002. "Concurrent Systems Design." In *Encyclopedia of Software Engineering*, 2nd ed., J. Marciniak (ed.), pp. 172–179. New York: Wiley.

Gomaa, H. 2005a. *Designing Software Product Lines with UML*. Boston: Addison-Wesley.

Gomaa, H. 2005b. "Modern Software Design Methods for Concurrent and Real-Time Systems." In Software Engineering, vol. 1: *The Development Process*. 3rd ed. M. Dorfman and R. Thayer (eds.), pp 221–234. Hoboken, NJ: Wiley Interscience.

Gomaa, H. 2006. "A Software Modeling Odyssey: Designing Evolutionary Architecture-centric Real-Time Systems and Product Lines." Keynote paper, *Proceedings of the ACM/IEEE 9th International Conference on Model-Driven Engineering, Languages and Systems, Genoa, Italy, October 2006*, pp. 1–15. Springer Verlag LNCS 4199.

Gomaa, H. 2008. "Model-based Software Design of Real-Time Embedded Systems." *International Journal of Software Engineering* 1(1): 19–41.

Gomaa, H. 2009. "Concurrent Programming." In *Encyclopedia of Computer Science and Engineering*, Benjamin Wah (ed.), pp. 648–655. Hoboken, NJ: Wiley.

Gomaa H. 2011. *Software Modeling and Design: UML, Use Cases, Patterns, and Software Architectures*. New York: Cambridge University Press.

Gomaa, H. and D. Menasce. 2001. "Performance Engineering of Component-Based Distributed Software Systems." In *Performance Engineering: State of the Art and Current Trends*, R. Dumke, C. Rautenstrauch, A. Schmietendorf, et al. (eds.), pp. 40–55. Berlin: Springer.

Gomaa, H. and D. B. H. Scott. 1981. "Prototyping as a Tool in the Specification of User Requirements." In *Proceedings of the 5th International Conference on Software Engineering, San Diego, March 1981*, pp. 333–342. New York: ACM Press.

Harel, D. and E. Gery. 1996. "Executable Object Modeling with Statecharts." In *Proceedings of the 18th International Conference on Software Engineering, Berlin, March 1996*, pp. 246–257. Los Alamitos, CA: IEEE Computer Society Press.

Harel, D. and M. Politi. 1998. *Modeling Reactive Systems with Statecharts: The Statemate Approach*. New York: McGraw-Hill.

Hatley D. and I. Pirbhai, 1988. "Strategies for Real Time System Specification," New York: Dorset House.

Hoare, C. A. R. 1974. "Monitors: An Operating System Structuring Concept." *Communications of the ACM* 17(10): 549–557.

Hoffman, D. and D. Weiss (eds.). 2001. *Software Fundamentals: Collected Papers by David L. Parnas*. Boston: Addison-Wesley.

Hofmeister, C., R. Nord, and D. Soni. 2000. *Applied Software Architecture*. Boston: Addison-Wesley.

IEEE Standard Glossary of Software Engineering Terminology, 1990, IEEE/Std 610.12-1990, Institute of Electrical and Electronic Engineers.

Jackson, M. 1983. *System Development*. Upper Saddle River, NJ: Prentice Hall.

Jacobson, I. 1992. *Object-Oriented Software Engineering: A Use Case Driven Approach*. Reading, MA: Addison-Wesley.

Jacobson, I., G. Booch, and J. Rumbaugh. 1999. *The Unified Software Development Process*. Reading, MA: Addison-Wesley.

Jacobson, I., M. Griss, and P. Jonsson. 1997. *Software Reuse: Architecture, Process and Organization for Business Success*. Reading, MA: Addison-Wesley.

Jacobson, I., and P.W. Ng. 2005. *Aspect-Oriented Software Development with Use Cases*. Boston: Addison-Wesley.

Jain, R. 2015. *The Art of Computer Systems Performance Analysis: Techniques For Experimental Design Measurements Simulation and Modeling*. 2nd ed. New York: Wiley.

Jazayeri, M., A. Ran, and P. Van Der Linden. 2000. *Software Architecture for Product Families: Principles and Practice*. Boston: Addison-Wesley.

Kang, K., S. Cohen, J. Hess, et al. 1990. *Feature-Oriented Domain Analysis (FODA) Feasibility Study* (Technical Report No. CMUSEI-90-TR-021). Pittsburgh, PA: Software Engineering Institute. Available online at www.sei.cmu.edupublicationsdocuments90.reports90.tr.021.html.

M. Kim, S. Kim, S. Park, et al. "Service Robot for the Elderly: Software Development with the COMET/UML Method." *IEEE Robotics and Automation Magazine*, March 2009.

Kobryn, C. 1999. "UML 2001: A Standardization Odyssey." *Communications of the ACM* 42(10): 29–37.

H. Kopetz, 2011. *Real-Time Systems: Design Principles for Distributed Embedded Applications*, 2nd ed. New York: Springer.

Kroll, P. and P. Kruchten. 2003. *The Rational Unified Process Made Easy: A Practitioner's Guide to the RUP*. Boston: Addison-Wesley.

Kruchten, P. 1995. "The 4+1 View Model of Architecture." *IEEE Software* 12(6): 42–50.

Kruchten, P. 2003. *The Rational Unified Process: An Introduction*, 3rd ed. Boston: Addison-Wesley.

Laplante P. 2011. *Real-Time Systems Design and Analysis: Tools for the Practitioner*, 4th ed. New York: Wiley-IEEE Press.

Larman, C. 2004. *Applying UML and Patterns*, 3rd ed. Boston: Prentice Hall.

Lauzac, S., Melhem, R., and Mosse, D. 1998. Comparison of Global and Partitioning Schemes for Scheduling Rate Monotonic Tasks on a Multiprocessor. In Proceedings of the EuroMicro Workshop on Real-TimeSystems. 188–195.

Lea, D. 2000. *Concurrent Programming in Java: Design Principles and Patterns*, 2nd ed. Boston: Addison-Wesley.

Lee, E. A., and S. Seshia. 2015. *Introduction to Embedded Systems: A Cyber-Physical Systems Approach – Second Edition*. lulu.com.

Lehoczy J. P., L. Sha, and Y. Ding. 1987. "The Rate Monotonic Scheduling Algorithm: Exact Characterization and Average Case Behavior," Proc IEEE Real-Time Systems Symposium, San Jose, CA, December 1987.

Leung, J., and Whitehead, J. 1982. On the Complexity of Fixed Priority Scheduling of Periodic, Real-Time Tasks. Performance Evaluation 2. 237–250.

Li Q. and C Yao. 2003. *Real-Time Concepts for Embedded Systems*. New York: CMP Books.

Liu C. L. and J. W. Layland. 1973. "Scheduling Algorithms for Multiprogramming in Hard Real-Time Environments," Journal ACM, 20,1.

Liskov, B. and J. Guttag. 2000. *Program Development in Java: Abstraction, Specification, and Object-Oriented Design*. Boston: Addison-Wesley.

Magee, J. and J. Kramer. 2006. *Concurrency: State Models & Java Programs*, 2nd ed. Chichester, England: Wiley.

Magee, J., N. Dulay, and J. Kramer. 1994. "Regis: A Constructive Development Environment for Parallel and Distributed Programs." *Journal of Distributed Systems Engineering* 1(5): 304–312.

Menascé, D. A., V. Almeida, and L. Dowdy, 2004. *Performance by Design: Computer Capacity Planning By Example*, Upper Saddle River, NJ: Prentice Hall.

Menascé, D. A. and H. Gomaa. 2000. "A Method for Design and Performance Modeling of Client/Server Systems." *IEEE Transactions on Software Engineering* 26: 1066–1085.

Meyer, B. 1989. "Reusability: The Case for Object-Oriented Design." In *Software Reusability*, vol. 2: *Applications and Experience*, T. J. Biggerstaff and A. J. Perlis (eds.), pp. 1–33. New York: ACM Press.

Meyer, B. 2000. *Object-Oriented Software Construction*, 2nd ed. Upper Saddle River, NJ: Prentice Hall.

Meyer, B. 2014. *Agile! The Good, the Hype, and the Ugly*. Switzerland: Springer.

Mills, K. and H. Gomaa. 1996. "A Knowledge-Based Approach for Automating a Design Method for Concurrent and Real-Time Systems." In *Proceedings of the 8th International Conference on Software Engineering and Knowledge Engineering*, pp. 529–536. Skokie, IL: Knowledge Systems Institute.

Mills, K. and H. Gomaa. 2002. "Knowledge-Based Automation of a Design Method for Concurrent and Real-Time Systems." *IEEE Transactions on Software Engineering* 28(3): 228–255.

Object Management Group (OMG). 2015. "MDA – The Architecture Of Choice For A Changing World." http://www.omg.org/mda/

Page-Jones, M. 2000. *Fundamentals of Object-Oriented Design in UML*. Boston: Addison-Wesley.

Parnas, D. 1972. "On the Criteria to Be Used in Decomposing a System into Modules." *Communications of the ACM* 15: 1053–1058.

Parnas, D. 1979. "Designing Software for Ease of Extension and Contraction." *IEEE Transactions on Software Engineering* 5(2): 128–138.

Parnas, D., P. Clements, and D. Weiss. 1984. "The Modular Structure of Complex Systems." In *Proceedings of the 7th International Conference on Software Engineering, March 26–29, 1984, Orlando, Florida*, pp. 408–419. Los Alamitos, CA: IEEE Computer Society Press.

Pettit, R. and H. Gomaa. 2006. "Modeling Behavioral Design Patterns of Concurrent Objects." In *Proceedings of the IEEE International Conference on Software Engineering, May 2006, Shanghai, China*. Los Alamitos, CA: IEEE Computer Society Press.

Pettit, R. and H. Gomaa. 2007. "Analyzing Behavior of Concurrent Software Designs for Embedded Systems." In *Proceedings of the 10th IEEE International Symposium on Object and Component-Oriented Real-Time Distributed Computing, Santorini Island, Greece, May 2007*.

Pfleeger, C., S. Pfleeger, and J. Margulies. 2015. *Security in Computing*. 5th ed. Upper Saddle River, NJ: Prentice Hall.

Pree, W. and E. Gamma. 1995. *Design Patterns for Object-Oriented Software Development*. Reading, MA: Addison-Wesley.

Pressman, R. 2009. *Software Engineering: A Practitioner's Approach*, 7th ed. New York: McGraw-Hill.

Quatrani, T. 2003. *Visual Modeling with Rational Rose 2002 and UML*. Boston: Addison-Wesley.

Rumbaugh, J., M. Blaha, W. Premerlani, et al. 1991. *Object-Oriented Modeling and Design*. Upper Saddle River, NJ: Prentice Hall.

Rumbaugh, J., G. Booch, and I. Jacobson. 2005. *The Unified Modeling Language Reference Manual*, 2nd ed. Boston: Addison-Wesley.

Sage, A. P. and Armstrong, J. E., Jr., 2000. *An Introduction to Systems Engineering*, John Wiley & Sons.

Schmidt, D., M. Stal, H. Rohnert, et al. 2000. *Pattern-Oriented Software Architecture, Volume 2: Patterns for Concurrent and Networked Objects*. Chichester, England: Wiley.

Schneider, G. and J. P. Winters. 2001. *Applying Use Cases: A Practical Guide*, 2nd ed. Boston: Addison-Wesley.

Selic, B. 1999. "Turning Clockwise: Using UML in the Real-Time Domain," *Communications of the ACM* 42(10): 46–54.

Selic, B., and S. Gerard. 2014. *Modeling and Analysis of Real-Time and Embedded Systems: Developing Cyber-Physical Systems with UML and MARTE*. Burlington, MA: Morgan Kaufmann.

Selic, B., G. Gullekson, and P. Ward. 1994. *Real-Time Object-Oriented Modeling.* New York: Wiley.

Sha L. and J. B. Goodenough. 1990. "Real-Time Scheduling Theory and Ada." *IEEE Computer* 23(4), 53–62.

Shan, Y. P. and R. H. Earle. 1998. *Enterprise Computing with Objects.* Reading, MA: Addison-Wesley.

Shaw, M. and D. Garlan. 1996. *Software Architecture: Perspectives on an Emerging Discipline.* Upper Saddle River, NJ: Prentice Hall.

Silberschatz, A., P. Galvin, and G. Gagne. 2013. *Operating System Concepts*, 9th ed. New York: Wiley.

Simpson H. and K. Jackson, 1979. "Process Synchronization in MASCOT," *The Computer Journal* 17(4).

Simpson H., 1986. "The MASCOT Method," *IEE/BCS Software Engineering Journal,* 1(3), 103–120.

Smith, C. U. 1990. *Performance Engineering of Software Systems.* Reading, MA: Addison-Wesley.

Software Engineering Institute, Carnegie Mellon University. 1993. *A Practitioner's Handbook for Real-Time Analysis: Guide to Rate Monotonic Analysis for Real-Time Systems.* Boston: Kluwer Academic Publishers.

Sommerville, I. 2010. *Software Engineering*, 9th ed. Boston: Addison-Wesley.

Sprunt B, JP Lehoczy and L Sha. 1989. "Aperiodic Task Scheduling for Hard Real-Time Systems," *The Journal of Real-Time Systems* 1 (1989): 27–60.

Sutherland, J. 2014. *Scrum: The Art of Doing Twice the Work in Half the Time.* New York: Crown Business.

Szyperski, C. 2003. *Component Software: Beyond Object-Oriented Programming*, 2nd ed. Boston: Addison-Wesley.

Tanenbaum, A. S. 2011. *Computer Networks*, 5th ed. Upper Saddle River, NJ: Prentice Hall.

Tanenbaum, A. S. 2014. *Modern Operating Systems*, 4th ed. Upper Saddle River, NJ: Prentice Hall.

Tanenbaum, A. S. and M. Van Steen. 2006. *Distributed Systems: Principles and Paradigms*, 2nd ed. Upper Saddle River, NJ: Prentice Hall.

Taylor, R. N., N. Medvidovic, and E. M. Dashofy. 2009. *Software Architecture: Foundations, Theory, and Practice.* New York: Wiley.

Ward P. and S. Mellor, 1985. *Structured Development for Real-Time Systems*, vols. 1, 2, and 3, Upper Saddle River, NJ: Yourdon Press, Prentice Hall.

Warmer, J. and A. Kleppe. 1999. *The Object Constraint Language: Precise Modeling with UML.* Reading, MA: Addison-Wesley.

Webber, D. and H. Gomaa. 2004. "Modeling Variability in Software Product Lines with the Variation Point Model." *Journal of Science of Computer Programming* 53(3): 305–331, Amsterdam: Elsevier.

Weiss, D. and C. T. R. Lai. 1999. *Software Product-Line Engineering: A Family-Based Software Development Process.* Reading, MA: Addison-Wesley.

Wellings, A. 2004. *Concurrent and Real-Time Programming in Java.* New York: Wiley.

Index

4+1 view model of software architecture, 59
action, 19, 105
  entry, 19, 108
  exit, 19, 108
  transition, 106
activity, 19, 110
actor, 14, 80, 299
  external system, 83
  generalized, 85
  input device, 84
  physical entity, 83
  primary, 81
  secondary, 81
  software engineering perspective, 81, 83
  specialized, 85
  systems engineering perspective, 81, 82
  timer, 84
actuator, 5
aggregation hierarchy, 16, 64
agile methods, 57
algorithm
  object, 128, 139
algorithm task
  demand driven, 244
analysis model, 144
analysis modeling, 53
analysis patterns, 185
application logic
  object, 128, 139
architectural communication patterns, 185, 197,
  229, 530, 540
architectural patterns, 185
architectural structure patterns, 185, 186,
  530
architectural styles, 185
association, 15, 62
  multiplicity of, 62
asynchronous message communication, 21,
  260
Asynchronous Message Communication pattern,
  183, 198, 540
Asynchronous Message Communication with
  Callback pattern, 201, 541

atomic operation, 40
attribute, 33
autonomy
  localized, 222
availability, 7, 315
  requirements, 88

behavioral pattern
  object, 129
Bidirectional Asynchronous Message
  Communication pattern, 199, 542
block, 61
  composite, 69
  external, 73
block definition diagram, 28, 61, 67,
  69
boundary object, 127, 129
  device I/O, 127, 129, 130
Broadcast pattern, 207, 543
broker, 203
Broker Forwarding pattern, 204
Broker Handle pattern, 544

Centralized Control pattern, 190, 531
class, 14, 33
  synchronization of access to, 274
class diagram, 15, 61
  subsystem, 166
classification
  of application classes, 127
client, 173, 194
  user interaction, 177
client subsystem, 179
COMET, 59
COMET/RTE, xx, 10, 51
  life cycle model, 51
communication diagram, 17, 18, 144
  concurrent, 20
  subsystem, 169
Completion Time Theorem, 327
  Example of Applying Generalized, 336
  Generalized, 333
  mathematical formulation, 329

component, 47
    composite, 167
    I/O, 223
    interface inheritance, 309
    mobile, 173
    plug-compatible, 308
component interface, 213
component performance, 223
component-based software architecture, 165, 212
    design, 212
composite component, 165, 212, 217
composite object, 172
composite state, 19, 114
composite structure diagram, 24, 167
composite task, 266
composition hierarchy, 16, 64
conceptual static model, 67
concurrency, 7
concurrent
    application, 37
    systems, 40
    task, 37
concurrent communication diagram, 22, 267
Concurrent Design Approach for Real-Time
        Systems (CODARTS), 58
concurrent processing
    runtime support, 43
concurrent sequence diagram, 22
concurrent software architecture, 164
concurrent task, 234
concurrent task design, 233
concurrent tasks
    implementation in Java, 295
condition, 19, 103
configuration
    requirements, 88
connector, 47, 215
    example of use for asynchronous
        communication, 289
    example of use for synchronous communication
        with reply, 290
    message buffer, 286
    message buffer and response, 287
    message queue, 284, 287, 288
constraint, 27
context modeling, 69
context switching, 39, 46
context switching overhead, 327
continuous data, 236
control
    object, 127, 137
control clustering, 254, 271
control object
    state dependent, 176
control subsystem, 176
coordinator
    object, 128, 138
coordinator subsystem, 177
coordinator task, 246
critical region, 40
critical section, 40, 43
cyber-physical system, 3

data abstraction, 35
    object, 136
data abstraction class, 275

data analysis subsystem, 179
data collection subsystem, 178
data distribution, 227
data replication, 227
database wrapper
    object, 136
deadline monotonic algorithm, 339
deadlock, 43
delegation connector, 217
demand driven tasks, 244
deployment
    application, 228
deployment diagram, 23, 169, 229
design
    rationale, 318
design anti-patterns, 185
Design Approach for Real-Time Systems
        (DARTS), 58
design for change, 319
design modeling, 54
    for software product lines, 308
design pattern, 184
design restructuring, 367
device I/O class, 268
discrete data, 236
Distributed Collaborative Control pattern, 191,
        532
distributed component, 212
distributed control, 7
Distributed Independent Control pattern, 191, 533
distributed service, 227
domain engineering, 298
domain–specific patterns, 185
duration, 5
dynamic interaction modeling, 54, 143, 145
    for software product lines, 304
    state dependent, 143, 150
    stateless, 143, 146
dynamic modeling, 54, 143
dynamic priority systems, 339
dynamic state machine modeling, 54

Earliest-Deadline-First scheduling algorithm, 339
encapsulation, 35
entity
    object, 128, 136
    class, 69
event, 5, 19, 101, 151
    external, 262
    internal, 263
    timer, 262
event sequence analysis, 315, 324
event sequence task, 354
event synchronization, 262
extend
    use case relationship, 94
external entities, 70

fault tolerant systems, 315
feature, 301
    alternative, 301
    common, 301
    group, 301
    prerequisite, 301
feature modeling
    in software product lines, 301

finite state machine, 100
functional requirements, 53

generalization/specialization, 37
generalization/specialization hierarchy, 16,
    65
generalized completion time theorem
    example of, 363
generalized real-time scheduling
    example of, 359
geographical location, 173
group message communication, 206
guard condition, 103

hardware/software boundary, 76
    specification, 76
hardware/software boundary modeling, 53, 72,
    73
hazard, 316
Hierarchical Control pattern, 192, 534
hierarchical decomposition, 113

I/O device
    event driven, 236
    hardware characteristics, 235
    interrupt-driven, 236
    passive, 236
I/O task
    demand driven, 240
    event driven, 236
    periodic, 238
    periodic timing considerations, 239
    sensor-based periodic, 238
idioms, 185
implementation, 165
include
    relationship, 94
    use case relationship, 92
incremental software construction, 55
incremental software integration, 56
information hiding, 34, 35, 43, 172,
    319
    class, 35
inheritance, 16, 36, 65
    as taxonomy, 65
    classification mechanism, 65
input class
    passive, 268
input object, 130
input/output (I/O)
    object, 130, 131
input/output subsystem, 178
interaction diagram, 17, 144
    descriptor form, 145
    generic form, 145
    instance form, 145
    use case based, 170
interface, 24, 33, 35, 165, 213
    abstract, 35
    external, 35
    provided, 26
    required, 26
    virtual, 35
Internet of Things, 9

Jackson System Development (JSD), 58

Kernel pattern, 189, 536
kernel system, 305

Layers of Abstraction pattern, 186, 535
load balancing, 8
localized control, 7
location transparency, 203

maintainability, 318
MARTE, xx, 11, 12, 28, 51
    stereotype, 234
MASCOT design method, 57
Master/Slave pattern, 193, 537
memory-locking, 44
message, 151
message communication, 181
    asynchronous, 182
    bidirectional, 181
    synchronous, 182
    unidirectional, 181
message sequence description, 145
middleware, 8
model-based software engineering, 51
model-based systems engineering, 51
model-driven architecture, 12
modifiability, 319
monitor, 43, 278
    condition synchronization, 279
    mutual exclusion, 278
Multicast communication, 207
multicore systems, 7, 234
Multiple Client/Multiple Service pattern, 196,
    538
Multiple Client/Single Service pattern, 194,
    539
multiple readers and writers, 225
multiple views
    of system and software architecture, 59
multiplicity
    of an association, 15
multiprocessor systems, 7, 45, 339
    global scheduling, 339
    partitioned scheduling, 339
multitasking
    kernel, 45
mutual exclusion, 40, 42, 224

nonfunctional requirements, 53, 88, 317

object, 15, 32
    active, 20, 37
    concurrent, 20, 37
    passive, 37
Object Access Pattern, 274
object and class structuring, 128
Object Management Group, 12, 578
Object Modeling Technique, 58
object structuring, 54
object-oriented analysis and design, 58
Object-Oriented Design, 58
Octopus, 58
OMG, 12
operating system
    kernel, 43
    services, 44
operation, 33

output class
    passive, 268
output object, 130, 131

package diagram, 20
performance, 315
    requirements, 88
performance analysis, 315
    example of tasks executing on multiprocessor
        systems, 365
    example using event sequence analysis, 346
    example using real-time scheduling, 351
    example using real-time scheduling and event
        sequence analysis, 354
    of software designs, 315
Performance Analysis
    Example Using Event Sequence Analysis, 337
    Using Event Sequence Analysis, 336
    Using Real-Time Scheduling Theory and Event
        Sequence Analysis, 338
Performance Analysis of Multiprocessor
    Systems
    using Timing Diagrams, 340
    with Event Sequence Analysis, 342
    with Mutual Exclusion, 342
performance modeling, 315
performance parameters
    estimation and measurement, 343
period, 6
periodic task, 242
platform transparency, 203
platform-independent model, 13
platform-specific model, 13
polling, 236
port, 214
    complex, 215
    provided, 215
    required, 215
priority ceiling protocol, 331
priority inheritance, 44
priority inversion, 331, 332
priority preemption task scheduling, 44
process, 38, 39
    heavyweight, 39
    lightweight, 39
process control, 6
producer/consumer problem, 41
profile, 26, 28, 565
provided interface, 214
proxy
    object, 127, 130, 133
proxy task
    event driven, 242
pseudocode
    periodic input task, 552
Publish/Subscribe pattern, 207
publisher, 207

quality of service, 164

rate monotonic algorithm, 325
rate monotonic priority, 332
reactive systems, 7
real-time control, 6
real-time embedded system, 3
    distributed, 7

real-time embedded systems
    characteristics, 5
Real-Time Object-Oriented Modeling (ROOM),
    58
real-time operating system, 44
real-time scheduling, 315
    aperiodic tasks, 330
    periodic tasks, 325
Real-Time Scheduling
    Advanced, 339
real-time scheduling theory, 324, 325
    task synchronization, 331
Real-Time Scheduling Theory
    Generalized, 331
Real-Time Structured Analysis and Design,
    58
real-time system, 3, 4
    hard, 4
    soft, 4
real-time systems, 315
required interface, 214
requirements modeling, 53
resource monitor task, 240
RFID, 9
run to completion semantics, 101

safety, 316
    requirements, 88
safety critical system, 317
scalability, 313
    requirements, 88
scenario, 145
scheduling algorithm
    priority preemption, 45
    round-robin, 45
scope of control, 175
security, 317, 318
security requirements, 88, 317
semaphore, 40
sensor, 5
separation of concerns, 172
    between tasks and nested classes, 267
    task and class, 274
sequence diagram, 17, 144
    concurrent, 20
sequential clustering, 253
    issues, 254
sequential software architecture, 164
server, 194
service, 173, 181, 194
    object, 128, 141
service component, 224
    concurrent, 224, 226
    sequential, 224
Service Discovery pattern, 205, 545
Service Registration pattern, 204, 546
service subsystem, 180
simple component, 165, 212
smart device, 236
software application engineering, 298
software architectural patterns
    documenting, 209
    software product lines, 309
software architecture, 47, 164
    deployment view, 169
    dynamic view, 168

multiple views, 166
structural view, 166
software context diagram, 174
software context modeling, 53
Software Cost Reduction Method, 58
software design method
    requirements for real-time embedded systems, 10
software evolution, 318
software maintenance, 318
software modeling, 61
software product line, 297, 323
    context diagram, 304
    engineering, 298
    evolution approach, 305
software quality attributes, 4, 55, 313
software reusability, 322
software system context diagram, 73, 74, 134
    associations, 74
spiral model, 57
state, 102
    composite, 113
    history, 116
state decomposition
    sequential, 113
state dependent control
    object, 128, 137
    task, 245
state machine, 101, 152
    class, 269
    developed from use case, 121
    diagram, 19
    flat, 113
    hierarchical, 113
    inheritance, 119
    integration, 124
    orthogonal, 117
state machine diagram, 100
state machines
    cooperating, 118
state transition, 101
    aggregation, 114
state transition diagram, 19, 100
state transition table, 100
statechart, 100
statechart diagram, 19
statecharts, 58
static modeling, 54, 61
    concepts, 62
    for software product lines, 303
stereotype, 26, 28, 70, 126
    architectural, 166
    concurrency, 234
    definition, 66
    MARTE, 166
    reuse, 303
    role, 166, 234, 303
structural element, 61
structural modeling, xx, 52, 61
    of the problem domain, 52
    of the system context, 52
structuring criteria
    component, 221
    I/O task, 235
    object and class, 126

subsystem, 175
    task, 235
Subscription/Notification pattern, 207, 226, 547
substate, 19, 113
subsystem, 172
synchronization
    multiple readers and writers, 277
    using mutual exclusion, 276
synchronization with monitor
    multiple readers & writers, 280
    writer starvation, 282
synchronized methods, 278
Synchronized Object Access pattern, 198, 263, 548
synchronous message communication, 21
    with reply, 21, 261
    without reply, 21, 261
Synchronous Message Communication with Reply pattern, 183, 200, 549
Synchronous Message Communication without Reply pattern, 202, 550
SysML, xx, 12, 27, 51, 61, 67, 70
system context diagram, 69, 70
    associations, 70
system deployment modeling, 53, 77
system modeling, 61
system quality attributes, 313
system testing, 56
Systems Modeling Language (SysML), 11, 12

tagged value, 27
task, 39, 233
    behavior specification, 264, 291
    event sequencing logic, 264, 291
    interface specification, 264
    multiple of same type, 248
    non-time-critical computationally intensive, 249
    periodic algorithm, 242
    sampling rate, 239
    scheduling, 45
    states, 45
    synchronization, 41, 44
task architecture, 233
task clustering criteria, 250
task communication and synchronization, 258
task interaction
    via information hiding object, 263
task inversion, 256
    multiple-instance, 256
task priority criteria, 248
task structuring criteria, 257
    internal, 242
TCP/IP protocol, 8, 186
temporal clustering, 250, 270
    issues, 252
testability, 320
thread, 39
throwaway prototype, 53
time
    blocked, 6
    elapsed, 6
    execution, 6
    physical, 6

time-critical task, 249
timer
    object, 128, 130, 139
timer event, 101
timing constraints, 4, 6
timing diagram, 29, 327, 336
traceability, 321
    requirements, 321
transition
    from analysis to design, 170, 181

UML, xx, 12, 51
UML tools, 30
Unified Modeling Language (UML), 11, 12
Unified Software Development Process (USDP),
    56
use case, 14, 79, 86, 299
    alternative in software product line, 299
    alternative sequences, 86
    base, 92, 95
    extension, 95
    extension point, 95
    inclusion, 92
    kernel, 299
    main sequence, 86
    model, 53, 79
    modeling, 79

optional, 299
    package, 98
    relationships, 92
    variation point, 300
use case diagram, 14
use case map, 59
use case modeling
    for software product lines, 299
use cases
    documentation of, 87
user interaction, 174
    object, 127, 130, 133
user interaction subsystem, 177
user interaction task, 246
Utilization Bound Theorem, 325
    Generalized, 333

visibility, 16
    private, 16
    protected, 16
    public, 16
Voice over IP, 187

white page brokering, 203
whole/part relationship, 64

yellow page brokering, 203, 205

Printed in the United States
by Baker & Taylor Publisher Services